IN GODS WE TRUST

\# 2914

IN GODS WE TRUST

New Patterns of Religious Pluralism in America

Second Edition, Revised and Expanded

Edited by
Thomas Robbins and Dick Anthony

Transaction Publishers
New Brunswick (U.S.A.) and London (U.K.)

Copyright © 1990 by Transaction Publishers,
New Brunswick, New Jersey 08903

Library of Congress Catalog Number: 89-4588
ISBN: 0-88738-800-0
Printed in the United States of America

Library of Congress Cataloging-in-Publication Data
In gods we trust : new patterns of religious pluralism in America /
    edited by Thomas Robbins and Dick Anthony. — 2nd ed.
        p.   cm.
    Includes index.
    ISBN 0-88738-800-0
    1. United States—Religion—1945–   2. Cults—United States.
  3. Religious pluralism—United States.   I. Robbins, Thomas,
  1943– . II. Anthony, Dick, 1939–
  BL2525.I5   1989
  306.6′0973′09045—dc20   89-4588
                                                              CIP

To the memory of the late Barbara Hargrove

Contents

List of Tables and Figures

Table

Figures

Acknowledgments

The following papers appeared originally in *Society* 26(1) (Jan./Feb. 1989): "Fundamentalism Revisited," by Frank Lechner; "Gender, Education and the New Christian Right," by Susan Rose; "Rural Ideology and the Future of Rural America," by Barbara Hargrove; "Virus as Metaphor: Religious Responses to AIDS," by Susan Palmer; "Religion and Power in the American Experience," by N.J. Demerath III and Rhys Williams. Some of these papers were published originally in *Society* in an abridged form or without tables, diagrams, and bibliographical references that appear in the present volume.

"The Apocalypse at Jonestown" by John Hall appeared originally in the first edition of *In Gods We Trust* but without the author's afterword which appears in the present edition. "Religion and the Legitimation of the American Republic" by Robert Bellah appeared in the first edition of *In Gods We Trust* and is reprinted here verbatim.

"Religion and Power" by James Beckford is a significantly abridged version of "The Restoration of 'Power' to the Sociology of Religion," which was originally published in *Sociological Analysis* 44 (1983):11–32 and subsequently reprinted in *Church-State Relations*, edited by Thomas Robbins and Roland Robertson (Transaction, 1987).

"Citizens and Believers: Always Strangers?" by Harvey Cox was originally written for and published in *Transforming Faith: The Sacred and Secular in Modern American History,* edited by Miles L. Bradbury (Greenwood Press, Westport, Conn., 1989), copyrighted by Miles L. Bradbury. The papers by Dr. Beckford and Dr. Cox are reprinted by permission of the authors and original publishers.

"The Limits of Modernity" by Irving Horowitz originally appeared in *Beyond Empire and Revolution: Militarization and Consolidation in the Third World,* by Irving Horowitz (Oxford University Press), and is reprinted by permission of Irving Horowitz.

"Civil Religion and Recent American Religious Ferment" by Dick Anthony and Thomas Robbins is a significantly revised and updated version of an earlier paper, "Spiritual Innovation and the Crisis of American Civil Religion," which was originally published in *Daedalus* (111 [1982]: 215–34) and was subsequently reprinted verbatim in *Religion and America*, edited by Mary Douglas and Steven Tipton (Beacon Press, 1982). It is reprinted by permission of *Daedalus*.

"Why Catholics Stay in The Church" by Andrew Greeley is reprinted from *America* by permission of the journal editor and Father Greeley.

The editors wish to thank Jean Peterson for her indispensable assistance in word processing, copying, and correspondence. We are also grateful to Irving Horowitz, Mary Curtis, Scott Bramson, and Esther Luckett for guidance and encouragement. Finally we would like to express our sadness at the passing of our contributor, Dr. Barbara Hargrove, who has been a major force in the sociology of religion for several decades and has provided an outstanding example of scholarly excellence and humane endeavor.

I
INTRODUCTORY

Introduction
Conflict and Change in American Religions

Thomas Robbins and Dick Anthony

American religion at the end of the 1980s seems to be simultaneously experiencing a revival and a crisis. New churches are proliferating, but the importance of overarching denominational structures may be diminishing. Some religious groups are experiencing a heady growth, while others, including some of the once-dominant mainline Protestant denominations, are declining and arguably are being "disinherited." Resurgent fundamentalists and evangelicals are flexing their political muscles, but religious conflict and controversiality is sharpening and the religious unity or harmony of the American people is a fading vision. Church-state tension is increasing and religiopolitical ideologies or variations of civil religion are polarizing. Young Americans of the Baby Boom generation are exhibiting a marked interest in religion, but their patterns of church shopping and church switching seem to reflect a consumerist orientation to religion that destabilizes particular commitments. Occult, New Age, and neopagan beliefs and practices are spreading, but they often seem to resist firm organization so that the survival of many new groups may be in doubt.

In this volume the editors have assembled a collection of papers that highlight some emerging patterns, with particular emphasis on change and conflict. We have assembled papers that collectively depict *American religion in transition* and promote the sociological analysis of emerging American religious patterns and movements.

The editors have divided this collection into sections dealing with topics, such as the resurgence of religious traditionalism, patterns of spiritual innovation, and religion and politics. But the boundaries separating these sections are tenuous and somewhat arbitrary. Many of the papers in our volume are *relevant to more than one section or topic*. Readers therefore should not be beguiled by our convenient topical constructions and separations.

Revival of the Social Science of Religion

The present revivalist, pluralizing, and politicizing trends in American religion are rendering the sociological and social-scientific study of religion increasingly popular and relevant. But this development hardly appeared to be the case when the editors were graduate students in the 1960s. Looking back, the transformation of the cultural and intellectual milieu with regard to the perceived significance of religion over the past two or three decades appears to be rather striking!

Religion was not considered to be a high-priority area of sociological and social-science inquiry in the 1960s. One usually had to be "in" religion to appreciate its study. The late Dr. Christina Larner noted in a lecture in 1982 that while the great classical sociologists of the nineteenth century, Marx, Weber, and Durkheim, were atheists, they "nevertheless attached importance to religion." In contrast, "the contemporary sociology of religion has become split off from mainline theory and has been mainly attractive to believing Christians" (Larner 1984, 110).[1]

The sociology and "scientific study" of religion appeared to be placid backwaters to the increasingly roiled currents of social science in the late 1960s and 1970s. The radical politics and student movement of the late 1960s and early 1970s had little immediate effect on the study of religion, while the broader sociological and social-science communities were riven with dissidence and dispute and with theoretical and philosophical ferment and radical debunking, all of which ultimately reflected the intensity of feelings over the Vietnam War and civil-rights crusades, and the resulting crisis of legitimacy which suddenly confronted the dominant political and socioeconomic institutions studied by social scientists.

Fall and Rise of Religious Controversies

American religious history has generally been turbulent and pervaded by conflict and controversy. Yet, as various scholars have recently noted, the period from the end of World War II until the early or middle 1970s was characterized by a *relative* mitigation of religious conflict and controversy. Cuddihy (1978) has analyzed the developments that by 1950 had led

Catholic, Jewish, and mainstream Protestant communities to water down their traditional exclusivist mystiques (for example, the One True Church, the meaning of Jewish "chosenness") in a process of assimilation to a broader American "religion of civility." Cuddihy speaks of the earlier situation of tense and antagonistic religious pluralism in the United States as "the era of 'cold war' and 'coexistence' between Protestantism, Catholicism, and Judaism, and between all of them and [American] civil religion, [which] gave way in post-World War America (1945–75) to a *thirty year period of religious ecumenism and theological detente*" (Cuddihy 1978, 28, our emphasis). By the 1960s, anti-Semitism and anti-Catholicism were conspicuously on the wane.

The intra-Protestant conflict between "fundamentalists" and "modernists" (now more frequently referred to as a conflict between "conservatives" and "liberals") also appeared to be somewhat muted in the post–World War II period. As Wuthnow notes, "it was the experience of World War II that had drawn conservatives and liberals closer to a common center" (1988, 143).[2] The onset of the Cold War and the felt need for Christian unity in the face of the "menace of communism" also tended to encourage the downplaying of theological differences among Christians (Wuthnow 1988).

In general, in the relatively consensual period lasting from the 1940s through the early 1970s it was widely assumed that, as one Christian writer affirmed in 1943, "the attempt to identify true religion with a specific theological pattern may be regarded as having failed" (quoted in Wuthnow 1988, 141). This period has been termed the "Eisenhower period" in American religious history (Robbins 1983, 1985a), an appellation which is intended to refer "to the former president's alleged statement that every American should have a religion and that he didn't care which religion the individual chose," which was frequently interpreted "as indicating that during this period, religion in general was viewed favorably and *particular religions were viewed as more or less interchangeable*" (Robbins 1985a, 172, emphasis in original).

Eisenhower, whose statement had probably been erroneously transcribed (Henry 1981), may not have meant to affirm theological indifference and the interchangeability of faiths. Nevertheless, the attitude that religion was vaguely good and that all religions deserve respect was widespread in the United States in the 1950s and 1960s (Herberg 1960; Turner 1983, 53–58). By the late 1960s various demographic trends as well as patterns of immigration, religious intermarriage, and denomination switching appeared to have undercut the sociocultural and religious "boundaries" separating different Protestant denominations, which throughout the 1950s and 1960s increasingly lost their distinctive demographic characteristics and cultural identities (Wuthnow 1988, 77–99).

Religions thus momentarily appeared less diversified and controversial in the 1950s and 1960s than had been previously or is presently the case. Of course there were "wild sects" in the 1950s and early 1960s (for example, West Virginia snake handlers), but they were assumed to appeal to a restricted southern, rural, and uneducated clientele. "Insofar as religion was found to be problematic, it was widely assumed to be 'safely' marginal" (Robertson 1985, 183). Fundamentalists were assumed to be restricted to the "Bible Belt," and the quiet nationwide growth of conservative evangelical and pentecostal Christian groups (Kelley 1972) was little noticed. Non-Christian religions (other than Judaism) such as Vedanta or Sufism appeared until the late 1960s to be restricted to bohemian artists and intellectuals (for example, beatniks), as well as certain alienated ethnics such as the "Black Muslims."

The relevance of religion to American politics seemed to be declining, particularly after the election of John F. Kennedy in 1960 as our first Catholic president. On the world stage, theistic religion seemed to be a less conspicuous political force than it appears to be today; for example, the most salient antagonists of American policy in the Mideast marched under the banner of secular ideologies such as Marxism and "Nasserism." Catholicism in Eastern Europe appeared quiescent and politically impotent; the Catholic Church also seemed to be "captive" in Latin America, the tame auxiliary of autocratic conservative regimes (while insurgent forces such as "Castroism" were Marxist and anticlerical).

In the United States, Christian churches tended in the decades after World War II to emphasize *individual piety,* an emphasis which "was consistent with broader individualistic orientations in American culture, as religious leaders themselves were quick to point out" (Wuthnow 1988, 57). A corollary of this emphasis was the view that the churches could best contribute to general social betterment by shaping the values of individual Christians rather than by direct social action. Both liberal and conservative Protestant leaders strongly affirmed the separation of church and state. When, under the impact of the movements for civil rights and against the Vietnam War, a number of (mainline) Christian leaders began to embrace political activism in the late 1960s, conservative Christian leaders such as erstwhile segregationist Jerry Falwell initially responded by reaffirming the primary responsibility of the churches for the "cure of souls" and the enhancement of individual piety, a nonpolitical attitude which was implicitly political but still *overtly* nonpolitical and nonconfrontational. Liberal activist clergy became dangerously isolated from the laity, which remained more conservative theologically and politically

(Hadden 1969). Large-scale conservative Christian activism—the Moral Majority—was not really evident until the mid-1970s.

Today the atmosphere is markedly changed compared to the postwar decades. Perhaps what stands out about the contemporary religious science is its *controversiality*, as Robert Wuthnow notes:

> On all sides American religion seems to be embroiled in controversy. Whether it be acrimonious arguments about abortion, lawsuits over religion in the public schools, questions over who is most guilty of mixing religion and politics, or discussions of America's military presence in the world, religion seems to be in the thick of it. Scarcely a statement is uttered by one religious group on the issues without another faction of the religious community taking umbrage. The issues themselves shift almost continuously, but the underlying sense of polarization and acrimony continues. (1988, 6)

Religion, Social Science, and Secularization

Increasingly controversial, newsworthy, and threatening, religion is now more interesting and relevant to persons who are not themselves religious or, in Max Weber's words, "religiously musical." Some formerly "nonmusical" persons have rediscovered the value of religion as a vital medium of social protest and mobilization which can be utilized to promote social change. Others have become alarmed at the destructive potentialities of religion in exacerbating ethnic, national, and class cleavages, or in allegedly deranging persons and promoting irrational and violent behavior (for example, Jonestown and "cults").

Modernization and Secularization Theory

But these thoughts are not entirely compatible with the thrust of much of the influential sociological writing about religion in the 1960s and 1970s, in which religion was "relegated to the margins of sociological activity," as noted by James Beckford in his contribution to this volume. In recent decades scholars have envisioned the fundamental process of *modernization* to be increasingly pushing religion, or at least theistic and supernaturalistic religion, into an increasingly isolated and marginal position in the advanced culture and society of North America and Western Europe. We refer here to what is often termed the *secularization thesis*, which "contends that modernity is intrinsically and irreversibly antagonistic to religion" and affirms that "As a society becomes increasingly modernized it inevitably becomes less religious" (Berger 1982, 14). As a society becomes more "modern," the authority and significance of religion is said to diminish through the continuous process of *rationalization,* or "the way in which society becomes increasingly subject to rules, regulations and a scientific outlook" (Lyon 1985, 24), and the ongoing "disenchantment of the world," or the waning of supernaturalist beliefs.

Particularly vital to this model is the posited *privatization* of religion in modern societies. Modern religion has been said to be relinquishing its influence on and concern with the dominant institutional structures of the society (for example, politics, welfare, education) and relegating itself to the private realm of intimate familial and small group processes (for example, "the family that prays together stays together") and to the nuances of personal identity and morale. Bryan Wilson writes:

> Religion becomes privatized. In a consumer society it becomes just another consumer good, a leisure-time commodity no longer affecting the centers of power or the operation of the system—even at the level of social control, socialization, and the organization of the emotions and motivations. Religion becomes a matter of choice, but whatever religion is chosen is of no consequence to the operation of the social system. (1976, 277)

Religion in modern society has thus often been said to be *marginalized*. "The forces of modernity are said to push the realm of feeling, symbol and the spiritual to the edge of society" (Lyon 1985, 58). Religion is driven from "the naked public square" (Neuhaus, 1984) and ceases to exert a major influence on institutional systems such as education (for example, no more prayers in public schools). Religiously based norms such as those prohibiting abortion or sodomy cease to be enforced by public authority. Religion "withdraws from public life," but even in the private realm religion's influence has been thought to be somewhat diminished; for example, sexual feelings become detached from the doctrine of original sin.

Reconsidering Religion: Religion and Power

The secularization thesis has certainly not gone unchallenged. It is challenged by various contributors to the present volume (for example, Hadden, Stark, Beckford). The theory has been vigorously, even ubiquitously debated (Wilson 1985). But James Beckford (1985a) argues that "the primacy accorded to debates about secularization processes" has not been beneficial to the sociology of religion; "the fact that sociological studies of religion have been dominated by considerations of its allegedly growing insignificance has created the impression that religion is not a topic worthy of serious study" (Beckford 1985a, 350). According to Beckford, "the dominant concern with secularization tends to separate the sociological study of religion from the study of other social processes, forces and conditions'' (Beckford 1985a, 350).

Beckford does not really claim that the influence of the secularization model has entailed an outright denial of the idea that religion can exert influence on other social institutions and on the total society. Rather, Beckford complains that religion has too frequently been seen influencing the total society only on a very general level and primarily through processes such as socialization and individual character formation. In his essay reprinted in the present volume, Beckford notes that sociologists have too often tended to see religion as ''the wallpaper of the social system''; that is, religion is always there in the background, but it has not been viewed, at least in the short term, as a contender for power, a contester of social policies, a mobilizer of protest, a promoter of change and innovation, or an interpreter not only of personal but of social and international stressful situations.

In the 1980s, various characteristics of religion, including its enhanced political relevance and its embodiment in dynamic movements that can transform the personal identities of converts, have influenced the sociology of religion toward a greater theoretical focus on *power*. '' There is nowadays,'' writes James Beckford in his essay in the present volume, ''a sharper awareness of the deliberate attempts being made to bring about certain effects in the name of religion.'' Sociologists of religion no longer see religion as interesting primarily ''as part of a general apparatus of socialization and social control supplying meaning through culture.'' Religion is acquiring a sociological importance ''in its own right as a sphere of activity where efforts are deliberately made to influence, manipulate and control peoples' thoughts, feelings, and actions in accordance with various religious values.''

Sociologists of religion studying religious movements are now increasingly directing their focus to the sense of *empowerment* as a core element of contemporary religious experience, for example, the empowerment of women in spiritualist groups (Haywood 1983). In this connection several papers in this volume, such as Janet Jacobs's paper on women's healing rituals and the paper by Mary Jo Neitz on feminist neopagan mystiques, deal with the theme of empowerment in contemporary feminist spiritual movements; for example, by identifying with *The Goddess,* devotees become aware of their capacity to transcend stereotypical feminine passivity.

The connection between religion and power is currently frequently made in contemporary media. Meredith McGuire, who has researched healing groups, writes:

A few years ago, when *Star Wars* gave us the phrase, "May the Force be with you," sociologists of religion were able to smile knowingly and perhaps tuck this example into a lecture on Durkheim's theory of religious "force." What I found extremely interesting was the readiness of the media to accept the imagery and plausibility of this blatantly religious conception, which bypassed conventional religious terms, yet could be easily translated into them. "The Force" was not an utterly remote power; rather, a human being in tune with it could tap it for enormous personal powers—with material effects and consequences for life and death. The notion of "The Force" in popular imagery bears remarkable resemblance to conceptions of power articulated by respondents in my own researches. (1983b, 3)

Beckford's emphasis on *power* in and through religion is hardly new (for example, Yinger 1946). His conception of a sociology of religion oriented more toward power has not been fully developed in the present contribution. But it is convergent with other current scholarly and intellectual currents. Thus as religiopolitical movements such as the New Christian Right, Catholic Liberation Theology, and Militant Islamic currents have gained prominence, political intellectuals and scholars have rediscovered religion, which is increasingly perceived as a fundamental medium of social protest and mobilization. As such, it increasingly becomes *the prism through which a variety of issues and stresses are interpreted and reacted to*. In recent decades various signs of increasing moral pluralism such as the spread of pornography, the legitimation of homosexuality, the "threat" of world communism, and the spectre of crime and drugs have been interpreted for their devotees by fundamentalist and Pentecostal preachers, including TV evangelists whose doctrines and rhetoric confer meaning and unity on anomic developments by integrating them into a single apocalyptic vision of a corrupt society on the eve of destruction (or possibly of redemption). The terrifying AIDS epidemic is also grist for the apocalyptic mill, as Susan Palmer's contribution to this volume indicates. The farm crisis of the middle and late 1980s also affords a basis for religious interpretation and mobilization, as shown in Barbara Hargrove's contribution, which depicts divergent populist-fundamentalist, New Age, and mainstream religious responses to agrarian distress.

Persistent Secularist Tendencies

The increasingly criticized secularization thesis still has much to recommend it. The privatization of religion or the latter's alleged modern retreat from the public realm may now be undergoing a partial reversal; yet overall, the influence of churches over key societal institutions and realms such as education, politics, or care for the impoverished (welfare) has probably waned since the nineteenth century (not to mention the Middle Ages). Substantial compartmentalization, or "structural differentiation," of religion from other institutions has prevailed. While diverse groups such as the evangelical Moral Majority or Catholic bishops opining on nuclear weapons and economic policies are endeavoring to break out of isolation and religious compartmentalization, other forces are working to maintain or strengthen this compartmentalization and even further diminish the area of religious authority and competence; for example, attempts to sue churches for "clergy malpractice" in the area of pastoral counseling for suicidally depressed persons who might otherwise be referred to secular psychiatrists. In the Middle Ages buying and selling were partially regulated by Christian conceptions of the "just price" and the religious disparagement of usury. Today the atmosphere is very different, and clerics who opine publicly on economic matters are likely to be sharply rebuked for economic incompetence and for their arrogant presumption in butting in on practical matters. As reported by Robert Wuthnow:

> [T]he Catholic bishops' pastoral letter on economic justice was roundly criticized by defenders of current economic policies. Writing in the *New York Times,* economist Leonard Silk took explicit issue with the bishops' religious arguments and suggested subjecting theses arguments to "higher standards" of efficiency and self-interest. Robert J. Samuelson [eminent economist], writing in the *Washington Post,* declared that the bishops were simply engaged in an act of "economic make-believe." Echoing the same sentiment, columnist George F. Will charged the bishops with "childlike innocence," "vanity," "flight from complexity," and a "comic sense of moral bravery." (1988, 258)

The Surge of Militant Traditionalism

Even in the quantitative terms of the alleged decline of religion, there is some evidence affirming continuing secularization processes. As the present editors noted in 1983:

> Until recently, the evidence regarding religious attitudes would seem to support the secularization thesis for both Western Europe and the United States. In Western Europe, church membership has declined throughout the twentieth century. In the United States, membership in mainline Protestant churches . . . [experienced] a brief upswing in the 1950s followed by a decline in the 1960s. But during that period there has been a shift in the content of beliefs within those mainline Protestant denominations . . . a decline in belief in the supernaturalistic motifs of those religions, which have been interpreted as having only 'symbolic' meaning. . . . [T]hese developments are compatible with the secularization perspectives . . . which imply some mode of rational humanism as the best hope for human progress. (Anthony, Robbins, and Schwartz 1983, 2)

But "recent trends challenge the secularization perspective":

> Liberal mainstream religion has not continued to grow during the late 1960s and 1970s. On the other hand, in the United States there has been a rapid growth in the conservative and fundamentalist Protestant churches while the liberal denominations have either declined or remained static. Even within Catholicism there are marked evangelical tendencies and Pentecostal or "charismatic" movements. The most dynamic parts of Judaism currently seem to be the neo-Orthodox revival and the growth of quasi-sectarian groups such as the [C]hassidim. (Anthony, Robbins, and Schwartz 1983, 2)

Does the growth of evangelical-conservative churches and Orthodox Jewish groups challenge the secularization thesis, as several of our contributors suggest? Or does secularization itself generate militant traditionalist reactions as well as spiritual innovation (Wilson 1976)? According to Gallup Poll data the share of adults who state religious preferences has *declined* by 6 percent over the last two decades. But, simultaneously, the number of religious bookstores has grown from 1,700 in 1972 to 4,100 in 1984, and sales of books, music, and other materials used by evangelical, fundamentalist, and Pentecostal groups are booming (Edmondson 1988). As with service industries, there is a new, *highly specialized religious market*. "Consumers now demand choice and diversity in all things including worship." Episcopalian, Presbyterian, and other large mainline Protestant denominations have experienced sharp losses of membership since the mid-1960s, "while the number of small fundamentalist, independent, and nondenominational churches has grown rapidly" (Edmondson 1988, 30). Such churches are growing in part because they appeal to the specialized needs of consumers who want to choose a particular church adapted to their particular needs; this is often a small, born-again church, "which will be more likely than large mainline churches to adapt their services to the specific needs of their congregation" (Edmondson 1988, 30). These patterns may be consistent with those theories of modernization that stress specialization and differentiation.

The members and leaders of mushrooming small independent churches tend to be theologically as well as politically conservative, yet there is marked diversity among such groups with regard to spiritual style and mode of worship. Many charismatics and Pentecostals believe in "gifts of the Holy Spirit," which manifest through speaking in tongues, prophecy, or miraculous healing, of which some staid fundamentalists disapprove (Ammerman 1987).

Finally, the rubrics of traditionalist resurgence and spiritual innovation might both be applied to the growth of *Islam* in the United States in recent decades. The numbers of American Moslems are presently being augmented by immigration from Asia, Africa, and the Mideast, and by the growing conversion of black Americans to Islam (*N.Y. Times,* Feb. 21, 1989, p. 1A). The latter more often tend to embrace varieties of Sunni orthodoxy rather than to become Black Muslims of the Nation of Islam sect or followers of controversial former Nation of Islam minister Louis Farrakhan. The growth of Islam in the United States is regarded warily by some Jews, who fear an attenuation of American support for Israel, and by some Americans who misperceive Islam exclusively in terms of the intolerance, violent rhetoric, and anti-Americanism of the Ayatollah Khomeini, the "Imam" of Iranian Shiíte Moslems. Although the growth of Islam in the United States undercuts the vision of some conservative evangelicals of a Judeo-Christian spiritual hegemony in the United States, the repugnance which so many American Moslems feel for rampant moral permissiveness in America, convergent with the attitudes of the evangelical "Moral Majority."

It is notable, however, that Farrakhan and other unorthodox leaders do have followings among blacks, particularly in prisons (Batiuk, 1988) and in crime and poverty ridden central cities. Islam may provide for some urban blacks a way expressing anti-establishment protest while simultaneously promoting the rejection of deviant styles involving drug use, alcoholism, etc. The current intensification of the problems of AIDS and "crack" in urban "ghetto" areas may conceivably set the stage for a Christian evangelical and/or Islamic revival among urban black Americans, who may be attracted to religious mystiques of purity and discipline.

Traditionalist Revival, Modernization, and the Study of Religion

Although the surge of traditionalist religion may be indicative of some shortcomings of models of secularization and modernization, it is no less significant that the *neotraditionalist surge is itself a consequence of modernization processes* and their unsettling impact. Fundamentalist churches, notes Ammerman (1987, 8), "are most likely to be found at the points where tradition is meeting modernity rather than where modernity is most remote." Fundamentalist churches thrive in suburbia, which is populated "at least in part by people who grew up in small-town religion and find the more agnostic urban world in which they now live untenable" (Ammerman 1987, 8).

We have quoted Beckford (1985a) to the effect that the primacy of the secularization model has had some unfortunate effects on the sociology and scientific study of religion. One such effect was the inadequate preparation of intellectuals and social scientists of the 1960s and early 1970s for the growth of certain kinds of groups that did not appear to fit a secularized culture. Acceptably *modern* religion was expected to "know its place" and not challenge the compartmentalization of life into separate religious and secular realms. It was not expected to highlight supernaturalist and intuitive-emotional (irrational) themes. Religions which did not conform to modern norms were expected to wane and, when they did not do so, were sometimes stigmatized as psychopathological conditions associated with brainwashing (Robbins and Anthony 1982).

The pervasive stigmatization of antimodern religious movements reflects the fact that the rise of such groups *had not been anticipated* by many intelligentsia influenced by the premise of progressive secularization. If the rise of guru groups and religiotherapeutic movements in the 1970s surprised some scholars, the resurgence of traditionalist Christian and Islamic movements in the 1980s has been particularly discordant from the standpoint of the secularization premise (Hadden and Shupe 1986), as Mary Douglas has noted:

> No one, however, foresaw the recent revivals of traditional forms. According to extensive literature, religious change in modern times happens in only two ways—the falling off of worship in traditional churches, and the appearance of new cults, not expected to endure. No one credited the traditional religions with enough vitality to inspire large-scale political revolt . . . thus no one foretold the resurgence of Islam. Its well-known expansion in Africa was not expected to presage anything for its strength in modern Arabia—but why not? Habituated as we are to Catholic bishops supporting reactionary forces in South America, who was ready to interpret their radical politics in other parts of that continent? The civil war conducted in Lebanon in the rival names of Catholicism and Islam was not on the syllabus of courses on religious change, any more than was the terrorism always threatening to turn the strife of Irish Catholics and Protestants into civil war. Perhaps these bloody events have been classified as religious continuity rather than change, or perhaps religious studies were too polite to talk about the bad religious things happening abroad. But the explicitly Catholic uprising in Poland, which evokes deep Western admiration, was as unpredicted as the rise of fundamentalist churches in America. (1982, 25)

"Religious studies," according to Douglas, "were taken unawares because of the rigid structure of their assumptions. Their eyes were glued to those conditions of modern life identified by Weber as antipathetic to religion" (1982, 25). Specifically, Douglas criticizes the assumptions of the *fundamental beneficence of religion*—"good for the human psyche"— which blinds intellectuals to the ugly, bigoted, and violent aspects of religion—and the assumptive *antithesis of religion and modernity*. The latter premise suggests that "moderns are utterly different from everyone else because of modernization" (Douglas 1982, 26).

The surge of militant neotraditionalist movements throughout the world has also impressed other scholars: "The near simultaneous birth of the Moral Majority in the United States and the stormy rise to power of Shiite Moslems led by Ayatollah Khomeini in Iran gave us cause to consider whether we were experiencing a *world-wide revolutionary tide of religio-political fundamentalism"* (Hadden and Shupe 1986, *xiii,* our emphasis). Hadden and Shupe feel that this surging tide has rather negative implications for the oversimplified "linear image of history" manifested by standard models of modernization and secularization, which proclaim an inexorable "process whereby modern societies are removed from the domination of religious institutions" (Hadden and Shupe 1986, *xii*). They suggest "that rather than some linear trend of secularization, we are currently riding the crest of a cyclical process in which progressive forces of secularization generate the alienation and discontent that facilitate intermittent religious revival and revitalization" (Hadden and Shupe 1986, *xv*).

A similar view has been developed in more detail by Stark and Bainbridge (1985), and is briefly summarized in Stark's paper on Mormon growth rates for the present volume, which also affirms "a model of alternating periods of secularization and revival." Stark's model concedes that "modernization does in fact seem to have stimulated a period of very rapid and extreme secularization. . . . Modernization has been causing major dislocations, often wreaking havoc with the dominant religious organizations in rapidly changing societies." These rapid changes have provided the context for the development of both new movements and revivalist, neotraditionalist surges. As Jeffrey Hadden (1987a) notes, the present political mobilization of conservative evangelicals has been preceded by decades of rapid secularization in the institutional realm, particularly in public education, for example, the banning of public prayers in public schools and the diminished attention paid to religion in school curricula (see also Hunter 1983a; Wuthnow 1988).

One of the basic responses of conservative Christians to the secularization and centralizing bureaucratization of the public sphere is the vast proliferation of *Christian schools* in the 1980s (Peshkin 1986; Rose 1988), which is discussed by Susan Rose in this volume. Through such institutions young Christians may be provided with "God-centered" education and insulated both from perceived insidious humanistic trends affecting curricula and from the seeming chaos of public schools in terms of violence, drugs, indiscipline, strikes, and sexual freedom. The hope, Rose notes, is to crystallize "close-knit networks of family, church, and school" which will mediate the transmission of traditional values and sustain autonomy from the broader culture, which is viewed as corrupted by false values. "It is not just evolution or sex education or lack of discipline that

Fundamentalists hold against public schools," notes Nancy Ammerman in her study, *Bible Believers,* it is also "the assumption that all problems can be solved by human effort and that variations in lifestyle should be respected" (Ammerman 1987, 190).

In his paper, "The Limits of Modernity," which is reprinted here, Irving Horowitz also sees the fundamentalist surge as partly a protest against modernization. In his view, both the modernizing disruptions and the antimodern protest have *global* dimensions, so that the conservative Christian revival in the United States bears some relation to the militant traditionalist Moslem movements in Egypt, Iran, and elsewhere, as well as to the Catholic revival in Eastern Europe.

Many social scientists, including Dr. Horowitz, are wary of the politicized surge of moralistic traditionalism in American religion, and warn of possible negative consequences in terms of "authoritarian-domestic politics" and a fundamentalist challenge to "the pluralistic value base of American society." Paradoxically, Horowitz also emphasizes the democratic and *antielitist* dimension of the worldwide fundamentalist surge. Contemporary modernizing, rationalizing, and secularizing forces tend to encourage the enhancement of the authority of experts (including sociologists), whose policies often tend to undercut traditional values and customs and promote centralized bureaucratic control of local institutions such as schools.

In both American society and Third World societies, argues Horowitz, the modernizing mystique of *development* has tended to be an elitist vision put forth in the name of the people, as the latter are often assumed to be incapable of comprehending modern complexities. Both the "cult of the individual" in the West and the militant traditionalist renewal represent demands for simplification, "for a world in which answers are known." The current surge of fundamentalism in American life "rests on an ideology based on solutions—the truth through Providence." On this level, "the fundamentalism of the Middle East may have a direct relationship to similar events in American society."

The important contribution by Frank Lechner provides a provocative complement to Horowitz's paper. Horowitz has implicitly used a broad cross-cultural definition of "fundamentalism" that transcends the specific tradition of American Protestant fundamentalism. Such a broad conception is also implicit in evocations (for example, by Hadden and Shupe 1986) of a worldwide fundamentalist surge. Lechner makes explicit a broad, cross-cultural conception of fundamentalism "as a value-oriented, antimodern, dedifferentiating form of collective action—*a sociocultural movement aimed at reorganization of all spheres of life in terms of a particular set of absolute values"* (our emphasis). The awkward term "dedifferentiating" is the key. In sociological modernization theory it is the *structural differentiation* of modern society which produces the compartmentalization of religion, which thus becomes set apart from other institutions (for example, businesses, schools) and restrictively privatized. As a dedifferentiating movement, fundamentalism seeks to reassert the cultural and *institutional* primacy of traditional values and their relevance to politics, economics, education, etc. Thus Christian fundamentalists in the United States want to "bring God back into the schools," and eliminate humanist or man-centered (as opposed to God-centered) textbooks. "Islamic fundamentalists" (not mentioned by Lechner) want to reinstate Koranic criminal punishments in the legal system and maintain the patriarchal submission of women. "Christian Reconstructionists" want to institutionalize Old Testament law in the United States (Boston 1988; Cavanaugh 1988).

Although it is antimodern in the sense of wanting to reverse structural differentiation in society, fundamentalism, in Lechner's sense, is also *a distinctly modern phenomenon,* which only exists because the society has indeed become highly differentiated, modernized, and secularized. While Mary Douglas may be correct in complaining that assumptions about secularization and modernization prevented social scientists from forecasting the revitalization of fundamentalism, from Lechner's perspective a surge of fundamentalism does not necessarily discredit these assumptions. Indeed, Lechner's analysis doubly vindicates the secularization-modernization model because he predicts that the new revivalism will, like past American revivals, manifest unintended modernizing and secularizing consequences and will ultimately enhance the very differentiation and moral and spiritual pluralism which upsets traditionalists (see also Lechner 1985).

One of the empirical problems confronting the thesis of a "worldwide fundamentalist religiopolitical surge" is the relative weakness of populist political mobilization based on television preaching in Britain (Wallis and Bruce 1986, 227–53) and Canada (Simpson 1987). The weakness of evangelical Moral Majority politics in Britain may be due to a number of factors, including Britain's greater cultural secularity and weaker religious revivalism in the twentieth century, compared to the United States. But a key role is certainly played by the more centralized and cohesive control of the media in Britain so that the latter have become somewhat homogenous, balanced, and *not accessible to the control of religious and political minorities.* "Even 'commercial' stations are not permitted to sell air-time" (Wallis and Bruce 1986, 250). Opportunities for political mobilization based on evangelical control of significant media are therefore lacking, although the decentralizing media policies of the Thatcher government may create future opportunities! Regulatory policies in the United States (see below) have been more permissive.

The "Electronic Church"

In recent years both evangelical political mobilization and several garish scandals have focused attention on TV evangelists. This topic has recently generated significant sociological research (Frankl 1984; Hadden 1987a; Hadden and Shupe 1987, 1988; Hadden and Swann 1981; Hoover 1988) as well as abundant media commentary and governmental investigations.

One sociological aspect of the scandals and flamboyant eccentricities that have surrounded such figures as Jimmy Swaggert, Jim and Tammy Bakker, and Oral Roberts is the volatile quality of *charismatic authority* (originally analyzed by Max Weber) and its resistance to routinization and institutionalized stability and accountability. TV evangelists are quintessential *performers;* the success of their operations depends upon their ability to entertain, to inspire, and to make persons feel good. The projection of the personalities and communicational skills of the performers is so central to their televangelical ministries that, given the vital element of fervent religious devotion, a setting is created in which it is rather difficult to consolidate institutional constraints and mechanisms of accountability which might guarantee the responsibility of operations and prevent financial mismanagement as well as reckless and unspiritual (for example, sexually promiscuous) behavior on the part of the preacher. Thus leading TV evangelists such as Swaggert have staffed their organizations with relatives (for example, Mrs. Swaggert, son Donny Swaggert) and flunkies, who are not in a position to restrain their "star."

The position of TV preachers is somewhat similar to that of gurus and cult leaders, who have been said to exercise charismatic authority uninhibited by institutionalized mechanisms of financial and behavioral accountability (Ofshe 1986). Financial corruption and other modes of deviance are augmented by the tendency toward the "deification of idiosyncrasy" whereby the whims and foibles of the charismatic leader are interpreted by adoring devotees as signs of special spiritual inspiration (Lifton 1979). The difference between televangelists and gurus, however, is that the former have more grass-roots supporters, in part because, notwithstanding their innovations, they are seen to exemplify the "Old Time Religion," and thus they wield considerable cultural power (see the contribution of Demerath and Williams to this volume) which cults do not possess.

It has also been suggested in the media that preachers such as Reverend Swaggert and Reverend Bakker get in trouble because they are charismatic not only in the sociological (Weberian) sense but also in the Christian sense of Pentecostalism and "gifts of the Spirit" such as speaking in tongues, prophecy, healing, and other actions associated with a flamboyant, emotional, and ecstatic style of worship and preaching. This mode of preaching is sometimes said to attract rather impulsive and emotional persons who achieve a release through their preaching but who find it difficult to be otherwise strictly ascetic. Perhaps more importantly, the legitimating mystique of charismatic ministries tends to stress that God or the Holy Spirit is working through the ministry and is responsible for its successes (the humble preacher is merely a medium for the work of the divine agent). This rationale can easily be distorted in an antinomian direction in which divine agency can be seen as endorsing the seeming transgressions of the minister.

As Jeffrey Hadden (1987a; see also his paper in this volume) has noted, the politico-legal foundation for contemporary televangelical empires was a 1960 policy directive of the Federal Communications Commission (FCC) that implied "that local stations could sell airtime for religious programs and still get 'public interest credit' in the eyes of FCC overseers" (Hadden 1987a, 16). Subsequently "evangelical and fundamentalist syndicators rushed in to compete" for airtime, thereby enhancing the value of the time slots. "As a result many local stations which had previously followed network policies of not selling airtime for broadcasting decided to cash in on the new demand." Gradually programs sponsored by Jewish groups or by the Catholic Church and mainline (liberal) Protestant denominations, which had been based largely on freely donated airtime, "have been virtually squeezed off the air" (Hadden 1987a, 17). The new evangelical shows are more emotional and revivalist than the disappearing mainline shows, and they devote more time to explicit on-air appeals for funds.

The substantial monies that have been accumulated have been utilized to build sizeable off-camera empires: colleges, cathedrals, hospitals, charitable projects, Disney-style theme parks, etc. Jerry Falwell's founding of the Moral Majority was a pioneering extension of this diversification into political mobilization. Further innovations have been made by Pat Robertson, whose "blending of religion, politics, and economic analysis on the *700 Club* has elevated his personal status as a respectable conservative spokesperson" (Hadden 1987a, 15). In his present contribution, Dr. Hadden reassesses a decade of evangelical political activism and probes the impact of Rev. Robertson's 1988 presidential campaign and the future prospects of the New Christian Right and televangelism.

Crisis of Fundamentalist Apocalypticism

Since World War II, according to psychiatrist Robert Lifton, the nuclear "imagery of extinction" has encouraged a surge of apocalyptic and cultic movements embodying a "symbolization of immortality" (Lifton 1985). In the early 1980s William Martin (1982) described the "growing interest in apocalyptic prophecy" and the discussion of the putatively imminent "last days" by televangelists such as Oral Roberts, Pat Robertson, Jerry Falwell, and Rex Humbard and by authors such as Hal Lindsey, whose popular book *The Late Great Planet Earth* (1970) has sold over twenty million copies. "No hard data are available, but millions of American evangelicals apparently believe that within the present generation . . . Jesus will return to lay the groundwork for a glorious thousand-year reign on earth" (Martin 1982, 30).

According to Ammerman (1987), a basic component of modern Protestant fundamentalism is "dispensational premillennialism," according to which the Second Coming of Christ will be preceded by the reign of Antichrist and the horrendous Great Tribulation. According to Lindsey (1970), during the Tribulation a totalitarian world government will establish a universal false religion and "will seek total control over humanity by requiring that every person wear a mark or number (probably 666—designated 'Mark of the Beast,' Revelation 13:16–18) in order to buy and sell" (Martin 1982, 32).

Hal Lindsey's writings, like the preachings of TV evangelist Jimmy Swaggert, represent the "pre-tribulationist" version of premillennial apocalypticism, according to which "saved" Christians *will not have to endure the tribulation* but will be "raptured," or beamed to Heaven shortly before the coming of Antichrist. In contrast, "post-tribulationist" premillennials believe that the Faithful will have to survive the tribulation, during which they will have to employ survival techniques to avoid starvation or imprisonment by demonic authorities. A kind of secularized post-tribulationism has also been popular in recent decades and is embodied in numerous books with titles similar to *How You Can Survive the Coming Financial Collapse*. On the other hand, the growth of computerization, the proliferation of credit cards, and the rise of giant shopping malls have been interpreted by some Christians as foreshadowing the coming demonic 666 control system. The spread of cults and New Age beliefs and practices have been seen, along with ecumenism in the churches, as anticipating the universal antireligion to be established by Antichrist.

Recently, in the late 1980s, some TV preachers, such as Pat Robertson or Jerry Falwell, seem to have been deemphasizing premillennial apocalypticism and the imminent fulfillment of biblical prophecies. In part this may be due to the inconsistency between the *fatalistic* implications of premillennialism (Christians cannot stop the advent of Antichrist, who will only be destroyed by a heavenly army) and the dynamic political mobilization of the New Christian Right. Implicit in the increasing political activism of evangelicals is a postmillennial outlook; that is, a view that *Christians can themselves build the Kingdom of God on earth* through gradual transformation of the sociopolitical status quo in a direction consonant with God's laws (Boston 1988). Sociologist Joel Barnhart (1988) and Jeffrey Hadden (1987a) and postmillennial "Dominion" theologian Gary North (1986) have recently noted that various evangelical and fundamentalist preachers such as Jerry Falwell are now *acting as if they were postmillennialists*. Barnhart (1988) feels that this situation reflects "the ambivalence of the American evangelical movement toward its own sociopolitical power and influence." Jeffrey Hadden suggests (1987a) that since premillennialism is an "eschatology of defeat and despair," the Christian Right will increasingly ignore premillennial prophecy, perhaps without explicitly repudiating it.

On the other hand, as Anthony and Robbins point out in their concluding contribution to this volume, some new movements have developed in the context of the conservative Christian political mobilization that make an open break with premillennialism and that envision *Christian activism creating the basis for the millennium and the construction of God's kingdom*. Many of these new groups and thinkers have been influenced by the Christian Reconstruction or Theonomy Movement (Cavanaugh 1988) and its leading theorist, R. J. Rushdoony, who envisions the eventual establishment of Mosaic law (including the stoning of adulterers and the death penalty for homosexuals!). More immediately significant may be the Dominion Theologies of Gary North, James Chilton, and others, which are less austere but a bit more apocalyptic in tone (Boston 1988). North (1986) denounces fundamentalist premillennialism as an escapist phantasy that would allow evildoers and New Age neopagans to rule the world while true Christians wait passively for the Rapture. But, "a new fundamentalism is appearing" (North 1986, 393). Some large evangelical congregations have accepted Dominion Theology (Moyers 1987).[3]

But the 1980s also present *opportunities* as well as challenges to doomsaying apocalyptic prophecy. In her provocative contribution, Susan Palmer discusses how various movements possessing different apocalyptic ideologies have interpreted, appropriated, and exploited the horrifying spectre of the AIDS epidemic. *Pestilence* has often been a key ingredient of apocalyptic and tribulationist visions! The AIDS crisis is likely to have a significant impact on religious ferment in the coming decade, and its influence may be seen not only in apocalyptic visions (Palmer 1988) but also in renewed religious legitimations for teenage celibacy and adult monogamy (or "pro-family" religion), and possibly in healing rituals.

Other Church Trends

The other side of the growth of conservative Christian groups during past decades has been the decline or stasis of the great mainline and liberal churches, such as Congregationalist, Presbyterian, Methodist, Episcopalian, etc. (Roof and McKinney 1987). The "Protestant puzzle" of the simultaneous retreat of some mainline groups and the resurgence of other conservative and supposedly antimodern traditions is discussed by Perrin and Mauss in their contribution. The authors attempt to evaluate the relative usefulness of various "explanations" for observed tendencies, including demographic factors, secularization theory, the impact of the counterculture of the 1960s and 1970s, and Dean Kelley's influential commitment thesis (Kelley 1972). The decline of liberal Protestantism is also discussed in this volume by McKinney and Roof, who see mainline denominationalism squeezed into a precarious middle ground between, on the one hand, New Age groups and other "privatized religious expressions" catering to "a therapeutic mentality," and on the other hand, the resurgence of a "more aggressive conservative Protestantism seeking to become the dominant culture-shaping force in America."

The proportion of Catholics in the American population has increased in the last few decades (Roof and McKinney 1987). But the Catholic Church has also experienced many defections. In his contribution, Andrew Greeley argues that rates of defection are diminishing and that the reasons why Catholics are now remaining in the church are increasingly unrelated to formal teachings and doctrine. The loyalty of most Catholics, which makes them "hang in there" (even if they want birth control), is largely ritualistic (sacramental), communitarian, and a matter of social identity; that is, being Catholic, like being American, helps make one at home in the world. One is part of a heritage.

On the other hand, American hispanics, particularly recent immigrants from Latin America, constitute one area in which the Catholic Church is losing ground to Protestant evangelical and pentecostal groups. Elsewhere Dr. Greeley has estimated that 23% of all Hispanic Americans are now Protestants, "and that approximately 60,000 Hispanic Americans a year join Protestant denominations" (Suro, 1989:14). The emotional power of evangelical revivalism and its emphasis on *miraculous healing* attracts Hispanic immigrants who are put off by the predominantly middle class hierarchical U.S. Catholic Church.

The Catholic Church in the United States is also a setting for divisive spiritual ferment and conflict. Diane Trebbi's short paper discusses feminist ferment in the church. But there are also dynamic conservative movements in American Catholicism. The Schismatic Church of Archbishop Lefevre, which opposes the reforms of Vatican II, has followers in the United States. There is also what Cuneo (1988) has termed the revivalist network within the American and Canadian Church. Nominally loyal to Vatican II, this network is linked to militant antiabortion protests and also challenges perceived clerical tendencies in the direction of support for feminism, homosexuality, social revolution, and other elements of cultural modernism. Rev. George Stallings heads a breakaway black Catholic group.

Catholic revivalists and Catholic Pentecostals, like Protestant fundamentalists and charismatics discussed by Lechner, Rose, and others are arguably reacting against modern tendencies toward cultural and moral pluralism and the compartmentalization of life into separate religious and secular spheres, which appears to traditionalists to shockingly limit the authority and relevance of sacred traditions in modern experience. The same might be said of the Chassidic Jewish group studied by Lynn Davidman, which she compares in her contribution to a more accommodative modern Orthodox synagogue. The struggles of American Judaism to adapt to modern secularizing, pluralizing, and compartmentalizing tendencies while preserving a vital residue of Jewish unity is discussed in this volume by Samuel Heilman, who discusses the divisions and conflicts within the American Jewish community.

Spiritual Innovation, New Age, and Quasi-Religious Movements

In his contribution, Rodney Stark views Mormonism as an innovative new religion or cult. As such it may have more in common, at least on one level, with "New Age" movements than with the Christian fundamentalist groups with which it shares many elements of social traditionalism and political conservatism. In their volume, *Understanding Cults*, Hexham and Poewe (1986) argue that Joseph Smith and other early Mormon leaders developed an innovative "mythology" which "placed human life within a framework of spiritual evolution" and which sought to integrate science and religion. It thus manifests some continuity not only with contemporary New Age movements but also to other nineteenth-century new religions such as Eddyism (Christian Science) and Theosophy.

Stark believes that the growth of Mormonism, as well as the development of many newer cults in the last two decades, requires a *revision*, though not a total abandonment, of secularization theory. Stark suggests a general "model of alternating periods of secularization and revival" (see also Stark and Bainbridge 1985). Secularization and modernization do indeed weaken the conventional faiths of a society, but this very circumstance tends to facilitate the emergence of new cults and movements which dynamically revitalize the religious milieu (see also Stark and Bainbridge 1985).

Two critical points might be noted. First, as Wallis and Bruce (1984b, 1986) have noted, the present defection from conventional churches exceeds the recruitment of new devotees to new groups. Second, Stark's revision of secularization theory does not really challenge the proposition that there has been a linear trend toward the compartmentalization and privatization of religion, and its consequent loss of influence in politics, education, social welfare, etc. Perhaps there is today a powerful attempt in the United States to reverse these trends; but it is the New Christian Right and the resurgent traditionalists who are in the vanguard of this movement, not, by and large, the exotic new cults. The Mormon Church, however, is also politically active and is alleged to operate a powerful, expanding politicoeconomic "empire" (Heinerman and Shupe 1987).

Dawning of the New Age

"Three decades ago, *reincarnation* would have been as unpronounceable as it was unknown. Add *guru, yoga, transcendental meditation* and a host of other words that are now common currency, and you will get some indication of the indirect influence of the consciousness revolution" (Burrows 1987, 88). Thus, a moderate evangelical critic of New Age spirituality acknowledges its present pervasiveness. A "multifaceted, multi-focused movement that is sociologically analogous in many ways to the evangelical community" has emerged. "The New Age Movement is not tied to any particular organization, has no overarching hierarchical structure, is diverse in both practice and belief—and although it has prominent spokespeople, has no official leadership." It consists of diverse beliefs, practices, and groups, which, however, may share "common world view assumptions about God or ultimate reality, humanity, and the nature of the human predicament" (Burrows, 1987, 88).

In the worldview which Burrows attributes to New Age spirituality, *ultimate reality* is unitary, or "oneness." "Ultimate reality or God is pure underdifferentiated energy, consciousness or life force." This force "manifests itself in creation as the dynamic interaction of polarities" such as good/evil, but these dualities "are not absolute," rather, "they are different facets of that single reality that unites all creation. In spite of appearances, all is one" (1987, 88).[4]

This worldview is sometimes called *monism*. The dichotomy of *monism* and *dualism* as conflicting worldviews permeating the present expanded religious pluralism is discussed in the final contribution by Anthony and Robbins. The dichotomy of monism/dualism is similar to the comparison by Hexham and Poewe (1986, 73–94) of the Hindu-Buddhist *Yogic* tradition and the Judeo-Christian-Islamic *Abramic* (or Abrahamic, from the Biblical

Abraham) tradition. Hexham and Poewe are also critics of New Age spirituality, which they see as an amalgam of Yogic and primitive magical or *Shamanic* beliefs and practices that are now challenging the partly secularized American Judeo-Christian tradition.

Humanity, in Burrow's typification of the implicit New Age worldview, is "an extension of God or ultimate reality . . . that divine essence is humanity's true, higher or real self" (Burrows 1987, 88). Fatuous or blasphemous *self-deification* is thus a charge frequently leveled against New Age spirituality (Groothuis, 1986). Humanity's predicament, according to Burrows, is viewed from the New Age perspective as *metaphysical ignorance,* or lack of spiritual enlightenment, that, however, can be dispelled by experiential knowledge of ultimate reality and the potentialities of consciousness. This knowledge can be obtained, in the view of many adherents, through "psycho-spiritual techniques that involve balancing polarities, manipulating energy and ridding consciousness of the fragmenting effects of reason and the predefining limitations of belief" (1987, 88). Evangelical Christians, on the other hand, affirm a more traditional definition of humanity's predicament in terms of man's sinful rebellion against God.

Finally, New Age mystiques often purvey an arguably somewhat post-millennial (see Susan Palmer's paper in this volume) apocalypticism whereby humanity is viewed as poised between two ages. "The perils of our time are interpreted not as the prelude to apocalyptic disaster, but to *evolutionary transformation*" (Burrows 1988, 88–89, our emphasis). The biological evolution of the human species is seen as shading over into the evolution of spiritual consciousness. Like nineteenth-century Theosophy and Christian Science, many New Age and quasi-monistic movements have "sought to integrate science, religion, and popular myth into an overall framework of evolutionary mythology that could fill the void left by the decline of traditional Christian views" (Hexham and Poewe 1986, 41).[5]

Hannigan (1988) argues that the ideology of the New Age milieux is characterized by an insistence upon the centrality of *self-healing* as the linchpin of global restructuring. A multiplicity of individual self-transformations will produce a "critical mass" effect which will lead to sociocultural healing and structural change. Similarly Beckford (1984) discusses the *holistic* imagery of "New Religious and Healing Movements," which embellishes the fundamental "holistic assumption that nature is one and indivisible" (1984, 269). As a "vehicle of the sacred," holistic imagery "provides a context of ultimate meaning for human life by stressing the interdependence between the bodily, spiritual and material dimensions of the human life-world" (1984, 270). Beckford argues that such holism is not

quite the same as spiritual privatism, mysticism, radical religious individualism, or the worship of humanity, which other scholars and critics have
identified as key features of contemporary religiotherapy movements.
Finally, Beckford notes that holistic imagery cuts across common distinctions between neo-Christian, neo-Oriental, and "Human Potential" movements, which may share some holistic themes.

Hannigan (1988) also emphasizes holistic elements in the New Age
movement, which tends toward holism, toleration of differences, and a
preference for *decentralization*. In this context it is difficult for any central
organized structure to develop within the broad New Age Movement (see
also Stark 1987). The values of toleration and decentralization encourage
maximum diversity and the multiplication of spiritual techniques. Vulgar
popularizations and sensationalist extremism cannot therefore be restrained, and the broader movement has some difficulty in attempting to
professionalize its services.

The sensationalist and extremist phenomena which Hannigan views as
obstacles to the mainstreaming of New Age spirituality include, most
conspicuously, the controversial phenomenon of *trance channeling* which
is discussed by Earl Babbie in his contribution, "Channels to Elsewhere."
This mediumistic phenomenon entails trance states in which "spirit entities," including both well-known and hitherto unknown personages from
the historical and prehistorical past, speak through the voice of the
channeler. Channeling is subject to differing interpretations both within
the New Age milieu and among critics. Babbie discerns common elements
in the varying messages which appear to be communicated by channeled
entities: the existence of a nonphysical realm, that God is within one,
reincarnation, and that "one creates one's own reality." These ideas bear
some relationship to the monist and yogic notions referred to above;
however, oriental monistic traditions are refracted through the prism of
American individualism and voluntarism in the New Age milieu.

Diffusion of the Sacred and Quasi-Religions

"The process of secularization," argues Richard Fenn (1978, 55), "increases the likelihood that various institutions and groups will base their
claims to social authority on various religious grounds while it undermines
consensus on the meaning and location of the sacred." Various groups and
movements turn to religious imagery and claims to enhance their social
authority. Secularization, in Fenn's view, produces a *diffusion of the
sacred*.

One key dimension of this diffusion is the phenomenon of quasi-religions
discussed by Greil and Rudy in the present volume. Quasi-religions are

viewed by their adherents or by others as "sort-of" religious; they "(often intentionally) ride the fence between the sacred and the secular." Many religiotherapeutic movements such as Scientology, est, Synanon, Silva Mind Control, and various meditation, yoga, and New Age groups are quasi-religions in Greil and Rudy's terms. The "triumph of the therapeutic" in contemporary culture has ultimately led to religiotherapy movements which take the increasingly therapeutic function of mainline church religion in modern society one step farther (Bellah et al. 1985), so that *the boundary between religion and professional psychotherapy loses its distinctness!*

This situation raises a number of tantalizing legal issues such as the prospect, referred to earlier, of clergy being sued for professional therapeutic malpractice. Perhaps the underlying issue here is whether participants in groups such as the Church of Scientology are really professional *clients,* so that state regulation is appropriate both with respect to taxation and to constraining abusive and unethical practice. At this writing the U.S. Supreme Court is considering whether fees paid by Scientology trainees for therapeutic "auditing" are tax deductible as religious donations.

On the other hand, Transcendental Meditation (TM) "has been to court to assert that it is *not* a religion." Its "religious" designation threatens its being taught in secular educational, business, correctional, and military contexts. The infiltration of quasi-religious New Age therapeutic practices into corporate, educational, correctional, and military settings has generated criticism and litigation (Basil 1988; Bordewich 1988; Brannigan 1989). New Age therapeutic techniques are also sometimes alleged to traumatize persons or even brainwash victims and enmesh them in psychopathology. The grain of truth in overblown brainwashing allegations pertains to the fact that many religiotherapy groups are what Greil and Rudy term "Identity Transformation Organizations" (ITOs), which seek to psychologically and/or physically "encapsulate" the participant to reinforce his new spiritual identity.[6] In his essay in this volume, Dick Anthony critically evaluates some recent court testimony about alleged cultist brainwashing.

Controversies over quasi-religious movements and the valuable privileges which are associated with a "church" status in the United States reinforce Beckford's emphasis on religion as a vehicle of *power* in contemporary society.

In their contribution, "Rebottling the Elixir," Shupe and Bromley discuss American quasi-religious corporations and commercial enterprises, which "sell hope as well as soap." Examples include Amway, Mary Kay Cosmetics, Fuller Brush Company, and Herbalife. The last is particularly interesting because it links the New Age holistic mystiques discussed by Beckford (1984) and the traditional *Gospel of Prosperity* which is part of the American Christian evangelical (and newer televangelical) tradition, and which Shupe and Bromley discuss.

Jonestown

The potential for destructive authoritarianism in contemporary American spiritual innovation may have been realized in the tragedy of the Peoples Temple settlement in Guyana, South America, where, on 18 November 1978, over nine hundred adherents of "Daddy" Jim Jones either committed suicide or were murdered. Jones's movement had emigrated earlier from California. Although Jones's group had originally been a legitimate congregation of the Disciples of Christ Church, his ideas had evolved in a Marxist and radical direction. According to Chidester (1988), Jones identified with the "Gnostic Savior" who liberates mankind from the realm of evil personified by the Judeo-Christian "sky-God" who legitimated the oppression of poor persons, blacks, and women (Chidester 1988).

Recently some important books have been written about this horrible event (Chidester 1988; Hall 1987; Moore and McGehee in press); however, John Hall's paper, "The Apocalypse at Jonestown," which appeared in the first edition of *In Gods We Trust* in 1981, was a pioneering analysis which highlighted the volatile mix of religious and political elements in Jones's Peoples Temple movement.

The tragedy of Jonestown raises the *evaluative* question with regard to contemporary spiritual innovation. Dick Anthony has recently developed a critique and defense of contemporary mystical exploration and innovative spiritual seeking, which acknowledges the pervasive fatuity and destructive authoritarianism that Anthony argues tends to arise in the context of rampant vulgarization of spiritual innovation. Anthony's formulation is linked to an evaluative or critical typology of contemporary American spiritual innovation (Anthony and Ecker 1987; see also Robbins, 1988b, 134–41), which is briefly discussed in the concluding contribution by Anthony and Robbins.

Religion, Politics, Church, and State

The debates over secularization and the spiritual meaning of modernization are also vital for understanding the increasing overt politicization of religion which appears to be a hallmark of the contemporary period. In their contribution, N. J. Demerath and Rhys Williams place the political impact of American religion in the context of patterns of differentiation and secularization in American society. "Organized religion has become but one voice among many trying to influence a bureaucratized government that has its own institutionalized agendas.'' In the face of American religion's apparent political resurgence, do institutionalized patterns of secularization, differentiation, and church-state separation continue to dominate and contain the political impact of religious ferment? The complex and nuanced analysis of Demerath and Williams culminates in a typology of religious influence settings that distinguishes between the direct *political efficacy* of religion at a given time and place and a religion's broader *cultural influence*.

This distinction is vital. Because of their zealous activists and (in some cases) their financial resources, ''cults'' such as the Unification Church may sometimes exert direct political influence. But they have little cultural *legitimacy* to fall back on. Thus government officials, such as IRS agents, may be quicker to investigate esoteric cults than Protestant evangelical leaders, whose broad cultural legitimacy as exemplars of the Old-Time Religion gives them greater grass-roots support.[7]

The critique of secularization models is vital to Harvey Cox's discussion of ''Citizens and Believers,'' reprinted here. It had been expected that while religion might persist indefinitely, ''it would be contained within the private or familial circle,'' and ''[I]t would have only a lessening impact on public policy formation.'' But this has not come to pass. ''Instead there has been a massive reappearance of religious personages and institutions in the public political realm in areas as disparate as Japan and Poland, Brazil and Iran, the United States and Israel.'' This development has led to various movements aimed at ''a re-fusing [re-combining] of religious and political values and rhetoric'' such as Third World Liberation Theology, the Jesse Jackson phenomenon, the linkage of revitalized Catholicism and national liberation in Poland, and the conservative Moral Majority in the United States. This surge of religiopolitical agitation highlights the increasing salience of the crucial inquiry: ''What is the appropriate role of those persons who are at once both believers and citizens?'' This is the problem of civil religion.

Vicissitudes of American Civil Religion

The term *civil religion* has generally referred to citizens' symbolic conception of their nation or government. American civil religion ''consists of Judeo-Christian symbols and values that relate the nation to a divine order of things; thus giving it a sense of origin and direction'' (Wuthnow 1988, 244). American civil religion was originally analyzed by Robert Bellah, (1970c) who has continued to be a prolific writer in this area (Bellah 1975). In his essay for the present volume he deals with civil religion in part as a *contested terrain;* different groups put forward conflict-ing "public theologies" expressing their needs and interests and their particular perspective on American civil religion. Thus, as James Beck-ford's paper notes, American civil religion becomes "yet one more occa-sion or site for power contests." Various groups such as the Christian Right or the American Civil Liberties Union seek to "acquire power for their particular (and often exclusive) version of the [civil religion] con-cept."

In their concluding essay Anthony and Robbins discuss Bellah's views and the interrelationship of puritanical moral absolutism, utilitarian indi-vidualism, and a messianic conception of the United States as a "chosen" nation with a redemptive world mission as elements of traditional Ameri-can civil religion (Bellah, 1975). But the authors suggest that the original mythic structure of our civil religion has broken down and its components are no longer as mutually consistent as they were in an earlier setting. Today's intense spiritual ferment responds to the erosion of the original ideological structure.

In his book, *The Restructuring of American Religion* (1988), Robert Wuthnow analyzes the emergence since the 1960s of *two distinct civil religions* in the United States. A conservative civil religion, many of whose adherents are evangelical Christians, views the United States as a specially "covenanted" nation with a mission to evangelize the world, in the sense of preaching Christianity and free enterprise capitalism and leading the resistance to the spread of communism. Competing with this vision is "a liberal version of American civil religion" which depicts the United States and its mission very differently (Wuthnow 1988, 250). In the liberal conception, America is also "chosen," in the sense that it is obligated to mobilize social compassion and to use its vast resources to work toward a resolution of urgent world problems of poverty, hunger, and social justice, some of which are said to have been worsened by prior, wrongheaded American policies. Neither competing version of American civil religion "can claim effectively to speak for consensual values." Each has its own constituency, and there are few shared assumptions common to both views. "Religion, therefore, becomes (as indeed it often has been charac-terized in the press) 'sectarian' rather than providing a basis of unity" (Wuthnow 1988, 256). Another provocative analysis of competing U.S. civil religions (Platt and Williams 1988) is discussed in the concluding chapter by Anthony and Robbins.

In the past decade, the fundamentalist, Pentecostal, and evangelical Protestants have tended to become increasingly politicized in support of conservative civil religion; yet, as Wuthnow and others have noted, this development has itself been largely a reaction to *the gradual drift in the*

1960s and 1970s of mainline denominational leaderships towards liberal civil religion and support for civil rights, nuclear disarmament, Third World liberation, redistributive economic policies, and feminism—the last has become a particularly divisive intrachurch issue (Wuthnow 1988). This drift has itself been part of the fallout of the iconoclastic cultural explosion and social protest of the 1960s and early 1970s: the traumas and enthusiasms of the civil-rights crusade, the Vietnam War protest, the Great Society reforms, the counterculture, etc.

Many of the present conflicts and issues which pertain to American civil religion might be termed "politicomoral" issues, for example, the politics of the Moral Majority. In his essay, Robert Bellah notes that our founding fathers were torn between the divergent conceptions of a "virtuous republic" that would endeavor to mold the character of citizens and a laissez-faire constitutional state that would be minimally interventionist in the moral realm. They opted largely for the latter model for the federal government, in part because it was assumed that powerful churches would sustain a firm *moral consensus* so that moral law could be upheld informally and extra-legally. The erosion of moral consensus and the growth of moral pluralism undercuts some of the original premises of a morally laissez-faire government. In this context morality is becoming increasingly politicized, and the state, particularly the judicial branch, is becoming the moral arbiter of American society. The expansion of the apparatus of government in recent decades reinforces this trend. As the state increasingly comes to deal with quasi-religious "quality of life" issues, including the definition of "life" itself, it really invites advocacy groups, religious zealots, and moral entrepreneurs to mobilize to direct public policy (Robertson and Chirico 1985; Wuthnow 1988). As Wuthnow (1988) notes, even when the state acts to expand individual choice and rebuff moral interventionists, as in the Supreme Court's 1973 *Roe v. Wade* decision restraining the states from prohibiting abortion, it is in effect politicizing morality and acknowledging that *moral choices are public issues,* not simply private matters. The factors currently enhancing the politicization of morality are discussed by Anthony and Robbins in their concluding essay.[8]

As Beckford notes in his contribution, "[M]orality can be as real as bread-and-butter; and is no less the staff of life for some people." In their respective papers both Cox and Horowitz affirm that the conception of a *technocratic value-free public-policy process* is essentially an elitist vision employed to exclude the noncredentialed from influence on decision making. But the public is not buying!

Religious Ferment and the Aspirations of Women

"Indeed, the absence of feminine symbolism for God marks Judaism, Christianity, and Islam in striking contrast to the world's other religious

traditions'' (Pagels 1979, 57). This may not hold as true for some of the
religiohistorical "also rans," that is, heterodox Christian groups and
teachings which did not survive. Some of the recently discovered gnostic
texts of the second century A.D. refer to God not as exclusively masculine
but "as a dyad who embraces both masculine and feminine elements"
(Pagels 1979, 58). Yet by A.D. 200, "virtually all the feminine imagery for
God had disappeared from the orthodox Christian tradition" (Pagels 1979,
68).

Elaine Pagels has noted the somewhat greater responsibility and authority accorded to women in the gnostic sects in the second and third
centuries compared to orthodox groups. "Among such gnostic groups as
the Valentinians, women were considered equal to men; some were revered
as prophetesses; others acted as teachers, travelling evangelists, healers,
priests, perhaps even bishops" (Pagels 1979, 72). The great early Christian
apologist and theologian, Tertullian, castigated overly activist women in
certain sects: "Those heretical women—how audacious they are! They
have no modesty; they are bold enough to teach, to engage in argument,
to enact exorcisms, to undertake cures, and, it may be, even to baptize"
(quoted in Pagels 1979, 72). But Tertullian ultimately joined the Montanists, a radical prophetic-Pentecostal movement that honored two prophetesses through whom the Holy Spirit was believed to speak! "If Montanus
had triumphed," declared a late-nineteenth-century Christian writer,
"Christian doctrine would have developed not under the superintendence
of Christian teachers most esteemed for their wisdom, but of wild and
excitable women" (quoted in Fox 1987, 409). Taking a similarly jaundiced
view in his classic, *Enthusiasm,* Monsignor Ronald Knox (1950) laments
the feminist impulse which has fueled the rise of heretical "enthusiastic"
sects in the history of Christianity, from Montanists through seventeenth-
century Quakers, Quietist mystics, and eighteenth-century French "Con-
vulsionists." "From the Montanist movement onwards, the history of
enthusiasm is largely a history of female emancipation . . . the sturdiest
champion of women's rights will hardly deny that the unfettered exercise
of the prophetic ministry by the more devout sex can threaten the ordinary
decencies of ecclesiastical order" (Knox 1950, 20).

In the nineteenth century in the United States, evangelical revivals were
associated with a "feminization of piety." "It was in the revival movement
that [American] women first developed the passive role of worshiper into
a more active ministry of prayer, public speaking, and exhortation to
conversion, giving them an appetite for greater participation" (Clark 1987,
374). But as new churches born in revivals institutionalized, they have
often tended to become hostile to female preaching.

The feminist element was particularly conspicuous in nineteenth-century new religions such as Christian Science, Theosophy, Spiritualism, and Shakerism. Such marginal groups tended to affirm "a perception of divinity with female as well as male qualities; little or no adherence to doctrines of original sin; the denial of the need for a traditional clergy; and a critical view of family and marriage, one which did not value domesticity as women's sole identity" (Clark 1987, 375). Some female-led movements such as Christian Science and Adventism were particularly concerned with questions of health and healing. Christian Science, according to Bednarowski (1980), promised to women a way of controlling or transcending their own putatively weak and fragile bodies, on account of which they had been consigned to second-class citizenship.

Yet many of these movements, such as the Shakers or Christian Science, suffered substantial declines after an initial spurt of growth based on conversions. The disproportionate number of women converts, many of whom were past the age of childbearing when they were converted, has rendered groups such as the Shakers and Christian Science *demographic losers* compared to more demographically balanced groups such as the American Mennonites (Stark 1987).

New Religious Roles for Women

Spiritual feminism thus has deep roots in American and Christian history, although it has often been restricted to the position of a deviant sectarianism or an intellectual fringe movement. "Spiritual feminism," notes Mark Silk, "swept through all the standard-brand churches during the 1970s. . . . The mainline denominations struggled to adjust to the revolution within their ranks" (Silk 1988, 158). An important part of the religious feminist current has been the drive to increase women's participation in church leadership roles. Substantial sociological research on women in clerical and seminary roles has accumulated in the 1980s (Dubois 1987; Lehman, 1985).

"It was not until the end of the 1970s, however, that women began to pursue careers as clergy in large numbers. Between 1972 and 1980, female enrollments in theological seminaries increased 223 percent while male enrollments grew by only 31 percent" (Wuthnow 1988, 228). The feminine influx into the seminaries has continued in the 1980s. Substantial resistance to further female mobility has been encountered (Wuthnow 1988), particularly in conservative Christian and (Orthodox) Jewish groups, where there is strong attachment to theological and scriptural proscriptions against women being in authority over men. In recent decades feminism has "deepened the divisions that were already becoming evident between religious conservatives and religious liberals" (Wuthnow 1988, 227).

Beyond "Our Father"

Beyond the drive for greater female authority and responsible participation in traditionally male-dominated and patriarchal religious traditions, there have been many efforts to transcend patriarchal religion and evolve a distinctly feminist spirituality. In 1973 Mary Daly published *Beyond God the Father,* which viewed Western religious traditions and faith as more or less hopelessly mired in patriarchy, a lost cause to be abandoned (Daly 1973). Not all spiritual feminists agree. In a passage quoted in Janet Jacobs's essay in this volume, "Women-Centered Healing Rites," feminist theologian "Carol Christ" lays out three basic views held by feminist theologians with respect to the question of whether sexist Western religious traditions can be reinterpreted and/or modified in a feminist direction, or whether they must be totally rejected.

What is objected to is the basic patriarchal conceptual matrix of the Abramic or Judeo-Christian-Islamic religions in which the godhead is "the Father," the messianic and prophetic figures are exclusively male, and the history of the faith involves the story of a chosen people descended from the biblical patriarchs. Feminist "alternative religions" and alternative conceptions of divinity have thus been flourishing for a decade and bear some relationship to fashionable New Age spiritual tendencies.

Radical feminist spirituality is rather diffuse and amorphous and encompasses a diverse conglomerate of "radical feminism, pacifism, witchcraft, Eastern mysticism, goddess worship, animism, psychic healing, and a variety of practices normally associated with 'fortune-telling' " (Lindsey 1985, 38). It manifests in various workshops and symposiums, meditation groups, and even "witches covens." Indeed, witchcraft has a special meaning for radical spiritual feminists: "It is a women's religion, a religion of the earth, vilified by patriarchal Christianity, and now, finally reclaimed" (Lindsey 1985, 38).

The development of feminist neopaganism and goddess symbolism is discussed in Mary Jo Neitz's essay for this volume, "In Goddess We Trust," which also discusses the role of "the Craft," (or witchcraft), in spiritual feminism. Dr. Neitz shows how contemporary feminist neopaganism developed from the interaction of a nonfeminist neopagan revival focusing on romanticized visions of pre-Christian mythology and nature worship with the modern political feminist movement. Radical feminist theologians now emphasize the significance of identification with the figure of the Goddess as a means of feminine empowerment and transcendence of stereotypical "feminine" passivity and submission. Janet Jacobs's paper discusses healing rites in which female participants chant "I am woman, I am power, I am infinite." Similar rituals have helped female victims of sexual abuse mitigate the effects of "powerlessness and low self-esteem associated with the trauma of victimization" (see also Jacobs, forthcoming).

As Mary Jo Neitz's contribution indicates, lively debates have transpired within the broader feminist movement regarding the significance of radical feminist spirituality and neopaganism, which has elicited severe criticism from some political feminists. Thus spiritual feminism has been castigated for escapist *irrationalism*. Such mystical irrationalism may conceivably lead to escapism that devalues the importance of tangible reforms to improve the social condition of women. The significance of lesbianism in spiritual feminism has also been debated (Neitz 1988a).

Like Shakers or Christian Science, spiritual feminist groups may ultimately be *demographic losers*. Disproportionate recruitment of women, many of whom will not be bearing more children, is not a characteristic likely to facilitate the long term survival of a religious group. Stark (1987) argues that ultimately successful groups tend to have a membership that resembles the total population (that is, not extremely skewed in terms of gender or age) and that is organized in terms of conventional social units, for example, nuclear families. Where will the second generation of feminist goddess devotees come from? From a feminist, or even just a liberal, standpoint it is unfortunate that it is the traditionalist, "pro-family" religious groups which are likely to be demographic winners, since negative orientations toward feminism, abortion, divorce, birth control, and working women are conducive to *large families* with many children to be rigorously socialized via Christian schools, evangelical summer camps, etc.[9]

The Appeal of Neotraditionalism for Women

A number of studies have documented the surprising fact that in this age of spiritual feminism and goddess mystiques, many women, after being involved in feminist, politically radical, or countercultural-hedonist milieus, are now going into religious movements such as evangelical-charismatic or Jewish Orthodox and Chassidic groups, which are socially conservative and formally support traditional patriarchal gender roles (Kaufman 1987; Neitz 1987; Rose 1987). This phenomenon is explored in the essays by Susan Rose, who reports on female converts to two charismatic groups, and by Lynn Davidman, who has studied women becoming members of both a conventional Orthodox Jewish synagogue and a Chassidic group.

One impression which emerges from the various studies of what might be termed neotraditionalist female religious converts is that even the formal inequality or expected submissiveness of women in traditionalist, patriarchal religious communities may afford women more power in inter-personal modalities than do the open-ended or normatively unstructured milieus of "sexual freedom" that many of the converts had previously experienced. Such "liberated" milieus seem to have operated to enhance tendencies toward the sexual exploitation of females by males, the latter having been implicitly encouraged to evade commitment and responsibil-ity. In traditionalist groups the women may obtain, as Davidman points out, the security of "clear definitions of female and male roles and the provision of norms for family life." Women who fear exploitation may gain a sense of security and even power from a strong "tradition with a moral ordering in which *women play a fundamental role*" (Kaufman 1987, 62, our emphasis).

In her paper, Rose emphasizes that beneath the facade of formal traditionalism there is really gender reciprocity, "negotiation" of gender roles, and family decision making in some charismatic Christian move-ments (see also Rose 1987). But *extreme* patterns of sexual inequality, abuse, and exploitation, which have manifested in some fundamentalist and charismatic Christian groups as well as in some guru or religiotherapy cults, often becomes a basis for female defection from such groups. Such exodus frequently arises when women devotees come to perceive a pattern of "unequal exchange" characterizing gender relations within the move-ment (Jacobs 1984). The women studied by Rose and Davidman may subsequently become disenchanted with their faiths and groups, but given the pro-family orientation of the latter, they may be too encumbered to be fully free to leave when second thoughts occur.

At present we have a period of enhanced interest in religion among women, perhaps a new "feminization of piety" as evidenced, among other things, by the female influx into seminaries. But there are contradictory trends. Some women are seeking to identify with pagan goddesses and to innovate in the direction of new symbols and rituals seen as means of emancipating women from passive dependency on men. Simultaneously, other women are seeking the emotional security of clear role definition and expected mutual commitment that ideally characterize gender rela-tions in traditional religious contexts, even at the cost of feminist libera-tion. Given these divergent trends it is not easy to generalize. But one provocative conclusion has been formulated by an eminent student of American religion, who affirms that the one "change in America's spiritual politics that is most likely to be remembered and felt decades from now [is] the women's movement, the changes in women's consciousness that are so deeply altering both ideas and practices in religious groups ranging all the way from evangelicism through Catholicism" (Marty 1988, 17).

Conclusion

To some degree the "women's picture" corresponds to the general portrait of contemporary American religion. Contradictory tendencies are blossoming concurrently: exotic spiritual innovation accompanies a powerful traditionalist surge; monistic relativism coexists with fundamentalist dualistic absolutism; pluralism and diversity are expanding while the Christian Right stridently reasserts the hegemony of the Judeo-Christian tradition.[10] A Soviet social scientist who has observed the American religious carnival comments:

> Everything is widespread at once—glossolalia, witches' Sabbaths, Zen Buddhism and fundamentalism. However, they have something in common. All of this is not standard American Protestantism. All of these movements, to one degree or another and in one form or another, contradict the American bourgeois system of values. (Furman 1981, 238)

Furman thinks that secularization in American culture has reached a point of no return. It is destroying civil religion, and it cannot be reversed by "pseudo-archaic" revivalism or a "pseudo-collectivist" flight from increasing "ideological and moral vagueness." "The processes of secularization and collapse of the system of values, are irreversible processes. . . . The present successes of the Protestant Right can not turn these processes back" (Furman 1981, 240). But disintegration is also hope, at least from Furman's Marxist standpoint. "All the fits of hysteria, all the pseudo-archaic religiousness contain elements of search for the new, for new forms and new means of integrating the individual and society" (1981, 241).

Throughout this essay we have sought to evaluate the implications of the various developments we have described for received theories of secularization and modernization. But the picture which emerges is ambiguous. Several elements such as the traditionalist revival, the increasingly conspicuous quality of religious *power,* and the apparently enhanced relevance of religion to politics and to vital social issues would appear to have negative implications for received models. Yet, as with the profusion of new movements and cults, there are theories which identify new developments as consequences (for example, reactions to secularization) (Robbins 1988b; Wilson 1976). Some recent trends, such as the decline of large mainline denominations and the proliferation of small, specialized independent congregations, along with an increasingly specialized market for church supplies (with a decline of the transdenominational mass market, see Edmondson 1988), seem to be in line with some elements of modernization and secularization, for example, structural differentiation. The proliferation of quasi-religions and the conflicts which they have generated seem to fit the "diffusion of the sacred" that Fenn (1978) associates with secularization. Even the growth of the electronic church might be interpreted to support the thesis of the basically privatized nature of religion in a highly differentiated society, in which disembodied media such as journals, books, and audio- and videocassettes increase in significance for the promotion of social movements compared to face-to-face interaction (Lofland and Skonovd 1981).

So the jury will have to stay out longer on secularization, but the American religious scene has certainly changed in the last few decades. The themes of religious conflict, religious power, the religiopolitical nexus, and religious menace are commanding increased attention and changing the way Americans look at religion.

Notes

1. We will argue that by the mid-1970s or 1980s this situation was altering due to the heightened "relevance" of religion (Robbins 1988a, 1988b), but Dr. Larner was presumably talking about the sociology of religion in several recent decades since mid-century or earlier.
2. Wuthnow (1988, 143) also notes that the Cold War and the spectre of Communist totalitarianism had the consequence of "silencing an important segment of the religious Left." A notable religious Left began to reemerge with the clerical opposition to the war in Vietnam in the late 1960s and early 1970s and today's Christian opposition in some quarters to American policy regarding Central America as well as clerical support for Liberation Theology, Latin American base communities, the Sanctuary Movement, etc. See Harvey Cox's paper in this volume.
3. Ammerman (1987) does not believe that most fundamentalists will relinquish the premillennial vision. The latter can be reconciled with activism in terms of emphasizing goals such as prayer in the schools which will allow more souls to be gathered for the Rapture. Fundamentalists also often see their political action as mainly *defensive,* that is, protecting their schools, families, and Christian way of life from intrusive humanist bureaucrats, social workers, educators, etc. As Susan Palmer points out in this volume, the label "postmillennial" might be applicable to some nonevangelical cults and optimistic New Age groups.
4. Of course some groups, following threads of Indian Hinduism, see ultimate oneness as *personified* in an Avatar such as Meher Baba (see the concluding essay by Anthony and Robbins) or in an exalted spiritual master or guru.
5. See Melton (1988) and Basil (1988) for additional perspectives on the definitive common elements of New Age spirituality. Melton highlights the premise of a latent *universal religion* that underlies variegated contemporary religious forms and labels. Of course this notion is anathema to many Christian evangelicals and fundamentalists, who affirm the unique truth of Christianity and are alert for signs of the coming universal false religion of Antichrist.

6. Some of the more eccentric born-again groups also fit this pattern. In their concluding essay, Anthony and Robbins refer to encapsulative groups as "civil religion sects" and "restored communities" (Berger 1982).

7. Although at this writing evangelist Jim Bakker is being prosecuted for fraud, an earlier investigation of Bakker's operation by the FCC in the early 1980s was aborted, allegedly partly because of the Reagan administration's desire to enlist evangelicals (who had high rates of nonvoting) as Republican voters. In contrast, Rev. Sun Myung Moon, a notorious leader of a "cult," was successfully prosecuted by the Reagan justice department despite the importance of the Moonie-subsidized *Washington Times* to the Reaganite political movement.

8. Tendencies toward the politicization of morality contribute to increasing proliferation of *church-state conflicts* in the late twentieth century, as does both the extension of the authority and apparatus of the state and the resurgence of religion (Robbins and Robertson 1987).

9. Chassidic Jewish groups such as the one reported on by Lynn Davidman in her contribution may also be likely demographic winners.

10. One area which has been neglected in this volume is the impact of *immigration* in transforming American religion; for example, American Moslems may outnumber Jews by 2030, and a substantial fraction of Hawaii's population is now Buddhist. Yet as immigration extends the limits of American religious pluralism, the Christian Right stridently reaffirms the centrality of our Judeo-Christian heritage.

References

Aidala, Angela, 1985

Ammerman, Nancy T., 1987

Anderson, Susan, 1985

Anthony, Dick, and Bruce Ecker, 1987

Anthony, Dick, Thomas Robbins, and Paul Schwartz, 1983

Barnhart, Joe, 1988

Basil, Robert, ed., 1988

Batiuk, Mary Ellen, 1988

Beckford, James A., 1984, 1985a, 1985b

Bednarowski, Mary, 1980

Bellah, Robert, 1970c, 1975

Bellah, Robert et al., 1985

Berger, Peter, 1982

Bloom, Allan, 1987

Borgeditch, Fergus, 1988

Boston, Rob, 1988

Brannigan, Martha, 1989

Bromley, David, and Anson D. Shupe, 1981

Burrows, Robert, 1987

Cavanaugh, Michael, 1988

Chidester, David, 1988

Clark, Elizabeth, 1987

Conway, Flo, and Jim Siegelman, 1978, 1982

Cuddihy, John, 1978

Cuneo, Michael, 1988
Daly, Mary, 1973
Davidman, Lynn, 1988
Demerath, N. J. III, and Rhys H. Williams, 1987
Douglas, Mary, 1982
Dubois, Ann, ed., 1987
Edmondson, Brad, 1988
Fenn, Richard K., 1978
Fox, Robin L., 1987
Frankl, Razelle, 1984
Furman, D., 1984
Greeley, Andrew, and Michael Hout, 1988
Groothuis, Douglas, 1986
Hadden, Jeffrey, 1969, 1987a, 1987b
Hadden, Jeffrey, and Anson Shupe, 1986, 1987, 1988
Hadden, Jeffrey, and Charles Swann, 1981
Hall, John R., 1987
Hannigan, John, 1988
Haywood, Carol, 1983
Heinerman, John, and Anson Shupe, 1987
Henry, Patrick, 1981
Herberg, William, 1960
Hexham, Irving, and Karla Poewe, 1986
Hoover, Stewart, 1988
Hunter, James Davison, 1987
Jacobs, Janet, 1984, forthcoming a
Kaufman, Debra, 1987
Kelley, Dean M., 1972
Kennedy, Paul, 1987
Kilbourne, Brock, and James Richardson, 1986
Knox, Ronald, 1950
Larner, Christina, 1984
Lechner, Frank J., 1985
Lehman, Edward, 1985
Lewis, James, 1986
Lifton, Robert J., 1979, 1983
Lindsey, Hal, 1970
Lindsey, Karen, 1985
Lindsey, Robert, 1986
Lofland, John, and L. N. Skonovd, 1981
Lyon, David, 1985
Martin, William, 1982
Marty, Martin, E., 1988
McGuire, Meredith B., 1983b, 1985
McGuire, Meredith B., and Debra Kantor, 1988
Melton, J. Gordon, 1987, 1988
Moore, R. Laurence, 1985
Moore, Rebecca and Fielding McGehee, in press
Moyers, Bill, 1981
Neitz, Mary Jo, 1987, 1988a

Neuhaus, Richard John, 1984
Nock, A. D., 1933
North, Gary, 1986
Ofshe, Richard, 1986
Pagels, Elaine, 1979
Palmer, Susan J., 1988
Peshkin, Alan, 1986
Platt, Gerald, and Rhys Williams, 1988
Richardson, James T., 1985b
Robbins, Thomas, 1983, 1985a, 1985b, 1986b, 1988a, 1988b
Robbins, Thomas, and Dick Anthony, 1982
Robbins, Thomas, and Roland Robertson, 1987
Robbins, Thomas, and Roland Robertson, eds., 1987
Robertson, Roland, 1985a, 1985b
Robertson, Roland, and Joann Chirico, 1985
Roof, Wade Clark, and William McKinney, 1987
Rose, Susan, 1987, 1988
Shupe, Anson, and David Bromley, 1980
Silk, Mark, 1988
Simpson, John, 1987
Spencer, Jim, 1987
Stark, Rodney, 1984, 1987
Stark, Rodney, and William Sims Bainbridge, 1985
Suro, Roberto, 1989
Turner, Bryan, 1983
Wallis, Roy and Steven Bruce, 1984b, 1986
Wilson, Bryan R., 1976, 1987
Wilson, John, and Harvey Clow, 1981
Wuthnow, Robert, 1983, 1988
Yinger, J. Milton, 1946

1

Religion and Power

James A. Beckford

Introduction

In the past decade, the notion of power in the sociology of religion has shown signs of emerging from an eclipse which had begun to take place in the 1960s. A variety of different notions of power is becoming apparent both in the everyday practice of religion in the Western world and in sociologists' interpretations of that practice. The first part of this chapter will chart the eclipse of power; the second will scan the signs of its emergence from obscurity; and the third will discuss the broad implications of this trajectory for the sociology of religion.

The chief significance of religion for most sociologists in the 1960s was that it was declining under the combined onslaught of secularization, rationalization, bureaucratization, alienation, massification, and depersonalization. Sociologists of religion responded in three main ways. The first was to concentrate on the supposedly declining functional capacity of religion to solve personal problems of meaning or identity. The second was to measure religion in all its empirical detail. The third response concentrated on the deviant and exotic fringe of religious phenomena, whose curiosity value was high, but whose relevance to what most sociologists saw as the major developments of the time was problematic.

An examination of the most favored textbook presentations of the sociology of religion in the 1950s and 1960s shows that the treatment of power was, at best, cursory, and, at worst, nonexistent. More often than not, it was actually precluded by explicit concern with religion's supposedly functional capacity to overcome so-called powerlessness. Yet, this had not always been the case. A more robust approach had characterized the work of earlier scholars such as Max Weber, H. Paul Douglass, or Reinhold and Richard Niebuhr. Furthermore, their keen awareness of the intimate associations between power and religion was later reflected in such classics as Liston Pope's *Millhands and Preachers* (1942) and J. Milton Yinger's *Religion in the Struggle for Power* (1946).

The orientation toward the functional capacity of religion to solve problems of meaning or identity was dominant throughout the late 1960s and 1970s, and the eclipse of the notion of power was largely a consequence of this orientation. I shall illustrate this thesis by reference to the highly influential works of Peter Berger and Thomas Luckmann who constituted religion as primarily a matter of knowledge susceptible of understanding in the same way as other cognitive products, in particular, language. If the sociology of knowledge was to serve as a new paradigm for the sociology of religion, then the recommended analytical strategy was to focus on *language* as the key to religious phenomena. Indeed, the religious enterprise was conceived as a search for knowledge about the taken-for-granted basis of the world's orderliness. Religious practice was seen as a matter of regenerating the self-evident knowledge of the ultimate order of things through social interaction. Religious meaning was thereby equated with the social perception of various kinds of order; and "theodicies" were said to protect the sense of order by virtue of "the redeeming assurance of meaning itself" (Berger 1967, 58).

Peter Berger

The limited use that Peter Berger makes of the concept of power tells us a lot about his deep assumptions about man and religion. The concept is virtually confined to statements about "the surrender of self to the ordering power of society" (Berger 1967, 54). "Concrete relations with individual others" are taken to be the source of "the masochistic attitude" in religion, through which "the self-denying submission to the power of the collective nomos can be liberating" (Berger 1967, 56–57). "Above all, society manifests itself by its coercive power" (Berger 1967, 11). "The institutions of sexuality and power first appear as thoroughly alienated entities, hovering over everyday social life as manifestations from an 'other' reality" (Berger 1967, 92).

It is highly significant that the experience of power in human relationships is not selected by Berger as one of the signals of transcendence. The reason for this surprising omission may be that he subsumes power under his concept of order which, in turn, is subsumed under the concept of meaning. There is clearly a strong connection (if not identity) between order and meaning in Berger's work, for which he has been criticized (Radcliffe 1980). His sense of power is also heavily influenced by this close connection. It seems to refer ultimately to the background noise of the social system—a pervasive sense of something constraining and "out there." Consequently, Berger pays little or no attention to power in human relationships or in the relationships between groups, social categories, and collectivities. His usage is very largely abstract and disembodied. Power is never treated as a phenomenon experienced by human beings directly: it merely underwrites the human condition in society.

Thomas Luckmann

The relegation of the concept of power to an abstract status or a background position in Berger's work on religion is taken one step further by Thomas Luckmann, whose *The Invisible Religion* (1967), in particular, helped to shape the dominant concerns of much sociology of religion in the 1960s and 1970s. This book is a treatise on the changing ways in which human beings are said to transcend their biological nature and thereby to generate identity and worldviews in a socialization process deemed to be religious:

> The historical priority of a worldview provides the empirical basis for the 'successful' transcendence of biological nature by human organisms, detaching the latter from their immediate life context and integrating them, as persons, into the context of a tradition of meaning.

Luckmann regards the worldview as performing "an essentially religious function" and thus constituting an "elementary social form of religion" (Luckmann 1967, 53). "Religious function" seems to mean the continuous provision of sense in human life and the preservation of "the coherence of meaning in the worldview" (Luckmann 1967, 70). Religion is therefore said to be "present in nonspecific form in all societies and all normal (socialized) individuals" (Luckmann 1967, 78).

Luckmann argued that specific contents or themes of religion vary with sociocultural circumstances. In the modern Western world the process of institutional differentiation allegedly created a "private sphere" in which individual consciousness was liberated from the dominant social structures, thereby giving rise to what Luckmann terms "the somewhat illusory sense of autonomy which characterized the typical person in modern society" (Luckmann 1967, 97). As a result, the "thematic unity of the traditional sacred cosmos breaks apart. . . . Once religion is defined as a 'private affair' the individual may choose from the assortment of 'ultimate' meaning as he sees fit—guided only by the preferences that are determined by his social biography'' (Luckmann 1967, 98–99).

As a consequence of Luckmann's focus on religion as *transcendence through worldviews,* the notion of power is excluded from the agenda. It seems to have no part to play in a theoretical scheme emphasizing the normality of transcendence through socialization, no matter whether in traditional or modern forms. In Luckmann's scheme religion is a social process in which meaning is conveyed from generation to generation by means of themes and symbols reflecting the texture of everyday social interactions. One may ask whether Luckmann's scheme can cope with events and experiences which threaten to overload the capacity of sacred meaning systems to make sense of existence. Is there nothing in life which cannot be handled by religion?

It is one thing to describe the mechanics of the way in which men may transcend their biological nature by means of sacred worldviews; but it is quite another to imply that the categories of transcendence can always cope with the flux of experience. It is really an empirical question whether men actually succeed in making sense of their lives in terms of them. This may be an instance of the ''oversocialized'' conception of religious man— to adopt Dennis Wrong's celebrated expression. To restore the balance, we need more studies of the *failure* of religion to achieve the functions so readily attributed to it by sociologists. Paradoxically, this would tell us more about the power of religion by exposing its empirical limitations. In this respect, Timothy Radcliffe's criticism of those who equate religious meaning with a sense of unitary order is entirely valid: ''[M]an is only driven to question the meaning of anything and everything because he finds himself at the intersection of many orders, employing many languages, playing many roles'' (Radcliffe 1980, 158). It is this pluralism, Radcliffe argues, that provokes the question of meaning.

Nobody seriously doubts the plurality of today's worldviews, and Luckmann is surely right to insist that modern man has a choice to make among them. But it would be wrong to infer that everybody actually makes such a choice to the exclusion of other worldviews or that the chosen worldview always succeeds in making sense of life.

The experiences of conflict, tension, and contradiction are no less meaningful simply because they frustrate the neat categories afforded by discrete worldviews. The creative bricolage, experimentation, alternation, revision, and special pleading which partly characterize our everyday reasoning are a significant element in religious thought and feeling. But theoretical schemes which tie meaningfulness too closely to perceived order have little place for such quintessentially human action.

In short, the orientation towards the sociological study of religion through meaning systems and language has been helpful in illuminating complex social, cultural, and mental processes through which religious values, ideas, thoughts, and feelings are transmitted. But it has also brought with it the negative implication that, since meaning systems and worldviews are expressed in terms that reflect particular social structures and roles, the meaning of religion is somehow contained in those terms.

To put this central point differently, the emphasis on the social construction of worldviews (unintentionally perhaps) *turned the purely formal processes of socialization into the sacred content of religion.* Social form was equated with sacred content. One might even go so far as to say that social form obliterated sacred content, albeit ironically in the name of freeing the sociology of religion from a fixation with formal religious organizations. In this connection we recall the earlier view of Reinhold Niebuhr for whom "the ultimate question is not whether life has a meaning . . . but whether or not that meaning is tragic" (Niebuhr 1940, 213). Perhaps "meaning" ousted "tragedy" as well as "power" from the dominant sociological perspectives on religion?

I do not mean to imply that no attention was paid in the late 1960s and early 1970s to issues transcending the identity- and meaning-conferring capacities of religion. Of course, there were clear signs of conflict and tension within religious groups, and sociologists were not slow to pick up on them. I am thinking of such timely studies as Hadden's *Gathering Storm in the Churches* (1969), Hammond's *Campus Clergyman* (1966), and Berton's *The Comfortable Pew* (1965). But sensitive as these books and others were to struggles within churches, the issues were only implicitly presented as struggles for power. They were mainly concerned with problems of organizational structure, innovative doctrines, ecumenical relations. The dominant questions were therefore about the churches' capacity to adapt their policies to changing circumstances and thereby to protect their mid-century material prosperity and moral influence.

Most sociologists of religion refused to swallow the bromides of the "end of ideology" thesis, but at the same time they nevertheless seemed to share an assumption that *religion was remote from power struggles.* Stormy weather was certainly forecast in the area of civil rights, and the pew was becoming a decidedly less comfortable place from which to contemplate persistent social problems in the early 1970s. But the difficulties were primarily diagnosed as matters internal to religious groups, that is, belief, doctrine, and organization.

The prospect of religious mobilization for direct political and legal action in the pursuit of more generalized power was still remote in the 1960s. And the challenge to the use of power in the name of religion was still weak in the United States, although contemporary events in other countries might have suggested the need to take more seriously the relationship between religion and power. I find it strange, for example, that, aside from the case of the Berrigans, the deep ideological fissures gouged at the time of the wars in Southeast Asia found such weak expression in organized religion.

Since I have been trying to argue that the notion of power remained in eclipse in the sociology of religion for about fifteen years, it has not been necessary to stipulate a precise meaning for the concept. Nor do I intend to do so now. But it is necessary for my purposes to recognize at this juncture that "power" has been defined in widely differing ways by sociologists of diverse theoretical persuasions (Lukes 1974; Wrong 1980). Conceptions of power which are now coming into use in sociology tend to differ from the conception of power that has generally prevailed in the sociology of religion over the past fifteen years or so. Let me be more specific.

So long as religion was constituted mainly as worldview or meaning system, power was conceptualized mainly as "functional capacity." It was used in such expressions as "the power of religion to provide meaning and identity" or "the power of radical ministers to overcome lay resistance to civil rights activism." But there are many other possible meanings of the term which are free from the teleological connotations of functionalism. I shall argue that different, and more widely differing, senses of the term "power" have been at work in more recent sociological analyses of religion. A wide variety of conceptualizations of power in sociology can be found in recent studies of religious phenomena. I shall review a small number of individual works which illustrate the diversity of connections between religion and power. I shall deal with them under the headings of religion and the experience of power as: confounding; convincing; contesting; controlling; cultivating; and curing.

Religion and the Power That Confounds

Let me begin with a brief review of some of the ideas of Peter Brown, who has revolutionized the study of the Christian religion in late antiquity. Recently, he has demonstrated the importance of the "the holy man" in the Eastern part of the late Roman Empire. In his books *Society and the Holy in Late Antiquity* (1981) and *The Making of Late Antiquity* (1978) he emphasizes that between the fourth and sixth centuries A.D., a period bridging the classical age and the middle ages, the focus of power in religious matters was disputed between the formal institutions of the church and the entirely informal practices of numerous individual holy men.

Holy men were mainly ascetics who claimed to enjoy unmediated access to God and, consequently, wide-ranging powers. They claimed the power to curse effectively, to heal physical and mental ailments, and to resolve disputes between people living in societies which were being slowly disengaged from Roman dominion. His own words are crystal clear and require no gloss:

> For some centuries the locus of the supernatural was thought of as resting on individual men. The rise of the holy man coincides . . . with the erosion of classical institutions; his decline . . . coincides with the re-assertion of a new sense of the majesty of the community. (Brown 1981, 151)

I want to emphasize three points. First, holy men were considered to be the repository or locus of supernatural power and were therefore in competition with the "vested hierarchy of church and state" (Brown 1981, 140). Second, the locus of spiritual power was as precarious as the society in which holy men flourished was fluid. And third, the manifestation of spiritual power was inextricably bound up with associated notions of suffering, evil, or misfortune. These observations underscore the importance of treating the notion of power in religion as variable, flexible, and contestable.

Power is not a fixed attribute or property of individuals, relationships or social systems. The distribution of power is best conceptualized as an emergent feature of changing circumstances. Brown makes the important point that the actual embodiment of religious power may be paradoxical, for in the Eastern Empire there were

> [M]en with 'reputation for power'; yet this power was thought to have been drawn from outside any apparent niche in the power structure of society. It was gained in the desert . . . beyond human sight, and depended upon a freedom to speak to God, the exact extent of which lay beyond human power to gauge. (Brown 1981, 183–4)

This view may correct the unfortunate tendency to think of power solely in terms of its prevailing form and distribution.

One further observation on Brown's work will lead us on to a different way of examining the intimate connection between power and religion. He emphasizes on several occasions the need for would-be holy men to affirm and confirm their spiritual power by speaking "authentically." In his own words, authenticity "demands histrionic and theatrical performances as a guarantee" (Brown 1981, 134). In societies in which the traditional formulas of religion have lost credibility and the extent of taken-for-granted agreement on the locus of the sacred is small, would-be "holy men" must continually re-create and maintain their authenticity by overt actions. In the case of the ascetic martyrs and holy heroes of Syria in the fifth century A.D., for example, this meant a constant struggle to demonstrate that their access to God was direct *and* mysterious. It was a struggle against competitors for the allegiance and reverence of ordinary mortals who sought their patronage.

In the sense in which Peter Brown makes such profitable use of the term, power has little to do with coercion or control. It concerns, rather, religious experiences which are riveting and confounding in the sense of going totally beyond normal comprehension. In fact, the elements of meaning and orderliness, of which so much was made in the functionalist sociologies, have little or nothing to do with this sense of the term "power."

Religion and the Power That Convinces

Richard Fenn's stimulating book, *Liturgies and Trials* (1981), also reasserts the centrality of power to an understanding of religion in its social dimensions. The book's express concern is with the place of language in the struggle between the forces of secularization and religion. Some of its main subject matter is taken from famous court cases in which the power of the state to impose its own secular criteria of technical justice has conflicted with the insistence of some people on a religious interpretation of their actions. The court records of cases concerning, first, the claimed right of Karen Ann Quinlan's father to suspend the extraordinary medical means of supporting her comatose life; second, the refusal of two employees of the Episcopalian Church to give evidence on the whereabouts of a Puerto Rican church member suspected of terrorism; and, third, the trial of the Catonsville Nine for burning the files of a local draft board, are examined for what they reveal about the power of the state, through the judiciary, to determine what can count as religious grounds for action.

Fenn's general thesis is that against the "overriding powers of the secular state, private commitments and sacred duties will not survive unless they are protected by liturgical words" (Fenn 1981, *xxiv*). The reason for this is that liturgy attempts to reestablish such powerful connections between words and deeds, between people, and between situations that the intentions and sincerity of speakers are guaranteed. "The liturgy is as close as humans ordinarily come to re-entering the closed linguistic garden of paradise" (Fenn 1981, *xv*). *Liturgy is therefore regarded as powerful:* it has the power to authenticate feelings, words, promises, and pronouncements. It functions as a last resort in attempts to resolve ambiguities in human speech on important matters. Thus, "oaths, sacraments, and signs are liturgical expressions of speech that have become unambiguous, serious and binding both on those who speak and on those who listen" (Fenn 1981, *xi*).

In the light of Fenn's specific interpretation of the power of religious language, the meaning of secularization takes on a special significance. It refers to the process whereby secular institutions reduce "authoritative declarations to mere assertions of personal opinion in the court or in the classroom" (Fenn 1981, *xxxiv*). The authenticity previously guaranteed to a speaker by religious language is ruled literally out of court. The only admissible expressions of religion are confined to a very narrow range of statements of a largely nondoctrinal kind. For example, the content of Karen Ann Quinlan's father's Roman Catholic convictions was ruled inadmissible in court. All that mattered was the question of whether he was a suitable guardian of his own daughter.

Religious terms allegedly lose their "prophetic power" when used in secular contexts because

> [T]he process of secularization . . . dissolves the powerful speech of the religious community, in which the same words are both sign and symbol, into the two distinct vocabularies and rules for speaking. One, in which words are taken literally, is a vocabulary of symbols that obey rules of relevance and reliability in secular courts and classrooms. The other is a liturgical language that creates . . . a community of common faith and hope. (Fenn 1981, 164–45)

Fenn's analysis of the Quinlan case and of the case of the Episcopal Church employees who refused to testify about a suspected terrorist on the grounds that it would be an infringement of their First Amendment rights turns on the issue of where the power lies to *define* religion in a secular society. One might wish to go further and to suggest that being religious nowadays entails a struggle to assert the power of religion over agencies whose effects are generally to exclude the relevance of religion to any but the most private and nonmaterial concerns.

The struggle to preserve the power of religious language also involves tensions *within* religious groups between the advocates of literalistic and metaphorical uses of language. Indeed, Fenn's view is that the secularization of religious language actually began within the religious community with the disposition to take religious pronouncements as "mere metaphors" or slippery symbols of "togetherness." The original power of prophetic speech has consequently been dissipated, or, as Fenn renders the point more poetically, "out of the metaphor's Trojan-horse belly come the soldiers of deviant interpretation and rival claims to the holy city" (Fenn 1981, 180). Thus, words which originally evoked commitment by speaking powerfully of common values and historical myths eventually degenerate into words which merely point to everyday objects.

This new and basically political approach to the sociology of religion represents a shift away from the kind of work which emphasized the largely subjective importance of religion as a set of precarious cognitions sustained by social interaction and conversation with significant others. The emphasis has been shifted towards a concern with the practical processes whereby religion is actually lived out at both the individual and collective levels in a struggle for power. The struggle is over the power to define situations, to affect the course of events, and, above all, to gain a hearing for religious testimony, declarations, and directions.[1]

This approach takes us into a realm of power defined by Steven Lukes (1974) as *the capacity to set the agenda,* that is, to decide what will, and what will not, count as relevant topics for consideration or criteria for evaluation. By this, he means that the exercise of power is frequently invisible and involves far more than simply having one's orders obeyed in the face of resistance from others. It involves, notably, being in a position to determine how critical issues are to be presented and understood by others.

Religion and the Power That Contests

A clear illustration of the shift towards a concern with the experience of religion as powerfully contesting the status quo can be seen in the ways in which the notion of civil religion has evolved in the last two decades or so. The "career" of the civil religion concept exemplifies a drift away from its organic, meaning-conferring functions as delineated by Robert Bellah in 1967 towards a concern with the struggles waged by numerous interest groups to acquire power for their particular (and often, exclusive) version of the concept. Studies by Michael Novak (1974) and by Roderick Hart (1977), for example, have opened our eyes to a kind of underground war being conducted by the advocates of various extremist interpretations of the sacred origins, mission, and millennial future of the American nation. These intense ideological struggles center on the perceived threats to America's sacred mission. And their participants make no secret of their conviction that the exercise of the power to contest is the only way to block the advance of the allegedly many-headed monsters of Antichrist and un-Americanism. These studies have destroyed the image of American civil religion as a peaceful and courtly preserve of elite groups and invisible opinion makers. It is becoming clear that the power to impose particular versions of civil religion is the object of continuous and occasionally naked conflict, although it must be conceded that the level of fervor rarely reaches the pitch of the Reverend Dallas F. Billington's exhortation to his flock to pray that God kill atheist leader Madlyn Murray O'Hair, for "[i]t is not wrong for you to pray God to destroy your enemy." (quoted in Hart 1977, 24).

The "Moonies" are one of the most visible and controversial of groups presently working hard to spread a sectarian version of American civil religion (see Robbins et al. 1976).

For me, a most poignant symbol of the current struggle to stake out America as sacred space was a violent confrontation that I witnessed in Berkeley between Eldridge Cleaver, speaking on a Unification Church–sponsored platform in October 1982 about "America's future and the world revolution," and sundry radical opponents claiming that he had sold his famous soul for a mess of Korean CIA pottage. Both sides made a bid to speak for "the real American people," the Constitution, and democracy. Yet, neither side was prepared to allow the other's legitimacy. And on their right flank the Moonies have formidable competitors in the various groups composing the New Christian Right. Far from signaling the end of ideology, then, it seems that American Civil Religion has become yet one more occasion or site for power contests which nowadays extend well beyond the clash of pulpit orators.[2]

Religion and the Power That Controls

The study of civil religion shades off naturally into the broader topic of religiously inspired movements for moral reform. But I shall not examine any particular study of the New Christian Right here. The reason for this is that so many studies of this phenomenon and of its most visible component, the Moral Majority, have appeared in recent years that it is unnecessary to belabor the obvious point that the relationship between religion and power is also crucial to this whole phenomenon.[3] I shall simply add the observation that, while electoral politics has understandably been the primary focus of attention, the phenomenon also includes issues bearing on what I would call "moral power." And this concept extends beyond the scope of purely electoral studies. By "moral power" I mean that, aside from influencing legislators and executives, this movement for the mobilization of large numbers of people in pursuit of the allegedly *inerrant* principles of biblical Christianity also disseminates or reinforces specific and categorical notions of right and wrong in all spheres of everyday life. The increased pressure on politicians may be the most novel aspect, but the longer-term impact may be more lasting in the moral life of the person in the street responsive to the blandishments, exhortations, and excoriations of, for example, the aptly named prime-time preachers or televangelists (Hadden and Swann 1981).

This is all the more likely to happen, of course, to the extent that the clergy of local churches are exposed to pressure from a newly militant laity to conform with the guidelines issued by the more conservative electronic churches. There are already signs that the moral power inspired in part by the New Christian Right is making itself felt in local politics on such issues as law and order, school-board syllabi, and zoning policies, but not without growing liberal resistance. The result is a struggle for the moral power to control wide swathes of life.

Unfortunately, studies of the New Christian Right tend to isolate the phenomenon from other developments in religion and morality. In particular, little attention has been paid to parallel campaigns being waged to control, for example, so-called cults. Admittedly, the scale of anticultism is meager compared with the Moral Majority, but it raises issues which touch upon some of the New Christian Right's central concerns: the family, education, and Americanism. Yet, at the same time, anticultism is also fed by currents of secular rationalism and liberal humanism. They are more exercised by perceived threats to the freedom of cultists' minds and the rationality of their thinking processes. There is therefore as much tension and disagreement with the New Christian Right as there is agreement. This is just one small example of the crosscutting lines of interest which indicate that the current struggles for moral power are anything but simple or one-dimensional. It is only when separate studies of the New Christian Right and of other phenomena, such as the Catholic campaigns for "respect for life," are juxtaposed that the complexities, tensions, alliances, and conflicts in the struggle to control moral sentiment are thrown into relief.

Let me add finally that there is little evidence to show that the present-day moral indignation of so many religionists represents a displacement of material deprivations or status frustrations (Wallis 1979) as in theories of "status politics." The truth is that morality can be as real as bread and butter; and is no less the staff of life for some people.

Religion and the Power That Cultivates

If we turn our attention to sociological studies of new religious movements (NRMs) in the last fifteen years or so, I think it is clear that the dominant perspective has been a mixture of functionalism and American phenomenology[4] that has tried to answer the question, "How have NRMs fulfilled the function of supplying meaning and identity to their followers?" I intend to sketch the outlines of a different interpretation that draws on a distinctive notion of power.

The sociocultural conditions engendering a loosening or relaxation of the bonds linking young adults to particular statuses, careers, occupations, geographical locations, etc., have been well enough researched to need no further comment here. The price that has been paid for the emergent autonomy of young adults as a social category has included the weakening of social ties to kin, locality, and workplace. For the vast majority of young adults this situation may amount to nothing less than the benefit of increased freedom of opportunity and action. Some young adults have taken advantage of their relative freedom to experiment with novel forms of consciousness, experience, social relations, and ideology. Indeed, some may even feel themselves under pressure to be experimental in outlook, and others may experience experimental failure. NRMs no doubt offer something useful to young adults in both categories, as the literature amply testifies. But it would be a great mistake to believe that the recruits to NRMs were exclusively unwilling or failed experimenters—just as it would be equally wrong to treat all NRMs and analogous enterprises as if they were alike in most respects. For there is enormous variety in the motivations to join NRMs, just as the movements themselves display a wide diversity of aims, values, and strategies. In a nutshell, my interpretation of the movements with which I am familiar is that they are seen by prospective and actual members alike as *sources of various kinds of power*. The expectation and the experience of many recruits is that membership empowers them to cultivate and to achieve a number of things more easily than through other means. The chance to cultivate various spiritual qualities, personal goals, or social relationships is the attraction.

I shall emphasize several points. First, there are frequent discrepancies between members' expectations and the actual possibilities for cultivation made available to them. Second, members' beliefs frequently bear only a passing resemblance to the "official" doctrines of NRMs (Balch 1980). Third, it is possible for members with very diverse motives and intentions to derive equally satisfactory benefits from membership of the same movement. Fourth, some members are prepared to tolerate high levels of discrepancy between their beliefs, experiences, and the movement's practices for the sake of exploring their potential for development in unforeseen and only dimly perceived directions (Straus 1976).

Of course, once members have invested time, resources, personal reputation, and even self-respect in the attempt to tap the power to cultivate all the things on offer from NRMs, they are unlikely to abandon them lightly. The models of cognitive dissonance and attribution theory would both confirm this general point. And one does not have to be a deprogrammer to realize how resistant some members can be to any and all efforts to induce them to abandon movements about which they may already have serious misgivings (Beckford 1985b). If one's understanding of human action is based on a narrow cost-benefit model, the tenacity of many NRM members can only signify pathology. But if one is sensitive to the importance of such human activities as willing, experimenting, striving for coherence (not necessarily consistency), and cultivating a sense of overall integrity, then both membership and apostasy can be understood in terms other than pathology. It must be appreciated that recruits to NRMs perceive in them (rightly or wrongly, clearly or confusedly) *the opportunity to tap sources of power*—power which will supposedly enable them to cultivate any number of personal ends and end-states.

Here, I wish to introduce an idea which helps to explain the popularity of so many collective experiments in new religious practices and experiences. Today's NRMs may offer relatively *safe* sites for experimentation with types of consciousness and modes of social relationships which entail quite serious risks. Indeed, these risks have alarmed not only anticultists but also more sophisticated commentators such as Christopher Lasch (1980). It is no small thing to abandon conventional routines, relationships, and habits of mind, and the evidence from serious studies of NRMs shows convincingly that young adults do not abandon themselves unthinkingly to experimental religion (see Barker 1984). Rather, they take a more or less calculated risk. By participating in a collective experiment—a movement— young adults share some of the risks with others and to some extent shelter under the patronage of people of presumably good will.

Let me make it absolutely clear that in my view many people seek the protection of new movements for reasons having more to do with adventurousness and risk taking than with weakness and retreatism. Ironically, some of the sources of power perceived in NRMs are precisely the conditions of success in the major economic activities and professions of modern societies. Many of the goals of training in the various branches of the Human Potential Movement, for example, are indistinguishable from the goals of executive training schemes in industry, commerce, and the armed forces (see Tipton 1982; Heelas 1986). Similarly, the communicative skills and self-awareness techniques engendered in a wide variety of meditative movements are also cultivated in many training programs in the spheres of therapy, education, and social welfare (see Swanson 1980; Westley 1983). There is scope, then, for a deeper interpretation of the relationship between sources and experiences of power in the NRMs and perceptions of the distribution of economic, cultural, and social power in the wider society.

Religion and the Power That Cures

I can illustrate this last point most economically by referring finally to the innovative work of Meredith McGuire, who has clearly identified the centrality of power to the theory and practice of Roman Catholic Pentecostalists. Her book, *Pentecostal Catholics* (1982), carefully documents the way in which "the discovery of a new source of power in their lives" (McGuire 1982, 174) led the subjects of her research to the practice of faith healing. Moreover, this practice is shown to be grounded in a coherent theory of disease and well-being. At its core is the ideal of achieving a balance of power between good and evil. There is the added insight that "the practices of faith healing . . . may be a political statement—a counter-assertion of power—against the dominant medical system" (McGuire 1982, 182).

McGuire's subsequent research on alternative healing groups in suburban New Jersey has shown that "[P]ower is a fundamental (if not *the* fundamental) category for interpreting healing. . . . [T]he treatment of illness is essentially the restoration of the balance of power—by weakening the antagonist's (disease-causing) power or by strengthening the victim's power" (McGuire 1983a, 229). Ritual language is a particularly effective transmitter of healing power (see Foltz 1987). In short, Meredith McGuire's work confirms my general argument about the importance of examining the relevance of power to the social dimensions of religion.

Conceptual Threads

Sensitivity to questions of power in all its diverse relations to religion is necessary for an adequate sociological understanding of religion. These questions can be likened to trace elements which show up the crucial lines of sympathy and antipathy, affinity and rejection between the various models of man, blueprints for society, and visions of world order which are currently competing for support and power on so many different sociocultural levels. Other examples of the newly apparent importance of the notion of power in religion could no doubt be added if space permitted. But enough has already been said to substantiate my main thesis that the sociology of religion is undergoing a reorientation of its main perspectives. What is urgently needed, of course, is a more careful analysis than I have provided here of the meanings denoted and connoted by "power" in relation to religion. Questions could then be asked about the bearing of discussions of power in general sociology on its specifically religious manifestations. In this way, a better integration might be achieved between sociological analyses of religion and of wider aspects of social structures and processes. The notion of power would then serve as a useful point of articulation.

In my opinion, the orientation towards power in sociological analysis makes it possible to give greater attention to the *intentional* production of foreseen effects (see Wrong 1980). In contrast to the predominantly cognitive view of religion as both product and condition of normal processes of socialization and interaction, there is nowadays a sharper awareness of the deliberate attempts being made to bring about certain effects in the name of religion. Religion is no longer considered interesting solely as a part of the general apparatus of socialization and social control supplying meaning through culture. Some sociologists have stopped looking at religion as if it were the wallpaper of the social system. It has now acquired distinct importance in its own right as a sphere of activity where efforts are deliberately made to influence, manipulate, and control people's thoughts, feelings, and actions in accordance with various religious values.

In conclusion, I must comment briefly on the relationship between the notions of *meaning* and *power,* lest it be objected that I have implied a contrast or opposition between them. It may also have seemed that I was advocating the abandonment of the perspective which has dominated the sociology of religion for the past fifteen years. But, in fact, my thesis is rather different. What I have proposed is that, in focusing on the capacity or function of religion to supply meaning, integration, and identity, the theoretical cart has been put before the empirical horse. Sociological interpretations of religious phenomena have been mistaken for their subjects' motives and intentions. In short, I agree that meaning and identity are important aspects of religion: but at the same time I dispute whether actors act out of consideration for them directly. Rather, I believe that *actors respond to perceived sources of power, and their responses may or may not supply the meaning and identity of which we have heard so much.* This is an empirical question: not something to be resolved by definition.

Doubt, despair, confusion, misgivings, rationalizations, agonizing indecisiveness, and evasiveness are no less common characteristics of the religious life than are meaningfulness and identity. Events connected with religion in many parts of the world at present have shown that the rumor of angels is a strident trumpet call to action in some believers' ears. (See, for example, Robertson and Chirico 1985; Dessouki 1982.) But until recently it was not much more than the background noise of the social system in the ears of many sociologists of religion. What I have therefore proposed is that empirical attention should, as a matter of priority, be focused on the reported experiences and the perceived manifestations of power and power struggles in religion. Until and unless this first step is taken, the meaning of religion for both individuals and societies cannot be adequately understood.

This is a substantially revised and abridged version of an article which first appeared under the title "The Restoration of 'Power' to the Sociology of

Religion'' in *Sociological Analysis* 44 (1) (1983): 11–32. I am grateful for permission to reprint it in modified form.

Notes

1. See Beckford 1979, 1985b; and Shepherd 1982 for studies of this kind of struggle in connection with the controversies surrounding cultism and anticultism.
2. See Robbins and Robertson 1987 for examples of comparable contests in other countries.
3. See, for example, the sensationalist report by Conway and Siegelman 1982; the judicious theological critique by Webber 1981; and the balanced collection of papers edited by Liebman and Wuthnow 1983.
4. See Robbins 1988b for an excellent overview of this whole field.

References

Balch, Robert W., 1980
Barker, Eileen V., 1984
Beckford, James A., 1979, 1985b
Bellah, Robert N., 1967
Berger, Peter L., 1967
Berton, Pierre, 1965
Brown, Peter, 1978, 1981
Conway, Flo, and Jim Siegelman, 1982
Dessouki, Ali E. Hillel, ed., 1982
Fenn, Richard K., 1981
Foltz, Tanice, 1987
Hadden, Jeffrey K., 1969
Hadden, Jeffrey K., and Charles E. Swann, 1981
Hammond, Phillip E., 1966
Hart, Roderick P., 1977
Heelas, Paul, 1986
Lasch, Christopher, 1980
Liebman, Robert C., and Robert Wuthnow, eds., 1983
Luckmann, Thomas, 1967
Lukes, Steven, 1974
McGuire, Meredith B. 1982, 1983a
Niebuhr, Reinhold, 1940
Novak, Michael, 1974
Pope, Liston, 1942
Radcliffe, Timothy, 1980
Robbins, Thomas, 1988b
Robbins, Thomas, et al., 1976
Robbins, Thomas, and Roland Robertson, eds., 1987
Robertson, Roland, and Joann Chirico, 1985
Shepherd, William C., 1982
Straus, Roger A., 1976
Swanson, Guy, 1980
Tipton, Steven M., 1982

Wallis, Roy, 1979
Webber, Robert E., 1981
Westley, Frances, 1983
Wrong, Dennis, 1980
Yinger, J. Milton, 1946

II
MILITANT TRADITIONALIST RESURGENCE

2

The Limits of Modernity

Irving Louis Horowitz

The postwar era witnessed a near-absolute commitment to the idea of development. In this sense, the aims if not the achievements of the First and Second Worlds became the received wisdom of the Third World. There have been occasional murmurs about the shortcomings, even evils, of "Western" development; but even in a nation such as India, where under Mahatma Gandhi such fears had a certain political currency, the idea of development has taken deep root. Hence, the present sense of the limits of modernity, found in nations as diverse as Iran, Poland, and the United States, must be seen as a largely unexpected, if not entirely unwelcome, reaction by those who have endured the dogmas of development while remaining untouched by the tremors of real development.

I

Let us address the question of the limits of modernity by briefly recalling the stages in the intellectual penetration of Western doctrines of development. The first phase took place in the 1950s and corresponded with the pronouncement of an American Century; it was the idea of development as modernization. Scholars and policy-makers came to view the problem of development in terms of a series of gaps: between elites sending messages and masses never receiving them; between the availability of air travel for some in contrast with those still living in a world of ox-drawn carts; between educational establishments that affected a narrow stratum of peoples in underdeveloped areas and a vast network of marginal classes of uneducated and illiterate peasants. The policy task was uniformly set in terms of an underdeveloped world in search of parity with a fully developed world.

The next phase took place in the 1960s, and was critical of this earlier point of view. It argued instead for indigenous development as an ideology; a model more appropriate to a Soviet model than an American model of development was advanced. The argument was that development is primarily a function not of modernization but of industrialization. Development should not be measured primarily in terms of creature comforts, commodity goods, or even personal health and welfare, but rather by rates and levels of industrial output and productivity. The developmental paradigm of the 1960s accepted the idea of development without qualification but denied that development had to do with modernism; instead, it argued that development had to do with industrialism. The argument in its more advanced, militant form claimed that commodity fetishism or modernization inhibited development by creating segmental stratification, an imbalance between social classes and social forces. The corollary is that industrialism overcomes commodity fetishism and creates national solidarity.

In many ways the decade of the fifties belonged to the "modernists," while the decade of the sixties belonged to the "industrialists." The developmental ideologies reflected the relative parity on a world scale of the United States and the Soviet Union in terms of acceptance of the idea that development has to do with rapid autonomy on a national level and rapid industrial buildup in economic terms. Whether it be in its American or Soviet, democratic or Stalinist forms, there was no disputing that development was good, that it was necessary, that it was in fact the name of the world game.

A new variant of the idea of development, which might be termed neo-Leninism, was introduced in the 1970s. This view of development was couched in new terminology, called "dependency theory" or the "dependency model." Its central concerns were not so much the nature of development but the sources of backwardness. These sources were held to occur anywhere but in the Third World itself. There was a global system called capitalism, which determined, through the cosmopolitan center, the character of the periphery (anywhere other than where the center was located). But even in this rather highly refined neo-Marxist perspective of the 1970s the idea of development itself was never challenged. It may have been argued that the sources of backwardness were not in domestic culture but in the international economy, not in the national capital but in overseas international capitals. But there was no disputing the virtue and the varieties of development. Commitment to the concept of social change was universal. It was expressed by modernists, industrialists, and *dependentis-*

tas in the economic realm, as well as by a whole panoply of people in serious intellectual circles whatever their ideological bias or their political commitment. There was almost no challenge to the notion of the essential virtue of development.

A review of dominant currents of thinking and acting regarding policy over the last three decades reveals that something profoundly new is happening today. Development—indeed, the very concept of development—is under attack. The virtue of planned progress is questioned. How has this come about? This counter-revolution is related to re-creation of the Malthusian paradox; its roots have to do with the pot-of-gold theory—its realization in fact for the first time.

From the time of the conquistadores, it has been believed, sometimes covertly, that somewhere there is a pot of gold that could make the risk of economic adventure worthwhile. But when the pot of gold materialized, it was in a totally unexpected context: it happened in the Middle East. The pot of gold turned out to be "black gold"—petroleum. A whole new level of wealth came into being, created not by development but in response to a crisis in development. One discovers oil; it simply exists, although oil rigs, drilling equipment, and special maintenance are required to reach it. Oil is not a dependable consequence of hard work. And oil exists in unequal proportions in geographical terms; in this respect oil is not like food, although both are a source of energy.

The material basis for criticism of the developmental hypothesis was the spiritual feeling that God had given former "have-nots" a monopoly of a rare source of energy required by the "haves." God, a spiritual engineer, arranged for the redistribution of world power, not just energy sources. One might argue that the energy crisis of the 1970s had an impact not unlike that of a major world war: it redistributed forms of power and sources of wealth no less than energy. This realignment was accomplished without war, but in a climate of quasi-animosity between more developed and less developed nations, not because of military activity (not very much of it in any event). The East-West balance of terror remained sufficiently stable to create a vacuum, in which Middle East OPEC nations were able to negotiate their demands with impunity.

II

The sense of the limits of modernity has structural no less than historical roots. An iron law of development is that people and leaders of less developed areas observe the material consequences of development, but not necessarily the extremely difficult and complex processes of "getting there." Leaders in the Middle East in particular, by virtue of the pot of black gold, can realize the fruits of advanced development without incurring the social and material costs of older developed societies. Hence, there arises a severe imbalance between advanced commodities and technology and the infrastructure in which they can be used, an imbalance that persists over time.

A second element in the revolt against modernity is inspired by socialist societies, especially Soviet society, in which materialism is not simply a fact of empirical life but the organizing belief system of the whole society. Given the extraordinary force of religious fundamentalism within Islamic societies, and to a lesser but still noticeable degree within Catholic societies, ranging from Poland in the Soviet orbit to Brazil in the Western camp, this emphasis on materialism leads not so much to a "new man" as to a rather bizarre recycling of old capitalist man: venality, greed, and dishonesty are not so much overcome by socialist systems as they are hidden from sight and filtered through much abused humanitarian rhetoric.

A third structural source of the new fundamentalism is the perception that economic development is a segmental activity; it is a phenomenon that stimulates growth, but it also creates wide disparities within the national culture. As a result, far from being an integrating mechanism, as it was in the industrial process, development may also function as a disintegrating machinery in preindustrial societies. Costs of development are borne disproportionately, and, worse, rewards are also disbursed disproportionately. Arguments by defenders of Western culture that such disparities are necessary to maintain innovation, industry, and invention tend to fall on deaf ears; they confirm the belief that the developmental ideologies are intrinsically materialistic, and hence evil.

A fourth factor is the concern that any authentic egalitarian model must reject notions of change that permit, even encourage, a variety of theories concerning political vanguards and/or intellectual elites. The urge toward development is too often seen as a revolution from above. The new fundamentalism claims that such developmental ideologies widen the sense and reality of disparities between elites and masses, proletariats and peasants, urban cosmopolitans and rural locals, and so on. In short, the developmental process encourages class differentiation and poses a serious threat to national hegemony in ethnic and religious terms.

Finally, the developmental model promotes a wide array of dualisms that may negate the value of the model. It so isolates the spiritual life from the political or material life as to foster needlessly sharp and antagonistic differentiations between church and state, clerical and lay forces. In political terms, therefore, the developmental impulse isolates a series of rational measures and models that deprive social life of spiritual meaning, or a sense of teleological purpose.

Thus, the ideological groundwork for an assault on modernity—criticism of development per se—is in no small measure a result of the quixotic nature of the developmental process itself, not simply or primarily a Third World conspiracy against modernization. Development has reached such "high" levels that it has come to depend, in a kind of economic irony, upon "low" forms of energy to make the engines of change work. Development has occurred with the assistance of advanced technology, computerization, and miniaturization; but, on the other hand, development can be frustrated by Bedouin tribes controlling major sources of the world's fuel energy. And without such energy this modernization process could not occur.

The empirical paradox took on a metaphysical character. Ultimately there was a crisis about what really counted. Providence, not socialism, was said to account for the monopoly of fuel energy in the hands of have-nots, energy without which the entire developmental process would come to a crashing halt. Such monopoly, furthermore, did not make it necessary for such nations to employ the equivalent of bows and arrows against atomic weapons. The disparity between military power and economic domination itself became a proof of Divine support for the anti-modernist vision.

A serious consequence of the theory of petroleum as a pot of gold is that it has limited commodity characteristics. An agricultural or commercial system creates a business civilization, but oil creates only revenues. As a result, an economy based on oil can afford the luxury of anti-developmentalism as an ideology, since it can import from abroad the sorts of managerial and organizational skills Western societies must generate from within. Beyond that, the pot-of-gold economy precludes the sort of developmental regimes found earlier among the Japanese Shogunate and the German Hohenzollerns. The maintenance of a pot-of-gold economy permits sheikdoms lacking mass support to retain power. But traditional tribal forms of rule can maintain their varieties of Islamic fundamentalism only for that period of time in which the petroleum pot can be replenished. The structural fragility and temporal limits of an economy based on petroleum cast a long shadow over the revolt against modernity in these cultures.

The basis of the ideology of the 1980s is a sense of the limits of modernity and development as such. Once a revolution in the distribution of goods was achieved, and once an absolute paralysis in the fueling mechanism or triggering mechanism of the advanced sector could be produced, if need be, a shift in the theory and practice of development became inevitable. For the first time the modern world is being attacked.

The decisive point is not the role of religion in the organization of state power but, rather, the uses of religious symbolism to confound the notion of development. In earlier epochs, whether in Italy, France, or England, religious fervor was used to organize state power to enhance the developmental process. What uniquely characterizes the current era is *the organization of religious forces either through or against the mechanism of state power* to frustrate the developmental process. This is an important difference. Religious fundamentalism has come to characterize the present period and current mood.

Religious fundamentalism is not only a Middle Eastern phenomenon. Poland is interesting in this regard. Few photographs of the workers' strikes of 1980 failed to show a group of workers displaying a crucifix or in the background a picture of the current Pope. The organizing premise, the ideological formation, was not only more money and less work—ordinary working class demands—but a strong ideological commitment to Christianity as an answer to the industrializing theories of Marxism. In both Iran and Poland, at some level the use of religion, or the use of traditionalism if one prefers, is aimed directly at the heart of the concept of development.

What shibboleths of development went unquestioned in the past? First, the need to sacrifice for the next generation and in the process to display a primitive accumulation of wealth. Demands were confounded. On the one hand came the call to sacrifice, on the other the assertion that material goods are not worth the sacrifice, that they are shabby, that they have no ultimate worth. A second shibboleth is that a society is defined by the character of its developmental process. The counter-argument is that society is not defined by the developmental process, but that the developmental process tends to wash away the unique characteristics of each society or each civilization. A conflict between traditionalism and modernity is emerging that threatens the developmental process itself. This is much more than a theological phenomenon. The zero-growth movement, the limits-to-growth movement, the idea of zero growth as a positive good—all assert that there are abstract values, goods, and services quite beyond those resulting from concrete development.

What potential do these movements have for frustrating further industrial innovation? How seriously should they be taken? What is the relationship between developmentally oriented regimes or developmentally oriented sectors within developing societies and the traditional elements or theocratic elements within these societies? In certain parts of Latin America a tremendous struggle may be taking shape between a military sector that is oriented toward development and a religious sector that is oriented toward traditional values. The issue is akin to the argument concerning indigenous folklore, about the relationship between the international environment and its folkloristic roots. The entire direction of the twentieth century is in question. The measurement of society or civilization by a gross national product, by levels of industrial output, or by levels of consumptive activity has come under tremendous criticism. At some level, the consequences will be a redefinition of what constitutes value as such; what constitutes the relationship of base and superstructure as such; and what constitutes the relationship of state power and religious power as a mobilizing force.

The ability of this new anti-modernization movement to survive is not likely to rest primarily on the structure of economic productivity but more decisively on the character of nationalist impulse. For the weakening of the modernizing sector also implies a lessening of the militarizing sector; and that means the essential pillar of power upon which modern nation-states rest is much more subject to external threat and military adventure. In Iran, the main danger to the rule of the religious mullahs came not from the modernizing forces, which were overthrown, but from rival regimes in the area such as Iraq or the Kurd separatists, who saw the opportunity to chip away at what has been a major force in the area. Whether religious fundamentalism can withstand an impairment of nationalism is an essential touchstone both of the depth of feeling involved in this revolt against modernity and the survival capacities of the counter-revolutionary regime which seizes power.

III

What is the impact on the United States of this revolt against modernity? This question concerns not only the United States but in part the Soviet Union as well. The postwar environment was shaped by the struggle between the United States and the Soviet Union, involving competing concepts of development between the Keynesian concept in the West of modernization based upon consumer satisfaction and the Marxist concept of industrialization based upon principles of national security and self-sufficiency. The entire postwar dialogue has been about which type of development should be implemented. No question has been raised about whether development is good per se, only about which form of development is admissible.

The rise of a special Third World segment, high in energy resources and otherwise low in developmental skills, has had a very profound impact on American society. For the first sustained period of time in its more than two-hundred-year history overseas reality is affecting everyday life in America. Unlike Europe, the United States has never been affected directly by war or famine or any other ravage. Even World Wars I and II, the Korean War, and the Vietnam War were essentially overseas events.

People lost loved ones, and war politicized the domestic climate of opinion, but essentially these wars had no mass impact on American life. The material life of American society remained largely unaffected by events that took place overseas.

This changed dramatically with the 1973 oil embargo; in the 1978–79 oil crises, the ordinary American felt that foreign affairs were real, more so than they had been at any previous time. The relationship between what went on abroad and what was going on at home became direct—in its reality, in its impact, and in its consequences. What began as a strategy and a tactic of Middle East regimes and the OPEC cartel became a world historic event in American life. For the first time Americans understood that they were not self-sufficient. Even the Vietnam War, which challenged the concept of American invincibility, had not shaken that feeling of self-sufficiency.

Every Soviet leader—Lenin, Stalin, Khrushchev, Brezhnev, Gorbachev—has aspired to the United States' level of self-sufficiency. The idea of self-sufficiency is the ultimate metaphysical payoff of the developmental process. Why develop? Why accelerate development? The answer is always that self-sufficiency is desirable. The nation will no longer be beholden to, no longer be dependent upon, other nations. The events within Middle Eastern societies like Iran or Saudi Arabia or other OPEC nations provide a framework within American life for challenging the developmental thesis in its essential form—the doctrine of national self-sufficiency.

At first the challenges to modernity took a secular form in the West, which might be identified as environmentalism, which asserted that the environment had to be preserved, even at the cost of economic growth. Industrial waste and industrial diseases were too high a risk factor; nature had its own value. Certainly, the early phases of the environmental movement were relatively innocuous. There was nothing particularly theocratic about it; the environmental impulse was, if anything, naturalistic. Environmentalism embodied a belief that somehow the relationship between environment and industrialism had to be dealt with in an entirely new way. Admittedly there were special problems involved: labor reallocation, increased fuel costs, increased costs of goods. The presumption was that these problems, as well as reduced industrial development and modernization, were worth it because nature had its own value.

The second round of the challenge to modernity moved beyond the environmental—beyond the purely secular. The rise of religious cults and of fundamentalist movements meant that the rejection of modernism had extended to a re-evaluation of the notion of what constitutes a good world. Limited growth was quickly translated into zero growth. Spiritual values were emphasized over material values. Millions of people within American society began to participate in religious fundamentalism. The origins of these sentiments were not so much anti-developmentalism as a spiritual answer to the externally imposed limits to further material growth. No growth became better than slow growth because it was easier to assert as a metaphysical first principle. The naturalistic impulses of the environmental movement of the seventies were transformed into an aggressive spiritual revolt against modern values, not infrequently involving the same fears of advanced technology and the same appeals to puritan values of self-discipline.

A third level was a kind of right-wing impulse toward anti-modernism, akin to isolation from the world at large and from America's problems in particular. What has evolved within the United States is unadorned anti-developmentalism akin to chiliastic visions in the Middle East, and no less demanding in ideological terms. What remains to be examined is how the new fundamentalism relates to engineering, science, and research. How does it connect with advanced forms of development within American culture and society?

At the very time a new kind of fundamentalism arises, new technological developments have occurred in data-base computation and in activities related to electronics, polymers, and biogenics. The world of science and information is accelerating at the same time that religious fundamentalism is expanding. Events in the West seem to parallel what is taking place in the Third World generally, and within the Middle East specifically. This leads to a two-track system, a religious track and a scientific track; as a result, development is increasingly linked to elite rather than to mass requirements.

There is a gigantic cultural struggle under way: the culture of development versus the culture of the spiritual; the culture of the traditional versus the culture of the modern. We are experiencing a new version of the nineteenth-century struggle between science and religion. It does not so much involve general ideological formations as it does the consequences of this ideology for development of power in the world. What are the consequences of this kind of traditionalism for Eastern Europe? For socialism and communism? For Western concepts of democracy?

One can only surmise what the consequences may be. There may be a kind of worldwide isolationism. Within the United States, we may experience a period in which these new movements—whether they be pentacostal, environmental, or libertarian—create dogged and determined neo-isolationism, while the nation protects itself through advanced technology and advanced systems design. The divisions between the scientific and the spiritual allow American society to develop what may be called capital-intensive militarization through advanced forms of scientific endeavor. On the other hand, they also encourage mass participation in theological and neo-isolationist movements, in reaction to this increasing sophistication. Among the masses, non-participation and non-commitment have become normative. Even under the most extreme provocation, U.S. political leadership, whether Democratic or Republican, must be cautious about extending its claims. The polarization of scientific and religious culture and the assault on development severely limit any claims the leadership can make on the masses.

A potential outcome of fundamentalism within the United States is authoritarian domestic politics. The character of American society is shaped by mass forces. Fundamentalist frameworks have to be expressed and could take the form of a protest not only against modernism but against presumed excesses of sexual liberation or excess personal freedom in general. At some level the new fundamentalism may challenge the pluralistic value base of American society. American society may not move in an authoritarian direction, but certainly it will if there is an economic slowdown coupled with a steady rate of high unemployment, and as a result this produces higher demands on the system. Within a stern moralistic value system, obligations to the system are emphasized over rights within the system. The consequence may well be an exaggerated turn to the Right. What limits such fundamentalism is the huge shift from rural to urban patterns, and the general secularization of culture in personal habits and decisions. Still, there is no incongruity between an authoritarian-bureaucratic orientation domestically and a neo-isolationist foreign policy; they may work very well in tandem. Shrinking power is increasingly focused on domestic rather than foreign policy.

Anti-modernity, anti-developmentalism, and anti-industrialism are phenomena that could lead to an American society increasingly insular in character, isolated from world patterns, and subjected to the same internal pressures that have led to "Finlandization" in Europe. A revolt against a complex present leads to policy-making unilateralism, disregard of the "other" side, and the sentimental view that all real problems are negotiable between "men of good will," whatever the nature of the social system.

The secular traditions, including French Enlightenment, German Enlightenment and romanticism, and American modernism, have all experienced a peculiar crisis. Requirements for personal achievement have become increasingly complicated. There is a systems overload within modern culture (and here I include the Soviet Union as well) because each generation must confront so much information, digest so much material, absorb so much innovation, and store so much scientific knowledge. The overload tends to produce an opposite result: namely, an impulse to disgorge or empty out. The developmental model came upon hard times not so much because of its negative consequences but through its positive results. Managing these developmental processes proved so complex that they became problems instead of advantages.

Take one small example. The phonograph machine is an entirely twentieth-century artifact. It began as a simple, hand-driven turntable, coupled with a record made of shellac which at best gave modest sound reproduction. Digital recordings are now so precise that recordings only three years old have become obsolete. The sophistication in equipment makes what we generated a decade ago appear primitive in comparison. Word processing equipment requires almost professional-level knowledge to assemble the equipment necessary to achieve the desired results. Similarly, in the developmental process, an enormous case of information overload occurs, resulting in an incapacity to enjoy the results of the developmental process or a much higher level of coping, as with a vast network of home computerization.

Anti-developmentalism becomes a critique of complexity as such. It is not only an attack on the notion of gross national product but a response to the difficulty of absorbing the language of mathematics and computer science or the methods of research and theories of evidence. The world of science and technology has become exceedingly difficult. The fact that significant numbers of people are unable to absorb large chunks of information has created a special problem within American culture, especially since it stands as the most advanced "modern" society. A rebellion thus arises not just against the developmental, but against complexity and difficulty. The failure to establish a firm set of answers produces frustration. A world in quest of certainty is denied answers. Instead, the developmental paradigm presents problems to be researched and policies to be evaluated. Teleological resolutions of life arise as a challenge to the new technology necessary to cope with the continuation of the developmental impulse.

It is extremely difficult to develop a scientific or technological style that encourages a developmental process within a society. In American society, no less than elsewhere, development has always been an elitist concept, a slogan put forward in the name of the people. But, basically, development remains a vision held by those at the top who have a sense of the national conscience and the national consensus. The cult of the traditional is a rebellion against such elitism. It is a demand for simplification, for a world in which answers are known. The current wave of fundamentalism in American life rests on ideology based on solutions—truth through Providence. In this sense, the fundamentalism of the Middle East may have a direct relationship to similar events in American society. The assault on modernity within American life and elsewhere should be taken with absolute seriousness. It affects the character of individual life, community values, and ultimately the nature of state power.

One Step Forward, Two Steps Backward

There remain several unanswered questions. Is this new moralism and religious revivalism simply a cyclical event in the United States, as short-lived as the "hang loose" ethic of the 1960s or the "environmentalism" of the 1970s, or will it be more durable? Will the isolationism that derives from such a moralism be any different from similar tendencies following World War I, with its Kellogg-Briand Pact outlawing war, U.S. rejection of League of Nations membership, and general dismantling of armed forces? These considerations pertain to temporal, cyclical aspects of what has herein been discussed in spatial and global terms.

While it is clear that there is a loose connection between the generational characteristics described above, it would be dangerous to reduce the new fundamentalism to such a common ancestry. What we are witnessing is not simply a challenge to modernity but an assault upon complexity, especially against scientific findings and formulas. The religious mood of exaltation and fervor, even if it remains a statistical minority, is a relatively painless way to knowledge. In place of many books is The Good Book; in place of relativism is moral certainty; in place of a series of questions begetting more questions are a series of answers stimulated by the rhetoric of certainty.

There has not been a serious, full-scale appraisal of the concomitant to the end of ideology: namely, the exhaustion of mythology. The scientific ethic—with its emphasis on experience and verification, information that is subject to testing and grounded in methods, data presented in a highly mathematical form—inevitably leads to a new elitism, based upon policy-oriented varieties of professionalism. There is a mushrooming of agencies based upon evaluation, measurement, policy-making—all of which debrief, debunk, and move people away from common inherited shibboleths. The new chiliastic religions and cults provide a wide variety of answers in a world of doubt, certainty in a world of uncertainty, and belief in a world of competing facts. The structure of scientific revolutions, no less than the structure of foreign policy, provide the motor force of this moral counter-revolution against economic development. The force of numbers, of masses, is potent. The power of mobilization has been crucial in the postwar climate from Gandhi to Khomeini. Such a force prevents limits to military might from being operative in the face of mass movements from below. The new moralism does not shy away from politics. Rather, it denies that politics is a complex game played by the rulers alone. Hence, the new fundamentalism perceives itself as supporting the restoration of traditional values, including the value that everyone counts in this new massive order of things.

Reaction to the novelty, or lack thereof, of this new fundamentalism, whether it is simply a cyclical reaction or a programmed restoration of the isolationist tendencies of earlier decades requires both analytic clarity and historical specificity. The old isolationism was essentially a political maneuver, a legislative and presidential tendency reflecting strong fears on the part of Americans of becoming linked to European embroglios: overseas adventures that would once again require shedding American lives to "bail out" European varieties of nationalism. Whether this scenario was accurate or not was less important than the fact that it was widely believed. The old isolationism was from the outset a political tactic reflecting cultural insularity. The American economy of the 1920s continued to expand and flourish. Indeed, perhaps no decade before or since saw such a startling expansion of American economic might and muscle. Hence, while the 1920s witnessed isolationist politics, it also revealed internationalistic economics. Political isolationism and economic imperialism confronted each other in uneasy truce. That a certain perceptual and linguistic confusion ensued, with a misperception of the relationship between a politics of non-involvement coupled with an economics of total dominion, doubtless makes the past seem like the present. But it would be a mistake to see history in mechanistic terms. The isolationism of the past was built upon a series of strategic considerations of growth; the isolationism of the present is built upon less precious metal: how to limit growth without inviting immediate collapse; or more prosaically, how to save the economic system without an absolute reliance upon the political structure.

The present isolationism involves economic considerations: high tariff walls against imports, protection for native manufactured goods, balanced export-import relations. But these aims reflect a growth in realization that economic control is in the hands of multinational corporations that do not move in lock step with American wishes any more than Dutch multinationals take their marching orders from The Hague. The globalization of capitalism comes at the expense and not necessarily with the aid of American capitalism. Thus, the new isolation often reflects less policy decisions than structural tendencies toward the realignment of the international economy. This realignment of the multinationals, coupled with the monopolization of vital energy resources by the OPEC powers, has meant that the new isolationism, unlike the old isolationism, is not something that can be turned off or on at will. The new isolationism is a reflection of a weakening, deteriorating global position. The old isolationism was a reflection of a certain quiet arrogance, a clear belief in the superiority of the United States way of life—a system capable of delivering the goods; it was the luxury of a secure imperial force. The new isolationism, by contrast, is a necessity, a consequence of a revolution of falling expectations, rather than the confidence of world supremacy. America searches for a place within the colonial cosmos, and abandons its pretentions to be at the head.

Are there measures at the policy level that could be implemented to turn this situation around? These policies must become essentially pedagogic: the creation of a scientific culture capable of fending off and withstanding the new religious revivalism. In this, the rising popular interest in intergalactic travel, space stations, planetary missions, may be seen to function as a counteractive myth, reinstituting the idea of the centrality of development into the myth of external progress. There is also a need for parallel, matching social myths. Here the problem is simply that the overwhelming myth of socialism so long dominant in the century after 1848 has broken down into fragments that cannot be reassembled. The collapse of the socialist alternative, certainly in its Soviet form at least, represents the failure of the last great secular myth. The return to traditionalism is in no small measure a function of this degeneration within the advanced societies. The industrial ideologies of both the First and Second Worlds have partially failed. Under the circumstances, new myths, of a more millennarian sort, have become widespread throughout the Third World.

The depth or breadth of this new fundamentalism, whatever varieties it takes, will be determined by the character and consistency of the response from the scientific and secular communities. The organizing values of social myths should not be minimized. The question is rather whether such myths have sustaining power. The struggle between developmental, modernizing, scientific ideologies and traditional, moralizing, theological ideologies has entered an advanced stage. We are not simply involved in a world of intellectual continuities and discontinuities but where there are quite practical and painful policy choices about whether to go forward, stand still, or move backward. The decisions taken will determine world socio-political priorities for at least the balance of the century.

This essay originally appeared in *Beyond Empire and Revolution: Militarization and Consolidation in the Third World,* by Irving Horowitz (Oxford University Press), and is reprinted by permission of Irving Horowitz.

3

Fundamentalism Revisited

Frank J. Lechner

Introduction

As fundamentalism reappeared on the public scene in America in the past decade, it was rediscovered by social scientists. This rediscovery was partly motivated by simple curiosity, which was shared by many Americans. Here were people making strong claims about a range of issues on seemingly traditional religious grounds, asserting a peculiar vision of American society, and demanding that Americans listen to their views on morality as well as public policy (cf. Falwell 1980). Sociologists of religion wanted to know more about the nature of this newly articulated vision, and about the way in which it might be realized. Moreover, the fundamentalist claims seemed to be receiving support from a substantial number of people, who identified with the core of a conservative Protestant religious tradition and, as participants in a significant social trend, could no longer be ignored in public discourse. Sociologists started to ask who they were, and what their influence was likely to be. But not only did they try to satisfy their curiosity and to chart the new trend, sociologists also faced a theoretical question. According to the conventional sociological wisdom, modernizing societies are undergoing a process of relentless secularization (see Wilson 1982), in which religion becomes increasingly irrelevant in the affairs of society; but then how was this apparent revival of conservative religion in the public sphere possible?

As the revived scholarly interest of sociologists has begun to produce a modest body of research dealing with such issues (Ammerman 1987; Hunter 1983a, 1987; Lechner 1985; Liebman and Wuthnow 1983), fundamentalism shows signs of waning. The New Christian Right is getting older; its dramatic "political rebirth" (Wuthnow 1983) is beginning to give way to a rather frustrating adolescence; a bid for presidential power has failed; the attempt to reshape public policy has had relatively little success. One objective of this chapter is to suggest reasons why this may be so. Clearly, the movement is in a crucial stage of its development, in which participants are faced with important dilemmas. For observers this presents an opportunity to take stock, albeit very selectively, of the events of the last decade involving fundamentalism and to pull together some of the main interpretations that have been put forth—before fundamentalism disappears from the public scene again. But although this chapter aims to contribute to this task, it is not meant to be a comprehensive overview. Rather, the chief purpose is to develop a few basic arguments about fundamentalism, based on some sociological theory and empirical evidence.

Let me briefly preview the main points of this chapter. First, I argue that we can think of "fundamentalism" not as a term describing certain kinds of conservative Protestants, but rather as a particular type of antimodern sociocultural movement. The New Christian Right is a special instance of a broader phenomenon. Second, I argue that in earlier periods of American history, when there were religious movements afoot that tried to revive a cherished faith and restore basic American values, these "revitalization movements" often had fundamentalist aspects, but produced unintended modernizing consequences. Contemporary fundamentalism clearly has some precedents in these earlier revitalization episodes. Third, fundamentalism is not simply an *antimodern* phenomenon. I argue that it is in many ways quite modern. Moreover, in spite of its apparent strengths in the past decade, I suggest that fundamentalism is subject to great inner tensions and is unable to realize a full-fledged fundamentalist program under modern circumstances. This does not mean fundamentalism is therefore unimportant. The rise, the unexpected public revival of fundamentalism tells us something important about the nature of American society, just as its failures and likely future demise tell us much about modernity.

Theoretical Considerations

There are different ways to think about fundamentalism. One is to define it in terms of a set of beliefs that certain conservative American evangelicals share.[1] Most simply put, it refers to the world view of people who think that the Bible is the inerrant Word of God and who have accepted Jesus Christ as their Lord and Savior. But fundamental*ism* goes beyond acceptance of such fundamentals of the faith. It involves at least the idea that the Bible and a person's relationship with Jesus provide answers to most personal and social problems—the biblically based world view is in principle all-encompassing. Moreover, fundamentalists are especially concerned about upholding a tradition, about maintaining the true faith in a defensive reaction against a perceived threat. On the basis of the fundamentals of faith and morality, they also wish to bring the wider culture back to its religious roots, to restore the Christian character of American society; the tenets of the faith are presumed to have implications for social change.

These important descriptive features of fundamentalism are recognizable to many conservative Protestants, and thus they have the advantage of being closely linked to the perspective of the people sociologists want to study. They already hint at some general characteristics of fundamentalism, ones that may link the American case to other forms of fundamentalism. Yet the disadvantage of such an approach to fundamentalism is that a critical, sociological examination of the self-conception of the people under study becomes more difficult. For example, the dilemmas fundamentalists often face and the unintended consequences of their actions are harder to analyze objectively if we begin by taking for granted the point of view of self-styled fundamentalists. Starting with specific descriptive features, such as the belief in inerrancy, also makes generalization more difficult; we cannot easily apply our findings in other contexts, and this is precisely something that sociologists want to be able to do. Moreover, sociologists often are interested in asking some general questions about particular phenomena. A simple example of such a general question is: *How is fundamentalism possible in an otherwise modern society?* But it is hard to formulate such questions properly unless you abstract from the specific characteristics of a particular case and try to identify some generic features of the phenomenon under study. In other words, rather than starting with historical description, a sensible sociological strategy is to construct a model of fundamentalism, and then to apply it to particular cases.

What would such a model of generic fundamentalism look like? Without going into an elaborate theoretical exercise, I simply suggest that we can think of fundamentalism as a value-oriented, antimodern, dedifferentiating form of collective action—a sociocultural movement aimed at reorganizing all spheres of life in terms of a particular set of absolute values. Leaving the technicalities of the model for another context (Lechner 1988), let me briefly clarify this proposal. First, fundamentalism is not just a set of beliefs; there is action involved. Fundamentalism is orthodoxy mobilized. People are acting collectively to bring about some sort of change. Second, they do so on the basis of a particular view of the desirable kind of society, of some ultimate values, of a comprehensive world view. The fundamentals form a pattern; the point of collective action is precisely to maintain and restore this pattern. Third, full-fledged fundamentalism embodies a profound critique of modern society, which is thought to undermine the sacred canopy provided by a revered tradition and to create social disorganization. The threat of modernity lies not so much in a new kind of theology, but rather in institutional differentiation, compartmentalization, and cultural pluralism—social life becomes horribly complex, and there no longer seems to be one true common culture. Thus, fourth, the response to this threat is to revitalize the true faith and to dedifferentiate— to make all institutions operate on sound value principles, to implement the sacred world view across the board and deprivatize religion.

This is what fundamentalism means in principle. As we will see, parts of conservative American evangelicalism fit this model in some ways. In practice, fundamentalism may rely on a literal interpretation of certain sacred texts (such as the Bible or the Koran); these may appear to provide a solid basis for the values the movement reasserts, though the so-called literal interpretations often involve some doctrinal innovation. Fundamentalism also may center on the claim that the movement is restoring a sacred past, a golden age in which modern discontents did not exist— again a plausible way to revitalize a set of values that are perceived to be threatened, though it often involves some historical myth-making. Fundamentalist movements also tend to be rooted in religious world views; links to a transcendent realm often strengthen their claims. These features are shared in part by American fundamentalism, but they are not necessary elements of fundamentalism generally. For example, the Cultural Revolution in China was a case of Maoist fundamentalism that did not rely on the idea of a golden past, though it did use sacred texts; it was also an antireligious form of fundamentalism. Clearly, then, there are different ways of being fundamentalist. My point is that thinking about fundamentalism in more general terms allows us to study the differences within the broad class of fundamentalist movements. The question for us is what makes American fundamentalism distinctive, both by comparison with other kinds of fundamentalism and by comparison with societies in which there is no such movement.

According to the analytical definition, fundamentalism is an antimodern type of movement. What makes cases of fundamentalism especially interesting for sociologists is indeed that they seem to go against the grain of modernization, of "modernity." These are tricky concepts and need to be treated with great caution. As in the case of fundamentalism, it is best to think of modernity as an analytical concept, not as a description of particular societies. An important reason is that, while contemporary societies may have some basic features in common, it is clear empirically that there are different ways of being and becoming "modern"; certainly we cannot assume, theoretically, that in the long run all societies will simply become like America. At the same time, sociologists (see, for example, Parsons 1971) have constructed a model of modern society. Among other things, it says that such a society is structurally differentiated—there is an intricate division of labor among many specialized institutions; that it is inclusive—people can become full members irrespective of race, religion, gender, or ethnic origin; that it has a pluralistic culture in which at best only some general values are shared by all—in particular, there is no one religious view that integrates the whole society. At least in theory, this model of modernity also has some typical implications for religion, which becomes one type of world view among others and increasingly segregated from the affairs of other institutions, more a matter of personal belief than of society-wide practice. Now the point is that fundamentalists typically reject this very pattern of modernity, this new kind of societal condition; religious fundamentalists, of course, especially object to its implications for religion. The question, then, is how an actual fundamentalist movement can occur in a society that in fact has become highly modernized.

The general concept of fundamentalism captures important aspects of real movements. In particular, the central focus of a fundamentalist movement is on the revitalization of a tradition, or of a set of values, from which radical social changes are presumed to follow. In practice, self-styled fundamentalists often think of themselves as engaged in exactly such a revitalization effort. Such revitalization movements have received some scholarly attention (Wallace 1966) because they seemed to be the typical way in which a collectivity can deal with fundamental cultural crises in which its basic values, its very identity, were at stake. The historian McLoughlin (1978) has argued that in American history there have been several periods in which many people perceived basic American values to be at stake, to which they responded, time and again, with religiously inspired and largely successful revitalization efforts. Given a solid core of values (such as individualism) that remains constant, American society has gone through several cycles of religious awakenings and revivals that translated into social reform, making the society live up to its own principles. Some of these points have been challenged. For example, McLoughlin may have overestimated the degree of cultural continuity in America; the cycles may be more apparent than real (Harper and Leicht 1984); and the revitalization and reform efforts may have been less successful than he thinks.[2] But it is quite clear that there have been recurrent, religiously motivated attempts to revitalize not only a particular faith but American values generally. The point to be derived from this historical argument is that contemporary fundamentalism shares at least some features with earlier American movements. The question is what makes the problems and prospects of this movement distinctive under modern circumstances.

A Historical Perspective

The theoretical preliminaries about fundamentalism, modernity, and revitalization, can be used to make a simple historical argument: In the revitalization episodes identified by McLoughlin, from the Puritan "Awakening" to recent years, we can see social changes taking place that constitute slow and very gradual steps toward modernity. The religiously inspired movements in most periods had at least some fundamentalist aspects, but in each case their actions had unintended modernizing consequences. This applies to contemporary fundamentalism as well: though it is antimodern in some ways, its implications are rather different. Strictly speaking we should reserve the term "fundamentalism" for the modern period; but the historical point is that it has proved to be difficult to be consistently and successfully fundamentalist in America. To exaggerate the point slightly: the more you try, the less you succeed. Since the main argument has been made elsewhere (Lechner 1985), I will only recapitulate it briefly here.

Consider first early American Puritanism. Though historians have relativized its stereotypical puritanical image, it is fair to say that the Puritan experiment had some fundamentalist features. The effort to revitalize the faith by building a "city on a hill," based on a sacred covenant, was intended to construct a hieararchical, organic, tightly integrated, community of "saints" (McLoughlin 1978; Miller 1938, 1961). Given the all-encompassing biblical prescriptions, differentiation obviously had to be limited; since there was one true faith with clear moral standards, pluralism was out of the question; in principle, full membership, requiring adherence to certain religious precepts, was defined in a rather exclusive fashion. But there was another side even to Puritanism. For example, the idea of a community under a covenant meant that society could be, indeed had to be, changed continuously to live up to high moral standards; the imperfection of the world was a stimulus for active reform. Membership in church and community was in principle voluntary and accessible to all; solidarity was to be based on consent and equality—which means a step toward a more inclusive community. Political authority not only was constrained by the covenant, it also was separated in principle from the church—a step toward differentiation in at least one sphere. Even these simple points suggest that, observed from the late twentieth century, Puritanism in some respects contained seeds of an alternative, more modern kind of society and world view.

In the First Great Awakening of the eighteenth century, the main emphasis was on conversion and saving souls, on personal piety, rather than on Puritan-style city-building (Ahlstrom 1972, chap. 18; Heimert 1966; McLoughlin 1978; Niebuhr 1959). Yet the thrust of the Awakening went beyond narrowly individualistic revivalism. For example, evangelism also required an attempt morally to reinvigorate society itself, real morality being rooted of course in evangelical Christianity. The Awakening did not directly legitimate any kind of pluralism, differentiation, or inclusion; rather, the newly converted were encouraged actively to further the coming millennium, to convert society itself, as it were. Although the attempt to turn society back to true religion is evidence of a fundamentalist impulse, it was in fact a rather modest one. In any case, the unintended consequences of the Awakening were more important. For example, the very concern with personal piety set the community of true believers further apart from the state, leading to disestablishment in some areas, and thus to what we would now call differentiation. The religion of the Great Awakening was a rather democratic religion, to be practiced in a voluntary church accessible to all; membership thus became more inclusive. There was not much of a blueprint for reintegrating society and religion. The Awakening also laid the groundwork for religious support for the revolutionary cause of liberty, for a culturally diverse republic with common citizenship and separation of church and state, in which the "theology" of the republic (the shared ultimate beliefs about America) was rather different from that of the denominations (Hatch 1977; Heimert 1966; Lidz 1979; Mead 1975, 1977). Thus the Awakening produced anything but a religiously homogeneous, undifferentiated society. Even in the eighteenth century, the sacred aspiration had already turned into a profane achievement (Clebsch 1968; Lechner 1985, 248).

The thrust of the nineteenth-century Second Great Awakening was perhaps more clearly fundamentalist than that of the first. Trying to reverse the consequences of the revolutionary victory and of creeping secularization, the objective was a republic of Christian virtue, in which the faith would be purified and society organized on the basis of Christian principles (Handy 1971; Hatch 1977, 97ff.; Miller 1961; Neibuhr 1959). Morality would be Christian again, and citizens would be good Christians. But the religious critique of early nineteenth-century secular accomplishments led to acceptance of the emerging more liberal kind of society. For example, while America was perceived as a *Redeemer Nation* and a *Righteous*

Empire (Marty 1970; Tuveson 1968), nineteenth-century evangelicalism in fact accommodated its public theology to the nonsectarian civil religion of the republic, acknowledging that the society was no longer covered by one sacred canopy. Religion itself became purely voluntary and disestablished, though church and state were not yet separated by a "wall" (Smith 1972). While being Protestant still was an advantage, citizenship never required religious qualifications, making the societal community more inclusive by differentiating it from the religious one. Evangelical religion was radically democratic in its emphasis on the freedom and responsibility of man; rather than providing a religious blueprint for a tightly controlled society, it was a model for democracy. While the contribution of religion to social life was still fully legitimate, it could no longer influence society strictly on its own terms; even the moral education to be provided by public schools was not specifically evangelical and was increasingly secular.

With the Third Great Awakening (to borrow McLoughlin's term) we come closer to the central topic of this chapter, for it is in this period around the turn of the century that we find a movement that, in its anxious defense of faith and tradition against the onslaughts of societal modernization, becomes more fully fundamentalist. For example, to reverse the liberalization of the churches at the end of the nineteenth century, conservative evangelicals and orthodox Calvinists asserted the importance of the fundamentals of the faith. The new emphasis on literalism and inerrancy was symbolically significant as a defensive reaction. In response to the involuntary culture shock experienced by conservative Protestants in an increasingly pluralistic society (Marsden 1980, 204), the Christian roots and the religious righteousness of the nation had to be reasserted (Handy 1971, chap. 3). From a Christian point of view, the new secular morality and cultural pluralism, separated from the one true religious tradition, could hardly be legitimate. As the role of religion appeared to be diminishing and secular ideas (like "progress") came to dominate the cultural scene, fundamentalists-to-be were critical of the societal change they saw around them, emphasized the need to build the Kingdom of God on Earth, and turned with renewed passion to the saving of souls. Only a return to biblical faith and personal piety, so it seemed to them, could reverse the liberalization of religion and society.

A few features of this emerging fundamentalist movement, described exhaustively by Marsden (1980), are worth emphasizing. First, it was, in fact a rather complex mosaic, including old-style orthodoxy and emotional Pentecostalism, militants and moderates, northerners and southerners. The exact strength of this coalition, a diffuse movement at best, is of course difficult to estimate, but at least initially it was not a marginal phenomenon. What came to be called fundamentalism had its intellectual origins at elite institutions, including major northern churches and universities. It could draw on solid Calvinist and evangelical traditions (cf. Sandeen 1970). Second, fundamentalism was more than simple conservatism. It was, indeed, a defensive reaction, possible only after society had become much more pluralistic, secularized and differentiated, and after significant liberalization on theological matters had penetrated the Protestant bastion. In this defense a theological tradition was mobilized, and plausible shared beliefs provided a sense of unity. Some of the old institutions—churches, schools, conferences, revivals—were turned to new, critical purposes. In the process of resistance, conservatism became fundamentalist. Third, although fundamentalists often regarded themselves as representatives of the American mainstream, they could not easily undo what secularization had wrought. The increasingly complex, industrializing, differentiated society would not turn back to God. Old-time religion had become one point of view among others, and religious beliefs could not be taken for granted as they once might have been. What was new in this situation was that fundamentalists had become the cultural opposition, that in the public arena the burden of proof was placed firmly on it by the early part of this century (as was most dramatically demonstrated in the 1925 Scopes "monkey trial"). Not surprisingly, in the absence of practical results and with continuing liberalization of mainline churches, fundamentalists, from the 1920s on, increasingly withdrew into subcultural institutions.

Yet the oppositional character of fundamentalism is only part of the story. For one thing, fundamentalism had much in common with the culture it came to oppose. The concept of separation of church and state, the importance of individual faith over church authority, the idea that churches were voluntary asociations, the emphasis on realizing high principles through active involvement in the world—these and other modern notions were very much a part of the evangelical heritage. Moreover, conservative Protestants had contributed much to the modernization that was occurring in society; after all, they had been part of the previously dominant elite. Even the opposition to theological liberalism (including critical analysis of the Bible) was not free of some ambivalence, since a certain kind of rationalism had been part of the Protestant traditions as well (Marsden 1980). Though the scientific method produced results (evolution theory above all) that clearly were perceived as challenges to the faith, fundamentalists still sensed a kinship with a cognitive style that Protestants like themselves had helped to pioneer in the past. The social and cultural antimodernism of the fundamentalist movement was real and important; at least in principle, it fits the outline of the fundamentalist syndrome sketched in the previous section. But the movement was in fact profoundly ambivalent because of its special kinship with the principles and structures of modernity. This very ambivalence may have added fuel to the fundamentalist fire.

The "modernity of fundamentalism" is not limited to this cultural kinship. In the beginning of this century, fundamentalism, as an identifiable force on the American religious scene, became increasingly peripheral and, as a result, more self-consciously separatist, in order to protect itself against a threatening modern center. In doing so, fundamentalists claimed a right to be different that could be extended to others as well. Living in subcultural institutions, in relatively sheltered communities, without directly challenging major national values, meant that fundamentalism in fact operated in terms of the shared secular rules of a pluralistic societal community. While the intention of fundamentalists may have been to effect some sort of dedifferentiation, or at least to limit the consequences of differentiation, they were in fact themselves differentiated-out. By their very practice, then, fundamentalists acknowledged, though in part simply because they had become a cultural minority, that social and cultural differentiation, guided by general secular principles, could make for a viable type of society. Thus an unintended consequence of fundamentalist action was to provide practical legitimation to the emerging new type of society.

What does this sketch of historical religiously inspired movements tell us about contemporary fundamentalism? Of course there is a certain risk in extrapolation. Certainly the modest modernizing consequences of, say, the First Great Awakening do not allow us to draw any clear-cut inferences about current events. But one lesson from this discussion is relevant: throughout American history there have been attempts by significant numbers of people, in loosely organized movements, to revitalize what they saw as the true faith, and to make this faith the guiding light of individuals and society alike. In many cases, these movements had some fundamentalist aspects. Contemporary fundamentalism, though operating with different purposes under new circumstances, has precursors. From a comparative point of view, fundamentalist-like revitalization activity indeed appears to have been more frequent in America.[3] But while the historical pattern is at least fairly clear, the reasons for it are not. Among them are the activist impulse in American culture to build the Kingdom of God on Earth, and the tradition of revivalist religion, making possible the mobilization of people for a larger cause. Of course the absence of a strongly integrated national religious organization and of government control also was important, especially from a comparative point of view; this provided a cultural free space for diverse forms of grass-roots action in America. All this remains quite relevant today.

Some of the basic reasons for the strange careers of fundamentalist-like revitalization movements also may be applicable today. Attempts to revitalize the true faith and make it the all-pervasive, all-encompassing sacred canopy have not been very successful in America. The explanation again requires comparative analysis, but at least the following points are relevant. In part it has to do with a peculiar element of American religious sensibility, recognizable in all the Awakenings, namely the great emphasis on individual faith and experience, to be enhanced by revivalism. While certain social or societal consequences may follow from the moral regeneration of individuals, it is clear that religious world views constructed around this central element are less likely to become full-fledged programs for societal control or even cultural dominance. In retrospect we can outline the thrust of religiously inspired action and world views, but the fact remains that these were rarely coherent ideologies or opposition movements. Apart from the distinctive content of American religion, there always was a distinctive relationship between religion and society as well. The point is that religiously inspired movements were indeed *re*vitalization movements, or were perceived as such by participants. In all cases the extent of their opposition to social trends was complicated by the extent to which they shared the ideas of the surrounding society. As I suggested above, the modern elements in Protestantism itself made the eventual fundamentalist antimodernism highly paradoxical. Most movements, in fact, appear to start from a position of partial cooptation, legitimating their claims in light of shared principles. And finally there are special features of the social context of American movements that make it difficult in principle to carry out anything like a coherent fundamentalist program. Most important is the fact that in a loosely integrated, decentralized, and over time increasingly pluralistic society, any attempt to assert the value of one world view as absolutely superior, and as the basis for societal reconstruction, is inherently problematic. In such a society fundamentalist-like efforts provoke important counterforces. Not only are comprehensive religious blueprints delegitimated on civil religious grounds,[4] they meet with institutional resistance as well. Even in the eighteenth century, the religion of the denominations did not become the religion of the republic, nor was the institutional framework of the new nation derived from any religious program put forth in the Great Awakening. Even modest institutional differentiation and the balancing of regional and group interests prevented any one religious world view from becoming nationally dominant at that time, or since.

Contemporary Fundamentalism

The "political rebirth" of fundamentalism (Wuthnow 1983) in the past decade is perhaps the single most interesting and surprising phenomenon in the American public arena. No longer satisfied with maintaining a subculture existing in splendid isolation, conservative Evangelicals increasingly asserted the value of their religious tradition, proposed solutions for social problems based on biblical precepts, and became active on the public scene in several ways. They used the media, most dramatically in the form of televangelism, not only to preach to the converted but also to mobilize people for action. They established organizations, such as the Moral Majority, to propagate a previously rather marginal world view. They built vigorous church-related institutions and, pushing a more clearly defined fundamentalist agenda, became dominant in the single largest Protestant denomination, namely the Southern Baptist Convention. They participated more actively in public debate on issues ranging from abortion to defense, and visibly contributed to political campaigns, most notably in the one mounted by a self-styled fundamentalist. All this was done in a fairly conscious way to establish fundamentalism as a cultural force to be reckoned with. As in earlier periods, religiously inspired people combined in a diffuse movement to remedy what they saw as dangerous secularization of culture and as a social crisis in a society that had lost its religious bearings. However, in spite of the drama of this political rebirth, I argue in this section that, like earlier religious movements in America, contemporary fundamentalism experiences inner tensions and produces unintended consequences, and that its practical effects and long-term significance are limited. In other words, the failures of fundamentalism are as important as its reappearance on the public scene.

If we consider the empirical characteristics of born again fundamentalism in the late 1970s and early 1980s, we find that the conventional, stereotypical views of fundamentalism are valid only in some respects. No longer a religiously marginal group, the new movement built on a postwar history of relatively high church growth for conservative Protestant churches (Roof and McKinney 1987, 150; Wuthnow 1988, chap. 8). Members of these churches, the primary population base for contemporary fundamentalism, constitute about 16 percent of the population; they are still concentrated in the South; they are highly committed to their churches; and of course they are theologically conservative (Roof and McKinney 1987, 82, 84, 101, 136; Hunter 1983, chap. 4). If we identify Evangelicals in terms of adherence to certain core beliefs, the proportion of the population is about 22 percent (Hunter 1983a, 140–41). Not surprisingly, then, they are a committed, growing, yet regionally concentrated minority. On the other hand, while their social status is still relatively low, they have made significant gains, especially in education (Roof and McKinney 1987, 111). Like conservative Protestantism earlier in this century, the contemporary Christian Right also is not as homogeneously fundamentalist (in the general sense used in this chapter) as might be expected; there is still considerable diversity on both doctrinal and political matters, as conservative Protestants would be the first to emphasize (cf. Gerstner 1975; Marsden 1975; Marty 1975; Quebedaux 1974, 1978; Wuthnow 1988, 194). In addition, among conservative American Protestants, doctrinal consensus does not necessarily translate into consistent and clearly articulated political beliefs (Kiecolt and Nelsen 1988), nor does it automatically produce support for organizations that claim to represent the world view of this religious community (Shupe and Stacey 1983). The army of God, still drawn in large part from the lower ranks of American society, is actually a rather loose coalition.

Identifying the empirical characteristics of conservative Protestants is one thing. Showing that there has been a political rebirth of fundamentalism is another. Of course the rebirth was in part a result of the way in which the public situation in America was socially defined, by self-styled fundamentalists as well as by critical observers and the media. This definition of the situation was not simply a matter of brilliant public relations; it was plausible in light of the increased and well-known public involvements of conservative Protestants previously mentioned. Through increased participation in politics, use of the media, legal action, and vigorous institution building, an effort was made to restore the Christian character of American culture and to provide a Christian solution for the social problems of modern society (as outlined in Falwell 1980; cf. Heinz 1983). By comparison with earlier periods, then, it makes sense to speak of a rebirth; however, as we will see below, this should not be confused with greatly increased power and influence.

But does this public revival qualify as fundamentalist in the generic sense—as a value-oriented, antimodern, dedifferentiating form of collective action? Let us look for the main features. First, the point of the whole effort is still to preserve a tradition, to maintain the faith, to uphold the fundamental ideas that unite the conservative Protestant community (cf. Gatewood 1969; Carter 1968; Marsden 1980, 227–28). Contemporary fundamentalism is indeed above all a cultural, value-oriented movement (cf. Harper and Leicht 1984). And characteristic of this new fundamentalism is precisely the idea that some sort of collective, public action is required—not only to maintain the tradition, but also to bring this tradition back to the center of modern society, in active response to the threat of modernity. Specifically, this requires restoration of the Judeo-Christian ethic as the core of American culture, and the application of Christian principles throughout American society. This would solve the moral chaos produced by unrestrained pluralism and the social disorganization produced by unrestrained differentiation. In principle, at least, the biblically inspired world view is all-encompassing and must be implemented across the board, in all spheres of life; a symbolic case in point is the effort to bring religion back into education. Thus in some actually rather limited ways the public resurrection of conservative Protestantism does qualify as fundamentalist.

But, as I suggested in the previous section, it is difficult to carry out full-fledged fundamentalism in America. This applies to its contemporary incarnation as well. The fact that there is no clear-cut unity among conservative Protestants on theological, moral, or political issues, in spite of fundamentalist claims to the contrary, of course hampers the development of a unified movement. This lack of unity, itself not unprecedented, is reinforced by some traditional features of the right wing of American Protestantism: its individualistic faith and its decentralized structure. With such internal features it is not surprising that there is less of a coherent program for the Christian reconstruction of America than one might suspect on the basis of fundamentalist claims. The focus in recent years has been on some rather specific symbolic issues: abortion, school prayer, drugs, and family. Though they were clearly part of an effort to remoralize American society, these issues as such hardly add up to a fully antimodern world view, and fundamentalist positions on them are shared by a majority of Americans. Nor do they suggest radical dedifferentiation. In fact, another feature of the tradition itself works against this, namely the old idea of separation, of preserving the autonomy of religion from government. While this recently may have become attenuated, and at least some Protestants may now favor greater involvement of government in religion, the old separationism clearly prevents a seemingly logical attack on the current wall of separation between church and state (Tamney and Johnson 1987). Perhaps most importantly, as suggested in the previous section, contemporary fundamentalism already incorporates much of the culture it claims to oppose; what was said about its precursors above applies even more today. It is, as I will emphasize below, a quintessentially modern phenomenon. But this means, again, that, contrary to the hopes of fundamentalist leaders, we cannot expect any kind of consistent, full-fledged fundamentalism in America.

This leaves us with the question of how even the watered-down version achieved national prominence in its political rebirth. We need to distinguish several aspects of the question—the fact that such a movement occurred at all, that it occurred in America, and that it took place when it did. A few deep factors account for the first two elements. In a general sense, of course, the nature of modern society is part of the answer. After all, fundamentalism is a reaction against the process of differentiation and secularization, against the new kind of society that is inhospitable to the old tradition. So modernity is a cause. But we cannot attribute the rebirth of fundamentalism to the "unkind forces" (Hunter 1983a) of modernity, since there are many modern societies that function quite well without it; there are no built-in discontents of modernity that necessarily give rise to antimodern movements. We need to look for some special features of American society as part of the answer. One is by now familiar: the long-standing pattern of dealing with perceived social and moral crises in the form of religious movements, often with fundamentalist characteristics. It is simply to be expected that they recur. In addition, the very tradition of revivalist Evangelicalism provides powerful cultural backing for any new movement that tries to address the social ills of modern society; in light of this tradition, at least quasi-fundamentalism is a plausible course of action (cf. Marty 1981, 9; Sandeen 1970). But plausibility is not enough. Sociological common sense suggests that there need to be resources and organizational structures as well—and clearly there were, in the old evangelical subculture with its growing membership and elaborate network of institutions (Wuthnow 1988, chap. 8). And finally, the secular liberalism of modern American society that is resented by fundamentalists in fact provides the opportunity for action. Several elements of the liberal tradition—the emphasis on religious liberty, separation of church and state, broad moral consensus, voluntarism in religion and community, weak central authority—in fact helped make renewed fundamentalism possible. Precisely in a truly liberal, pluralistic society, there is room for fundamentalism as well. Even seemingly radical opposition movements, especially those with cultural plausibility and organizational strength, can claim some legitimacy.

What about the timing? Why did we see the rebirth of fundamentalism in the last decade and not earlier? After all, the enemies of fundamentalism, secular humanism and liberal Christianity (Heinz 1983), were at least as threatening in the 1960s as a decade later. The apparent triumph of secularism also occurred earlier, as did potentially dangerous social change. It would be difficult to argue that America had become much more differentiated since the 1950s, giving fundamentalists that much more reason to revolt. Unfortunately, the question of timing has not received much attention; sociologists are better at dealing with long-term trends. Wuthnow (1983, 178–79; 1988, chap. 8) suggests that the blurring of the boundaries between private and public spheres, of individual morality and collective life since Watergate, stimulated fundamentalist participation in public life, since moral issues could no longer be separated from political ones, and in fact morality itself had become a political issue. Moreover, the various crises of the 1970s, defined as the "failures of modernity," could be seen by would-be activists as an opportunity to enhance their position (Simpson 1983, 202). We could add that the availability of a conservative political movement that actively solicited fundamentalist support was an additional factor, since it encouraged fundamentalist involvement in politics and became a vehicle for the expression of long-held concerns. And finally, it could be argued that what was different above all in the late 1970s was the different position of America in the world—that American society was no longer clearly the dominant power; this led to a reexamination of the national culture and identity. With the society not only turning further away from its own roots, but also under international pressure in a new uncertain global context, fundamentalists had all the more reason to participate in this national debate (cf. Robertson and Chirico 1985). But such precipitating factors, plausible as they may be, remain a matter of speculation. The question of timing is still open.

Judging the full effects of the rebirth of fundamentalism, though perhaps premature, is less difficult. We can discern some trends. First, if we judge the effects in terms of concrete achievements on issues that are of obvious concern to self-styled fundamentalists and conservatives generally, we can only say that success has been minimal. The legal treatment of abortion has not changed, in spite of symbolic support from a nominally conservative administration; "creation" laws in Arkansas and Louisiana have been struck down; initially favorable court rulings on school texts in Alabama and on the educational rights of fundamentalist children in Tennessee have been reversed on appeal; there still is no legally sanctioned prayer in the public schools. Fundamentalists may have contributed to the two Reagan victories, but they have not received much in return; after a second-place showing in the Iowa caucuses, Pat Robertson's 1988 campaign failed to generate any significant support, except among a small minority of highly committed fundamentalists (cf. Johnson, Tamney, and Burton 1988). More generally, there is no evidence that the fundamentalist rebirth constitutes an Awakening in the classical sense of a religious movement that also recasts the culture (cf. Hammond 1983). America is not in any sense a more Christian nation now than before. Thus by ordinary standards the public record of fundamentalism is one of failure.

Clearly, then, the "cognitive bargaining" between fundamentalism and modernity (Hunter 1983a) is rather one-sided. The structures of modernity have proved too strong. But simply making up a balance sheet, showing the failures of fundamentalism and the strengths of modernity, is not enough. There are more subtle consequences. For one thing, American democracy was at least temporarily enlivened (Hunter 1983b, 163). By becoming somewhat civilized participants in public debates, by putting new issues on the societal agenda, by advocating a radically different perspective, fundamentalists added to the quality of American pluralism. Thus a previously neglected group was reintegrated into the cultural

mainstream. But this reintegration also meant cooptation; the very participation in liberal society that was intended to change it, led to unintended
and still ongoing internal transformations in the fundamentalist camp.
Participation and modernization entail liberalization.[5] Operating in a secular, liberal environment fundamentalism could not help but abide by at
least some of the rules of the game. By playing it, fundamentalism ended
up legitimating the game in practice—especially modern pluralism. Needless to say, this produced great ambivalence on the part of fundamentalists. Perceiving themselves as good patriots to begin with, they also saw
what they had in common with the forces they opposed. The resulting
ambivalence further undermined the potential of a successful, full-fledged
fundamentalist movement. Thus not only does the record show failure and
ambivalence, the future holds further liberalization.

Conclusion

In conclusion I propose a few immodest theses and predictions to put
contemporary American fundamentalism in perspective.

In modern Western societies, conservative religions liberalize. Orthodoxy becomes subject to criticism. Attachment of members to church and
faith is loosened. The limited role of faith as world view and church as
organization, in a pluralistic and differentiated society, is increasingly
accepted and endorsed. Of course the generalization is not very valuable
without a clear time frame. And of course there are exceptions to the rule.
For example, some churches don't just liberalize, they disappear (as the
Catholic Church threatens to do in the Netherlands). Others occupy a
special niche in which they can preserve the old ways (say, Orthodox
churches in the United States). Still others are subject to recurrent injec-
tions of traditionalist fervor (as we have witnessed in recent years among
Southern Baptists). But such fundamentalist revivals, seemingly anomalous as they are, do not reverse the long-term trend, which is toward
liberalization. Even with the proper qualifications, the generalization
holds. The special characteristics of American society, discussed above,
that make full-fledged fundamentalism such a problematic project only
reinforce the point. In a decentralized, differentiated, pluralistic society,
where fundamentalists are a minority, internal and public liberalization are
to be expected. My prediction is that in retrospect the early 1980s will
appear as the high point of fundamentalist strength. Even the intradenom-
inational influence of fundamentalists, for example in the Southern Baptist
Convention, will be seen to have reached a climax, after which it started
to decline.

The American type of fundamentalist rebirth also does not constitute a reversal of, or at least a check on, secularization (Hunter 1983a). Secularization is indeed relentless. Modernity has no mercy. Clearly, as we saw, fundamentalism cannot succeed on its own terms in America. Although it is conceivable that fundamentalist proposals on particular issues that are supported by a large majority of Americans may have some success, a larger fundamentalist program cannot. Several predictions follow from this. First, just as we saw the political rebirth of fundamentalism in the past decade, we will soon witness the political death of fundamentalism *as* fundamentalism. Second, the process of cooptation to which fundamentalism is subjected in America does not rule out its reappearance. In fact, all other things being equal, it is to be expected that the historical pattern of recurrent fundamentalist-like movements will continue, and lead to another rebirth, in a different form, several decades from now. Third, liberalization and cooptation do not mean that fundamentalism will disappear altogether. While the fundamentalist movement will subside, there will remain a vigorous fundamentalist subculture, strong in the faith but modest in its claims for society at large. Just as fundamentalists have to live with pluralism, the continued subcultural existence of a certain form of fundamentalism is the price a liberal society pays for its pluralism. Similarly, while the society as such remains highly differentiated, precisely this differentiation makes possible niches in which an undifferentiated complex of Christian institutions (churches, schools, families, etc.) can flourish under a less extensive sacred canopy.

Fundamentalism is a quintessentially modern phenomenon. This is not so because modernity somehow naturally produces fundamentalist resistance; it does not. American fundamentalism owes more to features of American society and of the conservative Protestant tradition. But, clearly, to resist the very pattern of modernizing change is a modern thing to do, as is the adoption of a genuinely antipluralistic program. While fundamentalists would claim to be restoring a sacred tradition, in fact they are engaged in a necessarily innovative struggle, deliberately working for major societal change. In addition, American fundamentalism incorporates many modern tenets and ideas (cf. Opie 1965), including a special emphasis on the value of the individual and on religious liberty; its organizational structures, especially the voluntary denominations, are also modern inventions. The very effort to carry out a fundamentalist program adds to this modern character, since it requires the adoption of at least some modern (including legal and political) rules of the game; in the rational use of modern institutions contemporary fundamentalists would strike their historical precursors as exceedingly modern. But being modern in practice also means that the fundamentalist rebirth, legitimating its public efforts in terms of generally accepted principles and faced with a considerable array of countervailing forces, ends up endorsing the pluralistic form of modern society. Taken together, these modern features reinforce the predictions made above. They tell us something about the special character and the limitations of American fundamentalism. The attempt to deny or reject modernity altogether, as the model of fundamentalism would suggest, is necessarily blunted in America. For committed modernists this is a positive conclusion. But about fundamentalism in other kinds of societies we cannot be so sanguine. In fact, we can safely predict that where the particular institutional and cultural features of the American case are not present, and where the discontents of modernity are felt more keenly and defined more sharply, new and stronger fundamentalist movements are likely to emerge.

I would like to thank Laurel Kearns, Richard Lee, and Steven Tipton for their helpful comments. Work on this paper was supported by an Emory College Summer Faculty Development Award. This paper originally appeared in *Society* 26(1) (Jan./Feb. 1989), in a slightly abridged form and without the notes and bibliographic references included here.

Notes

1. This is not the place for elaborate discussion of definitional matters. I simply note that the term "fundamentalism" is obviously controversial, not only because it is difficult to find a useful operationalization of the concept on which everyone can agree, but more especially because conservative evangelicals resent the term because of the stigma associated with it and because they clearly want to separate themselves from what they consider to be extreme fundamentalists. With the term "fundamentalism" itself being the subject of debate, there is all the more reason to treat it in a slightly more neutral and abstract fashion, as I suggest below. For good scholarly discussion, mainly dealing with the historical-descriptive approach, see Hunter (1983a) and Ammerman (1987); see also comments in Lechner (1985).
2. For these and other criticisms, as well as a rejoinder by McLoughlin, see various contributions to a special issue of *Sociological Analysis*, 1983, 44(2).
3. This is a strong and plausible hypothesis. There is support for it in historical research, but the evidence is far from adequate. Of course historical proof would require rather careful specification of what qualifies as a religious movement in different societies; and measuring the frequency of movements comparatively would be a difficult task.
4. The term "civil religion" refers to a set of values and beliefs that constitute the core of American culture, are held by most Americans, and legitimate the American institutional structure. It is presumed to bind the society together. This is a rather contentious concept, in part because some scholars would argue that there are few such ultimate values that Americans actually share, and that even if they exist they can hardly integrate a large and diverse society. The point here is simply that if we accept the idea that there is such a religion, it clearly contains the notion that what is meaningful about social life is religious liberty,

the possibility of seeking religious truth in multiple ways. The civil religion defines America as a religiously open society, and this undermines strong fundamentalist claims.

5. Some evidence for this liberalization can be found in Hunter's (1987) study of evangelical college students. Though still conservative on the essence of the faith, they are moving slowly toward more liberal positions on several moral issues. In spite of drawbacks in the data, the clear implication is that a substantial segment of the future intellectual leadership of conservative evangelicalism will move further away from any kind of fundamentalist program.

References

Ahlstrom, Sydney E., 1972
Ammerman, Nancy T., 1987
Carter, Paul A., 1968
Clebsch, William A., 1968
Falwell, Jerry, 1980
Gatewood, Willard B. Jr., ed., 1969
Gerstner, John H., 1975
Hammond, Philip, 1983
Handy, Robert T., 1971
Harper, Charles L., and Kevin Leicht, 1984
Hatch, Nathan O., 1977
Heimert, Alan, 1966
Heinz, Donald, 1983
Hunter, James Davison, 1983a, 1983b, 1987
Johnson, Stephen D., Joseph B. Tamney, and Ronald Burton, 1988
Kiecolt, K. Jill, and Hart M. Nelsen, 1988
Lechner, Frank J., 1985, 1988
Lidz, Victor M., 1979
Liebman, Robert C., and Robert Wuthnow, eds., 1983
McLoughlin, William G., 1978
Marsden, George M., 1975, 1980
Marty, Martin E., 1970, 1975, 1981
Mead, Sydney E., 1975, 1977
Miller, Perry, 1938, 1961
Niebuhr, H. Richard, 1959 (orig. 1937)
Opie, John, Jr., 1965
Parsons, Talcott, 1971
Quebedeaux, Richard, 1974, 1978
Robertson, Roland, and Joann Chirico, 1985
Roof, Wade Clark, and William McKinney, 1987
Sandeen, Ernest R., 1970
Shupe and Stacey, 1983
Simpson, John H., 1983
Smith, Elwyn A., 1972
Tamney, Joseph B., and Stephen D. Johnson, 1987
Tuveson, Ernest Lee, 1968

Wallace, Anthony, 1966
Wells, David F., and John D. Woodbridge, eds., 1975
Wilson, Bryan R., 1982
Wuthnow, Robert, 1983, 1988

4

Gender, Education, and the
New Christian Right

Susan D. Rose

Contemporary evangelicals condemn the liberalism and secularization of American society, arguing that it issues a license of outrageous freedom to people of all persuasions. At the same time, they deplore the influence of "big government," arguing that it encroaches upon individual freedom. A politically and socially conservative movement, the New Religious Right wants to restore the common ground that once belonged to white, Anglo-Saxon, Protestants who professed a common core Christianity. Evangelicals believe that this old core, replete with patriarchal and patriotic beliefs, was destroyed when it expanded to include the interests of other religious, racial, ethnic, and special interest groups.

Their response has been to call for a return to the practices and values of "Old-Time Religion" and to the authority of the "traditional" American family (Falwell 1980). Advocating a "pro-family" stance, Evangelicals tend to oppose any legislation that would "undermine the traditional, patriarchal family." They lobbied against legislation in favor of women's and children's rights, shelters for battered women, mandatory child abuse reporting, and family planning clinics. And they supported the Family Protection Acts of 1981 that sought to deny any federal funding of educational materials that "in any way diminished, denied, or denigrated the traditional sex role norms as historically understood in the United States" (see Hunter 1983a; Rothenberg and Newport 1984; Hess 1984; and Hadden 1983).

At the same time, the evangelical movement resists reliance on secular agencies for psychological, social, and educational services. Instead of

99

playing the managerial role of the modern family, Evangelicals are attempting to establish their own "Christian" networks and communities wherein they can exercise greater control and autonomy.

Pollack argues that "the function which truly has been taken away from the family by other institutions is not education, health care, or homemaking, but the autonomy of setting its own standards" (Williams 1970, 557). It is this autonomy over setting up standards that Evangelicals are seeking when they establish their close-knit networks of family, church, and school. The major underlying reason for parents enrolling their children in Christian schools is "to exercise their right as parents to free their children from an educational environment which is perceived to be in direct conflict with the value system which they wish to instill in the lives of their children" (Ballweg 1980, *viii*). The establishment of the Christian schools is clearly linked to broader political and social issues. The evangelical hope is that they will serve both to "protect their children from the evils of the secular world," and to influence the values and direction of American society.

This chapter focuses on two different but interrelated subjects: the growth and meaning of the Christian School Movement, and gender roles and expectations. Drawing from the general literature on Evangelicalism and from case studies of two evangelical communities—one a working-class, fundamentalist Baptist community (referred to as Lakehaven) and one a middle-class, independent charismatic community (referred to as Covenant)—we will first explore the development and philosophy of Christian schools. In the second part of the chapter, we will examine how gender roles and expectations are played out within these contexts.

The Christian School Movement

Today, the Christian School Movement[1] is the fastest growing sector of private education, representing one of the most important mobilization efforts of Evangelicals to regain influence in our society. In an attempt to exercise greater control over the socialization of the young, parents of approximately one million children, or 20 percent of the total private school population, have enrolled their children in private, evangelical schools. By reuniting the three major socializing institutions of family, church, and school, Evangelicals hope to achieve a greater coherence in their own lives, bring their children up in the faith, and bring morality back to the United States. Many Evangelicals believe that Christian education is critical to the fight they want to win:

> The battle for the Christian school is thus the battle for the faith. We are in the most important and crucial war of religion in all history, the struggle between Christianity and humanism. (Rushdoony quoted in Gleason 1980)

From the mid-1950s, as America shifted from a Protestant nation to a three-religion country (Herberg 1955), Catholics became less inclined, and evangelical Protestants more inclined to enroll their children in private schools. Dr. Kienel, Executive Director of the Association of Christian Schools International, represents the views of many Christian school promoters when he writes that

> The unofficial partnership between the Protestant Church and the public school is in serious decline. Therefore, we are taking the initiative to reestablish quality, protestant education in our country. (Kienel 1980)

Evangelical Protestants, at one time the sponsors and regulators of the mainstream educational system, are now turning to alternative forms to exercise control over the education of their children. Their actions are motivated by their desire to restore religious authority in American society, to reinforce parental authority, and to provide an education for their children while protecting them from drugs, sex, violence, and the lack of discipline in the public schools.

By the 1960s, Evangelicals had begun to establish their own network of institutions in an attempt to reclaim lost territory:

> We have to reclaim America. . . . I believe that Americans want to see this country come back to basics, back to values, back to biblical morality, back to sensibility, and back to patriotism. (Falwell 1980, 17)

Marianne Brown, writing for the *Gospel Herald,* goes even further:

> The nation would consider utterly ridiculous the idea of sending its soldiers to Russia to be trained in order to later fight that nation. Just so, it is ridiculous to have children trained in the world to combat the forces of evil.

Evangelicals act in response to a series of perceived threats, including the general secularization of life and the legislatively mandated secularization of public schools. Court decisions prohibiting prayer (*Engel v. Vitale,* 370 U.S. 421, 1962) and Bible readings and devotions in public schools (*School District of Abington v. Schempp,* 374 U.S. 203, 1963) offended Evangelicals because these actions excluded God. As the Vietnam War and Watergate challenged the notion of America as the "Righteous Empire" (Marty 1970) and chipped away at the glorious image of flag intertwined with cross, Evangelicals were becoming convinced that even the best of civil religion had been lost; a righteous patriotism had been excluded from the public schools. Furthermore, court decisions desegregating schools (*Topeka v. Brown,* 1954), an increase in divorce and single parenting, as well as the civil rights, women's, and child rights movements of the 1960s and 1970s challenged the supremacy and legitimacy of the traditional, white Protestant, middle-class, patriarchal family and values.

Evangelical parents were looking for allies rather than adversaries. The professionalization of teachers distanced parents from the schools and created suspicions about parental competence and the wisdom of parental involvement (Lightfoot 1978). In response, many Evangelicals withdrew their support from public schools and established their own schools where they could hire teachers on the basis of personal character and religious commitment. In the Christian schools, character continued to count more than academic credentials or pedagogical expertise. These teachers, usually members of one of the sponsoring churches, could teach about the Bible and Christ, and reinforce the religious beliefs and values of parents and religious leaders. Theoretically, Christian schools consider teachers to be the handmaidens of parents who are considered to be the children's primary educators. In practice, however, we find that this is not necessarily the case. In Alan Peshkin's study of Bethany Baptist school and in my study of the Lakehaven Academy, the schools tend to dictate the rules to the parents who then choose either to conform or to withdraw their children from the school (see Peshkin 1986; Rose 1988).

As their alternative to public education, Christian schools are proposing authoritative, disciplined, and God-centered education that emphasizes character development and spiritual training. Affective and moral domains are considered at least as important, if not more important, than cognitive domains. Concerned with personal salvation rather than good works, Evangelicals value personal character and relationships over activities and accomplishments. When people at Lakehaven and Covenant were asked what they are preparing their children for, they responded:

> We want to introduce our students to certain disciplines of knowledge that will cause them to develop their God-given intelligence, gifts, and abilities to their potential and cause their true identities as God created them to develop. (Founder of Covenant)

> We want the individual child to find their identity and salvation in Jesus. (Covenant teacher)

> We want them to become men and women of God. (Covenant mother)

> To teach them to love the Lord. Academics will pass away. (Academy teacher)

> We want to guide and influence character growth. It is more important that they learn not to be selfish and not to lie; they'll eventually learn that $2 + 2 = 4$. (Covenant teacher)

While the Christian School Movement is not monolithic, one can identify a core educational philosophy. The following excerpts taken from the

Covenant Christian School Handbook represent the pedagogical orientations of the Christian School Movement in general:

> Mathematics: In light of the order God has produced in the material universe and its set relationships in space and time, we cannot overlook Mathematics as being an instrument for teaching our students concepts of order and logic that Creation itself portrays as a very attribute of God. Mathematics is an exact science and in this present age of "relative truth," it affords the Christian school an excellent opportunity to teach each student how to comprehend the orderly world around him, created by God who presents Himself as Absolute Truth (John 14:6).

> Science: Students should come to view Science not as a discipline that destroys the traditional values of Christian faith, but as a secondary interpretive aid to the Biblical revelation (i.e., understanding how creation works). Because the Biblical perspective is far deeper and more inclusive than the scientific viewpoint, reaching to the area of ultimate meaning, the Biblical revelation has the final priority.

> English: In the Kingdom of God our communications skills are a prerequisite for our walk, for to know God is to understand Him as He is revealed through the Word (John 1:1, 14 and 2 Timothy 3:16). We receive this revelation through listening or reading. Once we come to know Christ, that knowledge of Him must flow through us to others as we speak and write (Matthew 28:19–20). The Word is manifest in language. . . . Kingdom people must become skillful craftsmen in communication, language artists. Ineffective and unclear communicative endeavors hinder unity and one-mindedness (Genesis 11:6–7).

> Social Studies: Genesis 1 tells us that God created the heavens and the earth as well as every living and non-living thing in them. In light of this revealed fact, we need to accumulate and transmit to our children what God has created and how it may affect us who are a part of that Creation. We need a working knowledge of the world, its geography, and its people that will enable us to better be "in this world but not of it." We learn in our study of Scripture that the Lord God acted upon and in the world's history to shape and mold it according to His plan. He raised up kings and nations and tore them down always with a purpose in mind that was not at times clear to those participating.

In general, Christian schools stress the Christian history of America, the fight for religious freedom, the integral relationship between patriotism and Christianity, the religious foundation of the family, polity and educational system, and the religious character of traditional American leaders such as George Washington and Abraham Lincoln. They criticize secular humanism and values clarification in public education, and rally around the teaching of "basics" and moral education that once represented Protestant and patriotic sentiments.

Protests by blacks, women, gays, and the poor threatened to undo traditional gender, race, and class relations and roles, and challenged the

increasingly middle-class constituency of Evangelicals. The redistribution
of power among various religious, ethnic, and minority groups had strained
the limits of evangelical tolerance. Identifying themselves as "self-made,
hard-working, and too easily preyed upon by big government, labor,
minorities, and inflation" (Brumberg, 1980), many Evangelicals feared that
the "doctrine of entitlement" was going to entitle everyone to everything.
Their response has been to expose secular humanism as Satan's watchdog.
Their attack on the relativism of secular humanism is given expression by
television evangelist James Robison:

> Although it (secular humanism) ostensibly champions the dignity of man, it
> denies that he has a soul or is capable of salvation, and it leads inexorably to his
> degradation and a level of existence barely superior to that of animals. Its
> "creed book," the *Humanist Manifesto,* favors freedom of sexual choice,
> equality between men and women, abortion on demand, suicide, euthanasia,
> and one-world government. It is ultimately responsible for crime, disarmament,
> declining SAT scores, "values clarification," and the new math. And it seeks to
> limit free enterprise, distribute wealth to achieve greater equality, and place
> controls on the uses of energy and the environment. What is the origin of such
> consummate evil? It is spawned by demonism and liberalism, and that's a fact.
> (Quoted in Martin 1981, 226)

We are left here with quite a political and social bundle. And this bundle
is being carried into the courtroom as well as the classroom. Recent court
cases have debated whether Christian-school parents should be allowed to
censor educational materials in public schools (*Mozert v. Hawkins County
Board of Education,* Tennessee case) and whether secular humanism is a
religion, and if so, what role it has being taught in public school (*Smith v.
Board of School Commissioners,* Alabama case).

Central to their religious, political, and educational concerns is the
challenge to traditional sex role norms. They protest the "inversion" of
gender roles that are exhibited in some contemporary school textbooks,
where a father may be seen washing the dishes with his daughter and Mom
is dressed in a business suit. As expressed in Robison's statement, Evangelicals find gender equality to be a particularly disturbing idea. Instead,
they want to preserve the traditional, patriarchal family which maintains
parental authority over children, and male authority over women. One way
of trying to do this is to enclose their children within the Christian schools.

Gender and the New Christian Right

Contemporary Evangelicals continue to define men as the natural leaders of the family, church, and nation. According to established doctrine in

fundamentalist and many evangelical churches, women are supposed to submit to their husbands (Ephesians 5:22), and husbands are expected to love and provide for their wives. Men, as the "natural" leaders of the family, church, and society, have the responsibility to "cover" or protect their wives and children. They believe that this hierarchical ordering of relationships reflects God's natural order; if disrupted, the family, and in turn, society will fall apart (see Falwell 1980; LaHaye 1982).

The fact that many evangelical wives are working is usually condoned, however, since it often serves an economic necessity. But in no way should the wife challenge her husband's role as the primary breadwinner and head of household. Rather, the traditional, patriarchal family should be upheld:

> The Bible clearly states that the wife is to submit to her husband's leadership and help him fulfill God's will for his life (cf. Eph. 5:22–24; Col. 3:18). There can be no doubt as to the meaning of these passages. She is to submit to him, just as she would submit to Christ her Lord. This places the responsibility of leadership upon her husband, where it belongs. In a sense, submission is the wife learning to duck, so God can hit the husband. He will never realize his responsibility to the family as long as she takes it. If the wife wants her husband to be more of a leader, she must let go of the reins. Most men do not enjoy fighting their wife for control of the family, so they sit back and do nothing. In time, the wife has a nervous breakdown trying to run something God did not call her to run. (Hindson, Director of Counseling at Thomas Road Baptist Ministries quoted in Brumberg 1980, 222)

Furthermore, wives should be careful not to risk a reduction in their husband's self-esteem when they go to work outside the home. TV evangelist Robison elaborates: "The man's attraction is to a woman, not to a "professional person," and certainly not to a competitor whose success makes him feel inadequate as a provider" (in Martin 1981, 224).

Gender and sex quickly become intertwined as Robison addresses the primary issue of who should be in control; he argues that this sense of inadequacy may be generalized to the marriage bed, especially if the woman becomes sexually aggressive: "The masculine partner has traditionally been the initiator of sexual activity. It confuses and annoys men to find women behaving as pursuers rather than the pursued" (Martin 1981, 224).

Dr. Hindson, Director of Counseling for Falwell's ministries concludes: "Someone once said, 'Anything with two heads belongs in the zoo!' That includes your family. Two-headed households are as confusing as they are clumsy. . . . [W]hen no final authority exists in the family, confusion and arguing always result" (quoted in Brumberg 1980, 222).

In fundamentalist and many evangelical sermons, conversations, books, and family workshops, the values of the traditional American family and traditional sex role norms are extolled. And they find expression in the proposed legislation of the Family Protection Acts, which would deny any funding of educational materials that "in any way denied, denigrated, or diminished the traditional sex role differences as historically understood in the United States (see Hess 1984). Such traditional sex-role definitions described women as the vessel, the one who was soft, emotional, and the heart of the family, while the man was described as the fighter, the one who was strong, rational, and the head of the family.

While the above quotations represent the explicit ideology of the New Christian Right, we do find significant variations among practicing groups of Evangelicals. Two evangelical communities located in upstate New York, one a working-class, fundamentalist Baptist congregation (Lakehaven), the other a middle-class, independent charismatic community (Covenant) will serve to illustrate. While both the Lakehaven and Covenant fellowships share similar values about appropriate, "natural," and "God-ordained" gender traits and roles, their experiences and expectations are quite different. Their differences are grounded in the realities of their lives—in their personal, family, religious, and class backgrounds.

The Lakehaven Baptist congregation is largely composed of farmers, skilled and unskilled workers, factory workers, and truck drivers, while some members are teachers and secretaries. The Covenant fellowship is oriented more towards the arts, social work, teaching, middle management and engineering, although a number of members are secretaries and skilled laborers. The difference in income levels, however, is not what primarily distinguishes the two communities. In fact, the average salary range of both congregations in 1983 was $15,000–25,000. More critical are the substantial differences in educational and cultural background, the security of work, the degree of geographical mobility, and the age of their members.

Lakehaven Community

The Lakehaven congregation is primarily a working, lower-middle-class, agricultural community living in a rural area that is politically and socially conservative. American flags adorn Main Street which quietly runs through the town of eight hundred. The majority come from fundamentalist families. Some of Lakehaven's members have attended college, primarily Christian colleges, but the majority started working after high school on the farm or in a trade. Academic education is not a high priority; in fact, they tend to be suspicious of academics and intellectual endeavors. What is important to them is doing a good job at work and being responsible to one's family. The majority of people are near or at retirement age (approximately 40 percent), or in their twenties and starting young families. The middle-aged group (forty-to-sixty) are largely unrepresented.

Most grew up within a twenty-mile radius of the church and have experienced the security and watchfulness of a small-town environment. People know one another, and one another's families. They are aware of Uncle Tom's drunkenness and Aunt Sally's faithfulness. Weaving in and out of the familiar institutions of the family, farm, church, shop, and school, they understood one another well enough to depend on each other. There is no great need to analyze or articulate what someone thinks or feels, or what they do and why. Things are, for the most part, predictable.

People expect others to play their "proper" roles as the generations did before them. It is understood, although regretted by the women, that men do not listen to them or understand them—emotionally, spiritually, or intellectually. So the women turn to other women for comfort, understanding, and talk. But even here, the women do not spend hours analyzing the situation or their frustration; too much "idle" talk would be considered a frivolous indulgence. Besides, most of them are simply too busy given that all but one married woman in the congregation works outside the home as well as inside the home. Instead, feelings are summed up in short phrases that presume a common understanding: "That's the way men are. They just don't know how to express themselves." The simplification of the deeper, more complex realities that lie underneath thus absolves people of blame and guilt and having to work on their dissatisfactions. Rather than confronting one another, people tended to resign themselves to the belief that "anatomy is destiny" and that men and women are not supposed to see eye-to-eye. Thus, the men continue to ritually shrug their shoulders and repeat the age-old adage, "You just never know what a woman wants."

Although some of the young people want something more, something different, they are not very confident that they will be lucky enough to find it. When asked what they wanted of the future, a number of the Lakehaven high school boys spoke first of getting decent jobs—"one that's outside, that's not too confining or too boring." And one boy added, "I'd like to find a girl who I can talk with. I want a friend. It would help if she were pretty." The girls spoke first of family and wanting to marry "a good Christian man." This meant someone who was hard-working, even-tempered, and a nondrinker. One senior high school girl responded that she would like to get married a few years after high school to a "Christian man, mild-tempered; someone about six feet tall would be nice."

The mothers too wanted their daughters to marry a good Christian man, but they agreed with Pastor Mann that "good men" are hard to find. About twice as many women as men attend church which is an issue for both the church leadership and the lay women. Here, women are the keepers of the faith but they wish that their men would take religion more seriously. "Men sometimes pretend that they're interested in spiritual things while they're courting a girl, but then, once they 'catch her,' that'll be the end of their church going" (Pastor Mann). After marriage, the guys ride around with their buddies while their wives go to church:

> I can see it on their faces. On Sunday mornings I'd say, "Good morning, Where's John this morning?" and I could just see her face cringe. I knew she wanted to be able to say: "Oh, he's sick or he had to go to work," but she couldn't when he was out waxing his car or playing ball. I decided to stop asking for the most part. I don't want to make them feel too badly.

According to Pastor Mann, adolescent dreams often turned into bitter realities: "Many of them [the young girls] have dreams of the man on the white horse sweeping them away—well, reality can hit pretty hard. The romance doesn't last for long."

As with the working-class families presented by Lilian Rubin in *Worlds of Pain,* marriage is often a way for the young to get away from home, to assert their own independence, and escape bad family situations. But the tendency to marry young often aggravated the situation. In many cases the young couple could not afford a place of their own, particularly if they had young children. Therefore, they would live with one of their parents, which often increased the economic strain and tension in the family.

Therefore, the very recent trend of many of the Lakehaven young people in choosing to postpone marriage and attend college is supported by parents. Most of the recent graduates of the Lakehaven Academy (1985–1986) represent the first generation college-bound for their families, and they are proud that they are able to attend and achieve at community and Christian colleges. But parents' and teachers' encouragement is mixed with pessimism about their children's futures. The message is a mixed one. They tell their children that "they must learn to be punctual and obedient, to follow rules and respect authority, and *if there is a way,* to go to college" because "even a skilled laborer's or secretary's job is hard to find without a college degree" (Lakehaven mother, my emphasis).

Parents encourage their children to get more school and land a job before they get married so that they will be more economically self-sufficient. Otherwise, it "can put a real strain on the family and times are tough enough" (Pastor Mann). As one mother of a daughter who will be attending a Christian college in the fall put it, "George says [to their daughter], 'you are going to get yourself a college degree before you get married and start having children.' Somehow we'll find a way of putting her through college. It's just important that she be on her feet before she starts a family."

But many still marry young either out of choice or because of a pregnancy. In the case of unwed pregnancies, Pastor Mann believes that many people, including the girl's family and the father of the child, should be more supportive and accepting than many are. In many cases, the father will not take responsibility—something Pastor Mann thinks should be rectified but feels is not likely to change very much. Thus, it is primarily the girls who are "caught" and who must "pay the price for their sin." They must also take responsibility for the consequences: if they are to remain in the congregation, they must confess and ask for forgiveness before the whole congregation, and they must leave the academy.

Unwed pregnancies are not uncommon in this rural area nor unknown at the Lakehaven Christian school, which stands firm against abortion and birth control of the unmarried. Lakehaven Baptist parents tend to be suspicious of their young people's "blossoming sexuality" and afraid that their girls are going to grow up too quickly. By flaunting their femininity, they fear that their girls may get themselves and their boys "into trouble." A traditional image persists of the woman as temptress to the man who harbors uncontrollable sexual desires and impulses. Sexuality is not openly discussed. No sex education is offered in the school they sponsor nor is it commonly discussed in conversations or in seminars on family life that have become popular, along with sex manuals, for more middle-class Evangelicals. Instead, in this working-class culture which elevates romanticism and the glories of the traditional family, sexuality continues to be repressed.[2]

The women and men at Lakehaven are, for the most part, trying to "make do." Economics is the overriding issue, and they consider gender issues to be relatively moot. When I interviewed people about their expectations for men and women, husbands and wives, they interpreted these questions very generally. Their responses tended to be very similar for both men and women: "people should fulfill their responsibilities. They should take care of their family. Everyone has to pitch in."

But the segregation of the sexes in daily life serves to weaken the communal efforts of the family: "It's hard. The guys hang around with their buddies on weekends and after work. And the women, they have to watch the children and do the cleaning after they get home from work. Or else, they sit around and watch the soap operas."

Rather than glorify the uniqueness of female and male culture, the women tended to accept it as one of the unfortunate realities of life. More in tone and nonverbal expressions than in words, they described a chasm between men and women, an estrangement with which neither felt comfortable. Yet, they felt that there was no sense in belaboring the obvious.

While people at Lakehaven know that they do not like textbooks that invert traditional sex-role norms, such as a father washing dishes with his daughter or a mother leaving home in a professional business suit, they talk very little about female and male roles or relationships. Although gender differences were recognized and resentment was expressed, especially by women who felt strapped by doing unpaid labor and caring for children in the home as well as keeping a paid job outside of the home, this rarely was the topic of conversation.

As far as the Lakehaven women are concerned, they do not have many options. They are trying to get along as well as they can within a system that they seem unable to escape from; they inherited rather than actively chose to return to traditional relationships. Suspecting that their men are likely to let them down, they want to secure their families as well as they can.

The different ethos of female and male culture, a lack of understanding and communication between the sexes, and a strong sense of suspicion between the sexes was taken for granted. Inheriting the roles played by generations before them and passing them on to the next generation, the men and women of Lakehaven struggle to support one another in spite of their separateness.

Covenant Community

In contrast to Lakehaven, the middle-class Covenant men and women tend to encourage, even nurture the differences between men and women. Rather than being resigned to the segregation of men and women, they try to accentuate female and male culture. They fear that contemporary women have become too independent, and too manlike in their search for power and success. They are more concerned about their women "losing their femininity" or not becoming feminine enough than they are about premature sexuality.

While they believe that women are quite competent, they think that their energies should be channeled into appropriate (that is, feminine) directions: teaching, secretarial work, social work, nursing, and ultimately marriage and motherhood. Within the community they have created special women's groups for cooking, aerobics, and dancing. Covenant women are supposed to be sexually attractive and appealing to their men. Both within family seminars held at the church and within the school, they teach that sex is a gift from God. Within the sacredness of marriage, "sex can be a beautiful, creative experience that brings man and woman together'' (Covenant principal). What accounts for such differences from Lakehaven in spite of their similar evangelical beliefs?

Founded in 1969 by an ex-disk jockey and drug addict from New York City, the Covenant fellowship was an outgrowth of a radio ministry initially supported by Pat Robertson. A number of the members and early leaders had been involved in the countercultural movement of the 1960s and had experimented with drugs, alternative life-styles, and secular therapies. By the early 1970s, a theater company, national newspaper, rock band, and coffeehouse were key features of the ministry.

As of the early 1980s, Covenant continued to be a diverse community drawing people from all classes and many different geographical regions from the West to the East Coast, and from urban to rural areas. The majority, however, belong to the middle class and many are graduates of secular colleges. Many retain connections to academia through teaching or working (especially in computers, accounting, agriculture, or secretarial work) at nearby universities. Occupations represented include college professors, teachers, secretaries, farmers, skilled laborers, businessmen, and social workers. The fellowship is set in a rural township outside of a university town of 50,000 people.

With approximately 250 full (committed) members, the fellowship primarily consists of young families with small children, and single people; however, there are a few people over the age of forty and a number of single mothers. The founding members in the late 1960s were mostly in their late teens and early twenties, and the age of the leaders still reflects the youthfulness of the group: the elders are all in their mid-thirties, the oldest being thirty-six; and the mean age of fellowship members is twenty-eight. An emphasis on family life and the youth of the fellowship has led to a proliferation of young children; approximately half of the fellowship is under the age of fifteen.

The Covenant people have diverse religious backgrounds; many grew up in Protestant or Catholic families that they generally describe as "non-Christian"; others report no religious training. A few come from fundamentalist families.

Before joining the community, a number of women considered themselves to be liberated or feminist. One woman, who entered college in the early 1970s, related that at that time she was very political. She planned to start up health clinics for women after college: "I was quite political—pro-abortion, anti-Vietnam. I was more militant than anyone else I knew, except for the *really* militant ones who were the leaders of the movement [Women's movement]."

She went on to explain that the first time she visited Covenant with friends, the head elder was speaking about sex roles and involvement in the church:

> He was calling men back into the church, saying that all across the country it was the women who were leading the churches. He talked about the natural leadership roles of men—that were God-appointed. I was so offended! I hated him. I swore I'd never go back.

Why did she go back? In fact, why did many of these women and men choose to build a community such as Covenant that stressed the traditional family and sex role norms?

Many of the women describe themselves as consciously having chosen to return to and value traditional relationships:

> There are a lot of strong women here. Oh, we have some "run through the flowers ladies," but a lot of us are strong women. We had to step down in order for our husbands to rise to their God-given responsibilities and positions. We're still strong, but in different ways. For instance, we might not preach or make the major decisions in church, but we're there talking to our husbands and they listen. We are prayer warriors! (Covenant woman and an elder's wife)

Similar to other new religious groups that put much energy into thinking about and defining gender issues, in the end the Covenant people embraced traditional rather than innovative gender roles (see McGuire 1981; Aidala 1985). They adopted from the Bible a philosophy and praxis that they believed would build strong, healthy families. It was a traditional system of hierarchical responsibilities demarcated by a division of labor between men and women that had been espoused by many generations of fundamentalists and Evangelicals. Men would be responsible for the primary decision making, economic support of the family, discipline, and rationality; women would be responsible for the emotional support of the family, support of her husband, nurturance of the children, and care of the home. Drawing from Old Testament models of family life, they created an order with the husband at the top, and the wife and children following in line. The "only problem" with this, according to some women, was *the lack of strong, sensitive men* to head the godly institutions of church and family in a loving and responsible manner:

> We are looking for strong, sensitive men. In the early days of the community, we had a lot of emasculated men who joined the community. It seemed that a lot of men who joined the Kingdom community were weak—it was a result of the families they were coming from. If we wanted strong men, we had to build them up. Still today, many of the women are more together and stronger than a lot of the men—but they are young. They *marry in faith* that God will call their

husbands up and that their husbands will grow in the Lord and become stronger. For example, there was a marriage last weekend. Ruth married John. I wouldn't have. But she married him in faith—she almost had to carry him down the aisle—[she laughs]—and you listen to him say, ''I will be your strength.'' (Single woman in her mid-thirties, emphasis mine.)

Although humor and skepticism was, at times, expressed, all of the women with whom I talked echoed the philosophy of the church elders (all of whom are men, married, and middle-aged), their husbands, and evangelical spokesmen. Only after a number of months, when I began to test the validity of the research by repeating what I had heard and recorded, did new layers of meaning and contradiction unfold. In response to my saying, ''You have a number of strong men in this fellowship,'' one woman quickly and passionately responded: ''But it's not been without a cost— the death of women'' (Elder's wife). Sensing my surprise at her passionate response and a sentiment that clearly expressed the frustration and resentment towards roles (that from former talks and discussions appeared to be accepted and supported), she continued:

> The women are aware they have sacrificed. We had to step down in order to let them [men] step up to their ''God-appointed'' positions. We had to relinquish some of our power. We value it because it's part of God's order and government. Yet, we also get frustrated at times. If we had a concern, we'd go to—[one of the elders]. Well, there's nothing that's more of a slap in the face to a Kingdom woman, than to be told to: 'Pray about it.' (Middle-aged woman and wife of an elder)

Nancy clearly interpreted it as a put-down, a ''stalling mechanism. Telling women to pray is like relegating them to the backseat, or more specifically in the holy war against evil forces, to behind-the-line combat.'' While this is important in terms of its support of the men on the front lines and is consistent with the explicit ideology of female roles expressed in the fellowship, she expresses resentment. How does she deal with her anger? In part through suppression and rationalization, she compromises and quickly falls back to the standard discussion of men's and women's roles:

> I've seen visions of battle lines drawn and women are on the front lines with men. . . . I am a prayer warrior for my husband who is an educator. But we are a team and when he becomes a pastor, then I will be an equal as a pastor's wife. Until then I pray. He is my lord. He's not perfect, but he's my lord. He is the priest of this household, I the priestess.

Nancy then went on to reiterate that the sexes are by nature different; that women are ruled by the heart and men by the head. Therefore, they must play different roles. Men are better suited to leadership positions for they hold up better under stress. "Studies have been done by the air force to show this."

Discussion

The middle-class charismatic women expressed insecurities about the struggle for independence—especially in a system that systematically pays women less for equal work and makes it very difficult for single parents to make a reasonable livelihood and find child care. Even before the onslaught of articles describing the feminization of poverty, a number of these women (originally from middle-class backgrounds) knew that they and many of their friends were having a hard time making it, emotionally and financially. This was especially true for divorced mothers. Moreover, these women wanted to establish intimate relationships with men who were loving rather than abusive, strong rather than weak. So far, their interests are not so different from many women. But their choice involved more accommodation than resistance to the inequalities of the system. Their response was to maximize their chances and their interests within the confines of traditional marriage. Like Marabel Morgan and her "total woman," they decided to accentuate their femininity.

But elements of resistance were not absent. As Anyon (1983) argues, women rarely have completely or unconditionally accepted the patriarchal ideology of femininity that commands total submission of the wife to the husband. While women may be "successfully" socialized into behaving in "appropriate" ways that support the husband through sacrifice of her self, the behavior and attitudes of most women suggest neither total acceptance nor rejection but rather accommodation and resistance to the traditional ideology of femininity.

While their religious system legitimates male dominance, it also commands that a husband love and provide for his wife. Both mutual love and reciprocal responsibilities are emphasized; and according to the community ethos, "no matter how successful a man may be in his work or community, if his family is out of order—his wife unhappy or his family uncared for—he has failed." The Covenant women believe that it is necessary to sensitize and strengthen their men (as husbands and as "men of God") before they can liberate themselves. Thus, they hold back and accept their role as "transitional" women while they make of their husbands and sons "modern" men—men who will be *strong and sensitive,* and intimately involved in family, work, and religion (see Rose, 1987).

In asking about specific decisions that were made within the family, it became clear that issues were talked about and the vast majority of decisions were made jointly by husband and wife. These women may "follow" their husbands in terms of residence and employment, and proclaim their submission to them, but at the same time, the majority of them were active partners in decision making and their husbands were active in child care. While the husbands were not expected to be responsible for house care, they were expected to be emotionally and spiritually supportive of their wives.

Both communities stress the virtues of the traditional, patriarchal, American family, and for similar reasons—to secure the authority of and protection by men—but they have different means and motivations. The middle-class charismatics fear that women may become too independent and powerful, thus disrupting family commitments altogether. In contrast, the working-class Baptists fear that their women (and men) may become seduced too early by the temptations of sex and the secular world, and thus destroy both the morality of the legitimate family and the chances for a stable, economically secure family life.

These values are communicated to their children, but my sense is that it is done more through subtle forms of socialization than through explicit teachings in the schools. Neither of the schools sponsored by Covenant or Lakehaven has sex education classes that specifically address the questions of marriage and family, gender roles, or sexuality. While Bible readings may describe "appropriate" gender roles and selected texts represent more traditional gender roles and expectations, there is little explicit gender or sexuality instruction given at Covenant. In fact, there appears to be no more gender-specific treatment or instruction at Covenant than found at area public schools (where I also observed). The Lakehaven school, which uses Accelerated Christian Education (ACE), has students read individualized instruction packets that cover the basic academic subjects and health. The health materials focus on hygiene, family relationships, and obedience to parents and persons of authority. Because of the self-paced, individualized curriculum, no class discussions or lectures take place. But there is more enforced gender segregation in gym classes and recreation than at Covenant.

How do the adult orientations of these two fellowships influence the children they are educating in their schools? A cross-sectional survey of Lakehaven and Covenant students' attitudes revealed that the vast majority of both groups of students opposed women's rights, and supported the separation of male and female spheres of influence (work and government for men, and home for women). They also distinguished between female and male sensibilities: women were valued as "keepers of the heart," and men, as "guardians of the mind."

One part of the survey replicated questions used by the Behavioral

Research Institute in their National Youth Survey (1980). In contrast to the national sample of high school students, the combined sample of Lakehaven and Covenant students thought that:

1. Fathers should have greater authority in disciplining children than mothers.
2. Men are more reliable than women in emergencies.
3. It is the man's responsibility to earn the money for the family.
4. Women are physically weaker than men.
5. Women cannot do most jobs as well as men.

The only significant difference between the two Christian schools was that the Lakehaven students more strongly (p = .03) agreed that "a wife should submit to her husband."

Like their families and fellowships, both Covenant and Lakehaven students expressed general support for the traditional, patriarchal family, and opposition to the Equal Rights Amendment, shelters for battered women, mandatory child abuse reporting, and aggressive women. They believed that men were the "natural leaders" and that women should know their place, even though they recognized (like many of their parents) that some girls and women were stronger and smarter than some boys and men, and that some men had very nurturing feelings towards young children.

It is not possible to disentangle all the influences that affect students' values, thinking, and behavior but it appears that the process of socialization and the homogeneity of the children's environments may be more influential in establishing their gender identity and values than explicit educational instruction in these two Christian schools. By providing a relatively homogeneous, Christian environment, the schools are reinforcing the values of the children's parents, teachers, and religious leaders, and at the same time limiting their exposure to more egalitarian ideas about gender. The Christian schools tend to reinforce parental authority over expert control or peer culture, and traditional values over more egalitarian ones. The transmission of many of the most fundamental values—those of gender identity—often continue to be subtly transmitted rather than explicitly taught, even among those who have a clearly articulated agenda.

This paper appeared originally in *Society* 26, (1) (Jan./Feb. 1989) in a slightly abridged form and without the notes or bibliographic material included here.

Notes

1. The Christian School Movement is interdenominational and Protestant. Its constituency consists primarily of American Baptists, Assemblies of God, the

Brethren, Free Will Methodists, Nazarenes, Southern Baptists, and many independent Bible churches. Many of these denominations had sponsored post-secondary education for some time, but their ventures into elementary and secondary schooling is a relatively new phenomenon. Although its constituency is drawn from all socioeconomic classes, it is primarily a white, middle-class, grass-roots movement that took root in the 1950s and soared in the late 1960s and 1970s. Christian school students tend to come from families with an average income of $25,000 or more. In general, their parents tend to be more highly educated than the general population of public-school parents; almost all have completed high school and many are college educated (Donald Erickson, "Private Schools in Contemporary Perspective," Report No. TTC-14, Stanford, Calif.: Institute for Research on Educational Finance and Governance, 1980; Virginia Nordin and William Turner, "More Than Segregation Academies: The Growing Protestant Fundamentalist Schools." *Phi Delta Kappa* 61 (3) (1980): 391–93).
2. For a discussion of various evangelical views on sexuality, see Richard Quebedeaux, 1978 and 1974. Barbara Ehrenreich, Elizabeth Hess, and Gloria Jacobs also have a chapter on evangelical sexuality, "Unbuckling the Bible Belt," in *Re-Making Love: The Feminization of Sex* (New York: Doubleday, 1986).

References

Aidala, Angela, 1985
Anyon, Jean, 1983
Ballweg, George, 1980
Bernstein, Basil, 1976
Brumberg, Joan, 1980
Ehrenreich, Barbara, Elizabeth Hess, and Gloria Jacobs, 1986
Falwell, Jerry, 1980
Gleason, Daniel, 1980
Hadden, Jeffrey, 1983
Herberg, William, 1955
Hess, Beth, 1984
Hunter, James Davison, 1983a
Kienel, Paul, 1980
LaHaye, Timothy, 1982
Lightfoot, Sarah Lawrence, 1978
Martin, William, 1981
Marty, Martin E., 1970
McLoughlin, William G., 1978
McGuire, Meredith B., 1981
National Youth Survey, 1980
Peshkin, Alan, 1986
Quebedeaux, Richard, 1974, 1978
Rose, Susan, 1987, 1988
Rothenberg, Stuart, and Frank Newport, 1984
Rubin, Lillian, n.d.
Sklar, Kathryn, 1973
Williams, Robin, 1970

5

Rural Ideology and the Future of Rural America

Barbara Hargrove

In looking at ideological movements in rural America, I want first to paint a picture of the situation out of which they arise, and then to discuss, first, the movements of the far right (including religious ideologies) which are seeking to gain supporters in this time of distress, and second, some of the innovative ways of seeing the problem that are being provided by other religious perspectives. Some of the implications for the future should be evident by the time we have looked at these.

The current socioeconomic situation in rural America remains serious, despite statements to the contrary by optimists who consider the rural economy to have bottomed out. Not only that, it is tied to a changed global economy that has created, and continues to create, massive social dislocation and unrest. Peter Drucker, in an influential article in *Foreign Affairs* (1986), has described that changed economy as consisting of three facets, the first of which is the disengagement, at least in industrially advanced nations, of the primary economy from the industrial economy. That is, changes in the one seem to have little effect on the other, so that a lowering of farm prices, for example, is not reflected in the manufactured goods that farmers must buy. Similarly, the growth of a capital-intensive rather than labor-intensive agriculture parallels a similar movement in industry, so that urban centers of manufacture no longer can absorb excess labor migrating in from rural areas. In fact, says Drucker, capital seems to be disengaging itself from productive processes to have a sort of life of its own. All these trends, he says, are not going to reverse themselves. And all of them, I hold, affect the people of rural North America, not only farmers but also those engaged in other primary economic activity such as fishing, lumber, mining, and the like.

Changes in the economies of nations we term "developing" are easier to see, perhaps, and are often decried by religious groups advocating civil rights, local autonomy, justice, and the values of the local community. Large corporate organizations are found to be taking over the land from indigenous peoples, tearing out forests, despoiling the land, forcing former subsistence farmers to work at less than subsistence wages growing crops for export that do not feed the local population.

It is relatively easy for movements for social justice to be called for, if not implemented, under such conditions. What is less evident is the similarity of the process going on in rural North America to that just described in the Third World. More and more of the primary economy, and particularly agriculture, is being devoted to the production of cash crops; more and more of those crops are expected to go to the export market. The title to land is falling more and more to large corporate owners, many of whom are not primarily based in agriculture, but who deal in the international capital markets in whatever area will provide the greatest profits.

The primary—and crucial—difference is that in general, rural North Americans are being overtaken, not by outside forces that they can identify and hope to resist, but by a process in which they themselves believe and attempt to participate. It is no new thing to identify American agriculture with agribusiness. Especially in the Western states and provinces, North American farms followed the industrialization of the continent. Farmers followed the railroads to new lands, and set about to raise crops that could be shipped out on those railroads. In many cases, small cities existed, with their markets for agricultural products, before the farms were settled. The American farmer has been, to various degrees, in business from the beginning.

One result of this fact is that when things begin to go wrong with the rural economy, it is economic thinking that dominates the understanding of the situation. Farmers who lose their land are accused of being poor managers, and of course some are. However, in recent years, many of those who have gone into bankruptcy or foreclosure are the very ones who have been most adept at up-to-date management, bookkeeping, and market watching. They have been the first to follow the advice of bankers, market specialists, or agricultural extension agents.

That advice, being modern and understanding the turn of agriculture toward capital-intensive methods, has led these farmers to borrow money to buy new equipment, to use new technologies of fertilizing or weed and insect control, or to expand their acreage in order to develop a farm of sufficient size to be profitable.

One misapprehension of the average consumer of farm products, which of course includes us all, is that farm prices have increased in proportion to the increase of grocery prices. Instead, the reality is that many farm prices at the present time are not much higher than they were during the Great Depression, and this is true of some products of the other parts of the primary economy as well. Thus the farmer who has increased acreage in order to increase profits often finds that he or she has increased losses instead. This is particularly true at the interest rates that held recently, and one of the reasons that some people are saying the "farm crisis" is ending has to do with some drop in those interest rates. Unfortunately, that is not the only factor involved, and even these once again seem to be climbing.

A primary cause of current economic problems on the farm is the drop in the value of farm land. As even the latest methods of increasing production have failed to create profits, there has been a severe loss of interest in buying farm land. Indeed, in that past two decades, it has been impossible to believe that farm land at inflated prices would ever be able to produce a profit sufficient to pay back the investment unless, first, agricultural prices rose dramatically, and second, the land could be resold for profit if necessary. This was indeed the expectation, as national blue ribbon committees predicted a twenty-year global shortage of food, consequent rising prices, and consequent rising value of agricultural land. Instead, in the past couple of decades, food production in Third World countries has increased by over 20 percent, and global markets have dried up.

As the value of farm land has dropped, in many cases it is no longer sufficient to serve as collateral for loans taken out against it. In such cases, foreclosure can occur even if the farmer has never missed a mortgage payment, a fact generally unexpected and bitterly resented. Many farm lands are now held by insurance companies, banks, and other lending agencies, including the United States national farm credit system. In most cases, these corporations put the land under hired managers who are charged with obtaining from them the greatest possible amount of profit. Often this has meant destroying patterns of soil conservation and tillage, with the effect of rapidly increasing erosion and otherwise destroying the long-term viability of the land. In other cases, left with land that does not seem to offer the potentiality of profit, these corporations simply abandon the land, letting it grow to weeds and harbor insects that increase the dependence of neighbors on expensive methods of weed and insect control.

This is exacerbated in many areas of the arid West, where problems of irrigation are arising, including the drawing down of ancient underground aquifers to the point where it becomes too expensive to pump water to land that cannot be productive without irrigation; increased salinization of water that has been used for irrigation, picking up minerals from the soil before moving downstream to farms that may be poisoned by the water intended to make them fertile; and increased levels of toxicity in drinking water due to the runoff of pesticides, herbicides, and nitrogen fertilizers.

A final, and perhaps the most serious problem, though it is often overlooked as people concentrate on economics, is the effect of all this on rural communities. Part of that effect, of course, is economic. It is generally understood that for every five farms that are lost, one rural business is also lost. Rural towns are "drying up," are often populated primarily by retired folk living on fixed incomes who are not able to move. The tax base of the local area is eroded, so that social services are diminished, as well as such public works as road maintenance, fire and police protection, education, and the like, which make for the maintenance of the quality of life in any area. Local voluntary associations begin to collapse from lack of personnel to keep them going, and this of course includes the churches. At a time when people are most in need of consolation and support, many of the sources for such support are drying up.

It is from this bleak picture of rural America that we may now turn to the kind of ideological movements that are arising to speak to the situation. Not surprisingly, such movements run the gamut from left to right, but there are tendencies to move away from the middle ground.

Reactionary Movements in Rural Areas

Rural populism has had a long and varied history in America. It has tended not to fall neatly into dominant categories of the political right or left. Often its social agenda has been close to what we would categorize as the left, but its ideological base has often been that of the far right. This latter seems to be the case today, but in addition, much of the social agenda now seems to be rightist as well. One factor affecting this, it would seem, is the general rightward swing of recent American politics. Fringe groups most in evidence at the present time tend to be on the fringe to the right, just as when the national mood seemed more to the left—say, in the 1960s—we heard much more from the leftist fringe.

The sources of swings to the extreme are always found in the pain and dislocation of a population, and are most often in direct proportion to the perceived power of that population to be able to affect any solution. Rural people have often felt powerless against the forces of urbanization and industry, and as the farm population has dwindled to where it now composes less than 3 percent of the population of the United States, that powerlessness becomes even more poignant.

Current extremist movements in rural America at the present time have roots in early populist causes concerning the value of paper currency, as well as all too traditional prejudices against outside groups, in this case particularly the Jews and blacks. The broadest underlying ideology of such movements at the present time is that of Christian identity. This movement draws on old myths that have made the claim that northern European Aryan Christians are the real offshoots of Israel, and hence God's chosen people. This is true not just because Christianity has sometimes laid claim to having inherited the promise, but also because a claim is made that white Europeans are direct descendants of the ten lost tribes of Israel, and hence direct inheritors of the promise. The current Christian identity ideology has also added a new twist—the claim that people of color belong to "pre-Adamic" races, not fully human but created before God invested Adam and Eve with the divine image. Thus racial prejudice has been strengthened over earlier prejudice against immigrants.

The anti-Semitic bias of this ideology picks up old strains of prejudice against Jews as forming an international banking conspiracy, one that is now expanded to include members of the Trilateral Commission. This conspiracy is understood to underly supposedly illegal deviations from the United States Constitution, which is defined as a Christian document that never intended democracy but rather a Christian republic. In the words of one spokesperson for the movement, "In a democracy the majority is sovereign [but] in our Constitutional Republic the individual is King." (quoted in the *Monitor* 1987, 4).

The claims that arise out of this complex of religious, political, and economic ideas are that mortgages engaged in through the receipt of checks or paper money are illegal and hence can be abrogated by the borrower, that it is important to remove one's name and identifying papers from the public record in order to become a free and sovereign individual, that biblical prophecies of Armageddon apply to a battle between forces of righteousness and those of evil in the midland of America and hence all righteous folk should arm themselves for the coming apocalypse, and the like.

Biblical themes taken up by these movements include prohibitions against usury, which they apply to the interest, particularly to contemporary high interest rates, paid on loans. They also bring up the idea of the Jubilee year as laid out in the book of Leviticus, where every fiftieth year all debts are to be forgiven and all land returned to its original owners or their families. (Critics who say that means that the land should be given back to the Indians fail to recognize that no covenant of God would be possible for "pre-Adamic" races, any more than the original Canaanites were expected to be the beneficiaries of Israelite Jubilee returns.) At any rate, the bottom line is that for reasons both scriptural and constitutional, they claim that farmers' land cannot be taken away through the foreclosure process.

Not all these ideas are held by members of all the rightist movements gaining strength in rural America, and not all the people who subscribe to one or more of these ideas belong specifically to any such group. Probably the most ubiquitous and influential source of information in this ideological stream is a newspaper called the *Spotlight,* which is the organ of the Liberty Lobby, and claims a circulation of over 200,000. That claim may be inflated to impress potential advertisers, but the paper is also shared among people in rural communities in ways that may if anything make the figure too small. It has been called the *Wall Street Journal* of rural America (Ridgeway 1986, 22), and whether that is an accurate analogy, it is certainly to be found in the homes of many rural folk who are not on the whole given to extremism or political activism. It helps to structure their world and their understanding of the situation.

Secular "evangelists" of this movement have made a good deal of money out of the distress of farmers by selling schemes for defense in court against bankruptcies which are doomed to failure. They often infiltrate moderate groups which are trying to do what we might call "mainline" community organizing in rural areas, leaving people confused or destroying the reputations of reputable organizations.

There are two broad methodologies to be found in these movements. Some members of the movement believe in the importance of a wholly committed cadre, and do not seek wide support among the public at large. These groups include organizations like the Order, or the Covenant, Sword, and Arm of the Lord. The Posse Comitatus, with its various branches of similar names, may be somewhere between this approach and that of other groups. These include the recently organized Populist Party, which has taken over the now defunct American Liberty Party and is a joint effort with the Liberty Lobby; the LaRouche organization; and the like. These groups seek a wide support network, and find much of it in rural America, particularly in those areas of the continent most affected by the rural economic crisis. Needless to say, such groups are greatly alienated from mainstream American religion, though they find some support for their apocalyptic notions at least in the broader segments of American fundamentalism, including some of the more popular televangelists.

A New Rural Ideology

In contrast to this growth of interest in the far right in rural America, a new kind of ideology is emerging, something probably more closely related to the so-called New Age movement which is so excoriated by fundamentalists and those of right wing persuasion. This movement has closer ties to the liberal end of mainline religion, but must admit to being on the fringe here, even as the movements discussed before are on the fringe of the right. Here we find a combination of some biblical themes, feminism, paganism, Eastern spirituality, liberation theology, the ecology movement, and the new physics—an eclectic feast, to say the least.

The biblical themes may well begin where the rightists have left off, in the passages about the year of Jubilee, for in that passage the text provides two very different viewpoints from that of simply forgiving debt and returning land to former owners. One is in the prescription for a sabbath for the land every seven years, that seems to treat the land as a living being needing a rest, even as humans need rest. The Jubilee year is a sabbath of sabbaths, held at seven times seven years. This is only one of many places in the Bible where one can find a critique of the common modern understanding of the land as a commodity, to be exploited for human use without any other considerations. Here we come close to an understanding of nature that was more common in the suppressed religions commonly lumped together as paganism, including the religions of most of the American Indian nations.

The other part of the biblical text in Leviticus that is noted by this ideology is the rationale given for all the laws about the treatment of the land: "The land shall not be sold in perpetuity, for the land is mine; for you are strangers and sojourners with me." (Leviticus 25:23) Thus rather than the reigning individual, totally free to do with his (or her) land as one wills, this tradition is one of responsibility before God, and by extension, before other people as well.

In this ideology, what is most challenged is the whole complex of assumptions that make up the culture of modernity: the call of humankind to assume mastery over nature; the acceptance of technological developments that increase production without regard to other factors concerning the quality of life in rural areas or the long-term liveliness of the land; assumptions about progress and bigness; the equating of culture with urbanization and consequent devaluation of rural life; the acceptance of economic over social or religious values; the assumption of the basic separation of humankind from the rest of nature, particularly on the basis of our rational nature; assumptions about the competitiveness of a world created through a process of survival of the fittest; and the like.

New perspectives that fit into this mix and come from the new physics and other "hard" sciences challenge both the assumption of the separation of the human species from the rest of nature and that of the basic competitiveness of nature. The discovery of systems of cooperation, some sense of mentation in organisms much less evolved than humankind, some more knowledge of our midway status between smaller organisms and the cosmos, all lead to a greater appreciation for what theologians have sometimes termed our "creatureliness." Contemporary science casts considerable doubt on our expectation that we have a right to dominate nature, and of course the fears we have engendered of nuclear destruction have helped to make the doubt more acceptable.

This has allowed people to turn to other religious traditions, or to forgotten segments of the dominant Christian and Jewish traditions of the continent, for clues as to how to live more cooperatively with nature. It is not difficult to move from this perspective to questioning many of the methods of modern agriculture, including methods that have helped to increase rural debt and so to bring on the current economic crisis. The use of highly toxic insecticides and herbicides to allow the production of vastly higher yields on the land becomes questionable, not just because of its costs—particularly since some of those yields must be subsidized as surplus commodities—but also because of the long-term environmental imbalances that are created. The movement toward organic gardening has now expanded into patterns of organic farming that are becoming far more sophisticated, and that are creating networks of marketing and research that are beginning to have some impact on agriculture, albeit small.

In the meantime, many religious movements, some arising out of the ferment of the seventies, have turned to forms of spirituality that are more consistent with an attitude of cooperation and gentleness toward nature. Some are particularly concerned about the consequences to consumers of contemporary agricultural technology, as questions are raised about the toxicity and lack of nutrition and taste in crops produced by methods aimed at the highest levels of production and at the greater ease of mechanical harvesting, transportation, and storage. Other questions are raised as to the moral effects of violence toward nature, and its possible extension to violence in human life. Many religious groups question contemporary consumerism, and particularly the way in which food is wasted, cooked, or overconsumed.

Many of the facets of this movement are independent, often totally unaware of others that may be contributing to the same perspective. Recently there have been a number of attempts to get people together from these various perspectives, to make common cause, and some of those attempts are now reaching more fully into the American mainstream.

Mainstream Reactions

There has been some effect of these movements in what could be called the American mainstream. Reaction to the influence of the far right in American religion and politics has developed. Perhaps the best-known political shoring up came in the Democratic party after the surprising success of LaRouche candidates in last year's Democratic primary election. Police action has been taken among the most extreme of these groups, such as the Order, after a string of robberies and murders were traced to its doorstep. Rick Elliott, founder of the National Agricultural Press Association and publisher of the rightist *Primrose and Cattleman's Gazette,* has been indicted for defrauding farmers with false claims to fight their foreclosures in the courts. Others on this fringe have had much of their power taken away through legal action of one kind or another. But those whose activities have been less amenable to police or court action still manage to make their influence felt.

Perhaps more important has been the gradual awakening of the mainline churches to the challenge from both right and left. They find themselves accused of ignoring their rural constituencies and favoring city dwellers, and also of supporting a form of industrialization that may be leading not only to the despoliation of the land around us but to the destruction of a rural culture that had some good things to offer to the society at large.

Churches are beginning to link domestic political advocacy to themes previously linked to Third World concerns, themes of a religious demand for justice in the name of a just God. This includes advocacy in the legislative halls of states, provinces, and nations for relief from economic pressures that have become intolerable. Churches have joined farm groups to advocate legislation demanding longer notice of foreclosures and more options to farmers faced with them. They have joined with others to question many of the economic patterns that have resulted in the rural crisis. In this way they are helping to take away some of the appeal of the more radical groups on the right, who have been able in the past to claim that no one cared about the fate of the farmer.

At the same time, they have also joined with many of the causes and concerns of the groups on the left. They have been able to take seriously the links between agriculture in North America and in the Third World, both in terms of competitive markets and in relation to the "peonization" of American farmers who are more and more becoming tenant farmers, managers, or simply farm labor on land that they once owned. This concern is raised partly in the light of Jeffersonian ideals of a democracy based on the independent yeoman farmer; partly in fear of the monopolization of the market for basic commodities we all need to live; and partly for a concern for the quality of life, both urban and rural.

Early governmental policies concerning the use of rural land were based at least partly on that Jeffersonian ideal, and were created with an eye to providing a wide distribution of small farmers throughout the continent, with the possibility of developing lively and self-governing rural communities. More recent government programs have been based entirely, so it seems, on economic aspects of agriculture and agribusiness, with a tacit assumption that the quality of life in rural America is not the appropriate arena for governmental action. During the development of industry on the continent, it has been assumed that people driven off the land were needed to provide labor for a growing industrial sector. Now, industry is oversupplied with labor, and rural migrants tend to become urban problems, where religious organizations are enlisted with other agencies to treat the social ills of the pattern. Church denominations, facing the loss of many rural churches because of the shrinking of a population base in that portion of the society, and also with the costs of dealing with the urban homeless and unemployed, have a vested interest in seeking solutions to rural issues that might not require the removal of the rural population. The interest in some of these ideologies, particularly when tied to social justice issues that have been developed in relation to the Third World, has begun to grow.

In a number of areas of the continent, attempts are being made by church groups to link urban and rural congregations in ways where they may learn about one another's problems, joys, and fears, with the hope that some of the worst excesses of the current system may be raised and understood by those who are the dominant political forces of the time— the urban voters.

But the most important fallout from this situation may be the questioning of many common theological assumptions in American mainstream religion, particularly those related to what we have known as the Protestant ethic, or what Robert Bellah has called "utilitarian individualism." The need for questioning both a utilitarian ethic and rampant individualism is perhaps most clear in rural North America right now, but it is evident much more broadly in the society. It remains to be seen whether the rural situation may lead to broader religious movements that not only question that ethic but offer new alternatives.

This article, slightly expanded, appeared originally in *Society* 26(1) (Jan./Feb. 1989).

References

Drucker, Peter, 1986
Levitas, Daniel, and Leonard Zeskind, 1987
Paddock, Joe, Nancy Paddock, and Carol Bly, 1986
Ridgeway, James, 1986
Zeskind, Leonard, 1985

6

Virus as Metaphor: Religious Responses to AIDS

Susan J. Palmer

Although there is a tendency in the popular media to adopt a no-nonsense, demystifying approach to the disease AIDS (*The New York Magazine,* 19 April 1987), and to insist that the problem is one of public health not of morality, an examination of the literature of certain religious minority groups reveals a rich strain of "metaphorical thinking" about AIDS (Sontag 1978). For many of these groups, whether one classifies them as church, sect, or cult, AIDS has become a symbol of spiritual pollution or moral decay, and they insist that the issue is indeed a moral one and even, in some cases, a magical one.

Seven religious groups were chosen for this study: the Worldwide Church of God, the Jimmy Swaggert Ministries, the Jehovah's Witnesses, the Seventh Day Adventists, the Christian Scientists, the Unification Church, and the Rajneesh movement. The first two groups represent fundamentalist and evangelical churches within mainstream Christianity, the next three might be classified as Christian sects, and the last two conform to R. S. Ellwood's definition of a cult (Ellwood 1973). A perusal of their literature on AIDS reveals that the topic is usually discussed in connection with four main themes:

1. millenarian beliefs
2. sexual mores
3. magical approaches to illness
4. the strengthening/definition of boundaries between the group and the larger society

The differences between the groups' various attitudes to AIDS are striking. This study attempts to account for these differences and to interpret the meaning of the AIDS threat within each group. Finally, it is postulated that in each group AIDS is used as a symbol to reinforce its own particular standards of sexual behavior and ideal of family life. These in turn help to define the boundaries between the group and the larger society.

In order to understand how and why the disease AIDS is treated as a symbol in these groups, it is useful to turn to Peter Berger's thoughts on nomization. He suggests that "the most important function of society is nomization" which creates a shield against terror (Berger 1969, 22) to ward off the potent and alien forces of chaos. Thus the social order provides a shelter from marginal situations which reveal the "innate precariousness of all social worlds." Death is the marginal situation par excellence, not only because of its obvious threat to the continuity of human relationships, but because it threatens the basic assumptions of order on which society rests. Sexual deviance is another area which provokes anomic terror. Berger notes that the sexual program of a society is taken for granted not simply as a utilitarian or morally correct arrangement, but as an inevitable expression of "human nature." He cites the "homosexual panic" as an illustration of the terror unleashed by the denial of the program (Berger 1969, 24).

Religion, according to Berger, is "the human enterprise by which a sacred cosmos is established" and it plays a strategic part in world construction. Since the antonym to "sacred" is the "profane," to be in a right relationship with the sacred cosmos is to be "protected against the nightmare threats of chaos and anomy (Berger 1969, 26). Nomic constructions, designed to keep terror at bay, achieve their ultimate culmination— "literally their apotheosis" (Berger 1969, 27) in the sacred cosmos. Therefore since each religion projects its version of the human order—including its sexual program—onto the totality of being, it is understandable that a fatal, sexually transmitted disease that is contracted through what each church defines as sexually deviant behavior should become a symbol of the profane.

Disease is another marginal situation which society must respond to. Peter Conrad describes the anomic terror of the profane when he wrote of the American public's "overblown . . . irrational and pointless reaction to AIDS" (Conrad 1986, 51). He asserts that illness, unlike disease (which is a "biophysical phenomenon"), involves the world of subjective interpretation and meaning: "How a culture defines an illness and how individuals experience their disorder" (Conrad 1986, 51). He attributes the public's hysterical response to AIDS to the particular social features of the disease which combine to form a cultural image of AIDS that is socially devastating: "AIDS is a disease with a triple stigma: it is connected to stigmatized groups, it is sexually transmitted, and it is a terminal disease" (Conrad 1986, 54). Conrad touches briefly on the moral and religious aspects of the social meaning of AIDS and he points out that it belongs to that group of illnesses which reflect moral shame on the individuals who had the ill luck to contract them. He refers to Allen Brandt's observation concerning venereal diseases as also applicable to AIDS: "Venereal diseases . . . become the symbol for social disorder and moral decay—a metaphor of evil" (Brandt 1985, 92).

Susan Sontag explored the social meaning of illness in the nineteenth century's romantic obsession with tuberculosis and in the contemporary mystique surrounding cancer. She argues that metaphorical thinking about disease leads to placing the burden of guilt on the patient, and attributes this to our cowardly inclination to reduce ineluctable realities like fatal illnesses to mere psychological phenomena. *Illness as Metaphor* was published before the advent of AIDS in America, but Sontag's observations on why certain diseases invite "metaphorical thinking" are relevant to understanding the responses to the new plague documented in this study:

> Any important disease whose causality is murky, and for which treatment is ineffectual, tends to be awash in significance. First, the subjects of deepest dread (corruption, decay, pollution, anomy, weakness) are identified with the disease. The disease itself becomes a metaphor. (Sontag 1978, 59)

If one examines the literature on AIDS issuing from contemporary churches in the light of the theories of Berger, Conrad, and Sontag, it appears inevitable, when faced with a catastrophic event involving the issues of fatal illness, sexual morality, and the outcast status of AIDS victims, that each church must respond in an effort to bolster its own particular world construction and to reduce terror in its congregation. Since we live in a secular age in which reality is multifaceted, it is also inevitable that different churches should come up with different interpretations of the same set of events. The striking variety in the responses might be ascribed to the different belief systems found in these religious organizations. In cases where the response to AIDS does not reflect the group's major beliefs (for example, the Christian Scientists do not emphasize faith healing, and the Adventists do not emphasize the Last Days) it might more accurately reflect the church's relationship to its host society. In other cases the statements might say more about the type of leadership found in the religious organization; charismatic cult leaders Reverend Sun

Myung Moon and Bhagwan Shree Rajneesh are the most bold and inventive in working the AIDS symbol into their millenarian prophecies.

The primary method of data collection was the study of the literature which was sent, at my request, by the churches. A secondary method was to interview members of those churches which practiced healing rituals, body rituals to ward off disease, or instituted obligatory AIDS testing. Five of these groups have issued official, well-defined policies concerning AIDS and AIDS victims. Two groups insist on AIDS tests for their congregation, and one group, while exhibiting signs of metaphorical thinking about AIDS in its rituals and folklore, has not yet published a statement on the topic.

Religious Responses

The Jimmy Swaggert Ministries

Jimmy Swaggert's views on AIDS are expressed in an article which appeared in the *Evangelist* in 1987, and was enclosed in a letter sent to me by Swaggert's administrative assistant, dated 6 November 1987. It is entitled "Is AIDS a Judgement from God?" and Swaggert replies, "No, AIDS is not a plague sent by God [it] is a result of the evil, wicked, profligate lifestyle of the homosexual community." The evangelist then claims that AIDS "had its beginning in" or "originated with the homosexual community," so that every baby, every innocent individual contracting the disease "can thank the homosexual community for his death."

Swaggert goes on to provide an excellent illustration of what Berger would see as the "homosexual panic" arising from the denial of society's sexual program (Berger 1969, 24):

> The sin of homosexuality is one of the most filthy, rotten, degenerate, degrading, hellish lifestyles that's ever been incorporated into the human family. Its birth is in hell. . . . [I]t is a direct affront to the human race. . . . It is also the worst insult to God ever conceived of by hell.

Swaggert's advice to his congregation is to pray for a cure from the scientific community because, although "God can cure . . . few healings will result from this terrible disease." Unstricken homosexuals should "ask God to give [them] a wife and prepare to live for the Lord Jesus Christ." The stricken ones "can only ask God to have mercy . . . and prepare to meet God."

The Worldwide Church of God

The message preached by the late TV evangelist, Herbert W. Armstrong, was a curious blend of Christian fundamentalism and eccentric interpretation of biblical prophecy, based on the notion of British Israelism as the Master Key which unlocked the scriptures. Armstrong claimed to be the "only apostle for our time" divinely appointed to spread the "advance news" in the last days. His apocalyptic theory was that the Second Coming would occur in January, 1972, and "while Satan visited war and pestilence on the world, God's people would take refuge in Petra, Palestine until Jesus had given Satan his cosmic comeuppance and transformed the world into a kind of urbanized Eden" (Martin 1982, 59).

Members of the Worldwide Church of God (WCG) must observe dietary laws of the Jews and are forbidden to remarry if divorced, and must separate from their spouse and move one state away if they have already remarried before joining the church. Sickness is regarded as the penalty for sin and members cannot take medicine or see a doctor but must resort to prayer since healing is God's forgiveness.

In the articles on AIDS appearing in *The Plain Truth* it is clearly stated that the new plague is a punishment from God:

> Do not think that God is ignorant about all this! To the contrary, God is going to respond. . . . The Creator, for now, is letting human beings reap the natural consequences of their own ways of living. (*The Plain Truth* Nov. 1985, 40)

AIDS is linked to the biblical prophecy:

> The apostle Paul was inspired to write that 'in the last days perilous times will come.' . . . That includes serious diseases. (*The Plain Truth* March 1988, 6)

> Few realize the Bible prophesied the alarming social disease epidemics reported in this article. Note the prophecy of Deuteronomy 28: "The Lord will bring upon you and your offspring extraordinary afflictions . . . and sickness everlasting." (*The Plain Truth* Nov. 1985, 40)

The church's standards of sexual conduct are restated as based on divine authority:

> God's laws were designed to protect the family unit . . . disobeyed they bring unimaginable social curses! . . . God made the human body . . . [T]he male and female sex organs . . . are not made for lust, perversion or promiscuity. (*The Plain Truth* Nov. 1985, 40)

AIDS therefore is the consequence of flouting this authority:

> . . . the virus is not new in existence. Like many other disease pathogens [it comes] to the fore when God's revealed spiritual and natural laws of proper living are violated. (*The Plain Truth* March 1988, 6)

The origin of AIDS is traced back to Adam and Eve when "[t]he spirit and attitude of rebellion against God . . . had entered their minds." Since then, "God has allowed humanity 6,000 years to develop various cultures under Satan's sway—and experience the results." AIDS is one of the results, since

> Satan has worked in human cultures to pervert human attitudes, emotions and relationships. . . . Satan and his host work to implant in unwary human minds selfish moods, attitudes and feelings—including improper sexual feelings. (*The Plain Truth* March 1988, 5)

Finally, the WCG works the AIDS theme into its apocalyptic theory by anticipating the Second Coming as the only cure:

> To stop the growing plague . . . Jesus Christ must come with the full power and authority from God the Father to put down sin and establish the government and laws of God over all nations. (*The Plain Truth* March 1988, 6)

The Jehovah's Witnesses

The Watch Tower and Bible Tract Society have devoted the 22 April 1986 issue of their magazine, *Awake!,* to the AIDS problem. While there is no attempt to work the AIDS symbol into their apocalyptic theory, the Witnesses do use it to underscore their standards of sexual behavior. Besides outlawing sexual relationships before or outside marriage Witnesses must observe other rules of sexual conduct:

> The Witnesses are specifically forbidden to masturbate, laugh at dirty jokes, . . . go out on a date without a chaperon . . . give rein to unbridled passion whilst having sexual intercourse. (White 1967, 84)

For Witnesses, the AIDS threat serves as a reminder that their sexual program is divinely ordained:

> Yet it *is* more than a biological fact—morality *is* involved. The moral standards that society has chosen to flout did not originate with humans. A superior intelligence had them recorded long ago. (*Awake!* 22 Apr. 1986, 8)

The Jehovah's Witnesses' position on blood transfusions is well known, and, predictably, the fact that AIDS can be transmitted through blood is used to reinforce their position:

> First, avoid the sources of contamination . . . by living in harmony with the standards of conduct that Almighty God provided. Consider how these would

have protected the thousands now dying of AIDS. . . . Significantly, the Bible forbade humans to consume blood. It says: "keep abstaining from blood" Acts 15:28, 29. (*Awake!* 22 Apr. 1986, 8)

The article points out that homosexuals are "the most susceptible group" then quotes from the New English Bible: "Make no mistake . . . none who are guilty of adultery or of homosexual perversion . . . will possess the kingdom of God" (Corinthians 6:9).

As a comment on another susceptible group, heterosexuals with multiple sexual partners, the following biblical passages are quoted:

> Let marriage be honorable among all . . . for God will judge fornicators and adulterers. (Hebrews 13:4)

> Deaden, therefore, your body members that are upon earth as respects fornication, uncleanness, sexual appetite. . . . On account of these things the wrath of God is coming (Colossians 3:5, 6)

Although it is not stated overtly, in both articles the implication appears to be that AIDS is a form of divine punishment, that it is not a problem for His faithful servants, but rather a sign of those who "fall short of perfection in their behavior" who in the millennium will be "consigned to an everlasting oblivion from which there would be no release" (Beckford 1975, 6).

The Seventh Day Adventists

The *Adventist Review* of 24 July 1986 features an editorial entitled "AIDS: An Adventist Perspective." It explicitly states that AIDS is not a sign of God's wrath ("We shouldn't look upon people with AIDS as coming under the direct judgement of God") and that AIDS victims don't deserve the disease any more than an Adventist who gets sick because he doesn't exercise or he "pours on the salt and sugar." For Adventists the important issue, the moral stance in respect to AIDS lies in the treatment of its victims:

> . . . If Jesus were here today, how would he treat people with AIDS?

> Victims of AIDS are the lepers of our society. We know how Jesus treated the lepers of His day.

> We cannot bring healing to these modern lepers, but we should receive them in the spirit of Jesus. Although in many cases they are suffering as the result of their own actions, their offense is ultimately no worse than the respectable sins we indulge in . . . Their human condition, in current medical terms, is hopeless; but Jesus is their hope.

At present, Adventist hospitals are treating patients with AIDS. . . . The church, now hardly touched by the AIDS epidemic, will feel its impact. How we react to people with AIDS will reveal the genuineness of our Christianity. (*Adventist Review*, 5)

The *Adventist Review* cautions "We shouldn't be part of the panic over AIDS," and urges "Christian ministers [to] reach out . . . in support of AIDS victims and their families." While careful to avoid any homophobic comments, the AIDS threat is used to reinforce Adventist standards of sexual behavior:

Christians have long advocated the limitation of sexual intercourse to the marriage relationship and encouraged premarital abstinence . . . Now is the time to reinforce the idea that God gave His moral law as a means of protection for His children. (*Ministry* Sept. 1986, 23)

Of all the churches studied, the Adventists appear the least worried about contagion. Their literature insists that AIDS patients not be assigned separate pews in church and the following guidelines for those caring for AIDS patients at home are suggested:

An automatic dishwasher is adequate for cleaning dishes. . . . A patient may share the bathroom with other members of the family. Visibly soiled facilities should be cleaned. . . . Never share toothbrushes . . . razor blades when there is a possibility of a transfer of blood. (*Ministry* 1986, 23)

In summary, the Adventists' position on AIDS does not diverge very far from that of the American upper-middle class, as expressed in the many articles on the topic appearing in the *New York Times* over the last few years. The Adventists' refusal to fit AIDS into their premillennial theory, and their reasonable, "let's keep informed" attitude is perhaps due to their assimilation of American middle-class values and a deferred-reward thinking described by Gary Schwartz:

It promises success in this world and in the kingdom shortly to come to those who honor God's commands punctiliously. It equates the practical virtues which enhance one's chances for upward social mobility with the characteristics of God's elect, insuring that those who take God's stern warning seriously will also strive to prove they belong to this highly favored group. (1970, 212)

The Church of Christ, Scientist

Mary Baker Eddy's famous maxim, that disease is "invalid," sums up the Christian Scientists' view of AIDS. One member asserted during an interview that AIDS could be cured through prayer, but when asked whether there were any AIDS victims among the congregation replied, "There is no way of finding out. We don't go to doctors, so we wouldn't be tested." Nevertheless, in spite of their strong emphasis on faith healing, the only article produced by the church on AIDS presents a moral and patriotic stance rather than a magical one:

> AIDS . . . that fear should call forth wellsprings of compassion. The time has never been less ripe for an I-told-you-so misinterpretation of the Old Testament gloating over the wrathful punishment of sinners. Needed just now is a healing touch—the kind that restores immunity in all sorts of ways.

> But there are times when the most healing touch is a fresh breath of honesty and moral courage. What . . . must be faced is a simple fact: that the issue is deeply intertwined with a breakdown in sexual morality. (*The Christian Science Monitor* 13 Apr. 1987, 23)

A recent *Newsweek* article entitled "The Greying of a Church" notes the declining membership figures, and that the number of healers, or "practitioners," has decreased from 12,000 in the 1950s to 3,000 today (*Newsweek* 3 Aug. 1987, 60). Since the congregation is composed mainly of "aged faithful," it is perhaps understandable that the AIDS issue is not of pressing concern for Christian Scientists. It is perhaps a mark of institutionalization and secularization that this religion, which was once emphatically charismatic under Mary Baker Eddy, has adopted a more pedestrian tone towards the AIDS issue, and has chosen to view it as a sign of social disorder and moral decay rather than as a challenge for their charismatic healers:

> If the nation can bring to the AIDS situation a . . . honest compassion . . . the . . . most . . . healing touch . . . must center in a steady return from sexual license to moral uprightness—with a clear conviction that such a return is still vital to the nation's health, happiness, and survival. (*The Christian Science Monitor* 13 Apr. 1987, 23)

The Unification Church

This new religious movement, founded in 1954 in Korea by Reverend Sun Myung Moon, who claims to be the Second Coming, has produced no more than a brief paragraph on AIDS in their literature. However, the church recently instituted obligatory AIDS testing for its members before they participate in the Blessing (popularly known as the "Moonie mass marriages"). Reverend Moon announced during the last Matching Ceremony (in which he chooses the marriage partners under divine inspiration) that AIDS was a "sign of the Last Days." Four members who participated in this ceremony, which was held 27 and 28 March 1987 at the New Yorker Hotel in Manhattan, informed me of this announcement, which will eventually appear in their collection of Moon's published sermons.

Since Unification theology is concerned with the pollution of blood through sexual relations, it would appear to offer fertile ground for metaphorical thinking about AIDS. In Moon's theodicy, the Fall of Man was brought about through Eve's having sexual relations with an angel, Lucifer, and then transmitting her fallen state to Adam by seducing him in turn. For Unificationists, the consequence of the Fall is that we are all children of Satan and not, as was originally planned, of God. The Divine Principle (DP) notes that "sexual union between a human being and an angel is actually possible" (DP, 77). For Unificationists the path to redemption is to marry their divinely ordained spouse in the course of which their fallen nature is restored through becoming the children of Reverend Moon, the new Adam.

In spite of their concern over blood lineage, Unificationists may receive blood transfusions. One member explained, "We believe that although the spirit has been corrupted by Satan, the body remains uncorrupted." Since all members must observe a minimum of three years sexual abstinence before marriage, and three years after, they regard their standards of sexual conduct to be a protection against the disease. When asked if there had been any positive results to the AIDS tests, one member said she had heard that one man in New York had received a positive result, then had gone to a "spiritualist healer," and when he was re-tested the result was negative.

The Unificationists' repudiation of homosexuality makes them inclined to be unsympathetic towards homosexual AIDS victims. When asked what would become of these patients, eschatologically speaking, one Unificationist replied, "When they go to the Spirit World, they're in for a big shock!" Reverend Moon's position on this matter is based on an Augustinian notion of what is natural:

> It is the most unnatural kind of love. At the time of creation did Adam have any other men to love? Then it is in the Principle that woman must love a man and a man must love a woman. Homosexuality is unnatural, against God's law of Creation. (*Master Speaks* 4, 5)

The Rajneesh Movement (Friends of Rajneesh)

The new religious movement that grew out of the daily discourses of an Indian-born philosophy professor, Bhagwan Shree Rajneesh, has instituted the most rigorous precautions against AIDS, and exhibits the most elaborate metaphorical thinking about the disease of all the groups in this study. Rajneesh, throughout his career as a spiritual master, had occasionally dropped hints concerning disasters of a nuclear, geological, or environmental nature, but when he emerged from three-and-a-half years of silence in 1984, he announced with greater precision than usual that two-thirds of humanity would die of the disease by the end of the century. He quoted from Nostradamus's *The Centuries* and claimed that his red-garbed disciples would be among the survivors to build a new society based on meditative consciousness and ruled by women. Shortly after this event the Rajneesh Medical Corporation at Rajneeshpuram, the group's utopian city in Oregon, instituted various precautionary measures to protect the community: couples were obliged to wear condoms and rubber gloves during sexual intercourse and to refrain from kissing. Elaborate procedures for the preparation of food and waste disposal were introduced: cooks wore latex gloves, dishes were rinsed in Clorox, and doorknobs and telephone receivers were sprayed daily with alcohol. Birthday candles were not blown out, but clapped out (Palmer 1986; Fitzgerald 1986). "Super Sex Kits" containing condoms, latex gloves, Koromex jelly, and an information brochure were advertised in the *Rajneesh Times* and sold in local Rajneesh centers.

Rajneesh's statements concerning AIDS are illustrations of Sontag's ideas on illness as symbols of social disorder and inferior consciousness. Sontag points out that tuberculosis was once thought to be a pathology of the will. Rajneesh associates AIDS with a loss of will:

> Humanity is losing its will to live. If the mind loses the will to live it will be affected in the body by the dropping of resistance against sickness, against death. If the will to live disappears, the sex will be the most vulnerable area of life to invite death. As it appears to me, the disease is spiritual. (*Rajneesh Times* 18 Jan. 1985)

Like the other church leaders in this study, Rajneesh uses the AIDS threat to emphasize the sacred quality of his movement's sexual program, and by defining homosexual behavior as profane, or "against nature," he is asserting that Rajneeshee heterosexual relationships—which are deviant by mainstream standards—reflect a right relationship with the sacred cosmos and with Bhagwan, Himself:

> AIDS is the ultimate development of homosexuality and it has no cure. You have gone so far away from Nature that there is no way back. You have broken all the bridges behind you: That is the disease AIDS. (*Rajneesh Times* 16 Aug. 1985)

Rajneesh, unlike the other leaders quoted in this study, suggests that AIDS is caused, not by too much license, but by repression. In this way he resembles Wilhem Reich who described cancer as "the stagnation of the flow of the life energy of the organism," thereby contributing to the mystique surrounding cancer as a "disease of insufficient passion afflicting those who are sexually repressed, inhibited, unspontaneous, incapable of expressing anger" (Sontag 1978, 21). Rajneesh suggests in the passage below that AIDS is the outcome of society's repression of the individual's emotions and desires, and recommends cutting ties with the past and adopting a carpe diem attitude as a protection against the disease:

> Man is becoming mature, aware that he has been cheated by the priests, by the parents, by the pedagogues; he has been simply cheated by everyone, and they have been feeding him false hopes. The day he matures and realizes this, the desire to live falls apart, and the first thing to be wounded by it will be your sexuality. To me, that is AIDS. I am simply trying to teach you to live without your will, to live joyously. It is the tomorrow that goes on poisoning. Forget the yesterdays, the tomorrows. This is our day. Just by being fully alive in it is such a power that not only you can live, you can make others aflame, afire. If you are involved in the herenow, you are so completely out of the area where infection is possible. AIDS is to me an existential sickness. Only meditation can help. Only meditation can release your energy herenow. (*Rajneesh Times* 18 Jan. 1985)

AIDS tests are compulsory for devotees of Bhagwan Shree Rajneesh. The *Rajneesh Times* of 13 September 1985 reports that the whole community at Rajneeshpuram in Oregon was tested. Since the city was disbanded and Rajneesh returned to his former ashram in Poona, India, it has become a strict regulation that all members undergo an AIDS test every three months. The Montreal *Grada Rajneesh* newsletter of February 1987 announces:

> . . . [A]ll visitors to Rajneeshdam Neo-sannyas Commune in Poona will be required to bring a doctor's certificate—not more than three months old—showing the results of a recent AIDS test. Those whose tests show a positive result are requested NOT to come.

Conclusion

To undertake a detailed interpretation of AIDS as a symbol within the belief systems of each of the seven churches is, of course, beyond the scope of this study. However, it is possible to detect and comment on recurring themes which appear in connection with the AIDS topic in the literature reviewed above. Moreover, the wide variety of approaches to and definitions of the AIDS threat can, to some extent, be accounted for if one examines these statements in relation to each group's ideas on the millennium, healing, sexuality, and on their own identity vis-à-vis the larger society.

In table 6.1 the churches' responses to AIDS are presented under the following headings or questions:

1. Type of millennialism.
2. Is AIDS a sign of the end of the world?
3. Do homosexuals "deserve" AIDS for flouting Nature/God's Will?
4. Should AIDS victims be included in the congregation?
5. Is monogamy the solution?
6. Is AIDS a sign of inferior consciousness?

AIDS and the Millennium

Historians have traditionally divided American antebellum religions into two categories distinguished by their beliefs concerning Christ's Second Coming, premillennialists claiming He will usher in a thousand years of peace, and postmillennialists claiming He will return after the thousand year period to judge the living and the dead. Since the variety and complexity of apocalyptic theory in millenarian movements is overwhelming, a simpler method of classification is used that characterizes those groups that hold out no hope for this world and tend to regard society as evil and corrupt, richly deserving its impending destruction, as premillennialists, and characterizes those groups believing the world is on the threshold of unparalleled improvement as postmillennialists.

The most widespread premillennial theory is that developed by John Nelson Darby and published in the 1909 Scofield Reference Bible. In his scheme "the triggering action will be the 'Rapture' " (Martin 1982, 32) in which the faithful will be caught up to heaven. Then will follow the seven years of tribulation which will include plagues and pestilences. The false prophet will then ally with the Antichrist and wage war against Christ who will win the battle of Armageddon, at which point the saints will enter the millennium, "an age characterized by good weather, peace, and an end to crime" (Martin 1982, 32). The Worldwide Church of God's interpretation of AIDS as a fulfillment of prophecy and sign of tribulation (under "plagues and pestilences") is in accord with this tradition, and Jimmy Swaggert's gloating over the plight of homosexual AIDS victims can be better understood (if not forgiven) in this context. The Seventh Day Adventists espouse a premillennialist theory which predates the Darby-Scofield version and their refusal to work the new plague into their Adventism is perhaps due

TABLE 6.1
AIDS and Religious Organizations

Religious Organization	Type of Millennialism	End of World?	Homosexuals Deserve AIDS?	Victims Excluded?	Monogamy Solution?	Inferior Consciousness?
Jimmy Swaggert Ministries	premillennial	no	yes	no	yes	no
Worldwide Church of God (Church of Tomorrow)	premillennial	yes	yes	-	yes	no
Jehovah's Witnesses	postmillennial	yes	yes	yes	yes	no
Seventh Day Adventists	premillennial	no	no	no	yes	no
Christian Scientists	amillennial	no	no	no	yes	yes
Unification Church	postmillennial	yes	yes	yes	yes	no
Rajneesh Movement	postmillennial	yes	yes	yes	no	yes

to the embarrassments of overspecification they have suffered in the past. William Miller, a seminal figure in Adventism, confidently predicted Christ's appearance in 1843, which subjected him and over 50,000 Miller-ites to ridicule.

The kind of apocalyptic notions found in the speeches of Moon and Rajneesh resemble the type of postmillennialism found in utopian communitarians in the nineteenth century, such as the Shakers and the Oneida Perfectionists. These tended to deemphasize the "apocalyptic thrust of primitive chiliasm" (Kern 1981), and to claim the Second Coming had already quietly occurred and that their community was the living incarnation of the glorified Kingdom of God on earth. As a select vanguard of "saints," these communities played a paradigmatic, rather than a partici-patory role in ushering in the millennium. Since these groups held their own versions of perfectionism (as the doctrine of radical sinlessness) their members no longer considered themselves subject to civil or ecclesiastical law and needed to devise their own methods for the social regulation of sexual impulses. For the Shakers, renouncing "carnal concupiscence" through leading a celibate, sexually segregated but egalitarian lifestyle, combined with ritual shaking to cast out sin, was their attempt to live like "angels." The Oneidans believed Christ had quietly come again in A.D. 70; thus man was free of sin, but needed to live in a society based on communistic sharing of property and love in order to realize his perfection. To this end they practiced a form of pantagamy called "complex mar-riage," and a system of birth control through coitus reservatus called "male continence." Their notion that the loss of sperm resulted in weak-ness, disease, and premature death was prevalent in the Victorian age, and discussed in the writings of Sylvester Graham and Thomas Low Nichols (Kern 1982, 375).

The Rajneesh communes were also based on "free love" and on the rejection of exclusive, monogamous sexual relationships (Palmer 1986; Braun 1984). The Rajneeshee's use of condoms for the dual purpose of birth control and protection against disease could be viewed as a modern version of "spermatic economics." For the Oneidans and the Rajneeshee alike, sex was regarded as a form of communion with the divine, and a means of creating an elite community of "saints." In both pantagamous societies, parenthood was considered to be an obstacle to their spiritual aims. Thus, the Rajneeshee's preoccupation with AIDS could be seen as just another expression of the postmillennialist utopian's attempt to find a sexual solution to the problem of death. Since Rajneeshism is Hindu-derived one might ask where the Second Coming fits in. Although Rajneesh avoids Christian language, he claims to be the reincarnation of Gautama Buddha, and when he emerged from silence in 1984 he announced that God was dead, thereby elevating his own status to the next best thing.

Rajneesh's disciples "overcome" death through living intensely in the "herenow," and creating Rajneesh's "new man" through ritualized, pluralistic sexual relationships and wearing latex liturgical vestments in order to survive the AIDS holocaust. Rajneesh's "New Man," a sort of Nietzschean superman, could be seen as a modern, psychological version of Perfectionism in which not freedom from sin, but rather freedom from guilt and repression (à la Wilhelm Reich) is striven for. The notion that AIDS is caused by repression was expressed by a Rajneeshee in an interview:

> Everyone is saying this proves that making love is wrong—all those Christians and the bourgeoisie. Their solution is that everyone should go back to living in families, to monogamy. What they can't see is that the family is what drove all those people to rebel in the first place—to become homosexuals and junkies. So, returning to the family would only worsen the situation. There will be *more* hypocrisy, more homosexuality, more sneaky affairs with secretaries—and more AIDS!

The same informant described a postmillennialist's view of AIDS as a quiet separation of the wheat from the chaff:

> Perhaps this is Nature's way of clearing out the planet. In a way it's a beautiful thing. After all, we are overpopulated. The purpose of sex is no longer to increase and multiply; it's to decrease and decimate. Only the most aware and intelligent will be left.

The Jehovah's Witnesses can be classified as postmillennialists due to their teaching that Christ's Coming has already taken place (albeit invisibly) in 1874 in order to gather 144,000 corulers for the Kingdom of God. The Battle of Armageddon is projected far into the future, however, so that the intervening period allows time for evangelical activity and the gradual moral perfecting of individuals. Thus the Witnesses hold a "gradualist view of history and a relatively optimistic conception of the future" typical of postmillennialists (Beckford 1975, 201). Past experience with prophetic disconfirmation and an uncharismatic leadership today would account for their failure to extrapolate on the new plague within their apocalyptic theory. AIDS is rather seen as a branding of those who, due to immoral behavior, will be consigned to everlasting oblivion.

AIDS and Social Boundaries

The two churches that appear to be least worried about the possibility that their members might contract AIDS are the Seventh Day Adventists and the Christian Scientists. The former correspond to Beckford's "activist" type of church, which emphasizes the ethical correctness of members' lives, exhibits a low rate of turnover, and maintains harmonious relations with the secular authorities. The latter fits his "individualist" type, which permits a loose adherence to beliefs and is also on good terms with the larger society and has a low rate of turnover. Their compassion towards AIDS victims and their fearlessness regarding contagion is therefore consistent with the characteristics of Beckford's typology (Beckford 1975, 100).

The Jehovah's Witnesses, the Unification Church, and the Rajneesh Foundation all correspond to Beckford's "totalizing" type, which is characterized by a sectarian attitude, strained relations with secular authorities, strict adherence to belief, and a high rate of turnover. All three groups exhibit pollution fears in their taboos and rituals controlling body fluids, diet, and sexuality. These groups condemn AIDS victims and exclude them from their congregation. For Witnesses, all those who have contracted the disease through flouting sexual, blood, or drug rules will be consigned to everlasting oblivion. For Moonies, they are debarred from the marriage blessing, which is the major initiation ritual of the church, formalizing the devotee's relationship with the Lord of the Second Advent. However, in the Spirit World, restoration will eventually be possible, even for homosexual AIDS victims. For the Rajneeshee, those whose AIDS tests are positive are excluded from their community.

Mary Douglas's study of body rituals in primitive tribes contributes towards an understanding of these totalizing churches' attitudes to AIDS. She postulates that the human body is a "natural symbol" for the social body. Thus rituals guarding the entrances and exits of the body literally and figuratively reflect the social body and its concerns. She argues that, when the social boundaries or systems are threatened from internal or external sources, these threats are symbolized and acted out in body rituals (Douglas 1970, 1966). Both the Rajneesh movement and the Unification Church are examples of religious minorities that have suffered persecution at the hands of secular authorities: both leaders have been in prison, Moonies are accused of brainwashing their members, and the city of Rajneeshpuram was beleaguered by lawsuits and land use restrictions during its brief sojourn (1981–1985) in Oregon. If categorized as body rituals, the compulsory AIDS tests, the sexual and dietary practices of these two cults, and the Witnesses' injunctions against blood transfusions might be seen as reflecting a concern with the boundaries of the group separating it from the rest of society. The constant influx of new members might threaten the ideology and social reality as defined by the group, and thus AIDS testing and taboos governing the fluids and orifices of the body could be seen as an expression of feelings of marginality and what Douglas terms the "pollution fears" of a religious minority.

Religion and AIDS

Obviously, if a cure is found, the religious responses recorded above will become no more than curiosities. If, however, the virus does continue to spread and reaches epidemic proportions, the possible repercussions for religion are the following:

1. *The renewal of religion's function of preserving the sanctity of the family* The AIDS threat will continue to be used to reinforce individual churches' particular version of sexual relationships and family life, and to prove that these are divinely ordained, or reflect a higher order of nature or the cosmos.
2. *A resurgence of millenarian movements and healing cults* The advent of AIDS as we approach the year 2000 has stimulated the apocalyptic fantasies of some minority churches, and it is likely this will increase. Norman Cohn (1961) has described doomsday cults, such as the Flag-ellants, arising out of the period of the bubonic plague in medieval Europe. While established churches are slow to respond, present a divided front to the public, or are wishy-washy in their recommenda-tions for prophylactic measures (as, for example, the Catholic Bishops' policy on condoms, *Time* 28 Dec. 1987) the smaller, more socially deviant cults like the Rajneesh and the Unification movements are more decisive and extreme in their responses to the AIDS threat.

Indeed, Moon and Rajneesh have displayed an almost uncanny ability to predict future trends. In 1984 Rajneesh began insisting on condoms and AIDS testing. In 1987 singles clubs in New York began to institute obligatory AIDS tests for their members. The Moonies have already incorporated this practice into their holy weddings.

From those churches which hold that illness reflects a state of mind or is the outcome of an inferior consciousness, it appears likely that there will be a proliferation of healing mystiques and rituals, especially since AIDS victims will be living longer. Therapeutic cults originating in the Human Potential Movement, Spiritualist, and Pentacostalist churches will most likely respond to AIDS in this fashion.

Finally, if AIDS does continue to spread exponentially, and if increasing pressure is placed on public health, legal, and political authorities to solve the problem, religion might well offer the best protection for individuals and families. Churches are uniquely qualified to provide enclaves of safety due to their ability to exert a stringent control over their members' courtship patterns, sexual behavior and reproductive faculties.

Historian Laurence Stone, interviewed on "The Journal" by Jon Kalina, was invited to extrapolate on the social consequences of a widespread epidemic. He postulated the following developments:

> My guess is that a totalitarian state will emerge which will impose very, very severe restrictions on the victims and will also change sexual relationships, or drive people back into monogamous relationships whether they like it or not. ("The Journal" CBS 17 Dec. 1987)

It would appear unlikely that legal measures, public health rules, or even a totalitarian society can stem contagion or effectively segregate victims. In the end it will be those communities that can control the sexual behavior of their youth that will be the least threatened by AIDS. These include sects of established religions, such as the Chassidim, the Amish, and the Mormons, besides the new communal cults like the Krishna Consciousness Movement, the Happy-Healthy-Holy (3HO) and those already mentioned. Most of these communities have developed systems of supervising courtship and arranging marriages.

The reaction of the public, already described as "overblown" and "hysterical," will undoubtedly continue to be irrational if the number of victims increases. For this reason, minority churches with their apocalyptic visions, their healing rituals, their sexual and dietary taboos, are perhaps better equipped to handle irrational fears and feelings of guilt and pollution evoked by the disease than mere secular authorities. Due to their peculiar ability to provide nomic constructions in which disease becomes a symbol, they can offer their members an effective shield against the anomic terror of AIDS.

This chapter was originally published in *Society* 26(1) (Jan/Feb. 1989) in an abridged version, and without the table or bibliographic material included here.

References

Beckford, James A., 1975
Berger, Peter L., 1967
Brandt, Allen, 1985
Braun, Kirk, 1984
Cohn, Norman, 1961
Conrad, Peter, 1986
Douglas, Mary, 1966, 1970
Ellwood, Robert S., 1973

Fitzgerald, Frances, 1986
Kern, Louis, 1981
Martin, William, 1982
Palmer, Susan J., 1986
Schwartz, Gary, 1970
Sontag, Susan, 1978
Stone, Laurence, 1977
White, T., 1967

III
CHALLENGE AND RENEWAL IN MAINLINE GROUPS

7

The Great Protestant Puzzle:
Retreat, Renewal, or Reshuffle?

Robin D. Perrin and Armand L. Mauss

The dramatic changes in American Protestantism during the past two decades or so have presented social scientists with an interesting puzzle. Some major denominations have been declining noticeably in membership and support, while others have been growing just as dramatically. In addition, new religious movements, such as evangelicalism and charismatic renewal, have swept into many different kinds of denominations, enhancing the religious interest and commitment of some of their members, while antagonizing others. Finally, some entirely new religions never before known in North America (and not really Protestant) have brought great controversy to the religious scene, provoking charges that they are actually dangerous cults. What is happening? Is religion in retreat, as traditionally predicted by secularization theory, or is a religious renewal taking place despite the many other signs of secularization? Or is something else altogether going on, like a shuffling of membership from some denominations to others?

Prior to the 1960s there was little reason to question the vitality of American religion. From the beginning, most of this country's denominations have grown, often at a rate exceeding population growth rates (see Gaustad 1962 for a summary of growth from 1800 to 1960). What's more, the fifteen year period between 1950 and 1964 has often been referred to as a time of religious revival, with church membership rates increasing from 57 percent in 1950 to 64.4 percent in 1964 (Nash 1968). Certainly, there were few signs to suggest, as secularization theorists argued, that American religion would "wither in the bright sun of modern culture" (Marsden 1983, 150).

However, beginning in the mid-1960s something unexpected happened. Many of this country's culture-affirming mainline denominations began to experience membership declines for the first time. The declines were sudden, and in many cases quite dramatic (see table 8.1). Between 1965 and 1985, for example, the Episcopal Church declined 20 percent, the Presbyterian Church declined 24 percent, the United Methodist Church declined 16 percent, and the Disciples of Christ declined 42 percent. Certainly, if Edwin Gaustad (1962) could interpret the growth of the Disciples of Christ, which by 1965 had grown to 1.9 million, as "phenomenal," surely were he writing today he would consider the declines since 1965 (from 1.9 million in 1965 to 1.1 million in 1985) that much more phenomenal. To be sure, in twenty short years the disciples have lost 42 percent of the 1.9 million people it took them 160 years to accumulate.

However, while the mainline denominations more liberal in theology have declined, conservative denominations have continued to grow. Between 1965 and 1985, for example, the Assemblies of God, the Church of God (Cleveland, Tenn.), the Mormons, and the Jehovah's Witnesses more than doubled. In the same time span, the Seventh Day Adventists grew by almost 80 percent. Conservative denominations closer to the mainstream have also grown, although generally at a slower rate. The Church of the Nazarene has grown by 50 percent and the Southern Baptist Convention, the largest Protestant denomination in the country, has grown by 34 percent.

The growth of these established conservative denominations has not been the only sign of new religious fervor in recent years. Unusual religious cults and sects never known before 1960 have also flourished, whether Christian or non-Christian. These include various small and independent groups of so-called Jesus freaks (like the Jews for Jesus, the Love Israel Family, and the Children of God); the Unification Church (or the "Moonies"); the International Society for Krishna Consciousness (ISKCON or "Hare Krishna"); and the Church of Scientology. While the overall membership of these new entities has remained comparatively small, at least in North America, their growth rates were dramatic during the 1970s (Bromley and Shupe 1981).

Meanwhile, apart from the growth of denominations, old or new, a variety of general renewal movements have swept across the American religious landscape. One of these has been the evangelical movement, which has expressed itself not only within many of the established denominations, but also in ways that have cut across denominational lines (Hunter 1983a). An example of the latter is the Full Gospel Businessmen's Association. Even more noteworthy has been the proliferation of television

TABLE 7.1
Inclusive Membership Statistics: 1940–1985

Liberal Denominations	1940	1965	1975	1985	% Change 1965-1985
American Lutheran	1,129,349	2,541,546	2,415,687	2,332,316	-8.2%
Disciples of Christ	1,658,966	1,918,471	1,302,164	1,116,326	-41.8%
Episcopal	1,996,434	3,429,153a	2,857,513	2,739,422	-20.0%
Lutheran Church in America	1,988,277	3,142,752	2,986,078	2,898,202	-7.8%
Presbyterian	2,690,969	3,984,460	3,535,825	3,048,235	-23.5%
United Church of Christ	1,708,146	2,070,413	1,818,762	1,683,777	-18.6%
United Methodist	8,043,454	11,067,497	9,861,028	9,266,853b	-16.3%
Conservative Denominations					
Assembly of God b	198,834	572,123	785,348	1,235,403	+116%
Church of God (Cleveland, Tenn.)	63,216	205,465	343,248	505,775c	+147%
Church of the Nazarene	165,532	343,380	441,093	522,082	+52%
Jehovah's Witnesses	N.A.	330,358	560,897	730,441	+121%
Lutheran Church (Missouri Synod)	1,227,097	2,692,889	2,763,545	2,638,164	-2.5%
Mormon	724,401	1,789,175	2,336,715	3,860,000	+116%
Seventh Day Adventists	176,218	363,666	495,699	651,945	+79%
Southern Baptist Convention	4,949,174	10,770,573	13,600,126	14,477,463	+34%

Source: Data from *The Yearbook of American and Canadian Churches*
aData for 1966
bAssembly of God statistics for 1975 and 1985 are full membership statistics.
cData for 1984

evangelists, some of whom have been tarnished by scandal in recent years (Hadden and Swann 1981). Evangelism on the college campuses can be seen in such movements as Intervarsity, the Navigators, and Campus Crusade for Christ. Stressing a personal relationship with Jesus and conservative social and political values, the evangelical movement has also exerted considerable political influence through what has come to be called the "New Christian Right," including such political pressure groups as the Moral Majority, the Eagle Forum, and the Religious Roundtable (Liebman and Wuthnow 1983).

Another sign of increased religious fervor in recent years has been the charismatic renewal movement, which again has appeared in various Protestant denominations and even in Roman Catholicism (Anderson 1979; Poloma 1982). This movement emphasizes the seeking of spiritual experiences through ministrations of the Holy Spirit. Such experiences include glossolalia (speaking in unknown tongues), prophecy, healings, and other miracles (Wilson and Clow 1981). Movements of this kind have been seen before, not only in the United States but elsewhere (Gerlach and Hine 1970). Early in this century, such a movement led eventually to the establishment of new Pentecostal denominations, such as the Assemblies of God and various Holiness sects (Chalfant, Beckley, and Palmer 1987). Some of these older denominations have by now settled into somewhat more restrained forms of charismatic expression (Dayton 1987; Poloma 1982). Yet, independent Pentecostal evangelists, especially Oral Roberts, have also helped to maintain a charismatic tradition in American Protestantism, first via radio and then via television.

Starting in the 1960s, however, a neo-Pentecostal movement began, which greatly expanded the extent and variety of charismatic expression in American religion (Poloma 1982). Thus, the term "charismatic" now refers both to the older holiness and Pentecostal traditions and to the neo-Pentecostal movement of more recent decades. This more recent movement has itself generated new sects and independent churches, though it is too early to tell whether any of them will survive. Many of the Jesus-freaks groups of the 1970s clearly showed the influence of both the evangelical and the charismatic movements, attempting to substitute religious experiences for the experiences sought earlier through mind-altering drugs. A common slogan of those groups at the time was "Get High on Jesus!" (Petersen and Mauss 1973; Mauss and Petersen 1974).

Perhaps the most interesting and surprising impact of the neo-Pentecostal charismatic movement has been seen in some of the mainline traditional denominations, especially the Episcopal (Anglican), the Lutheran, the Presbyterian, and even the Roman Catholic (Poloma 1982). It is as though the spiritual needs of some of the members of those denominations have not been adequately satisfied by the more formal liturgies, and they have sought for more feeling and fervor in their religious expressions. While other members of these mainline churches have sometimes objected to such charismatic influence, they have generally been tolerant of it, and the clergy have often welcomed it. Indeed, the Roman Catholic church has implicitly endorsed charismatic activity among its members, even organizing special retreats and prayer groups for that activity (Poloma 1982).

The charismatics in these mainline denominations have, for their part, not usually sought to take over or to break off in schismatic sects. They have seen themselves more as an effort at renewal and resacralization within the churches than as an alternative to the churches, so they have continued to participate in the usual religious services of their denominations, while at the same time holding weekly or other regular meetings for the special bestowal of the gifts of the Holy Spirit. The adherents to this neo-Pentecostal movement, like the evangelicals, have generally been normal, solid middle-class people feeling a lack of fulfillment both in their traditional religious denominations and in the surrounding secular society. In social status, at least, they are somewhat different from the Pentecostals of earlier times and cannot be dismissed (as Anderson 1979 tends to do) simply as a deprived proletariat needing a safety valve for their radicalism so that they will be more docile workers.

Here, then, is the religious situation in America during the 1980s: the more conservative denominations, sects, and cults, whether old or new, are thriving and growing, whereas the more liberal or moderate mainline churches have stabilized in membership or are declining; and in the mainline churches, the most vital and promising prospects for future renewal seem to come from the evangelical and charismatic movements that have gained adherents across the various denominations. How do such developments in modern, secular America jibe with the traditional predictions of the secularization theorists in the social sciences? At first their predictions about the gradual and inevitable decline of religious influence in modern societies seemed to be confirmed as the mainline denominations began to lose members and resources. The more recent successes of the conservative evangelical and charismatic movements, however, now pose a serious theoretical problem for those who have been predicting the demise of traditional religion.

If science and religion are incompatible, why would the religious segment of American society most antagonistic toward science and modernism be thriving? Liberal religion has seemingly made enough accommodations during this century to coexist peacefully with science. Conservative and charismatic religion, on the other hand, has made fewer accommodations and has remained more antagonistic toward the modern world. The questions, then, for the secularization theorists, have been framed as follows:

Why is it that the "conservative," more Biblically oriented groups are doing comparatively well in a society which prides itself on modernism, rationality, and empirical thinking? (McGraw 1979, 146)

At least part of the secularization thesis is surely challenged by the sheer existence, if not the long term growth, of a population sector whose religious sentiments are at odds with the predicted "secular" view of the world. In the broadest terms, the question we address is how can this be? (Hammond and Hunter 1984, 221)

The query is simply this. If modernization secularizes and America is among the most modern societies in the world, how is it possible that Evangelicalism survives and even thrives in contemporary America? (Hunter 1983a, 4)

Explanations of the Trends

There are, of course, other indicators of religious vitality besides church membership. However, church membership is the most available indicator and is an important measure of "how citizens are voting with their bodies" (Marty 1979, 10). Thus, the declines in mainline denominations are considered cause for alarm and have attracted a great deal of attention.

Despite the attention, however, scholars have found it difficult to provide an explanation that can account both for the differential growth of the churches, and for the timing of the trends. In the pages that follow, we will outline these various explanations.

Dean Kelley's Thesis

The most significant early explanation of the trends came from Dean Kelley in *Why the Conservative Churches are Growing* (1972). The reason conservative movements have been able to grow, Kelley argued, is because they are strict and serious in the demands they make on members. It is this seriousness that attracts individuals who seek answers to the ultimate questions. People want more than a "smooth, articulate, verbal interpretation of what life is all about. Words are cheap; we want explanations that are validated by commitment of other persons" (Kelley 1972, 52). It is not the rationality, logic, credibility, or convenience that make religion meaningful; it is the fact that religion makes demands and those demands must be met by commitment. Members of conservative and charismatic churches, to the extent that they must give unswerving allegiance, be willing to work and suffer for their faith, abandon all else, and spread the Good News, will find meaning.

Mainline churches, therefore, are dying because they are theologically unsure of themselves and are less serious about what they do (or do not) believe. This lack of seriousness is evidenced by the fact that the liberal churches are seemingly unconcerned with members' moral conduct, do not actively seek new members, expect little in the way of commitment from their members, do not encourage emotional fervor, and have become very ecumenical in outlook. As the liberal churches have thus become increasingly "weak," they have become less effective at providing ultimate meaning.

One way to look at Kelley's thesis is through social exchange theory. All organizations offer incentives (rewards) in exchange for certain demands (costs). Liberal churches, Kelley argues, have become increasingly interested in appealing to a wide range of potential members by providing respectability, knowledge, fellowship, entertainment, etc. These are incentives that nonreligious organizations can also offer. While placing greater emphasis on what they think the people want, the liberal churches place less of an emphasis on the "one incentive unique to churches, that given preeminence by conservative churches: salvation" (Kelley 1972, 92). Conservative churches tend to cost more than liberal churches—more time, effort, sacrifice, involvement, anguish. Yet, they yield more meaningful rewards, the most important of which is a promise of a supernatural life after death and a stronger sense of closeness to God in this life.

Many theorists other than Dean Kelley have suggested that the liberal churches have become diluted to the point that they are uncertain as to what they believe. Rodney Stark recognized this in his research with Charles Glock on American churches in the 1906s. Reflecting upon this early research, Stark has recently written that he was struck by the fact that church intellectuals of the ecumenical movement "were reporting mainly their discovery that they now believed alike regardless of their denominational backgrounds, because they had come to believe so little" (Stark and Bainbridge 1985, 42).

Kelley's work proved very controversial, for it clearly placed blame on the churches themselves. No doubt liberal church leaders were reluctant to recognize their increasingly ecumenical theology as, to use Kelley's own words, "a recipe for the failure of the religious enterprise" (1972, viii). Furthermore, Kelley's thesis challenged the long-standing assumption that religion, to the degree that it wished to remain successful, would have to succumb to the secular pressures of science and modernism. Indeed, according to Kelley, such accommodation merely exposed the uncertainty of the churches, making them unable to attract people seeking clearly defined answers.

Kelley's book received immediate attention. Of course, the fact that the claims were being made by a well-respected Methodist minister and executive with the National Council of Churches ensured attention. Kelley was seemingly in a position to criticize; but there was more to it than that. "Kelley's thesis had a ring of plausibility. Liberal Protestant churches were indeed uncertain about theological issues, were reluctant to sell themselves, and had long ago given up any formal effort to oversee their members' moral conduct'' (Johnson 1985a, 41).

Surprisingly, Kelley's thesis has received little empirical validation. The research that has been done has generally approached the issue from one of two directions. First is the descriptive approach taken by Kelley himself. Kelley demonstrated that almost without exception, churches at the strict, demanding, serious, exclusive end of the scale are growing (for example, Mormons, Jehovah's Witnesses, Southern Baptists, Nazarenes, etc.) while churches at the more lenient, ecumenical, mellow end of the continuum are declining (for example, Presbyterian, United Methodist, Episcopal). Similarly, Dean Hoge (1979b) asked "expert judges" to rank various denominations on scales of ecumenism, conservatism, emphasis on evangelism, distinctiveness of life-style, etc. The factors that Kelley had stressed most were strongly correlated with denominational growth.

Similar support has also come from the work of Rosabeth Moss Kanter (1972). In work independent of Kelley's, Kanter made a remarkably similar argument in explaining the growth of nineteenth-century utopian communes. Commitment is maintained, she argued, via six mechanisms:

- Sacrifice is the extent to which members give something to be part of the group.
- Investment is the extent to which members invest their time and resources.
- Renunciation is giving up outside relationships that could undermine loyalty to the group.
- Communion is the development of intragroup relationships.
- Mortification is the transformation of identity to one defined by the group.
- Transcendence is the surrendering of oneself to a greater power.

Kanter demonstrated that the successful communes were those that effectively used these commitment mechanisms.

The second research approach bearing upon Kelley's contention has examined the sources of denominational growth. Implicit in Kelley's thesis is the assumption that conservative churches are growing at the expense of liberal churches. Several studies have examined this assumption but none have found support for it. The most damaging empirical evidence came rather quickly when Bibby and Brinkerhoff published a series of articles addressing the sources of growth of Canadian evangelical churches (1973, 1983; Bibby 1978). Growth for these churches came as a result of (1) switchers from other evangelical churches, (2) higher birth rates, and (3) higher retention rates. Bouma (1979) has similarly concluded that the growth of the Christian Reformed Church is largely a function of high immigration rates and high birth rates as opposed to its attractiveness to outsiders. The conclusion reached by these scholars is that Kelley's thesis can at best be applied to membership retention and not to the recruitment of outsiders. Furthermore, there is considerable evidence that switching patterns favor the liberal churches, and not the conservative ones (Hadaway 1978; Roof and McKinney 1987).

Perhaps the most telling theoretical criticism of Kelley's thesis is the fact that it is unable to account for the timing of the decline of liberal churches. The critical denominational conditions mentioned in Kelley's thesis did not appear overnight. Liberal churches were presumably very weak in the 1950s when they were growing. Kelley (1978) himself recognizes this as problematic and argues that the declines began in the 1960s as a result of increasing involvement of the liberal churches in social issues. The 1960s merely exposed the changed priorities of the churches, thus providing, in a sense, the final "straw that broke the camel's back." However, there is no evidence that social action had anything to do with the declines (Johnson 1985a).

The 1960s Counterculture

Kelley explains the appeal of demanding religion in social psychological terms, while providing evidence only at a structural level. As a result, while few have questioned the descriptive accuracy of Kelley's argument (that is, that strict churches are growing), many have remained unconvinced by the causes offered (that is, that strict churches grow because they are so strict, serious, and demanding). These scholars have preferred to look to factors external to the churches. Much of this research has been guided by the findings that liberal membership declines came at least partly as a result of "the failure of the offspring of their members to affiliate with a liberal religious body" (Johnson 1985a, 42).

What caused this youthful exodus? In retrospect the answer seems simple enough, for American culture seemingly never fully recovered from the 1960s. Indeed, in the eyes of many, the 1960s marked a turning point in American religion. The 1960s represented a time of significant changes in the values and attitudes of Americans. These changes were spearheaded by the large postwar Baby Boom generation which began reaching college age during the 1960s. Youth of the 1960s seemingly questioned many of the traditional conventions of their parents. They questioned traditional standards of morality, placed greater emphasis on personal freedom and individualism, and became increasingly skeptical of society's established institutions. As might be expected, the churches were among the institutions questioned by the youth of the counterculture movement (Perrin 1989). For many, in fact, the churches were perceived as "a part of the problem, not the solution. Closely identified with the establishment, these institutions were often blamed for the ills besetting the larger society" (Roof 1982, 141). Because the culture-affirming mainline churches were that much more identifiable as establishment, they were the most adversely affected. Indeed, as Martin Marty suggests, mainline religion is always among the casualties during cultural crisis:

> [M]ainline churches always have the advantage that in years in which the official culture is secure and expansive, they are well off . . . [but they] suffer in times of cultural crisis and disintegration, when they receive blame for what goes wrong in society but are bypassed when people look for new ways to achieve social identity and location. So they looked as good in the 1950s as they looked bad by the 1970s. (Marty 1976, quoted in Roof and McKinney 1987, 22)

A second explanation for why the liberal churches were more adversely affected by the counterculture has been offered by Dean Hoge (1979a). The value shifts, he argues, were greatest among the more educated middle-class youth, thus affecting the largely middle-class liberal denominations more than the traditionally lower-middle-class conservative denominations. Thus, conservative youth, who were less likely to be attending the college campuses where countercultural values were most pervasive, were more likely to remain in the churches of their parents.

Demographic Changes

Church involvement is strongly related to one's position in the life cycle, with participation being highest during young adulthood when school-age children are at home, and lowest during late adolescence and early adulthood. Thus, church membership and participation rates are highest when school-age children are at home (Nash 1968).

This process is summarized by Wade Clark Roof:

> In the years of late adolescence and early adulthood, young Americans are usually less involved religiously; but as they form families of their own and become parents, they tend to become more involved. Most want their children to have religious instruction, and they are apt to affiliate, or reaffiliate as is often the case, with a church or synagogue out of a feeling of responsibility to participate in the institution to which they send their children. (1982, 139)

The Baby Boom (generally considered to have occurred during the period 1945–1954) changed the age structure of society, creating demographic conditions conducive to growth during the 1950s. With the first of the baby boomers reaching school age in the 1950s, the churches experienced much growth. However, as these same baby boomers reached young adulthood beginning in the late 1960s and early 1970s, church participation levels dropped. Therefore, as a result of the demographic conditions created by the Baby Boom generation, the 1950s were as conducive to church growth as the 1970s were detrimental (Roof 1982; Roof and McKinney 1987).

Of course, the declining birth rates associated with the post-Baby Boom era had a more direct impact on the churches as well. After the birth rate peaked in 1958, relatively fewer children were born to church members, thus depriving the churches of an obviously important pool of new members.

To make matters worse, the counterculture and the resulting declines in church involvement of 1960s youth resulted in an older mainline constituency, thereby depriving mainline denominations of the young adults whose children would have populated the churches during the 1970s and 1980s. Therefore, declining birth rates, combined with declining numbers of young adults, resulted in fewer children being born in the churches during the 1970s (Roof and McKinney 1985, 1987).

Patterns of Switching

The religious history of the United States has led to unprecedented levels of religious pluralism and has resulted in a unique tendency for Americans to switch religious preferences. Given the possible link between switching and denominational growth and decline, the investigation of switching has been considered important by social scientists. Interest was further stimulated by the work of Dean Kelley. Kelley clearly implied that conservative growth was coming at the expense of the liberal churches. However, despite Kelley's claims, the most generally accepted and empirically validated pattern of religious switching has continued to favor liberal churches (Stark and Glock 1968).

Despite general agreement on this trend, Roof and McKinney (1987) have argued that recent patterns of switching, while still indicating greater net gains for liberal denominations, are not nearly as drastic as those reported earlier by Stark and Glock. Among the many factors contributing to the growth of liberal denominations during the 1950s were these favorable switching patterns. As these patterns have apparently become less favorable to liberal denominations in recent years, those denominations have begun to decline (Roof and McKinney 1987). In other words, there is an "apparent falloff in what was probably an important source of their [liberal] growth during the 1950s" (Johnson 1985a, 42).

Furthermore, the characteristics of the switchers make the patterns more complicated than perhaps Stark and Glock realized. For example, those switching into liberal denominations are comparatively old, thus further contributing to the aging of the mainline constituency (Roof and McKinney 1987). In addition, conservative denominations apparently pick up more committed converts (Hadaway 1978). Therefore, while liberal churches may enjoy somewhat larger net numerical gains from switching, conservative churches pick up "better" converts in the sense of institutional belonging and commitment (Roof and McKinney 1987). This pattern could well be interpreted as support for Dean Kelley's thesis, for Kelley clearly suggested that the most serious believer will be attracted to the most serious religion.

Significance of the Trends

There remain secularization theorists who argue that we are making far too much of the recent success of conservative religion. After all, it is not unreasonable to think that evangelicalism could grow while the larger universe of religion could shrink. "It is not unknown for evangelicalism to get warmer as the overall climate gets colder" (Martin 1983, 111). Yet, the majority of scholars make the assumption that secularization theories must be reexamined in light of the success of conservative religion. Indeed, not ten years after Rodney Stark and Charles Glock were writing, "the religious beliefs which have been the bedrocks of Christian faith for two millennia are on their way out; this may well be the dawn of a post-Christian era" (1968, 205), George Gallup was drawing a completely different conclusion in writing that American Christianity "may well be in the early stages of a profound religious revival" (1977, 80). Stark himself, almost two decades after predicting "the dawn of a post-Christian era," has recently written (in collaboration with Bainbridge, 1985, 2) that the result of the secularization trend has "never been the end of religion, but merely a shift in fortunes among religions as faiths that have become too worldly are supplanted by more vigorous and less worldly religions."

The Stark and Bainbridge theory of religion is a more elaborate and formalized restatement of the traditional church/sect theory originally introduced by Ernst Troeltsch (1931) and Richard Niebuhr (1929), and the related deprivation thesis of scholars like Glock (1973). Stark and Bainbridge assume, like so many scholars before them (including Dean Kelley), that religion is irreplacable as a provider of meaning and a source of answers to ultimate questions. Given these assumptions, it is difficult to imagine a world without religion. No doubt the form religion takes will change, but we fully expect religion to withstand the test of time.

There is less cause for optimism, however, for the future of America's liberal mainline. From a purely demographic standpoint, the prospects look bleak. As liberal constituencies continue to age, death rates will continue to rise, and birth rates will remain below those needed to grow. There is little reason to expect, furthermore, that liberal denominations will be able to attract appreciable numbers of outsiders. Liberal denominations have never actively sought new members. Furthermore, with increasing emphasis on ecumenism and blurring boundaries of institutional identity, potential recruits may have difficulty determining if the liberal denominations have anything unique to offer. As the boundaries between denominations blur, and perhaps more significantly, as the boundaries between the liberal denominations and secular institutions blur, the unique contributions of the churches become less apparent. Indeed, this could be liberal Christianity's most critical obstacle:

> If liberal Christianity merely accommodates itself to contemporary culture, it will cease being a religion, for religion must offer ultimate meaning. . . . Liberal Christianity must have a message for modern men and women; it cannot simply reflect contemporary values in sanctified form. There are enough social clubs in this world. Mysticism can be purchased from many a guru. If one is looking for ethics unadorned with metaphysics, the membership rolls of the Humanist Association are waiting to be filled. (Miller 1982, 268, 269, 70).

This is essentially the message of Dean Kelley. Liberal religion is dying because it has been watered-down to the point that it is hardly religious any longer. Evangelical and charismatic movements, on the other hand, continue to grow because they have maintained a serious message, one that demands commitment and participation, and, in turn, provides ultimate rewards. The demographic makeup of the conservative denominations, furthermore, suggests that conservative religion will continue to grow. Conservative constituencies are considerably younger than liberal constituencies, have higher birth rates, and are more successful at retaining the children they do have. As a result, all indications are that the shift in power which has characterized the past twenty years will continue.

References

Anderson, Robert M., 1979
Bibby, Reginald W., 1978
Bibby, Reginald W., and Merlin Brinkerhoff, 1973, 1983
Bouma, Gary, 1979
Bromley, David G., and Anson D. Shupe, Jr., 1981
Chalfant, H. Paul, Robert E. Beckley, and C. Eddie Palmer, 1987
Dayton, Donald W., 1987
Gallup, George Jr., 1977

Gaustad, Edwin Scott, 1962
Gerlach, Luther P., and Virginia H. Hine, 1970
Glock, Charles Y., ed., 1973
Hadaway, Kirk, 1978
Hadden, Jeffrey K., and Charles E. Swan, 1981
Hammond, Phillip, and James Davison Hunter, 1984
Hoge, Dean R., 1979a, 1979b
Hunter, James Davison, 1983a
Johnson, Benton, 1985a
Kanter, Rosabeth Moss, 1972
Kelley, Dean M., 1972, 1978
Liebman, Robert C., and Robert Wuthnow, eds., 1983
Marsden, George M., 1983
Martin, David, 1982
Marty, Martin E., 1976, 1979
Mauss, Armand L., and Donald W. Petersen, 1974
McGraw, Douglas, 1979
Miller, Donald E., 1982
Nash, Dennison, 1968
Niebuhr, H. Richard, 1929
Perrin, Robin D., 1989
Petersen, Donald W., and Armand L. Mauss, 1973
Poloma, Margaret, 1982
Roof, Wade Clark, 1982
Roof, Wade Clark, and William McKinney, 1985, 1987
Stark, Rodney, and William Sims Bainbridge, 1985
Stark, Rodney, and Charles Glock, 1968
Troeltsch, Ernst, 1931
Wilson, John, and Harvey K. Clow, 1981

8

Liberal Protestantism's Struggle to Recapture the Heartland

William McKinney and Wade Clark Roof

Two of the oldest, most prestigious Protestant denominations in America are considering proposals to move their national headquarters out of New York City. In June, the General Assembly of the Presbyterian Church (U.S.A.) will be asked to ratify a committee's recommendation that the offices of the newly reunited church be consolidated in Kansas City, and the United Church of Christ's General Synod will act on a proposal that the church move its offices outside the New York metropolitan area by 1991. The Presbyterian decision follows the reunion of the church's northern and southern branches, which have maintained separate offices in New York and Atlanta, and reflects a desire for a neutral site. The decision by the United Church of Christ comes in anticipation of the expiration of leases in areas of the city that have seen rapidly escalating rents. A possible shift to the Midwest for both groups follows a similar decision of the Evangelical Lutheran Church of America, a union body comprised of the nation's largest Lutheran churches, which will soon establish its national headquarters in Chicago. If the recommendations of the location committees of the Presbyterian Church and the United Church of Christ are approved, the Episcopal Church will be the only remaining Protestant denomination with its principal national headquarters in New York City.

One can almost predict the debate on the floor of the two churches' national governing bodies:

Iowa banker: "This will save the church a lot of money. Everyone knows how expensive New York is. To get good people to work in New

167

York we have to pay our national staff three times the average salary of our pastors, and that's not good for morale. By moving to Kansas City we'll make it possible again for people with families to join the national staff and to afford good homes in a good community.''

California accountant: ''I'm afraid the committee has underestimated the costs of this move. By the time we've paid severance pay, relocation expenses for employees, moving costs, and all the rest there won't be anything left for mission programming. It will take five years before everything comes together. And do you know what it costs to fly out of Kansas City?''

Houston pastor: ''I am in favor of the move. It brings the church closer to where our members are going to be in the future. I think New York is a fine place, but we're a new church and no longer that closely tied to the Northeast. The population is shifting to the Sunbelt, and our headquarters ought to be closer to the people.''

Philadelphia social worker: ''With all respect to places like Kansas City and the Sunbelt, which I'm sure are fine places, I just don't like our church turning its back on the older cities like New York. We have a history of concern for the poor, for the immigrants, for the homeless, and I don't like leaving this concern behind.''

Michigan pastor: ''It's about time we brought the national church closer to the people. New York is not America. Our national staff ought to be struggling with the issues faced by our church members in the towns and cities across our great country.''

The debate will likely turn on economic, demographic, and internal political grounds. Much will be said, pro and con, about geography and living costs, about population shifts and the religious vitality of the Sunbelt, about recapturing the heartland and getting close to the pulse beat of America. Overlooked, however, will be the deeper significance of the Presbyterian and United Church of Christ decisions, which lies less in the economic, demographic, and political attractions of individual cities than in what the recommendations imply about the changing relationship between religion and culture in America, and about the symbolic relationship between mainline Protestant religious groups and New York City.

The current mood seems to be worlds removed from an era not so long ago when the city was host to a more secure, more privileged mainline Protestantism. As recently as the 1950s, a New York headquarters location was a symbol of a position at the center of the culture. It said to members around the country and to mission partners around the world that the churches of the Protestant establishment possessed a vibrant and special relationship with the dominant forces of American society.

That establishment status found physical expression in a dynamic complex of religious and educational institutions on Morningside Heights. For many, the intersection of Claremont Avenue and 120th Street is the symbolic center of liberal Protestantism. On its northwest corner stands the Riverside Church, from whose pulpit distinguished preachers from founding minister Harry Emerson Fosdick to current senior minister William Sloane Coffin have spoken not only to a neighborhood congregation but to the city, the nation, and the world. On the northeast corner is Union Theological Seminary, a bulwark of liberal religious thought and home to some of the giants of American Protestant theology, including Reinhold Niebuhr and Paul Tillich, both of whom were highly influential public figures. Niebuhr as theologian and social critic captured audiences inside and outside the churches, and the more philosophically minded Tillich drew attention in the realms of culture and the arts. Union's proximity to Columbia University and the Jewish Theological Seminary symbolized an accommodating stance and a commitment to intellectual and interfaith dialogue in a world of religious and cultural pluralism, but with Protestant life and thought positioned very much at its center.

No event better signaled Protestantism's vitality and spirit of unity at the time than the opening, in October 1958, of the Interchurch Center at 475 Riverside Drive—on the southwest corner of Claremont Avenue and 120th Street. Thirty thousand people gathered for the occasion to watch President Dwight D. Eisenhower, amidst banners of thirty-seven Protestant and Eastern Orthodox churches and New York's most prominent clergy, lay the cornerstone of the "national home of the churches," an imposing if architecturally undistinguished edifice that was to become the headquarters for the National Council of Churches, for many denominational offices, and for various other ecumenically minded religious organizations. Pointing out that the United States is politically a free people because of its freedom to worship, the president observed: "Without this firm foundation, national morality could not be maintained." In the largest gathering ever to pay tribute to the developing solidarity of the Protestant churches, public officials, educators, industrialists, and church leaders were brought together in a remarkable display of institutional confidence and optimism. David Rockefeller brought greetings from his father, John D. Rockefeller, Jr., who provided the site for the Interchurch Center as he had for Riverside Church and Union Seminary, and predicted that "475 Riverside Drive" would soon be well known throughout the world.

Today, like the larger religious tradition in which they have their roots, all three institutions are struggling. The Interchurch Center faces the loss of key tenants, Riverside Church is beset by internal struggles and financial difficulties that will result in a budget deficit of $1.2 million in 1987, and Union Theological Seminary is exploring the construction of a luxury housing tower over part of its campus to raise the $2 million a year it needs to maintain current levels of programming.

At 475 Riverside Drive, as in local churches, seminaries, and church offices around the country, church leaders and lay people find themselves in the unusual position of wondering where things went wrong. What happened to the churches of the Protestant establishment whose religious and social preeminence was for so long a taken-for-granted aspect of American life? The answers lie less in the churches themselves than in the profound transformations in the nation's social and cultural life during these years. Beginning in the early 1960s, the nation was caught up in a series of traumatic events and dislocations—the assassination of President Kennedy, the civil rights movement, the youth counterculture, the Vietnam War, the deaths of Robert Kennedy and Martin Luther King, Jr., and Watergate—which greatly altered national mood and ethos. American life and institutions were deeply shaken. It was as if the old synthesis of religion and culture fell apart, or as Yale historian Sydney E. Ahlstrom put it in 1972, it was a time when the "old foundations of national confidence, patriotic idealism, moral traditionalism, and even of historic Judeo-Christian theism, were awash. Presuppositions that had held firm for centuries—even millennia—were being widely questioned" (Ahlstrom 1972, 1080).

For the Protestant establishment, these were years when its cultural authority was greatly eroded and the normative faiths for Americans generally were reordered. Old-line Protestantism had been so closely identified with the country's culture, so involved in its popular morality, that it became peculiarly vulnerable to the ills and hypocrisies that beset the larger society. Inequities of class, race, and gender; nativism and anti-Semitism; moralism and social control; imperialism and colonialism—all seemed to be blights upon the Protestant empire. "WASP" had become a four-letter word, and liberal Protestant leaders—recognizing that they were indeed mostly white, mostly Anglo-Saxon, and indubitably Protestant in their style and outlook—had little choice but to plead guilty.

The term "mainline" came into vogue to describe these older religious traditions, ironically, at just the time when their place in the sun was being challenged. Hit first by the cults and new religious movements of the 1960s that thrived on antiestablishment sentiments, these same churches were to face new and different challenges in the late 1970s with the rise of evangelicalism and the New Religious Right. In contrast to the buoyant 1950s when religious institutions were more securely positioned in the culture, in the decades that followed the religious establishment took much blame for what was wrong in the society. The mainline of religion—the normative, median-style, standard-brand religion—had become stale and could be dismissed as bourgeois and patronizing on the one hand, unfaithful and uninspiring on the other.

What has happened in the past three decades is but one chapter in the longer story of mainstream Protestantism's relation to its host culture. The major theme of that story is one of Protestantism's disestablishment. The first chapter—legal disestablishment—was complete by the early 1800s. Religion was placed on a voluntary basis and as a result its authority came to rest upon its continuing power to influence mores, ethos, and customs. Protestantism exercised that authority over the culture up until the 1920s and 1930s when its hegemony drew to an end. Historian Robert T. Handy has described this period as a "second disestablishment." Thereafter the old WASP order confronted a growing religious pluralism and was forced to accept the fact that America was a Protestant-Catholic-Jewish country. Following World War II there was a pervasive, highly generalized religious mood resulting in a close relation between religious belonging and the "American Way of Life," but since the 1960s, this easy relationship between religion and American life has fallen apart in what amounts to a third disestablishment. The result has been a further withering of shared religious values and meanings, an erosion of a common morality, and a decline in the influence of religion on the society. Having lost long ago its power to coerce, and more recently its power to influence, mainstream Protestantism wonders what it would have to say if indeed the American people were willing to listen.

These developments have given rise to a broad spectrum of religious and spiritual responses: highly privatized, mystical quests as well as a turn to more traditional faith. The former thrive upon the culture of religious individualism and take expression as do-it-yourself religiosity and selective picking and choosing of spiritual themes from such disparate sources as "possibility thinking," est, and New Thought. Such privatized religious expressions cater to a therapeutic mentality and preoccupations with self-fulfillment, but undercut communal belonging and corporate responsibility. At the opposite extreme, sectarian evangelical and fundamentalist movements marshal much support on behalf of traditional beliefs and moral values. Using the latest of media technologies, a new breed of televangelists—almost all of them southern and basking in sunbelt prosperity—gives voice to a new style, more aggressive conservative Protestantism seeking to become the dominant culture-shaping force in America. The conservative faiths have gained new energy and identity out of a struggle with what they call "secular humanism" and in protest against what neoconservative Lutheran theologian Richard John Neuhaus characterizes as the "naked public square"—that is, a public life lacking in religious symbols and values.

For the more liberal Protestant churches of the old center, it is a time of confusion. Most of the old-line denominations now find themselves in institutional disarray and suffering from a loss of identity. The optimism and confidence they once enjoyed have faded, provoking a crisis of morale and mission. A New York location was natural for religious bodies whose self-definition placed them at the heart of the political, cultural, and religious mainline. But today, no longer sure of their place, and at a time when the notion of a cultural and religious mainline has itself become blurred, a move to the nation's geographic heartland offers hope of finding a way out of the malaise which engulfs them. A struggle over symbolism and institutional identity would seem almost inevitable given their recent plight and the nation's current religious and ideological climate.

For the United Church of Christ and the Presbyterians, a struggle over an appropriate stance toward the culture has been a theme since the beginnings of their experience in America. The United Church of Christ was formed in 1957 from the union of the Congregational Christian Churches and the Evangelical and Reformed Church, the former tracing its roots to the settlement of New England in the seventeenth century and the latter to German immigration to Pennsylvania and the Midwest in the nineteenth century. The coming together of these two diverse churches was hailed at the time as a major breakthrough in ecumenicity and a harbinger of further church unions to come. Presbyterians came to America later than the Congregationalists, but hit their stride in the eighteenth century. Along with the Episcopal Church, the two churches were so firmly entrenched by the end of the eighteenth century that in 1793 Yale president Ezra Stiles could look ahead to an American future about equally divided among Congregationalists, Presbyterians, and Episcopalians.

Stiles's prediction did not anticipate the changes that would soon engulf both the nation and the churches. Congregationalism struggled with the loss of its established status in New England and found it difficult to adapt to life on the frontier and among immigrant groups in the nineteenth century. Presbyterians developed a taste for doctrinal and political controversy and divided into northern and southern branches over slavery and the Civil War. The "colonial big three" churches persisted as institutions but had to adjust to their social niche, and in time they were overtaken in numbers and influence by other religious groups.

Over the past quarter century it would be hard to find purer exemplars of liberal Protestantism than these heirs to the Puritan and Calvinist traditions. As founding members of both the National and World Councils of Churches, the two churches are mainstays of the ecumenical movement and its commitment to interfaith dialogue and cooperation. With memberships that are overwhelmingly white, Anglo-American, solidly upper-middle-class, and Republican in political party preference, they were nonetheless early supporters of the civil rights movements and remain committed to social justice for blacks and other minorities. At the national level the churches opposed the Vietnam War and were early supporters of women's rights, including freedom of choice in abortion and the ordination of women. They have taken up issues of gay rights, nuclear war, the environment, and one after another concern facing Americans. Along with decisions on the locations of headquarters, delegates to the two churches' conventions this summer will deal with a host of resolutions on public policy issues including the role of the United States in Central America and the morality of the American economy.

The persistently liberal cast to the social and economic agenda of these denominations has prompted critics inside and outside the churches to suggest that they are out of touch with a majority of their own members. Shifting the national offices out of the Northeast and to the Midwest is the latest, and certainly the most dramatic, of institutional responses designed to quell the critics. "It seems to be particularly tied in with a yen to get closer to the grass roots, closer to the needs and attitudes of the ordinary members," says James Wall, editor of the liberal *Christian Century,* published in Chicago. Past concentration of denominational headquarters in the East "has been a mistake, giving them a distorted view of the country," he adds, saying the move "is long overdue," needed for aligning them with more typical environments.

The decline in membership is a serious problem for mainline Protestantism. As many as ten of the largest Protestant bodies have suffered net membership losses over the past twenty-five years. Both the United Church of Christ and the Presbyterians have lost members since the mid-1960s. In two decades alone the United Church of Christ lost a half-million members, and the Presbyterians nearly nine hundred thousand, leading George Gallup, Jr., and David Poling to suggest that the two groups "cannot long exist as viable church organizations nationally if the declines of the seventies persist in the 1980s." (Gallup and Poling, 1980:10) Neoconservatives often attribute liberal Protestant membership losses to the social and political activism of its clergy and leaders and to what sociologist Peter Berger has described as a "theologically unappetizing mix of psychotherapy and politics" replacing more traditional religious content.

Our own research shows the reasons for the membership losses are a good deal more complex. Birth rates of liberal Protestant women, like those of Jewish women, have fallen below replacement levels. Differences in birthrates between liberal and conservative Protestants are striking: among women under forty-five years of age, the child-to-women ratio is 1.60 for liberal Protestants as compared to 2.01 among the conservatives.

Liberal Protestant churches also have aging constituencies. Compared with evangelical, conservative churches, their members are, on the average, almost four years older. A lopsided age distribution combined with lower fertility creates a serious demographic weakness which does not augur well for their future. We estimate that if the liberal churches had birth rates comparable to those of Southern Baptists and other conservative Protestants, they would be reporting annual membership increases rather than the declines of the past decades!

In addition to dismal demographics, the liberal Protestant churches have a problem recruiting new members and holding on to their young. Youth in the 1960s dropped out in large numbers, and they have yet to return in any significant way. Baby boomers prompted many Protestant churches to overbuild in the 1950s to accommodate growing church schools, but the expected return to churches as baby boomers raise their own children has yet to materialize.

Historically, liberal Protestantism has maintained its membership base through successful appeal to Protestants moving up the socioeconomic ladder. Socially and theologically, the liberal churches were attractive for upwardly mobile persons raised in more conservative traditions who desired a religious affiliation befitting their new social status. Thus Nazarenes often converted to Methodism, and Methodists moved up to the Episcopal Church. While some upward shifting still occurs, it is not the rich source of new members it was in the past. Two conditions have altered the religious situation in the period since World War II: the unprecedented social mobility of traditionally low-status religious groups, which made it possible for persons to retain their religious heritage while advancing economically, and the large numbers of liberal Protestant youth who have opted out of organized religion altogether.

For all these reasons, the position the liberal churches occupy in the religious economy is blurred today, and many church leaders and laity are confused. For an extended period of American history they have enjoyed their status as custodians of the culture. One might say they established the rules of the American religious game, that is, norms of voluntarism, tolerance, and fair play. With legal disestablishment, groups like the Congregationalists, Presbyterians, and Episcopalians were forced to admit other teams, but they continued to own the stadium and could choose which games to play. By the time of the second disestablishment they were further reduced to the nonimportant role of umpire. And now, for the first time in America, the once-privileged Protestant mainline is on the field of play and forced to compete with other teams to hold their standing. The third disestablishment in the present has altered the rules of the game:

liberal Protestantism is now a minority voice and one player among many in a more truly pluralistic religious and secular context.

Those who believe locating the churches' national headquarters outside New York City will reestablish a vital relationship with the culture are likely to discover that geography is really not the issue and that a move will not produce all that is hoped for. No one really expects that these old-line churches will ever regain the cultural dominance they once enjoyed, but pressures are on to get the Presbyterians and the United Church of Christ back in the religious game on a turf where they have a better chance of winning. For many of the leaders and members in these churches, relocation to the heartland signals a welcome move to the theological and ideological center, and it means getting closer to the people in those areas of the country now growing and experiencing a more robust religious life; both are believed to hold out the promise of a restored, more vibrant church. We think they are wrong—not in their quest for a revitalized church so much as the means of obtaining it.

Critically important is the historic public posture of these institutions. The distinguishing feature of these churches has long been their character as bridging institutions in American life—concerned with public well-being and not just the private religious life—compromising this character would run counter to their identity. In their recent book, *Habits of the Heart,* Robert Bellah and his associates observe that Americans speak two languages, both of which are derived in large part from the traditions that shaped the nation's early life: a rugged individualism and a commitment to community. They write: "if the language of the self-reliant individual is the first language of American moral life, the language of tradition and commitment in communities of memory are second languages that most Americans know as well, and which they use when the language of the radically separated self does not seem adequate" (Bellah et. al. 1985:154). These older religious traditions provide such communities of memory, distinctive for their emphasis upon social responsibility, and for reaching out to other religious as well as secular constituencies.

For all their current difficulties, we see in the liberal churches a residual capacity to provide a vocabulary of symbols, beliefs, moral values, and feeling responses for articulating a socially responsible individualism. They offer a language of communitarian ideals and national purpose, drawing from a theology which incorporates a vision of public order alongside that of personal commitment. Such language and vision are sorely lacking in contemporary America, in secular as well as in much religious rhetoric, at a time when a mediating posture on the part of a public-minded church could help to overcome divisions and strains within the country. By virtue of their heritage concerned with relating biblical faith and practice to the whole of life—cultural, social, political, economic—they offer an alternative to radical religious individualism on the one hand and sectarian withdrawal on the other.

The task ahead will be to preserve this vital balance—to self and community—and to affirm it in fresh and compelling ways. To do so will not be easy given the pressures upon the churches. The liberal churches have to sustain a sense of community, and thereby try to counter the drift toward religious privatism, yet at the same time they must hold out against pressures pulling them toward sectarianism. Rather than abandon their distinctive heritage we believe they should hold firm to the historic values for which they are known—to tolerance, to pluralism, to social and economic justice, and to a continuing renewal of public life. One reason for this is that their potential new members are not the religious conservatives but liberal, moderate-minded persons, many of them burned out evangelicals who are looking for greater openness and an affirmative spiritual climate.

But more than this, constructive dialogue with the culture and engagement with the concerns of the world are essential, we believe, to an enlivened public life in the United States. Public-minded Protestantism has much still to offer to debate over national life and the directions that lie ahead. Especially now when moral and ethical issues have become more sharply drawn among Americans, the liberal religious voice is needed more than ever.

References

Ahlstrom, Sydney, 1972
Bellah, Robert N., Richard Madson, William M. Sullivan, Ann Swidler, and Steven M. Tipton, 1985
Gallup, George, and David Poling, 1980

9

Why Catholics Stay in the Church

Andrew Greeley

The question is no longer why Catholics leave but why they stay.

The answer, should we be able to learn it, would tell us much about the resources available to American Catholicism and point towards policy directions the Church might take in years and decades ahead.

The current myths of the various conventional wisdoms still insist that Catholics are leaving the Church. According to the conservatives they are leaving because there have been too many changes. According to the liberals they are leaving because there are not enough changes. According to the national media each new document from Rome causes anguish for American Catholics as they are forced to choose between their own opinions and practices and the teachings of the Pope. According to the bishops and the Vatican, the simple laity are troubled and shocked by the strange doctrines and practices that they encounter in many parishes and dioceses.

None of these models stand the test of falsification by empirical data. Indeed if there is one fact that seems incontrovertible to me after almost three decades of research on American Catholicism it is that the laity in the United States have reacted to the changes and the traumas of the last quarter century with astonishing tranquility.

Consider:

1. In 1960 the proportion of those raised Catholic who no longer defined themselves as Catholics was 12 percent. In 1985, taking into accounting the changing age structure of the population, that rate had risen to 13 percent. (And the majority have affiliated with another church in conjunction with a marriage to someone of that denomination who was

more devout in their faith than the sometime Catholic was in his/her faith.)

2. While weekly church attendance declined from 1968 to 1975, that decline stopped in 1975. Moreover since 1975 most Catholics continued to go to church although somewhat less frequently. Eighty-seven percent of the Catholics in the country still attend church on at least some Sundays during the year.

3. Life-cycle projections indicate that the curve of the relationship between age and church attendance for those born as recently as the late 1960s is not different at levels of statistical significance from the curve for previous cohorts. When they are in their forties they will go to church as often as did their parents and as often as did my age cohort when we were in our forties.

The life-cycle relationship between age and religion is worth emphasizing. Young people are less likely to identify with a church and attend church less often not because they represent a significant social change—as most European Catholic sociology seems to think—but because they are young. This is not a theory of an opinion but a statistically demonstrated fact, documented in an article by Michael Hout and myself in the June issue of the *American Sociological Review*. As Hout observes, young people are less likely to vote, to affiliate with a political party, to make a definitive career choice, to choose a permanent sexual partner, to stay in a particular job. As they grow older—not much older—they make choices on all these matters. Even on a priori grounds it is absurd to suppose that religion would be any different than these other areas of their life.

The curve of church attendance begins to slope down in the late teens and early twenties (the result, as it seems to me, of inarticulate questions and doubts which arise in the middle teens), hits bottom in the middle twenties and then begins to rise in the late twenties, thirties, and early forties (at approximately the rate of 2 percent a year). This curve seems to be almost purely an age curve and is not affected (as one so often hears) by either marriage or child bearing—though in most cases it happens at the same time. (Unmarried men and women tend to drift back into the church at about the same time as their married age peers. Childless couples follow the same path back in as their age peers with children.)

As in so many other aspects of life adults do not seem to be able to remember their own behavior when they were in their late teens and early twenties and hence think that their children are different from them, when in fact in certain critical and fundamental ways they are not different at all.

The decision to remain Catholic (or to reidentify as Catholic) does not mean that the laity continue to be Catholic on the terms the institutional

Church requires: as is clear by now, they reject several major tenets of the Church's sexual ethic (though by no means all) and the right of the Church to lay down guidelines in certain areas of moral and political behavior.

Moreover, as is demonstrated in a recent research report by Bishop William McManus and myself, church contributions in terms of percentage of income have fallen to half of what they were in 1960 (from 2.2 percent to 1.1 percent, while Protestant contributions have remained steady at 2.2 percent), costing the Church at least sixty-five billion dollars during the period (six billion last year). Much of this decline is related to (as a matter of statistical statement and not personal opinion) a declining acceptance of authority and particularly of authority on matters sexual. (It does not follow that sexual teachings ought to be changed.)

The laity voted not with their feet but with their checkbooks.

Catholics therefore stay. They stay on their own terms but they stay. Moreover, anyone who associates with Catholic laity in moderately serious fashion knows that the anguish of the media or the troubled faith of the Vatican and the hierarchy simply do not exist for most of the laity. They are Catholic and that's that. In great part they simply tune out, as irrelevant and sometimes embarrassing noise, statements from the Vatican, the national hierarchy, their own bishop, and often even their parish priest.

Why?

Ah, my friends, if we can answer that, we'll have it all!

They stay despite enormous aggravations—poor preaching, inept and often tyrannical pastors, a vast array of extra canonical "rules" around the administration of the sacraments, bishops using funerals to talk about politics, homosexual and pedophile priests, poor preaching, tasteless priests (a pastor at a college announcing at Mass that he and his nun colleague were about to be married and then standing with his bride-to-be at the back of church to receive congratulations), poor preaching, compulsory and dull classes before your children can receive the sacraments, money sermons (on Mother's Day for example), poor preaching, denunciations of their teenagers, and almost every other dumb and insensitive thing clerical ingenuity can devise.

Poor preaching too.

Perhaps somewhere in the country there are "required" classes before your children's reception of the sacraments that are not incompetent, but I have never heard of them. Perhaps there are weddings that are not blighted in part by a horror story of what some stupid priest has said or done, but each year I hear more horror stories.

Perhaps there are other parishes which are as sensitive to the hunger of the alienated to return as is Msgr. Cahalane's parish as described recently in this journal [*America* 157(3) (Aug. 1–8, 1987)], but I don't know of many.

The laity identify the parish as the Church, it would seem, even when those who preside over the parish fail abysmally in their jobs.

As I read the data and listen to the laity, I draw the following conclusion: There is nothing more the Vatican, the bishops or we priests can do to drive the laity out of the Church. We did everything we could—and often continue to do it—and still they won't go! (For the statistical reasons to be discussed shortly, Hout and I believe that the impact of sexual teaching and institutional authority on Catholic behavior is spent and that should church attendance decline again it will be for some other reason, a reason that is difficult at this time to imagine.)

Hence, if one tries to predict American Catholic behavior for the middle run—into the next century and the next millennium—one can say with some confidence that the laity will continue to "hang in there" come what may.

After that? Especially if there is not a rejuvenation of the priesthood?

About such a scenario a cautious sociologist would not hazard a guess—except perhaps to say that the rejuvenation of the priesthood may depend (1) on the leaders Rome appoints and (2) on answers to the question of why the laity do indeed "hang in there." As to the first, there is little reason for hope. As to the second, the answers, I believe, can be found; but I'm not sure that anyone much cares.

Why, then, to ask the question again, do they stay?

Hout and I tried to find the beginnings of an answer. We noted that the shape of the curve of Catholic drift away from weekly church attendance in the late 1960s and the early 1970s was the same as the shape of the curve of their drift away from identification with the Democratic party. Looking more closely at the data we discovered that the curves were not only similar, they were related: among those who were strongly identified with either political party, the decline in weekly church attendance in the early 1970s was from 67 percent to 57 percent. Among those who were not only "independents" but "pure independents" not even leaning to one party or the other the decline was from 63 percent to 27 percent, almost four times as large.

There was a correlation then between political and religious "loyalty." Would we be justified in saying that there was a variable behind that correlation that might properly be dubbed "loyalty," a variable whose properties we could specify?

Using a model developed by the Swiss statistician, Georg Rasch, and refined by Otis Dudley Duncan (and with the latter's help) we (Hout, to be precise and give credit where credit is due) fit our loyalty assumption to extremely precise and rigorous testing. The model specified not only the distribution of data but also the distribution of data on religious and

political affiliation if there were the kind of "latent" structure we expected
and the direction of the relationship between the latent structure and both
political affiliation and religious devotion. The fit between the data and the
model, then, had to be extremely tight or the model would be rejected. We
were, however, not able to reject it. Therefore such a latent "loyalty"
structure best explains the relationship between the two known variables.

It seemed to us that this "loyalty" variable put a break in the decline of
Catholic church going (or, to honor the metaphor, on the increase in
unregular church going) in the middle 1970s. About a third of the regular
Catholic church goers who rejected the birth-control teaching (only 15
percent of Catholics accept it), it would seem, were so offended by the
birth-control decision that they stopped going to church regularly (though
usually not completely). But the other two thirds when apparently faced
with a choice between a drift to the margins of the Church and acceptance
of the birth-control encyclical, chose neither. They would remain regular
church goers, but on their own terms, rejecting the official teaching but
still showing up at church every week or nearly every week.

Whether one curtailed religious practice because of the birth-control
teaching or sustained practice and "resisted" the teaching was a function
of the level of one's "loyalty." The more "loyal" you were, the more
likely you were to stay and fight.

Having established that there is such a loyalty variable, Hout and I were
forced to speculate on its substantive properties (we are also attempting to
ascertain whether it also exists in the British Isles and in Canada). To
whom or what are Catholics loyal? Surely not to the Pope as such, because
they reject some of his teaching. Nor to their bishop insofar as he repeats
that teaching. Nor to their parish priest unless he is sensitive and competent. Nor to theologians whom they don't read. To what then?

Hout points out that political scientists have observed that no matter
how far from the political mainstream Americans might be, how much
they may be alienated from the national consensus, they still have difficulty
thinking of themselves as anything but American. Is it not likely, he asks,
that Catholics relate to their Church in a similar fashion? It is their
heritage, their birthright. In Hout's vivid words, "Even though the Pope
may not think so, they feel they are as Catholic as he is."

I can't think of a better summary of the picture I see in the data.

There are, I suspect, three substantive components to this loyalty:
identity, community, and sacramentality. I model them, not as distinct
factors, but rather as different aspects of one dense and polysemous
reality.

As Will Herberg pointed out more than thirty years ago, in a pluralistic
society like our own, religion is an essential component of your identity

and social location (so too, for many people and in many places, are your politics and your ethnicity). You have to be something and Catholicism is your heritage, it is a component of your selfhood. No one, not even the Pope, much less Cardinal Ratzinger or some bishop, is going to take it away from you!

Local community has always been a powerful part of the Catholic sensibility, manifesting itself in the United States in that singularly ingenious artifact, the neighborhood parish (and reinforced by that remarkable creator of community, with all its social capital—to use James S. Coleman's words—the parochial school). Despite the cliché among *Commonweal* type Catholics that the parish is no longer as important as it used to be, any serious consideration of suburban Catholicism indicates that it is still enormously important. However inept most suburban pastors may be, the laity continue either to hang in their own parish or find another one. It is hard to be a Catholic without a parish. But if you are determined to be a Catholic—and on the basis of the data most Catholics are so determined—you find one.

Finally, the sacramentality of Catholicism has tremendous appeal to the imaginative dimension of the personality. The various Catholic nostalgia books—fiction and nonfiction—of recent years all emphasize the ceremonies, assuming that they are lost and gone forever as they are in many parishes.

Did your parish have a May crowning?

Every night that John Powers's "Black Patent Leather Shoes" played in Chicago (for over three years), the audience joined in "Bring Flowers of the Rarest." Poor music perhaps, but rich, rich metaphor.

A woman in one of my novels sums up what hundreds if not thousands of those who drift back want, "I miss Midnight Mass and May crownings, First Communions and grammar school graduation, nuns in the school yard and the priest in back of church on Sunday. I want it all back, for myself and my kids."

Now she might add "the Easter Vigil," whose rich symbolism seems to appeal more to the laity with each passing year.

And a real-life person (a writer who might be said to be on the fringes of the Church) says the same thing: "As a Catholic child one is taught to believe in symbols, to understand that the world is form containing spirit, the union of body and soul in the eucharist. Metaphor becomes second nature, the first lesson, and we must struggle in order to be touched with grace."

The author of those words is able to reflect explicitly on the Catholic sensibility (David Tracy's analogical imagination); most people do not and cannot. However, they need not. You do not need to know what a metaphor is to be affected by it. You do not need to be able to define sacramentality to be swept up by it. You do not need to know that the Eucharist says it all, to sense the importance of Eucharist.

The Eucharist holds together all three components—identity (we are the ones who go to Mass), community (the Mass is priest and parish together), and sacramentality (when you receive communion, you assert the goodness of flesh and world). The Eucharist is the key to it all, but only the Eucharist rescued from the punctilious, precious, petty historicism and rubricism of the liturgists and from illiterate readers, off-key singers, clumsy church musicians, and dreadful homilists.

I am acutely aware as I write this article that rather few in the various church elites today care much either about my question or my answers. Whether the ordinary laity stay or leave is not a matter with which they are preoccupied (because the ordinary laity are not in the Third World or not "the poor" or not the people who write letters to the Vatican). And such issues as identity, community, and sacramentality (all summed in Eucharist) are deemed as utterly irrelevant. A tradition of incredible durability and strength, a resource of enormous richness and power, a sensibility of appealing and terrible beauty—it is all dismissed as simply not relevant.

And such a dismissal is perfectly legitimate if one condition holds:

The Spirit speaks through the magisterium and theologians and staff members of the National Conference, but She does not speak through the ordinary lay people of God.

This article is reprinted from *America* 157, (3) (Aug. 1–8, 1987) by permission of the journal editor and Father Greeley.

10

The Jews: Schism or Division

Samuel C. Heilman

"Split Widens on a Basic Issue: What is a Jew?" read the front page headline of the *New York Times* 28 Feb. 1986. The article that followed, written by Joseph Berger, went on to report that "the polemics have been marked by *uncommon* bitterness" (emphasis mine). It quoted a variety of rabbis and Jewish leaders who warned that "the dispute could result in deep and enduring divisions in the Jewish community," a schism that might ultimately lead to one group questioning the other's Jewishness, to the possibility that family pedigrees would be scrutinized by the more observant before they would allow "a son or a daughter to marry a less traditional Jew," to more restrictive and selective admission standards to Jewish day schools and summer camps, and even to erosion in the general Jewish support for Israel.

While the article went on to cite some students of Jewish life, among the sociologists and rabbis, who minimized the forebodings of permanent disunity and downplayed the prospects of growing and unbridgeable divisions within the Jewish community, the overall thrust of the report, and what made it front-page news, was the ominous possibility that was perhaps articulated best in a quotation from Haskel Lookstein, president of the New York Board of Rabbis, who suggested: "The extremism that manifests itself on both sides threatens to isolate Jew from Jew and to rend the fabric of Jewish peoplehood so that we will no longer be one people."

Often the discussion on the matter of schism focuses on the past experiences of the Jews and begins from the premise that history is the great teacher and an examination of it provides insight and instruction about possible future trends. But a reading of Jewish history makes it painfully clear that its lessons are not always unambiguously clear or monothematic. Indeed, while one reading of the facts leads to the pessimistic conclusion that differences that lead to separate marriage patterns ultimately result in schism and the separation of the unmarriageable population from the Jewish people at large, another analysis suggests that the membranes dividing Jew from Gentile have at times been at the very least semipermeable, allowing people to cross back and forth under a variety of circumstances and conditions. From this point of view, assimilation is not forever.

This paper will try to suggest a course between the extremes as well as a way of understanding the sociology underlying the concern over unity itself. First, however, a brief summary of some of the matters which divide the Jews is in order.

The Dividing Lines

Conversion and Patrilineal Descent

The most prominent current issue dividing Jews appears to focus around the question of "who or what is a Jew?" Although by no means the first time this matter has been a national concern (the book of Exodus recounts this as an issue even for the generation of those leaving the Egyptian bondage), the question of Jewish definition has undoubtedly become acutely problematic now because of a striking rise during this generation in the frequency of intermarriage between Jews and non-Jews. This increasing rate—ranging from approximately 25 percent on the average for American Jews to close to 40 percent in many communities, and in some places as high as 70 percent—has had several consequences. First, and most obviously, it has yielded a generation of children who have one parent who was not born a Jew, and who in only some cases (21 percent, as reported in a recent study of intermarriage by sociologist Egon Mayer) has been converted to Judaism. If the non-Jewish parent is the mother, then according to *halacha* (Jewish law), the offspring is not Jewish.

Secondly, where mixed marriages do lead to conversion, these conversions are not always carried out according to the most rigorous standards of Jewish law. In such cases, the convert (either a parent or a child or both) may not be considered a Jew by those who adhere to a strict interpretation of the law.

Complicating the matter even further are several social factors. Firstly, "many intermarried Jews take part in Jewish communal life. Many, if not most, have Jewish friends and family connections. Most retain residential, occupational, and educational bonds with other Jews. Many non-Jews married to Jews develop bases of communal contacts and are part of the Jewish community."¹ Simply stated, this means that a person raised as a Jew and tied to a network of Jewish relations and obligations, one who belongs to a synagogue or gets a Jewish education or gives to the United Jewish Appeal or identifies with the destiny of Israel may consider him or herself Jewish, regardless of whether or not he or she meets the Jewish legal, halachic demands for inclusion within the Jewish community. Thus, for example, a child with a non-Jewish mother but a Jewish father who has been brought up in a Jewish cultural and social environment, attended the synagogue, received some sort of Jewish education, and even had a bar or bat mitzvah, might consider him or herself a Jew, even though by the strict rules of the halacha, he or she is not.

Finally, someone born a non-Jew who enters the social and cultural milieu of Jewish life, either through marriage to a Jew or on his or her own, may decide to become a convert. As a neophyte to Judaism, the newcomer may often choose to enter through the path of least resistance— undergoing a conversion ritual that makes minimal demands upon him or her. Subsequently, the new convert becomes even more socially aligned and involved with the Jews. While from the social point of view, such integration appears to suggest a successful assimilation and demonstrates the capacity of the Jewish community to handle the potentially disruptive effects of intermarriage and conversion, it creates or fosters problems in other domains. Among these are the divisions between those on one side who accept the legitimacy of socially based definitions of Judaism and who seek to make entrance into Jewish communal life untroubled and those on the other side who are concerned with maintaining the integrity of the boundaries between Jews and others. Thus, the convert who has come into Judaism without undergoing the rigors of a traditional conversion under the auspices of an Orthodox Jewish court (beit din) may be stunned to discover that the legitimacy of his or her conversion is questioned by some segments (notably, the Orthodox and some Conservative Jews) of the community. Or, the child of a mixed marriage who has been raised as a Jew, but whose mother has converted by a process other than the most stringent one, may be dismayed to find out at some point in life that his or her Jewishness is called into question by more traditionally oriented members of the Jewish community.

Complicating these divisions even further are political and sectarian issues. Within America, the long-lasting and deep-seated rivalries among the various movements—Orthodox, Conservative, and Reform—for the mantle of American Jewish religious and spiritual leadership has, among other things, led to struggles over determining the definition of who and what a Jew is. In light of the growing attachments between Jews and non-

Jews, each sect of Judaism, through its rabbis and leaders, has made claims that assert its right to define and convert Jews.

On the one end are the Orthodox who point to their devotion to Jewish law and their apparent continuity with tradition as the source for their legitimacy. The fact that they still use the same criteria for defining a Jew that have been used for generations and that have been incorporated into the codes of Jewish law is presented as the basis of their claim for legitimacy.

On the other extreme are the Reform who argue in favor of a definition that recognizes social realities, that confronts the fact that Jews are increasingly involved with non-Jews; they therefore call for a definition that allows for the maximum integration possible. This means making conversion procedures less restrictive and more supportive and allowing for patrilineal as well as matrilineal lines of Jewish descent, a decision that the movement formalized in 1983.

Somewhere in the middle stand the Conservative Jews who seek to comply with the standards of the past with regard to defining Jews, to be conservative in making changes, but who have nonetheless accepted the principle that changes in Judaism have their origin in changes in the lives of Jews. They are thus caught between an attachment to traditional Jewish law and a desire to be in tune with contemporary needs of American Jewry. While prepared to struggle with the social realities of intermarriage, they are nevertheless unwilling to make what they view as radical changes in Jewish tradition. "I think (that accepting patrilineal descent is) a fundamental rupture with the idea of a Jewish community, and communal responsibility ought to prevent us from rupturing that unity," said the chancellor of the Jewish Theological Seminary of America, Ismar Schorsch. The Conservative dilemma is that the Jewish community to which they remain attached is not a monolith; to some of its adherents stability and loyalty to the past are essential, while to others communal responsibility specifically encourages change.

To recap, the matter of who and what is a Jew has become of increasing concern and a matter of public debate in the last number of years because of several factors:

1. The rise in the rate of intermarriage from around 10 percent to 15 percent in the 1950s to 25 percent or more in the 1970s and 1980s has alarmed Jews.
2. The offspring of mixed marriages occurring during the 1950s and 1960s are now coming of age, marrying, and taking their places in the Jewish community.
3. Orthodoxy, while not significantly increasing its demographic share in

American Jewry (whose population of 5.6 million is reported to be about 10 percent Orthodox, 33 percent Conservative, 23 percent Reform, and 35 percent unaffiliated but still identified as Jewish) has begun to feel an increased sense of security about its position in America. It has not disappeared, as many analysts a generation ago said it would; its adherents have acquired a modicum of financial and professional success, reflected in increased political power within Jewish life; its religious and educational institutions are flourishing, often encouraging a traditionalist (sometimes called right wing) swing among many who attend or have attended them; and it can point with triumph to numbers of newly Orthodox Jews *(baaley t'shuva)* who are rejecting assimilationist trends and choosing traditional Judaism as a way of life. Accordingly, Orthodoxy is publicly challenging the assimilationist and integrationist moves made by other Jews.

4. The rise of Orthodox power in the Israeli Likud government of Menachem Begin and the consequent hold this has had on defining Judaism there, coupled with greater American Jewish involvement with Israel (whereas prior to 1967 relatively few American Jews had direct contact with Israel, since then the number has increased dramatically), have brought the Israeli parliamentary question of "who is a Jew?" to this country.

5. The 1983 decision by the Reform movement to recognize patrilineal Jewish descent stimulated debate and discussion among American Jews.

6. Finally, the recent 1985 study of intermarriage and the Jewish future sponsored by the American Jewish Committee and carried out by Egon Mayer dramatically shed light on the facts which could no longer be ignored: Jews were marrying non-Jews in greater numbers and converts as well as offspring from mixed marriages and conversionary ones were an established part of the American Jewish community. The widespread dissemination of the findings throughout Jewish and non-Jewish media simply reinforced and focused public awareness on the issues.

Yet if the matter of converts and offspring of intermarriage appears to divide American Jewry, they are by no means the only bones of contention. A comprehensive look at the grounds of American Jewish disunity reveals a series of other points of conflict.

Divorce

Among the matters dividing Jews from one another is the matter of divorce. Although Jews have enjoyed a reputation for stable marriages, there has been an increasing incidence of separation and divorce among them. In 1971, the National Jewish Population Survey found that among the twenty-five-to-twenty-nine-year-old group, 15 percent of all the house-holds were separated or divorced. In the last twenty-five years, the Jewish Family Service caseload of divorce has grown from 5 percent to 30 percent. And while the general American population approaches a 50 percent divorce rate, the Jewish rate, although lagging behind, continues to grow.

Still, American Jews remain committed to marriage and the family, and they therefore tend to remarry in high numbers (indeed, more than other American religious groups). More than 50 percent of all divorced Jewish women remarry within five years.

While the Jewish law with regard to marriage is relatively flexible, divorce is a far more complex matter. Under the halacha, only a woman who has received a valid *get* (bill of divorcement), usually executed through the auspices of a Jewish court of law, is legally entitled to remarry. Should a Jewish woman remarry without such a valid get, her new marriage would, in the eyes of those who accept the authority of the halacha, be adulterous. Moreover, should she have a child from that new union, that child would, again in the eyes of those bound by the halacha, be considered illegitimate, a *mamzer*. In Jewish law, a mamzer may not marry a Jew. Nor may ten generations of offspring of a mamzer marry Jews. The mamzer is for all intents and purposes excommunicated.

To many, if not most, Orthodox Jews, civil divorces and those carried out through the aegis of non-Orthodox institutions are invalid. Conse-quently, all subsequent marriages and births lead to a population of people who are written out of the Jewish community as far as these Orthodox Jews are concerned. And thus divorce becomes, not only a problem for the Jewish family, but a source of disunity in the Jewish community.

The Status of Women in Judaism

While not nearly as divisive as the matter of conversion, patrilineal descent, or divorce and remarriage that may lead to structural rifts among Jews such that members of one group will find themselves unable to marry members of the others without compromising on their principles, there are other lines of cleavage in the Jewish community. Few matters have so exercised the contemporary Jewish community as has the matter of the status of women in Judaism. Although this is not the place to review the entire debate or the course of its development, it must be pointed out that in the last century and, even more, the last fifteen years, the traditional role of women in Judaism has undergone profound change. These changes have more or less paralleled the transformations in the status of women in the host societies of the West, within which most Jews reside. The keynote of that change has been the evolution the position of women from subservient to equal with men.

Among the non-Orthodox, this has resulted in offering women most if not all the same rights and privileges that Judaism has accorded to men. Although the effect of change among the Orthodox has been far less comprehensive and sweeping, it can be discerned nevertheless. In Orthodox circles, including even the most uncompromising, the rising importance of women is reflected in the nearly universal acceptance of the historically revolutionary principle that Jewish women should be provided intensive and advanced Jewish education like the men, something that in the past was largely unthinkable. But this change in the status of Orthodox women is symbolically far less than the non-Orthodox demand.

Accordingly, the status of women in Judaism has become a matter of dispute in the American Jewish community. The schismatic effect of this debate grows out of two symbolic issues, both of which the tradition opposes: (1) the counting of Jewish women along with men as part of the *minyan* (quorum) for prayer, and (2) the ordination of women rabbis. Both of these options have been rejected by Orthodoxy and accepted by all other sects, although with some resistance among the traditionalist wing of Conservative Jewry. Accordingly, these two points have become part of the ideological line dividing Jews.

Other Matters of Division

There are other matters of division. Among these is the distinction between those who do and those who do not observe Jewish dietary law *(kashrut),* sometimes leading to rifts such that members of one group will not eat in the homes of members of another that does not share its definition of what is and is not kosher. There is also the institutional division between Orthodox, Conservative, and Reform Jewry, which has nearly hardened into sectarian lines. And there is the division between those who receive an intensive Jewish education, with all it implies, and those who receive a meager one; those who choose the one option are coming less and less in contact and having less to share with those who choose the other.

The Implications of Division

Historians, in trying to reflect on the implications of these divisions have pointed to Jewish splits in the past. They cite the divisions that existed in the biblical period, both in the Mosaic time as well as the divisions between the Kingdoms of Judea and the ten northern tribes; rifts between the

Pharisees and Sadducees in ancient Palestine; the breach that occurred beginning in the eighth century in the heartland of Mesopotamian Jewry between Karaites and Rabbanites, who differed over the oral interpretations of Scripture; and the rupture between Sephardim, descendants of Jews who lived in the Iberian peninsula before the expulsion of 1492, and Ashkenazim, Jews of European origins, who differed markedly from each other in matters of detail and outlook. Finally, there are the lines of fracture that once bitterly divided Galician and Russian Chassidim from their Lithuanian-based opponents, the Misnagdim. But there are disputes about the precise outcome and implications of these divisions. Did they resolve themselves toward Jewish unity or did they lead to one group largely disappearing or becoming assimilated by the other? There are even questions about the segregation between Jews and Gentiles (Cohen 1988).

Lawrence Schiffman, a student of ancient Jewish life, opens a recent paper on this subject by arguing that "the conditions in which Judaism finds itself today are analogous to those in which it found itself" in earlier historical periods (Schiffman 1988). He goes on to suggest that the essential elements of modernization, which he lists as "enlightenment, emancipation, secularization and assimilation," occurred "before in Jewish history." And he contends that in the distant past, "Jews, just as they did in recent times, confronted a 'modern' society." From this he goes on to note that where the result of the division was that people did not intermarry, the consequence was schism. Hence, the argument runs, if the divisions today result in some Jews categorically not marrying other Jews, a similar outcome can be expected. Division will lead to schism.

A response to this argument, which epitomizes what may be termed the "pessimistic" perspective, needs to focus on two points: is the present age really analogous to the past, and do patterns of marriage still today (as apparently they once did) represent the sine qua non of religiocultural unity?

The Meaning of Contemporary Modernity

Consider first the essentials of the present age. While it is certainly true that each epoch has its own definition of modernity, and today's traditions were most certainly yesterday's innovations, there are particular features of contemporary modernity that distinguish it significantly from other "modernities" of the past. Modernity as we live and understand it today is "a syndrome, or complex, of qualities rather than . . . a single trait" (Inkeles and Smith 1974, 17). It is "a set of dispositions to act [and think] in certain ways" (Inkeles and Smith 1974, 16; see also Inkeles and Smith 1974, 17–25).

To begin with, no matter how modern the past may have been, it was essentially a world in which corporate, group, or tribal affiliations were paramount. Individual identity, except for the charismatic figures of history, is virtually unknown in the ancient or medieval worlds. In contrast, "in a complex modern society, . . . the tasks of life have become so completely individualized, (that) it is a question whether culture, in the sense in which anthropologists have conceived it, any longer exists" (Park 1930, 2:282). As individualists, moderns are distinguished by diminished relations to extended family life and local ties.

Furthermore, the individualism and its correlate, personal autonomy, at once liberated persons from absolute submission to received authority and shifted responsibility for action from the group to the individual. "A 'modern' man is an activist; he attempts to shape his world instead of passively and fatalistically responding to it. He is an individualist" (Kahl 1968, 37). People now believe that they can learn how to exert considerable control over their environment and look upon matters that their forebears may have considered matters of fate, rather as matters of choice. Thus, they believe that prevention of accidents is more a matter of carefulness than luck, that medicine is more effective than prayer in curing a sick person and that people need not resign themselves to their physical condition, that affairs can be planned in advance, and so on. It is the individual who is responsible for taking care, taking medicine, and making plans.

Second, these earlier epochs were epochs in which change—as measured by today's stands—was remarkably slow. The gap between what people actually did and what was expected of them—what W. F. Ogburn has called "cultural lag"—was far narrower than it is today. Stability rather than change was the predominant order of the day. One could expect affiliations, domicile, occupation, and almost everything else that mattered in life to hardly change at all throughout the course of one's life. In contrast, the syndrome of modernity encompasses an ethos of change and flexibility, which are viewed as far more adaptable than rigidity and inflexibility to the rapidly shifting conditions of contemporary conditions.

Third, the past was a time in which alternative ways of life were not available for the choosing; the circumstances into which one was born were more often than not the circumstances in which one would continue to live and die. If alternatives were known at all, they were not commonly accessible. Personal status was ascribed rather than subject to individual initiatives and achievements. Pluralism was unheard of as an acceptable alternative to a single way of life. People might have become something else, but in so doing they had to abandon for the most part what they had once been. They could not easily compartmentalize their existence.

In contrast, the modern world is one of mobility—geographic, social, and intellectual. As people move about, often rubbing shoulders with diverse attitudes, opinions, and lifestyles, they become—as moderns have—disposed to pluralism. That is, by virtue of this contact, moderns have in principle become open to the idea that there is more than one way to live. Along with this realization, which is a part of modern conscious-ness, has come the development of newer nonparochial loyalties coupled with the emergence of the far more cosmopolitan attachments.

But pluralism has meant not only an openness to other ways of life. Coupled with individualism and an ethos of encouraging change, it has meant that any given person can and often chooses to move among a variety of ways of life and share many affiliations. Whereas a person might have in the past thought of himself as loyal to a single way of life and cultural or tribal ties, the modern can conceive of himself in the more neutral category of citizen or individual, whose ties to particular groups and locales are often partial. People who at one time might have thought of themselves as either Germans or Jews can now think of themselves as both. In the most extreme expression of this development, people can cultivate newer nonparochial loyalties, coupled with the emergence of the far more cosmopolitan attachments, and finally define themselves as no longer tied to any particular corporate identity—even a hyphenated one— but rather as universalists, whose home is the planet Earth and whose people are all people. Moreover, as individualists and pluralists, moderns may choose to adopt all or some aspects of the other lives, values, beliefs, and opinions according to their personal needs.

Modernity, however, has not only affected individuals; it has trans-formed society. The modern society reflects the compartmentalization of individual life by creating divisions in all sorts of domains and at the same time frequently effacing those divisions. Thus, while contemporary life is marked by division of labor, partial affiliations, social cleavages, ethnic diversity, and neighborhood partitions; all these divisions are not viewed as absolute or unbridgeable. Jobs may be and often are changed. People move from neighborhood to neighborhood and community to community. Individuals go into and out of relationships of all sorts—including mar-riage. Precisely because they are partial rather than total, affiliations are often reshuffled. As already suggested, social status is not given at birth but subject to a variety of changes based upon achievements. Mobility is such a frequent feature of contemporary existence that few if any live in the same locality throughout their entire lives. And as marriages proceed across ethnic lines, even ethnicity is no longer pure or unequivocal, but rather becomes at most symbolic (Gans n.d., 1–20).

As such, no single affiliation becomes definitive for moderns. They can and do relate to groups and other individuals in a variety of different modalities. Thus, for example, if they are not related through marriage, they may be affiliated through some other activity, whether political, social, or situational. In the modern world, people can be part-time in lots of ways. They can be part Scotch, part German, part Indian and part Jew—all at once and with different facets of being and involvement. To the modern, the thought that on Christmas he might be Christian, on Hanukkah Jewish, and on the Fourth of July all-American is easily conceivable.

Modernity and Jewish Unity

What does all this mean for Jewish unity? It means, first, that we can no longer consider modern Jews only in terms of their corporate identity. Insofar as they have entered the modern world, they have entered it often as individuals and relate to one another as such. They are not only Jews; they are Jews and lots of other things. And sometimes they may choose to make their Jewishness primary, active, and salient; while at other times it remains secondary, dormant, or irrelevant to their lives. For many, it is only one aspect of their identity.

Second, contemporary Jews, like other moderns, view themselves as autonomous, often only partially affiliated with their Jewishness and other Jews. In the world which most historians describe, such a possibility was unthinkable. Yet in the modern world, partial affiliations and divided loyalties are perfectly normal and acceptable. In such a world, the idea that one either is a Jew or one is not is replaced by the notion that in some circumstances and ways one may be Jewish while in others one may not be. Compartmentalization is a fact of modern existence. Moreover, what may be true of one Jew is not necessarily true of all others.

Furthermore, as an active shaper of his own destiny, the modern Jew is less likely to look to others to evaluate the quality of his personal Jewish identity or even to decide if he is a Jew or not. While he may still feel the lingering ancient tribal tie and sense of history that has stamped much of Jewish identity, as a modern he is less inclined to accept the ascribed definitions that say that birth or formal conversion defines precisely who and what he is. Rather, he will rely on his own decisions as well as the objective markers that social norms determine.

For the contemporary Jew, corporate identity diminishes and ascription gives way to achievement and autonomy as the most powerful determinants of identity. Put more simply, who is a Jew may now be less a matter of immutable Jewish law and more a matter of shifting social and situational definitions. Whereas in the past, people may have relied on formal definitions of identity based upon corporate and cultural affiliations, today they may choose instead to be far looser and individualistic in those identities.

Thus, while in the past, without intermarriage the corporate boundaries separated and people found themselves locked in separate groups for all eternity, in the modern world of fluid and changing attachments, where it's every man for himself, intermarriage with other Jews may not be the only criterion for determining affiliation. In fact, in the world as it is now constituted, the question of who is a Jew may increasingly be answered by different people in different ways at different times and in different places.

Consider the following datum. Exploring the lines of fracture within the Jewish community, I asked a number of rabbinical students from each of the movements about their attitudes toward Jews from movements other than their own. In the course of my interviews, I asked questions about personal status, that is, questions about converts, children of mixed marriages, offspring of second marriages who might be considered mamzerim (illegitimate), and in general about who was a Jew. One might expect rabbinical students to take a corporate, religiocultural point of view. But that was not the case. While each interviews had a variety of responses to each of these questions of status, a common element that emerged in the answers of all my respondents—from the Reform, Conservative, Orthodox, and even those who affiliated themselves with most traditionalist wing of Orthodoxy alike—was the principle that in determining matters of personal status, one had to go on a case-by-case basis. The one lesson everyone (regardless of religious orientation) seemed to have learned from the situation of modernity was that wholesale corporate exclusion or inclusion was not desirable. While one might rhetorically say all sorts of things in a wholesale fashion about Jews from movements other than one's own, one had to be far more circumspect and individualized in the actual rendering of decisions on personal status.

Furthermore, decisions about how to characterize Jews required a sensitivity to shifting affiliations and perspectives. Thus, while some people were not necessarily ready to marry Jews from other movements—and had not been ready to do so for a long time—they were not prepared to say that there were absolutely no conditions under which they could carry on activities in common with these Jews they would not marry.

In fact, there were a whole array of activities which Jews of all movements whom I interviewed believed they could carry on as a unified people—such as, for example, social-action endeavors, activities aimed at combatting discrimination against Jews, or campaigns seeking to strengthen the quality of Jewish life. Moreover, they could imagine individual situations where Jews who were divided deeply in their communal orientations could nevertheless achieve personal rapprochement. Where communities or movements might be separate, individuals did not have to be. To be sure, the Orthodox envisioned such rapprochement as coming in the form of the non-Orthodox returning to the traditions and the non-Orthodox viewed it as coming with acceptance by the Orthodox of the legitimacy of Jewish pluralism. Yet, the idea that under certain conditions individuals could experience Jewish solidarity even if subcommunities could not suggests that Jewish unity in the future will be a de facto case-by-case compartmentalized reality rather than a de jure corporate one. In fact, Jews have been living this sort of reality for over two generations. In some ways they have been one and in others they have been divided.

Thus in the modern world, it is possible to imagine a series of Jewish affiliations in one domain and disaffiliations in another. People may be part of the Jewish community when it comes to supporting Israel or combating anti-Semitism;[2] they may experience Jewish solidarity as individuals even as they are divided communally. In short, they may be affiliated (and divided) in a whole variety of partial ways. Yet, whereas in the past such partial affiliations (and divisions) were neither possible, sufficient nor desirable, in the segment contemporary world they may be enough for considering people Jewish. The modern Jew is a relatively free-floating individualist. To define him in corporate terms, as most analysts concerned with the matter of unity and disunity do, or to subject him to authoritative and absolute definitions that come down from some higher authority is to misconceive his essence.

Moreover, because change is a part of contemporary existence, what is or is not Jewish today may not be identical with what it was yesterday or may be tomorrow. In the modern world, the lines of fracture could change and ties of individual affiliation could shift. Modernity as we know it has taught us that nothing any longer need be absolute. Insiders and outsiders can easily be redefined. Indeed, even the thorniest questions of who is a Jew or mamzerut (illegitimacy) have been handled by even the most stringent of rabbinic authorities on a case-by-case basis. Often what seemed an intractable problem has been solved by ingenious solutions—both halachic and social.[3] The basic rule of order simply remains a focus on the individual case—a rule perfectly at home with modernity.

The collision between the tradition and modernity which has in effect emancipated the individual, who now floats from place to place and who can sometimes be Jew and sometimes not, has of course had its disastrous consequences in some respects—particularly in increasing the level of anomie and ideological anarchy in contemporary life. But it has been beneficial for situations which formerly were locked in either/or realities. Very simply, being a Jew is no longer an either/or proposition. It is now a both/and one. People may be both Jews and non-Jews—as those who have accepted patrilineality have demonstrated. They may be both modern and Orthodox—as the Modern Orthodox have demonstrated. They may be both parochial or ethnic and cosmopolitan or universal—as many in the contemporary world have demonstrated. The either/or perspective comes from another era.

The implications for the definition of who is a Jew are clear. Division does not lead to schism any longer. For better or worse, contemporary Judaism has no choice but to tolerate great diversity and uncertainty, for diversity and uncertainty, pluralism, and a commitment to openness are its substance.

Notes

1. The case of Kitty Dukakis, a self-identified Jew married to a Greek Orthodox, is perhaps the most public example in point.
2. Indeed, it is in combating the broad-brush definitions of outsiders who are the enemy that Jews are most often one. Everyone whom I ever asked whether anti-Semitism fostered unity agreed that it did.
3. One thinks immediately on one extreme of Moshe Feinstein's brilliant halachic solution to the potential problems of mamzerut among the non-Orthodox or, on the other extreme, Reform and Reconstructionist patrilineal solutions to the high rates of intermarriage among its followers. While neither side accepts the solutions of the other, both are motivated by the goal of Jewish unity. As long as that motivation exists, there seems to me to be room for optimism.

References

Cohen, Shaye, J. D., 1988
Gans, Herbert, n.d.
Inkeles, Alex, and D. H. Smith, 1974
Kahl, Joseph, 1968
Park, Robert, 1930
Schiffman, Lawrence H., 1988

IV
SPIRITUAL INNOVATION AND THE NEW AGE

11

Modernization, Secularization, and Mormon Success

Rodney Stark

During the past century, only one social-science thesis has come close to universal acceptance among Western intellectuals—that the spread of modernization spells doom for religious and mystical belief. So persuasive and pervasive did the secularization thesis become that in recent decades even leading theologians have offered hymns to what Bonhoeffer called "man's coming of age." By the 1960s there was a virtual stampede by theological writers and seminary professors to embrace the triumph of science and reason over faith and revelation. In the extreme case, Harvey Cox (1965) won a ticket from Andover Newton to Harvard Divinity via his celebration of "the Secular City," an "age of no religion at all," and his dismissal of all contrary signs of religious vigor or revival as but dying spasms that "pose no real threat to the secularization process."

Looking back, the fact that "everyone knew" that secularization owned the future and that an age of reason was just around the corner should have been adequate reason for caution—especially since "everyone" was too eager for the predicted change to take place. In fact, the secularization thesis is at best a partial truth resting on biased assumptions. In any event, by now it must be evident to all but the most devoted ideologues that the thunderous religious activities taking place around the world are not dying spasms, but are the lusty choruses of revival and the uproar caused by the outbreak of new faiths.

It might be worthwhile one day to examine why it was that intellectuals (myself included) could so blind themselves to the self-evident durability of religion and its continuing importance for human culture—no matter how modernized. Yet, as Mary Douglas (1983) has noted, recent religious trends even took scholars of religion by surprise. Surely they at least should have been sensitive to the unique capacities of religions to answer the most fundamental questions of human meaning. As I have stressed at length elsewhere (Stark and Bainbridge 1980, 1985), to deny that the universe has purpose is not the same thing as giving an answer to the question: What is the meaning of the universe? It will be evident that only by assuming the existence of the supernatural is it possible to say that the universe does have a purpose. Hence, so long as people persist in wanting certain kinds of answers (or certain kinds of rewards such as life beyond death) religion almost must persist.

My purpose here is not to rehash arguments about the fundamental functions of faith. Instead, I want to isolate the important partial truth contained in the secularization thesis and to embed it in a more comprehensive and adequate theoretical model. More than that, I propose to test empirical implications of this model by examining the impact of modernization on conventional religion to Latin America and Europe and then show how this, in turn, creates the conditions under which new faiths find favorable market opportunities. In this connection I shall examine the basis for the recent extraordinary success of the Mormon Church in Latin America. Then I will replicate the results by analyzing Mormon membership in the nations of Western Europe.

Secularization, Revival, and Innovation

For the past several years I have been proposing a model of religious economies within which three key processes constantly interact (Stark 1981, 1985; Stark and Bainbridge 1980, 1981, 1985; Bainbridge and Stark 1982).

The model first raises the scope of conventional church-sect theory from the level of religious organizations to the level of whole societies. In so doing it equates the process by which sects are transformed into churches, and thus made more worldly, with the process of secularization at the societal level. In this way secularization becomes a universal feature of religious economies. That is, if sect transformation is a universal, then when viewed from the perspective of a whole society it ought to be the case that the dominant religious organizations always are moving towards ever-lower tension with their sociocultural environment (Niebuhr 1929; Johnson 1963; Stark and Bainbridge 1979). Sometimes this process is more rapid, as it seems to have been in the West during the past several centuries. Moreover, societies will differ on their overall level of secularization—sometimes the dominant religious organizations will not yet have moved into very low levels of tension, at other times secularization will be very advanced. But, just as church-sect theory tells us to expect sect formation to take place when a given religious body has become too churchlike, so too it leads to the prediction at the societal level that secularization will be a self-limiting process that will produce revivals—the appearance of new organizations offering a higher-tension version of the conventional faith: sects.

Applied to late eighteenth-century America, this linking of secularization and revival would suggest that the movement of the Congregationalists and Episcopalians towards ever-greater worldliness would not usher in a golden age of unitarianism soon followed by a triumph of humanism, but would instead prompt the explosive growth of the Methodists and Baptists, which is what actually took place. Indeed, as I examine the sweep of history within my competence I find it best described by a model of alternating periods of secularization and revival—except once every few centuries when something really new does take place.

Secularization doesn't always stimulate only an outbreak of sects aiming to restore otherworldliness of the conventional religious tradition. Rather, at periodic moments of extreme secularization, an opportunity exists for new religions successfully to break into the market. Put another way, only once in a while are the conventional religious organizations so weakened that they cannot easily withstand newcomers. From this viewpoint, the rise of Christianity was possible only because of the urgent failures of classical paganism and of the Judaism of the Diaspora to meet the needs of substantial segments of the religious market—for only when the entrenched competition is feeble can new faiths make serious headway.

Elsewhere, Bainbridge and I (1979, 1985) have conceptualized new religions as cult movements to indicate their deviant position because, unlike sects, they do not embrace the conventional religious tradition. Cult movements can appear in societies in two ways. Often they arrive by diffusion from another society as Buddhism came to China and Japan from India, as Christianity spread across Europe, or as Islam swept across North Africa and into Asia. Religions also appear that are entirely new everywhere—someone has or discovers a new religious insight and successfully recruits followers.

New religions (or cult movements) are extremely common. When and where the existing religious organizations leave even small groups of people ill-served, new faiths seize the opportunity. But, for all the thousands of new faiths that spring up, only once in a great while does one achieve significant success. This is because only rarely does the sect-formation process break down so completely that the conventional religious bodies cannot withstand vigorous competition, thus permitting a shift in religious traditions. However, as already suggested, the twentieth century seems to be one of these rare times when new religions can succeed. In this paper I plan to examine current trends in a movement that, during the next century, may well become a new world faith.

Modernization and Secularization

This is not the place to try to analyze in any depth why and how moments of opportunity arise when advanced secularization can facilitate major religious changes (although I plan to devote much future study to these questions). What matters here is to note that, whatever else is involved, modernization does in fact seem to have stimulated a period of very rapid and extreme secularization. This is the partial truth buried in the conventional secularization thesis I referred to above. Modernization really has been causing major religious dislocations, often wreaking havoc with the dominant religious organizations in rapidly changing societies. Although I shall not pursue a discussion here of why and how modernization has had this effect, I agree with the general outlines of the argument as proposed and ratified by a long line of scholars including Max Weber. Where I depart from this tradition is in its mistaking the decline of specific religious organizations for the final fall of religion in general. In making this error, modern commentators have, in my judgement, simply reenacted the failure of Roman and Greek intellectuals to understand the religious changes that ushered in the Christian Era. Intellectuals in classical times noted the fatal wounds inflicted on paganism by the rapid modernization taking place in their day. But, like modern intellectuals, they too mistook changes in the sources of religion for the demise of religion per se and thereby missed noting one of the most profound cultural shifts in Western history.

In any event, in this essay I wish to demonstrate something widely taken for granted, but hardly demonstrated: that modernization does have religious consequences. Indeed, I plan to test all major parts of the model outlined above. Specifically I should like to examine and test the following hypotheses which derive from the model:

1. The more modernized a society, the more secularized—the weaker and more worldly—are the conventional religious organizations of that society.
2. The less secularized the society, the greater the success of sect move-

ments—schismatic, higher tension organizations sustaining the conventional religious tradition.
3. The more secularized the society, the greater the success of new religions—of cult movements which represent an unconventional religious tradition.

Mormon Success

One of the great advantages of doing research on the Mormons is the extraordinary quality and quantity of the statistics they collect. In 1903 Richard T. Ely, a University of Wisconsin political economist, wrote in an essay on the Mormons in *Harper's Magazine:*

> So far as I can judge from what I have seen, the organization of the Mormons is the most nearly perfect piece of social mechanism with which I have ever, in any way, come in contact, excepting alone the German army (Ely 1903, 668).

And, as the German army in that era displayed its perfection not only in field tactics, but in scrupulous staff work, so too, has the Mormon Church maintained an appetite for detailed and exact information. Not only are their statistics constantly being updated, they are subject to periodic field audits, and are augmented by extremely professional research. This paper is based on official church statistics for 1980 as these appeared in *The Church Almanac for 1982*.

Recently, I published membership projections that indicate the Mormon Church almost certainly will become a major world faith during the next century (Stark 1984). Not only do the Mormons continue to grow at a rapid rate in the United States, but they are growing even faster in much of Asia and Latin America. Consider a typical, recent two-year period: 1978–80. During these two years Mormon membership in the United States grew by an impressive 10 percent. But their foreign missions grew by an incredible 32 percent! And, although they made significant gains in many mission fields, their most stunning gains came in Latin America—in South America overall they grew by 72 percent in this two-year period, while growing by 20 percent in Central America. In Chile they grew by 121 percent, in Argentina by 68 percent, in Brazil by 59 percent, and in Mexico by 21 percent. Granted that the absolute number of Mormons in Latin America is not yet large, with such growth rates it soon will be. Since 1980, Mormon growth in Latin America has held at these high rates and a primary concern of Mormon mission presidents has been to slow down growth so as to assimilate new members rather than to stimulate rates of conversion.

The Mormons do not have nearly as high membership rates in Western Europe as they have in Latin America. One reason is that their European congregations are much newer than might be supposed. Shortly after the founding of the church in 1831, the Mormons began to send out missionaries, many of whom went to Europe. Indeed, for a time Brigham Young led the Mormon mission in England. These efforts met with incredible success. The special census of religion conducted in Great Britain in 1851 reported more than thirty thousand Mormons—more than there were in the United States in that year! Thus the rate of Mormon conversion was much higher in Britain than in America in those days, and there is evidence of high conversion rates in Sweden and Holland, too (Stark 1984). Soon, however, Mormon membership in Europe plunged. By 1860 there were only 13,853 Mormons in Great Britain and by 1890 there were fewer than three thousand (Currie, Gilbert, and Horsley 1977). This decline was not caused by defections; instead, the British Mormons had gone off to Utah (which, in the 1980 census, is the state with the highest proportion claiming English ancestry). Similar patterns of immigration soon reduced the Mormon congregations in the rest of Europe. While immigration rapidly swelled the Mormon ranks in America, it had severe consequences for European conversion. Conversion is most rapid and effective when it moves through networks of preexisting interpersonal relations: early converts in turn bring their relatives and friends into the faith (Stark and Bainbridge 1985). However, the decision to encourage (and finance) European converts to come to America pulled them out of their social networks, thus breaking off the normal spread of Mormonism.

In the 1920s the Mormons ceased transporting converts to America and their foreign congregations were greatly strengthened thereby. However, the dislocations caused by the Great Depression and then by World War II delayed the rebuilding process in Europe. As recently as 1956 there were fewer than ten thousand Mormons in Great Britain. In 1980 there were more than ninety thousand. Clearly, the Mormons are on the brink of becoming a significant religious body in Europe, if we keep in mind that they have only really been active there for less than thirty years.

The Mormons offer the most appropriate opportunity for testing my model of how secularization is self-limiting as it generates new faiths to replace the old. Unlike the thousands of other new religious movements which seem doomed to oblivion, the Mormons appear to be on the brink of achieving a real breakthrough. I estimate that there may well be more than two hundred million Mormons on earth in a hundred years. But, during their rise to world prominence, they ought to be more successful some places than others, according to my model of religious economies. Thus, the Mormons ought to achieve their greatest successes in those nations where the conventional Christian denominations have been most weakened by secularization. This means, in turn, that the Mormons ought to flourish in the most modernized nations. Indeed, my model proposes that modernization causes the secularization of conventional faiths and that this in turn leads not to a secular society, but to the rise of new religious institutions better adapted to the new social and cultural situation.

This is not the conclusion to be drawn from the conventional secularization thesis. It proposes that modernization not only erodes traditional religious institutions, but that it renders populations immune to faith. That is, all religious organizations—church, sect, and cult—should face similar fates vis-à-vis modernization. Hence all should cluster where modernization has had (so far) the least impact, while all should be fading from view in the most modernized societies. What we have before us, then, is a reasonable instance of a critical test wherein two competing theses yield contrary predictions.

Using Nations as Units of Analysis

In this paper I shall test propositions about modernization, secularization, and Mormonism using seventeen nations of Latin America and thirteen nations of Western Europe as the units of analysis. My selections and strategies of analysis were based on many criteria that need to be discussed.

Since I have chosen to focus on Mormon membership rates, I must restrict the study to places where Mormons have made at least a minimum effort to missionize. That eliminates the nations of Islam as well the Soviet bloc and various communist nations of Asia.

However, I was unwilling to base a study on the remaining nations, lumping Europe, Latin America, and various parts of Asia together. I have found that research based on nations is tricky enough without facing extreme cultural heterogeneity. It is a sufficient challenge to confront an immense array of extraneous differences across cases without asking for trouble by mixing nations from different continents and cultural spheres. Instead, I will limit the analysis to sets of nations with relatively comparable cultures, shared history, and proximity. While these restrictions mean a study based on relatively fewer cases, they also keep the results from being an uninterpretable mess. Let me illustrate. In what follows I shall report huge positive correlations between various measures of modernization and the rate of Mormon membership, first on the Latin American data and then on the European data. Had I lumped the two continents together, and created a single data set, I would have found that Mormonism tends to do better in less modernized nations—a complete reversal of the real effect. This is because the data would not really have been reflecting modernization effects at all, but would merely be telling us that Europe is more modernized than Latin America and that Mormon membership is higher in the latter.

As I set about an analysis of Latin American nations it became clear that some ought not be included in the study. Thus, for example, many of the island nations are inappropriate: Cuba because Mormon missionaries are not permitted, Puerto Rico because it is not a nation, Haiti because it lacks Latin culture, and so on. So, I simply excluded them all, limiting the sample to nations of continental Central and South America. Still, four nations stuck out as deviant. Belize, once known as British Honduras, is an English-speaking nation, the majority of whose citizens are black and are not Catholic. In similar fashion, French Guiana lacks a Latin culture, as does Guyana where a quarter of the population is Hindu and another quarter Anglican, while only 8 percent are Catholic. Finally, Dutch-speaking Suriname has as many Hindus as Catholics and does not belong in a set of nations selected for a common Catholic, Latin culture and history. So I excluded these nations, too.

In the end I based my Latin American part of the study on seventeen nations. Admittedly this is a small N, but given the size of the correlations to be assessed they prove sufficient. Keep in mind that this is not a sample of anything and therefore tests of significance are without meaning. That is, whatever correlations I report are not statistics but are the actual population parameters, so the question of random fluctuation via sampling cannot arise. As a result I do not show significance levels for the correlations. Let me reassure the faint of heart that all correlations I treat as substantively significant also produce high, if meaningless, levels of statistical significance (.05 or higher, and usually .01 and higher). In this paper I report findings via Pearson's product-moment correlations. But I also have replicated all correlations with various nonparametric measures. In addition, I have checked scatterplots of each correlation in order to guard against results produced by an extreme case.

The European data set was easily defined. Adequate data were available for thirteen nations. All of the remarks directed towards the Latin American data above apply here, too. As will be evident, the results are so robust that many possible concerns become irrelevant.

Before proceeding to the analysis, another important methodological matter must be discussed: what might best be called the "ecological fallacy fallacy." Nowadays, it is impossible to publish a paper based on units of analysis larger than the individual without getting many admonitions to beware of the ecological fallacy—to be careful not to automatically impute correlations based on groups to the behavior of individuals composing those groups. Should one ignore this warning one might commit such foolishness as blaming high crime rates in poor neighborhoods on the large numbers of social workers active in these areas, since a substantial ecological correlation would exist between social workers and crime. I have spent too many years warning students in my graduate methods courses against this terrible fallacy. Now I regret ever having mentioned it. For, treated as a slogan to be spray-painted on the blank slate of impressionable sociological minds, concern for the ecological fallacy has simply diverted us from really doing sociology—that is, it has turned us from studying groups to studying individuals. The fact is that when I try to illustrate the fallacy I have trouble finding a real example apt to fool anyone (anyone who would attribute crime rates to social workers is either an idiot or has hung around too many welfare departments). Moreover, if we do not just randomly dredge for correlations, but instead attempt to test significant hypotheses, we are unlikely to fall into the ecological fallacy. Of course, when it is vital to make individual-level assertions we ought to consult individual, not ecological, data.

In the case at hand, I will attempt to show that the larger the ''unchurched'' or ''irreligious'' proportion of a nation's population, the higher the rate of Mormon conversion. Now, that can be true and important even if it is only an ecological effect, that is, even if it is not primarily the unchurched who are becoming Mormons. But, in fact, there is a very substantial body of research showing that new religious movements depend primarily on the presumably irreligious for their converts (Stark and Bainbridge 1985). To do ecological research, therefore, is not to dispense with the need for individual-level research. But it does seem a pity that for the past three decades sociologists have devoted most of their effort exclusively to individual-level trait research. The propositions on which this study is based have individual-level implications, but their most important implications can only be tested by using ecological units of analysis.

The best measure of secularization available for Latin America is the proportion of the population that is unaffiliated with a religious organization. These are the people who, when asked their religion, respond ''none.'' As it happens, recent data on religious affiliation, based on good nationwide surveys or on a census, are available for twelve of the seventeen nations. For the other five, David Barrett (1982) was able to assemble adequate bases for estimating the size of the secularized population. In a prior study (Bainbridge and Stark 1982) similar rates based on the Canadian census proved to be extremely sensitive barometers of church attendance. Thus, the irreligious population is simply the most visible tip of the phenomenon of secularization within societies, and an accurate basis for comparisons across areal units.

Modernization and Secularization in Latin America

Students of modernization have utilized a number of different measures of that phenomenon. But the most powerful of these (from among those available for Latin America) are the percentage of the labor force employed in agriculture (the more modernized a nation's agriculture, the smaller the farm labor force), the proportion of citizens who live in urban areas, and per capita income. Table 11.1 uses these measures to test the hypothesis that modernization does in fact erode the traditional religious institutions, causing an increase in the irreligious population.

The data very strongly support the widespread view among social scientists about the link between modernization and secularization—although, to the best of my knowledge, this is the first quantitative test of the hypothesis based on cross-national comparisons. The measures produce robust, nearly identical correlations with secularization.

Secularization and Revival

The second hypothesis derived from the model of religious economies is subtle. It predicts that in highly secularized societies sect movements will be weak. Indeed, what I am arguing is that a breakdown in the church-sect cycle is what causes societies to advance into a condition of extreme secularization. That is, sects function to revive the conventional religious tradition, to replace too-worldly organizations with new ones not so worldly. Thus, where sects are thriving, secularization will be minimized. The second level of table 11.1 shows that to be the case in Latin America. Evangelical Protestant sects have achieved their highest membership rates in the least-secularized nations. Indeed, in so overwhelmingly a Catholic milieu as Latin America, nearly all brands of Protestantism are more sectlike than churchlike. And this is reflected in the fact that the overall rates of Protestant membership also are highest in nations that are least secularized.

The third level of table 11.1 shows that sects do best in the least-modernized nations of Latin America, thus completing the mirror-image contrast between secularity and revival.

Mormon Success

The fourth level of table 11.1 tests the third hypothesis: that where secularization is most advanced, new religions will enjoy their greatest

TABLE 11.1
Correlations (r) in Latin America

Modernization and Secularization

	Secularization rate
% Employed in agriculture	-.43
% Urban	.45
Per capita income	.43

Revival and Secularization

Protestant sect membership rate	-.51
Protestant membership rate	-.45

Modernization and Revival

	Sect rate	Protestant rate
% Employed in agriculture	.40	.41
% Urban	-.50	-.45
Per capita income	-.35	-.36

Secularization, Modernization and Mormon Success

	Mormon membership rate
Secularization rate	.75
% Employed in agriculture	-.36
% Urban	.33
Per capita income	.24

success. This is, of course, the crucial basis of dispute between my theoretical model and the traditional secularization thesis. I dispute the claim that modernization is leading us to an age of no religion. I claim, instead, that it will, at most, lead us into an age of new religion. The immense positive correlation (.75) between the secularization rate and the Mormon membership rate is, in my judgement, strong evidence in support of my model. The Mormons are not recruiting best in the backwaters where magic, mystery, and piety persist, to paraphrase Anthony F. C. Wallace's (1966) famous assertion of the triumphant march of secularization. The Mormons do best, instead, where secularization is greatest. And, not surprisingly, that means the Mormons are strongest in the most, not the least, modernized nations of Latin America.

Assessing Path Models

My theoretical model of the secularization is not limited to predicting bivariate correlations. Instead, it clearly specifies how modernization, secularization, and Mormon success rates interact. Specifically, I postulate that modernization spurs secularization and it, in turn, creates the market for Mormon growth. What this means is that the relationship between modernization and Mormon success ought to vanish when secularization is controlled. This is a classic instance of what Paul Lazarsfeld liked to call "interpretation." When a third variable is the link between two other variables (the mechanism by which one influences the other) this can be demonstrated by holding the linking variable constant and finding that the original correlation between the other two disappears.

To test this prediction, a path model is very appropriate since the time order among the variables is fully specified. Because I have utilized three measures of modernization, it is appropriate to examine three separate path models. These are shown in figure 11.1.

The models fully conform to the theoretical predictions and explain a very impressive amount of the total variance in Mormon success. In each of the three models the whole impact of modernization on Mormonism is channeled through secularization. Frankly, these results far exceed what even an optimistic theorist could have hoped.

A European Replication

Many critics of my earliest publications testing the link between secularization and the rise of new religions pointed to Europe as the devastating exception. For there, I was told by Roy Wallis and others, the churches stand empty and no new faiths are stirring (Wallis and Bruce 1984a). Indeed, it is in America where conventional faith still runs high that new religious movements also abound. As it turned out, however, new religions are much more plentiful and successful in the most secularized nations of Western Europe—in Britain and in Scandinavia—than in the United States. It is simply that European intellectuals have ignored them, while Americans have paid attention to local religious novelty.

FIGURE 11.1
Path Models Based on Latin America

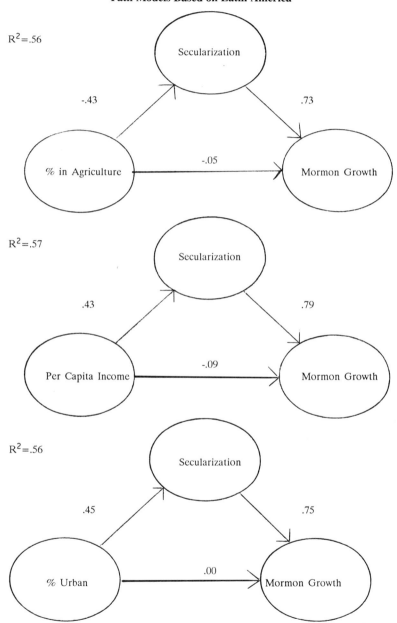

In the publications reporting these results for Europe (Stark 1985; Stark and Bainbridge 1985) I did not attempt to test the full model, giving no attention to modernization. Moreover, since completing those essays I obtained more adequate data on church attendance. In what follows, secularization is measured by the lack of weekly church attendance (Sigelman 1977; Barrett 1982). That is, the secularization rate is simply the percent not attending church weekly.

Turning to the data, we see that table 11.2 is almost identical with table 11.1. Per capita GNP, a good measure of modernization, is powerfully correlated with the secularization rate, as is the number of telephones per 1,000 residents. And, as in Latin America, the percent of the labor force employed in agriculture is strongly negatively correlated with secularization.

The second level in table 11.2 shows a strong negative correlation between secularization and revival. The latter is a measure based on the number of North American evangelical Protestant mission congregations in each European nation. The results show that American and Canadian evangelicals are doing much better in those nations of Europe where church attendance remains high—in the Catholic south. The third level in table 11.2 shows that modernization is very negatively related to the success of evangelical Protestant missionaries.

Table 11.2 also shows that secularization creates opportunities for Mormon growth—the Mormons have the highest membership rates in the most secularized parts of Europe: Britain and Scandinavia. Moreover, the Mormons thrive in the most modernized nations. But the table shows something else of interest. The rate of Asian and Eastern cult centers is based on counts of religious centers devoted to new religious movements from India and Asia (Stark 1985). While such movements gain immense publicity from their American activities, the fact is that they are much more successful in Britain and in northern Europe than they are here. Moreover, their pattern of success precisely reflects that of the Mormons— the correlation between the two rates is .78. Once again we see that new religions succeed only to the extent that weakness in the conventional faiths gives them the opportunity to do so. Put another way, empty Lutheran churches in Scandinavia are good news for Mormon missionaries as well as for gurus.

Figure 11.2 shows three path models of the process by which modernization generates secularization which in turn leads to successful Mormon recruitment efforts. In two of the three, the effects of modernization on Mormon growth is completely accounted for by secularization, and the amount of variance explained by each model is very impressive.

TABLE 11.2
Correlations in Europe

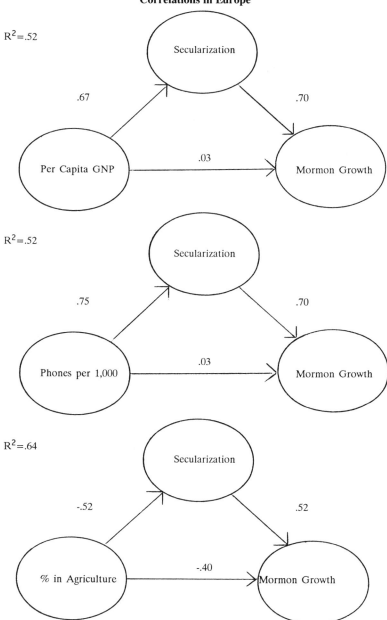

$R^2=.52$

Secularization

.67   .70

Per Capita GNP   .03   Mormon Growth

$R^2=.52$

Secularization

.75   .70

Phones per 1,000   .03   Mormon Growth

$R^2=.64$

Secularization

-.52   .52

% in Agriculture   -.40   Mormon Growth

FIGURE 11.2
Path Models Based on Europe

Modernization and Secularization

	Secularization rate
% Employed in agriculture	-.52
Per capita GNP	.67
Phones per 1,000	.75

Revival and Secularization

Rate of evangelical Protestant missions	-.57

Modernization and Revival

	Evangelical Protestant missions
% Employed in agriculture	.72
Per capita GNP	-.74
Phones per 1,000	-.70

Secularization, Modernization and Mormon Success

	Mormon membership rate
Secularization rate	.72
% Employed in agriculture	-.66
Per capita GNP	.55
Phones per 1,000	.56

Secularization, Modernization and Eastern Cults

	Asian and Eastern cult centers rate
Secularization rate	.87
% Employed in agriculture	-.61
Per capita GNP	.83
Phones per 1,000	.81
Mormon membership rate	.78

Conclusion

It would be rash to suppose that my model assumes there are no ups and downs in the levels of religiousness in societies or to suggest that I expect the immediate replacement of secularized religious organizations by new, more otherworldly and vigorous bodies. What I propose is that in the long run this is what happens. Even during periods when religious economies display extreme levels of secularization my model cannot predict just how soon a new faith will successfully fill the gap (or which new faith will do so). All it can predict is that in such times and places there will be an abundance of new faiths attempting to seize the opportunity for growth. Overwhelmingly these efforts will fail, for most new religious movements are ill-conceived and misdirected. What my model does predict is where such movements will cluster and where they will achieve their greatest relative success.

For these reasons it is irrelevant to cite the small absolute numbers attracted by the British branches of groups such as the Children of God or the Moonies—as Wallis and Bruce (1984a) recently did—in order to show that new religions are insignificant responses to the march towards secularity. Religious revolutions are not the work of hundreds of new religious movements. It only takes one. And that is why this paper has concentrated on the Mormons. They may be that rare phenomenon—a religious movement on its way to world significance. Indeed, I suggest it is time we ceased spending most of our limited scholarly effort on obvious failures such as the Children of God or Scientology and seize the opportunity to fully examine the rise of a world religion.

In my own work I have, in fact, turned to the task of creating a model of successful religious movements. I am no longer satisfied to ask when, where, and why new religions arise. Now I want to know which ones have a chance to succeed.

Note

I thank James T. Duke for calling to my attention the fact that Mormon growth rates are higher in more developed nations.

References

Bainbridge, William Sims, and Rodney Stark, 1982
Barrett, David B., 1982
Cox, Harvey, 1965
Currie, Robert, Dan Gilbert, and Lee Horsley, 1977
Douglas, Mary, 1982
Ely, Richart T., 1903
Johnson, Benton, 1963
Neibuhr, H. Richard, 1929
Sigelman, Lee, 1977

Stark, Rodney, 1981, 1984, 1985
Stark, Rodney, and William Sims Bainbridge, 1980, 1981, 1985
Wallace, Anthony F. C., 1966
Wallis, Roy, and Steven Bruce, 1984a

12

On the Margins of the Sacred

Arthur L. Greil and David R. Rudy

Introduction

This essay focuses on a class of religious phenomena that self-consciously place themselves on the frontier between the sacred and the secular, and that may therefore be appropriately referred to as "quasi-religions." In the first section, we attempt to define the term "quasi-religion" and to justify our interpretation of the proper use of the term. In the second section, we provide examples of some of the organizations which we think are appropriately classified as quasi-religions. We then go on to delineate some common features of these organizations and to employ these features as clues explaining why these organizations might position themselves on the border between the religious and the nonreligious. We conclude with a brief attempt to assess the significance of these quasi-religions and to summarize what the study of quasi-religion seems to be telling us about changes in the understanding of religion in contemporary America.

Defining Quasi-Religion

It will be immediately obvious that it is impossible to define quasi-religions without coming first to an understanding about what we mean by religion. The sociological debate over the proper definition of religion has typically pitted the supporters of functionalist definitions of religion against those who support a substantive definition of religions. Functional views of religion emphasize the essential element in religion as the provision of an "encompassing system of meaning" (Luckmann 1967, 53) or the ability to "relate man to the ultimate conditions of his existence" (Yinger 1970, 70). Substantive definitions of religion argue that the feature that is essential in distinguishing religion from other types of human activity is its reference to the sacred, the supernatural, or the "superempirical" (Robertson 1970, 47).

The advantage of functional definitions is that they allow us to look at beliefs and practices not commonly referred to as religious but which may nonetheless resemble religious phenomena in important ways. One major disadvantage of functional definitions is that they may have the effect of so broadening the concept of religion that it becomes meaningless. Another important disadvantage is that they force us to lump together supernatural and nonsupernatural belief systems whose sociological consequences may be quite different. Conversely, an advantage of substantive definitions is that they do not lump such phenomena together. Another advantage of substantive definitions of religion is that they accord more closely with American folk definitions, that is, with commonsense views of what a religion is.

Thus, one possible use of the term "quasi-religion" would be to effect a compromise between supporters of substantive definitions of religion and supporters of functional definitions of religion. The term "quasi-religion" could be used to refer to activities and organizations that involve expressions of ultimate concern or organizational dynamics similar to those of religious organizations narrowly defined (that is, functionally defined) but that do not involve a belief in the supernatural or superempirical. Employing the term in this way, running and the pursuit of health could both be described as quasi-religious in character. In similar fashion, radical political organizations, weight-loss groups, human potential groups, and companies like Amway could easily be classified as quasi-religious in that they share features in common with religious groups.

We have described the fact that substantive definitions of religion accord more closely with American folk definitions as an advantage, but this characteristic can equally be seen as a disadvantage for substantive definitions, since one might argue that it makes sociological analysis a slave to the commonsense definitions of reality that it is dedicated to seeing beyond.

"Religion" to most Americans, whether they see themselves as religious in this sense or not, refers to beliefs and practices focusing on a transcendent deity, standing above nature, controlling but not controlled by natural law. "Religion," in this view, usually centers around "churches" where people gather together to "worship" this transcendent deity, usually called "God." The transcendent worldview implicit in the American folk definition of religion is that there is an empirically available natural world governed by laws. Someone who believes that there is another, unseen, world not governed by such laws is called "religious." "Nonreligious" people are people who do not believe in an unseen world. The immanentist view that all of life, the seen and the unseen, is governed by laws which can be understood and applied by people is made anomalous by the definition of "religious" as meaning "making reference to the transcendent deity of the Judeo-Christian tradition." Substantive definitions of religion tend to buy into this American folk definition of religion with its equation of religion and transcendent religion. The very belief that it is possible to distinguish between the sacred and the secular, between the supernatural and the natural, or between the superempirical and the empirical implicitly assumes the validity of a transcendent world view.

The error made by proponents of both substantive and functionalist definitions is to assume that religion is a phenomenon that exists independently of people's conceptions of it. Both substantivist and functionalist definitions are objectivist in intent. Both try to draw a line through reality and then determine objectively whether a given phenomenon falls on the religious side or the nonreligious. We would substitute a subjectivist approach to understanding what is a religion and what isn't. From our point of view, the proper focus of the study of religion is what people do when they think of themselves as "doing religion." Our point isn't so much that the task of separating the religious from the nonreligious is impossible as that it is fundamentally uninteresting. If people see what they (or others) are doing as religious (or as not religious) it doesn't really matter much what the sociologist thinks, because people will respond differently to things they define as religious from the way they respond to those things they define as nonreligious, regardless of how the sociologist may categorize them.

This view of the proper definition of religion leads us to a different conceptualization of the category "quasi-religion" than the one presented above. Quasi-religions are neither religious entities that seem to be secular nor secular entities that seem to be religious. Rather, quasi-religions are entities whose status is anomalous given contemporary folk definitions of religion. Quasi-religions are organizations which either see themselves or are seen by others as "sort-of" religious (Rudy and Greil, forthcoming).

Quasi-religions are collectivities in which organizational and ideological tension and ambiguity regarding the group's worldview, perspective, and regimen are profitably used to facilitate affiliation as well as commitment. Quasi-religious organizations (often intentionally) ride the fence between the sacred and the secular. Leaders as well as members have at their disposal the option of emphasizing the religious nature, the nonreligious nature, or the ambiguity of their organization and its regimen in different sorts of circumstances. Examples of quasi-religious organizations, in the sense that we use the term, can be found both among self-help groups and among new religious movements, especially Human Potential, New Age, and Occult groups.

Illustrations of Quasi-Religions

Alcoholics Anonymous

A number of students of Alcoholics Anonymous (A.A.) have noted analogies between the structure, activities, dynamics, and ideology of A.A. and those of religious organizations (Gellman 1964; Greil and Rudy 1983; Jones 1970; Rudy and Greil forthcoming; Whitley 1977). A few among many of the religious characteristics of A.A. are a conception of the sacred, ceremonies and rituals, creedal statements, conversion experiences, and the presence of an A.A. philosophy of life. While these religious features of A.A. are obvious, what is also obvious is the denial by A.A. members and in A.A. literature that A.A. is a religion. However, the way in which denial is usually expressed is ambiguous to say the least. The A.A. literature and A.A. members frequently express the view that A.A. is not religious but spiritual. The heart of the A.A. program, the Twelve Steps, repeatedly mentions a "Higher Power." However, in A.A.'s view, the "Higher Power" can indicate anything from a traditional Judeo-Christian God to the group itself. Such views allowed members with extremely divergent views of God and religion to band together under one umbrella.

Compassionate Friends

Other self-help groups are characterized by similar ideological ambiguity. Compassionate Friends, a self-help group for parents who have experienced the death of a child, was founded by clergymen. It has specific ritualistic meetings, and it emphasizes that the group sharing of "experimental knowledge" allows members to transcend the human condition. Through sharing and empathy, members of Compassionate Friends may develop "an ongoing source of meaningfulness and purpose in life" (Videka-Sherman 1982, 76).

As in other quasi-religions there is an attempt to interpret some aspect of existence, in this case, the child's death, within a general religious framework. However, specific theological explanations are avoided because group members come from diverse religious traditions, and, therefore, specific theological explanations are seen as potentially disruptive.

Thus the literature of Compassionate Friends declares, "We espouse no specific religious or philosophic ideology." (Klass 1982, 317).

Organizations generally associated with the human potential movement, such as Silva Mind Control, est, Lifespring, Transformational Technologies, etc., are easily conceptualized as quasi-religions. Although it is now defunct and its founder, Werner Erhard, has moved on to other projects, such as the Forum and Transformational Technologies, est remains one of the best known of the human potential groups. In est, people attended arduous four-day workshops whose basic message to participants was that they are in control of their own experience.

Like other organizations within the human potential movement, est understands "itself to be communicating epistemological, psychological, and psychosomatic facts about human existence, not teaching religious beliefs or moral systems" (Tipton 1982, 180). And yet, as with the self-help groups we have described above, there is an emphasis on linking together within a community context so that one can transcend typical existence. The quasi-religious nature of human potential movement organizations is expressed by the idea of the "transpersonal." This term, frequently seen in the human potential literature, refers to a variety of experiences in which the individual transcends typical human experience. While members of human potential groups often say that God is not a meaningful concept for them and eschew use of the term "religion," they frequently employ the term "spiritual" to describe their experiences. All of the cosmos is related or connected, and through greater awareness and perception one can become, if you will, spiritualized. As one spokesperson for the Forum claimed, after an introductory session, "this is very similar to a religion" (Amano 1986, 21).

Spiritual Frontiers Fellowship

One example of a quasi-religious group within the occult tradition is Spiritual Frontiers Fellowship (SSF) which sees itself as a scientific religious philosophy aimed at uncovering the nature of "spiritual laws" (Wagner 1981, 22). SSF members learn to solve personal problems by such means as mediation, prayer, positive thinking, spiritual formulas such as "giving one's problem to God" or "putting it in the White Light," and making proper use of spiritual laws. But SSF members are not expected to take the efficacy of such practices on faith. Rather, they are encouraged to be skeptical of any concept until it has been verified in their own experience (Wagner 1981, 20). The study group Wagner observed was not called a congregation but a class. The participants were called, not members, but students. The ideas they discussed were not called beliefs, but theories, concepts, and ideas (Wagner 1981, 21).

Scientology

Scientology began life in 1949 as Dianetics, which presented itself as a "modern science of mental health." The basic premise of Dianetics was that normal minds are more troubled and less effective than they might otherwise be because they are held back by memories of past painful events, called "engrams." The purpose of dianetic therapy was to restore these engrams to consciousness and thus erase them from the "reactive mind," allowing the "analytical mind" to develop to its full capacity. A person whose reactive mind had been erased was known as a "clear."

In 1952, the founder of Dianetics, L. Ron Hubbard, created Scientology. Scientology differs from Dianetics theoretically, technologically, and in terms of its self-presentation. Theoretically, Scientology added the concept of the "Thetan," a being of pure spirit that allowed itself to become matter, that has been reincarnated in successive human bodies, and that represents one's true self. Technologically, the meaning of "clear" was changed to achieving a better understanding of one's true nature as a Thetan, and the process of becoming clear was aided by the use of the "E-meter," a variation of a lie detector test which was used to detect tension in those being audited. In terms of presentation of self, Hubbard declared Scientology to be a religion. Hubbard has been accused of cynically creating a religious front in order to avoid paying taxes, to protect himself from charges of fraudulent use of the E-meter, and to gain legitimacy from the wider community.

Scientologists describe Scientology as an "applied religious philosophy." At the same time, much of Scientology's ethos is decidedly secular. The principles of Scientology are presented as axioms, not as creedal statements, and services are rendered for a fee to people called customers. Although scientology is a religion, some official pronouncements still describe it as a science. In 1963, Hubbard described scientology as "the science of how to change conditions. . . . And it is the ONLY science of improvement Man has that really works" (cited in Straus 1985, 4).

Hubbard has distinguished between Scientology proper, which includes therapeutic techniques, and Para-Scientology, which includes the more religious aspects of Scientology theory. He advises ministers to steer away from Para-Scientology when dealing with potential converts. Rather, he advises, they should emphasize that man has a spiritual side and that Scientology solves social problems (Wallis 1977, 106).

Transcendental Meditation

While Scientology has been to court repeatedly to argue that it *is* a religion, Transcendental Meditation (TM) has been to court to assert that it is *not* a religion. On the face of it, it seems obvious that TM is religious in nature, derived as it is from the Hindu religious tradition. Yet, at least until 1979, when the U. S. Court of Appeals affirmed a lower court decision that TM was in fact religious in character and could therefore not be taught in public schools, the organization tried to present a secular face to the public. TM presented itself as a rationalized, streamlined method of achieving greater happiness and personal efficacy through the practice of meditation (Ellwood 1973, 231). Although no attempt was made to disguise the fact that TM was derived from a religious tradition, TM presented itself as a body of scientifically validated techniques and was successful in its attempts to have articles attesting to its efficacy placed in respected scientific journals. TM was offered as classes given for a fee to students who were expected to take their knowledge and employ it in their everyday lives as one might be expected to do with material learned in any other class.

But the face TM presented to the public was not entirely secular. Classes began with a traditional invocation performed by the teacher (Bainbridge and Jackson 1981, 139). And while introductory lectures were designed to appear secular and scientific, advanced lectures intended for core members contained explicitly religious elements, including excerpts from the Bhagavad Gita (Bainbridge and Jackson 1981, 140). In 1977, TM signaled the beginnings of a more religious public presentation with the announcement of the development of "Siddhis," performances "of higher states of consciousness described in the yoga system of Patanjali" (Bainbridge and Jackson 1981, 152). TM now promised that meditation could give initiates the ability to become invisible, to levitate, and to move objects through the exercise of mental powers. Although TM's growth is nothing like what it was in the 1960s and 1970s, the group still exists.

Common Features of Quasi-Religious Organizations

Because of space constraints, we have limited ourselves to thumbnail sketches of the salient features of these organizations. In these sketches, we have tried to highlight the ambiguity inherent in the presentations these organizations make to adherents, prospective adherents, and the general public. All of them present themselves as "sort-of" religious and/or "sort of" secular, and this qualifies them as quasi-religions. While these groups represent such a wide array of beliefs, practices, and organizational structures that it would be virtually impossible to say anything that would apply to all of them, we do think it is possible to point out some salient characteristics possessed by most of them.

First of all, it may be noted that none of these groups sponsors activities which take the forms commonly associated with religion in the American folk definition of that term. None of these groups have services; rather, they offer classes, do sessions or hold meetings. None of these groups focus their attention on a concretely defined supreme being. A.A.'s "Higher Power" might be God, but then again it might not. Scientology's theology deals more with abstract forces than with deities. SSF talks about understanding spiritual laws and about finding divinity within oneself, not about a personal relationship with God.

Less obviously, but perhaps more importantly, all of these groups see that primary goal as providing a therapeutic service. While the goal of presenting revealed truth is seldom absent, this goal is subordinated to the goal of helping people to make their lives better. Thus, a pragmatic theme pervades the ideologies of these organizations. What is true is not as important as what works.

In A.A., for example, the most important thing is achieving sobriety and helping others to achieve it. Members are constantly urged not to try and understand everything but rather to get on with the program, or cure. In A.A. one frequently hears old-timers saying, "Utilize, don't analyze." In the Occult and New Age groups, too, the most important thing is what works. Jach Pursel, the channel through whom the entity Lazarus speaks, responded in the following way when asked if he really believes in Lazarus:

> I suppose Lazarus could be a different part of me, a "higher" part of me or something. And, ultimately, I'd say, well, if you want to think that, fine. Because what really matters is the value you gain from it. And if talking to another part of me can help you improve your life, then have at it (cited in Alexander 1987, 24).

But at the same time that practical personal betterment is presented as the ultimate goal, it is typically made clear that spiritual growth and the transcending of the limits of oneself are necessary means to that end. In A.A., one must give oneself over to the Higher Power before one can achieve sobriety. In Compassionate Friends, bereaved parents learn to cope with their grief through transcending the human condition. A major goal in SSF is to achieve spiritual growth by identifying oneself with the divine inner self (Wagner 1983, 113).

Thus, many (if not most) quasi-religious organizations qualify as what we have called Identity Transformation Organizations (ITOs) in other work

(Greil and Rudy 1984). ITOs are organizations which encourage adherents to undergo radical shifts in worldview and identity. ITOs attempt to encapsulate the individual within the confines of the organization in order to ensure that he or she is surrounded by definitions of the situation favorable to the formation of his or her new identity. To become committed to the extent required by ITOs, people must come to identify their goals and interests with those of the organization. Kanter (1972, 102) has described the commitment mechanisms of mortification, through which a person becomes more committed to the organization by subordination of his or her own ego to the will of the group, and of transcendence (1972, 113), through which a person comes to feel a kind of "institutionalized awe" for the power of the group.

It should perhaps be pointed out that a number of quasi-religious organizations including Scientology, TM, and many New Age and human potential groups are ITOs from the perspective of the core members who work full-time or longer for the organization and who define themselves in terms of its ideology but not from the perspectives of clients, who may attend one workshop, lecture, or course and then go their own ways. For example, the human potential group (MSIA) offers a series of courses called "Insight." Insight I and Insight II are secular in tone, but Insight III introduces advanced students to the mystical teachings of founder Jean-Roger (Mains 1987).

Related to the practical bent of quasi-religious organizations is their presentation of their ideologies as being based on scientific evidence. We have already seen that TM, Scientology, and SSF claim to have solid scientific grounding. A.A. claims scientific backing for its assertion that alcoholism is a "physical, mental, and spiritual disease." And listen to the words with which a participant in the New Age movement describes the healing power of crystals:

> The crystals emanate an electromagnetic field that has an ability to couple with the field of the human body. The crystal, the most perfect geometric form, helps the human form go into a more harmonious alignment. When trauma occurs, the body begins to discharge positive ions, thereby realigning the symmetry in the human form (Dullea 1986, B10).

Religious Versus Secular

The groups we have been describing are self-consciously ambiguous about whether they are religious or secular. Presumably, this is because members or leaders see both benefits and drawbacks to being associated with the term "religious." In this section we look at some of the reasons why organizations might choose to present themselves as religious as well as some of the reasons why they might choose to present themselves as secular. As we progress in this discussion, the relationship between the organizational features described in the previous section and the ideological ambiguity that defines quasi-religions should become clear.

Advantages of the Religious Label

There are some obvious practical advantages for organizations that are successful in labeling themselves religious. First of all, the religious label carries with it financial advantages in the United States (Richardson 1985a). Religions can solicit tax-deductible contributions. The property they own is tax-exempt. They are exempt from certain regulations dictated by civil rights and labor legislation. For example, religions, unlike other organizations, may take religion into consideration in hiring employees. L. Ron Hubbard has often been accused of declaring Scientology to be a religion primarily for financial reasons. The Internal Revenue Service has rejected Scientology's claims to tax-exempt status on the grounds that it is organized to make a profit and that profit-making activities, even if conducted by religious organizations, are taxable. An additional reason why organizations such as Scientology and Synanon might find it to their advantage to be classified as religious is that, "while non-profit charities are required to file annual financial reports with state and federal agencies, churches are not obliged to do so" (Ofshe 1980).

There are some nonfinancial practical reasons why a group might want to claim the religious label as well. If an organization is defined as a religion, then its clergy are exempt from military service and its members can claim conscientious-objector status more easily. If an organization is defined as a religion, its leaders can be defined as clergy and may legally marry people. Most significantly, an organization which is considered to be a religion can conduct healing and therapy practices without fear of scrutiny by regulatory agencies. In 1963, the Federal Drug Administration (FDA) raided the Founding Church of Scientology in Washington and seized several examples of E-meters, charging that Scientology was making false claims about their therapeutic efficacy (Wallis 1977, 192). Scientology argued successfully before the U. S. Court of Appeals that, because it qualified as a religion, the E-meter was not subject to FDA regulation.

But perhaps the most important practical reason for claiming the religious label has to do with the legitimacy conferred upon groups who can lay claim to it. Religious organizations and religious leaders are held in high esteem by many, and any organization that is successful in getting itself seen to be religious can benefit from the respectability that the label implies. Among the reasons L. Ron Hubbard gave to followers for incorporating Scientology as a church in England was the fact that "parliaments don't attack religions" (cited in Straus 1985, 6).

In addition to practical reasons, organizations may have existential reasons for representing themselves as religious. That is to say, if we may put it crudely, that groups may claim the religious label because it feels right to them. We stated earlier that many quasi-religions are ITOs, and that ITOs create an atmosphere of institutionalized awe, giving members a sense of reality that exists beyond themselves. Such institutionalized awe is almost inevitably expressed in superempirical terms. The sense that one is nothing compared to the power and majesty of the group is generally experienced and expressed through religious idiom. This observation is, of course, reminiscent of Durkheim's (1965) classic argument that the source of reverence for the sacred is to be found in the awe inspired by participation in the collectivity.

In other words, members may describe their group as spiritual or as religious because the experiences they have within the group strike them as being close or identical to what they understand religious experience to be. These considerations may help to explain why core members of certain groups see the group as religious while fringe members do not. As adepts get more involved in an organization, they may experience heightened levels of transcendence and institutionalized awe and may come to feel that religious symbolism provides the most suitable means of expressing this (Bird and Westley 1985; Wallis 1985).

Disadvantages of the Religious Label

We now discuss some of the practical and existential considerations that might pull quasi-religions away from a religious self-definition. We begin with some practical reasons for avoiding the religious label.

The United States is a pluralistic society in which the prototypical form of religious organization is the denomination. For an organization to present itself as a religion is tantamount to presenting itself as one denomination among many. Organizations may, like TM, try to avoid the religious label in order to have the broadest possible base for recruitment. Therapeutic groups like A.A. and Compassionate Friends may fear that being too closely identified with a particular creedal statement might alienate some individuals who would benefit from membership.

Furthermore, the very term "religion" may be viewed negatively by some, especially those who do not espouse the transcendent worldview that is recognized by the American folk definition as real religion. Thus, a spokesman for the human potential group the Forum explains that one reason for speakers to avoid identifying the Forum as a religion is that some people might "be turned off by the word religion" (cited in Amano 1986, 21).

While religions may get tax exemptions and other special considerations from government, there are some services that government may not provide to entities identified as religions because of the Constitutional prohibition against the establishment of religion. As stated above, once TM was declared to be a religion, it was unable to offer instruction in the public schools. Many of A.A.'s recruits are referred to A.A. by the courts. Arguably, courts would be much less likely to refer those convicted of driving while intoxicated (DWI) and other offenses if A.A. were thought to be a religious organization.

While being labeled "religious" may bestow a certain kind of legitimacy on an organization, being labeled "nonreligious" may bestow a different kind of legitimacy. For an organization's offering to be accepted as legitimate therapy, the organization may have to distance itself from its more religious tendencies. Being labeled "non-religious" may also confer financial benefits. For example, religions do not qualify for third-party medical payments while therapies do. Many human potential organizations offer their services to corporations interested in increasing worker productivity. Certainly, businesses are more likely to hire a secular consulting firm than a religious sect.

There may be existential reasons for rejecting the religious label as well. Members frequently join quasi-religious organizations for therapeutic benefit. Because of the this-worldly orientation of many quasi-religious organizations, leaders and followers who associate religion with otherworldly concerns may not feel the label fits. Religion in America is often compartmentalized. That is to say, religion is often relegated to a particular sphere of life (such as going to church on Sundays) and insulated from other spheres (such as work). Quasi-religious organizations might, therefore, stay away from the religious label because they may see it as their mission to reform all of members' lives and not just part. Adherents of quasi-religions often think of their beliefs as being scientific and may find the religious label inappropriate because they think of religion as unscientific. Finally, adherents of quasi-religious belief systems may think of religions as being mutually exclusive. One cannot be a Catholic and a Presbyterian, but a member of SSF can be a Presbyterian (Wagner 1983, 31). Such a person might conclude that if Presbyterianism is a religion SSF must not be.

Significance and Implications

Just how important are quasi-religious organizations in the contemporary United States? As one might expect, reliable statistics on membership in quasi-religious organizations are not available, but impressionistic evidence suggests that the appeal of some of these organizations may be great.

Hurley (1988, 64) reports that A.A. had 804,000 American members in 1986. Moreover, he asserts that there are twelve million people in five hundred thousand self-help groups, some (but certainly not all) of which would qualify as quasi-religious organizations. Scientology claims a membership of over six million, but outside observers usually estimate membership to be below one million (Hopkins 1986, 53). Bainbridge and Jackson (1981, 144) report that by 1977, almost a million people had been initiated into TM. Melton (1981, 279) calls the occult religions the most important segment of American alternative religion. Shirley MacLaine's books on New Age themes have sold over eight million copies (Friedrich 1987, 64), and one quarter of all Americans say they believe in reincarnation, a central New Age belief (Friedrich 1987, 69). Lifespring, Arica Training, and est can each boast that two hundred thousand people have been trained (Friedrich 1987, 68; Wallis 1985, 139). In a survey of the Montreal area, Bird and Reimer (1982) found that 31.7 percent of their sample had had some involvement in "new religious and para-religious movements," most of them in groups we would classify as quasi-religious.

If, as we suspect, quasi-religious organizations are coming to play a larger role on the American religious scene, this would indicate that the American folk definition of religion is beginning to lose its hold over us and that the line between religion and nonreligion is getting fuzzier.

What do the appeal of quasi-religions and the blurring of the distinction between religion and nonreligion have to tell us about religious trends in American society? This subject is worthy of a discussion as long as the discussion that has preceded it, but here—due to space limitations—we confine ourselves to a few suggestive comments. The appeal of quasi-religion suggests that large numbers of people are not finding satisfaction with the transcendent worldviews offered by many of their traditional religious options. This may be due in part to the fact that globalization has resulted in greater exposure to religious ideas outside the Judeo-Christian tradition. It may also be due to the increased privatization of American society, which may have the effect of leading people to look for the sacred within themselves instead of outside themselves (Westley 1983). The practical—in many cases, magical—orientation of the quasi-religions suggests that there are a number of Americans who feel out of control, who feel that the est trainer is right when he tells them, "Your lives don't work, assholes" (Tipton 1982, 177). The appeal to science found in many of the quasi-religious ideologies suggests that, although modernization may have led to alienation and loss of meaning, the new quest for meaning is heavily influenced by the modernization and secularization of contemporary society against which it revolts.

References

Alexander, Brooks, 1987
Amano, J. Yutaka, 1986
Bainbridge, William Sims, and Daniel H. Jackson, 1981
Bird, Frederick, and Bill Reimer, 1982
Bird, Frederick, and Frances Westley, 1985
Dullea, George, 1986
Durkheim, Emile, 1965 (orig. 1912)
Ellwood, Robert S., 1973
Friedrich, Otto, 1987
Gellman, Irving, 1964
Greil, Arthur L., and David R. Rudy, 1983, 1984
Hopkins, Joseph, 1986
Hurley, Dan, 1988
Jones, Robert Kenneth, 1970
Kanter, Rosabeth Moss, 1972
Klass, Dennis, 1982
Luckmann, Thomas, 1967
Mains, Jeremy, 1987
Melton, J. Gordon, 1985
Ofshe, Richard, 1980
Richardson, James T., 1985a
Roberts, Keith A., 1984
Robertson, Roland, 1970
Rudy, David R., and Arthur L. Greil, forthcoming
Straus, Robert A., 1985
Tipton, Steven M., 1982
Videka-Sherman, Lynn, 1982
Wagner, Melinda Bollar, 1981, 1983
Wallis, Roy, 1977, 1985
Westley, Frances, 1983
Whitley, Oliver R., 1977
Yinger, J. Milton, 1970

13

Rebottling the Elixir: The Gospel of Prosperity in America's Religioeconomic Corporations

David G. Bromley and Anson Shupe

One of the significant consequences of the Protestant Reformation was the cultural linking of religiosity and economic activity. While there has been a long-standing debate among scholars as to the causal relationship between religious belief and economic behavior, the historical connection between the two has not been seriously disputed. In American culture one linkage between religiosity and economic success has been the Gospel of Prosperity. The Gospel of Prosperity is based on the belief that Americans have a special covenant with God—that in return for obeying His mandates and creating a Christian nation that will eventually carry His message and the American Way of Life to the entire world, God will raise up Americans, individually and collectively, as His most favored people. Ironically, perhaps, it is because religion has been disestablished, formally separated from economy and polity, that the Gospel of Prosperity has had such cultural significance. In the face of institutional differentiation, which has diminished the capacity of religion to provide the kind of social and cultural integration so often observed in premodern groups, the Gospel of Prosperity has operated as one significant means through which religion, work, and family have been harmonized.

In this chapter we begin by briefly tracing the evolution of the Gospel of Prosperity through American history. We then consider two historical examples (Ford Motor Company and Fuller Brush Company) and three contemporary examples (Mary Kay Cosmetics, Herbalife, and Amway) of economic enterprises in which the Gospel of Prosperity was integral to the founder's vision of these respective corporations. While these five groups differ on a number of organizational dimensions, each incorporates several central themes of the Gospel of Prosperity. Four such themes are highlighted here:

1. *Transcendent Purpose* relating an economic product or service and/or the method of its production or distribution to a higher cultural purpose. Specific forms of economic activity are viewed as offering unique opportunities to meaningfully change the world, and participants are conceived as pioneers or missionaries who take the leadership in creating this new world.
2. *Service* linking individual success to collective good. Individual economic prosperity is understood as a natural outgrowth of achievement which simultaneously serves self-interest and the interests of others.
3. *Achievement* expressing freedom and moral responsibility through individual initiative and achievement. Individual accomplishment constitutes a moral imperative and meaningful form of participation in the community.
4. *Cultural Integration* linking and harmonizing work, family, and religion. Economic activity contributes to the strengthening of the family and is an expression of divine purpose.

The Gospel of Prosperity in American History

The Gospel of Prosperity is older than either the Constitution or the Republic. The English Puritans with their somber Calvinism brought the seed of it originally to the New England colonies in the early 1600s. As McLoughlin notes: "The Puritan Awakening in effect gave America its own culture core, its sense of being a differently constituted people, covenanted with God on a special errand in the wilderness" (1978, 30).

The First Great Awakening in the early-to-mid 1700s transformed the Puritans' sense of a very limited, elect group predestined to either heaven or hell into the Arminian, more democratic ideal that all persons hold within their grasps the opportunity of salvation. Along with this major shift in theology, popular thinking moved away from the Puritans' harsh premillennialism toward a more optimistic postmillennialism. That is, the Arminian new light doctrine of free will created the possibility of improving not just individuals but also entire societies. Says McLoughlin:

> Revitalization of the individual led to efforts to revitalize society. Having a new sense of harmony with God, the new-light convert was impelled to work in conjunction with God's power to help his fellow men have it likewise. The regenerate could not rest content with the world as it was; they wished to make it what it ought to be. (1978, 75–76)

Thus the Puritans conceived of America as a Promised Land for a few. The First Great Awakening democratized this promise so that all persons might share in the covenant. Moreover, the latter began a growing tradition that this land might serve as God's flagship in evangelizing the world, with the bounty of God's providence the reward for its citizens.

The Second Great Awakening, beginning in the early 1800s, further reinforced this theme. Heavily evangelical like the first, the Second Great Awakening spread the notion of America having a special covenant with God in which doing His will was repaid with earthly blessings for the Republic. It merged the growing sense of national identity with postmillennialism's evangelical Christianity. The doctrine of manifest destiny and a sense of an American empire became popularly accepted. Such a sense served as a powerful political rationale undergirding the U.S. Government's attempts to pacify the constantly expanding frontier regions. This same fervent sense of divine destiny likewise fueled the abolition movement as well as various Bible-tract and missionary societies.

But it was in post–Civil War America, specifically in the industrializing north, that the Gospel of Prosperity came to assume its more modern form. Individual prosperity, regardless of the condition of the nation's masses, became equated with private virtue and integrity in the sense of being its reward. Many Americans considered this era to be the actual realization of the fruits of their having kept their covenant with God to preserve the union. Historians of the late nineteenth and early twentieth centuries continually return to the themes of complacency and prosperity when they describe popular culture of the time. Along with general affluence, in other words, developed a popular theology to apologize for it and even glorify it. For example, Hudson writes:

> For many Americans the years following the Civil War marked the beginning of a period of unrivaled prosperity. Rapidly as the population increased, the nation's wealth multiplied three times as fast. Those who benefited by this tremendous economic expansion were confident that they were living in the best of all possible worlds. (1981, 305)

This became the gilded age in which laissez-faire economics and its prophets such as Adam Smith, Herbert Spencer, Francis Wayland, William Graham Sumner, and Andrew Carnegie were lionized. Carnegie (1900, 6), in fact, wrote a famous essay entitled "The Gospel of Wealth" which equated the accumulation of personal wealth with virtue (and the absence thereof with sin). Clergymen unabashedly apologized for capitalism's stratification system and inequities. One, the Right Reverend William Lawrence of Massachusetts, even claimed in 1901 that "Godliness is in league with riches'' (cited in Gabriel 1949, 601). Evangelist Russell H. Conwell extolled readers of his best-seller, *Acres of Diamonds:* ''I say that you ought to get rich, and it is your duty to get rich'' (cited in Marty 1970, 150). Many of these religious authors displayed what Ahlstrom calls an ''explicit, even crass concern for wealth and success'' (1972, 1,032). Another historian concludes: ''For post–Civil War American Protestantism, the gospel of wealth became a formula which permitted the Church to make peace with popular materialism'' (Gabriel 1949, 65).

This trend continued across the span of the nineteenth and twentieth centuries. For example, a number of religious writers, both theologically liberal and conservative, continued to popularize the gospel of prosperity into the period between World War I and the Depression. One of the most widely read was Bruce Barton. Son of a Congregational minister and a successful advertising executive, Barton wrote a series of best-selling books that tried to reconcile new economic practices (such as installment buying, stock speculation, and affluent lifestyles) with traditional Victorian virtues (such as thrift and restraint). In particular, his *The Man Nobody Knows: A Discovery of the Real Jesus,* published in 1925, reconciled spiritual and materialistic values to the satisfaction of millions of readers by turning Jesus Christ into the founder of modern business. Christ was a ''modern executive,'' his twelve disciples ''the first corporation,'' and the modern American corporation ''the greatest missionary society in the world'' (Barton 1925; Montgomery 1985).

Thus, there is a legacy extending into the American culture of modern times that has persistently attempted, with varying degrees of success, to reconcile the material with the biblical emphasis on the spiritual and transcendent.[1] Its roots are as old as Calvinism but have been modified over time. For the Puritans as well as the converts touched by the First and Second Great Awakenings the blessings of God's providence were to be showered on an obedient, biblical nation. By the early twentieth century, however, when the United States had emerged as the world's foremost industrialized nation, little perception of incompatibility between personal wealth and virtue survived in mainstream American consciousness. While American society overall might indirectly benefit from an individual's prosperity and moral fortitude, it was to individuals—an unequally, befitting the vicissitudes of a competitive capitalistic opportunity structure—that blessings would directly accrue.[2]

Historical Forerunners to Contemporary Religioeconomic Corporations

In the early twentieth century one important cultural link between the spiritual or transcendent and material success was forged through harmonial philosophy, which was founded on the assumption of human perfection-ism. Ahlstrom (1972, 1,019) defined harmonial philosophy as "those forms of piety and belief in which spiritual composure, physical health, and even economic well being are understood to flow from a person's rapport with the cosmos." Individuals could think their way to wealth by appropriately using their God-given faculties. However, individual success in accumulating wealth was not enough. "True success" involved using such wealth in the service of great humanity. As Bruce Barton put it, true success "comes through making your work an instrument of greater service, and larger living to your fellow men and women" (1925, 189). Service was thus both the means to true success and its purest expression.

The early twentieth century witnessed the rapid development of mass production techniques and the corresponding development of marketing, advertising, and public relations (Huber 1971, 190–195) as expanded productive capacity created the imperative for stimulating consumption. Success was justified in terms of providing service. Such service involved finding means for making better products, making them at a lower price, or distributing them more efficiently. In discussing the sympathy of the American religious tradition for this interpretation of service, Huber quotes Andre Sigfried:

> The idea of service, which has become so popular in America, springs from the Puritanical idea of wealth sanctified by labour. . . . Money thus became not only the symbol of creative power but a sort of moral justification. Efficiency was looked upon as a Christian virtue, and one could no longer separate what had been accomplished for God from what had been contributed to the development of the country. (1971, 224)

Both Henry Ford and Alfred Fuller, leaders in the development of mass production and marketing techniques respectively, were influenced by harmonial philosophy and incorporated its precepts into personal philosophies which reconciled spirituality with material success.

Ford Motor Company

Henry Ford, founder of the Ford Motor Company, has been elevated to loftier mythic levels than any other business leader.[3] Ford's rise from humble rural beginnings to a fabulously wealthy, world-famous corporate giant is in itself the stuff of American Horatio Alger legend. While employed as chief mechanic at Detroit's Edison Illuminating Company, Ford finished his first prototype vehicle in 1896. By 1908 he was selling his famous Model T cars at $850 apiece. When other automobile manufacturers were producing more expensive vehicles for a restricted class of wealthier customers, Ford deliberately engineered a relatively inexpensive, durable car aimed at a broader market. More than any other car maker, Ford brought the automobile to the level of affordability for the general public.

Ford saw a grander purpose in his technological and production innovations. For him the affordable Ford automobile offered a new way of conceiving and organizing industrial production and, more broadly, of making the world a better place. As he once remarked:

> I do not consider the machines which bear my name simply as machines. If that was all there was to it I would simply do something else. I take them as a concrete evidence of the working out of a theory of the business which I hope [is] more than a theory of business—a theory towards making the world a better place to live. (Collier and Horowitz 1987, 70)

As two of his cobiographers conveyed this vision:

> The Model T was more than a car; it was a calling, the vehicle Ford believed would take the auto industry to the promised land of efficiency and utility. ''I will build a motorcar for the multitude,'' he said in prophetic tones. ''It will be large enough for the family but small enough for the individual to own and care for. It will be constructed of the best materials, by the best men to be hired, after the simplest design that modern engineering can devise. But it will be so low in price that no man making a good salary will be unable to own one—and enjoy with his family the blessing of hours of pleasure in God's great open spaces.'' (Collier and Horowitz 1987, 52).

This latter quotation is particularly interesting in that Ford clearly ties the larger purpose of increased efficiency and utility with service to individuals and families. Indeed, Ford became legendary among proponents of the Gospel of Prosperity for achieving wealth through service. In his writings, Barton specifically cited Henry Ford as an outstanding example of one whose wealth emanated from service to humanity.

> Have you ever noticed that the man who starts out in life with a determination to make money, never makes very much? . . . He may gather together a competence, of course, a few tens of thousands or even hundreds of thousands, but he'll never amass a really great fortune. But let a man start out in life to build something better and sell it cheaper than it has ever been built or sold before—let him have *that* determination, and give his whole self to it—and the money will roll in so fast that it will bury him if he doesn't look out. (1925, 166–67)

Ford also viewed his industrial innovations as creating the basis for individual achievement. Greenleaf observes that:

Convinced that the broadening of economic opportunity under the institutions of private enterprise was more effective than philanthropy as an instrument of social amelioration, Ford asserted that charity would be unnecessary if every employer conducted his business to serve the aims of social justice. It was thus that Ford came to regard his company (and, by extension, all forms of productive business organization) as a cure for poverty and misery far superior to the humanitarian projects of reformers. The abolition of poverty, he said, "is the only legitimate purpose of business. . . . I want to abolish poverty from America. (1968, 16)

Ford not only set out to advance individual opportunity through the eradication of poverty, he also pioneered employee profit sharing and other employer—employee innovations that were designed to increase the consumptive capacity of workers.

Ford envisioned benefits for families as well as individuals resulting from the increased productivity and income of workers. With this end in view and in his typically autocratic, paternalistic style, Ford intervened very directly in the family lives of his workers. For example, he established the Ford Sociological Department, recruiting as its head a former dean of Detroit's St. Paul's Church. This department sent investigators to the homes of factory workers to advise them on hygiene, help manage their household finances, and enroll them in Ford-financed English lessons if needed. These "social workers" took inventories of families' needs and made progress reports to the company.[4]

Henry Ford was not a personally religious man. Nonetheless he was deeply influenced by harmonial philosophy. Indeed, he saw himself as having thought his way to success simply by having developed a new technology that was useful to others. One of the best-selling positive-thinking books of the day, *In Tune with the Infinite,* by Ralph Waldo Trine (1897), which stressed this theme, was one of his personal favorites, and he frequently passed along copies to friends and acquaintances (Huber 1971, 126). As a result of his success and his linking of that success to individual achievement and transcendent purpose, in the eyes of many Americans Ford embodied the Gospel of Prosperity. As a result, Ford was elevated to the status of a cultural hero. Indeed, in 1924 there was a grass-roots movement to nominate him for president of the United States. Greenleaf sums up the qualities which made Ford so popular.

In considerable measure, Ford's popularity was based on his success in epitomizing the middle-class creed whose matrix was a village and yeoman outlook that extolled hard and useful work, self-reliance, and thrift. That creed was a commitment to the values of competitive individualism, the free marketplace, the legitimacy of a reasonable profit on a socially useful commodity or service, the promotion of progress through technological efficiency, and the broadest possible diffusion of material abundance in a society without extremes of poverty and wealth. (1968, *vii*)

Fuller Brush Company

Fuller Brush Company was the grandfather of the contemporary direct-sales companies discussed in the following section of this chapter, and hence is a particularly instructive example of the Gospel of Prosperity. Its founder, Alfred C. Fuller, was born to a devout Methodist family of eleven other children in rural Nova Scotia in 1885. With but a minimal formal education, Fuller tried a succession of low-paying manual-labor jobs before discovering a market and a knack for selling household cleaning brushes. The business grew rapidly, and, although Fuller himself never attained the heroic status of Henry Ford, Fuller Brush soon became a household name across America. In the early 1900s Fuller improvised on the design and production of brushes for various household uses. Further, Fuller set out to improve the image of door-to-door salesmen through such innovations as establishing regular sales routes to build repeat business instead of relying on high turnover and encouraging greater consideration for the largely female clientele. Thus his primary innovations were in marketing.

More important for our purposes Fuller infused a transcendent element into his company's philosophy that derived directly from harmonial philosophy. Although raised a Methodist, Fuller later converted to Christian Science as an adult. As Moore (1986, 115–16) has noted, "Christian Science was one important nineteenth-century product of harmonial philosophy." Consistent with this mode of thought, Fuller did not claim for himself any extraordinary ability. Indeed, he readily acknowledged his own personal inadequacies: "Anyone who believes that he was not sufficiently endowed by nature and education to make a great success should consider what has happened to me. My life is proof of the tremendous power available to everyone to vault above his own deficiencies" (Fuller and Spence 1960, 1). Instead of taking personal credit for his financial success, Fuller attributed it to a suprahuman force: "The only conclusion I can reach from my own experience is that there is a tremendous power somewhere that can lift any person, however mediocre, to great opportunity, affluence and happiness (Fuller and Spence 1960, 3). His writing is full of references to "harnessing" this transcendent power for worldly success.

Fuller saw his mission as much grander than marketing brushes. From his perspective there was a larger and more noble purpose, making the world a better place. He writes: "The ultimate goal is not merely to make money, but to secure the future of many persons, the nation under which they prosper, and the world at large.'' (Fuller and Spence 1960, 237). His vision of Fuller Brush was one of a war against major domestic evils of his day, dirt and drudgery, and clearly linked economic success with family well-being. Consistent with this vision, his salesmen became in his eyes not merely door-to-door entrepreneurs but rather ''missionaries of new ideas.'' Regarding himself as the prophet of a household-products revolution, Fuller could later write about his initial efforts as a crusade to improve the housewives' lot and also bring to his sales a nobility that made them more than simply commissions and profits:

> Here were thousands of persons who needed brushes. In the buoyant elation of my adventure, I considered myself a reformer, eager to attack the dirt and domestic labor of the city, destroying the one and alleviating the other. I was a benefactor to the housewives, a crusader against unsanitary kitchens and inadequately cleaned homes. Never before, I daresay, had any door-to-door salesman brought this sense of dedication with his wares. (Fuller and Spence 1960, 87)

The crusade against domestic dirt and drudgery offered his salesmen the opportunity to serve humankind, and Fuller emphasized that selling without such commitment would not yield personal economic success:

> [T]he successful seller must feel some commitment that his product offers mankind as much altruistic benefit as it yields the seller in money. The salesman is an idealist and an artist; in that respect he differs from the huckster, who is just out for profit. As years passed, this missionary spirit infected the growing organization. Thousands of young men gripped sample cases and went out to the homes of America to sell the Fuller line. Those who thought only of financial return failed promptly; those who, like myself, were enthused with mission as well, prospered materially far beyond their dreams. (Fuller and Spence 1960, 87)

It is noteworthy that by the 1980s Fuller Brush, its founder deceased and the company part of a large corporate conglomerate, was struggling. The firm's sales force had dwindled to fifteen thousand with revenues around fifty million dollars (Gelfand 1983, M51–M53). During the 1980s the company began a comeback. It did so by product diversification (the expanded product line included, for example, cleaning products, eating utensils, and jewelry), recruiting a predominantly female sales staff (80 percent versus about 30 percent during the firm's early years). These changes moved the company closer to the contemporary consumption-oriented direct-sales companies.[5]

Contemporary Religioeconomic Organizations

Over the last two decades a number of religioeconomic groups such as Amway, Herbalife, Mary Kay, Shaklee (Smith 1984), and Tupperware (Peven 1968; Taylor 1978) have grown dramatically and become household names like their historical counterparts. The three organizations discussed here are all direct-sales organizations. Juth-Gavasso defines direct selling as "a method of distribution of goods and services from producer to consumer which utilizes independent salespersons in place of normal retail outlets" (1985, 59). There are four essential elements: salespersons make face-to-face contact with clients, salespersons either initiate contact or respond to an inquiry from the customer, contact typically occurs at the customer's home, and items are sold for personal use.

Mary Kay Cosmetics

Mary Kay Ash was born into a family of modest means. Her mother worked as a restaurant manager and was forced to support her father, who was an invalid. After completing high school, she did not have enough money to enroll in college; instead she got married. Several years after their marriage, during World War II, her husband was drafted. Upon returning from his tour of duty he abruptly asked for a divorce. Left suddenly with three children to support, she took a job selling Stanley cleaning products for Stanley Home Products at "home shows." Mary Kay Ash experienced almost immediate success in her new occupation and within a short time she became Stanley's "queen of sales." She later resigned from her job at Stanley and went to work for World Gift Company and advanced to the position of national training director. In 1963 she resigned after a policy dispute. Quickly becoming bored, she began contemplating starting her own company "based on the Golden Rule, for women who are willing to pay the price and have the courage to dream" (Kingan 1982, 13). Shortly thereafter she began that venture by purchasing rights to a locally produced skin cream. The firm grew rapidly, with annual revenues climbing from $198,000 in her first year of operation to well over $200,000,000 by the early 1980s.[6] The sales force, composed primarily of part-time workers, has climbed to over 150,000.

Sales of Mary Kay products are organized through "beauty shows" at which a small number of invited guests are offered a beauty-care program and makeup lesson. The ultimate objective, of course, is the sale of various beauty-care products. In the direct sales tradition, "beauty consultants" also recruit new consultants and receive a commission on the sales of their recruits. As with early counterparts, Mary Kay representatives are taught to think in terms of service to others rather than sales. Ash has stated:

> At our beauty shows we do not like a beauty consultant to think, "How much can I sell these women?" Instead we stress, "What can I do to make these women leave here today feeling better about themselves? How can I help them have a better self-image?" We know that if a woman feels pretty on the outside, she becomes prettier on the inside too. She'll go home a better wife, a better mother, and a better member of the community. (Ash 1984)

Serving others by improving their self-concept has a similar outcome for the beauty consultants, particularly when these women lack personal confidence. As Mary Kay put it:

> Women often come to us all vogue on the outside and vague on the inside. We offer them encouragement and goals and praise them to success. In a short time they respond beautifully and a tight little rosebud becomes a glorious flower. (Kingan 1982, 14)

There are more tangible rewards as well, of course, as serving others yields individual economic success. Mary Kay makes certain that this message is not lost on sales personnel. Successful representatives are rewarded with mink coats, diamond rings, gold pins, silver coffee services, and, the ultimate symbol of success, a pink Cadillac. "The awards are presented in a setting reminiscent of the Miss America pageants—in a large auditorium, on a stage in front of a large cheering audience, and with all participants dressed in glamorous evening clothes" (Trice and Byer 1984, 660). Kingan described one such rally:

> A whirlwind of excitement fills the convention center. Thousands of women are taking their seats, eagerly anticipating the evening ahead. An orchestra is playing themes from popular musicals. Water fountains surge thirty feet high, reflecting lights that change color in time with the music. Backstage, more women are lining up, dressed in the most elaborate evening gowns. Suddenly, a figure in white, trimmed with fur and diamonds, emerges onto the runway. The audience quickly rises. The applause is thunderous. "Are you ready?" she asks, as the cheers for her, Mary Kay, become deafening. "Here it comes, the most exciting night of your life . . . when dreams come true!" (1982, 12)

These awards link work, liberation, and (conspicuous) consumption. Indeed, Ash's favorite award is a diamond-studded bumblebee pin. The bumblebee's body is too heavy for its wings, she observes, and should be unable to fly. However, the bumblebee is unaware of this limitation and flies easily. There is a metaphorical lesson for her beauty consultants here. As Ash put it: "They come to us not knowing they can fly. Finally, with help and encouragement, they find their wings—and then they fly very well" (Tunley 1978, 22).

Individual achievement, however, is clearly linked to God and family for Mary Kay Ash, who is a devout Baptist. She tells her consultants that the priorities in their lives must be "God first, family second, career third" (Tunley 1978, 18). She preaches that careers for women can offer liberation through financial independence both for them and for their families. For example, one of Mary Kay's more successful consultants offered testimony to the family benefit deriving from her Mary Kay career at one of the frequent awards ceremonies:

> One of the top winners was an Arkansas farm wife. After the cheering stopped, the woman called her husband up on-stage and asked him for a match. Then she reached into her pocketbook for a document, lit the match and touched fire to paper. "This," she said triumphantly, "is the mortgage to our farm. We've been trying to pay it off forever. Thanks to Mary Kay, we've finally done it!" (Tunley 1978, 18)

Indeed, from Ash's perspective individual accomplishment always occurs within the context of the traditional family and should not supersede spousal responsibilities. Ash reports that in her own life "Every night on my drive home from the office I forget that I'm chairman of the board, and remember that I'm Mel's wife," and she "beams when Mel tells people that he's 'chairman of the chairman of the board' " (Tunley 1978, 22).

Herbalife International

Herbalife was founded by Mark Hughes in 1980, while he was still in his mid-twenties. Hughes had previously been a distributor for Seyforth Laboratories' Slender Now diet products, and rose to be one of that firm's top hundred salespersons. After the financial collapse of Seyforth, Hughes briefly sold exercise equipment and diet products for another now-defunct firm before founding his own company. Hughes traces his interest in founding a weight loss–nutritional supplement company to his mother's death from an amphetamine overdose related to her compulsive dieting. By his own account, he wanted to market a safe, nutritious plan that would also help people become happier. Herbalife markets more than a dozen nutritional products: weight-loss formulas, digestion aids, natural herbal stimulants (including one to ease menstruation), soaps and fiber supplements, herbs that fight premature aging, children's vitamins, arthritis pain relievers, skin creams, shampoos, and antistress tabs to fight depression and moodiness. Since 1980 company sales have skyrocketed. The company earned two million dollars its first year in business and about five hundred million dollars by 1985 (Paris 1985).

Herbalife management proclaims a larger purpose for the firm than simply selling herbs. Sales Director Lawrence Thompson was very explicit about Herbalife's suprabusiness purpose. In Dallas he proclaimed to distributors: "Herbalife is more than just a business. It's a way of life. We believe in what we're doing." He compared the company to a crusade and elevated the activities of its sales force far beyond mere herb pushing. "It's one thing to make a lot of money," Thompson somberly told his responsive sunbelt audience. "It's another thing to make a lot of money and know you're doing good." Founder Mark Hughes echoed a similar theme to a Dallas rally in early 1986: "Go out and sell these products and we'll make this world a better world for people to live in!" If the sales staff is in fact "making the world is a better place" by selling Herbalife products, then sales become service. Salespersons are offering customers good nutrition and helping them lose unwanted weight. Thompson told a rally at Dallas County Convention Center in February 1986: "Our distributors care about the people that they sell the product to." He told another audience that Herbalife is "a people business, a people company sharing the most precious gift—good health—with other people."

Service to others, of course, brings rewards to the salesperson, which are not difficult to achieve. Indeed, company leaders tell distributors that products do not really have to be sold as they sell themselves when clients recognize their life-enhancing value. Speaking through a live satellite transmission from Hartford, Connecticut, Lawrence Thompson stated: "The public wants Herbalife products. This is the most incredible business opportunity that you ever dreamed of." Sales representatives are admonished simply to "link themselves to the products" for the kinds of four- and five-figure commissions that Thompson repeatedly describes as "awesome." The method for achieving this success is simple: use the product, wear the button ("Lose Weight Now! Ask me how."), talk to people. At high-intensity motivational rallies Herbalife users and distributors offer testimonials on how Herbalife has changed their lives.

Amway Corporation

After graduating from high school, the founders of Amway, Rich DeVos and Jay Van Andel, traveled to Central and South America together. Upon their return they became distributors for Nutrilite, a food supplements company. In 1949 they formed Ja-Ri Corporation, which eventually came to include a sales organization of over two thousand distributors. In 1959 when Nutrilite was on the verge of financial collapse, DeVos and Van

Andel moved to establish their own company. In that year they formed the Amway Sales Corporation and Amway Services Corporation. By 1964 the three companies were consolidated into Amway Corporation, with Van Andel as chairman of the board and DeVos as president. Amway began by marketing two of the first biodegradable detergent products. The business grew quickly. In 1959 retail sales totaled about five hundred thousand dollars; by 1978 sales totaled five hundred million dollars; and by the early 1980s sales had surpassed the one billion dollar mark. Currently Amway is one of the three hundred largest industrial corporations in the United States, and it is the second largest direct-sales organization, surpassed in retail sales revenue only by Avon Products. In addition to dramatically diversifying its product line and expanding its production/distribution facilities, the corporation purchased the Mutual Broadcasting System in 1978 (which includes over nine hundred radio stations), initiated a ten-million-dollar satellite system, developed a multimillion-dollar hotel project in Grand Rapids, and purchased the Peter Island Yacht Club and Resort in the British Virgin Islands where successful distributors are fêted.

Among the religioeconomic organizations discussed in this paper, Amway certainly constitutes the archetypal case. The link between transcendent purpose, individual success, service to humanity, family, and religion are clearest. Amway leadership emphasizes the organization's commitment to the larger purpose of ensuring "freedom." A former Amway employee quoted Rich DeVos as follows:

> [N]o business will prosper unless it has a mission larger than itself. You can't merely manufacture "widgets" and expect that by itself to be rewarding. There must be a cause; and the cause we have in our business is the preservation of free enterprise and individual freedom. (Smith 1984, 129)

For the leaders of Amway the organization is restoring the vision that made America unique among nations, a vision that has somehow been lost. From its perspective Amway seeks not only to rekindle that vision but also to provide a means by which the American dream can actually be realized in the present era. Charles Conn describes Amway as the way to recapture the golden era.[7]

> America—the Land of Opportunity. The place where an individual has always had an honest shot at the Big Time. However poor the start in life, there is an opportunity to break out to a richer life. That is the American Way, the tradition of hungry, hard-working men and women breaking out of the life of the have-nots, to take their places among the haves. That tradition has in recent years felt the squeeze of new grim realities. The golden promise of the New World has receded a bit, and some argue that it is gone altogether—that for a person to begin with nothing and work his way into the ranks of the wealthy is virtually a

thing of the past, a casualty of our times. People just don't have an honest chance to do that anymore, they say. . . . In Amway, the tradition of breaking out is still alive and well. (Conn 1982, 35)

Members' perceptions of Amway's uniqueness are also captured in everyday conversation; distributors frequently will refer to themselves as being in "the business" and refer to the Amway marketing system as "the plan."

As in the other religioeconomic organizations discussed here, one serves one's own interests best by serving others. In Amway, leaders and members view "the business" as a means of serving others by offering them a real opportunity to achieve the American dream. As one distributor testified:

> We believe it's God's purpose in our lives. We can help people on a material level (as well as ourselves) plus help them in their personal growth and spiritual growth. We are excited about what Amway stands for concerning our country. Not only will Amway provide the opportunity for increased personal income, but at the same time we can be involved in making positive changes in people's lives. (Johnson 1987, 117)

The reward for hard work and service is economic success, and Amway both promises and celebrates wealth at frequent meetings and rallies that take on the appearance of religious revivals. Juth-Gavasso has described a 1984 Michigan rally attended by about two thousand people, typical of such occasions, at which the focus clearly was on displaying the symbols of material success:

> A master of ceremonies (another distributor or an Amway Corporation representative) opens the event with miscellaneous facts or stories about successful distributors and the growth of Amway. The featured speaker(s) are introduced and enter the stage area amid cheers, applause, and the theme music from *Rocky*. The Guests speak for about an hour delivering what may be termed their variation of "How we got involved in Amway and became successful." In addition, the speakers usually have with them color slides depicting some of their material possessions (homes, boats, cars) and pictures of the places they have traveled (Hawaii, Hong Kong) in conjunction with their Amway business. (1985, 177–78)

The message of Amway literature and rallies alike is simple—individuals can be whatever they wish if they are willing to exert the energy and effort to realize their own dreams. Amway offers the vehicle for members to formulate and achieve these goals and dreams. The economic success attained through Amway in turn is equated with one of the most fundamental American values, personal freedom. Charles Conn (1982, 2) invoked the vision of a life in which individuals are truly free, which translates into personal choice. He acknowledges that all Americans possess constitutionally guaranteed civil liberties, but points out that there are other "uncommon freedoms" which can only be earned through individual achievement. As he puts it:

> [T]hese common freedoms, by themselves do not make an individual fully liberated. There is another set of freedoms, rare and uncommon freedoms, that only a few individuals enjoy. These are the freedom *to be* what one wishes to be, to live where one wishes to live, to support the causes one believes in, to explore the full and exciting range of one's potential. Not many people ever experience that kind of freedom. It is rare, uncommon freedom that must be won; it must be earned; it is the result of one's own individual effort and vision. (1982, 2)

The Gospel of Prosperity is very explicit in the Amway message. For example, at a 1988 rally in Richmond, Virginia, Bill Britt, head of one of Amway's largest distributorships, quoted from the Bible in justifying economic success (Allen 1988, 1): "Remember the Lord thy God, for it is He that giveth thee power to get wealth" (Deuteronomy 8:18). It is not only the leadership that employs religious discourse; many members frame their activities in spiritual terms as well. Johnson's survey of distributors found that 80 percent reported having strong or very strong religious convictions and 12 percent indicated that the most important reason for their involvement in Amway was that it permitted them to "get closer to God and promote religious values" (Johnson 1987, 114–16).[8]

Strong families are also part of the Amway vision. Amway strongly encourages husband-and-wife business partnerships within the context of traditional, male-headed families. Members testify that Amway brings together spouses who otherwise might well find it necessary to pursue separate careers, thereby permitting husbands and wives to integrate work life and home life. Parents and children too can share a mutual sense of value that prevents the fragmentation and distance that characterizes parent-offspring relationships in mainstream American society. For example, after interviewing members of one husband-wife team, Conn commented:

> One senses that the Payne sons, like so many Amway children, do not take for granted what they have because they have *seen* the work required to produce it. They can hardly avoid learning that rewards follow performance, because the work of Amway, unlike that of dentistry or law or whatever goes on all around them. . . . "Amway means to me the freedom to have a home that's really a home, with a family that is there full-time, all of us working together and reaping the rewards together. We don't have a situation anymore where I have my life,

and my wife has hers, and the kids have theirs, and we don't know what the others are doing. We have a family now, a real family, and the life we have in Awway we can all share together." (Conn 1982, 194)

In addition, Amway itself is portrayed as a family in which members nurture their common vision of life, share their involvement in "the business," and care for one another in quasi-familial fashion. Conn quoted one member as saying, "It was in this business that I really learned how to live. . . . I've had people in Amway who showed me for the first time in my life what love really was. I've had people help me when there was nothing in it for them" (1982, 189).

For leaders and committed members the world is filled with opportunity, and Amway is the organizational vehicle through which those opportunities can be realized. The mood therefore is ebullient; the American dream is still alive and attainable if only the opportunity is seized. Rich DeVos effused this optimism in a media interview:

This is an exciting world. It is cram-packed with opportunity. Great moments await around every corner. It is a world that deserves an upward look. . . . I believe in life with a large "yes" and a small "no." I believe that life is good, that people are good, that God is good. And I believe in affirming every day that I live, proudly and enthusiastically, that life in America under God is a positive experience. (Birmingham 1982, 60)

Summary and Conclusions

The Gospel of Prosperity has very deep roots in American culture. The notion that Americans are a chosen people and that their individual and collective prosperity are the bounty of that covenantal relationship has long been a major element of the national identity. In this chapter we have examined four themes—transcendent purpose, service, achievement, and cultural integration—central to the expression of that gospel throughout American history. In each of the historical and contemporary religioeconomic corporations considered in this chapter several of these themes have been prominently featured.

The close cultural connectedness between religiosity and economic activity following the Protestant Reformation provided a major source of cultural cohesiveness and sense of transcendent purpose that fueled the development of capitalism during the latter nineteenth and early twentieth centuries. By the end of the nineteenth century, however, as economic and technological development achieved a legitimacy in its own right, there was a corresponding erosion of religious authority. In institutionally differentiated urban-industrial society, religion became one among a constellation of institutions, lacking its former moral and integrative force. The balance almost shifted to the point that rather than economic activity being mandated and legitimated by religious faith, economic progress confirmed religious faith. Further, the Gospel of Prosperity was individualized so that individual success came to be seen as the reflection of private virtue.

With the advent of the industrial revolution, there was increasing separation between family and work, unprecedented regimentation of workers, poverty, and social dislocation. Solutions to the human problems attending industrialization were sought in further development of the process itself, through advances in efficiency and productivity. During this era taking full advantage of the economic opportunities created by an industrial economy was viewed as the best means for ensuring the collective good, fostering individual achievement, expressing religious commitment, and strengthening families. Personal achievement was a moral imperative and work became a primary means for engaging in public life. The dominant view was that America could be made better and stronger through the combined efforts of countless individuals each aspiring to and achieving the capacity of their God-given abilities. It was in this cultural context that economic entrepreneurs such as Henry Ford and Alfred Fuller were lionized. Although these men differed in their expression of conventional religiosity, both were deeply touched by harmonial philosophy. For many Americans both came to embody the Gospel of Prosperity in the industrial age because they created and communicated a vision of corporate development as reflecting divinely inspired progress.

By the mid-twentieth century America had moved into the postindustrial era in which the economic landscape was dominated by large, bureaucratically structured corporations and consumption became more pivotal than production to economic prosperity. Increasingly the viability of the earlier version of the Gospel of Prosperity, which stressed production over consumption and work as both a moral imperative and an expression of one's true self, failed to resonate with the realities of the times. As Long has observed, the transformation of America into a corporate society, and the transformation of independent small businessmen into suburban-dwelling corporate employees "required the devising of new life strategies for coping with a new range of occupational possibilities." She goes on:

[T]he decision to give up the entrepreneurial ideal of unlimited aspiration in favor of a balance between work and privatized familial happiness is not merely a revolt against the old, but also an accommodation to the constraints of the new. The corporate-suburban definition of success meshes very well with the occupational and organizational structure coming into being after World War II. Certainly, it would be futile for everyone to attempt to reach the few pinnacles of success in a world of increased monopolization and conglomeration: the

times called for a redefinition of success that allowed for satisfaction with a life
a few notches down from the top. Seeing success in terms of a healthy balance
between different activities may have been a useful formulaic shift to justify
abandonment of a frustrating and increasingly unrealistic desire to be the best.
(1985, 89)

The "balance between work and privatized happiness" has proven
elusive, however. Not only has the "entrepreneurial ideal" become more
remote but also the family has come under increasing pressure. The role
of mother and homemaker has progressively lost cultural viability, and
women (even those with young children) have begun entering the labor
force in greater numbers as a product both of economic necessity and of
gender role redefinition. Particularly over the last two decades, families
have become more vulnerable economically through rising inflation, rapidly escalating housing and educational costs, and the emergence of a
service-oriented economy with lower-paying jobs.

In response to these tensions, contemporary religioeconomic corporations have offered a vision of America in which boundless economic
opportunities would once again be available, individual accomplishment
would be unfettered and would alone determine one's financial rewards, a
transcendent purpose would be served through individual achievement,
and familial bonds would be strengthened. Specific versions of this vision
and corresponding symbolic touchstones have been offered, of course.
Mary Kay has emphasized the opportunity for women to contribute to the
family economy while maintaining their primary identities as wives and
mothers while Amway has stressed the opportunity for husbands and
wives to become partners in a family business. Herbalife has stressed the
values of health and fitness, Mary Kay beauty, and Amway freedom. All
three, of course, have promised a direct avenue to affluence and have
celebrated wealth in revivalist-style gatherings. In a broader sense, all of
these organizations sought to rekindle a vision of the American dream,
one which was plausible to mid-twentieth century Americans through
incorporation of the goal of self fulfillment.

In closing, we should note that we have examined religioeconomic
corporations from a cultural perspective, attempting to understand their
cultural plausibility. Obviously the social viability of these organizations,
their ability to construct organizational auspices for sustaining viable lifestyles consistent with their visions, is another matter altogether. The
enormously high rate of turnover in these organizations (Juth-Gavasso
1985), the public disaffection expressed by some of the former faithful
(Butterfield 1985; Kerns 1982), well documented organizational deviance
(Juth 1985), and the rather paltry economic returns actually garnered by

most individuals working for such organizations suggest that the idyllic dream is belied by a more troubled reality. Nonetheless, the fact remains that literally millions of Americans have experimented with such enterprises. For the purposes of the present essay, we would conclude, simply, that the Gospel of Prosperity remains a potent cultural theme, for in very different times and circumstances Americans have shown a persistent proclivity to seek to create moral order in their lives by reconfiguring and invoking the themes of transcendent purpose, service, achievement, and life-style integration that are its hallmarks.

Notes

1. For a discussion of the historical tension between biblical religion and utilitarian individualism see Tipton 1982 and Bellah 1976.
2. The economic success assumed a variety of different forms. Prior to the early twentieth century one version involved the concept of "stewardship" in which individuals were perceived to have a right or obligation to accrue wealth but not a corresponding right to retain it. Some portion of wealth accumulated through the use of God-given qualities should be given for the common good.
3. Virtually every item in the Ford legend is historically erroneous. Daimler and Benz, of course, invented the modern automobile, not Ford. Indeed, the first Ford was built by Charles B. King, but King sold out because his contraption looked so poor beside the French models. The automobiles that Ford took to exhibit in London to counter the French threat were Cadillacs built by Henry Leland, not Fords. It was Leland, also, who standardized automotive parts, having learned the technique from Colt and Whitney. Mass production was the brainchild of Olds and Walter Flanders; the assembly line was devised by Frederick Taylor and perfected for Ford by C. W. Avery. Neither the Model A, Model T, nor V8 was designed by Ford; and, the capping blow, Ford had so little faith in his company that he was willing to sell out to Durant of General Motors in 1908 for three million dollars (Friedman 1971, 45).
4. For a more Marxist interpretation of Ford's intervention in worker and family life, see Hoare and Smith 1971. Seeking to explain this intervention, Gramsci comments that "the instrument used to select and maintain in stability a skilled labour force is suited to the system of production and work." Once higher wages have been granted, Gramsci observes, "It is necessary for the worker to spend his extra money 'rationally' to maintain, renew and if possible, increase his muscular-nervous efficiency and not to corrode or destroy it."
5. However, Fuller Brush also retained certain features of its original organizational form. Salespeople worked established routes and on commission. Utilizing this traditional form of organization clearly limited income potential. Further, despite its new products the organization was conceived in an era when the housewife's crusade against dirt was central to her mission. As one long-time salesman acknowledged, "These days . . . it's hard for a Fuller salesman to earn much more than $15,000 a year."
6. May Kay Cosmetics was not as adversely affected by the slowing of sales of cosmetics during the early 1980s as other industry giants since a higher proportion of its business was in skin-care products rather than cosmetics.

7. Conn's writings are probably best interpreted as Amway apologetics. He has written a series of books containing enthusiastic descriptions of the organization and endorsements of Amway by current distributors, although he is not himself a distributor. His books are widely read and distributed in Amway circles, he has spoken at Amway meetings and rallies, and one of his books was coauthored with Rich DeVos.

8. It should be acknowledged that Amway distributors are relatively independent. Operating styles, and therefore the extent to which religious beliefs and practices are integrated into Amway meetings, varies. Some distributorships clearly have taken advantage of and been formed through religious networks, such as the Mormon Church, for example. However, even in distributorships which are not explicitly religious, nondenominational prayer meetings or religious services are common.

References

Ahlstrom, Sydney, 1972
Allen, Mike, 1988
Ash, Mary Kay, 1981
Barton, Bruce, 1925
Bellah, Robert, 1976
Birmingham, Frederic, 1982
Butterfield, Stephen, 1985
Carnegie, Andrew, 1900
Collier, Peter, and David Horowitz, 1987
Conn, Charles, 1982
Friedman, Albert, 1971
Fuller, Alfred C., and Hartell Spence, 1960
Gabriel, Ralph H., 1949
Gelfand, Howard, 1983
Greenleaf, William, 1968
Hoare, Quintin, and Geoffrey Smith, ed. and trans., 1971
Huber, Richard, 1971
Hudson, Winthrop, 1981
Johnson, George, 1987
Juth, Carol, 1985
Juth-Gavasso, Carol, 1985
Kerns, Phil, 1982
Kingan, Adele, 1982
Long, Elizabeth, 1985
Marty, Martin, 1970
McLoughlin, William G., 1978
Montgomery, Edrene, 1985
Moore, R. Laurence, 1986
Paris, Ellen, 1985
Peven, Dorothy, 1968
Smith, Rodney, 1984
Taylor, Rex, 1978
Time, 1982

Tipton, Steven M., 1982
Trice, Harrison, and Janice Byer, 1984
Trine, Ralph Waldo, 1897
Tunley, R., 1978

14

Channels to Elsewhere

Earl Babbie

Imagine for a moment that you are on a very long escalator, descending in search of the basement ballroom of San Francisco's stylish Hyatt-on-Union-Square hotel. You emerge into a plush lobby area, outside the large ballroom. Though you had taken the precaution of arriving an hour before the doors opened, you find you are not alone. In fact, you are confronted with three lines of fifty to seventy-five people each, queued up at the closed door to the ballroom.

The people around you are a mixed group, running the gamut from the well-dressed upper-middle class, even chic, to the funky and counterculture. They are predominantly white and the median age appears to be the mid-thirties. Men and women are about equally represented. They seem rather quiet given the size of the gathering; no one seems particularly unhappy with the wait for the door to open. There is a general sense of contentment, even serenity, in the air.

Once the ballroom has been opened and the audience—ultimately over four hundred—have found seats, gotten a drink of water, and made that last trip to the bathroom, a young man moves to the front of the room, takes a seat on the platform, and soon he is talking to the audience about life, work, relationships, and similar topics. He discusses anger, guilt, worry, depression, and other emotions—giving examples of how people commonly manage and mismanage them in everyday life.

In general, the presentation is lighthearted and entertaining. From time to time the audience bursts into laughter, apparently recognizing times they had done something similar to what the speaker has just described. While people may exchange whispers with their neighbors from time to time, the audience is, on the whole, extremely attentive to what is being said.

Who is this young man who will keep his large audience entranced for an entire weekend? Jach Pursel[1] actually seems rather ordinary. Sporting thick glasses and a beard, stocky of frame, unassuming and friendly in demeanor, he is hardly the image of a charismatic spellbinder. As he leaves the platform at the conclusion of the weekend session, no adoring throng of devotees greets him. In fact, he is soon nearly anonymous in the crowd filing out of the room, saying hello to a few friends he meets, waiting his turn at the door.

The answer to this puzzling situation is actually quite simple. While the body on the stage belonged to Jach Pursel, the voice identified itself as a being called "Lazaris." And while Pursel is from California, Lazaris is from somewhere else.

In the terminology associated with this phenomenon, Jach Pursel is known as a "channel"—a vehicle through which "entities" from other planes of existence choose to address human beings. In a more familiar metaphor, Jach is the telephone through which Lazaris places his long distance calls: very long distance calls.

What Is Channeling?

In this chapter, I want to explore the phenomenon of channeling in the context of the sociology of religion. First, as we shall see, channeling's content is relevant to a number of ontological issues traditionally addressed by religion, and I want to point to a few areas of agreement and of disagreement. Second, the sociological study of channeling raises a number of methodological issues inherent in the sociological study of religion; I will discuss some of those and suggest ways in which a genuinely scientific study of channeling can make our understanding and practice of science more robust in the bargain. Third, the phenomenon of channeling raises certain ontological questions which lay near the heart of sociology itself. While my ongoing research into channeling has not yet provided me with answers to these questions, it has forced me to address them more directly than ever before.

Description

So what is channeling? Most typically, it involves a person—called the "channel," "trance channel," or "medium"—closing his or her eyes and going into a trance: either a light trance in which the channel remains at least somewhat conscious of what goes on or a deep trance in which the medium has no later recollection. Then, after anywhere from a few seconds to a few minutes, the channel begins speaking. The voice may be similar to the channel's normal voice or quite different, but it asserts that it originates with some consciousness other than that of the channel.

In some cases, the channeled entity claims to be the consciousness of some historical figure: Jesus, Nostradamus, John Lennon. Elwood Babbitt, a well-known channel, is said to have channeled John F. Kennedy, Sam Clemens, Winston Churchill, Gandhi, and Abraham Lincoln. The one time I heard him, Babbitt channeled General George Patton.[2]

In the past two or three years, a fair amount of publicity has been drawn to J. Z. Knight, a young woman from Washington state, who channels an entity named Ramtha, who claims to have lived thirty-five thousand years ago. Not only was Ramtha a mighty warrior, he claims to have invented war itself. Some entities like Jach Pursel's Lazaris say they have never had a physical existence. Others claims to have had past physical lives, but not on Earth. Overall, the majority of entities I've interviewed claim to have had incarnations on earth.

Typically channels remain seated with their eyes closed during a session, but the entire range of possible variations seems realized in practice. Some, like Ramtha, stride about with eyes open. Babbitt sometimes stands and walks about with eyes closed. Katherine Torres's eyes flutter constantly as she channels Malachi, an entity who speaks with an Eastern European accent. Some channeling sessions involve dramatic embellishments, such as lowered lights, music, quartz crystals, and so forth. Other sessions are pretty unadorned and matter-of-fact. While most entities communicate through the channel's voice, some engage in automatic writing (as in the case of Ruth Montgomery and others) and some channel art and music.

I'll talk about the content of what the entities say a little later, but it is worth noting here that while some limit their comments pretty much to what a cynic might label New Age platitudes, others delve deeply unto concrete technical matters. Jach Pursel's Lazaris and Duane Packer's Da-Ben, for example, do not hesitate to talk their way into the innermost workings of quantum physics—a topic neither Pursel nor Packer is expert in. While I am not qualified to judge the accuracy of what they say in that area, there is no question of their easy confidence in dealing with complex, technical topics.

The channels and entities engage in a variety of activities. A few, as I've already indicated, conduct workshops and seminars for audiences running in the hundreds. Many meet with smaller groups and also offer one-on-one consultation. Some of those I interviewed mentioned their work with AIDS patients: dealing with both the spiritual and physical aspects of the disease. Most channels are prepared to offer audio—and a few, video—tapes of past sessions, and some can provide written materials ranging from short pamphlets to full books.

My research to date, in collaboration with my wife, Sheila, has involved about two dozen in-depth interviews with channels and their entities, plus numerous more casual interactions with entities and/or interviews with channels, and observations at other public channelings. We've either interviewed or observed entities in action from Hawaii, Oregon, and California to Massachusetts, Connecticut, and Rhode Island. In addition, we've read the transcripts or listened to the tapes of countless other channeling sessions.

While none of this constitutes a representative sampling of the phenomenon, I feel grounded enough in the subject to make a few exploratory comments. Before turning to the methodological and ontological questions I mentioned earlier, let's briefly review the history of channeling.

An Historical Perspective

The phenomenon of channeling is not new. It abounds in the anthropological literature on animism and shamanism among preliterate cultures around the world. The ancient Greek oracles channeled spirit entities. Contemporary Voodoo practitioners in Haiti and the West Indies are frequently possessed by spirits of various kinds.

Within the Judeo-Christian tradition it's at least as old as the assertion that the Bible was written by God rather than by the men who actually penned the words. Other modern religious traditions include instances of channeling as well.

Some writers trace modern channeling to 1848 and the origination of Spiritualism on a Hydesville, New York, farm (Nelson 1969). During the first three months the Fox family occupied the house, the two young girls, Kate and Margaretta, complained to their parents about rappings and other strange noises in their bedroom during the night. No one knew what to make of the noises, much less what to do.

On the night of 31 March, Kate took matters into her own hands. Snapping her fingers a few times, she called out "Here Mr. Splitfoot do as I do" (Nelson 1969, 4). This was followed by a rapping equal to the number of times she had snapped her fingers! Soon, Kate was able to hold up a number of fingers and get that number of raps in response. Family and friends were called in to observe the strange phenomenon.

Eventually the Foxes developed a communication system that allowed them to get more complex information through the rappings. The entity identified itself as Charles Roena, a peddler, who had been murdered in the house four or five years earlier. Roena's claim to have been buried in the cellar prompted a series of excavations. In 1848, the Foxes claimed to have found human hair and bones. Arthur Conan Doyle, the creator of Sherlock Holmes, became satisfied that the claims were genuine when a skeleton was uncovered in 1904 (Nelson 1969, 4).

From the start Spiritualism provoked heated criticism from both the established churches and from science. Nonetheless, it spread broadly around the country, with a growing number of spirit entities rapping messages to human mediums, speaking directly through them, painting pictures, healing the sick, levitating, and performing similar activities.

By 1853, *Home Journal,* a Spiritualist publication, estimated there were forty thousand Spiritualists in New York alone. Adherents included physicians, ministers, judges, and other learned individuals. Horace Greeley was a believer. It is widely reported that Abraham Lincoln had a medium on his staff throughout his years in the White House.

By 1870, Spiritualism had begun to decline in popularity. Ironically, this seems partly due to an attempt by organized Spiritualists to identify and expose fraudulent practitioners. This effort at self-policing may have created a view among the general public that all mediums were fakes.

Channeling spirit entities became popular again during the 1890s and once again in the séances of the 1920s and 1930s. More recently, Jane Roberts's series of *Seth* books in the 1970s brought the phenomenon to the attention of a new generation of Americans, laying the groundwork for the current phenomenon.

Current Status

In March 1986, I attended the weekend Lazaris workshop described at the outset of this paper. At the time, I was somewhat aware of the *Seth* books and J. Z. Knight's channeling of Ramtha. My decision to undertake organized research on the topic was accompanied by the comment, "If I look hard enough, I may be able to uncover as many as ten or twelve people doing this at the present time." Today, my best estimate is that there are thousands of people channeling spirit entities. Some channels, such as Sanaya Roman (channeling Orin) and Duane Packer, mentioned earlier, give classes to train people to channel and have written books on the topic. The flow of channeling-class graduates keeps the number of channels increasing.

While some channeling is still limited to small circles of friends, some— like Ramtha and Lazaris—hold workshops attended by hundreds of participants and seen via videotape by thousands more. All told, at least tens of thousands of people are participating directly in the channeling phenomenon. Millions more watched Ramtha and Lazaris on the Merv Griffin show and in similar appearances. Shirley MacLaine has brought the topic to additional millions in her recent books, *Out on a Limb* (1983), *Dancing in the Light* (1985), and *It's All in the Playing* (1987), as well as through a much-publicized television special in 1987.

The current wave of channeling differs in many ways from its forerunners. In particular, the mediums of the 1920s and 1930s—often working with "Spirit Guides"—primarily contacted the recently dead on behalf of relatives, asking Uncle Irving where he had left the combination to the safe or the deed to the farm. A given medium, then, would be channeling a variety of spirits over time. Jerry Primm, a medium in Portland, Oregon, who channels Jubal (previously incarnated as an Ethiopian prince at the time of Christ, a more contemporary Baptist minister, and others), told me that the earlier mediums suffered a great deal in the process, since the spirit entities typically left a residue of their personality with the mediums. In fact, Primm initially channeled a variety of entities and said that he would find himself acting strangely the next day. It was particularly troublesome whenever he channeled female spirits, as he would find himself acting very differently afterward. Now Primm only channels Jubal. While some contemporary channels (like Babbitt, for example) channel a number of different entities, a great many limit themselves to only one.

And whereas the mediums of the 1920s and 1930s dealt mostly with the recently dead, many of today's entities are either long dead,[3] of non-Earth origins,[4] or never-physical beings.[5] And where Uncle Irving was pretty personal in his communications to relatives back home, the current entities lean toward grander topics: ontology, cosmology, the evolution of the Earth, quantum physics, and the like.

Let's turn now to the three issues I mentioned earlier:

1. the relevance of channeling content to religion
2. the methodological challenges to studying channeling
3. the ontological implications for sociology in general

Content Relevant to Religion

While there is considerable variation in the messages being received from contemporary entities, there is also a good deal of agreement. Let me outline some of those, pointing to differences, where appropriate.

Existence of Nonphysical Domain

By definition, I suppose, all the entities are agreed on the existence of a nonphysical, spirit world, though they differ in the details of its organization. Typically, however, they speak of some spirit entities who are rather closely linked to our physical plane and others who are more distant. In the former category are many of the recently dead. Some of these are more closely linked to our plane than desirable, unaware of their deaths and continuing to haunt their old homes. There is also common talk of an astral plane of mischievous, even malevolent, entities who interact with the Earth plane. Poltergeists would fit in this latter category.

Some of the more distant entities are described as angels, with religious overtones, while others are said to occupy dimensions and realities so far removed from our day-to-day experience as to be literally inconceivable to us.

Hand in hand with the view that the spirit domain is real is the view that our physical reality is actually illusion. Lazaris uses the metaphor of a hologram to characterize our existence: it seems real and solid to us, but is pure illusion when viewed from the outside. Lazaris says we are no more physically real to him than Princess Leia's hologram was to those who watched the movie *Star Wars*.

God Is within Each of Us

A common theme voiced by the entities I've studied is that God resides within each of us—as distinguished from the common view of an anthropomorphic god somewhere "out there"—or, more specifically perhaps, "up there." Thus, their focus is less on the proper relationship between a person and God and more on living life appropriate to one's god-ness. By the same token, there is little or no talk of salvation and a lot on awakening or enlightenment.

Reincarnation

The entities are, in my search so far, unanimous in supporting the view that each of us lives many lifetimes. And this is typically cast within a content of long-term evolution toward the full experience of our god-ness. Thus, it is generally held that a person is currently on this earth in a particular physical and social circumstances for the purpose of learning some lesson that is important to his or her spiritual evolution. In some cases, it may be a lesson one failed to learn in an earlier life, or it may be related to karma—good or bad—accrued through a previous lifetime.

Moreover, it is often held that an earthly form was chosen for the purpose of learning that particular lesson. Unfortunately, the person is likely to have lost sight of his or her purpose for being here and get caught up in illusionary concerns for such appearances as money, grades, tenure, status, and the like.

When a person dies, within this general belief system, he or she will continue spiritual evolution while residing in the spirit world and may again choose to take up an earthly existence to continue his or her work.

We Create Our Own Reality

Commensurate with the view of God residing within us and the view that our physical reality is an illusion is the view that each individual creates his or her own reality. This applies most specifically to our life experiences and altogether denies the notion of victimhood or martyrdom. If someone is experiencing difficulties at work or in a relationship, for example, the entities I've studied are quite consistent in suggesting that he or she look to him or herself for explanations and solutions—rather than blaming problems on the others involved.

By the same token, there is much talk of individual responsibility. And while there are some differences, many of the entities I've studied are pretty dogged in their refusal to tell people what to do. Asked whether one should quit a job or get a divorce, and the entity is likely to tell the questioner that he or she must make the final decision, although the entity may offer guidance on how and where to look for an answer. (Those willing to make people's decisions for them were often identified by other entities as astral beings.)

For some observers, this assertion of individual responsibility for one's circumstances has produced the same confusion engendered by similar assertions within the human potential movement. The suggestion that a particular poor person take personal responsibility for his or her poverty is often regarded as a conservative political posture that "the poor are to blame for their poverty." In my interviewing of channels and entities, it is clear that something quite different is intended.

To begin, the use of the term "responsibility" carries no sense of blame or guilt but might more accurately be interpreted as simply an "ability to respond." Those I've interviewed on this topic suggest there is power in the assumption of personal responsibility, whereas the assumption that someone or something else is responsible for circumstances implies that nothing can be done about it. Moreover, when an individual takes matters into his or her own hands—from the point of view of creating one's own reality—there is nothing to prevent those actions from addressing fundamental social change, solving social problems, or whatever one chooses.

It is my observation, however, that the idea that individuals create their own reality is a difficult one to comprehend. It has an even more confusing aspect, moreover: the notion of "multiple, simultaneous realities." Many of the entities say it is possible for you to create and experience one reality and for me to create and experience quite a different one—even though you seem to still be in my reality and I still seem to be in yours.

The independent creation of differing realities extends into some interesting domains. For example, there is a good deal of talk in New Age circles these days about "Earth changes" prophesied to occur around the end of this century. Some people (and some entities) expect a genuine cataclysm: earthquakes, tidal waves, volcanic eruptions, floods, and the like (with or without a nuclear holocaust) while others take a far more benign view. Lazaris and others suggest that each of us will actually get/create pretty much what we expect.

A similar discussion can be heard with regard to life after death, for example in one situation where an entity was asked to contact three recently dead individuals, it was reported that each was experiencing a very different situation. One, a fairly traditional Protestant, was experiencing a rather gray, somber afterlife; another more free-spirited soul was experiencing an afterlife of blissful excitement. I have been told by entities that while no one actually goes to a Christian hell, some who believe in it very strongly spend some time teetering on the edge of it, experiencing the terror of eternal damnation.

Without going through a detailed comparison of these views with the teachings of established religions, I think it is clear that channeling—should it grow even more popular—potentially competes with establishing religions as a source of metaphysical and cosmological information.

Sometimes, the entities talk about established religions, and not always positively. In particular, fundamentalist Christianity and Islam sometimes come under fire as religions that have become more committed to their forms than to the genuine spirituality that originally prompted their creation. One entity told me that both Christianity and Islam depended on enemies for their very existence and thus constituted a threat to humanity.

Other entities are clearly more aligned with established religions, like the two angels interviewed in October 1986, and most of the entities speak favorably and lovingly of Jesus.

It bears repeating that there are many variations on these themes and one should not claim to now know "what the entities are saying." Still, the views I've been describing are quite widely agreed to—or so it seems to me. My caution about how things "seem" to me points to the next topic I want to discuss: the methodological difficulties involved in studying channeling.

Methodological Issues

Most simply put, the question is: how does one study—scientifically—something that contradicts fundamental elements of science itself. Consider, for example, the view that each of us creates our own reality—that there is no such thing as one, solid, immutable reality that we each may experience somewhat differently. Though we don't talk about it a lot, day-to-day sociology implicitly assumes the existence of our conventional, physical reality. Here are some other fundamental conflicts between channeling and science.

Time is fundamental to science, but the entities I've interviewed all seem to agree that our conventional notion and experience of time is as much an illusion as physical reality. As I've indicated above, from many an entity's-eye view, all the different times we talk about exist simultaneously.

The entities are also generally agreed that our notion of the individual is also an illusion. And many object to the apparent need for them to create the illusion of individuality and personality in order to interact with humans. Some, like Lazaris, prefer "we" to "I" as a self-referent, and others even refuse to use a name. Another, channeled by Peggy Graham, simply calls itself the Group. Even though sociologists typically focus our attention on aggregates, we do assume they are aggregates of individuals.

Whereas replication is boilerplate scientific methodology, it becomes problematic in the study of channeling, where the impact of the observer is said to be as important as any other variable in the mix. Thus, if two observers attend the same event and one claims to have seen a ball of white light while the other claims not to have seen it, both the entities and a conventional scientist would probably agree that the difference was a function of differences in the two observers. There the agreement would end, however, with the scientist demanding to know whether the ball of light really appeared or not (and perhaps preferring to think it didn't), whereas the entities would say there was no "really" that existed separate from the observers.

When I discussed criteria for scientific proof with Lazaris, he suggested that the idea of proof might be incompatible with channeling. At the very least, he indicated his unwillingness to prove his reality to people since that would detract from their ability to create their own reality, as discussed earlier. In fact, he warned me to distrust entities that were concerned about proving themselves.

There are numerous other conflicts between scientific and channeling points of view. The issue I wish to raise is what a sociologist ought to do in that situation. The easiest solution, perhaps, is to dismiss the existence of the entities and all their "peculiar" notions as simply false—as conscious deceptions on the part of the channels and/or as figments of their imaginations. If we were to begin with this position, then it would be relatively simple to proceed "scientifically." Wherever the science and channeling disagreed, science would win. For example, we'd demand replicability regardless of what the entities said.

Not only would this approach solve the problem fairly neatly, I suggest it represents the way scientists have most often handled such conflicts in the past. This is the way we deal with the Flat Earth Society, who suggest the world is—you guessed it—flat! Unfortunately, that's also the way an earlier generation dealt with the "nuts" who said the earth was round.

There is another relatively easy solution, one that anthropologists are very familiar with: scientists sometimes "go over the hill." They begin to identify with the people they are studying and give up their commitment to scientific principles. In this instance, you could solve the conflict between science and channeling by saying that science is defective and that the entities offer the truth.

My own commitment in this research is to see if it's possible to resolve the apparent conflict by finding a vantage point from which the integrity of both science and channeling can be respected. Perhaps we can take a lesson from the tolerance of quantum physics for ambiguity with regard to the wave and particle theories of light. While I cannot say I have reconciled the two apparently contradictory points of view, I can report that the exercise has made my appreciation of certain scientific concepts far more robust.

The notion of objectivity is a case in point, as I've grown increasingly conscious of my feelings in the course of my data collection. Whenever I find myself warming up to an entity, notice myself relaxing, feeling safe, and experiencing a real fondness, for example, the scientist in me also notes that my objectivity is slipping. That's not necessarily bad, by the way, but it's important to note the slippage of objectivity in that situation.

What I've just described hardly represents a methodological breakthrough; any sociologist worth his or her salt should be willing and able to do it. But, it was an eye-opener for me to realize that I was also guilty of nonobjectivity when I found myself being very uncomfortable with the idea that Commander Ashtar was beaming people aboard—and I was very uncomfortable when I met people who claimed to have been beamed up previously. I was sure they were crazy. Plainly put, I was being no more objective when I felt negative than when I felt positive.

I've come to see in all this the extent to which we mistake cynicism for objectivity. And while skepticism is fundamentally useful to a scientist, I suggest, cynicism is as limiting a point of view as total faith in the reality of the entities. Here's a rule of thumb I've developed for myself.

Whenever I find myself generally believing or generally disbelieving something, I ask myself what evidence would change my mind. If I find I cannot conceive of any evidence that would change my mind, I recognize that I am being as irrational as any other kind of true-believer (or true-disbeliever).

This research also forced me to look more deeply into the operation of paradigms and the possibility of paradigm shifts. I have by no means mastered this, but, again, I have made some headway. It now seems to me that the first step in the rigorous testing of a new paradigm is, ironically, to accept it as stated!

Having tentatively accepted the paradigm, we may then proceed to examine its internal consistency, the extent to which it can predict empirical matters, and so forth. The primary error we generally make, I think, is to demand that the new paradigm make sense within the axioms of the established one it seeks to replace. This approach to the study of channeling has made it possible for me to discuss criteria of validity with the entities, without insisting that they be the conventional criteria of science.

Some of the entities have suggested that elegance is an important criterion, similar to our notion of parsimony. Several have said that empowerment was critical: does the information received from an entity empower the recipient in dealing with his or her life? Synchronicity is another criterion mentioned more than once: is there an increase in the number of convenient "coincidences" in life (for example, people calling you right after you think "What ever happened to old———?'').

I am particularly interested in seeing if these criteria of validity offered by the entities have anything to offer us in the conduct of more conventional research. It seems at least possible to me that I will learn something in the study of channeling that can be applied with value to the study of, say, voting behavior. At the very least, I know that the challenge I face in dealing with channeling—in terms of objectivity, paradigms, and the like—will make me more effective in the study of religion. It's more than a little embarrassing to recognize the unthinking and unyielding points of view I have brought to that endeavor in the past.

Ontological Issues

I want to conclude this chapter by pointing to a fundamental ontological issue within sociology that has been brought to the surface for me in the study of channeling. For the first time in my professional life, I find it necessary to answer an absolutely basic, philosophical question in order to address a rather more mundane, empirical one.

Here's the basic, no-kidding-around empirical question raised by the study of channeling: when Jach Pursel closes his eyes, goes into a trance, and then begins speaking, who is *really* speaking? Is it Jach Pursel, or is it really an entity calling itself Lazaris?

As I have grappled with that question and asked myself how I would go about answering it with any sophistication, it has become evident that the prior question to be answered is "Who is Jach Pursel?" Or, by the same token, "Who is Earl Babbie?"

Though sociologists have done extensive work on the topic of self-concept, we haven't addressed the issue of what a self really is. And although philosophers and theologians have addressed this basic, ontological issue in far more depth, they have yet to arrive at definitive answers.

Until we can distinguish what a human being is, how can we say with integrity whether the voice heard in a channeling session is that of a human or some other order of being? This is the kind of delicious dilemma that has so far made my research into channeling endlessly fascinating.

The study of channeling provides an opportunity for the researcher to face up to the difficulty of transparadigmatic thinking in general. Certainly since Thomas Kuhn's classic, *The Structure of Scientific Revolutions* (1962, 1970), social scientists have often talked of past paradigm shifts, but it is far more difficult to deal with such shifts in the present or future.

In my research and speaking on channeling, I've concluded that most of us view paradigm shifts as follows:

• We recognize how totally paradigms determine what we see and experience.
• We recognize, therefore, how revolutionary paradigm shifts are.
• We can appreciate how difficult and even painful it has been for people to deal with paradigm shifts in the past.
• And we are relieved that all that's finished. We now know everything and don't have to consider any new paradigms.

Kuhn and others provide us with ample historical examples of these aspects of paradigm shifts. While we certainly believe Copernicus was right, for example, in arguing that the earth revolved around the sun and not the reverse, we can understand how difficult it must have been for sixteenth-century Europeans to give up such a profound and basic belief in the nature of the solar system. Similarly, we can appreciate the difficulty people had in first confronting the Darwinian notion of evolution—and can, perhaps, understand how some religious fundamentalists still resist the idea today.

It is more difficult, however, to relate the Copernican and Darwinian examples to the disparity I described between the basic views associated with channeling and conventional scientific paradigms. To the scientist, science somehow seems to stand above the interplay of paradigms rather than as a competitor within it. (Of course, religious fundamentalists feel that way about their religious paradigms, as does everyone about his or her most basic worldviews.) My research on channeling has provided a continuing opportunity to confront this dilemma and discover new aspects of the methodological enterprise itself.

Notes

1. His first name is pronounced "Jack."
2. For the remainder of this paper, I am going to indulge a literary convenience of speaking of the entities as though they exist and are being channeled as claimed; thus I say Babbitt channeled Patton but retain an open mind as to what was really happening. I recommend that you approach the topic with an open mind also, and I'll discuss that more directly later.
3. For example, Jesus, St. Germain, Ramtha.
4. For example, Commander Ashtar, who speaks of beaming a limited number of humans up to his spaceship to save them from earthly disasters in the near future.
5. For example, Lazaris, Orin, Wil.

References and Additional Readings

Kardec, Allan, 1978 (orig. 1874)
Kautz, William H., and Melanie Branon, 1987
Klimo, Jon, 1987
Kuhn, Thomas S., 1970 (orig. 1962)
MacLaine, Shirley, 1983, 1985, 1987
Nelson, G. K., 1969
Roman, Sanaya, 1986
Roman, Sanaya, and Duane Packer, 1987
Lazaris, 1987

15

The Apocalypse at Jonestown
(with Afterword)

John R. Hall

The events of November 1978 at Jonestown, Guyana have been well documented, indeed probably better documented than most incidents in the realm of the bizarre. Beyond the wealth of "facts" that have been drawn from interviews with survivors of all stripes, there remain piles of as yet unsifted documents and tapes. If they can ever be examined, these will perhaps add something in the way of detail, but it is unlikely they will change very much the broad lines of our understanding of Jonestown. The major dimensions of the events and the outlines of various intrigues are already before us. But so far we have been caught in a flood of instant analysis. Some of this has been insightful, but much of the accompanying moral outrage has clouded our ability to comprehend the events themselves. We need a more considered look at what sort of social phenomenon Jonestown was, and why, and how the Reverend Jim Jones and his staff led the 900 people at Jonestown to die in mass murder and suicide. On the face of it, the action is unparalleled and incredible.

The news media have sought to account for Jonestown largely by looking for parallels in history. Yet we have not been terribly enlightened by the examples they have found, usually because they have searched for cases that bear the outer trappings of the event but have fundamentally different causes. Thus, at Masada, in 73 A.D. the Jews who committed suicide under siege by Roman soldiers knew their fate was death, and they chose to die by their own hands rather than at those of the Romans. In World War II Japanese kamikaze pilots acted with the knowledge that direct, tangible, strategic results would stem from their altruistic suicides, if they were properly executed. And in Hitler's concentration camps, though there was occasional cooperation by Jews in their own executions, the Nazi executioners had no intentions of dying themselves.

Besides pointing to parallels that don't quite fit, the news media have portrayed Jim Jones as irrational—a madman who had perverse tendencies from early in his youth. They have labelled the Peoples Temple a "cult," perhaps in the hope that a label will suffice when an explanation is unavailable. And they have quite correctly plumbed the key issue of how Jones and his staff were able to bring the mass murder/suicide to completion, drawing largely on the explanations of psychiatrists who have suggested the concept of "brainwashing" as the answer.

But Jones was crazy like a fox! Though he may have been "possessed" or "crazed," both the organizational effectiveness of the Peoples Temple for more than fifteen years and the actual carrying out of the mass murder/suicide show that Jones and his immediate staff knew what they were doing.

Moreover, the Peoples Temple only became a cult when the media discovered the tragedy at Jonestown. As an Indiana woman whose teenager died there commented: "I can't understand why they call the Peoples Temple a cult. To the people, it was their church. . . ."[1]

It is questionable whether the term cult has any sociological utility, for as Harold Fallding has observed, it is a pejorative term most often used by members of one religion to describe a heretical or competing religion, of which they disapprove (1974, p. 27).[2] Of course, even if the use of the term "cult" in the press has been sloppy and inappropriate, some comparisons—for example, to the Unification chruch, the Krishna Society, and the Children of God—have been quite apt. But these comparisons have triggered a sort of guilt by association. In this view, Jonestown is not such an aberrant case among numerous exotic and bizarre religious cults. The only thing stopping some people from "cleaning up" the cult situation is the constitutional guarantee of freedom of religion.[3]

Finally, the brainwashing concept is an important but nevertheless incomplete basis for understanding the mass murder/suicide. There can be no way to determine how many people at Jonestown freely chose to drink the cyanide-laced Flav-r-ade distributed after word was received of the murders of U.S. Representative Leo Ryan and four other visitors at the airstrip. Clearly, over 200 children and an undetermined number of adults were murdered. Thought control and blind obedience to authority—brainwashing—surely account for some additional number of suicides. But the obvious cannot be ignored—that a substantial number of people, brainwashed or not, committed suicide. Since brainwashing occurs in other social organizations besides the Peoples Temple, it can only be a necessary but not a sufficient cause of the mass murder/suicide. The coercive persuasion involved in a totalistic construction of reality may explain in part *how* large numbers of people came to accept the course proposed by their leader, but it leaves unanswered the question of *why* the true believers among the inhabitants of Jonestown came to consider "revolutionary suicide" a plausible course of action.

In all the instant analysis of Jones' perversity, the threats posed by cults, and the victimization of people by brainwashing, there has been little attempt to account for Jonestown sociologically or as a religious phenomenon. The various facets of Jonestown remain as incongruous pieces of seemingly separate puzzles, and we need a close examination of the case itself in order to try to comprehend it.

In the following discussion, based on ideal-type analysis and *verstehende* sociology (Weber, 1977, pp. 4–22), I will suggest that the Peoples Temple Agricultural Project at Jonestown was an apocalyptic sect. Most apocalyptic sects gravitate toward one of three ideal typical possibilities— preapocalyptic Adventism, preapocalyptic war, or postapocalyptic otherworldly grace. Insofar as the Adventist group takes on a communal form, it comes to approximate the postapocalyptic tableau of other-worldly grace. Jonestown, I argue, was caught on the saddle of the apocalypse: it had its origins in the vaguely apocalyptic revivalist evangelism of the Peoples Temple in the United States, but the Guyanese communal settlement itself was an attempt to transcend the apocalypse by establishing a "heaven-on-earth." For various reasons this attempt was frustrated. The Jonestown group was drawn back into a preapocalyptic war with the forces of the established order, and thus "revolutionary suicide" came to be seen as a way of surmounting the frustration, of moving beyond the apocalypse to heaven, albeit not on earth.

In order to explore this idea, let us first consider the origins of Jonestown and the ways in which it subsequently came to approximate the ideal typical other-worldly sect. Then we can consider certain tensions within the Jonestown group with respect to its other-worldly existence in order to understand why similar groups did not (and are not likely to) encounter the same fate.

Jonestown as an Other-Worldly Sect

An other-worldly sect, as I have described it in *The Ways Out* (1978), is a utopian communal group that subscribes to a comprehensive set of beliefs based on an apocalyptic interpretation of current history. The world of society-at-large is seen as totally evil, in its last days, at the end of history as we know it. It is to be replaced by a community of the elect—

those who live according to the revelation of God's will. The convert who embraces such a sect must, therefore, abandon any previous understanding of life's meaning and embrace the new world view, which itself is capable of subsuming and explaining the individual's previous life, the actions of the sect's opponents, and the demands that are placed on the convert by the leadership of the sect. The other-worldly sect typically establishes its existence on the "other" side of the apocalypse by withdrawing from "this" world into a timeless heaven-on-earth. In this millennial kingdom, those closest to God come to rule. Though democratic consenuality or the collegiality of elders may come into play, more typically a preeminent prophet or messiah, who is legitimated by charisma or tradition, calls the shots in a theocratic organization of God's chosen people.

The Peoples Temple had its roots in amorphous revivalistic evangelical religion, but in the transition to the Jonestown Agricultural Mission it came to resemble an other-worldly sect. The Temple grew out of the interracial congregation Jim Jones had founded in Indiana in 1953. By 1964 the Peoples Temple Full Gospel Church was federated with the Disciples of Christ (Kilduff and Javers, 1978, p. 20). Later, in 1966, Jones moved with 100 of his most devout followers to Redwood Valley, California. From there they expanded in the 1970s to San Francisco and Los Angeles, which were more promising locales for liberal, interracial evangelism. In these years before the move to Guyana, Jones largely engaged himself in the manifold craft of revivalism. He learned from others he observed—Father Divine in Philadelphia and David Martinus de Miranda in Brazil—and Jones himself became a purveyor of faked miracles and faith healings (*Newsweek,* December 4, 1978, pp. 55–56). By the time of the California years, the Peoples Temple was prospering financially from its somewhat shady tent meeting–style activities and from a variety of other money-making schemes. It was also gaining political clout through the deployment of its members for the benefit of various politicians and causes.

These early developments make one wonder why Jones did not establish a successful but relatively benign sect like the Jehovah's Witnesses, or, alternatively, why he did not move from a religious base directly into the realm of politics, as did the Reverend Adam Clayton Powell when he left his Harlem congregation to go to the U.S. House of Representatives. The answer seems twofold.

In the first place, Jim Jones appears to have had limitations both as an evangelist and as a politician. He simply did not succeed in fooling key California religious observers with his faked miracles. And for all his political support in California politics, Jones was not always able to draw on his good political "credit" when he needed it. A certain mark of political effectiveness is the ability to sustain power in the face of scandal. By this standard, Jones was not totally successful in either Indiana or California. There always seemed to be investigators and reporters on the trails of his various questionable financial and evangelical dealings (Kilduff and Javers, 1978, pp. 23–25, 35–38).

Quite aside from the limits of Jones' effectiveness, the very nature of his prophecy directed his religious movement along a different path from either worldly politics or sectarian Adventism. Keyed to the New Testament Book of Revelations, Adventist groups receive prophecy about the apocalyptic downfall of the present evil world order and the second coming of Christ to preside over a millennial period of divine grace on earth. For all such groups, the Advent itself makes irrelevant social action to reform the institutions of this world. Adventist groups differ from one another in their exact eschatology of the last days, but the groups that have survived, e.g., the Seventh Day Adventists and Jehovah's Witnesses, have juggled their doctrines that fix an exact date for Christ's appearance. They have thus moved away from any intense chiliastic expectation of an imminent appearance to engage in more mundane conversionist activities that are intended to pave the way for the Millennium (Clark, 1949, pp. 34–50; Lewy, 1974, p. 265).

Reverend Jones himself seems to have shared the pessimism of the Adventist sects about reforming social institutions in this world—for him, the capitalist world of the United States. It is true that he supported various progressive causes, but he did not put much stake in their success. Jones' prophecy was far more radical than those of contemporary Adventist groups: he focused on imminent apocalyptic disaster rather than on Christ's millennial salvation, and his eschatology therefore had to resolve a choice between preapocalyptic struggle with "the beast" or collective flight to establish a postapocalyptic kingdom of the elect. Up until the end, the Peoples Temple was directed toward the latter possibility.

Even in the Indiana years Jones had embraced an apocalyptic view. The move from Indiana to California was justified in part by his claim that Redwood Valley would survive nuclear holocaust (Krause, Stern, and Harwood, 1978, p. 29). In the California years the apocalyptic vision shifted to CIA persecution and Nazi-like extermination of blacks. In California also, the Peoples Temple gradually became communalistic in certain respects. It established a community of goods, pooled resources of elderly followers to provide communal housing for them, and drew on state funds to act as foster parents by establishing group homes for displaced youths.

In its apocalyptic and communal aspects, the Peoples Temple more and more came to exist as an ark of survival, Jonestown—the Agricultural

Project in Guyana—was built, beginning in 1974, by an advance crew that by early 1977 still amounted to less than 60 people, most of them under 30. The mass exodus of the Peoples Temple to Jonestown really began in 1977 when the Peoples Temple was coming under increasing scrutiny in California.

In the move to Guyana, the group began to concertedly exhibit many dynamics of an other-worldly sect, although it differed in ways that were central to its fate. Until the end, Jonestown was similar in striking ways to contemporary sects like the Children of God and the Krishna Society (ISKCON, Inc.). Indeed, the Temple bears a more than casual, and somewhat uncomfortable, resemblance to the various Protestant sects that emigrated to the wilderness of North America beginning in the seventeenth century. The Puritans, Moravians, Rappites, Shakers, Lutherans, and many others like them sought to escape religious persecution in Europe by setting up theocracies where they could live out their own visions of the earthly millennial community. So it was with Jonestown. In this light, neither disciplinary practices, the daily round of life, nor the community of goods at Jonestown seem so unusual.

The disciplinary practices of the Peoples Temple—as bizarre and grotesque as they may sound—are not uncommon aspects of other-worldly sects. These practices have been played up in the press in an attempt to demonstrate the perverse nature of the group, in order to "explain" the terrible climax to their life. But, as Erving Goffman has shown in *Asylums* (1961), sexual intimidation and general psychological terror occur in all kinds of total institutions, including mental hospitals, prisons, armies, and even nunneries. Indeed, Congressman Leo Ryan, just prior to his fateful visit to Jonestown, accepted the need for social control: ". . . you can't put 1,200 people in the middle of a jungle without some damn tight discipline" (quoted in Krause, Stern, and Harwood, 1978, p. 21). Practices at Jonestown may well seem restrained in comparison to practices of, say, seventeenth-century American Puritans who, among other things, were willing to execute "witches" on the testimony of respected churchgoers or even children. Meg Greenfield observed in *Newsweek,* in reflecting on Jonestown, that "the jungle is only a few yards away" (December 4, 1978, p. 132). It seems important to recall that some revered origins of the United States lie in a remarkably similar "jungle."

Communal groups of all types, not just other-worldly sects, face problems of social control and commitment. Rosabeth Kanter (1972) has convincingly shown that successful communal groups in the nineteenth-century United States often drew on mechanisms of mutual criticism, mortification, modification of conventional dyadic sexual mores, and other devices in order to decrease the individual's ties to the outside or to personal relationships within the group and thus to increase the individual's commitment to the collectivity as a whole.

Such commitment mechanisms are employed most often in religious communal groups, especially those with charismatic leaders (Hall, 1978, pp. 225–26). Other-worldly communal groups, where a special attempt is being made to forge a wholly new interpretation of reality, where the demand for commitment is especially pronounced, in a word, where it is sectarian—these groups have tremendously high stakes in maintaining commitment. Such groups are likely to seek out the procedures that are the most effective in guaranteeing commitment. After all, defection from "the way" inevitably casts doubt on its sanctity, no matter how it is rationalized among the faithful. Thus, it is against such groups that the charges of brainwashing, chicanery, and mistreatment of members are leveled most often. Whatever their basis in fact, these are the likely charges of families and friends who see their loved ones abandon them in favor of committing material resources and persona to the religious hope of a new life. Much like other-worldly sects, families suffer a loss of legitimacy in the defection of one of their own.

The abyss that comes to exist between other-worldly sects and the world of society-at-large left behind simply cannot be bridged. There is no encompassing rational connection between the two realities, and therefore the interchange between the other-worldly sect and people beyond its boundaries becomes a struggle either between "infidels" and the "faithful" from the point of view of the sect, or between rationality and fanaticism from the point of view of outsiders. Every sectarian action has its benevolent interpretation and legitimation within the sect, and a converse interpretation is given from the outside. Thus, from inside the sect, various practices of "confession," "mutual criticism," or "catharsis sessions" seem necessary to prevent deviant world views from taking hold within the group.

In the Peoples Temple, such practices included occasional enforced isolation and drug regimens for "rehabilitation" that were like contemporary psychiatric treatment. From the outside, all this tends to be regarded as brainwashing, but insiders will turn the accusation outward, claiming that it is those in the society-at-large who are brainwashed. Though there really can be no resolution to this conflict of interpretations, the widespread incidence of similar patterns of "coercive persuasion" outside Jonestown suggests that its practice there was not so unusual, at least within the context of other-worldly sects, or total institutions in general for that matter.

What is unusual is the direction that coercive persuasion or brainwashing took. Jones worked to instill devotion in unusual ways—ways that fostered the acceptibility of "revolutionary suicide" among his followers. During "white nights" of emergency mobilization, he conducted rituals of proclaimed mass suicide, giving "poison" to all members, and saying they would die within the hour. According to one defector—Deborah Blakey—Jones "explained that the poison was not real and we had just been through a loyalty test. He warned us that the time was not far off when it would be necessary for us to die by our own hands" (cited in Krause, Stern, and Harwood, 1978, p. 193). This event initially left Blakey "indifferent" to whether she "lived or died." A true believer in the Peoples Temple was more emphatic. Disappointed by the string of false collective suicides, he said in a note to Jones that he hoped for "the real thing" so that they could all pass beyond the suffering of this world.[4]

Some people yielded to Jim Jones only because their will to resist was beaten down; others—including many "seniors," the elderly members of the Peoples Temple—felt they owed everything to Jim Jones, and they provided him with a strong core of unequivocal support. Jones apparently allowed open dissension at "town meetings" because, with the support of the seniors, he knew he could prevail. Thus, no matter what they wanted personally, people learned to leave their fates in the hands of Jim Jones and to accept what he demanded. The specific uses of coercive persuasion at Jonestown help to explain how (but not why) the mass murder/suicide was implemented. But it is the special use, not the general nature, of brainwashing that distinguishes Jonestown from most other-worldly sects.

Aside from brainwashing, a second major kind of accusation about Jonestown, put forward most forcefully by Deborah Blakey, concerns the work discipline and diet there. Blakey swore in an affidavit that the work load was excessive and that the food served to the average residents of Jonestown was inadequate. She abhorred the contradiction between the conditions she reported and the privileged diet of Reverend Jones and his inner circle. Moreover, because she had dealt with the group's finances, she knew that money could have been directed to providing a more adequate diet for everyone.

Blakey's moral sensibilities notwithstanding, the disparity between the diet of the elite and that of the average Jonestowner should come as no surprise: it parallels Erving Goffman's (1961, p. 48ff.) description of widespread hierarchies of privilege in total institutions. Her concern about the average diet is more to the point. But here, other accounts differ from Blakey's report. Maria Katsairs, a consort of Reverend Jones, wrote her father a letter extolling the virtues of the Agricultural Project's "cutlass" beans that were used as a meat substitute (Kilduff and Javers, 1978, p. 109). And Paula Adams, who survived the Jonestown holocaust because she resided at the Peoples Temple house in Georgetown, expressed ambivalence about the Jonestown community in an interview after the tragedy. But she also remarked: "My daughter ate very well. She got eggs and milk everyday. How many black children in the ghetto eat that well?"[5]

The accounts of surviving members of Jones' personal staff and inner circle, like Katsaris and Adams, are suspect, of course, in exactly the opposite way to those of people like the "Concerned Relatives." But the inside accounts are corroborated by at least one outsider, *Washington Post* reporter Charles Krause. On his arrival at Jonestown in the company of U.S. Representative Leo Ryan, Krause noted that "contrary to what the Concerned Relatives had told us, nobody seemed to be starving. Indeed, everyone seemed quite healthy" (Krause, Stern, and Harwood, 1978, p. 41).

It is difficult to assess these conflicting views. Beginning early in the summer of 1977, Jones set in motion the mass exodus of some 800 Peoples Temple members from California. Though Jonestown could adequately house only about 500 people at that time, the population climbed quickly well beyond that mark. At the same time the population mushroomed beyond the agricultural potential of the settlement. The exodus also caused Jonestown to become top heavy with less productive seniors and children. Anything close to agricultural self-sufficiency thus became a more elusive and long-range goal.

As time wore on during the group's last year of existence, Jones himself became more and more fixated on the prospect of a mass emigration from Guyana, and in this light, any sort of long-range agricultural-development strategy seemed increasingly irrational. According to the *New York Times,* the former Jonestown farm manager, Jim Bogue, suggested that the agricultural program would have succeeded in the long run if it had been adhered to.[6] But with the emerging plans for emigration, it was not followed and thus became merely a charade for the benefit of the Guyanese government.

This analysis would seem to have implications for the *internal* conflicts about goals at Jonestown. Jim Jones' only natural son, Stephan Jones, and several other young men in the Peoples Temple came to believe in Jonestown as a socialist agrarian community, not as an other-worldly sect headed up by Jim Jones. Reflecting about his father after the mass murder/ suicide, Stephan Jones commented: "I don't mind discrediting him, but I'm still a socialist, and Jim Jones will be used to discredit socialism. People will use him to discredit what we built. Jonestown was not Jim Jones, although he believed it was."[7]

The seniors, who provided social security checks, gardened, and produced handicraft articles for sale in Georgetown in lieu of heavy physical labor, and the fate of agricultural productivity both reinforce the assessment that Jim Jones' vision of the Peoples Temple approximates the other-worldly sect as an ideal type. In such sects, as a rule, proponents seek to survive *not* on the basis of productive labor, as in more "worldly utopian" communal groups, but on the basis of patronage, petty financial schemes, and the building of a "community of goods" through prosyletization (Hall, 1978, p. 207). This was the case with Jonestown. The community of goods that Jones built up is valued at more than $12 million. As a basis for satisfying collective wants, any agricultural production at Jonestown would have paled in comparison to this amassed wealth.

But even if the agricultural project itself became a charade, it is no easy task to create a plausible charade in the midst of relatively infertile soil reclaimed from dense jungle. This would have required the long hours of work that Peoples Temple defectors described. Such a charade could serve as yet another effective means of social control. In the first place, it gave a purposeful role to those who envisioned Jonestown as an experimental socialist agrarian community. Beyond this, it monopolized the waking hours of most of the populace in exhausting work, and it gave them a minimal—though probably adequate—diet on which to subsist. It is easy to imagine that many city people, or those with bourgeois sensibilities in general, would not find this their cup of tea in any case. But the demanding daily regimen, however abhorrent to the uninitiated, is widespread in other-worldly sects.

Various programs of fasting and work asceticism have long been re-garded as signs of piety and routes to religious enlightenment or ecstasy. In the contemporary American Krishna groups, an alternation of nonsugar and high-sugar phases of the diet seems to create an almost addictive attachment to the food that is communally dispersed (Hall, 1978, p. 76; cf. Goffman, 1961, pp. 49–50). And we need look no later in history than to Saint Benedict's order to find a situation in which the personal time of participants was eliminated for all practical purposes, with procedures of mortification for offenders laid out by Saint Benedict in his *Rule* (1975; cf. Zerubavel, 1977). The concerns of Blakey and others about diet, work, and discipline may have some basis, but probably they have been exagger-ated. In any case, they do not distinguish Jonestown from other-worldly sects in general.

One final public concern with the Peoples Temple deserves mention because it parallels so closely previous sectarian practices. The Reverend Jim Jones is accused of swindling people out of their livelihoods and life circumstances by tricking them into signing over their money and posses-sions to the Peoples Temple or to its inner circle of members. Of course Jones considered this a "community of goods," and he correctly pointed to a long tradition of such want satisfaction among other-worldly sects. In and interview just prior to the tragedy, Jones cited Jesus' call to hold all things in common.[8] There are good grounds to think that Reverend Jones carried this philosophy into the realm of a con game. Still it should be noted that in the suicidal end, Jones did not benefit from the wealth in the way a large number of other self-declared prophets and messiahs have.[9]

Like its disciplinary practices and its round of daily life, the community of goods in the Peoples Temple at Jonestown emphasizes its similarities to other-worldly sects—both the contemporary ones labelled cults by their detractors and historical examples that are often revered in retrospect by contemporary religious culture. The elaboration of these affinities is in no way intended to suggest that we can or should vindicate the duplicity, the bizarre sexual and psychological intimidation, and the hardships of daily life at Jonestown. But it must be recognized that the settlement was much less unusual that some of us might like to think. The practices that detractors find abhorrent in the life of the Peoples Temple at Jonestown prior to the final "white night" of murder and suicide are the core nature of other-worldly sects. Therefore, it should come as no surprise that practices like those at Jonestown are widespread, both in historical and contemporary other-worldly sects. Granted that the character of such sects—the theocratic basis of authority, the devices of mortification and social control, and the demanding regimen of everyday life—predisposes people in such groups to respond to the whims of their leaders, no matter what fanatic and zealous directions they may take. But given the widespread occurrence of other-worldly sects, the other-worldly features of Jonestown are insufficient in themselves to explain the bizarre fate of its participants. If we are to understand the unique turn of events at Jonestown, we must look to certain distinctive features of the Peoples Temple— traits that make it unusual among other-worldly sects—and we must try to comprehend the subjective meanings of these features for some of Jonestown's participants.

Persecution at Jonestown

If the Peoples Temple was distinctive among other-worldly sects, it is for two reasons. First, the group was more thoroughly integrated racially than any other such group today. Second, the Peoples Temple was distinctively protocommunist in ideology. Both of these conditions, together with certain personal fears of Jim Jones (mixed perhaps with organic disorders and assorted drugs), converged in his active mind to give a special twist to the apocalyptic quest of his flock. Let us consider these matters in turn.

In Peoples Temple, Jim Jones had consistently sought to transcend racism in peace rather than in struggle. The origins of this approach, like most of Jones' early life, are by now shrouded in myth. But it is clear that Jones was committed to racial harmony in his Indiana ministry. In the 1950s his formation of an interracial congregation met with much resistance in Indianapolis, and this persecution was one impetus for the exodus to California (Kilduff and Javers, 1978, pp. 16–17, 19–20, 25).[10] There is room for debate on how far Jones' operation actually went toward achieving racial equality, or to what degree it simply perpetuated racism, albeit in a racially harmonious microcosm (Kilduff and Javers, 1978, pp. 86–7; Krause, Stern, and Harwood, 1978, p. 41). But Peoples Temple fostered greater racial equality and harmony than that of the larger society, and in this respect it has few parallels in present-day communal groups.[11] It also achieved more racial harmony than is evidenced in mainstream religious congregations. The significance of this cannot be assayed easily, but one view of it has been captured in a letter from a 20-year-old Jonestown girl. She wrote to her mother in Evansville, Indiana that she could "walk down the street now without the fear of having little old white ladies call me nigger."[12]

Coupled with the commitment to racial integration and again in contrast to most other-worldly sects, the Peoples Temple moved strongly toward ideological communism. Most other-worldly sects practice religiously inspired communism—the "clerical" or "Christian" socialism that Marx and Engels railed theories of Marx, Lenin, and Stalin. By contrast, it has become clear that, whatever the contradictions other socialists point to between Jones' messianism and socialism (Moberg, 1978), the Reverend Jim Jones and his staff considered themselves socialists. In his column, "Perspectives from Guyana," Jones (1978, p. 208) maintained that "neither my colleagues nor I are any longer caught up in the opiate of religion. . . ." (reprinted in Krause, Stern, and Harwood, 1978, p. 208). Though the practices of the group prior to the mass murder/suicide were not based on any doctrinaire Marxism, at least some of the recruits to the group were young radical intellectuals, and one of the group's members, Richard Tropp, gave evening classes on radical political theory.[13] In short, radical socialist currents were unmistakably present in the group.

It is perhaps more questionable whether the Peoples Temple was religious in any conventional sense of the term. Of course, all utopian communal groups are religious in that they draw true believers together who seek to live out a heretical or heterodox interpretation of the meaningfulness of social existence. In this sense, the Peoples Temple was a religious group, just as Frederick Engels (1964a; 1964b) once observed that socialist sects of the nineteenth century were similar in character to primitive Christian and Reformation sects. Jim Jones clearly was more self-consciously religious than were the leaders of the socialist sects.

Though he preached atheism and did not believe in a God that answers prayer, he did embrace reincarnation. A surviving resident of Jonestown remembers him saying that "our religion is this—your highest service to God is service to your fellow man." On the other hand, it seems that the outward manifestations of conventional religious activity—revivals, sermons, faith healings—were, at least in Jim Jones' view, calculated devices to draw people into an organization that was something quite different. It is a telling point in this regard that Jones ceased the practice of faith healings and cut off other religious activities once he moved to Jonestown. Jones' wife, Marceline, once noted that Jim Jones considered himself a Marxist who "used religion to try to get some people out of the opiate of religion."[14] In a remarkable off-the-cuff interview with Richard and Harriet Tropp—the two Jonestown residents who were writing a book about the Peoples Temple—Jones reflected on the early years of his ministry, claiming: "What a hell of a battle that [integration] was—I thought 'I'll never make a revolution, I can't even get those fuckers to integrate, much less get them to any communist philosophy.' "[15]

In the same interview, Jones initimated that he had been a member of the U.S. Communist party in the early 1950s. Of course, with Jones' Nixonesque concern for his place in history, it is possible that his hindsight, even in talking with sympathetic biographers, did not convey his original motives. In the interview with the Tropps, Jones also hinted that the entire development of the Peoples Temple, down to the Jonestown Agricultural Project, derived from his communist beliefs. This interview and Marceline Jones' comment give strong evidence of Jim Jones' early communist orientation. Whenever this orientation began, the move to Jonestown was predicated on it.

The socialist government of Guyana was generally committed to supporting socialists seeking refuge from capitalist societies, and they apparently thought that Jones' flexible brand of Marxism fit well within the country's political matrix. By 1973 when negotiations with Guyana about an agricultural project were initiated, Jones and his aides were professing identification with the world historical communist movement.

The convergence of racial integration and crude communism gave a distinctly political character to what in many other respects was an otherworldly religious sect. The injection of radical politics gave a heightened sense of persecution to the Jonestown Agricultural Project. Jim Jones himself seems both to have fed this heightened sense of persecution to his followers and to have been devoured by it himself. He manipulated fears among his followers by controlling information and spreading false rumors about news events in the United States (Moberg, 1978, p. 14). With actual knowledge of certain adversaries and fed by his own premonitions, Jones spread these premonitions among his followers, thereby heightening their dedication. In the process, Jones disenchanted a few members who became Judas Iscariots and who in time brought the forces of legitimated external authority to "persecute" Jones and his true believers in their jungle theocracy.

The persecution complex is a stock-in-trade of other-worldly sects. It is naturally engendered by a radical separation from the world of society-at-large. An apocalyptic mission develops in such a way that persecution from the world left behind is taken as a sign of the sanctity of the group's chosen path of salvation. Though radical and political persecution are not usually among the themes of other-worldly persecution, they do not totally break with the other-worldly way of interpreting experience. But the heightened sense of persecution at Jonestown did reduce the disconnection from society-at-large that is the signature of other-worldly sects.

Most blacks in the United States have already experienced persecution; and if Jim Jones gave his black followers some relief from a ghetto existence (which many seem to have felt he did), he also made a point of reminding those in his group that persecution still awaited them back in the ghettos and rural areas of the United States. In the California years, for example, the Peoples Temple would stage mock lynchings of blacks by the Ku Klux Klan as a form of political theater (Krause, Stern, and Harwood, 1978, p. 56). And, according to Deborah Blakey, Jones "convinced black Temple members that if they did not follow him to Guyana, they would be put into concentration camps and killed" (quoted in Krause, Stern, and Harwood, 1978, p. 188).

Similarly, white socialist intellectuals could easily become paranoid about their activities. As any participant in the New Left movement of the 1960s and early 1970s knows, paranoia was a sort of badge of honor to some people. Jones exacerbated this by telling whites that the CIA listed them as enemies of the state.

Jones probably impressed persecution upon his followers to increase their allegiance to him. But Jones himself was caught up in a web of persecution and betrayal. The falling-out between Jones and Grace and Tim Stoen seems of primary importance here. In conjunction with the imminent appearance of negative news articles, the fight over custody of John Victor Stoen (Grace's son whom both Jones and Tim Stoen claimed to have fathered) triggered Jones' 1977 decision to remove himself from the San Francisco Temple to Guyana (Krause, Stern, and Harwood, 1978, p. 57).[16]

We may never know what happened between the Stoens and Jones. According to Terri Buford, a former Jonestown insider, Tim Stoen left the Peoples Temple shortly after it became known that in the 1960s he had gone on a Rotary-sponsored speaking tour denouncing communism.[17] Both sides have accused the other of being the progenitors of violence in the Peoples Temple.[18] To reporters who accompanied Representative Ryan, Jones charged that the Stoen couple had been government agents and provocateurs who had advocated bombing, burning, and terrorism.[19] This possibility could have been regarded as quite plausible by Jones and his staff because they possessed documents about similar alleged FBI moves against the Weather Underground and the Church of Scientology.[20] The struggle between Jones and the Stoens thus could easily have personified to Jones the quintessence of a conspiracy against him and his work. It certainly intensified negative media attention on the Temple.

For all his attempts to curry favor with the press, Jones failed in the crucial instance: the San Francisco investigative reporters gave much coverage to the horror stories about the Peoples Temple and Jones' custody battle. Jones may well have been correct in his suspicion that he was not being treated fairly in the press. After the mass murder/suicide, the managing editor of the *San Francisco Examiner* proudly asserted in a January 15, 1979 letter to the *Wall Street Journal* that his paper had not been "morally neutral" in its coverage of the Peoples Temple.[21]

The published horror stories were based on the allegations by defectors—the Stoens and Deborah Blakey being foremost among them. We do not know how true, widespread, exaggerated, or isolated the incidents reported were. Certainly they were generalized in the press to the point of creating an image of Jones as a total ogre. The defectors also initiated legal proceedings against the Temple, and the news articles began to stir the interest of government authorities in the operation. These developments were not lost on Jim Jones. In fact, the custody battle with the Stoens seems to have precipitated Jones' mass suicide threat to the Guyanese government. Not coincidentally, according to Jim Jones' only natural son, Stephan, the first "white night" drills for mass suicide were held at this point. Stephan Jones connects these events with the appearance of several negative news articles.[22]

With these sorts of events in mind, it is not hard to see how it happened that Jim Jones felt betrayed by the Stoens and the other defectors, and persecuted by those who appeared to side with them—the press and the government foremost among them. In September 1978 Jones went so far as to retain the well-known conspiracy theorist and lawyer, Mark Lane, to investigate the possibility of a plot against the Peoples Temple. In the days immediately following, Mark Lane—perhaps self-servingly—reported in a memorandum to Jones that "even a cursory examination" of the available evidence "reveals that there has been a coordinated campaign to destroy the Peoples Temple and to impugn the reputation of its leader." Those involved were said to include the U.S. Customs Bureau, the Federal Communications Commission, the Central Intelligence Agency, the Federal Bureau of Investigation, and the Internal Revenue Service.[23] Lane's assertions probably had little basis in fact. Although several of these agencies had looked into certain Temple activities independently, none of them had taken any direct action against the Temple, even though they may have had some cause for so doing. The actual state of affairs notwithstanding, with Lane's assertions Jones had substantiation of his sense of persecution from a widely touted conspiracy theorist.

The sense of persecution that gradually developed in the Peoples Temple from its beginning and increased markedly at Jonestown must have come to a head with the visit of U.S. Representative Leo Ryan. The U.S. State Department has revealed that Jones had agreed to a visit by Ryan, but that he withdrew permission when it became known that a contingent of Concerned Relatives as well as certain members of the press would accompany Ryan to Guyana.[24] Among the Concerned Relatives who came with Ryan was the Stoen couple; in fact, Tim Stoen was known as a leader of the Concerned Relatives group.[25] Reporters with Ryan included two from the *San Francisco Chronicle,* a paper that had already pursued investigative reporting on the Peoples Temple, as well as Gordon Lindsay, an independent newsman who had written a negative story on the Peoples Temple for publication in the *National Enquirer* (This article was never published) (Krause, Stern, and Harwood, 1978, p. 40). This entourage could hardly have been regarded as objective or unbiased by Jones and his closer supporters. Instead, it identified Ryan with the forces of persecution, personified by the Stoens and the investigative press, and it set the stage for the mass murder/suicide that had already been threatened in conjunction with the custody fight.

The ways in which the Peoples Temple came to differ from more typical other-worldly sects are more a matter of degree than of kind, but the differences profoundly altered the character of the scene at Jonestown. Though the avowed radicalism, the interracial living, and the defector-media-government "conspiracy" are structurally distinct from one another, Jim Jones incorporated them into a tableau of conspiracy that was intended to increase his followers' attachment to him but ironically brought his legitimacy as a messiah into question, undermined the other-worldly possibilities of the Peoples Temple Agricultural Project, and placed the group on the stage of history in a distinctive relationship to the apocalypse.

Jonestown and the Apocalypse

Other-worldly sects by their very nature are permeated with apocalyptic ideas. The sense of a decaying social order is personally experienced by the religious seeker in a life held to be untenable, meaningless, or both. This interpretation of life is collectively affirmed and transcended in other-worldly sects that purport to offer heaven-on-earth beyond the apocalypse. Such sects promise the grace of a theocracy in which followers can sometimes really escape the "living hell" of society-at-large. Many of the Reverend Jones' followers seem to have joined the Peoples Temple with this in mind. But the predominance of blacks, the radical ideology of the Temple, the persistent struggle against the defectors, and the "conspiracy" that formed around them in the minds of the faithful gave the true believers' sense of persecution a more immediate and pressing aura, rather than an other-worldly one.

Jones used these elements to heighten his followers' sense of persecution from the outside, but this device itself may have drawn into question the ability of the supposed charismatic leader to provide an other-worldly sanctuary. By the middle of October 1978, a month before Representative Ryan's trip in November, Jones' position of preeminent leadership was beginning to be questioned not only by disappointed religious followers, but also by previously devoted seniors, who were growing tired of the endless meetings and the increasingly untenable character of everyday life, and by key proponents of collective life, who felt Jones was responsible for their growing inability to deal successfully with Jonestown's material operations.

Once these dissatisfied individuals circumvented Jones' intelligence network of informers and began to establish solidarity with one another, the conspiracy can be said truly to have taken hold within Jonestown itself. If the times were apocalyptic, Reverend Jones was like the revolutionary millenarians described by Norman Cohn (1970) and Gunther Lewy (1974). Rather than successfully proclaiming the postapocalyptic sanctuary, Jones was reduced to declaiming the web of "evil" powers in which he was ensnared and to searching with chiliastic expectation for the imminent cataclysm that would announce the beginning of the kingdom of righteousness.

Usually other-worldly sects have a sense of the eternal about them— having escaped this world, they adopt the temporal trappings of heaven, which amounts to a timeless bliss of immortality (Hall, 1978, pp. 72–79). But Jim Jones had not really established a postapocalyptic heavenly plateau. Even if he had promised this to his followers, it was only just being built in the form of the Agricultural Project. And it was not even clear that Jonestown itself was the promised land. Jones did not entirely trust the Guyanese government, and he was considering seeking final asylum in Cuba or the Soviet Union. Whereas other-worldly sects typically assert that heaven is at hand, Jones could only hold it out as a future goal—one that became more and more elusive as the forces of persecution tracked him to Guyana. Thus, Jones and his followers were still within the throes of the Apocalypse as they conceived it—the forces of good fighting against the evil and conspiratorial world that could not tolerate a living example of a racially integrated American socialist utopia.

In the struggle against evil, Jones and his true believers took on the character of what I have termed a "warring sect," fighting a decisive Manichean struggle with the forces of evil (Hall, 1978, pp. 206–207). Such a struggle seems almost inevitable when political rather than religious themes of apocalypse are stressed. And it is clear that Jones and his staff acted at times within this militant frame of reference. For example, they maintained armed guards around the settlement, held "white night" emergency drills, and even staged mock CIA attacks on Jonestown. By so doing, they undermined the plausibility of an other-worldly existence. The struggle of a warring sect takes place in historical time, where one action builds on another and decisive outcomes of previous events shape future possibilities. The contradiction between this earthly struggle and the heaven-on-earth Jones would have liked to proclaim (e.g., in "Perspectives from Guyana") gave Jonestown many of its strange juxtapositions—of heaven and hell, of suffering and bliss, of love and coercion. Perhaps even Jones himself, for all his megalomaniacal ability to transcend the contradictions that others saw in him, and that caused him to be labeled an "opportunist," could not endure the struggle for his own immortality. If he were indeed a messianic incarnation of God, as he sometimes claimed, presumably Jones could have either won the struggle of the warring sect against its evil persecutors or delivered his people to the bliss of another world.

In effect, Jones had brought his flock to the point of straddling the two sides of the apocalypse. Had he established his colony beyond the unsympathetic purview of defectors, Concerned Relatives, investigative reporters, and government agencies, the other-worldly tableau perhaps could have been sustained with less repressive methods of social control. As it was, Jones and the colony experienced the three interconnected limitations of group totalism that Robert Jay Lifton (1968, p. 129) described with respect to the Chinese Communist Revolution—diminishing conversions, inner antagonism of disillusioned participants to the suffocation of individuality, and increasing penetration of the "idea-tight milieu control" by outside forces.[26] As Lifton noted, revolutionaries are engaged in a quest for immortality. Other-worldly sectarians short-circuit this quest in a way by the fiat of *asserting* their immortality—positing the timeless heavenly plateau that exists *beyond* history as the basis of their everyday life. But under the persistent eyes of external critics and because Jones himself exploited such "persecution" to increase his social control, he could not sustain the illusion of other-worldly immortality.

On the other hand, the Peoples Temple could not achieve the sort of political victory that would have been the goal of a warring sect. Since revolutionary war involves a struggle with an established political order in unfolding historical time, revolutionaries can only attain immortality in the widescape victory of the revolution over the "forces of reaction." Ironically, as Lifton pointed out, even the initial political and military victory of the revolutionary forces does not end the search for immortality. Even in victory, revolution can be sustained only through diffusion of its principles and goals. But, as Max Weber (1977, p. 1,121) observed, in the long run it seems impossible to maintain the charismatic enthusiasm of revolution; more pragmatic concerns come to the fore, and as the ultimate ends of revolution are faced off against everyday life and its demands, the question for immortality fades, and the immortality of the revolutionary moment is replaced by the myth of a grand revolutionary past.

The Peoples Temple could not begin to achieve revolutionary immortality in historical time because it could not even pretend to achieve any victory against its enemies. If it had come to a pitched battle, the Jonestown defenders—like the Symbionese Liberation Army against the Los Angeles Police Department S.W.A.T. Team—would have been wiped out.

But the Peoples Temple could create a kind of immortality that is not really a possibility for political revolutionaries. They could abandon apocalyptic hell by the act of mass suicide. This would shut out the opponents of the Temple. They could not be the undoing of what was already undone, and there could be no recriminations against the dead. It could also achieve the other-worldly salvation Jones had promised his more religious followers. Mass suicide bridged the divergent public threads of meaningful existence at Jonestown—those of political revolution and religious salvation. It was an awesome vehicle for a powerful statement of collective solidarity by the true believers among the people of Jonestown—that they would rather die together than have their lives together subjected to gradual decimation and dishonor at the hands of authorities regarded as illegitimate.

Most warring sects reach a grisly end. Occasionally they achieve martyrdom, but if they lack a constituency, their extermination is used by the state as proof of its monopoly on the legitimate use of force. Revolutionary suicide is a victory by comparison. The event can be drawn upon for moral didactics, but this cannot erase the stigma that Jonestown implicitly places on the world that its members left behind. Nor can the state punish the dead who are guilty, among other things, of murdering a United States

Congressman, three newsmen, a Concerned Relative, and those many
Jonestown residents who did not willingly commit suicide.[27]

Though they paid the total price of death for their ultimate commitment
and though they achieved little except perhaps sustenance of their own
collective sense of honor, those who won this hollow victory still cannot
have it taken away from them. In the absence of retribution, the state
search for the guilty who have remained alive and the widespread outcry
against cults take on the character of scapegoating.[28] Those most responsible are beyond the reach of the law. Unable to escape the hell of their
own lives by creating an other-worldly existence on earth, they instead
sought their immortality in death, and left it to others to ponder the
apocalypse that they have unveiled.

In addition to the references cited in this article, it is based on personal
interviews by the author conducted in Georgetown, Guyana, and in California
during the summer of 1979.

Notes

1. *Louisville Courier–Journal,* 23 December 1978, p. B1.
2. Fallding does not want to "plunge into relativism," so he tries to retrieve the
   term "cultism" for sociological use by defining it as ascribing sacred status to
   anything in the profane, actualized world. But this just displaces the problem
   of "false religion" onto the definition of "profane," which itself can only be
   defined within a religious perspective!
3. Even the constitutional guarantee is under fire. Prior to the Jonestown events,
   the U.S. Justice Department (texts in Krause, Stern, and Harwood, 1978,
   pp. 171–85) had carefully examined the legal issues involved in investigating
   religious sects, and determined against such action. But since Jonestown, there
   have been suggestions, for example by William Randolph Hearst, in the *San
   Francisco Examiner* (10 December 1978, p. 28), and a law professor, Richard
   Delgado, in the *New York Times* (27 December 1978, p. A23), that totalitarianism in the name of religion should not qualify for constitutional protection.
   Also, the *Washington Post* (16 December 1978, p. 3) reports that mainline
   churches have been reexamining their stands on freedom of religion in light of
   the Jonestown events.
4. *San Francisco Examiner,* 6 December 1978, p. 10.
5. *San Francisco Examiner,* 10 December 1978, p. 9.
6. *New York Times,* 24 December 1978, pp. 1, 20.
7. *San Francisco Examiner,* 10 December 1978, p. 9.
8. *San Francisco Examiner,* 3 December 1978, p. 16.
9. The list of these religious swindlers, if it is kept by God's angels someplace,
   must be a long one indeed! Some would want to suggest that even in the end,
   Jim Jones plotted to make off with the loot. One theory holds that he planned
   to escape with his personal nurse at the conclusion of the cyanide poisonings.
   But this theory seems far-fetched to the *New York Times* (25 December 1978,
   p. 15) reporter who attended the Guyanese coroner's inquest where it was

proposed. It did not account either for the bequeathing of Temple assets to the Communist party of the Soviet Union or for the suicidal "lost hope" that Jones expressed in the taped portion of the mass murder/suicide episode.

10. *Time,* December 4, 1978, p. 22.
11. Only one contemporary, explicitly interracial communal group immediately comes to mind—Koinonia Farm in Georgia, a Christian group founded in the 1940s.
12. *Louisville Courier–Journal,* 23 December 1978, p. B1.
13. *San Francisco Examiner,* 8 December 1978, p. 1.
14. *New York Times,* 26 November 1978, p. 20.
15. *San Francisco Examiner,* 8 December 1978, p. 16.
16. Kilduff and Javers (1978, pp. 77–78) cite the imminent appearance of negative news articles as a cause of Jones' departure.
17. *New York Times,* 1 January 1979, p. 35.
18. *San Francisco Examiner,* 6 December 1978, p. 1; *Louisville Courier–Journal,* 22 December 1978, p. 5.
19. *San Francisco Examiner,* 3 December 1978, p. 14.
20. *New York Times,* 6 December 1979, p. 16; *Columbia (Mo.) Tribune,* 6 January 1979, p. 6.
21. "Letter to the Editor," *Wall Street Journal,* 5 January 1979, p. 21.
22. *San Francisco Examiner,* 17 December 1978, p. 5.
23. *New York Times,* 4 February 1979, pp. 1, 42.
24. *San Francisco Examiner,* 16 December 1978, p. 1.
25. *New York Times,* 1 January 1979, p. 35.
26. The Peoples Temple perhaps had already begun to undergo the third of Lifton's limitations—the "law of diminishing conversions"—before the move from San Francisco to Guyana.
27. On the trip into Jonestown with Ryan, Peoples Temple lawyer Mark Lane told reporter Charles Krause (1978, p. 37) that perhaps ten percent of Jonestown residents would leave if given a chance but "90 pecent . . . will fight to the death to remain." The U.S. State Department originally suppressed the tape recording of the mass murder/suicide, but I have listened to a pirated copy of it, and the event clearly involved a freewheeling discussion of alternatives, with vocal support as well as pointed resistance voiced for the proposed "taking of the potion." (*New York Times,* 10 December 1978, p. A28; 25 December 1978, p. A16).
28. *Washington Post,* 16 December 1978, p. 3; *New York Times,* 27 December 1978, p. A23.

References

Benedictus, Saint, 1975 (orig. written c. 525?)
Clark, Elmer T., 1949
Cohn, Norman, 1970, 1st ed., 1957
Engels, Frederick, 1964a (orig. 1850), 1964b (orig. 1883)
Fallding, Harold, 1974
Goffman, Erving, 1961
Greenfield, Meg, 1978
Hall, John R., 1978

Jones, Jim, 1978
Kanter, Rosabeth, 1972
Kilduff, Marshall, and Ron Javers, 1978
Krause, Charles, Lawrence M. Stern, and Richard Harwood, 1978
Lewy, Gunther, 1974
Lifton, Robert Jay, 1968
Marx, Karl, and Frederick Engels, 1959 (orig. 1848)
Moberg, David, 1978
Weber, Max, 1977 (orig. 1922)
Zerubavel, Eviatar, 1978

Afterword

The editors have offered me an opportunity to revise "The Apocalypse at Jonestown," and I have declined, for two reasons. First, nothing we have learned since has called into question the factual basis of the essay (and even if it had, there would be something to be said for so indicating here, and preserving the text based on its own historical moment). Second, because the essay was one of the earliest efforts to understand Peoples Temple in a reasoned way, maintaining the original text will preserve a benchmark by which we may chart the development of new understandings about Peoples Temple.

Since this article was completed in the early summer of 1979, much more has been written about Peoples Temple. Others (Barker, 1986; Robbins, 1988b) have traced research since 1978 on "cults" in general and on Peoples Temple. Ten years after the events that led to the murders and mass suicide, it is appropriate to briefly take stock. Scholarly writers— Lindt, 1981–82; Smith, 1982; Weightman, 1983; Hall, 1987; and Chidester, 1988—all have been struck by how the popular writings and movies about Jonestown have served motives other than seriously trying to understand what has turned out to be an ambiguous tragedy. The thrust of research has displaced the mass-mediated conception of Peoples Temple as essentially the produce of brainwashing by a crazed megalomaniac. Rebecca Moore (1985, 1986)—a sister of two women who died in Jonestown—has offered poignant testimony that the people of Jonestown mostly were not zealots, but human beings with religious and political commitments, who cared about life and other people. Moore's portrait in itself does not explain what happened, but it directs attention to other approaches than the popular accounts.

A number of studies have revealed the Temple as the product of dynamics that long have been more widely understood more generally by sociologists, and these studies have yielded new sociological insights. Especially important are the explorations of Peoples Temple that draw on

Weber's model of charisma (Johnson, 1980) and on Berger and Luck-mann's insights about the socially constructed nature of reality (Weight-man, 1983). In addition, comparative analysis suggests structural conditions under which protopolitical religious movements run into trouble with external authorities. Comparing Peoples Temple and the seventeenth-century Russian Old Believers, Thomas Robbins (1986a; forthcoming a) has argued that mass suicide seems most likely under circumstances when members of a deviant politicoreligious movement see that movement as significantly threatened by a superior, and politically legitimated, external force. Another comparison—with Bishop Hill, a relatively benign nineteenth-century communal group of Lutheran immigrants—shows how family separations between believers and their unconverted and apostate relatives fuel religious conflict between a sect and the outside (Hall, forthcoming b). The conditions of a Jonestown may be rare, but they have a structural basis in charisma, in the isolated group's construction of reality, and in conflicts with society at large.

Then there is the question of group commitment by followers in an other-worldly apocalyptic sect: a reanalysis of Rosabeth Kanter's data on nineteenth-century communal groups (Hall, 1988b) establishes the strong capacity of other-worldly sects, compared to other types of groups, to marshal high degrees of commitment among their members. In Peoples Temple, Jones did so in large part on the basis of struggles with the Temple's detractors, and for their part, these detractors mounted an opposition so strong that the apocalypse at Jonestown must be understood as an outcome of the unfolding and interactive struggle *between* the Temple and its opponents (Hall, 1987, 1988a).

The events surrounding Peoples Temple without question were unique. Yet they cannot be understood without reference to the cultural context in which they occurred. Chidester (1988; see also Weightman, 1983, chap. 5) has described the public reactions of "cognitive distancing" after the murders and mass suicide at Jonestown. In order to understand the character of these reactions, it is necessary to plumb the depth of cultural connections between Peoples Temple and the society in which it existed before Jonestown. Peoples Temple grew out of a confluence of nineteenth- and twentieth-century movements in the United States, specifically, (1) black religious and political movements contending with the legacy of slavery, (2) the split between fundamentalists and Pentecostals and liberal Protestants, and (3) left-liberal political movements. Moreover, Peoples Temple borrowed profusely—in matters of organization, social control, public relations, and politics—from the contemporary culture that surrounded it (Hall, 1987).

It is the deep affinities with culture in the United States that gave

Peoples Temple its special potency as a religious movement, and, precisely because of these broad affinities, not just tainted groups and individuals, but modern society in general had to be cleansed of any connection to the Temple after the mass suicide; thus, the dediction with which purveyors of popular culture have established Jim Jones as a scapegoat and Peoples Temple as a negative cult. Jonestown has become a modern myth (Hall, 1987, chap. 12).

For all the scholarly work already done, the construction of the myth means that the subject of Jonestown will loom before us for many years. Partly because the U.S. government so far has suppressed key documents about the role of its agencies, speculation abounds about the involvement of the CIA (Hall, 1987, pp. 305–6; see, for example, Meirs, forthcoming), and conspiracy theories seem to have attained a life of their own in popular thought, as an odd counterpoint to mythmaking in the mass media. Equally substantial, in my view, are the problems of understanding the consequences of the Temple's specific history for U.S. history more widely. Effects of events often are more difficult to trace than their causes, and this is especially true of Peoples Temple. Yet the events cut a wide swath, touching many people and organizations, and a number of social movements. Now these effects are beginning to be assessed (see Moore and McGeehee, in preparation).

"The Apocalypse at Jonestown" identified Peoples Temple as an organization directed toward establishing a radical break in history. For themselves, the people of Jonestown did so in the chilling act of murder and mass suicide. Yet the mass suicide was a moment of ending and beginning in the broader history of the United States as well. Clearly it marked the ebb tide of New Left politics. After Jonestown came a new conservative era which left the once broad coalition of left-liberal political groups badly splintered, with radical social movements marginalized while liberals reacted defensively to the rise of Ronald Reagan. How much Peoples Temple directly affected this wider sea change is a question that should be considered in depth. At the least, the story of Jonestown became a cautionary tale that caused a good deal of self-reflection on the left. In some quarters, it may have offered tactical lessons as well.

More directly, the mass suicide changed the conditions under which religious social movements like the Krishna sect and the Unification Church existed in the United States, and it seems to have offered an object lesson to law enforcement agencies on how to deal with religiously inspired last stands. Yet we have to be struck by the very prevalence of standoffs between authorities and groups like MOVE in Philadelphia and the Covenant, the Sword, and the Arm of the Lord (CSA) along the Arkansas-Missouri border, both in 1985, and, in early 1988, a Mormon family in

Utah. Apparently the seeds of the apocalypse are still among us. It is not too much to hope that future research on Jonestown and other such movements will help us learn to see beyond seemingly isolated incidents of social-movement conflicts with society at large to the broader cultural dilemmas that they reveal.

John R. Hall
June 1988

References to the Afterword

Barker, Eileen V., 1986
Chidester, David, 1988
Hall, John R., 1987, 1988, forthcoming a, forthcoming b
Johnson, Doyle Paul, 1980
Lindt, Gillian, 1981–82
Meirs, Michael, forthcoming
Moore, Rebecca, 1985, 1986
Moore, Rebecca, and Fielding M. McGeehee, forthcoming
Robbins, Tom, 1986a, 1988b, forthcoming a
Smith, Jonathan, 1982
Weightman, Judith M., 1983

16

Religious Movements and Brainwashing Litigation: Evaluating Key Testimony

Dick Anthony

Introduction

This paper addresses a complex interdisciplinary controversy that has profound practical implications for defining the limits of religious pluralism in the Western world. As part of the cultural turmoil of the 1960s, exotic new religions, often of foreign origin, began attracting significant numbers of youthful converts. Such conversions tended to accentuate the sharp divergences in worldviews which divided the cultural innovators from mainstream cultural traditions and to give such value conflicts formal organizational boundaries. Parents and other relatives of these converts became alarmed as they saw the generation gap that they had assumed would be a passing phase in their family's life assume the proportions of a permanent rift between them and their offspring. Their children became as strange and difficult to understand as if they were visitors from Mars.

Very soon after this scenario began to develop, deprogrammers such as Ted Patrick and Joe Alexander began to offer themselves for hire as would-be emancipators who would—for a fee—kidnap such converts and subject them to intense counterindoctrination designed to reconvert them to mainstream value orientations. This procedure, which was sometimes—but not always—successful, was designated as "deprogramming," the term itself being inseparably linked to the psychological/legal theory that was intended to justify it.

According to the "brainwashing theory" of conversion to new religions, converts have been "programmed" to claim adherence to an alien set of beliefs as the result of diabolically effective psychotechnological manipulation by the unscrupulous agents of the religious group. As the story goes, converts have no authentic interest in the groups they have joined and their true selves subsist in a kind of suspended animation while their bodies function essentially as robots controlled by their cultic masters. This theory of cultic conversion was formulated primarily by Margaret Singer, a psychologist who had done research on communist mental coercion during the Korean War; L. J. West, a psychiatrist who had also studied communist mental coercion; and John Clark, a Massachusetts psychiatrist.

The legal implications of this theory were developed by Richard Delgado in a series of law-review articles (1977, 1979–80, 1982, 1984). Delgado argues that the constitutional protection of the freedom of religious belief and conduct does not legitimately apply to the brainwashed members of cults. He maintains that beliefs are not truly beliefs in the first place unless they are arrived at as the result of a process of autonomous internal reflection. Because cult members adhere to their doctrines as the result of external manipulation by others rather than such inner reflection, their views are more akin to the programs run on a computer than to the authentic beliefs of a real person.

Since such mechanical commitments do not truly constitute beliefs in the first place, the constitutional protection of religious belief from governmental interference does not apply. Rather, the government has the obligation to aid in the rescue of cult converts from the coercive imposition of externally derived commitments. The government should grant conservatorships to converts' relatives so that converts can be deprogrammed of their inauthentic beliefs, and returned to their rightful states as autonomous persons. If this remedy is not available, then the courts should allow testimony by cultic brainwashing experts such as John Clark or Margaret Singer in civil suits for psychological damages caused by the alleged brainwashing.

The psychiatric/legal theory of brainwashed cultic conversion became the central doctrine of a social movement that sociologists have designated the "anticult Movement" (Bromley and Shupe 1981). A variety of specific institutions developed within this loose general movement, for example, the Citizen's Freedom Foundation (later the Cult Awareness Network), the Human Freedom Center, the American Family Foundation, designed to accomplish the aims of the movement in a more organized way. The purpose of this paper is not to track the development of the anticult movement in general, but rather to sketch the history of the brainwashing argument as a legal tactic of the movement and to evaluate its scientific status in relation to still unresolved legal questions.[1]

The Focus on Margaret Singer's Testimony

Although Singer, West, Clark, and Delgado have been jointly responsible for developing the unified psychiatric/legal brainwashing argument,
Singer has been its primary activist agent in terms of testifying in legal
trials. Indeed, Singer's testimony in civil suits based on her brainwashing
argument may constitute all by itself the most effective tactic of the anticult
movement. She has testified in thirty-seven of these suits and acknowledged that in 1987, for instance, she worked at least one-half-time in these
activities (Singer 1988a).[2]
Moreover, the theory that she expresses in these suits, which she
designates the "Systematic Manipulation of Social and Psychological
Influence" (SMSPI), has never been published and thus has not been
available for scholarly evaluation and critique. Indeed, review of her
testimony in these cases reveals that her trial testimony differs quite
significantly from the views expressed in her publications on this topic.
Consequently, her claim that the point of view she expresses in this
testimony represents a synthesis of the views of leading authorities has
never been evaluated by other scholars. The only available means for
evaluating this claim is the painstaking review of her trial and deposition
testimony and the systematic comparison of it to the views expressed by
scholars such as Lifton and Schein on the one hand and her own published
views on the topic on the other. This is the approach to evaluating the
anticult brainwashing paradigm that has been taken in this article.

The Legal-Scientific Interface: The Frye Standard

The Frye Standard governs the admissibility of expert testimony in most
federal and state courts. This rule asserts that expert testimony interpreting the facts in a specific case must involve the application of a theory that
has widespread acceptance in the relevant scientific community. The point
of it is to ensure that the respect that the layperson usually gives to a
technical argument provided by an expert certified by the court is not
misplaced. If not for this rule, an expert with opinions based on eccentric-
ity or prejudice rather than legitimate scholarly research might have an
undesirable impact on juries. Juries are for the most part composed of
laypeople who do not have adequate training to distinguish authentic
scholarly theories from the private prejudices or quirks of individuals who
happen also to have academic or professional credentials.
Margaret Singer maintains that her theory, SMSPI, summarizes and
integrates the best research on mental coercion conducted by the most
authoritative researchers, especially Robert Lifton and Edgar Schein. In

this article, I argue that Singer's testimony in brainwashing/cult cases does not reflect the views of these recognized mental-coercion scholars but is rather an application of the pop-psychological brainwashing paradigm that their research repudiated.

Indeed, Dr. Singer's claim that the "systematic manipulation of social and psychological influence" can coercively deprive individuals of free will in the absence of physical force or threats of force is without empirical foundation, and has not been confirmed by legitimate research published in fully refereed professional journals. There is no accepted body of scholarly research that has ever demonstrated the existence of such "induced loss of capacity" to form and retain political or religious commitments. In particular, the most widely accepted and authoritative scholarly research on mental coercion in the Chinese thought reform and Korean prisoner of war (POW) situations demonstrated that coerced conversions did *not* occur.

Consequently, Dr. Singer's testimony fails to satisfy the Frye requirements of admissibility for the following reasons:

1. It conflicts with established theories and findings within the coercive-persuasion-research tradition.
2. Although Singer purports to be able to empirically draw the line between conventional social influences and the influence of new religions, on the basis of non-physically coercive brainwashing, the consensus of authoritative scholarly opinion in the field considers it impossible to unequivocally distinguish coercive persuasion from conventional social influence on any other basis than the presence or absence of physical force.

The Molko and Leal Decision

The recent California Supreme Court decision in the Molko and Leal case involved two former Unification Church members who sued the church for brainwashing. Singer was the primary expert witness for the plaintiffs. The decision demonstrates that confusion over this issue (Singer's confusing of the pop-psychological brainwashing model with legitimate mental coercion research) can produce unfortunate and far-reaching consequences for the separation of church and state. Writing for the majority, Justice Mosk states:

> Some highly respected authorities conclude brainwashing exists and is remarkably effective (see, for example, Lifton 1961; Schein 1961). . . . To the contrary, other authorities believe brainwashing either does not exist at all (see Coleman 1984, 322, 323) or is effective only when combined with physical abuse or

physical restraint (see Scheflin and Opton, 1978, 23). We need not resolve the controversy; we need only conclude that the existence of such differing views compels the conclusion that Molko and Leal's theory indeed raises a factual question—viz., whether Molko and Leal were brainwashed—which, if not prohibited by other considerations, precludes a grant of summary judgment for the Church. (*Molko and Leal v. Holy Spirit Association* 1988, 1,109, 1,110)

Obviously, then, Mosk has accepted Singer's view of Lifton's and Schein's theories. Like Singer, Mosk has interpreted Schein and Lifton as advocating two common misconceptions associated with the brainwashing argument: (1) that brainwashing is remarkably effective, and (2) that it does not require physical coercion. On the contrary, both Schein's and Lifton's research on communist thought reform demonstrated both (1) that it was remarkably ineffective and (2) that the boundary between it and ordinary processes of social influence is defined by the presence of physical coercion. Nevertheless, Mosk, clearly misled by Singer's claim to represent their views, interprets Schein and Lifton as being opposed to the views that they in fact hold. Based on this misunderstanding, Mosk reasons that legitimate authorities disagree on these issues, thus creating a triable issue of fact that should be left up to a jury to decide.

Following such reasoning, the court overturned lower-court rulings that Singer's brainwashing testimony is inadmissible because it constitutes a constitutionally impermissible judgement on the truth or falsity of religion. This article attempts to clear up the confusion between the pop-psychology brainwashing model and legitimate research upon communist thought reform that led to Justice Mosk's and the California Supreme Court's unfortunate decision. In the conclusion, we will show that Singer's brainwashing testimony does indeed constitute a forbidden judgement on the truth or falsity of religion based not upon scientific research but rather upon firmly held religious prejudice that predated her involvement in the anticult movement.

The Brainwashing Hoax[3]

In describing the "systematic manipulation of psychological and social influences" as "coercive persuasion" (Singer 1983, 5,139–140, 5,142), Dr. Singer self-consciously grounds her theory on a body of scientific inquiry into purported "mind-control" techniques that became notorious during the Korean War (Singer 1983, 5,438). Seeking to explain why some American prisoners held in Korea and China appeared to adopt the belief system of their captors, the popular press at that time advanced the notion that the free will and judgement of these individuals had been overborne by sophisticated Pavlovian techniques of mind control, or "brainwashing.'' The brainwashing model was thus formulated by Edward Hunter, a journalist, who was also a covert employee of the CIA, in order to explain communist influence on Korean POWs and Western civilian prisoners in China (Hunter 1951).[4] The brainwashing model poses a sharp distinction between religious or political conversions based on internal motives, that is, "free will," and those based upon external circumstances, that is, "brainwashing." Hunter claimed that brainwashing is so effective as a technique of extrinsic mental coercion that a person could be turned into a robot:

> The intent is to change a mind radically so that its owner becomes a living puppet—a human robot—without the atrocity being visible from the outside. The aim is to create a mechanism in flesh and blood, with new beliefs and new thought processes inserted into a captive body. What that amounts to is the search for a slave race that, unlike the slaves of olden times, can be trusted never to revolt, always to be amenable to orders, like an insect to its instincts (Hunter 1960, 309).

Hunter's robot brainwashing model of mental coercion was accepted in its major outlines and elaborated upon by a variety of journalists, psychologists, and psychiatrists (see, for example, Merloo 1956; Hunter 1951, 1960; Sargent 1957, 1974; Farber, Harlow, and West 1957; Huxley 1958). However, careful researchers on mental coercion such as Robert Lifton and Edgar Schein repudiated the suggestion that external events can completely overwhelm free will, or that conversions can be sharply divided between those that are based totally on internal motives and those that are externally coerced.

Moreover, because the term "brainwashing" was so closely associated with the robot model of extrinsic mental coercion, Lifton and Schein repudiated not only the robot concept, but the term "brainwashing" as well. Schein, for instance, proposed "coercive persuasion," as opposed to "brainwashing," as the appropriate focus of study:

> The experiences of the prisoners do not fit such a model . . . hence we have abandoned the term brainwashing and prefer to use the term coercive persuasion. Coercive persuasion is a more accurate descriptive concept because basically what happened to the prisoners was that they were subjected to unusually intense and prolonged persuasion in a situation from which they could not escape; that is, they were coerced into allowing themselves to be persuaded. (Schein 1961, 18).

Lifton also repudiated both the robot model of extrinsic conversion and the "brainwashing" term:

Behind this web of semantic (and more than semantic) confusion lies an image of "brainwashing" as an all-powerful, irresistible, unfathomable, and magical method of achieving total control over the human mind. It is of course none of these things and this loose usage makes the word a rallying point for fear, resentment, urges towards submission, justification for failure, irresponsible accusation, and for a wide gamut of emotional extremism. One may justly conclude that the term has a far from precise and a questionable usefulness. (Lifton 1961, 4)[5]

Singer, in contrast, has testified in various cases that the terms "brainwashing" and "coercive persuasion" are synonymous:

Q: Dr. Singer, do you use the terms "Brainwashing" and "Coercive Persuasion" synonymously?
A: Yes. (Singer 1983, 5,368)[6]

Singer also repeatedly testifies that conversions to new religions are based upon totally extrinsic reasons, which she characterizes as the "systematic manipulation of social and psychological influences" (Singer 1983, 5,279). Singer's paradigm thus involves the transfer to cults of the brainwashing model of mental coercion that had already been demonstrated to be of no scientific value in its original purpose of explaining communist influence on Western prisoners in Korea and China (Singer 1983, 5,372). Singer testifies as follows:

Q: (By Mr. Silverman) . . . Is the end result of such a process the overpowering, if you will, of the person's will or freedom of choice in making critical decisions?
A: Yes. (Singer 1983, 5,275)

And later in the same trial:

Q: Is it the opposite of a sort of a free, voluntary, knowing consent of what's going on, as far as their life is concerned?
A: Yes. (5,277)
Q: And in your experience is that control at times virtually total?
A: Yes. (5,278)[7]

The main problem with Singer's extrinsic conversion model is that it has never achieved any sort of scholarly or scientific credibility. As noted above, legitimate scholarly research on communist mental coercion evaluated the brainwashing model and found it to be without explanatory value.[8] Although Singer claims that her version of the brainwashing paradigm—SMSPI—is a synthesis of the views of legitimate experts on communist mental coercion, primarily Lifton and Schein, in fact her argument is point-for-point a presentation of Hunter's journalistic robot brainwashing paradigm that was systematically evaluated and repudiated by those very researchers.

Singer's theory is thus contradicted by research data in eight primary areas:

1. the area of conversion
2. the area of predisposing motives
3. the area of physical coercion
4. the continuity of social and psychological techniques of influence with those in conventional institutions
5. the area of conditioning
6. the area of psychophysiological stress or debilitation
7. the area of deception
8. the area of dissociation/hypnosis/suggestibility

We discuss each of these eight categories below.

True Conversion to Communism Did Not Take Place; Only Coerced Behavioral Change Occurred

Dr. Singer has repeatedly testified that her modern theory of SMSPI is based primarily on studies conducted on repatriated prisoners after the Korean War, as well as the Russian purge trials of the 1930s and the revolutionary universities of mainland China (Singer 1983, 5,254, 5,272). Singer has failed to point out, however, that true conversion to communism did not occur in either the Korean POW situation, or in the Chinese incarceration of Westerners on the mainland (Lunde and Wilson 1977).

According to Edgar Schein, "[i]deological change may be defined as a reorganization of political beliefs, which could vary from acquiring mild doubts concerning some aspects of the democratic ideology to the complete abandonment of this ideology and a total embracing of communism. The latter I shall label *conversion*" (Schein 1958, 327). Thus, Schein was careful to distinguish between acts of trivial collaboration to avoid punishment or gain amenities, and genuine ideological conversion. Although collaboration was prevalent, genuine conversion was rare. "Considering the effort devoted to it," Schein concluded, "the Chinese program was a failure" (Schein 1958, 332).[9]

Moreover, there was a wide range of individual variation with respect to such behavioral collaboration, with those who extensively collaborated being a small minority. Thus, of the 3,500 POWs held in Chinese camps, "fewer than 50 collaborated on propaganda statements for the Koreans" (Scheflin and Opton 1978, 89).

What sensationalistic journalists had interpreted as conversion turned out upon closer scrutiny to be simply coerced behavioral collaboration accompanied by little, if any, internal attitude change towards communism. Thus, "the much-ballyhooed Communist program of 'brainwashing' was really more an intensive indoctrination program in combination with very heavy-handed techniques of undermining the social structure of the prisoner group, thereby eliciting collaboration that in most cases was not based on ideological change of any sort" (Lunde and Wilson 1977, 348).

True conversion not having occurred in the original POW context, Dr. Singer's testimony exaggerates and distorts the findings of the original POW studies on the efficacy of mind-control techniques. Indeed, the so-called mind-control techniques elaborated upon by Dr. Singer "are neither mysterious nor new, nor have they nearly the effectiveness attributed to them by popular writers" (Bromley and Shupe 1981, 100; see also Richardson and Kilbourne 1983, 29, 32–32).

The Contribution of Preexisting Internal Predisposing Characteristics to Whatever Meager Attitude Changes Were Found

If extrinsically induced conversions did not occur, what, then, determined the minimal amount of internal attitude change and behavioral collaboration that did occur? This question was intensively investigated in separate studies by Lifton and Schein, who both found that preexisting motives were important in the influence process (Lifton 1961, 117–32, 207–22; Schein 1961, 104–10). This contradicts the "extrinsic conversion" brainwashing paradigm, which avoided acknowledging the predictive role of such preexisting motives by assuming that communist doctrines are so inherently spurious and irrational that only coercive characteristics of the influence process per se could have accounted for previously sane individuals having been influenced by it.[10] In rejecting such assumptions, Schein explicitly noted that

> [T]he assumption that the captor-induced beliefs are completely in conflict with the prisoner's may be applicable to a few cases but certainly is not an accurate description of the situation of those cases who were influenced by the process . . . those cases in which influence resulted from a gradual shifting of the cognitive frame of reference, the adoption of new standards of evaluation, and the discovery of new perceptions of self and others (none of which were necessarily in fundamental conflict with the person's own value system). (Schein 1961, 202)

Because the "ego-alien" character of communist doctrines constituted a key dimension of the brainwashing paradigm, Lifton's and Schein's discovery of preexisting motives for conversion among those who were influenced constituted a key reason for its repudiation by recognized scholars.[11]

Physical Coercion Draws the Line between Thought Reform and Conventional Institutions

Of critical significance to these cases is the fact that incarceration and physical maltreatment, rather than any sort of exotic psychotechnology based upon conditioning, were the primary elements which characterized communist indoctrination of Western prisoners. Physical conditions were so unpleasant that prisoners had substantial inducement to comply behaviorally with the wishes of their captors so that treatment would improve.

What was reprehensible about communist persuasion efforts was that they used means that were objectionable on grounds entirely independent of their effect on the efficacy of propaganda, which was not substantial. In other words, coercive persuasion was coercive in an obvious physical sense since it rested upon incarceration and physical mistreatment. This contrasts with any suggestion of some exotic or distinctive form of psychological persuasion that was coercive because of its efficacy in accomplishing conversion for external reasons.

In her testimony, Dr. Singer has repeatedly emphasized that coercive persuasion is best achieved without the use of force or threats of force (Singer 1983, 5,151–52, 5,158, 5,185).[12] However, Schein, Lifton, and other authoritative researchers on communist coercive persuasion emphasized that the line is drawn between coercive persuasion in the strict sense, on the one hand, and other forms of social influence on the other, on the basis of incarceration accompanied by physical maltreatment.[13] Schein considered this point to be so important that he made it part of his definition of coercive persuasion (Schein 1961, 125–27), and he emphasized it elsewhere as well (Schein 1959).[14] Lifton also heavily emphasized the role of extreme external force or physical coercion (1961, 65–85) and asserted that it was intrinsic to the thought-reform process (1961, 13).[15] Moreover, in the Patty Hearst trial, Lifton testified that physical coercion is the distinctive feature which constitutes the dividing line between thought reform and normal social influence processes.

In Lifton's cross-examination, the prosecutor attempted to use his writings on nonphysically coercive parallels to thought reform to show that there was nothing legally meaningful about the thought-reform process to which Miss Hearst was subjected. The following interchange occurred:

Q: Doctor, in your writings on thought reform, have you observed anywhere in those writings that the thought reform—that psychological sources and the thought reform process are not unique, but represent exaggerated expressions of things present in varying degrees of all kinds of social organization?

A: Well, your paraphrase isn't entirely accurate. What I said was that there is no single psychological current in thought reform that's unique. These currents one finds in thought reform, I think that was clear from what I explained this morning, that have to do with guilt or threat or fear of death, self betrayal, there's not one of those phrases that doesn't have some relationship to everyday life. What is *unique* is the whole pattern and especially *the combination of that pattern with life or death coercion.* (Lifton 1976, 327–28, emphasis ours)

In a recent U.S. Court of Appeal decision that was upheld by the U.S. Supreme Court,[16] Judge Krupansky emphasized the centrality of physical coercion to Lifton's model of thought reform. As emphasized by Judge Kropansky:

[T]he "brainwashing" techniques employed by the Chinese as studied by Dr. Lifton were scientifically implemented, and scientifically monitored around the clock. The techniques were professionally structured into a planned, systematic, progressive program calculated to totally pervert and/or destroy an individual and to change his behavior and his beliefs. Essential to effective metamorphosis of the prisoner was an environment of physical captivity, a realization of the futility of escape or rescue, and the use of force or the ever-present threat of force and even death. (Kropansky 1987)

The Continuity of Social and Psychological Dimensions of Mind Control with Conventional Institutions

Lifton and Schein each emphasized that except for the issue of physical coercion, influence processes in the communist setting had much in common with those in conventional American social institutions (Schein 1961, 269–82; Lifton 1961, 438–61). Lifton states:

The psychological forces we encounter in thought reform are not unique to the process; they represent an exaggerated expression of elements present in varying degrees in all social orders. The extreme character of thought reform offers a unique opportunity to recognize and study them. Any culture makes use of somewhat analogous pressures of milieu control, guilt, shame and confessional, group sanction, and loading the language, in order to mold common identities and beliefs. (Lifton 1957, 249, emphasis ours)

Both Schein and Lifton discussed a continuum of "coerciveness in influence processes," with coercive persuasion, or thought reform, in the strict sense defined in terms of physical coercion at one pole of the continuum, and more individualistic, autonomous decisions at the other end (Schein 1961, 277; Lifton, 1961, 435, 438).[17] Influence processes in most conventional institutions lie in the middle of the continuum, resembling those in thought reform except for the lack of physical coercion. Lifton and Schein see social and psychological processes analogous to those in communist thought reform as operating, for instance, in college fraternities (Schein 1961, 274), Catholic orders (Lifton 1961, 141–435; Schein 1961, 260–61, 270–73, 281), self-help organizations such as Alcoholics Anonymous (Schein 1961, 274), mainstream Christian denominations (Schein 1961, 276, 282), the armed services (Schein 1961, 271), psychoanalytic training institutions, (Lifton 1961, 451; Schein 1961, 202, 276), mental hospitals (Schein 1961, 260–61, 273) and conventional child-rearing practices (Lifton 1961, 436). [Interestingly, Singer herself has argued that social and psychological influence tactics identical to those in thought reform are commonly used to ensure ideological conformity in families (Singer 1988c).]

Schein even went so far as to maintain that no social relationship is entirely free of a coercive element. He states:

> It should be clear that the term coercion is applicable to the entire continuum of forces ranging from small constraints imposed by the very nature of the moral order governing interpersonal relationships to very sizable constraints which derive from a combination of physical and social forces such as those found in Chinese Communist group cells. (Schein 1961, 277)

Because of the continuity of conventional institutions with communist thought reform when only nonphysical, social, and psychological influence techniques are taken into account, the overwhelming majority of scholars have soundly rejected the attempt to extend the POW mind control hypothesis to the practices of new religious movements. For example, James (1986, 241, 254) has written that it is "absurd to compare this [recruiting practice of new religions] to the fear of death in prisoners held by the Chinese and North Koreans"; Kilbourne and Richardson (1984, 244) that "applications of so-called brainwashing or thought reform models to new religions . . . have major difficulties"; Barker (1984, 134) that comparison "cannot be taken seriously"; Saliba (1957, 51) that the "model of the Chinese prisoner of war camp . . . is highly deficient since members of the new religious movements are not abducted or physically detained"; Anthony and Robbins (1981, 263, 264–65) and Robbins and Anthony (1980; Reich, 1976, 400, 403) that the comparison is "far-fetched."

Surprisingly, in the DIMPAC report, a confidential report to the American Psychology Association of which she is the senior author (see the subsection "The Scientific Status of Singer's Argument" in this chapter), Singer also acknowledges that because of the lack of physical coercion in cults, the brainwashing model adds nothing to our understanding of their conversion processes. She states:

> [T]he threat of physical coercion found in Korean War brainwashing is rarely present in cult conversions, . . . brainwashing represents one end of a continuum of influence [defined by physical coerion] and is not mysterious, . . . the individual's personality and actions play a significant role in his or her conversion. . . . In summary, it seems that the only confident conclusion one can draw from the many studies of religious cults is that a large variety of people join diverse groups for many reasons and are affected in different ways. (Singer, et al. 1987, 26, 27)

We find then that in her private communications (the report quoted is stamped "confidential" on its title page), Singer acknowledges that the brainwashing theory of cultic conversion has the very same defects that we have claimed so far for her courtroom testimony. In the passage above, she acknowledges that the brainwashing model is defective with respect to the variables of effectiveness, predisposing motives, and physical coercion.

The interrelated dimensions of the brainwashing paradigm. Abandoning Lifton's and Schein's emphasis upon the role of physical coercion in mind control, Singer substitutes the brainwashing paradigm with its four interrelated dimensions: (1) conditioning,[18] (2) psychophysiological stress/debilitation, (3) deception/defective thought, and (4) suggestibility/hypnosis/dissociation.

Schein, who was Singer's original mentor with respect to research on mind control in the Korean War, produced detailed criticisms of each of these four dimensions of the brainwashing paradigm based upon his research on Chinese Communist thought reform. It is puzzling and ironic that Singer has adopted these very dimensions as the crux of her explanation of conversion to new religions; she had formerly assisted Schein in conducting the very research that led to their condemnation as being without scientific value with respect to the mind-control phenomenon.

Conditioning

Singer has explicitly argued that the line is drawn between brainwashing and the influence processes in conventional institutions on the basis of conditioning procedures. She states:

> If intervention against cults that use coercive persuasion is consistent with the First Amendment, the problem arises that *a line must be drawn between cults and other organizations.* . . . Such differentiation simply entails examining the

intensity and the pervasiveness with which mind influencing techniques are applied. . . . [F]ew, if any, social institutions claiming First Amendment protection use *conditioning techniques as intense, deceptive, or pervasive as those used by many contemporary cults.* (West and Singer 1980, 3,252, 3,253, our emphasis)

Accordingly, Singer's brainwashing paradigm, the SMSPI, is essentially a conditioning paradigm. As she develops it in her courtroom testimony (for example, Singer 1983) it has two divisions: (1) the characteristics of the institutions that conduct the brainwashing, which she labels the "six Cs," and (2) the characteristics of the individuals who have been brainwashed, which she labels the "five Ds."

The six Cs are: (Characteristic One) Get Control Over the Social and Physical Environment and Time; (Characteristic Two) Create a Sense of Powerlessness; (Characteristic Three) Manipulate Rewards and Punishments to Suppress Old Behavior; (Characteristic Four) Manipulate Rewards and Punishments to Elicit New Behavior; (Characteristic Five) A Closed System of Logic; (Characteristic Six) People in Uninformed State, Conduct Changed One Step at a Time in Such a Way that They Are Unaware of Changes.

The five Ds are: (1) deception, (2) debilitation, (3) dependency, (4) dread, and (5) desensitization (Singer 1983).

Characteristics one through four of the six Cs section of SMSPI are straightforward conditioning assertions, in particular characteristics three and four which each contain the characteristic conditioning jargon "manipulate rewards and punishments." Singer has explicitly testified that these are conditioning propositions and that thought reform is based on conditioning (Singer 1986b, 15, 17). In addition, D2 (debilitation), D3 (dependency), D4 (dread) of the five Ds section of SMSPI are the primary dimensions of the DDD paradigm of communist mind control developed by Farber, Harlow, and West (1957). The DDD perspective was explicitly critiqued by Singer's mentor, Edgar Schein, as essentially a conditioning argument (Schein 1961, 205–11). Indeed, the title of the article by Farber, Harlow, and West, "Brainwashing, Conditioning, and *DDD* (Debility, Dependency, and Dread)," makes clear that the DDD argument is based on conditioning principles.

Singer has also testified (1986b, 12–14) that characteristic 5 (closed system of logic) and characteristic 6 (special uninformed state) of the six Cs section, as well as D1 (deception) of the five Ds section, of SMSPI all refer to the theme of deception. She argues that these deception variables were both the precondition and the effect of the DDD conditioning processes and that they were taken for granted as part of the context of brainwashing by Farber, Harlow, and West. According to Singer, she is merely making explicit the deception concept that was really always part of the DDD paradigm. Finally, Singer also argues that the desensitization variable was taken for granted as part of the brainwashing syndrome by Farber and his collaborators (Singer 1986b, 12). Since all of the propositions of SMSPI, then, were originally either an explicit or an implicit part of the Farber, Harlow, and West argument, SMSPI is really a restatement of their DDD model and, like it, is essentially a conditioning paradigm.[19]

Singer's mentor, Schein, and other scholars, on the other hand, explicitly repudiated the scientific value of conditioning explanations of conversion by proponents of the brainwashing paradigm. Schein devoted substantial effort to explicitly critiquing the Farber, Harlow, and West conditioning/brainwashing argument in his book *Coercive Persuasion* (1961, 205–11). His critique was essentially that their DDD theory is vague, "circular," and unscientific; it flunks the main test of a scientific theory, which is to provide a systematic explanation for variation in the phenomenon at issue. Specifically, the DDD theory does not account for why most of the people who are exposed to communist mental coercion are not influenced by the alleged brainwashing.

As we discussed above, Lifton and Schein found that predisposing motives accounted for the small percentage of people who displayed some degree of attitude change as a result of thought reform. Brainwashing/conditioning theories such as DDD and SMSPI remain vague and unscientific ideological positions rather than scientific theories because they do not take into account individual differences in response to attempts at persuasion.

Psychophysiological Stress–Debilitation

The debilitation concept seems particularly ill-suited to an analysis of conversion to the new religions. Converts are clearly not debilitated in any sense that would be diagnosed as such by medical doctors. This seems even more obviously true of them at the time of their initial conversions, at which point, according to Singer's repeated testimony, they have already completely lost their free will. The communists' prisoners, on the other hand, were so severely debilitated that over a third of them died of this condition. (See note 9.) This scarcely seems comparable to any conceivable debilitation that, as Singer testified in *George v. ISKCON,* could be produced by a typical Hindu vegetarian diet (Singer 1983). Nevertheless, Singer testifies that debilitation sufficient to undermine free will "is *always* present when someone is controlled by a thought-reform program" (Singer 1986b, 10, emphasis ours).

In both the brainwashing perspective and the views of legitimate scholars such as Schein and Lifton, extreme physical mistreatment was intrinsically involved in communist mental coercion.[20] However, these perspectives differed radically with respect to how they conceptualized the role played by physical mistreatment. According to brainwashing perspectives, physical mistreatment, for example, poor nutrition, fatigue, drugs, torture, etc., produced a state of physiological brain dysfunction and a resulting suspension of critical rationality accompanied by mental confusion. This state of "cortical inhibition" set the stage for religious or political conversions on the basis of more primitive mental processes involving defective thinking, conditioning, and/or dissociation.

According to mainstream mental coercion experts such as Edgar Schein, on the other hand, extreme physical mistreatment played quite a different role in communist mental coercion than that described in brainwashing arguments (Schein 1961, 199–205). Such extreme physical maltreatment, because of its painful and life-threatening character, created a desperate desire to leave the environment in which the coercion was taking place. (After all, these prisoners observed a large percentage of their comrades die from the severity of the very same physical conditions they themselves were suffering.) The communist captors demanded either collaborative behavior or actual conversion to communist doctrines as a precondition of improvement in their physical treatment or their release from captivity. As part of their desire to improve their physical situation and/or be released from captivity, prisoners paid careful attention to the political doctrines that were being presented to them as part of the indoctrination process. In some cases, a degree of attitude change resulted. In more cases, collaborative behavior resulted unaccompanied by attitude change. In either case, the change resulted from the prisoner's desire to improve his physical condition and not from defective thinking, conditioning, or dissociation.

This account of the role of extreme physical maltreatment in mental coercion takes for granted the prior condition of physical incarceration. If the prisoner were physically free to leave the situation, he could bring the physical mistreatment to an end without being forced either to attend to strange political doctrines or comply with his captors' demands. In this regard, Schein considered involuntary physical imprisonment so central to communist mental coercion that he made it part of the definition of "coercive persuasion," that is, "a situation from which a person could not escape" (1961, 125–27).

Singer, on the other hand, in her testimony in various trials, follows the view of the brainwashing theorists on the role of debilitation in most respects, linking it closely to the other themes of the paradigm, that is, defective thinking, conditioning, and dissociation. Her treatment, as exemplified by her SMSPI paradigm, follows closely the Debilitation, Dependency, and Dread argument developed originally by Farber, Harlow, and West (1957). However, even they and the other brainwashing theorists described debilitation as resulting from such severe physical mistreatment (for example, see Farber, Harlow, and West 1957, 27) that Singer's assertion that equivalent conditions are present in new religions seems a particularly far-fetched aspect of her testimony.

Defective Thinking–Deception

Singer argues that deception is the new ingredient that substitutes for physical coercion in cult situations, which makes them even more coercive than the original brainwashing situations. As mentioned above, inspection of the original brainwashing literature reveals that this emphasis on deception is not new; it was always part of the robot paradigm of mental coercion. Indeed, Singer has acknowledged this in her deposition in *Kropinski v. Transcendental Meditation* (Singer 1986b, 12–14). Through physical debilitation, so the robot argument went, the communists were able to diminish their captives' capacity for rational thought and then through repetitive exhortation plus conditioning and hypnosis fool or deceive them into believing ideology that was patently false.

According to the robot paradigm of mental coercion, as originally formulated by Edward Hunter (1951), the themes of overpowered will, defective thinking, and deception were intricately intertwined, indeed almost indistinguishable from each other. Hunter and other robot theorists argued that modern voluntary decisions about political and religious commitments are normally made through a process of clear thinking using inductive procedures similar to those described in a positivistic model of science. Certain religious and political doctrines are so transparently counterfactual that individuals would never form or retain commitments to them through the operation of free will, which is equated with the scientistic use of reason. Proponents of such false and implausible doctrines develop indoctrination techniques that put reason to sleep and then use conditioning and hypnotic procedures to accomplish conversions on the basis of more primitive psychological functions.

In keeping with this robot model of extrinsic conversion, Singer repeatedly testifies that coercive persuasion involves a reduction or lapse in rational/critical thinking (for example, Singer 1983, 5,275).[21] But the prisoners Schein studied had been quite alert and rational during the communist influence process. The degree to which prisoners were influenced was the product of the intellectual appeal of their captor's arguments (Schein 1961, 202–3, 238–39). Schein states:

There is always a certain amount of distortion, sharpening, leveling, and false logic in the beliefs and attitudes which other people acquire. Because people are ambivalent on many issues it is easy to play up some "facts" and play down others when our value position or feeling changes. Coercive persuasion involves no more or less of such distortion than other kinds of influence, but *our popular image of "brainwashing" suggests that somehow the process consists of extensive self-delusion and excessive distortion. We feel that this image is a false one;* it is based on our lack of familiarity with or knowledge about the process and the fact that so much publicity was given to the political influence which resulted in a few cases. (1961, 239, emphasis ours)

Elsewhere Schein says simply:

The essence of coercive persuasion is to produce ideological and behavioral change in a fully conscious, mentally intact individual. (1959, 437)

The distinctive features of the communist-influence situation were, therefore, that the prisoners were held against their will, and were forced to consider thoughts and ideas to which they would not otherwise have been exposed. Whatever small degree of influence did occur, then, would probably have occurred even if the prisoners had been exposed to such doctrines through a noncoercive mechanism.

Despite such strong conclusions from the preeminent authority on coercive persuasion, Singer persists in the belief that she can distinguish new religious practices such as chanting, vegetarianism, and belief in reincarnation, as being coercive in a way that the beliefs and practices of mainstream institutions are not (West and Singer 1980, 3,245, 3,251–53). However, any attempt to establish a clear-cut difference between the religious practices of new religions and those of other types of religious or secular organizations places upon Singer the preliminary requirement of being an authority on religious practices such as conversion, an expertise which she has repeatedly disavowed in various trials (1983, 5,341, 5,343, 5,372).

Singer's insistence that cults utilize "second generation" thought reform techniques (1983, 5,140–41, 5,254–55) in which deception has replaced physical coercion (1983, 5,288) does not square with her assertion that SMSPI is nothing new or distinctive relative to the research conducted by Lifton and Schein upon "first generation" techniques. In reality SMSPI is neither a distinctive description of so-called second generation coercive persuasion, nor a synthesis of principles of coercive persuasion discovered by Lifton and Schein. Rather, SMSPI is simply a restatement of the discredited pop-psychology robot model of brainwashing.

Dissociation-Hypnosis-Suggestibility

Dissociation is defined as "segregation of any group of mental processes from the rest of the psychic apparatus: dissociation generally means a loss of the usual interrelationships between various groups of mental processes with resultant almost independent functioning of the one group that has been separated from the rest" (Campbell 1981, 181). In the history of psychology, "dissociation" preceded "repression" as the primary explanatory concept for mental disease. It in turn succeeded the concept of "possession" by the devil as psychological explanations for mental disease replaced religious ones. (See Ellenberger 1970, 53–110, for a discussion of the relationship of the concept of "dissociation" to those of "repression" on the one hand and "possession" on the other.) Dissociation remains an important concept in contemporary psychopathology with respect to its role in defining a specific class of psychological disorders.

According to the *Diagnostic and Statistical Manual of the American Psychiatric Association* (third edition) (American Psychiatric Association, 1980), "dissociative disorders (or hysterical neuroses, dissociative type)" are disorders in which the "essential feature" is "a disturbance or alteration in the normally integrative functions of identity, memory, or consciousness" (1980, 253). They include multiple personality disorder, psychogenic fugue, psychogenic amnesia, depersonalization disorder, and atypical dissociative disorder. Singer, herself, wrote the description of atypical dissociative disorder.[22]

Atypical Dissociative Disorder puts into the official psychiatric diagnostic system the anticult category of "floating," and as such represents a real coup for Singer in her efforts to mobilize the forces of mainstream psychology and psychiatry against the new religions. It specifies that "brainwashing" is synonymous with "thought reform," "coercive persuasion," and "indoctrination while the captive of terrorists or cultists." Since Singer is responsible for its wording, then, she must also take responsibility for its treatment of "coercive persuasion" and "thought reform" as synonymous to "brainwashing" (see the subsection "The Brainwashing Hoax" above).

According to the concept of floating, brainwashed individuals enter into a dissociated state in which their higher mental faculties have been put to sleep and in which their normally unconscious primitive emotional processes dominate their mental functioning. These primitive mental processes are controlled in turn by external agents, normally, according to Singer's testimony, members of the cults in which the person has been mentally imprisoned. Deprogramming revives the person's dormant rational faculties and frees the individual from the control of the cult, but the person remains subject to transient ego-alien intrusions of his or her formerly dominant false self, that is, episodes of floating. The old identity as a cult member, the zombie-like cult persona in which primitive emotion rather than scientistic rationality is in control, thus continues to alternate with the authentic rational self in the post-cult recuperation period.

As can be seen from this description, the concept of floating, and of atypical dissociative disorder that gives it official status as a mental disease, implies not only that the cult convert is in a dissociative state as a psychopathological aftermath of his or her cultic brainwashing, but also that the dissociative state was an essential dimension of his or her brainwashing in the first place. Indeed, this is how the hypnosis/suggestibility/ dissociation dimension of the brainwashing argument is most frequently utilized by Singer in her trial testimony. That is, dissociation is treated both as a cause and an effect of brainwashing, and is also nearly inextricably intertwined with the other dimensions (that is, deception–defective thought conditioning and debilitation) of the brainwashing paradigm as well.

In effect, then, Singer is arguing that brainwashed cult converts have been *hypnotized* and remain in a hypnotic trance throughout their stay in the cult.[23] In the history of psychology, hypnosis has traditionally been defined as a type of dissociation in which the dissociated state is produced by means of a hypnotic trance, usually or often induced by a person or persons other than the person affected.[24] Thus, Singer is essentially contending that the brainwashed convert has been placed under the hypnotic control of the cult and is functioning in a somnambulistic trance. In this respect, as in others, she is following the DDD brainwashing model of Farber, Harlow, and West that served as the basis for her SMSPI paradigm. Farber, Harlow, and West also argued that brainwashing is based on a mental state equivalent to "hypnosis" (1975, 278).

Frequently, Singer makes the hypnosis assumption explicit, as in her testimony in the *Wollersheim v. Scientology* (Singer 1986a) and the *Kropinski v. Transcendental Meditation* (Singer 1986b, 15–17) cases in which she argued that the central religious rituals of these movements ("auditing," in the case of Scientology, "mantra," meditation in the case of transcendental meditation) are the groups' devices for establishing hypnotic control over converts. Even when Singer doesn't make the hypnosis accusation this explicit, however, she nevertheless gets it in through the back door by way of the accusation that she makes in all her cultic/brainwashing testimony that the ex-converts are presently suffering from atypical dissociation disorder as the result of their prior membership.

In the *George v. Krishna* trial, for instance, Singer testified that George had been fully brainwashed and lost control of her will to the group while she was still living at home with her parents. She had contact with Krishna devotees only on weekends but practiced the central Hare Krishna ritual, the chanting of a mantra, in her parents' home. Thus, Singer testified that the chanting of the mantra was sufficient in and of itself to accomplish George's brainwashing because of the dissociated state it induced in her.

The following quote from Singer's testimony in that case expresses the essence of Singer's articulation of the brainwashing paradigm as she intertwines the vaguely interrelated concepts of dissociation, conditioning, and deception-defective thought:

> [Robin George] shows *dissociative features* of two kinds. She has her mind get off the track, and go blank for two reasons now: One is the *impact of continuous chanting where she was trained not to think* while she was with the Krishnas. This was very *reinforced and conditioned* into her, and it has *stayed as a kind of overlearned habit* in her thinking so when she gets a little bit anxious she starts spacing out. She no longer does the chanting, but *that part of the chanting,* the spacing away from and *not thinking* and not reflecting, turns on now. So that she does sort of space out a bit. (Singer 1983, 5,325, emphasis mine)[25]

This quote, which combines references to conditioning, deception–defective thought and dissociation, demonstrates how the interrelated aspects of the brainwashing paradigm tend to blur together into an inseparable smear of pejorative connotation in Singer's testimony. In turn, the related concepts of dissociation, trance states, hypnosis, heightened suggestibility, etc., become inextricable aspects of the brainwashing paradigm as employed by Singer and others.

It is the consensus of authoritative scholarship on communist mental coercion, however, that the interrelated concepts of hypnosis, dissociation, and abnormal suggestibility[26] play no role whatsoever in communist mental coercion. Schein states:

> Given these considerations, it is difficult to see how Merloo and Huxley can be so sure of the effectiveness of *brainwashing* and of their interpretation of it as a process based on *hypnosis and Pavlovian psychology [conditioning]*. The chief problem with the hypnotic interpretation is that the relationship between hypnotist and subject is to a large degree a *voluntary* one, whereas the coercive element in coercive persuasion is paramount (forcing the individual into a situation in which he must, *in order to survive physically* and psychologically, expose himself to persuasive attempts). A second problem is that as yet we do not have an adequate theoretical explanation for the effects seen under hypnosis, and hence there is little to be gained by using it as an explanatory concept. Third, and most important, all hypnotic situations that I know of involve the deliberate creation of a *state resembling sleep or dissociation*. The essence of coercive persuasion, on the other hand, is to produce ideological and behavioral

changes in a *fully conscious, mentally intact individual.* (Schein 1959, 437, emphasis mine)

Schein could hardly be more definite in his assertion that the concepts of hypnosis and dissociation, with their associated concepts of conditioning and defective thought, have no role whatsoever in communist mental coercion. He also states completely explicitly that hypnosis, far from contradicting an assumption of voluntariness, in fact requires a completely voluntary relationship in order to work. In addition, he asserts that the involuntary character of thought reform consists of *both* physical and mental coercion, and that it is incompatible with hypnosis, which requires a voluntary relationship. Finally, he asserts that dissociation, with its intrinsic linkage to defective thought, was absolutely contradicted by his finding that the communist prisoners were completely alert and rational during the influence process.

In this brief passage, then, Schein unequivocally demystifies and repudiates the brainwashing paradigm. Consequently, Singer's testimony in anticult brainwashing trials is fundamentally contradicted by the very mental coercion theories that she claims to be applying.

Conclusion: Psychology as Religious Prejudice?

Edgar Schein, Singer's original mentor with respect to research on mind control, took pains to point out repeatedly that there is nothing intrinsically morally objectionable about the social and psychological techniques used in communist thought reform. The extreme physical coercion intrinsic to the process was, of course, reprehensible, but Schein emphasized that, with that exception, so-called mind control practices are endemic in conventional American institutions and that there is nothing wrong with this. (At one point Schein even went so far as to suggest that American institutions would do well to study communist indoctrination techniques so as to pick up a few pointers.)

Does this mean that Schein had no objection to communist thought reform other than the fact that it is physically coercive? Not at all: Schein was quite opposed to the communist influence process on grounds other than its phycial coerciveness. What Schein objected to about this process was not the social and psychological methods of influence but rather the *ideological content* transmitted by means of those methods. Schein states:

And do we not put criminals with the wrong attitude in the midst of others with the right attitude in the hope that they will learn the right ones through the pressure of the group? Let me remind you, I am not drawing these parallels [between communist and American techniques of influence] in order to condemn some of our own approaches, rather my aim is just the opposite. I am trying to show that Chinese *methods* are not so mysterious, not so different and not so *awful, once we separate the awfulness of the Communist ideology and look simply at the methods of influence used.* (Schein 1962, 97, emphasis ours)[27]

Singer, on the other hand, claims to have no interest whatsoever in the content of the beliefs of the groups that she is accusing of brainwashing. For instance, in her testimony in *George v. ISKCON,* she asserted:

I don't use the term "religion" when I am studying the practices of organizations, because it's irrelevant to me what the content of the organization is. (Singer 1983, 5,452–53)

In her testimony, then, she is at pains to point out that, unlike Schein, her objection to nonphysically coercive mental coercion is to the conduct through which the influence is transmitted, that is, the practice of brainwashing, rather than the doctrines that are being transmitted by means of that conduct. This claim, that she is objecting to conduct and not belief, does not survive any sort of close scrutiny, however. It seems to be transparently untrue and to have been advanced in the first place as a means of evading the absolute constitutional protection of religious belief from governmental interference. As the Court of Appeal asked rhetorically in the Katz decision—a decision that forbade the use of Singer's argument to gain governmental support for deprogramming in California: When the court is asked to determine whether change [of religious commitment] was induced by faith or by coercive persuasion is it not in turn investigating and questioning the validity of that faith? (Katz 1977, 987).

Indeed, when her testimony is scrutinized carefully, her supposed interest in conduct alone slides quickly into an obvious condemnation of the theologies of the groups she is opposing. Her mental coercion paradigm (SMSPI) is carefully phrased in terms of coerced behavior rather than coerced belief, with "behavior" referring to the activity of believing rather than the content of belief. In application of this paradigm to concrete instances of conversion, however, she commonly slides from reference to change in behavior to change in belief without any indication that she is aware of the transition. Thus, in the case of *Christofferson v. Scientology,* the following exchange occurred:

Q: Well, had she suppressed her old behavior, completely suppressed her old behavior by some point in time that you can give us a reference to?
A: My point that I was making yesterday, and I thought it was quite clear, is that management tries and works at getting certain types of *old behavior suppressed.* And it was—what I was trying to convey to you—what is so insidious about this type of attack upon a person's personality and sense of

self is that the attack is made to stop using your *old value systems, your old belief systems.* And she was being subjected continuously to that type of suppression of her old belief system, etc. (Singer 1985b, 2,934-2,935, emphasis ours)[28]

In *George v. ISKCON,* moreover, she testified that Robin George's conversion to ISKCON was not a "true" conversion:

Q: Is it your basic contention that Robin George was in the Hare Krishna movement as a result of *coercive persuasion rather than true conversion?*
A: It is my opinion.
Q: The answer to that is yes?
A: Yes. (Singer 1983, 5,498, emphasis ours).

The major thrust of her testimony in this and other cases, as well as her publications on mental coercion in cults, is that coercion rather than "true conversion" is the normal or typical mechanism by which belief is initiated and maintained in the doctrines of so-called cults. Conversion has been defined in a prominent dictionary of psychology as "a rapid, often dramatic change in religious beliefs" (Chaplin 1985, 105). The practical thrust of her testimony, then, is that belief in new religious doctrines is false belief and that the doctrines themselves are false doctrines.

In her publications, as opposed to her trial testimony, Singer's view of cults as false religions becomes more explicit. She states:

Just as there are "spiritual counterfeits," I am saying there are also "therapeutic counterfeits." (Singer 1984, 12)

Elsewhere she says quite explicitly that her objection to cults is based on her judgement that participation in the new religions involves belief in false doctrines.

Cults offer certain pseudo-philosophical, spiritual, and psychological dimensions to the lives of these persons. . . . Cults pare down multidimensional reality into an oversimplified pastiche of cosmic truths that explain everything. (Singer 1978, 16)

Surely, when Singer refers to the type of religion she opposes as "pseudo-philosophical" and "an over-simplified pastiche of cosmic truths," there can be no doubt that she is contending that religious doctrines are false rather than confining her objection to conduct, as she contends in her testimony. Conduct cannot meaningfully be referred to as "pseudo-philosophical" or an "over-simplified pastiche of cosmic truths."[29]

In her publications as opposed to her testimony, then, Singer drops all pretense of being uninterested in religion per se and states quite boldly that she is opposed to a certain class of religion characterized by belief in a certain type of doctrine, that is, those that are "spiritual counterfeits," "pseudo-philosophical," or "an over-simplified pastiche of cosmic truths." It turns out that her objection to this type of false religion was present even before she had done any research on cults. In fact, she acknowledges that it was her antipathy to that type of religion that motivated her campaign against cults, and that this value judgement preceded her research rather than resulting from it. She states:

> I became particularly interested in the new cults as they sprang up because it was an era in which many *liberal political advances* had been achieved; *scientific reasoning* had come to the forefront of our thinking and *rationalism* had become widely accepted. Yet, I saw many young adults turning to extremely authoritarian social groups, dropping the *world of science, liberalism and rationalism* and entering a *world of magic and primitive thinking.* What were the processes that might help to explain the phenomenona from an individual, psychological, social historical, religious and legal standpoint? (Singer 1978, 14, emphasis ours)[30]

Singer believed then, in advance of any actual research that she conducted on them, that these groups are obviously undesirable on their face.[31] And what were the obvious values that these groups contradicted in Singer's mind? The "world of science, liberalism and rationalism." But why do these groups so obviously contradict scientific reasoning? Singer says that these groups embody a "world of magic and primitive thinking." But for the religious scholars who study these groups it is not at all obvious that they embody magic or primitive thought. (For instance, some of them represent religious traditions, for example, Buddhism or Hinduism, which are regarded as among the most sophisticated responses to the mystery of existence.)

Rationalism, liberalism and science cohere into a uniform value perspective and thus constitute a "world" primarily within the worldview of "positivism," a tradition in philosophy and the human sciences that seeks to propagate a norm of optimal mental functioning modeled upon a particular view of physical science.[31] According to the positivist viewpoint, scientific generalizations must be based upon pure induction from incontrovertible observations of the material world, i.e. physical facts. (The positivist view of science as based on pure material induction is no longer widely held by scientists or philosophers, but that is a story for another time.) Materialistic induction, then, is the only valid form of gathering true information about reality, and all human values should be based upon mental functioning modeled upon a positivistic norm of science. Because religion traditionally depends upon nonmaterial sources of information and private mental states that are not universally shared (and thus not incontrovertible), supernaturally based religion has no legitimate place within the positivist worldview.

Careful inspection of Singer's writings on her cultic brainwashing thesis, then some of which appear in very obscure anticult publications, reveals that Singer believes that the doctrines of the new religions contradict rationalism, liberalism, and science because she is committed to a general value perspective, that is, positivism, which maintains that it is true by definition that any value perspective generated on the basis of inner intuitive experience embodies magic and primitive thinking.[32] Singer regards the new religions as unscientific and thus embodying primitive thought not because they reject science, which for the most part they do not, but rather because they do not accept the domain of physical science as defining the whole universe of human meaning. Singer's evaluation of the whole class of experientially grounded new religions as "spiritual counterfeits" amounts to nothing more than a naked value conflict over the ultimate scope of science in human life.

Moreover, Singer appears to believe that the theologies of the new religions are inconsistent with "many liberal *political* advances" and thus lie outside "the world of science, *liberalism* and rationalism" because she believes that citizenship in the United States requires commitment to a sort of scientistic civil-religious orthodoxy that is the apogee of progress. Deviation from this politico-religious orthodoxy, Singer appears to feel, is un-American. For instance, in discussing her reasons for extending her cultic brainwashing thesis to "human potential" and "transpersonal" psychotherapies and quasi-religious therapeutic movements such as est and Lifespring, Singer states that the doctrines transmitted by these movements are "contrary to the general scientific understanding of causality" and that consequently they are impermissable because they do not "stay within *the general tenets of our larger social order* which is a democracy and *which operates by the theories of scientific causality*" (Singer 1984, 6 and 12, emphasis ours).[33]

With this statement Singer has clarified not only why she feels that the "world of magic and primitive thinking" of the new religions fundamentally contradicts "the world of science," but also why science, liberalism, and rationalism cohere into a uniform value perspective that should define the limits of permissable variation for religious doctrines in the United States. In Singer's mind, the concept of democracy seems to be synonymous with that of a social order united by uniform belief in a national ideology based upon the "theories of scientific causality." For Singer, the positivist doctrine of basing ultimate values upon science is not merely the superior theological option among inferior but permissable competing alternatives. Rather, belief in positivism as a civil religious orthodoxy is an underlying requirement that sets the limit for religious pluralism in the United States.

In Singer's vision of the United States as a positivist democracy, then, wherever there is apparent conflict between science and religion, religion *must* yield in favor of the doctrines espoused by science. Singer appears to believe not only that science should increasingly replace religion in the sphere of value formation but that this progressive replacement of the influence of religion by that of science should be enforced legally. Her testimony in more than thirty-seven cases has put teeth in this proposition and come uncomfortably close to making Singer's vision of a legally obligatory positivist civil religion the law of the land. (Singer has apparently confined her testimony to cases involving the new religions and conservative Christian groups because, in her view, the mainstream liberal denominations have for the most part accepted the reality of secularization and the hegemony of science in value formation.)

However, Singer is clearly familiar with the present constitutional requirement that religious doctrines be unconditionally free from governmental regulation (West and Singer 1980, 3,251–53). Consequently, as we have seen, her unequivocal critique of religious doctrines per se is denied in her testimony and is revealed only in obscure anticult publications such as the *Spiritual Counterfeits Newsletter* (Singer 1984). In this light, her puzzling shift from the more scholarly mental coercion theories that she once shared with Schein (e.g., Schein, Cooley, and Singer 1960) to the pop-psychological brainwashing paradigm upon which she bases her testimony in anticult brainwashing cases can be seen as little more than an attempt to pass off her explicitly ideological objections to a class of religious doctrines as a disinterested scientific analysis of coercive behavior.

How ironic that Singer's defense of the hegemony of science in human values relative to religious perspectives that she believes embody "magic and primitive thought" should be based upon an argument that is itself so intrinsically unscientific. Nevertheless, in a religiously pluralistic society such as our own she has every right to criticize religious groups from this perspective and to attempt to persuade others not to join them. Religious prejudice is itself constitutionally protected as long as it is confined to thought and speech.[34] What is fundamentally unacceptable, however, is that the courts, by failing to unmask the unscientific character of Singer's argument and thereby allowing her to testify, in effect have given her religious bias the force of law. Because of the antireligious crusade of one person, the courts have come close to definitively establishing certain religious organizations, that is, those that have accepted the hegemony of science in the sphere of ultimate values, and to prohibiting those that have not.

The Scientific Status of Singer's Argument: Recently, the relevant professional organizations have taken public stands on the scientific status of Singer's brainwashing argument. The American Psychological Association (APA) and the Society for the Scientific Study of Religion (SSSR) are the professional organizations most relevant to evaluating Singer's position. Both have officially gone on record firmly declaring the scientific unacceptability of her brainwashing theory.[35]

The APA Position: At the vote of their board of directors, the American Psychological Association filed an amicus curiae brief in the *Molko and Leal v. the Unification Church* case before the California Court of Appeal. It argued that Singer should not be allowed to testify on her brainwashing theory of cultic conversion because the theory lies outside the boundaries of scientific acceptability. The brief incorporated two main arguments: (1) Singer's research for SMSPI is inherently unscientific as it violates normal methodological standards designed to ensure objective and unbiased conclusions; (2) her conclusions are contradicted by voluminous research, published in mainstream refereed journals, on factors influencing conversion to the new religions as well as upon the mental health consequences of such involvements.

On both the latter points, that is, conversion and the psychological consequences of conversion, the scholarly evidence overwhelmingly contradicts Singer's SMSPI paradigm. Compounding this problem from a scientific standpoint is Singer's invariable habit, both in her publications and in her testimony, of totally ignoring the abundant, painstakingly collected evidence contradicting her theory on conversion to new religions. Acknowledging the existence of contrary evidence is considered to be so basic to the scientific method that a perspective that avoids this principle is usually not considered to be scientific at all.

Soon after the APA had filed this brief with the court, Singer and her allies conducted an intensive lobbying campaign within the organization to get the board of directors to reverse its vote. (This account of the development of APA's position on Singer's testimony is based primarily on Singer's own account that she provided in her deposition in *Miller v. Lifespring,* Singer 1988a, 2:238–53.) Singer and her cohort argued that it was premature for the APA to take a position on the scientific status of Singer's theory because its merits still were in the process of being evaluated by the APA's Board for Social and Ethical Responsibility (BSERP).

At the request of Singer and some of her colleagues, the APA had previously formed a committee to produce a task force report on "Deceptive and Indirect Techniques of Persuasion and Control'' (the DIMPAC report). The goal of the DIMPAC committee was to produce a version of Singer's cultic brainwashing argument that was state-of-the-art in terms of its scholarly quality. Singer envisioned that if she could get the APA to endorse this version of her argument, it would lay to rest any questions about its scientific acceptability. She also testified that she had hoped that the APA would publish this report in one of its official journals, preferably the *American Psychologist*.

In response to the argument that it was premature to take an official position until Singer's committee had a chance to tell their side of the story through the DIMPAC report, and until the APA's Board for Social and Ethical Responsibility had had time to evaluate the report, the APA board of directors agreed to withdraw their sponsorship of the brief in *Molko and Leal*.[36] When Singer submitted her report, BSERP sent it to four reviewers for anonymous peer review as to scientific merit. Their unanimous opinion was that the DIMPAC report failed to meet normal standards of scientific acceptability. Consequently, the APA decided that it would reject the report because of its unscientific character and it ordered the DIMPAC committee not to publish or circulate the report without indicating that APA had rejected it as being without scientific merit.[37]

This would seem to be a strong judgement on the unscientific status of Singer's brainwashing argument. Singer herself recognizes that this is so. As she complained in her *Miller v. Lifespring* deposition:

> I was so mad at them at that point because of the injustice and the sheer nonsense of it all that it is only within recent times that people are coming to see the impact broadly on legal testimony. It is as if the original amicus brief has been filed many months after the APA took their name off it. (Singer 1988a, 243)

Singer has a defense of the scientific stature of her position, however, even in the face of this devastating blow to its scientific credibility. She testified that APA's review process for the DIMPAC report was not legitimate because the reviewers lacked Singer's special expertise in the mental coercion research literature. Singer states that the reviewers

> are not competent to judge the whole area of undue influence, large group awareness trainings, thought reform, brainwashing. They are not experts in that whole area at all, and they just wrote pejorative reports, and they then from the APA office sent something back saying: your report has been rejected, and we are closing down the committee or something. (Singer 1988a, 243)[38]

What Singer is saying here is that APA's grounds for denying the scientific validity of her testimony, that is, poor methodology and conflict

with scholarly research on new religions, is not sufficient to invalidate
SMSPI because mental coercion research requires specialized expertise.
According to Singer, only someone who is intimately familiar with this
specialized area is competent to evaluate arguments within it.

These may be the assumptions behind Justice Mosk's eventual ruling
that granted Singer's position in the Molko and Leal case a degree of
scientific credibility. He seems to have decided that the arguments against
Singer's testimony raised in the APA amicus brief involved a dispute
between two equally reputable scholarly traditions, that is, mental coercion scholars such as Singer, Schein, Lifton, etc., on the one hand versus
experts on new religions per se on the other.

What has not been done, before the study reported in this article, is to
carefully evaluate Singer's argument in relation to the very mental coercion
research tradition that she claims supports her position. The results should
speak for themselves. Singer's claim of a special scientific expertise in
understanding conversion to the new religions, based upon her former
research upon mental coercion in the Korean War, turns out upon examination to be of no scientific or scholarly merit.

The Current Legal Situation: Robert Shapiro, in the best law-review
article to date upon the legal implications of the cult/brainwashing theory,
has argued that only a vision of a theory that maintains that a person has
totally lost the capacity to meaningfully form and evaluate religious or
political commitments has direct legal implications (Shapiro 1983). In other
words, according to Shapiro, a person must have ceased to be a person at
all and in effect have become a robot as the result of the proselytization
practices of new religions before those practices are legally actionable.

Mainstream mental coercion research such as that of Lifton or Schein
has no legal implications where physical coercion is not involved because
this research demonstrated that people subject to communist mental
coercion did not lose their capacity to meaningfully form and retain
religious or political commitments, that is, they did not become robots.
Consequently, Lifton explicitly argues against the use of his research for
legal purposes with respect to conflicts arising as the result of conversion
to the new religions. He states:

> From my perspective, then, cults are not primarily a psychiatric problem, but a
> social and historical issue. . . . I do not think that pattern is best addressed
> legally. . . . Not all moral questions are soluble legally or psychiatrically, nor
> should they be. I think psychiatrists and theologians have in common the need
> for a certain restraint here, to avoid playing God and to reject the notion that we
> have anything like a complete solution that comes from our points of view or
> our particular disciplines. (Lifton 1987, 218, 219)

Singer, on the other hand, has in her testimony in legal trials made Schein's and Lifton's research appear to be legally relevant only by covertly substituting for their arguments the cartoonlike brainwashing paradigm that their research explicitly evaluated and repudiated. What is most surprising and scandalous about this fact is that the courts, and the scientific and professional organizations upon whom the courts rely for advice in technical matters of this sort, have been letting her get away with the presentation in courts of law of simplistic concepts from the worlds of propaganda and science fiction as if they were serious scholarly arguments. That the courts would enable her to do this on a topic where constitutional protection of a basic freedom, that is, of religion, is at stake, and where the standard of evidence is supposedly higher, makes this lapse even more difficult to understand.

What is undeniable is that the result of this lapse on the part of the courts has been a serious and sustained curtailment of the religious freedom of the members of the various new religions. Singer's argument and courtroom testimony effectively prohibit religious rituals and practices so central to these movements that they could not dispense with them and retain their identities as religious entities. Moreover, the judgements for punitive damages in these cases have been so large that they put the very survival of these relatively small religious traditions at stake.

The Singer/Delgado cultic/brainwashing theory has clearly become the most effective weapon of religious prejudice in our history. While professional organizations such as the American Psychological Association and the Society for the Scientific Study of Religion have recently begun mobilizing against it, it is not clear at this time whether these activities have not been too little and too late to have substantial legal consequences. The Molko and Leal decision by the California Supreme Court has for the time being legitimated Singer's brainwashing theory as a scientific argument in California. This decision is presently being appealed to the U.S. Supreme Court. If it should be affirmed at that level it will likely have the force of law in our country for at least a generation as the Supreme Court is slow to reverse itself once it has made a definitive decision.

At least at this point, it looks as if the "brainwashing hoax" has been even more successful in its second career as a propaganda device than it was during its original heyday during the era of McCarthyism.

Notes

1. Dick Anthony has been for over a decade an outspoken critic of the use of "brainwashing" and allied concepts in legal actions against religious movements. (See: Anthony and Robbins 1978b, 1981; Anthony 1980; Anthony,

Robbins, and McCarthy 1980; Anthony, Robbins, and Schwartz 1983; Robbins and Anthony 1979a, 1980a, 1980b, 1980c, 1980d, 1980e, 1980f) and he has recently begun to serve as a consultant to lawyers representing several movements enmeshed in related litigation.

He has also published and continues to publish material that is critical of the ideas and practices of many new religious groups, including some groups that he is helping to defend against brainwashing litigation. See for instance, *Spiritual Choices* (Anthony, Ecker, and Wilber 1987), which provides a comprehensive overview of his research on the mental-health consequences of various types of new religions.

In his view, the civil liberties problem created by the use of the unscientific brainwashing argument, and its use to circumvent the constitutional separation of church and state, presents at least as great a challenge to religious and personal integrity in this country as do the practices of the groups that are being attacked. He believes that the appropriate corrective to religious excesses under our system of government is the give-and-take of dialogue and critique within the free marketplace of ideas rather than totalistic governmental control, in particular, governmental control based upon misleading and unscientific theories.

2. Singer supplied a list of cases in which she has testified in *Miller v. Lifespring* (Singer 1988b). She lists thirty-seven cases there but does not include pending cases in which she has already been listed with the court as an expert. She also acknowledges in her deposition in that case that in 1987 she spent at least twenty hours per week working as an expert in these cases (Singer 1988b).

In addition to her testimony in brainwashing cases, Singer, according to her own report, (Singer 1988a, 1:57–58, 1:69–75, 3:44–65) devotes much of the rest of her professional time as well to anticult activities. She holds no full-time academic appointment and her private psychotherapy practice is largely devoted to her own brand of specialized directive and supportive psychotherapy with ex–cult members. See Singer 1978, for a description of this specialized therapy. It seems primarily to consist of her discussion of her views on the evils of the cults with her clients. At least one ex-client described her counseling of him as "deprogramming," a term he uses not as criticism but as praise (Wollersheim 1985).

In addition, Singer is a very active participant in the activities of the various specific anticult organizations, for example, she serves on the board of advisors of the Cult Awareness Network, on the editorial board of the *Cultic Studies Journal,* on the board of advisors of the American Family Foundation, and she was on the board of directors of the now-defunct Human Freedom Center in Berkeley. She gives many talks on the effects of cults to the members of these organizations as well as serving on the inner councils that plan their activities. Sociological studies identify these organizations as the leading ones of the anticult movement (for example, Bromley and Shupe 1981) and identify Singer as one of the movement's three most influential leaders (for example, Richardson 1986:176).

When specifically questioned in legal settings, Singer acknowledges her participation in the activities of these anticult organizations (Singer 1988a, 1:57–58, 1:69–75, 3:44–65). However, she routinely denies any knowledge of the existence of the anticult movement per se and also denies membership in it. For instance, when she was asked if the American Family Foundation, an organization in whose affairs she is intimately involved, is an "anticult move-ment" organization, the following exchange occurred:

> A: I don't know what the anticult movement would consist of.
> Q: Well, you consider yourself a member of the anticult movement, do you not?
> A: No, I've never so designated myself (Singer 1988a, 1:58).

However, in spite of her professed ignorance of what the anticult movement "consists of," in a "confidential" report to the American Psychological Association, Singer knowledgeably discusses research by other scholars upon the effects of participation in the anticult movement on ex-members of the new religions (Singer et al. 1987, 22). In this report she uses the term "countercult" movement, rather than the term "anticult" that was used by the scholars whose articles she is discussing, and in spite of the fact that all the published scholarly descriptions of the movement use the term "anticult." Could her denial of any knowledge of the existence of the anticult movement, and of her own role within it, be based on nothing more than a private and unjustified preference for the alternative term?

Nevertheless, her professed ignorance of the anticult movement in her legal testimony, as opposed to her publications, seems suspiciously disingenuous and misleading. It contributes to the illusion in juries' minds that her testimony is that of a disinterested scientist rather than that of the activist leader of a social movement which has as its raison d'être the elimination of the religious groups about which she is testifying.

3. Surprisingly, we are obligated for this phrase, "the brainwashing hoax" to L. J. West, the senior author of Singer's primary theoretical publication on her cultic/brainwashing hypothesis (West and Singer 1980). In discussing the brain-washing theory of communist influence on Korean POWs, West, in later years, repeatedly acknowledged that this theory was a "hoax." In "Psychiatry, 'Brainwashing,' and the American Character" (1964), for instance, on p. 842 West refers to "the great 'brainwashing' hoax." At a later point in the same article, after describing the evidence invalidating the brainwashing paradigm, West states: "Thus, the 'brainwashing hoax' is conclusively refuted" (844). Elsewhere, West states: "Perhaps the most insidious domestic threat posed by the shibboleth of 'brainwashing' is the tendency of Americans to believe in its power and in our own weakness" (quoted in Scheflin and Opton 1978, 77).

4. "Brainwashing" is defined as "the forcible application of prolonged and intensive indoctrination sometimes including mental torture in an attempt to induce someone to give up basic political, social, or religious beliefs and attitudes and to accept contrasting regimented ideas" (Webster's 1981). According to Edward Hunter, the term "brainwashing" was derived from the Chinese phrase *hsi nao,* which literally means "cleansing the mind," and describes the process whereby the vestiges of the old order were washed away in the process of reeducation to assume one's proper role in the new communist order. Scholars, however, questioned this etymology and suggested that Hunter had coined the term for propaganda purposes. According to these scholars, the Chinese Communist program of reeducation was commonly referred to as *szu-hsiang kai-tsao,* which is variously translated as "ideological remolding,"

"ideological reform," or "thought reform" (Lunde and Wilson 1977, 341, 343 n. 6).

Hunter's career as a psychological warfare specialist who was a covert employee of the OSS and the CIA is well documented. See, for instance Scheflin and Opton (1978, 226–32) and their detailed establishment of this point on the basis of secret testimony before congressional committees. Scheflin and Opton state: "The facts surrounding Hunter's work strongly suggest that his popularization of the brainwashing concept was a part of his [CIA] job" (p. 227). In this connection, Walter Bowart, author of the book *Operation Mind Control* (1978) states unequivocally that "the word brainwashing and the official governmental explanation of what happened to the Korean POWs was propaganda."

Several histories of the brainwashing concept also contend that L. J. West, who helped to give Hunter's concept of communist brainwashing a brief illusion of scholarly acceptability (Farber, Harlow, and West 1957), was also employed by the CIA. Lee and Schlain (1985), for instance, state that West was a CIA "contract employee" (24) who did mind control research under its aegis and who later served as part of a "network of doctors and scientists who gathered intelligence for the CIA" on the popularization of LSD (25–26) as well as on the counterculture of the 1960s (189–90). (On West's employment by the CIA, see also Scheflin and Opton 1978, 149–50; Schrag, 1978, 5; and Huxley 1977, 131 and 186).

Parallels between the use of the brainwashing concept as a propaganda device for invalidating foreign ideologies in the cold war, anti-communist, and the counterculture new religions contexts are suggestive and intriguing. West, of course, is senior co-author of Margaret Singer's primary theoretical publication describing her cultic brainwashing thesis (West and Singer 1980).

5. Lifton's views on the undesirability of the term "brainwashing," and the mind-control model it stands for, have not changed. In a recent book he writes: "I do not use the term *brainwashing* because it has no precise meaning and has been associated with much confusion" (Lifton 1987, 211).

6. Singer has repeatedly claimed in her testimony that "brainwashing," "thought reform," and "coercive persuasion" are synonymous terms, for example:

> Q: In this term that equates to "brainwashing" that you have called "coercive persuasion," you didn't invent that term, did you?
> A: No, sir.
> Q: And you have seen where they are synonymous, one with the other?
> A: Yes. (Singer 1983, 5,140)

Furthermore, in the description, which Singer wrote, of Atypical Dissociative Disorder in the Diagnostic and Statistical Manual of the American Psychiatric Association (1980, 260), "brainwashing" is defined as synonymous with "coercive persuasion," "thought reform" and "indoctrination while the captive of terrorists or cultists." See note 22 below.

In her deposition in *Wollersheim v. Scientology* Singer was asked whether she really intended to say that these terms are equivalent when she wrote that description:

> Q: In that parenthetical phrase [in the description of Atypical Dissociation Disorder] are you using brainwashing, coercive persuasion, and thought reform interchangeably?

A: In that particular passage, its implied that they are interchangeable or at least closely related.

Q: In a more technical sense, does brainwashing—strike that—can brainwashing be distinguished from thought reform processes?

A: No, sir.

Q: In a more technical sense can coercive persuasion be distinguished from either brainwashing or thought reform?

A: Please read me that.

(The preceding question was read by the reporter.)

The Witness: No, sir. Not if you are totally familiar with what's implied in the correct usage of each of the terms. (Singer 1986a, 585, 586)

7. On the other hand, in her publications Singer has acknowledged that brainwashing's putative capacity to overwhelm the will, and the term "brainwashing" itself—which is closely linked to that supposed capacity in the public mind— are fallacious. She writes:

> "Brainwashing" is the least satisfactory of the common names for the [mind-control] phenomenon. It conjures up, at least for the non-professional reader, ideas of mindless automatons deprived of their capacity for decision-making. (Ofshe and Singer 1986, 20)

This quote raises the question: Why, if the term "brainwashing" is misleading for the nonspecialist because it implies the inaccurate stereotype of "mindless automatons" does Singer repeatedly state that the term is synonymous with more scholarly terms such as "coercive persuasion" or "thought reform" in her courtroom testimony when she is addressing a jury that is composed of such nonspecialists? One can only conclude that Singer *intends* to evoke the misleading stereotype of "mindless automatons" in the jury's mind, or at least to collaborate with the plaintiff's lawyer's attempt to evoke that stereotype.

8. Moreover, scholars argued that the brainwashing theory of coerced conversion to communism was a central, pseudoscientific, propaganda device of McCarthyism and other extremist forms of anticommunism, for example, the John Birch Society and the Christian Anticommunist Crusade, in the 1950s. As such its utilization as a weapon of political persecution was denounced by prominent scholars of the phenomenon at the time. Richard Hofstadter argued that the brainwashing argument was a symptom of what he called the "paranoid style" that characterizes social movements centered around the unjust persecution of individuals or groups for adherence to "false" doctrines. Hofstadter writers:

> The paranoid's interpretation of history is . . . distinctly personal: decisive events are not taken as part of the stream of history, but as the consequences of someone's will. Very often the enemy is held to possess some especially effective source of power: he controls the press; he directs the public mind through "managed news"; he has unlimited funds; he has a new secret for influencing the mind *(brainwashing);* he has a special technique for seduction (the Catholic confessional); he is gaining a stranglehold on the educational system.

> This enemy seems to be on many counts a projection of the self: both the ideal and the unacceptable aspects of the self are attributed to him. A fundamental paradox of the paranoid style is the imitation of the enemy. (1964, 32, emphasis ours)

Writing of this same phenomenon, Edgar Schein states:

> One of the most interesting aftermaths of the Korean conflict in 1950–1953 has been the preoccupation of many Americans with "brainwashing." The word itself has become popular as a term for all sorts of persuasion and, within the appropriate context, as an explanation for any behavior which we do not understand. . . . [W]e have begun to question where the limits of the integrity of the human mind lie, and increasingly to entertain concepts like "brainwashing" which express graphically our loss of confidence in our capacity as individuals to master our world. When things go wrong, it is far less ego-deflating to say that we have been brainwashed than to recognize our own inadequacy in coping with our problems. (1959, 430, 431)

Chodroff, another prominent scholar of communist mental coercion, states:

> At any rate, the intensity of the furor over brainwashing suggests public uneasiness, possibly due to the mobilization of conflicts over unacceptable feelings of powerlessness and dependency widespread in contemporary American life, as well as reaction formations and other defenses against such feelings. (1966, 386)

Moreover, Robert Lifton asserts that the "brainwashing" concept is "a rallying point for fear, resentment, urges toward submission, justification for failure, irresponsible accusation and for a wide gamut of emotional extremism" (Lifton 1961, 4). He criticized McCarthyism as a "bizarre blend of political religion and extreme opportunism" and asserted that it had "many uncomfortable resemblances" to the communist thought reform process "including most of the characteristics of ideological totalism" (Lifton 1961, 457).

Finally, Robbins and Anthony have noted that the anticult movement is merely the current expression of a recurrent type of antireligious movement in American history that they (following the historian David Brion Davis 1960) refer to as "counter-subversion movements." In the nineteenth century such movements attacked Catholics and Mormons, among others, and like the current anticult movement used mind-control theories as central persecutory rationales (Robbins and Anthony 1979a, esp. 83–86).

9. In all, 7,190 American servicemen were captured during the war. Of this figure, 2,730 died, 21 refused repatriation, and 11 were retained against their will by the communists, but were subsequently released (Secretary of Defense 1955, 78–81). Nearly 4,500 POWs survived the camps and were repatriated; of that number, the military questioned the conduct of 565 servicemen (25). Only 14 servicemen were ever tried by court-martial, and only 11 convictions were obtained (Lunde and Wilson 1977, 341, 343 n. 6).

10. See, for example, Biderman: "The popular political conception, particularly evident in discussions of the behavior of military prisoners, is that Communist doctrine per se is ego-alien, that it is fundamentally alien to human nature and social reality. The acceptance of Communist beliefs is consequently regarded as *ipso facto* evidence of insanity or a warped, evil personality, or both" (1962, 547, 560).

11. Surprisingly, in her publications as opposed to her trial testimony, Singer quite explicitly acknowledges that individual differences in predisposing motives

rather than the efficacy of proselytization strategies by new religious movements tend to determine who does or does not join. She states:

> [T]he individual's personality and actions play a significant role in his or her conversion. . . . In summary, it seems that the only confident conclusion one can draw from the many studies of religious cults is that a large variety of people join diverse groups for many reasons and are affected in different ways. (Singer et al. 1987, 26, 27)

In her publications, moreover, Singer describes the same "seeker" profile as characteristic of those who join the new religions that has been described by more neutral scholars:

> What to believe in, what to think, and what to do with one's self in relation to the world have been made specially difficult tasks for *certain young adults*. The cults' supposedly sublime principles and ultimate states of awareness offer clearcut, black-and-white answers to young adults who are *seeking* relief from many age-appropriate developmental crises in a period of history characterized by philosophical relativism and rapid sociological and technical changes. The disillusions, revolutions, and upheavals in families, governments and societies in recent years have seemingly made *certain persons more vulnerable than others to the lure of the cults*. (Singer 1978, 16, emphasis ours)

Singer even acknowledges that family conflicts *precede* and motivate the convert's religious seeking rather than *being caused* by the cults as she testifies in these trials: "Some families foster a combination of indecisiveness and rebelliousness that makes the cult seem like a perfect solution (West and Singer 1980, 3,250).

12. In her publications, Singer acknowledges that coercive persuasion, strictly speaking, requires physical coercion. She states: "As generally used 'coercive persuasion' connotes a substantial reliance on physical abuse and imprisonment" (Ofshe and Singer 1986). See also note 17 below wherein Singer describes the same continuum of influence, with physical coercion defining the extreme end, as that described by Lifton and Schein.

As indicated above, however, in her trial testimony Singer repeatedly contends that the use of thought reform on Chinese civilians who were not imprisoned during the process demonstrates that thought reform does not always require physical coercion (e.g., Singer 1983, 5,520). This would seem to indicate that Singer believes that the scholars who originally did research on communist thought reform interpret the thought reform of unimprisoned Chinese civilians as an exception to the general rule that thought reform requires physical coercion. (Robert Lifton, for instance devotes a substantial portion of his major work on thought reform to an account of the thought reform of Chinese civilians who were, for the most part, not formally imprisoned during the process [1964, pt. 3, 243–399])

The obvious problem with this interpretation of Lifton's and other thought reform scholars' research, however, is that Communist China has no tradition of civil liberties or free speech, in fact quite the reverse. Ideological conformity is mandated by the state and dissent is punished by imprisonment or worse.

(The recent massacre of hundreds and perhaps thousands of student dissidents in Tiananmen Square, as well as the order that soldiers should summarily execute any remaining protesters on the spot, is a vivid reminder that physical pressures to conform still enforce ideological uniformity in China.) The Chinese civilians studied by Lifton and other scholars were clearly aware that physical coercion was the bottom line reality behind "requests" that they participate in thought reform reeducation processes.

In this connection, Robert Lifton has expressed himself very clearly on the issue of whether physical coercion was an intrinsic part of the thought reform of Chinese civilians. He states: "it was the combination of *external force or coercion with an appeal to inner enthusiasm through evangelistic exhortation* which gave thought reform [of Chinese civilians] its emotional scope and power" (1964, 13, emphasis in original).

In her publications, as opposed to her trial testimony, Singer acknowledges quite explicitly that physical coercion was an intrinsic part of the thought reform of formally unimprisoned civilians in China. She states: "In non-prison settings, participation was usually obtained without having to resort to physical abuse, although *it was often obtained from persons knowing that imprisonment was a possible consequence of resistance*" (Ofshe and Singer 1986, 7). (One wonders about the identities of the civilians who were, Singer imagines, naive enough *not* to have known "that imprisonment was a possible consequence of resistance"? Hermits in caves? Children who hadn't yet learned to speak?) Furthermore, in describing the differences between the conversion processes in new religions and the thought reform of Chinese civilians, Singer states:

> We term as "second generation of interest" those examples of coercive influence and behavior control programs which are currently creating public concern [i.e., cults]. They can be distinguished from "first generation" programs [i.e. thought reform of Chinese civilians] in several ways. One of the significant differences is that the organizations and residential communities within which [cult] programs are carried out *lack the power of the State to command participation. Further, they lack the right of the State to back demands for compliance and conformity with the use of force.* This results in a radically different method of generating the initial involvement of targets with "second generation" organization. (Ofshe and Singer 1986, 9, emphasis ours)

Singer could hardly be more unequivocal in contradicting her own testimony that the thought reform of civilians in Communist China did not involve physical coercion. Furthermore, she acknowledges that the *"lack"* of "the use of force" in the new religions' recruitment processes "results in a *radically different method* of generating the initial involvement of targets" (emphasis ours) in the new religions as compared to the thought reform of formally unimprisoned Chinese civilians. But in her testimony, she had contended that it was the ostensible similarity of the lack of physical force in the recruitment processes between both the formally unimprisoned Chinese civilians and cults that established the possibility that the cults were using thought reform for the purpose of recruitment. Again we are struck with the remarkable disparity between the views Singer expresses in her testimony and those she expresses in her publications.

13. In this article, we are emphasizing the conflicts of Singer's views with Lifton's and Schein's because they are generally considered the most authoritative experts on communist mental coercion, and Singer repeatedly claims that her paradigm of cultic brainwashing, SMSPI, is based primarily upon the results of their research. However, the other leading researchers on the phenomenon generally agree with Lifton and Schein, and consequently disagree with Singer's testimony, on the issue of physical coercion as well as on the other points to which we are referring. On the issue of physical coercion being essential for coercive persuasion see for instance Somit (1968, 139–40) and Chodroff (1966, 387–92). Even L. J. West, Singer's collaborator on her cultic brainwashing theory (West and Singer 1980) has argued elsewhere that physical coercion is essential for brainwashing (West 1976, 250; Farber, Harlow, and West 1957, 272, 273–4).

    Scheflin and Opton, in the most complete contemporary book on mind control, sum up this research on the role of physical coercion in defining coercive persuasion by stating:

    > Brainwashing exists only when a person has been compelled to believe *subjectively* a set of principles originally alien to him. Furthermore, the means used to accomplish this change must have been aggressive or violent. Otherwise any successful attempt at persuasion, such as education or advertising, would be brainwashing. (1978, 85–86, emphasis in original)

14. In his table summarizing essential features of the coercive-persuasion process in China (1961), Schein lists: "Physical pain induced by prolonged standing or squatting in cell or during interrogation; Physical pain and injury due to wearing of manacles and chains; Physical pain due to prevention by authorities of defecation except at two 2-minute intervals during the day; Cuffing and beating by cellmates, occasionally by interrogator (p. 125); Threats of death, of non-repatriation, of endless isolation and interrogation, of torture and physical injury, of injury to family and loved ones—induction of anxiety and despair" (p. 127).

15. Lifton asserted that *both* physical force and psychological techniques were required for true thought reform to occur. He states:

    > [I]t was the *combination* of external force or coercion with an appeal to inner enthusiasm through evangelistic exhortation which gave thought reform its emotional scope and power. (1961, 13, emphasis ours)

    Lifton's research demonstrated that thought reform is essentially a process of forcing compliance to the wishes of the captors through the use of extreme physical threat, rather than a process of actual conversion to new political or religious opinions:

    > Thought reform succeeded with all Westerners in the first of its aims, the extraction of an incriminating personal confession, because *it made this confession a requirement for survival*. It fell far short of its more ambitious goal of converting Westerners into enthusiastic Communist adherents; for although none could avoid being profoundly influenced, virtually all prison-

ers showed a general tendency to revert to what they had been before prison, or at least to a modified version of their previous identity. (1961, 150)

Lifton *repeatedly* makes the claim that true thought reform requires extreme physical threat. For instance, he states that the "dominant message" of the thought reform milieu is "only those who confess can survive" (1961, 74).
        Finally, Lifton also considers physical incarceration a requirement for true thought reform.

In thought reform, coercion is greatest during the early stages *of the prison process;* but it is an essential ingredient of all varieties of thought reform and of all phases, however much it may temporarily be shunted to the background. (1961, 439, emphasis ours).

16. In the recent case of *United States v. Kozminski* (1987), the Sixth Circuit Court of Appeals squarely addressed the question of "involuntary conversion" by psychological coercion in a federal prosecution for involuntary servitude under 18 U.S.C. 1584. The government's expert witness, Dr. Harley Stock, attempted to establish the government's case by "incorporating the well-established [theory] of 'captivity syndrome' " (1,194).

According to Dr. Stock, "captivity syndrome" has ten necessary features: "(1) Prolonged captivity; (2) continuous around-the-clock supervision, such as guarding; (3) an isolated environment; (4) removal of all supports; (5) an attack on personality; (6) a lack of privacy; (7) assault upon the total personality; (8) a systematic use of reward and punishment; (9) a tearing of the fabric of the personality; and (10) the building up of a new personality." (1,194)

In ruling such testimony inadmissible, the court noted:

This testimony was offered to show that Fulmer and Molitoris were the victims of psychological coercion and had been "brainwashed" into serving the Kozminskis. This evidence is inadmissible because a foundation was not laid to establish its conformity to a generally accepted explanatory theory. (1,194)

17. Amazingly, in a secret publication Singer affirms the same continuum of influence described by Lifton, Schein, and other authoritative researchers. The Report of the Task Force on Deceptive and Indirect Techniques of Persuasion and Control (DIMPAC REPORT) (Singer et al. 1987) is a report to the American Psychological Association of which Singer is the senior author. It is stamped "confidential" on its title page and has never been publicly released. (See the concluding section of this chapter.)
        The report states: "The threat of physical coercion found in Korean War brainwashing is rarely present in cult conversions. . . . Brainwashing represents one end of a continuum of influence [defined by physical coercion]" (26). At a later point she explains: "On one extreme of the continuum lie nondirective techniques, such as reflection and clarification. On the other [brainwashing] extreme we find physical restraint and punishment and pressured public confes-

sions'' (48). In a table on a later page designated the "Continuum of Influence" she divides this continuum into four types of increasingly coercive influence: (1) Educative/Therapeutic; (2) Advisory/Therapeutic; (3) Persuasive/Manipulative; (4) Controlling/Destructive (66). The specific techniques of influence are grouped under the four categories of increasing coercion with "brainwashing" being represented by the fourth and most coercive category. Again we find "physical restraint/punishment" as one of the techniques required for a group to fall under the brainwashing category.

18. Conditioning theory was the dominant theoretical position in academic psychology at the time that the brainwashing theory of communist mental coercion was formulated. Conditioning theory was also known as "behaviorism." It was closely associated with logical positivism, the dominant orientation in the philosophy of science at that time. Conditioning theory's main emphases were: (1) human beings have no unique qualities relative to animals. Consequently most of the research done on conditioning was done on rats; (2) determinism: free will is an illusion; (3) human behavior is totally controlled on the basis of external stimuli; internal mental and emotional processes are illusory: they have no true existence and no truly causal effect on behavior (Zuriff 1985).

19. Singer has acknowledged that she is primarily indebted to L. J. West for SMSPI (Singer 1986b). At the time that Singer was originally collaborating on mental coercion research with Schein after the Korean War, West was also conducting research on mental coercion with his collaborators Farber and Harlow. Unlike Schein and Singer's research, however, which utilized concepts from clinical and social psychology, Farber, Harlow, and West employed a version of the robot brainwashing paradigm focused around conditioning theory.

West is the coauthor of Singer's only substantial academic publication on brainwashing in cults (West and Singer 1980). Strangely, however, that article mentions neither the DDD paradigm nor SMSPI, its contemporary expression, even though Singer had been using that paradigm for some time as the primary framework for her testimony in court cases when she and West wrote the article. Undoubtedly, West and Singer are too academically sophisticated to use an outmoded mental coercion argument based on conditioning principles in a publication subject to scrutiny and critique by their peers, which, of course, raises the question of why Singer uses an outmoded conditioning argument to influence a technically unsophisticated audience unlikely to recognize its obvious flaws from an academic point of view, that is, juries, when she does not use the same argument for an audience competent to recognize its limitations.

20. Schein referred to brainwashing theories that heavily emphasized the role of physical mistreatment as psychophysiological stress theories (1961, 199–211). Debilitation, on the other hand, was the term for psychophysiological stress used by one specific brainwashing theory, the DDD paradigm of Farber, Harlow, and West (1957), that served as the most direct influence on Singer's SMSPI model. Consequently, Singer utilizes the term "debilitation" rather than the phrase psychophysiological stress.

21. In her publications, also, Singer contends that belief in new religious doctrines constitutes "primitive thought" (Singer 1978, 14). As with the other themes of SMSPI, Singer's contention here is the same as that made by Farber, Harlow, and West. They argue that Korean War brainwashing was based on "*primitivization* in language, thought, and those integrative and mediating symbolic

processes essential to reasoning and foresight" and involves an "impoverish-ment of thinking" (1957, 275, emphasis ours). Farber, Harlow, and West also contend that brainwashing involves "the collapse of certain ego functions" and compare the brainwashed state to "post-lobotomy syndrome," to "a distur-bance of association and a concreteness of thinking similar to that sometimes seen in schizophrenia," and to the condition of "brain-damaged individuals" (1957, 275).

22. According to Singer's deposition testimony in *Wollersheim v. Scientology* (1986a, 585, 586), Singer wrote the description of atypical dissociative disorder and approved its final wording after editing. The full text of this "residual category" is:

> This is a residual category to be used for individuals who appear to have a Dissociative Disorder but do not satisfy the criteria for a specific Dissociative Disorder. Examples include trance-like states, derealization unaccompanied by depersonalization, and those more prolonged dissociated states that may occur in persons who have been subjected to periods of prolonged and intense coercive persuasion (brainwashing, thought reform, and indoctrina-tion while the captive of terrorists or cultists). (American Psychiatric Asso-ciation 1980, 260)

Note that Singer equates the term "brainwashing" therein with the terms "coercive persuasion" and "thought reform."

23. Singer herself has not published on hypnosis per se and so is not really an authority on the subject in a theoretical sense. However, she has a great practical interest and experience in using it and in teaching its use to would-be therapists. L. J. West, coauthor of the Cults and Quacks article (West and Singer 1980) is also an enthusiastic practitioner of hypnosis.

24. Chaplin's *Dictionary of Psychology* describes hypnosis as: "a sleeplike state induced artificially by a hypnotist and characterized by greatly heightened suggestibility" (1985, 216). Suggestion in turn is defined as "the process of inducing another to behave according to one's wishes or uncritically to accept one's wishes without the use of force or coercion (455).

25. This quote perfectly illustrates Singer's negative evaluation of chanting, the central Hare Krishna religious practice. She explicitly states that dissociation is an intrinsic, inextricable part of the practice: "She no longer does the chanting, but that part of the chanting, the spacing away from and not thinking and not reflecting, turns on now." Thus, there is no possibility that the Hare Krishna movement could avoid deceptive mental coercion, in her view, and go on with their religion. In the Hare Krishna worldview, this chanting is the very heart of their religion, the means whereby the transformation of consciousness occurs that results in awareness of the experienced data that grounds their doctrines as a form of knowledge.

26. Schein argues that abnormal suggestibility is the root allegation in the brain-washing paradigm because it amounts to a simple semantic variation on the allegation of defective thought. Abnormal suggestibility as the root allegation in brainwashing, then, gets linked to more specific allegations such as condi-tioning, debilitation, and dissociation in constructing the full-fledged brain-washing argument. However, Schein found in his research that abnormal suggestibility played no part in whatever influence occurred. He states:

The psychophysiological stresses entered into the unfreezing process in generally lowering the prisoner's resistance, but the assumption is not tenable, in our opinion, that such lowering of resistance is equivalent to the production of a state of uncriticalness and high suggestibility. The most that could be said is that these stresses facilitated unfreezing and the induction of a motive to change. But the prisoner could not be said at this time to have been mentally incapable of exercising critical judgement (though it might have seemed that way to him retrospectively). On the contrary, in some cases the prisoner gained in such a crisis situation some very clear notions and insights concerning himself and his total situation (Schein 1961, 202).

27. Elsewhere in the same article Schein states:

If we find similar methods being used by the Communists and by some of our own institutions of change, we have a dilemma, of course. Should we then condemn our own methods because they resemble brainwashing? I prefer to think that the Communists have drawn on the same reservoir of human wisdom and knowledge as we have, but have applied this wisdom to achieve goals which we cannot condone. These same techniques in the service of different goals, however, may be quite acceptable to us. (Schein 1962, 90)

28. Such a dissolution of her distinction between coerced conduct and false belief is typical and can be found throughout her writings and testimony. For instance, she states that

the person doesn't realize and doesn't have as a concept or construct in their thinking the idea that they are being subjected to an orchestrated and designed program to change their *conduct,* and eventually change their expressed *behavior,* and eventually change their expressed *opinions and values.* (Singer 1985a, 237, emphasis ours)

29. Other leading anticult-movement psychotherapists who are associated with Singer echo her objections to cults as involving belief in false doctrines. John Clark serves with Singer on the editorial board of the *Cultic Studies Journal.* He states: "Seekers . . . are trying to restore themselves to some semblance of comfort in a fresh, though *false,* reality (Clark 1977, 3, emphasis ours).

L. J. West is coauthor with Singer of two publications on cultic brainwashing (West and Singer 1980; Singer et al. 1987). He states: "Cults are as much a perversion of the *meaning* of religion as the quack is a perversion of the *meaning* of the medical oath" (West 1982, 13, emphasis ours).

Surely, any doubt that Singer and her cohort are engaged in an evaluation of the general truth or falsity of these religious doctrines cannot survive familiarity with these quotes.

30. The reader should not be misled by Singer's use of the term "authoritarian" in this passage to characterize the grounds for her antipathy to the new religions. She is not using the term in a technically precise way (for example, as in *The Authoritarian Personality,* Adorno et al. 1950) to refer to extreme or clinically deviant attitudes to authority. She has testified that her use of the term "authoritarian" vis-à-vis religious groups is not based on any generally ac-

cepted scholarly research, literature, or methodology, and she was unable even to name any textbooks that could provide the basis for a scholarly use of the term (Singer 1985a, 31). She also testified that according to her definition of the term, the Roman Catholic Church is an "authoritarian organization" (180). (She claims that her knowledge of the nature of the Catholic Church is based on her experience as a member of the church during her childhood, although she has not participated in its activities since her youth.) Apparently, in her mind, any religious tradition with a substantial emphasis upon religious rituals and the religious experiences resulting from their use is thereby to be considered "authoritarian."

31. When Singer complains of cult converts' migration from one "world" (that of science) to another (that of magic and primitive thinking), surely it is the transformation in their world*views,* i.e., their *beliefs* about the world, about which she is complaining and not merely of a change in their *conduct.* Moreover, Singer was able to comprehend the unfortunate character of this transition between viewpoints "as they [the cults] sprang up" and this evaluation thus motivated rather than resulted from her research on these groups.

When she asked the question "what were the processes that explain the phenomena," she had already decided that the phenomena that needed explaining were widespread conversions from a good worldview to primitive ones. By her own account, then, her opposition to the worldviews of the cults preceded rather than resulted from her eventual scientific discovery that the transition in their converts' viewpoints had resulted from their having been brainwashed. Consequently, her testimony in these cases, that she is indifferent to the *content* of cultic religious beliefs and that her opposition to cults has resulted solely from her research having demonstrated the coercive manner of the *transmission* of those beliefs, would seem to have been contradicted by the above quotation.

32. Positivism began in the nineteenth century as a movement, in philosophy and the human sciences, that argued that human intellectual and social development is progressing through three stages: the theological, the metaphysical, and the positivist or scientific. In the theological period, which lasted from the beginning of history through the end of the middle ages, humanity was guided in personal and social life primarily by religion. In the metaphysical period, which lasted until the dawn of positivism in the early nineteenth century, humanity was guided by rationality of a general philosophical or metaphysical type and the sphere of religion was greatly reduced. In the positivist period, which began in the nineteenth century and is to stretch on indefinitely into a glorious future, we are to be guided in every sphere by the sciences, especially the human sciences. Religion in a supernatural sense is to completely disappear in the positivist period (Becker and Barnes 1961).

In psychology, the positivist philosophy of history reached its fullest expression in conditioning theory, also known as behaviorism, the theoretical orientation upon which Singer's SMSPI paradigm, like other brainwashing arguments, is based. (For an excellent discussion of the relationship between positivism and conditioning theory, or behaviorism, see "Positivism, Realism, and Behaviorist Psychology," Mackenzie 1977.) American behaviorism originated very explicitly as a critique of and replacement for evangelical Christianity with its heavy experiential emphasis and its focus on the conversion experience. (See Fuller 1986, chapter 6, and Cohen 1979, chapter 1 for discussions of the antagonism of behaviorism towards evangelical Christianity.) To the behaviorist, evangelical Christianity is more offensive than the more secularized and rationalized forms of religion because it is more heavily influenced by affective, subjective processes. The behaviorist believes that intense religious experiences tend to be based upon semiconscious emotions, which are more "primitive" than the scientific rationality which is the optimum guide in human affairs. In an excellent chapter summarizing the conflict between behaviorism and evangelical Christianity in America, Robert C. Fuller writes:

> Behaviorism was in fact as much a crusade as it was a science, and foremost among the outmoded institutions it sought to replace was [evangelical] religion. (Fuller 1986, 138)

We can see, then, that for Singer, with her positivist and behaviorist commitments, the uprush of interest in the new religions in the 1960s, with their heavily experiential emphasis, appeared to be a socially regressive phenomenon. Rather than relying on science in general and psychology in particular for the guidance of human life, young people who were the cream of the crop with respect to their social and academic backgrounds were turning to the evangelical Christianity and Oriental religions that she believes involve immersion in a "world of magic and primitive thinking" (Singer 1978, 14).

33. Positivism in American social and behavioral science has frequently been associated with the "idea of progress" and with a chauvinistic form of American patriotism that regards the United States as at the apex of world history (Nisbet 1980, chap. 8). Although explicitly repudiating American Puritan traditions that emphasized the importance of religious conversion in subdividing humanity into the elect and the damned, positivistic social science has tended to merely replace religion with science in planning for the establishment of the United States as a "new Israel," the fulfillment of a utopian vision of a materialistic heaven on earth. According to Vidich and Lyman, positivistic social scientists

> sought substitutes for the . . . theologies of Puritanism . . . and set about the task of providing moral underpinnings to [*laissez faire*] economic ideology, which would mean ordering society within the framework of a *progressive evolutionary schema* and coping with its diversity by supplying rationales *for the existence of morally inferior economic actors, races, and ethnic groups.* Firmly believing that the destiny of American civilization rested on the superiority of its moral character, [positivistic social scientists] set out to rationalize the earlier Puritan conception of the elect. Included in [the positivist's] theory is the notion *that this character had to be protected from morally inferior groups in the society.* (1985, 77, emphasis ours)

One of the major premises of behaviorist theory is the notion that the person is a totally empty vessel into which surrounding social groups may pour any content they wish. According to Vidich and Lyman, J. B. Watson "claimed that if behaviorist behavior scientists were given control over socialization of children and authority to design the *entire social environment,* they could construct utopia" (1985, 97, emphasis ours). In this regard Watson states:

Give me a dozen healthy infants, well-formed, and *my own specified world* to bring them up in and I'll guarantee to take any one at random and train him to become any kind of specialist I might select—doctor, lawyer, artist, merchant, chief and, yes, even beggar-man and thief, regardless of his talents, penchants, tendencies, abilities, vocations, and race of his ancestors. ([1924] 1970, 104, emphasis ours)

The behaviorist notion of the total passivity of the human organism relative to influence by the social environment suggests both great peril and great promise depending on the evolutionary stature of surrounding groups. Watson claimed that social conditioning could just as easily create beggars and thieves as doctors, lawyers, merchants or chiefs. For the behaviorist, then, it is important that the ideological climate surrounding the organism be homogeneous with respect to its evolutionary level. Watson promised to create utopia only if he could totally control social conditioning within "my own specified world." We can see, then, that for Singer, with her positivist and behaviorist commitments, the uprush of interest in the new religions in the 1960s, with their heavily experiential—and thus, for her, irrational—emphasis, appeared to be not only a socially regressive phenomenon, but also a horribly seductive influence from which, like addictive drugs, young people must be protected at all costs.

From the positivist viewpoint, cultures such as those of the Far East that have, until recently at least, not been in the forefront of scientific and technological progress, are mentally, morally, and religiously inferior to the culture of the United States. (Such ethnocentric prejudice relative to Oriental culture has traditionally been very widespread in the United States [Said 1978]; it has presented very real problems not only to immigrants from Asian countries but also with respect to its use to justify Western imperialistic practices in the Asian nations themselves [Pannikar 1965].) Imagine Singer's horror, therefore, when the primitive philosophies of such backward nations began to seduce substantial percentages of American youth into the Oriental world of magic and primitive thinking.

Given the behaviorist's belief in the necessity of an ideologically uniform environment if utopia is to be achieved, in Singer's mind the responsibility for their converts' regression from the category of the elect to the category of the damned belongs totally to the exotic new religions rather than to the helpless victims who are attracted to them. Within the totalist worldview, error has no rights. (Robert Lifton, himself, has criticized the positivist worldview as "totalist" [1964, 382 and 458–62].) After all, Singer seems to be saying, if these primitive foreign religions hadn't come here in the first place, our young people wouldn't be converting to them, would they?

34. By referring to Margaret Singer's argument as one involving religious prejudice I by no means intend to imply that all critical evaluations of religion from the standpoint of psychology or the other human sciences are prejudiced. On the contrary, I believe that the human sciences have a very useful role to play in aiding people to choose between competing religious alternatives in a religiously pluralistic society and in helping religious organizations to evolve in a positive direction. Indeed, I have spent the last twenty years doing research evaluating the mental-health consequences of involvement in the various new religions with precisely these aims in mind. See *Spiritual Choices* for the most

complete summary of this research (Anthony, Ecker, and Wilber 1987). Interestingly, *Spiritual Choices* received a very positive review in *Cultic Studies Journal,* the most prestigious periodical of the anticult movement (Brauns 1988). Singer serves on the editorial board of this journal. Apparently even Singer's cohort agrees that my research on the mental health consequences of the new religions is of practical utility to prospective converts.

This does not mean, on the other hand, that evaluations of religion that claim the mantle of psychology or the other human sciences automatically are free from normal human ethical obligations, for example, the obligation to be unprejudiced when encountering racial or religious diversity. A prominent dictionary of psychology defines prejudice as "an attitude, either positive or negative, formulated in advance of sufficient evidence and held with emotional tenacity." (This description is usefully expanded in the section on the definition of prejudice in Gordon Allport's landmark study, *The Nature of Prejudice,* 1958, 6–10).

To be unprejudiced in the religious sphere, then, does not mean to refrain from evaluating religious positions but rather that such evaluations be based upon adequate empirical examination conducted, initially at least, in a spirit of honest and open curiosity about the phenomenon at issue. Critical evaluations of religion in psychology and the human sciences must earn the right to be considered unprejudiced through the caliber of the empirical research upon which they are based. By this standard Singer's testimony in anticult brainwashing trials clearly reflects religious prejudice rather than scientific objectivity.

In addition, because of the global and ineffable nature of the experiential data upon which religious doctrines are based, a researcher who would avoid religious bigotry would do well to present even the results of properly conducted research in a spirit of dialogue rather than a spirit of authoritarian condescension. No one automatically deserves the last word in conversations about religion simply because of disciplinary or professional status. I believe that researchers on religious positions from the standpoints of the various human sciences have at least as much to learn in a general human sense from proponets of the positions they are evaluating as vice versa. The spirit of Singer's encounter with the new religions clearly conflicts with this point of view.

35. The Society for the Scientific Study of Religion (SSSR) submitted an amicus curiae brief in the *George v. Krishna* appeal before the California Court of Appeal. It argued that Singer's testimony should have been forbidden by the trial court because of its unscientific nature. The brief is based primarily upon an as yet unfinished book-length manuscript by the present author that had been reviewed by a committee appointed by the executive council of SSSR.

The SSSR brief contains a less elaborate version of the argument in the present article as well as brief sections reviewing: (1) the methodological problems with Singer's "research" for SMSPI, (2) the conflicts of SMSPI with most research on the new religions (James Richardson drafted this section); (3) the conflicts of Singer's diagnostic testimony with the criteria specified by the American Psychiatric Association's *Diagnostic and Statistical Manual III* (1980).

The author would like to thank James Richardson, Thomas Robbins, and David Liberman for their substantial help in translating a long and complex argument into the brief forms found in the SSSR amicus brief and in this article. The members of the SSSR executive council also helped to shape the argument for its presentation in a legal context in the amicus brief. As is usual in such cases, whatever is valuable about this argument owes much to the input provided by others while the defects remain my own.

36. The APA released a letter giving its reasoning for this decision. It emphasized that it was not recanting the opinions expressed in the brief but only refraining from making this position definitive until BSERP had had a chance to evaluate the DIMPAC report for scientific acceptability. The full text of the APA's motion follows:

Motion of the American Psychological
Association to Withdraw as Amicus Curiae

On February 10, 1987, the American Psychological Association ("APA") joined with numerous behavioral and social scientists, as individual *amici*, in submitting a brief *amicus curiae* in the above-captioned case. Since that time, it has come to the attention of APA's Board of Directors that one of its constituent Boards had, previous to that date, established a task force to study the issues addressed in the *amicus* brief. That task force has not yet reached any final conclusions.

Accordingly, the Board of Directors now believes it was premature, for organizational reasons, to endorse the positions taken in the *amicus* brief prior to completion of the task force study. For this reason, and because the APA review process will take some time to complete, APA respectfully moves this Court to withdraw as signatory of the *amicus* brief rather than risk delay in the adjudication of this case.

By this action, APA does not mean to suggest endorsement of any views opposed to those set forth in the *amicus* brief. Nor does APA mean to suggest that it will not ultimately be able to subscribe to the views expressed in the brief.

Additionally, in this motion APA does not speak for the individuals who are co-signers of the brief, they continue to participate as *amici,* and their endorsement of the positions taken in the *amicus* brief remains unaffected. This motion does not withdraw the brief; it merely withdraws APA's participation as an *amicus.*

APA regrets any inconvenience its motion may cause this Court.
Dated: March 27, 1987
Los Angeles, California

37. The American Psychological Association released a memo on May 11, 1987, from its Board of Social and Ethical Responsibility addressed to Singer's DIMPAC committee. It stated:

BSERP thanks the Task Force on Deceptive Methods of Persuasion and Control for its service but is unable to accept the report of the Task Force. In general, the report lacks the scientific rigor and evenhanded critical approach necessary for APA imprimatur.

The report was carefully reviewed by two external experts and two members of the Board. They independently agreed on the significant deficiencies in the report. The reviews are enclosed for your information.

The Board cautions the Task Force members against using their past appointment to imply BSERP or APA support or approval of the positions advocated in the report. BSERP requests that Task Force members not distribute or publicize the report without indicating that the report was unacceptable to the Board.

38. Note that again Singer takes it for granted that "brainwashing" and "thought reform" are synonyms, even though in the very same deposition she had denied that she ever does so on her own volition.

References

Adorno, T. W., Else Frenkel-Brunswik, Daniel J. Levinson, and R. Nevitt Sanford, 1950
Allport, Gordon, 1958
American Psychiatric Association, 1980
Anthony, Dick, 1980
Anthony, Dick, and Thomas Robbins, 1978b, 1981
Anthony, Dick, Thomas Robbins, and James McCarthy, 1980
Anthony, Dick, Thomas Robbins, and Paul Schwartz, 1983
Anthony, Dick, Bruce Ecker, and Ken Wilber, 1977
Barker, Eileen V., 1984
Becker, Howard, and Harry Elmer Barnes, 1961
Biderman, Albert, 1962
Bowart, Walter, 1978
Brauns, Timothy, 1988
Bromley, David G., and Anson D. Shupe, 1981
Campbell, Robert J., 1981
Chaplin, J., 1985
Chodroff, Paul, 1966
Clark, John, 1977
Cohen, David, 1979
Coleman, John, 1984
Davis, David Brion, 1960
Delgado, Richard, 1977, 1979–80, 1982, 1984
Ecker, Dick Anthony, and Thomas Robbins, forthcoming
Ellenberger, Henre F., 1970
Fuller, Robert R., 1986
Farber, I. E., H. F. Harlow and L. J. West, 1957
Fuller, Robert C., 1986
Hofstadter, Richard, 1964
Hunter, Edward, 1951, 1960
Huxley, Aldous, 1958, 1977
James, Gene G., 1986
Katz v. Superior Court, 1977
Kropansky in United States v. Kozminski, 1987
Lee, Martin, and Bruce Schlain, 1985
Lifton, Robert J., 1957, 1961, 1976, 1987
Lunde and Wilson, 1977

Mackenzie, Brian D., 1977
Merloo, Joost A. M., 1956
Molko and Leal v. Holy Spirit Association, 1988
Nisbet, Robert, 1980
Ofshe, Richard, and Margaret Singer, 1986
Pannikar, K. M., 1965
Reich, Walter, 1976
Richardson, James, 1986
Richardson, James, 1988
Richardson, James T., and Brock Kilbourne, 1983
Robbins, Thomas, and Dick Anthony, 1979a, 1979b, 1980a, 1980b, 1980c, 1980d, 1980e, 1980f, 1981a, 1981b
Said, Edward W., 1979
Saliba, Edward, 1985
Sargent, William, 1957, 1974
Scheflin, Alan, and Edward M. Opton, 1978
Schein, Edgar, 1958, 1959, 1960, 1961, 1962
Schrag, Peter, 1978
Secretary of Defense, 1955
Shapiro, Robert, 1983
Singer, Margaret, 1978, 1983, 1984, 1985a, 1985b, 1986a, 1986b, 1988a, 1988b, 1988c
Singer, Margaret Thaler, Harold Goldstein, Michael D. Langone, Jesse S. Miller, Maurice K. Temerlin, and Louis J. West, 1987
Somit, Albert, 1968
United States v. Kozminski, 1987
Vidich, Arthur J., and Stanford M. Lyman, 1985
Watson, John B., 1924 (1970)
Webster's Third New International Dictionary, 1981
West, Louis J., 1964, 1976, 1982
West, Louis J., and Margaret Singer, 1980
Wollersheim, Larry, 1985
Zuriff, G. E., 1985

V
RELIGIOUS FERMENT AND THE ASPIRATIONS OF WOMEN

17

Women-Church: Catholic Women Produce an Alternative Spirituality

Diana Trebbi

Introduction

The first document produced by the Second Vatican Council of the Catholic Church, the *Dogmatic Constitution on the Church,* presents a profound revision of the self-understanding of the church. In chapter 2, the church is defined as "the People of God," in line with council members' desire to emphasize the human and communal aspects of the church, rather than the institutional or hierarchical aspects. This new ecclesial pronouncement had the effect of raising the social expectations of groups previously understood as subject to hierarchical control: notably, laypersons, including all members of religious orders who did not possess the status of clergy.

Perhaps the most radical result of the social ferment spawned among groups of Catholics after the council of 1963–65 is the Catholic women's movement. Spurred on by the secular women's movement developing concurrently in the United States of the 1960s, Catholic feminists emerged for the first time as an identifiable group in the United States. Today, the coalition known as Women-Church includes a large proportion of Catholic feminists among its leadership and membership. A correct understanding of Women-Church requires some historical background of developments that preceded its emergence in the United States of the 1980s.

The Question of Women Priests

In 1975, the Detroit Conference on Women's Ordination spawned a new current among Catholic women seeking ordination to the priesthood. The

Women's Ordination Conference became the first major Catholic feminist organization with both a religious and a lay membership. Its single agenda was that of securing women's ordination, an issue that gave scope to laywomen as well as nuns to apply talents which otherwise lay untapped by the official church. Theologian Elizabeth Schussler Fiorenza and historian Rosemary Ruether, both Catholic laywomen, bent their outstanding scholarship to the task of convincing theologians, hierarchy, and laity that women priests are consonant with the Christian message. Soon, a few male liberal theologians began to publish articles and books, arguing that there did not exist any scriptural barriers to women's ordination, nor were there any in the traditions of the church. This immediately attracted the attention of the Vatican, which pressured some of the more widely known male theologians to desist from publishing on the subject of women priests. Attempts to suppress free inquiry only fueled the debate, and it still rages. Women in greater numbers than ever before were encouraged to earn the M.Div., the seminary degree that prepares one for priestly orders. But the pope forbade Vatican officials to engage in dialogue on the subject of women's ordination.

The single issue that has impelled Catholic feminist organizations to coalition formation has been attempts on the part of Rome to suppress public discussion of women's ordination.

The divergent interests of the major Catholic women's organizations are subsumed in times of crisis, when they act in coalition on various issues. This has been facilitated by interlocking directorates. Members of executive committees of the National Coalition of American Nuns, for instance, are also on the core commission of the Women's Ordination Conference, and on the board of directors both of Catholics for the ERA and the National Assembly of Religious Women. This has made it possible to share communication systems and expand the number of adherents needed to keep the question of women's ordination before the ecclesial community.

In January 1977, the Vatican issued a *Declaration* that reasserted its position of refusing the possibility of women's ordination (Vatican 1977). In attempting to reinforce the belief that only males were eligible for priesthood, the document had the effect of galvanizing the U.S. Catholic women's movement. Each year after 1977, on 27 January, the date of the letter's publication, members of various Catholic women's organizations join the Women's Ordination Conference in protesting the exclusion of women from priestly orders. Groups such as the National Coalition of American Nuns, Catholics for the ERA, and the National Assembly of Religious Women stage protests, usually outside major cathedrals. The protests have escalated to outdoor liturgies led by women, which are presented outside the cathedrals, while inside, the ordination of male seminary graduates is in progress. The Women's Ordination Conference has now established local chapters throughout the United States. Newsletters and books carry articles by a growing number of Catholic women theologians, psychologists, and sociologists, who seek to provide a theory of justice for men and women in the church, based on both scriptural and humanist notions of equality. These publications provide a voice for single and married laywomen, nuns, and lesbian and Third World Catholic women, and women of other religious traditions.

The Emergence of Women-Church

In 1977, the year of the Vatican *Declaration* on women's ordination, a group calling itself Chicago Catholic Women asked to meet with a number of bishops, because they feared the Vatican document would result in a repression of women's groups. Since the Chicago group contained some of the most articulate and highly visible leaders among religious feminists, it was soon able to attract wide network support. A new, larger group became known as Women of the Church Coalition. It sponsored its first general meeting, known as Woman-Church in Chicago in 1983. Seven women's organizations sponsored the event; four U.S. bishops were co-sponsors. Twelve hundred participants attended, from thirty-seven states. The meeting was scheduled just before a major gathering of bishops in Washington, D.C. At the final liturgy of Woman-Church, the assembly witnessed the anointing of two prominent Catholic feminists, Theresa Kane and Elizabeth Schussler Fiorenza, at a "missioning" ceremony, before they departed to address the bishops on the question of Catholic women's low ecclesial status. The Woman-Church meeting achieved a reaffirmation of female solidarity and its principal effect was to revitalize the Catholic women's movement.

The second meeting of the Chicago coalition occurred in 1987 in Cincinnati, Ohio. In the intervening four years, the organization had changed its name again, to Women-Church. The event, known as Women-Church Convergence, was sponsored by a coalition of twenty-five women's groups. Three thousand women from the United States and fifteen foreign countries gathered for three days of intensive discussions on the condition of Catholic women. It was clear at Cincinnati that the visible segment of Catholic feminists had grown larger. It was also clear that a transformation has occurred among religious feminists during the past fifteen years regarding the notion of ministry. Ministry is no longer a means of serving others to improve their lives. Ministry now involves a commitment to transform all oppressive relationships and structures, including the oppression of Catholic women. This new emphasis impels Women-Church to seek out allies among women of other religious persuasions and from secular feminist groups: among principal speakers were Protestant theologian Cheryl Gilkes, Eleanor Smeal of NOW, Gloria Steinem of *Ms. Magazine,* and Jewish feminist Drorah Stetel. Also evident was Women-Church's hardened position vis-à-vis clergy and hierarchy. The theme of the meeting was "Claiming Our Power!" It was scheduled at the same time as the Synod on the Laity in Rome. As one keynote speaker observed: "*This* is the real Synod."

Brief Sociological Analysis of Women-Church

Women-Church is a social and religious movement in the making; therefore, it is possible for the sociologist to gather the empirical data needed to demonstrate how pressures for change develop within an institution professing to be the repository of a divinely inspired religious tradition.

Ruether envisions Women-Church as a type of "spirit-filled community," having historical precedents. These communities have shown a pattern of tension with the institutional churches within which they attempted to operate. Tension certainly existed around the revivalist movements of the Second Great Awakening of early nineteenth-century America. In revivalism, men and women members of Protestant sects with talent for preaching were deemed called to that ministry and were affirmed by a believing community. This tended to break down distinctions between laity and clergy, a development not welcomed by mainline churches (Ruether 1985, 19–21). Similarly, Women-Church leadership takes the post-Conciliar understanding of "church" as "the People of God" and is attempting to show that the new definition cannot refer to a patriarchal structure. Its principal claim is to represent a church based on a "discipleship of equals" that can incorporate the charisma of Christ more authentically than the present hierarchy and clergy.

Women-Church is modeled on the basic Christian communities that have sprung from Latin American models of Liberation Theology. Like those communities, it is committed to struggle for redress of social injustices on local, national, and international levels. The issue of women's ordination, which combines the ideologies of liberation and equality, acted as a catalyst to forge Women-Church in the form we know today. Given its prophetic view of Scriptural messages, Women-Church is perceived by the hierarchy as a threat to the effectiveness of its control over its flock, that is, the lay stratas of the church.

Does Women-Church Have a Future?

It is difficult to predict the future course of Women-Church. The nuns and single women among its membership might invite the label "demographic loser" in the long term. However, a sizable proportion of the organization is made up of married women, and many of them have children. But few men are numbered in Women-Church; therefore, the family structure among members is lacking. Furthermore, one cannot predict what may be the future adult worldviews of children of present-day Catholic feminists.

In attempting to present its claims to members of the hierarchy, Women-Church is engaged in a dialogue with a much more powerful partner. It is to be seen what concessions can be wrested from the U.S. bishops in the struggle between unequal powers.

While Women-Church presents itself as the emerging vehicle for liberation from social and religious injustice towards women, some nun and lay groups among its membership have been observed to experience institutional injustices differently. Nuns reported a pervasive status ambiguity in relation to clergy ranks and to other laywomen; while laywomen, especially married women, felt the most powerless and invisible among status groups in the church. One source of alienation identified by married laywomen stemmed from official Vatican condemnation of birth control; while nuns found that myriad rules and regulations imposed on their religious orders by male cardinals in effect kept them in subordinated roles (Trebbi 1986).

There is also some ambivalence in the movement regarding its relation to biblical origins. Some feminist theorists feel that the church's tradition can be useful to underpin movement claims. Others reject Christianity as hopelessly patriarchal, and lean toward the goddess-worshipping traditions antedating Judaism.

What Women-Church has accomplished is to create a special space for women to reconstruct a religious culture around feminine experience and to theorize on that experience. Although its future may be in doubt, at present it is a clear call for the liberation of men and women from sexism in the church.

References

Vatican, 1977
Ruether Rosemary R., 1985
Trebbi Diana, 1986

18

In Goddess We Trust

Mary Jo Neitz

Witchcraft as a Mystery Religion

Witches work with symbols, myths, and ritual to speak to the unconscious. According to Starhawk, a well-known priestess and writer in the movement:

> Symbols and ritual acts are used to trigger altered states of awareness, in which the insights which go beyond words are revealed. . . . [T]he inner knowledge literally *cannot* be expressed in words. It can only be conveyed in experience, and no one can legislate what insight another person may draw from any given experience. (1979, 7)

Witches share the symbol of the Goddess, but that symbol has different meanings to different witches. For many neopagans the Goddess is a romantic symbol. They see the Goddess as a symbol of "nature," of course, but nature at its prettiest. The Goddess is always beautiful. She is often represented with pre-Raphaelite imagery: young, thin, delicate Caucasian features; everything about her flows—her clothing, if she is wearing any, her long wavy hair (for example, in the style of the Rider Waite tarot deck). Her body is often adorned with intricate jewelry, and she may be pictured with animals near her. Some covens even require that, since she becomes the Goddess in ritual, a priestess must retire when she is no longer "young and beautiful."

For feminist witches the symbol of the Goddess is very different. Rather than seeing the Goddess as a symbol of all that is beautiful in life, feminist witches see the Goddess as a symbol for the empowerment of women.

Among feminist witches there is appreciation for the diversity of goddess symbols available, and an interest in exploring the figure of the crone, the wise old woman, and even in the crone's connections to goddesses who bring the gift of death (see the Mother Peace tarot deck for appropriate images). Even insofar as the Goddess says something about nature for both, what it means has often been different.

Eleven women make a circle in a small dark room lit only by candles in the four corners. A pretty scarf lies on the floor in the middle of the circle. It is covered with small items: a pine cone, a feather, some leaves, a few stones, a couple small crystals, some pieces of jewelry. There is a small clay figurine of a very fat woman, naked, reclining on a couch. Some incense is burning in a bowl. The women begin to move around the circle. Some of them carry gourd rattles or tambourines which they shake as they chant: "Isis, Astarte, Diana, Hecate, Demeter, Kali, Inanna"—the names of the goddesses over and over. The chant continues, the dancing becomes more vigorous, the energy builds.[1]

A woman stands in front of a shelf in her bedroom. She has covered her shelf with a white linen cloth. This is her altar. Two white candles are on either side of the altar; a rose, a clay goblet made by a potter friend, a snake skin that she found one day in her garden, a round mirror, a crystal given her by a friend are all arranged on the cloth. For this ritual the goblet is filled with a mixture of water and wine, and a small dish of salt is placed on the altar. The woman has just emerged from a bath and is naked. She takes the salt and puts it on the floor—the salt of the earth. She lights the candles and says, "Blessed be, thou creature of fire." Next, she dips her fingers into the chalice and touches her forehead, saying, "Bless me, Mother, for I am your child." Again dipping her fingers, she touches her eyes, and says, "Bless my eyes to see your ways." Repeating the dipping motion each time, she touches her nose, lips, her breasts, her genitals, and her feet, blessing each part of her being as she touches her body. She stands for a moment, on the salt, and feels the energy flowing through her. Then, giving thanks, she puts out the candles.[2]

The dance begins with all facing outward, alternating male and female, and holding hands. We begin dancing widdershins, the direction of death and destruction, sing, "thout, tout a tout, throughout and about," which are the words the Witches of Somerset used to begin their meetings. The men dance with the left heel kept off the ground, in the hobbling gait of the bullfooted god, the lamed sacred king. The priestess who leads the dance lets go with her left hand and leads the dance in a slow inward spiral. . . . When the spiral is wound tight, the priestess turns to her right and kisses the man next to her . . . to awaken him to a new life. The priestess leads the new spiral outward, sunwise, the direction of birth and creation, and she (and each other lady) kisses each man she comes to. The spiral thus unwinds into an inward-facing circle, dancing sunwise. In this dance, widdershins is transformed into sunwise, destruction into creation, death into rebirth and those who dance it pass symbolically through Spiral Castle.[3]

In the last twenty years in the United States we have seen the emergence of religious groups oriented either entirely or primarily toward a female rather than male deity. For many involved in such groups the female deity represents "mother nature," and honoring her is a way to begin restoring the balance to a society threatened with extinction by technological rationality. Their religious rituals often recall symbols and practices from ancient times. Some groups are for women only, others involve men and women.

What I call the goddess movement encompasses many different groups and perspectives. Participants share the symbol of the Goddess and a repudiation of the dominant Judeo-Christian tradition, but the movement has no unifying organization, written scriptures, or dogma, no defining ritual practice. In outlining the goddess movement here I focus on two currents in modern society, neopagans and feminists, and the intersection of the two in modern witchcraft.

The first section focuses on what is shared by those who come to participate in the goddess movement: the emphasis on experience of ecstasy through goddess symbols and rituals. Because of this concern with symbols and rituals I argue that the goddess movement can best be examined as a cultural movement. Next, I examine briefly the controversial words "pagan" and "witch" to see why these names are used in the contemporary goddess movement. Then I describe the incorporation of the English witchcraft revival into the neopagan movement and the development of women's spirituality within the feminist movement. Finally, I discuss the relations between feminist and neopagan witches. It is my contention that although the goddess movement began among neopagans, it is its growth within the feminist movement that makes it a vehicle for cultural change in our society.

There is not even consensus on whether the symbol of the Goddess stands for a powerful potential inside of every person (even every living thing), or whether the symbol of the Goddess points to some being outside of the self. One gets both interpretations among witches. One woman explained her feelings to me this way:

> Something I have always found appealing in this religion is its multi-level symbolism. . . . It is that everything is alive. If you go back far enough, like Jane Ellen Harrison writes in her stuff, [in prehistoric times] you can see the development of the idea of the absolute sacredness of everything and relating to that constantly, all the time. And then, [you can imagine] the jump from that to a tree goddess living in a tree to a separation in ourselves of what is divine, and even to naming it as goddess. So to me the ideal religious way of thinking is a kind of pantheism.

> But I grew up in the patriarchy, and I also feel a need to relate to a personalized goddess a bunch of the time. I don't want to fight it myself. I need that. It's a healing process for me, even though I don't think it religiously, theologically, is

the ideal way to think. At this point in the patriarchy, to have a very powerful, loving intense image of the goddess—whoever she is to each one of us—I think that is a great way of counteracting two thousand years of patriarchal tradition. So I really embrace that, too.

For this woman, one conception of the Goddess is intellectually compelling, the other emotionally powerful. Yet, she did not feel that the movement, or even that she herself, had to choose between the different conceptions.

For Starhawk, what is important is the experience of the Goddess: "Ecstasy is at the heart of witchcraft—in ritual we turn the paradox inside out and become the Goddess, sharing in the primal throbbing joy of union," (1979, 25). She cites Eliade who notes that "Shamanism is not only a technique of ecstasy, its theology and philosophy finally depend on the spiritual value that is accorded to ecstasy." Starhawk adds,

> Witchcraft is a shamanistic religion, and the spiritual value that is placed on ecstasy is a high one. It is the source of union, healing, creative inspiration, and communion with the divine—whether it is found in the center of a coven circle, in bed with one's beloved, or in the midst of a forest, in awe and wonder at the beauty of the natural world." (1979, 26)

Starhawk finds symbols in nature, symbols in Geertz's sense of "models of and models for" (Geertz 1973, 93). For her, the metaphor for human existence is the cycle of birth and rebirth that she sees everywhere in nature. This is the spiral dance from which her book takes its title: "whirling into being, and whirling out again" (1979, 3). The process of birth and death and rebirth in the natural world for witches symbolizes their understanding that the world is born, not made, and it is born of the Goddess. The symbol is descriptive of nature's cycle; for many, but not all, witches it also suggests a stance toward the world.

Symbols are different from beliefs. The witchcraft can be described as a mystery religion: ritual comes first and myths are second. It is possible to be a practicing witch and an atheist: it is not necessary to "believe in" any goddess in order to accept the power of goddess symbols or to experience that power in ritual. Following Jung, some witches have worked out an interpretation of the Goddess which sees her as an archetypal figure based in the early human experience of nurturance from a mother. Such an interpretation gives "the Goddess" primary significance, without being theological (for example, Walker 1987).

In recent years sociologists studying social and religious movements have tended to focus on organizations. Because organizations are tightly bounded—in comparison with cultural aspects of movements—they are easier to study. The sociologist can say who the population is, can take a representative sample, or can stratify the sample as he or she wishes. The sociologist can examine the resource base of the organization and study what the people do together. Cultural aspects of movements are more diffuse: one cannot always say who is using a symbol and who is not.[4] Yet cultural changes can have enormous effects on a society.

A way of looking at social movements that attempts to recognize cultural changes looks for "the quickening of action, the change in meanings, and the understanding that something new is happening in a wide variety of places and arenas" (Gusfield 1981, 322). Here we are concerned with a change in meanings—the appearance of goddess symbols—among two distinct networks of people. First introduced within the neopagan movement, developments in the feminist movement greatly extend the goddess symbol and its capacity for cultural transformation.

Witches and Neopagans: Why These Words?

Before the neopagan movement, the word "pagan" had commonly been used to mean one of two things. People used it to refer to polytheistic religions of native or tribal people. When used to refer to individuals in modern culture, it referred to antireligious hedonism. Writing in *The Green Egg,* the most important neopagan publication of its time, Tim Zell began using, in 1967, the words "pagan" and "neopagan" to describe the new polytheistic nature religions (Adler 1986, 293–96).

In the mid-1960s the witchcraft revival was also using the word "pagan," but to refer to the pre-Christian folk religions in the old Celtic settlements of Europe, and their own practices. According to Adler, "It took a catalyst to create a sense of collectivity around the word *pagan,* and in the United States the Church of All Worlds and its *Green Egg* filled this role" (295).

The word "witch" comes from the Old English, *wicce/wicca* (female and male forms). According to the common derivation in witchcraft circles, this came from *wik,* meaning to bend or to shape; witches are those who are skilled in the "craft" of "bending or shaping" reality (for this and other possible derivations see Adler 1986, 11). For those who support this etymology, the words "witch," "wiccan," and "the craft" are used interchangeably. Witches I have met in the United States sometimes make a distinction between the pagans who celebrate the holidays and the witches, the priestesses and priests who practice the craft of working magic.

Witches are aware of the negative connotation of the word "witch" in this culture. Furthermore, the negative connotations may be more important as the movement grows more public. Although Wiccans have used the word "witch" since Gerald Gardner started the modern revival of Wicca in England in the 1940s, until recently witches were quite secretive. It is still the case that many witches adopt a "craft name" to be used in settings where they are identified with being a witch; their legal names may never be revealed even to coven members of long standing.

Pagans themselves are ambivalent about using the word "witch" to describe themselves. Among 195 respondents to a questionnaire distributed at three large gatherings in 1985, Margot Adler found that two-thirds of her respondents considered themselves witches although most of them used the word with care in public settings. According to Adler, "Many people told me, 'When I have a limited amount of time to explain my viewpoint, it's just a lot easier to omit the word "witch" ' " (1986, 461). For Adler, "[t]he most important argument against the word *witch* is that it just doesn't communicate the reality of Pagan experience to most of the public, whereas a less loaded word often does" (462). A substantial minority feel that the word has such negative associations in the public culture that it cannot be reclaimed.

But many feminist witches have a special interest in reclaiming the word witch and its associations with healing and female power. Early feminist guerilla theater groups used WITCH as their acronym (see Morgan 1970). Revisionist feminist historians developed the argument that the women who were burned during the European witch trials were traditional wise women skilled in magical and practical healing arts (see Ehrenreich and English 1973).

In addition, theorists like Mary Daly began to advocate that feminists invert patriarchal language: she broke words into their parts and radically reinterpreted them (for example, in the title of her book *Gyn/Ecology* where the word for the medical specialty becomes the worldview through which women will save the earth), and she takes words which had been used to describe women in negative ways and bends the traditional understanding only slightly to arrive at a positive meaning. Thus for Daly, the witch is "one who is in harmony with the universe; wisewoman, healer; one who exercises transformative powers." (1987, 180)

Using the word witch may be reclaiming a part of oneself. To quote Adler:

> The number of people who understand the word *witch* in a Jungian archetypal sense and who feel the word's connection with the hidden, primal forces of nature probably number in the millions. That is why, in the end, the arguments against the word *witch* are usually tactical, and the arguments for the word *witch* are usually spiritual. The arguments against the word are never quite able to counter the deep feelings expressed by those who consider the word a part of their essence. (1986, 463)

Furthermore, for feminists the danger of the label may add to its attraction, increasing the possibility of identification with "witches" labeled and executed in the sixteenth century, victims of patriarchal officials.

Neopagans and the Witchcraft Revival

Adler suggests that what is unusual about neopagans is that like modern liberals they are antiauthoritarian and nondogmatic, but unlike modern liberals they use rituals and ecstatic techniques. Although Adler's book describes neopagan groups that do not consider themselves to be witches, witches currently dominate the neopagan movement both in terms of numbers and in terms of levels of activity within the movement (Adler 1986, 282).

The current witchcraft revival can be traced to Gerald Gardner, in England in the 1940s. Gardner claimed to have been initiated in 1939 into one of the few covens that had lasted through the centuries. He saw himself as reviving the ancient religion of the British Isles. Gardner's witchcraft is a nature religion oriented to the Goddess of birth and rebirth and her consort, the Lord of the Forests. Gardner's story about his initiation has fallen into disrepute (Kelly 1983). There is much specula-tion—both within and outside of the neopagan movement—about where Gardner got his rituals, but he seems to have put together a group of people and a system that was reasonably attractive and coherent enough to be transmitted. After the repeal of antiwitchcraft laws in England in 1951 he published a series of books. Kelly (1983) and Adler (1986, 80–86) argue that Wiccan traditions, especially the basic form of ritual used by witches today, originate with Gardner: casting a circle, consecrating participants, calling the spirits of the four directions, invoking deities, raising group energy, working spells, sharing a ceremonial meal, and unwinding the circle.[5]

Witchcraft as it came out of England was romantic and nostalgic. It looked backward to a time before the twentieth century and the two World Wars, before Britian was an empire, before patriarchy—before things went "so dreadfully wrong" in the world. Moving to the United States the witchcraft revival encountered other creative, eclectic, neopagan groups. Some of them looked to other pasts than the Celtic one of Gardner and his followers. Others took models from the future—from science fiction texts such as Heinlein's *Stranger in a Strange Land* (see Adler 1986, 233–337).

Witchcraft also found affinities with other groups engaged in radically nostalgic fantasy, such as those involved in playing the game Dungeons and Dragons and members of the Society for Creative Anachronism. In the 1960s witchcraft in the United States seemed to be a form of "deep play" (Geertz 1976, 432–42). With its rich symbols, sensual stimulation, and potential for complex forms, coupled with a lack of dogmatism, witchcraft provided a place for the imagination to play. People who began by playing at witches felt themselves becoming witches, and found themselves committed to an identity that carried with it real risks.

The vision of restoring the balance of nature began to seem less nostalgic, if not less radical, as the ecology movement grew in the 1970s and the antinuclear movement mobilized in the 1980s. Although individual neopagans take different positions on any political issue, as a group neopagans became much more concerned with ecology and antinuclear issues between 1975 and 1985 (see Adler 1986, 399–417). Neopaganism attracted people involved in these issues: goddess rituals now take place at political demonstrations and political rituals have become part of pagan festivals.

Feminists and the Goddess Movement

Feminist theologians, grass-roots groups, and an informal publishing network all played a part in birthing goddess spirituality in the women's movement. Theologians both offered a critique of patriarchal nature of dominant religious traditions (for example, Reuther 1975; Schussler Fiorenza 1983; Gross 1977) and developed theological alternatives that placed women's experience at the core (for example, Goldenberg 1979, Christ 1987). Equally important were the many study groups, circles, and covens that began to meet in the 1970s and that continue to grow in number today. Feminist (womanspirit) circles began to develop ties through publications and festivals. Local feminist papers entertained debates on women's spirituality issues, and calendars and advertising pages helped individuals to find others who shared their beliefs and practices. On a national level the magazine *Womanspirit* stimulated the sharing of information and debate about women's spirituality. In what follows I will examine examples showing how each of these modalities provided a vehicle for the developing goddess movement.

Goddess Theology

In the early 1970s feminist members of the American Academy of Religion formed a women's caucus, an early forum in academia for the sharing of the feminist critique. Carol Christ was among the first of these trained theologians to become involved in the goddess movement. Her work bridged the feminist and academic contexts. Her essay, "Why

Women Need the Goddess,'' is perhaps the most influential article by a theologian in the goddess movement. In it she explores the ways that goddess symbolism has the potential for responding to particular needs of contemporary American women and for providing new models.[6]

Most significant, she states, is that "the symbolism of the goddess is the acknowledgement of the legitimacy of female power as a beneficent and independent power" (1987, 121). This symbol contrasts with the characteristic depictions of women—as passive, often as dependent, even as victims—in western religious traditions.

The second reason goddess symbolism is important is that it affirms the female body. The denigration of women in many cultures has been tied to women's bodies. Women have been seen as "closer to nature" and, like nature, in need of subjugation by male culture (see Ortner 1972; Griffin 1978). Male culture has viewed menstruation and female sexuality as dangerous, the latter even as evil.[7] The goddess symbols carry a vision of life that is cyclic rather than linear; cycles of birth and death, cycles of ovulation and menstruation are invested with a renewed sanctity.

Giving birth and menstruation are celebrated as "women's mysteries" in feminist goddess circles. At the end of one such ritual women mark each other with menstrual blood, reciting words from Carol Erdman's poem: "This is the blood that promises renewal. This is the blood that promises sustenance. This is the blood that promises life" (*Womanspirit,* winter 1974). This kind of ceremony, while not a common practice, represents a radical inversion of the way that menstruation is usually viewed in our culture. (See Christ 1987, 123; also Neitz 1988b).

The Wiccan traditions speak of the Goddess in her three aspects, the maiden, the mother, and the crone, often represented by the waxing moon, full moon, and waning moon. This, too, captures a cycle, and, by honoring the crone, such symbols bring honor to women whose bodies are waning.

Third, in witchcraft circles the symbol of the Goddess offers a "positive evaluation of the will":

> The basic notion behind ritual magic and spellcasting is energy as power. Here the Goddess is a center or focus of power and energy: she is the personification of the energy that flows between beings in the natural and human worlds. (Christ 1987, 127)

A woman is encouraged to "know her will, to believe that her will is valid, and to believe that her will can be achieved in the world" (128).

This is contrary to Christian demands for the submission of one's will, and the association of willfulness with sin. Most spiritual disciplines require the devotee to learn to subvert his or her will. We can imagine that such practices indeed encourage spiritual growth in elite young men—the archetypical saint is the arrogant/willful/perhaps wealthy young man who must give up his material power and become humble to find his spiritual path—but we might question whether such practices are what women in patriarchal cultures, socialized to be submissive to men as a tactic for daily survival, need for spiritual wholeness.[8]

Carol Christ argues this perspective does not encourage unrestrained willfulness:

> In the Goddess framework will can be achieved only when it is exercised in harmony with the energies and wills of other beings. . . . [A]wareness of waxing and waning processes in the universe discourages arbitrary ego-centered assertion of will, while at the same time encouraging the assertion of individual will in cooperation with natural energies and the energies created by the wills of others. (1987, 128–29)

Finally, the goddess symbolism is preparing the way for a reevaluation of women's bonds and heritage. One bond to be celebrated is that between mothers and daughters (Christ 1987, 129). In a ritual I have now witnessed several times in different parts of the United States, women sit in a circle and each woman, in turn, gives her name and her mother's name and her mother's mother's name—as far back as she can go. Most women can only go back to two women before themselves. The ritual is simple but profound: participants hear that even the names of their foremothers are lost to them.[9] At the end of her essay Carol Christ envisions a future where the goddess symbols will strengthen not only individual women, but also women's bonds with each other.

The contributions of Carol Christ and other women theologians (see Christ and Plaskow 1979; Spretnak 1982) do not account for the presence of a goddess movement in the United States today, but they do contribute to its vitality. These women shared their scholarship in the feminist journals, and they were inspired by the creative rituals in the women's circles at the grass roots.

Grass-Roots Women's Circles

At the same time that the feminist theologians were working out intellectual formulations, small groups of women without formal training in theology or religion were beginning to form womanspirit circles. These women are likely to say that their religion "comes out of their experience." As several have said to me, "I am a witch because I have a woman's body." In the early 1970s "having a woman's body" combined with some experience in the women's movement, plus a desire for spiritual experience led some women to experiment with new religious forms. In what follows we will examine one such group, Ursa Maior, a group whose history is better documented than most. Like many similar groups, this one began with a study group. The founding statement for the group took the form of a description of the course "Women, Goddesses, and Home-made Religion" offered through a San Francisco Bay area "free university" in 1974. The statement began:

> We are women who feel a need to explore our spirituality together. Because we cannot identify with male deities or participate in male-dominated religions, we have never had space for our spirituality to blossom. We have felt it ebbing away or being taken from us. We wish to hold on to what is ours, so we have come together to create a space for our spirituality to grow.

The women read about matriarchies in prehistory (for example, Briffault 1931; Diner 1973; Davis 1971; see Webster and Newton (1987) for a review of this literature). They found goddesses in ancient religions: not only the more familiar figures from the Greek and Roman pantheons—Demeter, Diana, Gaia, etc.—but also Inanna from Sumer, Brigid from the Celts, Isis from Egypt. In addition to their historical study the women wanted to recreate a practice of woman-centered spirituality. They experimented with raising energy through dancing and music, and they began to develop their own rituals, some of which they shared with other women at spiritual gatherings. They continued meeting after the end of the official class, now calling themselves a circle or coven.

By 1975 they had reclaimed the title of witches. In part they identified with the prepatriarchal goddess religions. But they also accepted a feminist interpretation of the European witch trials, that the witches were not evil women, but rather independent women and healers who "threatened established social norms." Yet, while they identified with these women from the past they also saw themselves as beginning something new, and related to the day-to-day experience of modern women. One woman reported:

> [W]e're all very mundane. . . . Sometimes it takes a lot of energy just to make it from day to day. Our group offers me just about unequivocal support. It's a way to recharge my energy, to come out refreshed and ready to cope with the world. We create rituals to affirm what's happening in our own lives. Our rituals are rooted in our own lives and experiences, not in books (Barbary MyOwn, quoted in the Hayward California *Daily Review*, 9 October 1975).

The coven name expressed a sense of who they were in relation to one another. Barbary MyOwn and Hallie Mountain Wing described their group in an article for the journal *Womanspirit:* "We have taken the name Ursa Maior, after the great she-bear, or the Big Dipper, constellation which resembles our structure in that it appears to be seven distinct stars but it is actually a web of complex galaxies" (June 1976, 25). But the name "Ursa Maior" also captured a bit of their vision of the role that they as a group might have—the constellation is easily recognized, and it points to the North Star, the guide in the night sky.

The group lasted a little more than two years. In that time the group created a number of rituals based in their common experiences as women, and yet seen as magically transforming those experiences. Focusing on the need for positive rituals in their lives, the women used ritual to accomplish three different goals: (1) recognizing issues that need resolution; (2) healing in the broad sense of changing negative occurrences or feelings into positive ones; and (3) celebrating positive occurrences or aspects of their lives.

As an example, here is one of several rituals coven members described in various issues of *Womanspirit.* It begins with the story of Inanna, a Sumerian goddess who

> decided, because she was curious and courageous, to visit the underworld. She goes there by *setting her mind* from the great above to the great below, where she was held captive but escaped. Inanna shows us a strong woman confronting the unknown which is scary, but necessary to our growth. (Barbary MyOwn, *Womanspirit,* June 1976, 88)

The women participating in the ritual split into pairs. In each pair one woman was to "journey below" while the other one stayed above. The women who were journeying below lay on the floor like spokes in a wheel, their feet in the center of the circle. Their partners held them while they journeyed inward. As part of the ritual the women-above covered the faces of the women-below with wet plaster bandages.[10]

According to Barbary MyOwn's account:

> The plaster acted as a sensory deprivation device, shutting out the world. For some women this felt claustrophobic or scary, and the women-above recognized this by their breathing or bellies and touched them or talked to them to help them. The women-below were told that someplace in the underworld there was a special place of power for them which they would recognize. When they found this place they would feel at home. . . . Slowly the women-above began singing to the women-below—singing their names and great mythic stories about them. . . . Each woman-below was encouraged to leave any bothersome thoughts or obstacles behind in the underworld and surface above, being reborn in a new circle of friends coaxing her home. As the plaster masks hardened they were peeled from the women's faces leaving new layers of skin below. Each goddess,

looking at her own face, expressed surprise—"That's not how I have ever seen myself. She's so beautiful! Is that really me? It is—it's my *face!* I'm so beautiful." (*Womanspirit,* June 1976, 89)

A ritual like this uses mythic material, but uses a new form and modern materials (plaster bandages rather than eye of newt). The object of the ritual, spiritual rebirth, is a common one in religious traditions. The visit to the underworld is designed as an opportunity to encounter and confront fears or bad feelings. In addition, in this case, the spiritual rebirth is accompanied by a new appreciation for one's physical body. And the masks are physical objects which could be incorporated into future rituals.

Ursa Maior, although perhaps better known than many feminist circles, shares a number of characteristics with other such groups. Many circles and covens arise out of a class or a study group. They tend to be small; five to eight members is the norm. They tend not to be tied to any one goddess or pantheon or tradition. And, while individual members may have long involvement with a community of people who are pursuing spiritual paths, the groups themselves coalesce and dissolve when intensity cannot be maintained or interests shift.

A Magazine Like a Consciousness Raising Group

One way that women pursuing a spiritual path know about each other and share discoveries is through newspapers and other publications.[11] More than any other publication from 1974–1984, *Womanspirit* filled this role. Jean Mountaingrove, coeditor and copublisher, has described the beginnings of *Womanspirit* as an emergent process: "I found feminism in 1970 and realized that I had to question everything." Then forty-five, she left her city life and moved with her two children to a rural commune in Oregon. In this mountain setting she discovered a special grove of trees where she felt a "very special spiritual presence." She says "I returned there frequently and always felt the same opening of my heart. I had my own meaning for the Goddess at first and called her 'Mother'." Yet this experience of the Goddess did not make her an authority in the usual sense.

At a woman's gathering Jean Mountaingrove participated with other women in a consciousness-raising session on their personal religions. In 1973 some of the women in that group decided to organize a women's gathering focusing on spirituality. Among the women who attended the gathering was part of the editorial staff from the journal *Country Women.* They invited Jean Mountaingrove and her partner Ruth to work with them on a special issue which was the precursor to *Womanspirit.*

In a recent interview Jean Mountaingrove said that she learned about witchcraft in the process of doing the magazine:

> I was the original visionary who started this magazine process, and I was abysmally ignorant. I didn't know about witches. I couldn't tell an Equinox from a Solstice. . . .
>
> There were so many women who wanted to say something. I wanted the early issues to be like a CR [consciousness raising] group. I wanted it to be a place where all women could be heard. I did not feel like I was an expert at all. . . . We tried to bring material together and find out what was going on. If I had known what was going on I would have written a book. . . . [S]ince I did not know I started a magazine. (*Of a Like Mind,* Lammas 9988 (1988), 4–5)

For ten years *Womanspirit* published women's accounts of their feelings and experiences in the spiritual dimension of their lives. In that respect it was like a consciousness-raising group. Women theologians argued with one another. Women shared their research about matriarchies and Goddess worshippers in other cultures. Women from all over the country shared rituals that worked for them. The journal did not advocate one perspective over another. It was both a forum for women's thoughts and feelings and a tool for women interested in practicing some kind of women's religion.

Through *Womanspirit* and other journals and newsletters, as well as through women's festivals and spiritual gatherings, a Goddess-oriented women's spirituality movement began to gain momentum. Women who called themselves witches have been and continue to be important in the movement, but not all choose to describe themselves that way. Some of those who are oriented to the Goddess feel that the word "witch" is too exclusive to describe their spirituality. They accept the view that the Wiccan or witchcraft tradition is the pre-Christian religion of Northern Europe, and they do not see themselves practicing in that tradition. Some feel that, given that we live on the North American continent, we should look to the traditions native to this land. Others feel that their own approach is more personal or eclectic. As was discussed above, others feel that it is important to reclaim the word "witch" in order to counter a negative cultural stereotype that can too easily be used against any woman, regardless of her religious practice.

Through a collective process—one in which not all of those involved realized they were participating—the goddess movement brought together elements of feminism with elements of neopaganism. Yet the relationships between the movement and feminists and the movement and the neopagans have been problematic, particularly so during the late 1970s. The first responses of at least some neopagans and feminists to the emerging feminist goddess movement were hostile.

Connections with Feminists and Neopagans

Today many women who become involved with the goddess movement do so with very little knowledge of the rest of the neopagan movement. Jade, one of the organizers of the Re-Formed Church of the Goddess, a woman-only Wiccan church in Wisconsin, told me that women now "discover the Goddess on their own" and become involved in women's religion. If they find out about the neopagan movement "they are angry that someone else got there first, and that it was a man."

In general, feminist circles and covens have a different character than do the neopagan circles and covens. First, feminist covens have no men. Feminists covens are less structured: they are less likely to have formal training and initiation; they are less likely to require specific clothing or words in a ritual; they are less likely to use titles or differentiate between skill levels or experience. Feminist covens are more likely to make use of women's experiences of their bodies as in rituals marking menstruation, birthing, and menopause.

In the 1970s women who thought of themselves as feminists had more contact with the neopagans simply because there were fewer exclusively feminist resources available for women who wanted to learn about witchcraft. However, women who came out of feminism and women who came out of the craft had differing conceptions of what a feminist craft might be like. Both used the term "Dianic" to describe a tradition where the Goddess is primary. In the early 1970s two different models were available. Morgan McFarland in Dallas led Dianic covens and trained others to serve the Goddess as priestesses and priests. Although the Goddess was primary, two of the covens had men as members. For many witches, McFarland's Dianic group was a radical departure: by doing rituals in groups with no men she dispensed with the belief, central to the Gardnerian legacy, that raising energy involves balancing male and female forces.

But McFarland's version of Dianic Wicca was not radical enough for feminists who took for granted that the energy in their circles was female. Zsuzsanna Budapest founded the Susan B. Anthony Coven in Los Angeles in 1970, claiming the label "Dianic" for women-only, feminist covens. This usage became the more common one.

If the feminists who were drawn to the Goddess approached the craft with care, some feminists who were not witches condemned the whole endeavor. In 1976 and 1977 a series of articles in *Off Our Backs,* the feminist monthly newspaper, debated the pros and cons of the women's spirituality movement.

The initial blast came July 1976 in a report on "Through the Looking Glass, a Gynergetic Experience," a conference held in Boston in April 1976. Morgan McFarland opened the conference with a ritual exemplifying all the pomp and ceremony neopaganism offers. The report called the conference pompous, divisive, didactic. In the next issue the "Letters" column of *Off Our Backs* was filled with responses, along with an interview with Ruth and Jean Mountaingrove in which they defended the women's spirituality movement against charges of escapism.[12]

In December *Off Our Backs* published two reports on the New York Women's Spirituality Conference, "Celebration of the Beguines," held Halloween weekend. The reports were positive but specific to particular lectures and workshops. In July another article renewed the attack. Writing from a Marxist perspective, Marcy Rein wrote that feminists needed political analyses of women's problems and concrete solutions. She dismissed women's spirituality as utopian. Hallie Iglehart responded in September that women's spirituality did promote political change. The end of the exchange came in November with a long letter from Merlin Stone, author of several books on ancient goddess religions. Stone took an offensive position: on the basis of her cross-cultural studies, she accused the attackers of women's spirituality of sexism, racism, and homophobia.

By the 1980s the battle between the political feminists and the spiritual feminists diminished. In part this was because both realized that religion had the potential to be either repressive or liberating.[13] In part the fighting diminished because witches put their energy behind political actions such as ERA and antinuclear issues. But, perhaps most important, by the 1980s women's spirituality and feminist witchcraft had permeated the common everyday culture of the radical feminist community, to the extent that goddess symbolism and as well as certain practices are taken for granted.[14]

For some women close to the feminist separatist community, the recognition of oneself as a lesbian was soon followed by identification with the witches. Among feminists, the same word is used to describe both processes: women "come out" as lesbians and they "come out" as witches. Even when a woman shares her identity as a witch with a very small group of friends, she is likely to describe it as having "come out as a witch."

Neopagans do not "come out." Although the psychological process of identifying as a witch may be much the same, most neopagans still think of becoming a witch in terms of a formal initiation into a secret society after a period of study. Some neopagans were angry about feminist disregard for their traditions (that is, initiation, hierarchy, and the importance of balancing male and female energy). What neopagans called "their traditions," feminist sometimes called "sexist" and "homophobic."

In the 1980s tensions between the two have abated. The hostility directed at feminist witches by some neopagans is rarely evident today. Neopagan witches still talk about the importance of balancing male and female energies, yet many pagan festivals now feature all-male and all-female circles. The Gardnerian rule about only admitting heterosexual couples to covens has been relaxed. Most feminist witches have little interest in doing rituals in groups with both women and men, but they may cooperate in area councils or projects with neopagans.

In the 1970s individual women got their training from neopagan individuals or sources, then had to fight for the legitimacy of their separate domain. At this point feminist women often have many opportunities to learn a form of the craft tailored to their needs. The neopagans are perhaps more likely to borrow from the feminist craft than the other way around.

Starhawk and Margot Adler are two women who helped lessen the distance between the two movements in the 1980s. *The Spiral Dance* and the first edition of *Drawing Down the Moon* were both published on All Hallow's Eve in 1979. In different ways the two books have brought many people to the goddess movement. Adler's lively accounts, her inclusive polytheism, and her undogmatic enthusiasm introduced a neopagan world previously unknown to most people. *The Spiral Dance* has sold over fifty thousand copies, and some say a thousand covens and spiritual groups have begun with reading it (Adler 1986, 228). Neither is identified primarily with the feminist craft—Adler is a Gardnerian and Starhawk is part of the faery tradition—yet both are feminists. Both are respected by feminists and mainstream witches, go to both kinds of gatherings, and talk to both kinds of witches.

Conclusion

Witchcraft is not a religion in the sense that many people use the word to indicate an established organization with a formal set of rules governing group interactions as well as individual behavior. Most witches want little to do with such an organization.[15] But it is a religion in the sense that Geertz describes religion as a cultural system: "Religion is a system of symbols which acts to produce powerful pervasive and long-lasting moods and motivations" (1973, 90).

Rituals, such as those presented at the beginning and throughout this paper, suggest attitudes toward the body, toward birth and death, toward nature at variance with modern culture. The 1980s have witnessed changes within the neopagan community itself: more explicit political activity directed toward ecological issues, nuclear issues, feminist concerns and gay and lesbian issues. It is not the case that certain positions on these issues are a necessary consequence of the belief in the Goddess. As we have seen, it is impossible to say what "believing in the Goddess" means even for all witches, and not all witches believe in the Goddess. Yet, it may be the case that the combination of ritual without dogma is a potentially liberating form.

The work of the anthropologist Victor Turner suggests that rituals create a special frame outside of ordinary interaction, and that within that frame it is possible to germinate the seeds of social transformation:

> Yet in order to breathe, to live, and to generate novelty, human beings have had to create—by structural means—spaces and times in the calendar or in the cultural cycles of their most cherished groups which cannot be captured in the quotidian, routinized spheres of action. These liminal areas of time and space—rituals, carnivals, dramas, and latterly films—are open to the play of thought, feeling, and will; in them are generated new models often fantastic, some of which may have the power and plausibility to replace eventually the force-backed political and jural models that control the centers of a society's on-going life. (1969, *vii*)

The symbols of the goddess movement in themselves represent cultural change. For many the rituals are new forms of play. For others the rituals express their deepest hopes for social transformation as well.

What is suggested by the history of the goddess movement is that symbols become transforming in the context of a broader social movement. Gardnerian witchcraft introduced new symbols and forms of ritual enjoyed for themselves, an elaborate game for most participants. In the encounter with feminism the goddess symbols resonated with the experience of some women, who then used the symbols in a way that challenged not only the Judeo-Christian tradition, but much neopagan practice. While relatively few people are directly involved in the goddess movement the attitudes toward women and nature that are embodied in the goddess symbols are a part of a more widespread social and cultural change.

I would like to thank the following people for their comments on earlier drafts of this paper: Margot Adler, Deborah Bender, John Hall, Jade, Peter Mueser, and Jim Spickard.

Notes

1. "The Goddess Chant" is by Deena Metzger with music by Caitlin Mullin. See Starhawk 1982, 227.
2. The ritual is adapted from Zsuzsanna Budapest's self-blessing ritual. The entire

ritual is published in *The Holy Book of Women's Mysteries, Part II*. See also Christ and Plaskow 1979, 269–72. Margot Adler reports a very similar self-blessing ritual written by Ed Fitch in the 1960s (Adler 1983, 468–70).

3. Taken from Aidan Kelly, "Why a Craft Ritual Works," *Gnostica*, 4 (No.7):33 (March-April-May 1975).

4. For example, Kelly reports three different measures of activity in the neopagan movement and comes up with a "ball park estimate" of approximately 50–100,000 active participants (1987, 1–2). I believe that these estimates all leave out most of the feminist witches.

5. In his investigations in the United States, Gordon Melton claims that he has not found anyone who claims to have been initiated before the early 1950s—when Gardner's book was published (personal communication). I have met a few witches who claimed to come out of "family traditions" that existed for generations. These people are unlikely to go to festivals, and practice mostly folk magic in relative isolation. For the most part they do not belong to the neopagan movement.

6. First printed in a special issue of the feminist journal *Heresies*, the article has been reprinted in anthologies and college textbooks, is included in the Unitarian Universalist course on the Goddess "Cakes for the Queen of Heaven," and xeroxed copies pass from woman to woman.

7. For example, see the profound misogyny of *Malleus Maleficarum*, the sixteenth-century witch-hunters' guide, which is obsessed with "sexual crimes" of women.

8. Contrast for example the recent treatment of Augustine's battle with his will and consequent rejection of sexuality in Pagels 1988 with the traditional depiction of Saint Maria Goretti, the early-twentieth-century Italian saint. Her "martyrdom" took the form of her "choosing death" rather than submitting to sexual intercourse. One mark of her saintliness was that on her deathbed she forgave her murderer, who then converted to a pious life.

9. Many people can go back four or more names when they list their fathers.

10. Plaster-impregnated bandages, used for setting bones, are available from surgical supply houses. They are prepared for the ritual by being cut into strips and dipped in water. At the appropriate time they are spread on a face which has been greased with Vaseline, with a breathing hole left for the mouth.

11. One listing is in Adler 1986, 474–507.

12. The summer 1976 issue of *Womanspirit* published the conference proceedings. A description of McFarland's ritual can be found in Adler 1986, 222–25.

13. For example see Kim Womantree, "Hexes to Holy Wars: Nonpolitical, 'Pure' Spirituality Has Never Existed," *Big Mama Rag* 10 (3):14–15, March 1982.

14. An illustration of the complexity of the interaction between traditional Wicca and feminism can be found in Robin Morgan's essay "Metaphysical Feminism" (1977, especially 302–6). The essay is part of Morgan's celebration of emerging women's culture, including both spiritual practices and art forms. In this essay she talks about her own process of "coming out as a witch." At the same time she expresses uneasiness about some of what is done in the name of feminist witchcraft. (In 1973 at the West Coast Lesbian Feminist conference Morgan announced that she was an initiated wiccan priestess, and ended her speech with the traditional "Charge of the Goddess." The whole speech is reprinted in 1977, 170–88.)

15. Witches in fact have been notoriously resistant to rules and organization. Adler

gives an account of the various efforts to create an umbrella group of witches (1986, 99–107).

References

Adler, Margot, 1986
Briffault, Robert, 1931
Christ, Carol, 1987
Christ, Carol, and Judith Plaskow, 1979
Daly, Mary, 1978
Daly, Mary, with Jane Caputi, 1987
Davis, Elizabeth Gould, 1971
Diner, Helen, 1973
Ehrenreich, Barbara, and Dierdre English, 1973
Geertz, Clifford, 1973
Goldenber, Naomi, 1979
Griffin, Susan, 1978
Gross, Rita, ed., 1977
Gusfield, Joeseph, 1981
Kelly, Aidan, 1983, 1987
Kramer, Heinrich, and James Sprenger, 1971 (orig. 1484)
Morgan, Robin, 1970, 1977
Neitz, Mary Jo, 1988b
Ortner, Sherry, 1972
Pagels, Elaine, 1988
Ruether, Rosemary Radford, 1975
Schussler Fiorenza, Elizabeth, 1983
Spretnak, Charlene, ed., 1982
Starhawk, 1979, 1982
Turner, Victor, 1969
Walker, Barbara, 1987
Webster, Paula, and Esther Newton, 1975

19

Women-Centered Healing Rites:
A Study of Alienation and Reintegration

Janet L. Jacobs

Introduction

Over the last two decades the rising feminist consciousness in the United States has led to changes in the sociopolitical spheres of contemporary life. Within the area of women and religion these changes are reflected in a variety of responses to male-dominated religious thought and practice. The challenge to patriarchal religion posed by feminist theologians is evident in three diverse approaches to existing tradition, which Christ has outlined as follows:

> The views held by feminist theologians fall into three main types: in type 1, tradition contains an essentially nonsexist vision or intentionality that becomes clear through proper interpretation; in type 2, tradition contains elements of an essentially sexist vision: the nonsexist vision must be affirmed as revelation, while the sexist vision must be repudiated . . . and in type 3, tradition contains an essentially sexist vision and must therefore be repudiated and new traditions must be created on the basis of present experience and/or nonbiblical religion. (1982, 238)

The type 1 approach is most closely associated with the work of Russell (1974, 1976) and Trible (1973), while the second approach (type 2) is identified with the scholarship of Reuther (1972, 1985) and Fiorenza (1979). The type 3 orientation, the most revolutionary of the three perspectives, is represented in the work of Christ (1982, 1985), Starhawk (1979, 1982) and Budapest (1986) who hold a more radical view on the nature of male

dominance in religious tradition. These feminist thinkers, unlike the reformist theologians identified with the first two approaches, maintain that
any faith that is premised on the imagery of a patriarchal god symbol is
antithetical to the emergence of a feminist religious consciousness. As
such they advocate the development of the feminine principle in the
concept of the divine and a religious structure that is nonhierarchal in
nature.

Despite the differences that characterize feminist religious studies, both
the reformist and revolutionary orientations incorporate healing as a means
through which female spirituality can be reconstructed and expressed. The
significance of healing to the contemporary women's spirituality movement has its origins in the roles that women once assumed as healers,
midwives, and wisewomen, social and spiritual roles that were marginalized and stigmatized by the church establishment in the pre-Renaissance
period and by the simultaneous development of the medical profession as
a male-defined science (Ehrenreich and English 1978; Reuther 1985).
Within this historical context, one aspect of the feminist movement has
been to reclaim the healing powers of women through the creation of
female-centered rituals that bring participants together to heal themselves
as well as others who are seeking a meaningful spiritual identification.

While Ruether maintains that feminist healing rites involve the "opening
up of the self to the healing life forces of creation and redemption" (1985,
150), Glendinning focuses on the relationship between healing and political
action:

> For women to heal themselves is a political act. To reclaim ourselves as whole
> and strong beings is to say no to the patriarchal view of women as weak and
> "misbegotten." To call upon the natural healing ways is to say no to the
> patriarchal obsession with controlling, directing and enacting "cure." To heal
> ourselves is a reclamation of the power we all have as living beings to live in
> harmony with the life energy. (1982, 291)

It is within the framework of women healing themselves that the study
presented here was undertaken. The research focuses on a women's
spirituality group that met over a period of eighteen months to create and
participate in life-affirming rituals. Membership in the group was fluid and
was comprised primarily of students and faculty at the University of
Colorado, the majority of whom shared a feminist consciousness and a
desire to build community with each other while validating the existence
and belief in female creativity and power. In an earlier report of this
research (Jacobs, forthcoming a), the effect of ritual healing, specifically
on victims of abuse, was assessed. The results of that analysis strongly
suggest that ritual healing reduces the effects of powerlessness and low

self-esteem associated with the trauma of victimization. The work presented here elaborates further on these findings through a comprehensive examination of the role that ritual assumes in altering the effects of spiritual, social, and political alienation, thus empowering women to make changes both in their inner psychic lives and in their outer social responses to male-dominated society.

The Collection of Data

Data collection for this research began in the fall of 1985 with the formation of a women's spirituality group at the University of Colorado in Boulder. A core group of six women arranged the time and place for the rituals which were conducted two or three times a semester over the next year-and-a-half. Participants ranged in age from eighteen to forty and were drawn from faculty, students, and friends who formed the basis of a grassroots spirituality movement on the Boulder campus. This movement was loosely defined and maintained no direct affiliation with any particular feminist tradition such as the Wiccan witchcraft orientation favored by the revolutionary theologians. Nonetheless, the women adopted the same group processes described in the work of Starhawk and Budapest, collectively creating seasonal rituals according to the ancient pagan calendar, as well as healing rituals to address the specific needs of group members. It is the latter form of ritual that primarily will be addressed here. Over half the women in the group had been victims of abuse, including incest, battering, and rape, and of the forty participants, more than half attended the rituals on a regular basis.

The research method used in this study included participant observation at the rituals, in-depth interviews with the participants, written questionnaires, and follow-up interviews at three and six months after the group began meeting. The interviews were open ended and were intended to ascertain religious background, the meaning of spirituality in the participants' lives, and the significance of ritual to the process of change and personal development. The written questionnaires focused on frequency of attendance at the rituals, the motivation for joining the spirituality group, and the strengths and weakness of the ritual process as perceived by the respondents.

For the most part, the healing rites were organized around four sequential activities. These included bonding among group members, the acknowledgement of social and individual suffering, the release of anger and painful emotion, and a guided meditation in which the symbol of the Goddess was invoked as a source of strength and healing. Typically, the rituals were initiated by the formation of a circle that represented the creation of sacred space. Once the circle had been demarcated, the group performed a shared activity such as anointing each other with fragrant oil. Then the group joined hands, chanting repeatedly, "I am woman, I am power, I am the infinite within my soul." By anointing each other and chanting together, the participants welcomed everyone into the group, establishing bonds of connectedness and trust. With this act of community accomplished, the group was then ready to proceed to the second stage of ritual, the acknowledgement of suffering.

At this point in the healing process, individual members of the group would state their reason for attending the ritual. One by one each woman would acknowledge her source of suffering whether it be a personal form of tragedy or a more global sorrow for the suffering of others. Often in this act of acknowledgement, mothers, sisters, lovers, and friends would be invited into the circle as spiritual participants in the healing rite. Following these public expressions of hurt and sadness, the ritual release of emotion, particularly anger and rage, was initiated. At this stage in the healing rite, anger was validated through the symbolic smashing of eggs or the burning of names of perpetrators of violence. The release of anger in this manner created a highly charged moment in the ritual in which there was a clearly cathartic release of emotion through the collective discharge of personal rage (see Jacobs, forthcoming a).

Before entering the final stage of the ritual, the meditative imaging, the group would once again hold hands and chant in order to refocus the emotional energy aroused by the release of emotion. Once the group was refocused, the ritual concluded with one or two participants leading the others through a guided meditation. During the imaging, the women were typically asked to imagine themselves as the Goddess, in whatever form was meaningful for the participant, and through this imagery to envision an act of strength directed at a source of harm identified by the woman. For the abused respondent, this imaging often involved confronting her perpetrator and taking revenge, as the following example illustrates:

> I saw myself as Erishkigal, goddess of the underworld. I was bending over the man who had raped me as a child. He was on his knees and I was threatening him with a knife just as he had threatened me.

At the close of the guided meditation, the leader would direct the participants to name the Goddess in themselves and to keep that name as a private resource of power that could be taken from the ritual circle as a reminder of female strength and resourcefulness. When the ritual was over the women embraced one another and broke the circle with the sharing of food and drink, often staying together to discuss the feelings and changes they experienced during the healing rite.

The data gathered during the ritual participation and in the discussions and interviews that followed suggest that alienation is at the root of the women's spirituality movement, alienation both from the dominant patriarchal culture and from the female self which is devalued and denigrated within this culture. Through the spiritual community created by ritual participation and the focus on the goddess symbol, both forms of alienation are attended to within the context of ritual healing. Each aspect of ritual, the development of community and the significance of the goddess symbol, will be elaborated below.

The Collective Spiritual Community

Among the participants, the effects of alienation from the dominant culture were expressed as disenchantment with and exclusion from patriarchal religious traditions that treated women as inferior and worshipped a male god that was often used as a legitimation for violence and control. As one woman described her disaffection from Christianity:

> I am at a point in my life where I am having trouble with theology. I think the essence of most theology is good and valid, but having grown up within the Christian theology of the great male god, I am real offended by that. I am offended by the sense you can name this life force and put it in a male body with male characteristics. I have never been comfortable with these limitations.

For the women in the group, religious traditions were not seen as separate from the secular society but as manifestations of dominant cultural values and beliefs that are male constructed. As such, the alienated religious consciousness expressed by the participants is symptomatic of the sense of powerlessness and estrangement that women experience within a larger social system that excludes females from positions of authority and subordinates the lives of women to the control and domination of men.

In assessing the impact of this form of alienation and the role that spirituality may play in alleviating the intrapsychic and social tensions produced under systems of domination, it is useful to draw on the work of Durkheim, whose classic study of suicide (1951) laid the groundwork for understanding the role that religion can play as an integrating force in society. In his study of suicide in nineteenth-century Europe, Durkheim found that members of groups such as Catholicism and Judaism, who had unifying religious communities, were less likely to take their own lives than their Protestant counterparts, whose religious tradition did not provide a strong sense of connection to other believers. Although Durkheim's emphasis was on the moral authority exercised by the minority religious denominations, the value of his research today would seem to be in his discovery of the importance of religion and ritual as a source of community and connection among alienated groups who might otherwise be led to states of despair and hopelessness that derive from their sense of power-lessness and isolation. Within this view of religious community, the healing ritual becomes a source of social integration and identification with other group members who are experiencing similar feelings of alienation. In the following account, a respondent describes the sense of connection that the ritual provided:

> I think the process of bonding with other women is extremely important. One of the most powerful things that happened to me in the first ritual was seeing other women as human beings, having compassion for them rather than a sense of the competitiveness we are made to feel in patriarchal society.

Both Reuther and Starhawk address the importance of this integrative aspect of the women's spirituality movement. In her work with ritual, Starhawk refers to the "culture of estrangement" that makes the healing journey an arduous path in a society where "power over" is the dominant form of social institutions, necessitating the formation of spiritual alterna-tives that stress power from within individuals who act collectively to heal themselves from the divisive effects of cultural and political alienation. Similarly, Reuther articulates a need for feminist religious communities that reject patriarchal social, political, and religious systems. Accordingly, she discusses the role that a feminist spiritual community plays in validat-ing women's experience:

> [T]he first step in forming the feminist exodus from patriarchy is to gather women together to articulate their own experience and communicate it with each other. Women assure each other that they really are not crazy, that they really have been defined and confined by systematic marginalization of their human capacities. They develop words and analysis for the different aspects of the system of marginalization, and they learn how to resist the constant messages from patriarchal culture that try to enforce their acquiescence and collaboration with it. (1985, 49)

In the rituals studied here, the act of publicly naming the source of suffering for each participant gives language and expression to the experi-ence of marginalization that Reuther describes. This acknowledgment of shared pain and victimization helps to dissolve the boundaries created by the isolation of one woman from another, and thus begins the process of building a spiritual community based on connectedness rather than alien-ation. This sense of connectedness is further enhanced by the use of the goddess symbol, which affirms women's strength within a cosmology of female power and autonomy that challenges male hegemony.

The Reintegration of the Female Self through the Symbol of the Goddess

Building community through ritual participation offers one means through which social integration takes place among women. The second form of integration evident in women's spirituality is the connection that is created through identification with a symbol of female power as this is expressed through the imaging of the Goddess. In her discussion of the significance of the Goddess for women (1982, 1985), Christ maintains that it is through goddess symbolism that women can celebrate their power, their bodies, and their connection to one another, including the bond between mother and daughter. With respect to the self-integrating aspects of women's rituals, it is the mother-daughter bond in particular that appears to be most significant for healing the effects of self-alienation. As alienation from the female self is manifested in the most primary of female connections, the mother-daughter relationship, the merging and identification with the Goddess that takes place during the guided meditation can be understood as the symbolic reintegration of daughter and mother and thus of the daughter with her feminine self.

In analyzing the types of visionary experiences that the women in the group reported, a pattern of maternal images emerges that supports the notion of mother-daughter bonding through a meditative process that symbolically creates powerful mother goddesses who protect and care for their suffering daughters. Two examples from the visionary accounts will help to illustrate this phenomenon. In the first example, a twenty-two-year-old graduate student describes both the fear of being abandoned by the mother Goddess, Hecate, and then the relief of being saved by her. Her vision was revealed in the following manner:

> In my vision Hecate led me down a stairway to a circle of women who were dancing. It was a slow plodding dance. I started talking to them, asking them if they had anything to teach me. I could see their faces moving and they were gesturing but there were no noises coming out. So I asked Hecate to translate but she went into another cavern and I followed her. In the cavern was a corpse but its heart was still beating. Hecate left me and ran out of the room. I was terrified and ran after her. Then she got down on her hands and knees and was looking in the cavern for something in the dark. So I got down and was looking beside her and then she found this amulet—this gold amulet with a bronze sun symbol in the middle. So she gave it to me and I put it around my neck and then she took me back upstairs and I felt much better. She had taken care of me after all.

As the account suggests, the respondent's vision expresses fear of isolation from other women (not understanding their gestures and silent language) and fear of the death of self (the corpse in the cavern). The woman is saved in her vision by the amulet that Hecate gives her for protection, leading her out of darkness and fear and into the light and warmth of the sun.

In the second example, the respondent articulates an awareness of herself as her own mother, a merging identification that she discovers through the connection to the Goddess:

> The immediate effect of the ritual was that I felt incredible. I feel like I really empowered myself and that I have some strength to rely on. I had heard about that, mothering yourself. But I really never understood it before. In the healing ritual we were to call out the name of our vision of strength and I called out me and I realized that I was my mother and I could take care of myself.

The significance of the maternal imagery as it emerges through the unconscious association with the goddess symbol can have varied meanings and interpretations. Within the psychoanalytic framework of object relations theory (Pollack 1975), the merging of female deity, mother, and daughter might be explained as the daughter's reattachment to the first object of primary love, the mother, through the spiritual representation of the Goddess. What is of particular significance, however, for the ritual participant is that bonding to the mother is experienced within a reconstructed vision of maternal power wherein the Goddess/Mother is imaged as a powerful force of protection against the violence and alienation of patriarchal culture.

In this regard, the visions created by the participants represent a collective unconscious desire on the part of women to create through mythology what is denied them in reality, a mother-daughter relationship that is not informed and controlled by paternalistic interests and female violation. As such, these visions seem to contain elements of the ancient myth of Demeter (seventh century B.C.), which has recently been embraced by feminist psychologists (Bolen 1984; Hall 1980) as an archetype of female strength that resides within the unconscious realms of the feminine psyche. In this myth, Persephone, the daughter of the goddess Demeter, is kidnapped by the lord of the underworld where she is forced to live with him and "taste his seed." At the loss of her daughter, Demeter rages at the gods and in her revenge withholds life on Earth until the god Zeus orders Hades to return Persephone to her mother.

The story of Persephone and Demeter is a myth that enacts the separation of the daughter from the mother in a scenario of abduction and rape that is all too familiar to the daughters of modern patriarchy. In the ancient myth, however, the mother goddess exerts her power to withhold life and thus avenges the act of male aggression and has her child returned to her, although Persephone is changed forever by the ordeal and must now spend a portion of each year in the underworld. In the depiction of the avenging mother goddess, it would seem that the myth of Demeter captures the universal desire for maternal protection in a world where such protection and female autonomy is rarely actualized. The reality of incest, rape, battering, and lesser forms of male control and violence suggest that unlike the goddess Demeter, mothers are rarely powerful enough to protect their daughters from the abuses of patriarchal culture. The effect of their powerlessness is the sense of betrayal and loss that women often express toward their mothers. Rich (1976) articulates this alienation between mother and daughter in her discussion of the myth and reality of mother-hood:

> Few women growing up in patriarchal society can feel mothered enough; the power of our mothers, whatever their love for us and their struggles on our behalf, is too restricted. And it is the mother through whom patriarchy early teaches the small female her proper expectations. The anxious pressure of one female on another to conform to a degrading and dispiriting role can hardly be termed "mothering" even if she does this believing it will help her daughter to survive. (1976, 246)

The research presented suggests that through ritual and imaging of the Goddess, women are seeking to heal the mother-daughter relationship within the context of spiritual metaphor and a woman-centered cosmology. Through the reconstructed vision of the Goddess/Mother, participants reunite with the most primary of all human relationships, an intrapsychic union that reaffirms not only the positive bond between mother and child but the acceptance of the female self as worthy and empowered. For, in the alienation that exists between mother and daughter, there is also the estrangement of the daughter from her own gender identity—as the young female child is made aware of the powerlessness of the mother she also must accept the powerlessness of a gender by which she herself is identi-fied. The woman-centered ritual thus heals two forms of alienation that characterize women's experience: the effects of social isolation that sus-tain "the culture of estrangement" and the effects of self-alienation that result from the nature of mother-daughter relationships that develop under systems of male dominance and the pervasive threat of male violence.

The Politics of Women's Healing

In concluding the analysis and discussion of women-centered healing rites, it seems appropriate to consider the role that women's spirituality plays within the overall framework of feminist goals for social change and political equality. As essentially a grass-roots movement among women who are seeking a female-centered spiritual orientation, the women's spirituality movement represents creativity and initiative among women who are seeking to redefine and perhaps reinvent a spiritual cosmology that validates and incorporates notions of female power and interrelatedness. By challenging existing doctrine, practice, and conceptions of divinity, goddess-centered rituals break down assumptions that maintain the consciousness of estrangement and the attending psychological dependence on an all-powerful male god figure. In this regard, Christ argues that while the emergence of the Goddess does not guarantee equality for women, it does offer a means through which women can rethink issues of power and autonomy. As such she writes:

> [M]ost feminists who are interested in the symbols of God-She and the Goddess have an intuitive sense that the reemergence of God-She and the Goddess will not be without enormous social and political consequences. . . . They say that the Goddess and God-She have made them more comfortable in accepting their own power and the power of other women, and that the unconscious needs for male approval have lessened as the Goddess and God-She symbols begin to transform the hold of the male-father-saviour on their minds. (1985, 250)

Added to the significance of the symbology is the social act of participating in communal rituals that bond women together and reaffirm the possibility for achieving social change through the independent and creative action of women. The dynamic seems to be one of personal transformation that empowers participants to engage in political actions that are inspired by the spiritual vision of healing and wholeness. Two examples of this phenomenon became evident in follow-up studies of the spirituality group. After the group stopped meeting, five of the women continued to be involved in women's spirituality but in a less personal and more political form. Three of the women organized a community-wide ritual to protest violence against women that has now become part of the "Take Back the Night" celebrations during Violence Awareness Week at the University of Colorado. Two other participants were jailed for their civil disobedience at the Nevada test site where nuclear bombs are detonated underground. Protesting nuclear destruction, these women were part of a group that performed rituals on the test site, naming themselves after the goddess Pele. In describing this political action, one of the women said:

> We arrived at ground zero and before they came to arrest us we formed a circle and took flowers and green plants from our backpacks. We also had seeds with us and the ground there is like a desolate crater. We planted our seeds and laid

the flowers and greenery around us, chanting and visioning the rebirth of the earth which had been destroyed by nuclear explosions. We knelt down and felt the dry earth in our hands and we felt our connection to life and the possibility of recovering our mother earth for us, for everyone, for all our children.

In both cases of ritualized political action, the women reported that they chose this method of protest because of their involvement in the women's spirituality group:

> After doing rituals with other women, I became aware of the incredible power we can generate with each other. Taking that power out of the realm of individual healing and bringing it to the public arena in the form of public ritual is empowering and makes a statement that we are not only victims but we are in the process of transforming society as well—however slowly and painstakingly.

As ritual thus reduces the effects of alienation, reintegrating individuals who have been marginalized and devalued by culture, it may also lead to changes that are realized both in the personal lives of participants and through the desire to transform society as a whole. In the latter situation, those involved in women's spirituality may become engaged in acts of courage that seek to heal and change that which is perceived as harmful and destructive to human life.

References

Bolen, J. S., 1984
Budapest, Zsuzsanna, 1986
Christ, Carol P., 1982, 1985
Durkheim, Emile, 1915, 1951
Ehrenreich, Barbara, and Deirdre English, 1978
Fiorenza, E., 1979
Glendinning, C., 1982
Hall, N., 1980
Jacobs, Janet, forthcoming a
Pollack, G. H., 1975
Reuther, Rosemary R., 1972, 1985
Rich, A., 1976
Russell, L. M., 1974, 1976
Starhawk, 1979, 1982
Stein, D., 1987
Trible, P., 1973

20

Women's Search for Family and Roots: A Jewish Religious Solution to a Modern Dilemma

Lynn Davidman

Introduction

This paper presents an analysis of the attraction and resocialization of contemporary, secular young women into a traditional religious world-view: that of Orthodox Judaism. In the past fifteen years, paralleling the growth of Christian fundamentalism, there has been an increase in the number of women and men who become attracted to Orthodox Judaism (Aviad 1983; Kaufman 1985). I focused this study on the young, educated middle-class women who are making this choice, since their attraction to this traditional religion raises two interesting and related questions. Why and how are old religious traditions reconstructed in the modern world, when many of the predictions and much of the evidence pointed toward the increasing secularization of modern Western societies? (Berger 1969; Wilson 1966, 1982). Secondly, given that Orthodox Judaism prescribes for women the traditional role of wife and mother in a nuclear family, why does it appeal to contemporary women who appear to have a relatively wide range of role choices, particularly since this is a time in which the feminist critiques of traditional roles, and of religion's place in maintaining these roles, are so widely available? (for example, Daly 1968, 1973; Heschel 1983).

This paradox of contemporary women's attraction to Orthodox Judaism raises questions that compel us to reexamine our commonly held assumptions concerning the changing of women's roles and the secularization of religion in modern society. The study presented here aims to contribute to our understanding of these larger questions through an in-depth, comparative analysis of one particular instance of these tensions: the case of women *ba'alot teshuvah* (women who become newly Orthodox Jews as adults).

This paper presents some of the findings of my study of the "conversion" of secular Jewish women to Orthodox Judaism (Davidman 1986, 1989, 1990).[1] The study focuses on individuals, institutions, and their interactions: it provides an analysis of the women who become ba'alot teshuvah and the process of their socialization into Orthodox Jewish worldviews. Here I will present these interrelated dynamics of conversion and proselytization specifically as they relate to issues regarding women's roles. A major finding of the study is that gender and family themes are prominent both in the women's accounts of the factors that attracted them to Orthodox Judaism and in the teachings that shape their socialization as religious women. In other words, there is a fit between the women's motives for joining and the methods of indoctrination. I will show that the women's decision to join a religious community was actually shaped by their desires for a family and for clarity about gender roles, and subsequently that the religious institutions' attempts to recruit them included a major emphasis upon these dimensions.[2]

This finding is consistent with those reported in other studies of young adults who join contemporary religious communities. Debra Kaufman, in her study of women ba'alot teshuvah who were already integrated into Orthodox Jewish communities, found that the search for clear definitions of female and male roles and the provision of norms for family life were important dimensions in the women's accounts of their attraction to Orthodoxy. Janet Aviad's research on newly Orthodox American and Israeli Jews also pointed to the significance of Jewish models of family life in Orthodoxy's appeal to young assimilated Jews. Similarly, studies of fundamentalist and charismatic Christian communities report that the clarity about gender roles and the emphasis on family life offered by these religious groups are significant features in their appeal to young adults who grew up in a culture in which these norms were in flux (Ammerman 1987; Neitz 1987; Rose, 1987). A theoretical analysis of the significant relationship between gender-role ambiguity in modern society and the attraction of religious communities is provided by Angela Aidala in her report of her research comparing young adults who join secular and religious communes. She suggests that modern moral pluralism and gender-role ambiguity enhances the appeal of religious movements that present *explicit gender ideologies,* which are operationalized in close-knit communities, to young people who have become frustrated and disoriented by the gender-role uncertainty in the wider society (Aidala 1985).

Methods of the Study

In order to explore the range of the phenomenon, I chose to compare two groups of women within two settings that are well known for their outreach work, and that represent very different approaches to Orthodox Judaism (Glaser and Strauss 1967). One setting is a large modern Orthodox synagogue in New York City that is widely known and emulated for its extensive programs for recruiting and resocializing newcomers into Orthodox Judaism. I will refer to this synagogue as "Metropolitan Synagogue." The modern Orthodox are a subgroup within the Orthodox community that advocates a combination of religious observance with active participation in the secular world. Members of this synagogue dress and appear like other white middle-class Americans. They participate widely in the cultural offerings of New York and hold professional positions even as they are committed to observing Jewish religious laws and rituals. For my research I spent five months in the spring of 1984 doing participant observation (attending Beginner's Services every Saturday and adult education classes several nights a week) and conducting in-depth interviews within this synagogue community.

The other setting is a residential institute sponsored by the Lubavitch Chassidim to introduce women to traditional, Lubavitch-style Judaism, through an intensive program of classes and everyday living of Judaism. I will refer to this institution as "Pardes Sara." As a group, Lubavitch Chassidim are much more insular than modern Orthodox Jews and have much stronger boundaries with the secular society. They maintain a distinctive style of dress (the men wear black suits, beards, and *yarmulkes* (skullcaps); the women wear long sleeves and long dresses; the married women always have their heads covered). They generally do not celebrate American holidays and instead maintain a calendar of their own community celebrations. I spent one month in the summer of 1983 living at Pardes Sara and participating in the daily round of activities, including ten hours of classes a day, meals, and conducting formal and informal interviews. I conducted a total of forty-five interviews in the two settings.

Profile of the Recruits in Each Community

A striking and significant characteristic shared by nearly all of the women recruits in both communities studied is that they are single. This pattern was found in other studies of newly Orthodox Jews (Aviad 1983) as well as in many studies of individuals joining other contemporary religious groups (for example, Barker 1984; Richardson, Stewart, and Simmonds 1979; Parsons 1986): in general a higher proportion of people embrace a new religious way of life when they are single than when they are already married. This is due to the fact that young adults in the transitional stages in their lives—specifically, the transition to adulthood—are more likely to experience the impact of major structural changes and the "lack of fit between institutionalized guides for thought, feeling, and behavior, and changed conditions and events" (Aidala 1985, 289). These individuals, then, would be more likely to be attracted to groups that provide explicit norms for major areas of their lives, including gender roles and family organization. For both groups of women in this study one life-cycle stage emerged as the most common time for this conversion to Orthodoxy: the transition to adulthood in terms of the desire to establish a family.

Yet in spite of this essential commonality, there were many important differences between the women attracted to the two Orthodox communities. The women attracted to Metropolitan Synagogue tend to be older, more highly educated, and more professionally established than the women who come to the Lubavitch institute. The large majority of ba'alot teshuvah at Metropolitan Synagogue are between the ages of twenty-nine and forty. Nearly all have college degrees, and many have advanced degrees beyond the B.A.: there were several M.A.s, M.B.A.s, Ph.D.s, and one M.D. in the group. Nearly all of these women work in well-paid positions in business or the professions. At the Lubavitch institute the majority of women are younger. Nearly all are under thirty years old: a third of the women are teenagers and half are between the ages of twenty and twenty-five. The large majority of women there had completed only twelfth grade. Almost none of these women are professionals. These women were much more likely to describe themselves as "spiritual seekers," in contrast to the women who join the modern Orthodox synagogue. Many had tried other religious groups, such as Christian fundamentalism or Eastern religions, before ending up at Lubavitch. Their accounts included more stories of troubled family backgrounds, divorce, family violence, suicide attempts, and difficulty with male-female relationships.

The differences in age, education, occupation, and background between the type of woman attracted to each community is understandable: the enormous changes demanded by the Lubavitch socialization process makes it more attractive to those individuals who are less well established, and therefore have less to lose in taking on such a radically new way of life.

The Metropolitan Synagogue Women

Ordering One's Life: The Search for Family

Nearly every woman I interviewed specifically mentioned a longing for family and a committed relationship as an important factor in her attraction to Orthodox Judaism. The dominant theme that comes through in my interviews is *not* the search for God or metaphysical truth or spiritual experience. In fact, half of the women at Metropolitan Synagogue were not even sure they believe in God! Yet every woman I spoke with spontaneously highlighted the salience of her desire for a family.

These women are at a stage in their life cycle in which the majority of their contemporaries are already married and having children. Their desire to form families of their own is often on their minds when they choose to enter the synagogue. As one woman, a thirty-five-year-old bank executive, expressed it: "Probably at this point in my life I would prefer to be married, and that may be part of the reason why I'm in this kind of community. Family is a value here."[3] Within traditional Judaism a great deal of emphasis is placed on family life. Many of the rituals specifically take place at home, in a family setting. The nuclear family was highlighted and glorified continuously in both communities I studied.

Many of the Metropolitan Synagogue women I interviewed live alone in studio apartments in high-rise buildings. They had moved into these apartments several years ago, when they were in their twenties, expecting to get married soon and move out. Yet six or eight or ten years later they find themselves still single, and still living alone in small apartments. There aren't that many opportunities in their lives to meet compatible men and they have given up on, or never even considered, Manhattan's renowned singles bars. One thirty-two-year-old woman expressed precisely the experience of many of the others: "I would really like to meet someone, but New York City is an island, a desolate island of singles."

So what we have here is a group of women who are grappling with issues many adult single women face today. Recent studies indicate that the demographics are seriously weighted against single women over twenty-five. There is an "undersupply of available men" and "the older the woman the strikingly fewer the men." This results in an "ever-increasing number of women over twenty-five without potential marriage partners" (Richardson 1985, 2, 3). The women I interviewed found themselves in the same situation as many of their cohorts: their lives had not worked out in the way they had grown up assuming they would, that is, they would meet someone, fall in love and get married, certainly by the time they were thirty. As single women in their thirties they were having a difficult time finding husbands in the urban secular environment in which they lived. These women therefore actively sought out a setting in which they could change their situation, a context in which they might find men to marry and in which the norms explicitly encourage marriage.

One thirty-four-year-old businesswoman said she had hoped that since the synagogue is a religious institution, the milieu might be more conducive (than the secular Manhattan singles world) to forming stable relationships. "Meeting men has not been easy in New York. You know, the same old shtick, they don't want to get married. I thought the men here would be different." A recent *New York Times* article entitled "Singles Seek Social Life at Houses of Worship" quotes a woman who is a new member of this synagogue: "It's a much more civilized place to meet than in a singles bar. . . . How bad can a place be when every guy's opening line is 'Good Shabbos'?" (Kerr 1985, 82). The women imagine that the synagogue operates as a gatekeeper, screening out the undesirables who would not be excluded from most secular settings. The religious institution thus has the latent function of allowing eligible women and men to mix. The religious dimension and the study of Judaism are not central for these women; the relationships are.

The women express not only the desire to get married; they also want children. And this wish is felt to be made more urgent by the ticking of the biological clock. A thirty-six-year-old woman who works in publishing clearly expressed this sentiment voiced by many of the others: "Most women, especially women who are in their thirties, are finding that it's extremely important to be a mother or to at least be married and to try and build a family." Several of the women told me that they were inspired to live in a more Jewish way in their daily lives in order to have something to pass on to their children. So strong are their desires for a warm, close-knit family life that their accounts of their decisions to join an Orthodox community include children they do not yet have. One such twenty-nine-year-old woman, in response to the question "how would you articulate what being Jewish means to you?" said,

> Raising my children Jewish. Keeping these traditions alive for my children. For me Judaism means I will raise my children to be a little more Jewish than I was, so that at least I'll know for them that Judaism won't die out.

Families within the Community

The women's emphasis on family is also expressed in the way they talk about finding a community. The language the women use when they describe the feeling of community is replete with metaphors associated with family and particularly with mothering—such terms as "warm," "nurturing," "loving," and "closeness" are used frequently. Many of the women state explicitly that they have found in the religious community a substitute or extended family. As a thirty-eight-year-old advertising executive expressed it:

> One of the reasons for my involvement in a place like Metropolitan Synagogue is a substitute for a family. I have used something like Metropolitan Synagogue, which is all-encompassing and very supportive and warm and all, as a substitute family, and got involved with religious Judaism for that reason.

In addition to feeling that the community has become their extended family, the women are also attracted by the positive value attached to family in the community, and by the happy families they see as role models. The newcomers are deliberately exposed to some of the most prominent and "special" families in the community, since they are frequently the ones who open their homes for hospitality. The contrast between these bustling households, as they prepare for Sabbath and holiday meals, and the women's own more quiet and solitary lives, makes the Orthodox way of life very attractive. As is evident in this quotation from a thirty-six-year-old saleswoman, the ba'alot teshuvah talk about the families they see in glowing terms: "It's nice being with the families. I've met some really wonderful people and the relationships are so nice, between the husband and the wife and the kids." Thus the role models for their socialization into membership are the nuclear families into whose homes the recruits are invited.

Clarity about Gender

Since nearly all of these women have for years been active participants in the world of work, successfully competing with men for professional positions, I wondered how they felt about the sexual division of roles in the synagogue. Orthodox Judaism defines the synagogue, that is, the public domain, as the sphere of the men, and assigns women primary responsibility for the home, the private domain. The women in this community are excluded from full participation in public ritual life. Yet nearly all of the women interviewed stated that they do not mind the traditional gender differentiation which underlies these definitions of male and female roles. They make distinctions between the various areas of their lives: they do not object to their lack of access to full participation in the synagogue, but would strongly object to it in the workplace. A forty-year-old film producer expressed this sentiment precisely:

> Now if you said to me, Stephanie, you can't work on this project because you're a woman, I wouldn't like that. Work seems to be an area where it doesn't seem fair to me and I do feel I want to be an equal, but outside of work I don't feel that way.

The women resolve the possible cognitive dissonance between their needs for equality and their desire for what the synagogue has to offer by separating the two spheres of public and private life. Since many of these women have struggled for and achieved equal access in the public sphere, they are actually glad to have a private sacred sphere in which they do not have to be "out there" asserting themselves.

In fact, several of the women stated quite clearly that the community's clear delineation of separate roles for men and women is a welcome contrast to the blurring and confusion about these roles in secular society. As a thirty-five-year-old bank executive said,

> In modern urban society the idea of the family, or the idea of children, the idea of certain basic things like that, and certain basic ideas about why there are men and women is considered really old hat and ridiculous and in a lot of ways I really think the traditional values are much more important.

The articulation of distinct roles and obligations for men and women provides a conception of order for a central part of their lives, one that is experienced as highly disordered in contemporary society.

The Lubavitch Women

The Search for Family

The accounts of the women who join the Lubavitch community reflect these same themes of desire to form a family, attraction to the warm, nuclear families in the community, and search for clarity about gender roles. Nearly every woman I interviewed, even the women under twenty years of age, highlighted her desire to get married. Many explicitly stated that this was part of their agenda in joining the Lubavitch community and in coming to Pardes Sara. One twenty-one-year-old college student specified:

> I came to Pardes Sara because here's a place where I can get what I want to learn. The stuff that helps me put myself together just in terms of the fact that marriage is one of my main goals now. At Pardes Sara you learn about what it is. That's what goes on here.

A very troubled nineteen-year-old woman expressed the same desire: "The Rabbi told me that in Lubavitch I could be married to a nice guy and they would straighten me out first. I very much want to get married."

These women are particularly attracted to the Lubavitch system of courtship and marriage, in which the community strictly regulates dating through matchmaking and the total prohibition of premarital physical contact between women and men. An important factor in their attraction to this system is that many of them have had sexual relationships in which they had been hurt. One twenty-one-year-old secretary described a typical scenario:

> I was never very good at playing the dating game but I tried like anything to make it work. It didn't work. . . . I went to college and I met this guy at college and we started dating and I started to care about him and then I got screwed, literally screwed by him. If I could go back to being sixteen years old again I'd do it all over . . . but I'd make a lot of changes.

In having had negative sexual experiences, the Lubavitch recruits are probably no different from the large majority of contemporary single women who, it is very likely, have also been hurt at some point in their relationships with men. I am certain that many of the women who are attracted to Metropolitan Synagogue had also had sexual relationships in which they had been hurt. Yet since I asked very open-ended questions in my interviews, the women had the opportunity to recount those experiences that they understood as most relevant to their attraction to Orthodoxy. The absence of such stories among the women who join Metropolitan Synagogue indicates that they do not construe these experiences as so decisive in their decision to join an Orthodox synagogue. Indeed, once they join the synagogue most remain sexually active. In contrast, the prominence of such experiences in the accounts of the women who come to Pardes Sara indicates that within their own self-understanding these experiences play a major role in their attraction to a religious community that demands they surrender control over their sexuality. *They actually seem relieved to follow the community's norms and to be given external reasons for not being sexually active.* This finding is similar to that of Aidala who reports that recruits to religious communes were attracted by the "religious ideology [that] promised easy resolution of uncertainties regarding sexuality and patterns of gender relating." For these young adults who had been troubled by the lack of clarity about these norms in the broader culture, "in many ways the simplest solution to confused and unanchored sexual feelings is total abstinence" (Aidala 1985, 292).

Models of Family Life

As at Metropolitan Synagogue, an attractive feature of the Lubavitch community is that it provides numerous models of warm, nuclear families and affirms the value of family, thus validating the women's desires. The women express enormous admiration for the families they meet within the religious community. They view these families as prototypes for the families they wish they had, and would like to create. As one sixteen-year-old high school student enthused:

> What else turned me on? The family life? I loved it . . . they had bunches of kids and they were so neat. How they raise their children and they never get into problems. The problems that I had. I know that if I was brought up in a family like that I would never have those kinds of problems. So their system is very good, it makes the kids grow up really healthy. And they're close to each other and they have a sense of community and it's nice. Family life in Lubavitch keeps you out of trouble. . . . The Lubavitch families seem so perfect.

The women's glowing descriptions of family life within the religious community are at least partly an idealization based on a sense of deprivation in the women's own experience. Many of the women present stark contrasts between the Lubavitch families they had come to know and their own troubled family lives. I imagine that the difficult familial experiences recounted by the women at Pardes Sara is an important factor in their readiness to join a religious community that assumes such strong control over its members' lives. The community provides the closeness, guidance, firm boundaries, and foundations for identity they feel they never received from their own families.

Additionally, as we saw at Metropolitan Synagogue, the community becomes a substitute or extended family. Until the Lubavitch ba'alot teshuvah marry and form their own families, the community provides for each recruit a *mashpiah,* a sponsor, who in some ways acts as a substitute parent. The amount of personal attention and solicitude provided by the sponsors, and the social control entailed in having someone so closely supervising one's conversion, lead to a rapid transformation of the new recruits in this community.

Clarity about Gender

A major element of a person's identity is a clear definition of her or his gender role. Like many of the ba'alot teshuvah at Metropolitan Synagogue, the women who come to Pardes Sara have been unable to find within the wider society a satisfactory articulation of their role as women. Their accounts highlight the confusion about gender roles in contemporary culture and emphasize that Orthodox Judaism is attractive precisely because it delineates distinct roles for women and men. Recent studies of individuals who join Orthodox Jewish, fundamentalist Christian, and other contemporary religious movements also find that the articulation of clear norms for gender roles and family life is a major attraction of these religious communities (Aidala 1985; Bromley, Shupe, and Oliver 1982; Rochford 1985). Many of the women I interviewed highlighted the contrast between secular views of womanhood and the Orthodox Jewish conception. A twenty-one-year-old college dropout described this distinction:

> Society cries, "women's lib! Don't get tied down and caught up in a rut of old-fashioned norms. Be a modern woman! Use birth control." Being "just" a wife and mother, we are taught, isn't satisfying, even degrading. We must go to college, find careers, and find our own identity. I think that with all of this identity finding we have lost the true identity we had all along. . . . We *are*, first and foremost, women. . . . We are meant to cleave to a man and be one together with him; we *are* meant to raise a family and yes, even find fulfillment in it. This was God's plan from the beginning and nothing's changed as far as He's concerned.

These women are reexamining some of the presumptions that come from our secular society in terms of gender roles. They find within traditional Judaism new ammunition for rejecting contemporary norms. While the ideas of the dominant culture emphasize that women should be free to choose whatever roles they wish, the Lubavitch ba'alot teshuvah echo the rabbis of this community, who insist that in fact contemporary women are not free to choose, because women's role at home is devalued. They articulate a profound critique of the feminist position that women can be truly fulfilled only in the public arena of work.

The Lubavitch community is much more insular than Metropolitan Synagogue and sets up much stronger boundaries with secular society. Therefore they attract people who are looking for a much more radical alternative to everyday life and for a guarantee of security at any cost.

Why This Choice?

If, as I found, the women's attraction to Orthodox Judaism is fundamentally based upon a desire for family and clear definitions of femininity and masculinity, why do they make this choice in particular? One factor seems to be the compatibility between Orthodox Judaism and certain aspects of their childhood experiences. Many of the women recounted positive memories of religious grandparents. Participating in Orthodox Jewish services and community life evokes for them feelings of warmth and belonging evocative of their childhood experiences with their grandparents. Other women described negative memories from their childhoods of feeling a lack of a positive sense of religious or ethnic identity in contrast to their friends. Orthodoxy is attractive to them precisely because it offers that which they always felt was missing. In addition, the women who make this choice define themselves as traditional in many ways. They were not active in the student protests of the 1960s, have traditional values about marriage and family, and the large majority of them do not identify as feminists.

Perhaps most importantly, joining an Orthodox Jewish community provides them with opportunities and benefits that are not so readily available in secular society. The religious community legitimates their desire to form families and provides models of family life as well as explicit definitions of femininity and masculinity. Religion is actually one of the few remaining institutions that provides such explicit, clearly defined, and comprehensive norms for private life. Orthodox Jewish ideology, like that of other contemporary fundamentalist religious groups, provides "systematic explanations which define the 'true' nature of women and men and provide spiritual and practical guidance for male/female relations" (Aidala 1985, 295). In addition, while their choice may seem deviant to secularists, from the recruits' point of view it offers many benefits even if the particular goal of marriage doesn't work out: a sense of roots, a community that becomes an extended family, and a clear and explicit definition of self.

Socialization into Membership

Since the women come to these religious communities seeking assistance in forming families and clarity about gender, the teachings concerning women's roles, marriage, and the family are an important part of the socialization process. Women who join an Orthodox Jewish community are taught not only to be practicing Jews but also their appropriate roles as women: i.e., wives and mothers within nuclear families. Thus the order the community projects and attempts to impose in this area is a major attraction of this way of life.

What we see here is the mutual influence and interaction of the settings and the women. These women come to Orthodox Judaism with certain needs. They are attracted to these settings in particular because they feel these particular religious communities will be able to meet their needs. The institutions, in turn, recruit them through emphasizing these same themes. The women are seeking marriage partners and models of family life. These institutions thus offer socialization for marriage in a world in which conventional routes to marriage have eluded many women.

The Metropolitan Synagogue

In keeping with the values of traditional Judaism, and in response to the plethora of singles attracted to the Metropolitan Synagogue (50 percent of the twelve hundred people who attend Saturday services are single), the rabbis in this community are clearly interested in promoting nuclear families. The importance of family life in Judaism is repeatedly stressed. Even in teachings about other aspects of ritual observance, such as the Sabbath or holidays, the discussion inevitably included references to the nuclear family setting within which many of these rituals are performed. The message here is very similar to what is taught in the Lubavitch community: people are incomplete unless they are married. The rabbis try to convey the image that in contrast to the secular society, the synagogue is a good place in which to find a marriage partner.[4] This has become a selling point of the synagogue. One woman told me that when she told the Beginners' rabbi about her engagement his response was, "Great! That's good for our statistics." Within the synagogue community there is a great deal of informal matchmaking going on and the rabbis occasionally even introduce men and women to each other. Recently they have added a singles newsletter to their program. The institution is obviously responding to and trying to meet the needs of the single women and men who are attracted to it.

Yet, as we will see, the Lubavitch have clearly established norms for ensuring that its members get married: they arrange marriages for them and do not allow people to date casually. They thus set up an alternative to prevailing patterns of dating and mating. The modern Orthodox community, in contrast, has a much looser social structure: the rabbis and other members of the community generally do not exercise very strict social control over members' lives. Since the people in this community do remain rooted in the secular world, there is no attempt made to completely restructure their dating and mating practices. They are not limited to dating only other members of the community. Essentially, then, although it is discouraged, they are able to carry on, even as members of the synagogue community, the same patterns of male-female relationships, including premarital sexuality, that prevail in the wider society.

On this issue the rabbis of the Metropolitan Synagogue send out mixed messages. On the one hand the rabbis explicitly teach the traditional Jewish laws concerning sexuality, that premarital and extramarital sexual activities are clearly forbidden. Yet even while cautioning members against prohibited sexual activity, the rabbis are aware that the newcomers to this community are not likely to change their sexual behavior. These adults remain very involved in the secular world in many ways, and since the synagogue is an open institution, the community is not in a position to enforce such a drastic change from contemporary mores. This is implicitly acknowledged, sometimes in humorous ways. One evening in bible class the rabbi was going over the relevant laws, and explained that one of the reasons premarital sexual relations are forbidden is that only married women are required to immerse themselves in a *mikveh* (ritual bath) following their menstrual period. It is only after this immersion that men are permitted to have sexual relations with them. An excerpt from my field notes relates the ensuing conversation:

> A woman in class asked, "You're saying that the only thing prohibiting sexual relations between single men and women is mikveh?"
>
> The rabbi answered, "*Only mikveh*. If a woman doesn't go to mikveh she's considered a menstruant. If you have sexual relations with a menstruant the punishment is excision. If you eat bread on Passover the punishment is excision."
>
> A man asked, "But if she goes in the ocean—"
>
> The rabbi responded, "Look, if you're making plans, she could also put on a wedding ring and cover her hair and go to a mikveh."
>
> A woman then asked, "Is it better to go to the mikveh and lie, or not acknowledge that a person is a sexual being?"
>
> The rabbi said, "I'll answer these questions on an individual basis."

The humorous tone in which this interchange was carried out is one means of dispelling the tension that might arise over the discrepancy between the community's norms and the recruits' behavior. Since the rabbis here know how difficult it would be to change the newcomers' sexual attitudes and behaviors, they either ignore the discrepancies, or engage in light joking about it.

Conceptions of Women's Roles

The presentation of women's role in Judaism within the modern Orthodox community resembles their teachings on other aspects of Jewish religious observance: it represents an attempt to challenge and reverse contemporary values and assumptions, even while upholding modern attitudes and behavior patterns. This conception of women's roles blends traditional, essentialist understandings of women's nature with contemporary egalitarian ideas. Although a majority of women within this community work outside of the home (particularly the new ba'alot teshuvah, who are predominantly single and have no other means of support) the Beginners' rabbi teaches that Judaism assigns women primary responsibility for the care of the home and family. As he stated one Saturday morning in services,

> Men and women have roles and basic areas of responsibility. That's incontrovertible. Nothing can be used to rationalize that away. . . . The woman basically is ascribed the responsibility for the raising and nurturing of children. The men are assigned the responsibility for the cognitive education of the children.

By asserting that women's roles are determined by their ascribed characteristics, the rabbi is articulating a traditional conception of women's nature. His emphasis on the importance of women's nurturing capacities can be seen as an attempt to reverse contemporary trends, which press for equality in the public realm and, at least rhetorically, in private life as well.

This conception of women and the importance of the home is reminiscent of the nineteenth-century "cult of true womanhood," in which, at a time of great social upheaval, women's ability to create a warm, loving haven away from the heartless world was lauded by preachers and social philosophers alike (Welter 1966). At that time, the upheavals wrought by industrialization resulted in widespread confusion about gender roles and male/female relations (Ehrenreich and English 1978). Similarly, as Jessie Bernard (1975) has summarized, American society in the late 1960s and early 1970s saw major shifts in institutional structures that resulted in widespread confusion about gender roles and relationships between the sexes. The rabbi frequently made clear his perception that we are in a time of great crisis; society and the Jewish community urgently need women's capacity to set up a peaceful, comforting home that can serve as a refuge (Lasch 1977).

On the other hand, I want to emphasize that the rabbis in this community also uphold contemporary norms in their teachings about women's roles. The adult education program includes a course entitled "Feminism and Jewish Law." Offering such a course implies that the two elements— traditional Jewish law and feminism—can and should be reconciled. The Beginner's rabbi frequently asserted that while traditional Judaism does believe in certain forms of division of roles by sex, it is not opposed to modern egalitarian ideals.

> There's nothing in Judaism that says men and women can't share household responsibilities. That a man can't change a baby. Or that a woman can't work. Judaism—Jewish people—adopted the norms of the culture, and now that is changing, and there is no reason that it can't change in Judaism. But the primary responsibility for children *is* assigned to the mother.

What he's suggesting here, then, is *not a radical alternative to modernity, but a compromise with it,* including even a few modern feminist ideals such as equality in the workplace and shared labor at home.

During my stay in the community I observed many instances in which the tradition was creatively reinterpreted to show how attuned it is with feminist thinking. For example, the *niddah* laws (laws of family purity) which have been highlighted by feminists as reflecting negative attitudes toward women's sexuality, are reinterpreted in a way that incorporates feminist ideas. In services one Saturday, the Beginners' rabbi emphasized how these laws actually benefit women, by encouraging men to see women as individuals, and not as sex objects.

> I would say that the relationship of impurity has to do with sexual attitudes: it has to do with not being seen as a sexual object, which I think is a totally pro-woman attitude. You have to love me for what I am, and not for what you can get off me, and that's the laws of *tum'ah* (ritual impurity) and *taharah* (ritual purity) in Judaism. . . . Take a look at what's going on out there, how women have been objectified. Do you see women in Judaism objectified as sexual objects? On the one hand you can say it's keeping women down on the farm by keeping their heads covered. On the other hand, you could say, hey, it's by maintaining a certain attitude towards women which is not to objectify them as a sexual object.

Thus the rabbi incorporates a modern feminist analysis of the sexual objectification of women to reinforce a traditional religious critique of current sexual norms. While the rabbi's intention here is to oppose modern trends, he actually presents a very contemporary analysis that asserts that people are to be valued for their own individuality: "Love me for what I am."

We can see that in their teachings concerning women, marriage, and male-female relations, the representatives of this community do not completely attempt to reverse the prevailing norms of the wider society. Instead, they maintain a precarious balance between upholding the implicit assumptions of the wider culture and advocating a retreat to a more traditional way of life. They engage in a creative reinterpretation of the tradition that blends elements of contemporary feminism and individualism with a more traditional conception of sex roles. They also propose a model of socialization that involves gradual change through steps and stages. This represents a significant contrast with the Lubavitch community, whose teachings directly challenge and attempt to replace modern American ways of life in both the public and private spheres and advocate a swift and dramatic transformation.

The Lubavitch Community

Promoting Traditional Families

Since within this community the most significant means for women to fulfill God's will is through marriage and childbearing, teachings on marriage and the family were a major emphasis in all of the classes in the Lubavitch resocialization center. This was an explicit part of the agenda, as the rabbi who is the main teacher announced on the first day of the session: "Anything that we learn that's got any value has to be useful to you in your *Yiddishkeit* (traditional Jewish observance) and in your marriage. If it's useful in only one of them, you're in trouble." Thus the institution directly addresses the needs and desires of the women coming there: they are seeking to get married, and the rabbi clearly tells them that traditional Jewish observance is synonymous with marriage for them.

A central theme in all of the rabbi's teachings concerning marriage replaces the ideal of romantic love with a sense of relationships as based on duty, obligation, and commitment. As Robert Bellah and his coauthors point out in their recent study, *Habits of the Heart,* white middle-class Americans believe in love as the basis for enduring relationships. "They tend to assume that feelings define love and that permanent commitment can come only from having the proper clarity, honesty, and openness about one's feelings" (Bellah et al. 1985, 98). The rabbi at Pardes Sara reverses this order. Rather than relying on feelings as the basis for forming permanent relationships, he advocates the primacy of commitment over feeling. Love should not be seen as the reason for marriage, but the *result* of it.

> In order for love to exist—to have the desire for closeness—you need to already have a relationship, and that relationship permits or cultivates the emotion of love. Until the guy proposes it's not love. Only when the guy proposes, when he's made the ultimate sacrifice for you, is that love. . . . Love comes only *after* marriage. You can never love somebody before marriage. In most relationships outside of marriage the love isn't love at all but the comfort we feel with *ourselves.* . . . Through *conviction* you create a relationship that in the end will reward you with love.

Traditionalists fear that the "expressive individualism" that underlies our culture's preoccupation with feelings will threaten family life. The Lubavitch Chassidim are similar to evangelical Christians in their attempt to reverse the current primacy of emotion over obligation in relationships. An evangelical minister cited by Bellah sounds exactly like Rabbi Levine:

Most people are selfish . . . looking at relationships for themselves only. . . .
Scriptures teach there is a love we can have for other people that is selfless. We
have to learn it. It's actually a matter of the will. (Bellah et al. 1985, 94)

Even when it might be inconvenient for oneself, or go against one's
immediate preferences, marriage requires putting the commitment to one's
partner first. This view of marriage encourages permanence and commitment by emphasizing the primacy of roles over individual selves. The
rabbi teaches the women to fit their selves into the prescribed roles, and
thus to uphold the institutional arrangements of the community.

Restructuring Courtship

One of the practical implications of these teachings is the restructuring
of the women's courtship behavior. The Lubavitch Chassidim maintain a
very different pattern of courtship than that which prevails in the wider
society. Adolescent boys and girls are not permitted any casual interactions or dating. At the age of eighteen or nineteen, when the woman is
deemed ready for marriage (early twenties for a man), a third party
arranges a *shidduch* (a meeting between a woman and a man). They are
encouraged to go out only a few times, and then decide on the suitability
of the person as a marriage partner. The couple is allowed no physical
contact prior to marriage. This is similar to the pattern that prevails in the
religious communes studied by Aidala and other students of contemporary
religious movements (Aidala 1985; Bromley and Shupe 1979).

When new recruits adopt the way of life of this community, they come
under the community's auspices in this realm. The sacrifice of their control
over their dating and sexual relationships is a commitment mechanism,
one that is frequently employed in utopian communities (Kanter 1972, 77–
78). During the socialization process at the institute they are completely
isolated from men (except, of course, the rabbis) while they are taught the
new norms. The community's regulation of behavior in this realm is
complete and thorough—they are told they are not even allowed to shake
hands with men. Once they join the community there is generally a waiting
period of at least a year to ensure that their commitment to Chassidism is
solidified before they are deemed ready to go out. Then the recruits will
follow the prescribed pattern of dating only men who have been selected
for them as possible marriage partners.

These are obviously enormous changes to make in women who have
been brought up in an era of sexual freedom and who have already
experienced sexual relationships with men. The rabbi fosters their acceptance of these restrictions by weakening their commitment to their past

lives and suggesting that they can begin life anew—they can reclaim their native "innocence" and start again. He suggests,

> I think that innocence is a native condition and that there's an intrinsic need to be innocent. Innocence means that you're created a certain way and that you've never corrupted that condition. You never tampered, a virginal territory. Untouched. That's the way it was created and that's the way it remained. That's innocence. And if God says, "I created you kosher," then to have eaten nonkosher means that you've been tampered with. You introduced an ingredient that didn't belong. Discoloration. You're no longer virginal and that hurts.

Although in this quotation the rabbi explicitly points to the violation of kosher laws as his example of lost innocence, his use of the words "virginal," "tampered," and "untouched" suggests that he is also talking about sexuality. Here he promotes the goal of resocialization by reinforcing the women's already existing discomfort about their past sexual activities. Many of them did indeed feel "tampered with" and were concerned with whether they could erase that taint now that they were embracing a new way of life. The women are attracted to these teachings because they reinforce their preexisting desire to avoid or be protected in their sexual relationships.

Conception of Women's Roles

"When a woman comes into Yiddishkeit she has to rethink her whole being as a woman." Thus the rabbi at Pardes Sara communicates that within this community, the process of resocialization to Orthodoxy demands a radical reconceptualization of femininity following a radical break from the outside world, as in a total institution. A great deal of the rabbi's time in class was spent breaking down contemporary understandings of women's role, male-female relations, and marriage, and presenting the Chassidic alternative. This type of resocialization is more attractive to those with more radical, that is, more extreme needs.

The Chassidic interpretation of women's proper role rests upon an essentialist view of women, the idea that *women have a unique and distinct nature,* rooted in their biology, and expressed in all aspects of their being. Woman's greater involvement in childbearing is taken as a metaphor for her essential nature. As the rabbi said:

> That's why, for many women, to relearn devotion, to replace narcissism with devotion, is really a very natural thing because it's more feminine to be devotional than to be narcissistic. . . . Biologically, a man does not give of himself in any real sense to have children. A woman does. So right there before we even get into any profound mystical stuff, just the way our bodies are built,

a woman is, by nature, going to give of herself. . . . For the woman it's almost inevitable, natural.

As with other aspects of obedience to Jewish law, the women are taught that any deviation from this conception of women's roles is a violation of their own inner nature.

For a woman to wait to have children is wrong, because she's violating herself. It seems to be that that's part of the definition of being a woman and when you tamper with the definition you're tampering with yourself. Psychically that's got to be damaging.

In contrast to contemporary society which teaches that women are free to choose their roles, and that they may reasonably elect to fulfill several different primary roles either simultaneously or in succession, the message here is that women's inherent nature is consistent with the demands of a traditional feminine role.

Conclusion

The attraction of certain modern women to Orthodox Judaism, and the attempts of each group to resocialize them into its worldview, particularly its conception of women's roles, must be understood against the backdrop of the changing conceptions of gender and family patterns in the wider society. Studies of other contemporary religious groups have also found that an important function of these groups is the provision of clear-cut norms for gender roles and the legitimation of nuclear family life. Religious groups vary in the specificity of their guidelines for members' lives. The two communities presented here differ in their attitudes toward modernity and consequently in the extent to which they specify and enforce norms for gender roles, sexual behavior, and family life. Thus they each appeal to women with varying needs for structure and guidance: the insular Lubavitch community appeals more to those women who are less rooted in the secular world (that is, jobs, apartments, relationships) than does the more liberal modern Orthodox community. This is similar to Aidala's finding that the "ideological rigidity of religious groups . . . appeal[ed] to individuals most in need of certainty regarding problematic sex and gender issues" (1985, 297) and that "differences in ideology and practice regarding sex and gender issues are important factors in the differential appeal of movements to various audiences" (1985, 310).

Religion remains one of the few institutional arenas in contemporary society in which one can still find comprehensive guidelines for how to conduct one's private life. While secularization theory suggests that it is a sign of decline that religion, which once was all-pervasive, is now relegated to private life, in fact it still performs a very important social role. This is one factor which may account for its surviving and even flourishing in contemporary society. Secularization theory had predicted that religion would become irrelevant in the modern world because it would be replaced by more rational modes of thought and worldviews. The data reported here suggest (as does Neitz 1987) that individuals who choose religion in modern society are in fact being highly rational—they have examined the various alternatives and decided that the religious groups either provide better explanations or offer opportunities that are unavailable elsewhere. Thus religious realities continue to appeal to individuals because they offer solutions to the dilemmas and ambiguities that pervade contemporary life.

This study actually addresses the age-old question: what do women want? A major finding is that these women, at least, want what women have always been believed to want: meaningful relationships with others, particularly within the context of a nuclear family: they want a husband and children. For the large majority of women in my study religion was pursued as a context in which they could form a family and find positive models of traditional family life.

Recent feminist research has demonstrated that there are unanticipated consequences of feminism that are actually difficult for women. Lenore Weitzman, for example, has shown how contemporary divorce law, modeled on the image of a liberated professional woman, actually results in poverty for large percentages of divorced women (Weitzman 1985). Betty Friedan has argued that feminists need to move into a second stage: that the goals of the first stage—equality in the public sphere—have been won and that the women's movement has failed to energize many contemporary women because it ignores what women really want—fulfilling private lives in families (Friedan 1981). I don't agree with Friedan that the goals of the first stage have been won. Yet I also see that women are still struggling to find meaningful love and relationships and that the movement toward sexual liberation has in some ways not freed women that women who want relationships with men now are free only to say yes. The women I met in the course of this research still want nuclear families and private life is very important to them. Traditional religion is attractive to them because it legitimates their desires for a family, provides models for it, and even helps them find partners. Religion offers a valuable certainty concerning gender roles and family life that is unavailable elsewhere. This is a significant factor in its continued appeal to modern secular individuals.

I wish to thank the following foundations for their generous support of my research: Barnard College Alumnae Fellowships; Brandeis University Center for Modern Jewish Studies; Memorial Foundation for Jewish Culture; Woodrow Wilson Women's Studies Fellowships. I would also like to thank the following people for their comments on an earlier draft of this essay: Vicki Caron, Chuck Lidz, Sonya Michel, Shulamit Reinharz, Tom Robbins, Shelly Tenenbaum, and Alan Zuckerman.

Notes

1. I am using the term "conversion" here not in the conventional sense, since nearly all of the women are Jewish from birth, but to connote a radical change in their worldview and behavior, a "transformation of self concurrent with a transformation of one's central meaning system" (McGuire 1982, 49).
2. Although the question can be raised whether the similarity between the women's accounts and the modes and message of their socialization is simply a result of the women's reconstruction of their conversion accounts following socialization, I was careful to interview women at all stages of this process, including women who had just begun to explore Orthodox Judaism. These women reflected the same concerns as did women who had been in the religious communities for over a year.
3. The quotations presented in this article are all verbatim excerpts from the transcripts of the interviews conducted in this study and from my field notes.
4. While some of the women (and men) who join this synagogue do meet partners within the synagogue community, they are clearly a minority of the members. Many adults who join do eventually get married, but it is only occasionally to someone they met at the synagogue.

References

Aidala, Angela, 1985
Ammerman, Nancy T., 1987
Aviad, Janet, 1983
Barker, Eileen V., 1984
Bellah, Robert N., et al., 1985
Berger, Peter L., 1969
Bernard, Jessie, 1975
Bromley, David, and Anson D. Shupe, 1979
Bromley, David G., Anson D. Shupe, and Donna Oliver, 1982.
Daly, Mary, 1968, 1973
Davidman, Lynn, 1986 (revised 1989), 1990
Ehrenreich, Barbara, and Deirdre English, 1978
Friedan, Betty, 1981
Glaser, Barney, and Anselm L. Strauss, 1967
Heschel, Susannah, ed., 1983
Kanter, Rosabeth Moss, 1972
Kaufman, Debra, 1985
Kerr, Peter, 1985
Lasch, Christopher, 1977
Luker, Kristen, 1984
McGuire, Meredith, 1982

Neitz, Mary Jo, 1987
Parsons, Arthur, 1986
Richardson, James T., Mary White Stewart, and Robert B. Simmonds, 1979
Richardson, Laurel, 1985
Rochford, E. Burke Jr., 1985
Rose, Susan, 1987
Weitzman, Lenore, 1985
Welter, Barbara, 1966
Wilson, Bryan R., 1966, 1982

VI
RELIGION, POLITICS, AND CIVIL RELIGION

21

Religion and Legitimation in the American Republic

Robert N. Bellah

Just over a decade ago I published an essay (1970) that I have never subsequently been allowed to forget. In that essay I suggested that there is such a thing as civil religion in America. My suggestion has roused passionate opposition as well as widespread acceptance. Opposition to the idea has shown little unity. Some of my opponents say there is no such thing, that I have invented something which does not exist; others say there is such a thing but there ought not to be; still others say there is such a thing but it should be called by another name, "public piety," for example, rather than civil religion. Unfortunately for me my supporters are in even greater disarray. The term *civil religion* has spread far beyond any coherent concept, or at least beyond anything I ever meant by it. Perhaps the commonest reaction is a puzzled, "Yes, there seems to be something there, but what exactly is it?" Among professional specialists in American studies there is another reaction: "We knew it all the time. What Bellah says is nothing new." And then there is perhaps a vague reference to Tocqueville. But with one or two exceptions, little in the way of conceptual clarity has been forthcoming from specialists. I would like to try once again to clarify this most troublesome problem.

I am partly to blame for the confusion by the choice of the term *civil religion,* which turned out to be far more tendentious and provocative than I at first realized. Yet the choice of the term was fortunate in that the controversies it generated are fruitful. More neutral terms such as *political religion, religion of the republic,* or *public piety* would not have generated the profound empirical ambiguities that the term *civil religion* with its two thousand years of historical resonance inevitably did.

What would be more natural than to speak about civil religion, a subject which has preoccupied theorists of republican government from Plato to Rousseau? The founders of this republic had read most of those theorists and were consciously concerned with the problem, even though they did not use the term. The difficulty comes from the fact that for most of those two thousand years there has been a profound antipathy, indeed an utter incompatibility between civil religion and Christianity. There is even a question, which we cannot explore here, whether there has not been a historic antipathy between republican government and Christianity. Most Christian political theorists down through the ages have preferred monarchy as the best form of government (Christian religious symbolism is much more monarchical than republican), and the great republican theorists— Machiavelli, Rousseau, even Tocqueville—have wondered whether Christianity could ever create good citizens. Augustine in the opening books of the *City of God* denounced Roman "civil theology" as the worship of false gods and the Roman Republic as based on false ideals and therefore as finally no commonwealth at all. Rousseau, in arguing for the necessity in a republic of a civil religion other than Christianity, wrote:

> Christianity as a religion is entirely spiritual, occupied solely with heavenly things; the country of the Christian is not of this world. . . . Imagine your Christian republic face to face with Sparta or Rome: the pious Christians will be beaten, crushed, and destroyed. . . . But I am mistaken in speaking of a Christian republic; the terms are mutually exclusive. Christianity preaches only servitude and dependence. Its spirit is so favorable to tyranny that it always profits by such a regime. True Christians are made to be slaves, and they know it and do not much mind: this short life counts for too little in their eyes.

Yet at the beginning of our history we were that contradictory thing, a Christian republic. (Samuel Adams even called us a Christian Sparta.) Or were we? Christianity was never our state religion, nor did we have in Rousseau's strict sense a civil religion, a simple set of religious dogmas to which every citizen must subscribe on pain of exile. So what did we have? What do we have now?

Tension between church and state lies deep in Christian history. The idea of a nonreligious state is a very modern and doubtful one. Through most of Western history some form of Christianity has been the established religion and has provided "religious legitimation" to the state. But under that simple formula lie faction, intrigue, anguish, tension, and on occasion massacre, rebellion, and religious war. Through much of history the state has dominated a restless church, exploited it, but never removed its refusal of final allegiance. On occasion the church has mastered the state, used it for its own ends, temporalized its spiritual loyalties into a kind of religious nationalism. In all this Christianity is no different from other religions that I have characterized as being at the historic stage. Even religions that are much more intrinsically political, such as Islam or Confucianism, have for most of their histories been involved in uneasy and unhappy alliances with state power. Relative to the first four caliphs all Muslim rulers have been viewed as at least faintly illegitimate by the religious community. Relative to the ancient sage kings all Chinese emperors have lacked fundamental legitimacy in the eyes of Confucian scholars.

The very spirituality and otherworldliness of Christianity has provided a certain avenue for reducing the tension not always open to other historic religions: the differentiation of functions, the division of spheres. Yet no solution has ever dissolved the underlying tensions described by Augustine and Rousseau. The tendency has been for every solution to break down into religion as the servant of the state or vice versa.

There have been great periodic yearnings in Western history to overcome the dichotomy, to create a society that would indeed be a Christian republic, where there would be no split in the soul between Christian and citizen. Savonarola had such a dream in fifteenth-century Florence, as did the Anabaptists in sixteenth-century Germany and some of the sectarians during the Civil War in seventeenth-century England. Most of these experiments were highly unstable and illustrated rather than refuted Rousseau's argument for mutual exclusiveness. Yet John Calvin in sixteenth-century Geneva created a city that was Christian and republican in an organic way that had few precedents (and that stood curiously behind Rousseau's own republican theorizing). Church and state were not fused; formal distinctions were sharply maintained. Yet Christian and citizen were finally two ways of saying the same thing. The New England Colonies in the seventeenth century were Christian republics in a comparable sense. In Massachusetts, for example, only Christians could be citizens, though the church did not control the state and both were governed by their members. Even though the reality of this experiment had evaporated by the early eighteenth century, the memory was still strong in the minds of the founders of the republic.

The civil theology of the youthful Hegel in Germany during the decades after the French Revolution shows that the yearning for the union of Christian and citizen was still vigorous at the end of the eighteenth century. These youthful speculations stand behind Hegel's mature political theory as well as Marx's thought about man and citizen.

Could there be a sense in which the American republic which has neither an established church nor a classic civil religion is, after all, a Christian republic, or should we say a biblical republic, in which biblical religion is indeed the civil religion? Is that what Sidney Mead (1975) means by saying that we are "a nation with the soul of a church"? The answer, as before, is yes and no. The American solution to the problem of church and state is unprecedented, unique, and confused. Let us turn from external speculation and from the introduction of tendentious terms like *civil religion* to the way in which the tradition has understood itself.

Today the almost Pavlovian response which provides a solution to all problems in this area is *the separation of church and state*. That phrase, especially when it is intensified with the unfortunate Jeffersonian image of the "wall of separation," seems to offer a clear solution when in fact it creates more difficulties than it eliminates. The phrase *separation of church and state* has no constitutional standing. The first clause of the first amendment states that "Congress shall make no law respecting an establishment of religion." That clause has a long history of interpretation which I do not intend to review here, but it certainly does not mean nor has ever meant that the American state has no interest in religion, and it certainly does not mean that religion and politics have nothing to do with each other. To the extent that the "wall of separation" image leads to those conclusions it distorts the entire history of the American understanding of religion and leads to such absurd conclusions as that religious congregations should have no tax exemption and legislative bodies should not be opened with prayer. To attribute such intentions to the founders of the republic is not only a historical error but a political error about the nature of the republic. Inspection of the second clause of the first amendment, "or prohibiting the free exercise thereof," should begin to dispel the distortions of the extreme separationists position.

The Constitution, while prohibiting a religious establishment, protects the free exercise of religion. It is this second clause to which that other common phrase *religious freedom* refers, a phrase that has often been used to sum up American teaching about religion. This phrase too has a significant Jeffersonian source, for Jefferson pointed to his authorship of a bill for "establishing religious freedom" in Virginia as one of the three things he most wanted to be remembered for. The phrase *establishing religious freedom,* which is not constitutional but which explicates the free exercise clause, suggests positive institutionalization in this area. It is religious freedom or free exercise which is the controlling idea. Prohibition of the establishment of a particular religion is required because it would be an infringement on religious freedom. Even so, today it is not uncommon for the religious freedom concept to be swallowed up in the separation concept because freedom here as elsewhere is interpreted in purely negative terms, as the liberal philosophical tradition tends to treat it. Religious freedom becomes merely the right to worship any God you please or none at all, with the implication that religion is a purely private matter of no interest or concern to political society. I will argue that "establishing religious freedom" means much more than that—that it has a powerful positive political significance. But the difficulty of interpretation is not entirely in the mind of the analyst. It is not just a question of reading late twentieth-century ideas about religion into the minds of the founders, though there is much of that. The difficulty is rooted in certain fundamental unclarities about the American political experience and the nature of the America regime, unclarities that go right back to the formative period of the republic itself.

The basic unclarity rests on whether we are a republic in recognizable relation to the republics of classical and modern times and dependent on that inner spirit of republican character and mores that makes for republican citizenship—or whether we are a liberal constitutional regime governed through artificial contrivance and the balancing of conflicting interests. What we wanted was to have our cake and eat it too, to retain the rhetoric and spirit of a republic in the political structure of a liberal constitutional state. In so doing we blurred every essential political consideration including the place of religion in public life. We artfully used religion as a way of evading the incompatibilities in our political life. For as long as the religious bodies remained vital and central in our public life the evasion was (at least partially) successful. Today when religion, more even than our other institutions, is uncertain about itself, the evasion is no longer tenable. But I am getting ahead of myself.

The great political philosophers from Aristotle to Machiavelli to Montesquieu (who had such an influence on the founders of the republic), all believed that a political regime is an expression of the total way of life of a people—its economics, its customs, its religion. The way of life correlates with the type of person the society produces and the political capacities inherent in that person. As Montesquieu said, a despotic society will have despotic customs—the arbitrary use of power, dependence of inferiors on superiors, slavery—that will produce a person primarily motivated by fear, just the right kind of subject for a despotic polity. But a republic will have republican customs—public participation in the exercise of power, political equality of citizens, a wide distribution of small and medium property with few very rich or very poor—customs that will lead to a public spiritedness, a willingness of the citizen to sacrifice his own interests for the common good, in a word a citizen motivated by republican virtue. It would be as absurd to expect a people long inured to despotism to create a successful republic as for a republican people to tolerate a despotic regime. And yet these patterns are not fixed. There is constant flux and a tendency toward degeneration—good customs become corrupted and republicn regimes become despotic. Since republics go against "gravity," it is essential if a republic is to survive that it actively concern itself with the nurturing of its citizens, that it root out corruption and encourage virtue. The republican state has an ethical, educational, even spiritual role, and it will survive only so long as it reproduces republican customs and republican citizens.

The much newer form of political organization we are calling "liberal constitutionalism," though it grew in the very seedbeds of modern republicanism, developed a markedly different idea of political life, partly in response to a newly emerging economic order. Though formulated by some of the toughest minds in the history of modern philosophy—Hobbes, Locke, Hume, Adam Smith—this tradition gave rise to the most wildly utopian idea in the history of political thought, namely that a good society can result from the actions of citizens motivated by self-interest alone when those actions are organized through the proper mechanisms. A caretaker state, with proper legal restraints so that it does not interfere with the freedom of citizens, needs do little more than maintain public order and allow the economic market mechanisms and the free market in ideas to produce wealth and wisdom.

Not only are these political ideas—republicanism and liberalism—different, they are profoundly antithetical. Exclusive concern for self-interest is the very definition of the corruption of republican virtue. The tendency to emphasize the private, particularly the economic side of life in the liberal state, undermines the public participation essential to a republic. The wealth that the liberal society generates is fatal to the basic political equality of a republic. And yet the American regime has been from the beginning a mixture of republican and liberal concepts. However, the republican moment emerged first, out of the revolutionary struggle itself, and crystalized in a document, the Declaration of Independence. The liberal moment emerged second, during the complex working out of interests in the new nation, and crystalized in the Constitution. Even that division is too simple, for there are liberal elements in the Declaration and republican elements in the Constitution, but it does suggest that from the very beginning the balance has never been easy or even. For our purposes it is interesting to note that the Declaration has several central references to God and the Constitution none at all. It is time to turn to religion as a means of mediating the tensions within the American regime.

Superstructural Role

In the early republic religion had two vital locations: the superstructure and the infrastructure of the new political regime. It is to the superstructural location of religion that the Declaration points. By superstructural I mean a locus of sovereignty taken to be above the sovereignty of the state.

Perhaps the most striking recognition of this superordinate sovereignty comes from the hand of Madison in 1785 during the debate on the bill establishing religious freedom in Virginia:

> It is the duty of every man to render to the Creator such homage, and such only, as he believes to be acceptable to him. This duty is precedent both in order of time and degree of obligation, to the claims of Civil Society. Before any man can be considered as a member of Civil Society, he must be considered as a subject of the Governor of the Universe: And if a member of Civil Society, who enters into any subordinate Association, must always do it with a reservation of his duty to the general authority; much more must every man who becomes a member of any particular Civil Society, do it with a saving of his allegiance to the Universal Sovereign.

Here Madison confines himself to the superordinate sovereignty of God over the individual citizen which precedes the sovereignty of political society over him.

The Declaration of Independence points to the sovereignty of God over the collective political society itself when it refers in its opening lines to "the laws of nature and of nature's God" that stand above and judge the laws of men. It is often asserted that the God of nature is specifically not the God of the Bible. That raises problems of the relation of natural religion to biblical religion in eighteenth-century thought that I do not want to get into here, but Jefferson then goes on to say: "We hold these truths to be self evident, that all Men are created equal, that they are endowed by their Creator with certain unalienable Rights, that among these are Life, Liberty and the pursuit of Happiness. That to secure these rights, Governments are instituted among Men, deriving their just Powers from the consent of the governed. That whenever any Form of Government becomes destructive of these ends, it is the Right of the People to alter or abolish it." Here we have a distinctly biblical God, who is much more than a first principle of nature, who creates individual human beings and endows them with equality and fundamental rights.

It is significant that the reference to a suprapolitical sovereignty, to a God who stands above the nation and whose ends are standards by which to judge the nation and indeed only in terms of which the nation's existence is justified, becomes a permanent feature of American political life ever after. Washington and Jefferson reiterate, though they do not move much beyond, the language of the Declaration in their most solemn public addresses such as their inaugural addresses or Washington's Farewell Address. This highest level of religious symbolism in the political life of the republic justifies the assertion that there is a civil religion in America. Having said that, we must also say that American civil religion is formal and in a sense marginal, though very securely institutionalized. It is formal in the sparsity and abstraction of its tenets, though in this it is very close to Rousseau's civil religion. It is marginal in that it has no official support in the legal and constitutional order. It is in this connection that we must again point out the absence of any reference to God, and thus of any civil religion, in the Constitution of the United States. Belief in the tenets of the civil religion are legally incumbent on no one and there are no official interpreters of civil theology.

The marginality of American civil religion is closely connected with the liberal side of our heritage and its most important expression, the Constitution. This side has led many to deny that there is a civil religion or that there ought to be in America. And indeed from the point of view of liberal political ideology there need not and perhaps ought not to be. The state is a purely neutral legal mechanism without purposes or values. Its sole function is to protect the rights of individuals, that is to protect freedom. And yet freedom, which would seem to be an irreducible implication of liberalism on etymological grounds alone, no matter how negatively and individualistically defined, does imply a purpose and a value. Pure liberalism is a reductio ad absurdum and a pragmatic impossibility—one reason why a pure liberal state has never existed and why in America the rhetoric and to some extent the substance of republicanism have always existed in uneasy tandem with liberalism.

From the point of view of republicanism civil religion is indispensable. A republic as an active political community of participating citizens must have a purpose and a set of values. Freedom in the republican tradition is a positive value which asserts the worth and dignity of political equality and popular government. A republic must attempt to be ethical in a positive sense and to elicit the ethical commitment of its citizens. For this reason it inevitably pushes toward the symbolization of an ultimate order of existence in which republican values and virtues make sense. Such symbolization may be nothing more than the worship of the republic itself as the highest good, or it may be, as in the American case, the worship of a higher reality which upholds the standards that the republic attempts to embody.

And yet the religious needs of a genuine republic would hardly be met by the formal and marginal civil religion that has been institutionalized in the American republic. The religious superstructure of the American republic has been provided only partially by civil religion. It has been provided mainly by the religious community itself entirely outside of any formal political structures. It is here that the genius and uniqueness of the American solution is to be found. At the 1976 Democratic Convention Barbara Jordan called for the creation of a national community that would be ethical and even spiritual in content. It is in a sense prepolitical, but without it the state would be little more than a mechanism of coercion.

The first creation of a national community in America preceded the revolution by a generation or two. It was the result of the Great Awakening of the 1740s, a wave of religious revivalism that swept across the colonies and first gave them a sense of general solidarity. As the work of Nathan Hatch has shown, this religious solidarity was gradually given a more political interpretation from within the religious community itself in the 1750s and 1760s with the emergence of what he has called "civil millennialism," namely the providential religious meaning of the American colonies in world history. It is the national community with its religious inspiration that made the American Revolution and created the new nation. The national community was, in our sense of the term, the real republic, not the liberal constitutional regime that emerged in 1789.

The liberal regime never repudiated the civil religion that was already inherent in the Declaration of Independence and indeed kept it alive in our political life even though the Constitution was silent about it. From the point of view of the legal regime, however, any further elaboration of religious symbolism beyond that of the formal and marginal civil religion was purely private. From the point of view of the national community, still largely religious in its self-consciousness, such elaboration was public, even though lacking in any legal status. Here we can speak of public theology, as Martin Marty has called it, in distinction to civil religion. The civil millennialism of the revolutionary period was such a public theology and we have never lacked one since.

The problems of creating a national community in America did not decrease with the establishment of the constitutional regime but in a sense became more severe. With the formation of the new nation centrifugal forces that were restrained during the revolutionary struggle came to the fore and a sense of national community declined. To some extent a national community in the new nation was not fully actualized until after the trauma of the Civil War, though that event set in motion new problems that would later create even greater difficulties in maintaining a genuine national community. But, as Perry Miller has pointed out, to the extent that we did begin to create a national community in the early national period it was again religious revivalism that played an important role. I would not want to minimize the role of Enlightenment thought in complicated relation with the churches that Sidney Mead has so brilliantly emphasized. Enlightenment religion and ethics were also a form of public theology and played a significant role. Yet Jefferson's hope for a national turn to Unitarianism as the dominant religion, a turn that would have integrated public theology and formal civil religion much more intimately than was the case, was disappointed and public theology was carried out predominantly in terms of biblical symbolism.

Even though I have argued that the public theology that came out of the national community represented the real republic, I do not want to idealize it. As with all vigorous young republics it had an element of self-intoxication that has had ominous consequences for us ever after. The "chosen people" or "God's new Israel" symbolism that was eliminated from the formal civil religion was common in the public theology though it also had its critics. Public theology provided a sense of value and purpose without which the national community and ultimately even the liberal state could not have survived, but what that value and purpose were was never entirely clear. On the one hand they seemed to imply the full realization of the values laid down in the Declaration of Independence, but certainly not fully implemented in a nation that among other things still legalized slavery. On the other hand it could imply a messianic mission of manifest destiny with respect to the rest of the continent. It may be a sobering thought that most of what is both good and bad in our history is rooted in our public theology. Every movement to make America more fully realize its professed values has grown out of some form of public theology, from the abolitionists, to the social gospel and the early Socialist party, to the civil rights movement under Martin Luther King, and the farmworkers movement under Caesar Chávez. But so has every expansionist war and every form of oppression of racial minorities and immigrant groups.

The clearest and purest expression of the ethical dynamism that I have located in the realm of public theology broke through at one crucial moment in our history into civil religion itself in the person of our greatest, perhaps our only, civil theologian, Abraham Lincoln. Basing himself above all on the opening lines of the Declaration of Independence, in the Gettysburg Address he called us to complete "the great task remaining before us," the task of seeing that there is a "new birth of freedom" and that we make real for all our citizens the beliefs upon which the republic is based. In the Second Inaugural Address Lincoln incorporated biblical symbolism more centrally into the civil religion than had ever been done before or would ever be done again in his great, somber, tragic vision of an unfaithful nation in need above all of charity and justice.

It has not been my purpose here to evaluate the whole checkered story of civil religion and public theology in our national history but only to point out that they have been absolutely integral to one aspect of our national existence, namely our existence as a republican people. So far I have spoken only of the superstructural role of religion in the republic. Now I would like to turn to the infrastructural role.

Infrastructural Role

In the classical notion of a republic there is a necessity not only for the assertion of high ethical and spiritual commitments, but also for molding, socializing, educating the citizens into those ethical and spiritual beliefs so that they are internalized as republican virtue. Once again, when we look at the liberal constitutional regime we find a complete lacuna in this area. The state as a school of virtue is the last thing a liberal regime conceives itself to be. And yet here too what the liberal regime could not do the national community as the real republic could.

Partly the problem was handled through federalism. What would not be appropriate on the part of the federal government could be done at lower jurisdictional levels. Just as religion was much more open and pervasive at local and even state levels through most of our history than it ever was at the federal level, so the state as educator, and educator in the sphere of values, was widely accepted at lower jurisdictional levels. Robert Lynn (1973) has brilliantly shown how the McGuffy readers purveyed a religious and republican ideology, including a powerful stress on the common good and the joys of participation in public life, during much of the nineteenth century.

And yet, as important as public schools have been, the real school of republican virtue in America, as Alexis de Tocqueville saw with such masterful clarity, was the church. Tocqueville said religion is the first of our political institutions. It was a republican and a democratic religion that not only inculcated republican values but gave the first lessons in participation in public life. More than the laws or physical circumstances of the country, said Tocqueville, it was the mores that contributed to the success of American democracy, and the mores were rooted in religion. As a classic theorist of republican government would, Tocqueville saw that naked self-interest is the surest solvent of a republican regime, and he saw the commercial tendencies of the American people as unleashing the possibility of the unrestrained pursuit of self-interest. He also saw religion as the great restraining element that could turn naked self-interest into what he called ''self-interest rightly understood,'' that is, a self-interest that was public spirited and capable of self-sacrifice. In this way Tocqueville showed how religion mitigated the full implications of American liberalism and allowed republican institutions to survive. Late in his life he began to doubt that such a compromise would work in the long run, and his doubts have been all too fully confirmed by our recent history. Yet for its time and place Tocqueville's analysis was undoubtedly right. It gives us an essential clue to understand this strange, unique, and perhaps finally incoherent society in which we live.

What Tocqueville saw about the role of religion in such a society as ours was understood by the founders of the republic. It is significant, for example, that John Adams, during his first year as our first vice-president under the new liberal constitutional regime said: "We have no government armed with power capable of contending with human passions unbridled by morality and religion. Our constitution was made only for a moral and a religious people. It is wholly inadequate to the government of any other." And Washington in his Farewell Address wrote: "Of all the suppositions and habits which lead to political prosperity Religion and morality are indispensable supports. In vain would that man claim the tribute of Patriotism, who should labour to subvert these great Pillars of human happiness, these firmest props of the duties of Men and citizens. The mere Politician, equally with the pious man ought to respect and cherish them." Perhaps the recognition by our first and second presidents of the necessity of religion and morality, of the basis in the mores and religious beliefs of a people, for a successful republic, in the rather negative, circuitous, and almost apologetic terms of the above quotations, expresses the uneasy compromise between republicanism and a liberal regime that I am describing as characteristic of the new nation. But it also suggests that the relation between the way of life of a people and their form of political organization was fully understood by the founders of the republic.

It is inevitable having recently celebrated the two-hundredth anniversary of our republic that we should look around us to see how well our heritage is understood and how much of it is still operative in our public life. We might have hoped that a political campaign in that bicentennial year would have been educative in the high republican sense of the term. We have had such campaigns in the past. In the Lincoln-Douglas debates the deepest philosophical meaning of our republic and history was plumbed by two men of enormous intelligence and sensitivity to the crucial issues. Alas, we did not get that in 1976. Perhaps the Illinois farmers who drove into the towns from miles around to hear the Lincoln-Douglas debates were a different kind of people from the millions in their living rooms in front of the television screen. Perhaps there were other reasons. But in 1976 what we got was vague and listless allusions to a largely misunderstood and forgotten past, and an attitude toward the present that seems to be determined, above everything else, not to probe beneath the thinnest of surfaces. And yet the great themes I have been probing here were present in that campaign, present not in any articulate form but present in the uncertainty, the groping, the yearning for something that has so slipped out of memory as to be almost without a name. It is the ethical purpose of our republic and the republican virtue of our citizens, or rather the loss of them, that haunted that campaign.

Our rhetoric speaks in the terms of another day, another age. It does not seem to express our present reality. Yet our politicians and their constituencies are surprised and troubled by the lack of fit, less concerned to find a new rhetoric than to find an easy formula to make the old rhetoric apt again. Such an easy formula is the assertion that we must restrain, control, and diminish government, as though the enormous growth of our government were some fortuitous thing and not a sign and symptom of the kind of society in which we live.

To ask the questions the 1976 campaign did not ask is to ask whether under the social conditions of late twentieth-century America it is possible for us to survive as a republic in any sense continuous with the historic meaning of that term. If we discover that the republican element in our national polity has been corroded beyond repair, then we must consider whether a liberal constitutional regime can survive without it. Finally we must ask, if both our republic and our liberal constitutional regime lack the social conditions for survival, what kind of authoritarian regime is likely to replace them, remembering that republican and liberal regimes have been in the history of the planet few and brief. Perhaps we can even discern, beneath the battered surface of our republican polity, the form of despotism that awaits us. Of course it would be my hope to discover how to do what Machiavelli says is that most difficult of all political things, reform and refound a corrupt republic. But we must not flinch from whatever reality is to be discovered.

Corruption

I have mentioned corruption. Corruption is a great word, a political word with a precise meaning in eighteenth-century discourse even though its use has become narrowed and debased with us. Corruption is, in the language of the founders of the republic, the opposite of republican virtue. It is the thing that destroys republics. It might be well for us to remember what Franklin said on the last day of the Constitutional Convention, on September 17, 1787. Old, sick, tired, he had sat through that long hot Philadelphia summer because his presence was crucial to the acceptance of the new document. He was the very symbol of America. He rose on that last day to call for unanimous consent in hopes that that too might help the document be accepted, and he said:

> In these sentiments, Sir, I agree to this Constitution with all its faults, if they are such; because I think a general government necessary for us, and there is no form of Government but what may be a blessing to the people if well administered, and believe further that this is likely to be well administered for a

course of years, and can only end in Despotism, as other forms have done before it, when the people shall have become so corrupted as to need despotic Government, being incapable of any other.

We see in those words the sentiments of an old republican, aware of the compromises contained in the new Constitution, but hoping almost against hope that the republican virtue of the people would offset them, at least for a time.

Corruption, again using eighteenth-century vocabulary, is to be found in luxury, dependence, and ignorance. Luxury is that pursuit of material things that diverts us from concern for the public good, that leads us to exclusive concern for our own good, or what we would today call "consumerism." Dependence naturally follows from luxury, for it consists in accepting the dominance of whatever person or group, or, we might say today, governmental or private corporate structure, that promises us it will take care of our material desires. The welfare state—and here I refer to the welfare that goes to the great corporations, to most of us above the median income through special tax breaks, and the workers whose livelihood depends on an enormous military budget, as much as to the "welfare" that goes to the desperately poor to keep them from starving—the welfare state, then, in all its prolixity, is the very type of what the eighteenth century meant by dependence. And finally political ignorance is the result of luxury and dependence. It is a lack of interest in public affairs, a concern only for the private, a willingness to be governed by those who promise to take care of us even without our knowledgeable consent. We would need to explore throughout our society the degree and extent to which corruption in these forms has gone in order to assess whether there is strength enough in our republic for its survival.

We would also need to look at religion, following the brilliant sociological analysis that Tocqueville made of the role of religion in our public life, a role that all the founders of the republic discerned. To what extent do our religious bodies today provide us with a national sense of ethical purpose? Certainly here there are some notable recent examples. Religious opposition to the Vietnam War was certainly more effective than the opposition of those who spelled America with a *k*. And if we have made some significant progress with respect to the place of racial minorities in our society in the last twenty years it is due in major part to religious leadership. Yet is the balance of American religious life slipping away from those denominations that have a historic concern for the common good, toward religious groups so privatistic and self-centered that they begin to approach the consumer cafeteria model of Thomas Luckmann's invisible religion? And to what extent is the local congregation any longer able to serve as a school for the creation of a self-disciplined, independent, public-spirited, in a word, virtuous, citizen? Have not the churches along with the schools and the family—what I have called the soft structures that deal primarily with human motivation—suffered more in the great upheavals through which our society has recently gone than any other of our institutions, suffered so much that their capacity to transmit patterns of conscience and ethical values has been seriously impaired? I am not prepared to say that religious communities, among which I include human-ist communities, are not capable even today of providing the religious superstructure and infrastructure that would renew our republic. Indeed it is to them that I would look as always before in our history for the renewing impulse, the rebirth that any ethical institution so frequently needs. But the empirical question as to whether the moral capacity is still there on a sufficient scale seems to be open.

If we look to the scholarly community, there is not a great deal to be proud of. We have left the understanding of our basic institutions as we have left everything else, to the specialists, and with notable exceptions they have not done a very good job of it. We have never established a strong academic tradition of self-reflection about the meaning of our institutions, and as our institutions changed and our republican mores corroded even what knowledge we had began to slip away. On the whole it has been the politicians more than the scholars who have carried the burden of self-interpretation. The founders were all political thinkers of distinction. Lincoln's political thought has moments of imaginative gen-ius—his collected works are still the best initiation into a genuine under-standing of the regime under which we live. Even as late as Woodrow Wilson and Calvin Coolidge we had presidents who knew our history in intricate detail and understood the theoretical basis of our institutions. In contrast we have never produced a political philosopher of the first rank. The only profound work of political philosophy on the nature of the American polity was written by a Frenchman. Still we have produced works of the second rank that are not without distinction, though they are usually somewhat isolated and eccentric and do not add up to a cumulative tradition. Such works are Orestes Brownson's *The American Republic* and Raymond Croly's *The Promise of American Life*. But in a barren time we must be grateful for such works as we have. If we turn to these works we will be referred once again to the great tradition with which I began this paper. For example on the last page of Croly's book he quotes the European-American philosopher George Santayana as saying: "If a noble and civilized democracy is to subsist, the common citizen must be some-thing of a saint and something of a hero. We see, therefore, how justly flattering and profound, and at the same time how ominous, was Montesquieu's saying that the principle of democracy is virtue." How ominous indeed! It is in that context that we can understand the bicentennial epigram written by Harry Jaffa, one of the few political scientists who continues the great tradition today: "In 1776 the United States was so to speak nothing; but it promised to become everything. In 1976, the United States, having in a sense become everything, promises to become nothing."

One would almost think the Lord has intended to chastise us before each of our centennial celebrations so that we would not rise up too high in our pride. Before the centennial he sent us Grant. Before the bicentennial, Nixon (in whom we can perhaps discern the dim face of the despotism that awaits us—not a despotism of swastikas and brownshirts but of gameplans and administrative efficiency). It is not a moment for self-congratulation, but for sober reflection about where we have come from and where we may be going.

References

Bellah, Robert N., 1970a, 1970b
Hatch, Nathan O., 1977
Lynn, Robert Wood, 1973
Mead, Sidney E., 1975
Miller, Perry, 1965

22

Religion and Power in the American Experience

N.J. Demerath III and Rhys H. Williams

Over the past quarter-century, the religious component of world politics has captured increasing attention. The Iranian revolution has highlighted a resurgence of a militant Islamic traditionalism in countries as diverse as Nigeria, Pakistan, and Indonesia; violence between Hindus, Moslems, and Sikhs threaten to tear India apart; Catholicism is both a troubled and troubling force in Latin America and Eastern Europe. But what of the United States, a nation that claims to be founded in the name of religious freedom and indeed may be the most religiously pluralistic country on earth?

There are at least three reasons to suppose that religion has been losing political power here ever since the nation's inception. First, America's much-heralded "separation of church and state" is embedded in its founding principles and codified in the First Amendment of the United States Constitution's Bill of Rights: "Congress shall make no law respecting an establishment of religion or prohibiting the free exercise thereof." Generally referred to as the "establishment" and "free exercise" clauses, the two have become an important part of the American creed and self-conception. The "separation" phrase comes from a letter written by Thomas Jefferson in 1802 rather than the Constitution itself, but it has become a shibboleth familiar to most Americans and often guides their perceptions of reality, if not always reality itself (cf. Demerath and Williams 1987). Thus the nation's legal foundation prohibits a formal alliance between religion and government; and religion has been losing its political influence ever since.

But there is another reason for doubting American religion's political potency that does not rely on the Constitution. Ask Western social scientists for the major trend affecting religion over the past 200 years and more, and the answer is likely to involve some version of "secularization." The term has several definitions but one common theme involves the retreat of sacred influences from the secular arena. Even without Constitutional barriers to a religious establishment, there is considerable question whether organized religion any longer has the clout or credibility to support such a presence. As the church has moved from its former position at the very core of society to a position of peripheral parity with other social institutions, religion and religious beliefs have become less public and more private. As such, they no longer have the authority to dictate policy in realms such as politics.

Of course, secularization must not be equated with obliteration. There are inevitable ebbs and flows of the religious tide, and specific religious movements often seize public attention at various times and over various issues. As we will suggest later, these movements may be more a sign of religion's dimunition than its revival. Meanwhile, secularization is related to the larger historical process of institutional differentiation. Whereas secularization entails a religious retreat from other social realms such as politics, differentiation involves the increasing autonomy of all social institutions in their relations with each other. Thus the economy has grown more separate from the family; education has grown more separate from the church; and of course, religion has grown more separate from politics—and vice versa.

As institutions become increasingly separate and distinct, the values that orient appropriate behavior within them have become increasingly specialized. For example, the norms and values applicable to political behavior are different from those concerning religious behavior. Therefore, an alliance of secularization theory with broader interpretations of societal differentiation suggests that religion's day in American corridors of power is over, at least as an institutionalized force. Not only have political organizations and religious organizations grown more separate, but the values and behaviors needed for each have become more distinct.

Quite apart from what has happened within the sacred sphere, the secular itself has changed. More specifically, power in the United States has become more and more autonomous behind the government's double insulation of law and bureaucracy. The rise of the welfare state since World War II, and the decline of ideological differences between the major political parties has meant the diminution of the spoils system. Organized religion has become but one voice among many trying to influence a bureaucratized government that has its own institutional agendas. Sheer bureaucratic inertia may be the most powerful force in contemporary American government; and the federal bureaucracy, at least, is thoroughly secularized. Religious groups do exert moral claims, but they do so mainly from the sidelines rather than as principal figures within the main arena. Further, the rationalization of the procedures of government (and social control generally) has meant that the nonrational, transformative power of religion has less influence on the day-to-day workings of the political system. One can be religious on one's own time, but when attending to governmental business, one uses the values and procedures appropriate to the secular world (see Wilson 1982). This is also a symptom of institutional differentiation, religious secularization, and constitutional separation.

A Religious Revival in American Politics?

The preceding theoretical arguments aside, current popular images of American religion suggest that it has risen from the ashes to become again a potent political force. A recent president (Carter) publically proclaimed his "born again" faith; the Moral Majority, a lobbying coalition of largely fundamentalist Protestants with a conservative religious and political agenda, is actively involved in several election campaigns; the College of Roman Catholic Bishops in the United States releases pastoral letters on nuclear disarmament and the economy; a number of clergy inject the abortion issue directly into political campaigns; Jews continue to exert political pressure on the United States government on behalf of Israel; and religiously based groups lead political pressure campaigns against pornography, the content of popular TV, nuclear arms, and United States foreign policy from South Africa to El Salvador. The 1984 presidential campaign featured church-state issues to such a point that several major news magazines ran cover stories on it, and Mondale and Reagan competed in pledging fealty to both the "separation of church and state" and their own personal religious commitments.

The 1988 presidential season provided evidence of both decline and continuing vitality of religion in politics. On the one hand, evangelical religion was subverted by internal divisions, external suspicions, and a sense of "peace and prosperity" that was as uncongenial to the conservative Right as to the liberal Left. On the other hand, the primaries featured campaigns by two ordained ministers. While Jesse Jackson's religion was eclipsed by his race, Pat Robertson's showing provided a critical test of the short-run strength and long-range weaknesses of campaigns that are religious at their core. If the general election campaign between Bush and Dukakis was less religiously overt than in 1984, the controversy surrounding the Pledge of Allegiance was laden with religious and church-state overtones.

Within the formal apparatuses of the federal government, church-state and religion-politics issues abound. The secretary of education pushes for tuition tax credits for religious schools; Congress considers school prayer and human-life amendments to the Constitution. Perhaps most important, the Supreme Court has recently issued several judgments on church-state issues, deciding in favor of crèches on public property, chaplains in state legislatures, and tax credits for parents' private (and parochial) school expenses. While the Court also rejected a Louisiana law mandating the teaching of creationism, this will probably not be the last case they hear on the subject. Now that President Reagan has elevated Justice William Rehnquist to Chief Justice and has nominated a replacement for Justice Lewis Powell, the Court may be considerably more conservative (that is, "proreligious") by the time it considers other church-state cases currently in the queue in the appellate system.

These references are all to events at the level of national politics, but religious-political interaction may be even more pronounced at the municipal level. Many communities play out their own versions of these issues with religious-based activism gaining headlines on issues ranging from pornography and Christmas crèches to homeless shelters. Public health departments receive heated protests from prolife groups if city-provided health services deal with contraception or abortion. Public school commissions are pressured by conservative Protestants objecting to the "secular humanist" content of textbooks. Even though the "creation science" movement has suffered recent defeat in the Supreme Court, the war is far from over. Fundamentalists have recently tried a new tactic: rather than proposing that religion be inserted into the schools, they charge that public school curricula are now imbued by "secular humanism," which is itself a surrogate religion and thus unconstitutional. A Federal District Court in Mobile, Alabama, recently upheld this argument. Although the decision was reversed in the Federal Circuit Court of Appeals, it is almost surely on its way to the United States Supreme Court for a final decision.

Whatever the outcomes of these legal battles, it is not clear that Court decisions alone will halt practices already long-established in many communities. Research on the responses of local school boards to the school prayer decisions of the early 1960s shows that compliance is problematic and highly dependent on local factors (viz. Dolbeare and Hammond 1971). This again suggests a religiously conscious society in which putative secularization seems belied by deep and continuing religious commitments. It is hardly surprising that newspaper editorial pages give frequent space to the relations between religion and politics, or even that recent sociological assessments write specifically of a political rebirth of American religion (see, for example, Wuthnow 1983 and Johnson 1986).

Resurgence or Retreat?

At this point, then, we are confronted with a puzzle or a paradox. It seems possible to read the American religious-political scene in two quite different ways. On the one hand, recent events and headlines suggest that religion has experienced a political resurgence of major proportions. On the other hand, broader theoretical assessments caution that this may involve more smoke than fire as the trend continues to be dominated by separation, secularization, and differentiation. How can one decide between or, better yet, reconcile these contending images? Actually there are several possibilities, none mutually exclusive.

For one, things are not always as they seem. For example, election analysts continue to disagree over the impact of the Moral Majority in President Reagan's 1980 and 1984 presidential campaigns. There were larger nonreligious groups pursuing the same conservative religious ends, and one must be wary of assigning undue credit to any of the several factions involved. Johnson and Tamney (1982), Shupe and Stacy (1982), and others have demonstrated that the so-called New Christian Right rode, rather than created, the current conservative wave; the votes for Ronald Reagan were more often economically motivated than religiously based. The lackluster performance of Moral Majority–backed candidates in 1984 as compared to their successes in 1980 indicates that the 1980 "mandate" may have been generally tinged with a "throw the rascals out" sentiment, rather than a religious platform. What is more, a sizable faction of the evangelical community are not fundamentalists, and many are life-long Democrats by no means sympathetic with Falwell's pro-Republican movement (cf. Hunter 1983a). While religious-moral issues may have the kind of emotional salience that turns more people out to vote, the content of the votes themselves suggest that religion was only one among several competing priorities.

There is also some question as to President Reagan's own religiosity; he may not be the religious zealot his most ardent friends and foes portray him. While some picture him as a fervent—though private—fundamentalist, others interpret his privacy quite differently. The fact that he neither attends church regularly nor donates significantly to religious groups may indicate that he is not as religious as his political rhetoric would suggest (cf. Flake 1982). It is arguable that he best represents the secularizing citizen—those who appreciate religion for its moral impact but have strayed from the ritual and doctrinal commitments of their forebears.

Reagan may even have attracted votes on this basis. Whereas Jimmy Carter's born-again aggressiveness may have frightened voters, Reagan's more relaxed embodiment of religion as morality rather than dogma may be reassuring to those troubled by religious uncertainty and guilt.

Despite the public professions of support from the Reagan administration, the federal government was not wholly on the side of the angels. While some commentators describe a possible new religious establishment within the government, many religious groups are wary of government constraints on their free exercise. Federal agencies such as the Internal Revenue Service and the Departments of Labor and Justice have put increasing pressure on cults, sects, and by implication all religious groups, to justify their special status, tax exemptions, and dispensations (Robbins 1984, 1985b). Of course, mainline religions have been targeted less often than those on the margins, such as the Unification Church (whose leader, Reverend Sun Myung Moon was imprisoned for tax evasion), or the Hare Krishnas (against whom there have been successful lawsuits concerning "brainwashing"). In the mid-1970s, before televangelism became more established, even the PTL Club was subject to a brief Federal Communications Commission investigation for financial irregularities (the investigation was ultimately called off by a 4–3 vote, despite a staff report identifying financial abuses). Following the recent discrediting of the Bakkers and a return to more marginal standing, the PTL Club is now the subject of a pending congressional investigation.

But all of this may say more about the political influence of a religious group's constituency than about its cultural centrality, per se. For example, the Immigration and Naturalization Service has recently prosecuted clergy and laity from several churches offering sanctuary to Central American refugees. Even though many of these churches are mainline (for example, Presbyterian, Episcopalian), their political stand has engendered the administration's wrath.

Such governmental pressures are sufficiently threatening to all organized religion that many mainstream churches and church councils have opposed governmental action against such religious marginals (see, for example, the published proceedings of the Government Intervention in Religious Affairs Conferences: Kelley 1982, 1986). As these examples attest, relations between religion and government are palpably uneasy. It makes a real difference whether one is focusing on the religious rhetoric of office seekers on the political stump or actions taken towards religion by those within the bowels of the government bureaucracy.

Another framework for reconciling our two images of religion in politics involves the difference between the long term and the short run. Gradual processes such as societal differentiation and religious secularization are by no means entirely consistent or linear. In fact, it is reasonable to suppose that there will be periods of reversal within the trend, partly in response to the trend itself. Thus, many of the most celebrated evidences of religious politicization reflect efforts to resist the tides of change. They are assertions of an older religious sensibility and an older set of values centering on the sanctity of the so-called traditional family, the individual, and a prior social structure. While this would certainly describe groups such as the Moral Majority and the Religious Roundtable, it applies as well to Catholicism's concern over abortion, and in a slightly different sense, to American Jewish support for Israel in a changing Middle East. Each of these groups is acting more in opposition to a trend than setting a trend in its own right. Each is providing short-run response to long-range developments. While these short-run dynamics are frequently dramatic and the stuff of newspaper headlines, they should not obscure the larger processes to which they are reacting.

In much the same way, it is important to distinguish minority from majority phenomena. Processes affecting the American religious community generally may not affect every segment of that community in the same way. Any country as complex as the United States will have groups who appear to fly in the face of dominant patterns. Minority religious movements, like minority political factions, are often important responses to the significant needs and grievances of those who feel disadvantaged and disenfranchised. Minority movements can exercise disproportionate influence through their greater intensity and mobilization, not to mention their misperception as larger than they really are. However, it is important to place these movements in a larger context, rather than assume that they are defining that context through their own actions. One irony of the rise of the Christian Right, and its attempts to institutionalize some form of "Christian politics," is that this occurs at a time when growing American heterogeneity and conflict have rendered highly problematic the very idea of a consensual American "Christian culture."

Consider too the difference between positive and negative power, that is, between the capacity to initiate new policies and the ability to veto change and innovation. There is little question that religion has more of the latter power. Without suggesting that there is anything intrinsically negative about the religious spirit, religious movements have generally been far more effective in opposing change than in promoting it. This is especially true within local communities, where even small minorities of religiously concerned activists have been able to postpone and sometimes preclude community measures ranging from fluoridation and sex education clinics to racial integration.

Clearly religion is not to be dismissed as a source of power on the

American political scene. However, there is a last basis for reconciling our conflicting images which merits more detailed development. It is possible to distinguish two quite different forms of power in the political process, one by direct political means, and the other through indirect cultural influence. This distinction has been largely unexamined, but it offers considerable help in making sense of previous research on American power configurations.

The Power of Culture and Its Agents: Highlighting the Empirical Literature

We have mentioned three reasons (separation, secularization, differentiation) why one would expect religion to wield low political power post–World War II. Such is in fact the case, both at the national and community levels. Nationally, studies of power elites and policy decision making rarely mention religion at all. In the literature ranging from C. Wright Mills (1956) through the more recent assessments of William Domhoff (1980) and others, the omission of religion is conspicuous. Even the so-called pluralists fail to include religion as a vital actor in their own broadened conception of the pertinent elites. Political scientists assessing the policy process mention religion only to note its decline in influence; the failure of political science to deal with religion and politics in any comprehensive matter was highlighted in a recent issue of the journal *PS* (Fall 1986). While students of voting do cite religious affiliation as a significant variable, they often tend to interpret its effects less in terms of theology and ecclesiastical influence than in terms of ethnic, class, and regional factors lurking beneath the symbolic surface.

If there is one single theme that dominates the assessment of religion's declining influence, it involves the shrinking impact of mainstream Liberal Protestantism. Despite the Constitution's prohibition of "an establishment of religion," there is little doubt that American government and politics were dominated by a coalition of Congregationalists, Unitarians, Episcopalians, Presbyterians, and Methodists well into the twentieth century. But with the continued development of other religions, especially Catholicism, the rise of true religious pluralism meant the decline of religious power. This was partly due to the countervailing checks and balances among contending religious groups. It was also because of the increasing sensitivity of government and the courts to religious entanglements of any sort. Meanwhile, the decline of the Protestant mainstream has continued, both in terms of influence and sheer numbers. It is worth noting that Catholicism and Evangelical Protestantism are now moving in the same direction, as both are far more "emancipated" today than in the past (cf. Hunter 1983a; McNamara 1985).

In some ways the most revealing literature concerning religion and power deals not with national politics but rather with the local community. Here is where lives are actually lived, and here is the more direct test of religious influence in the everyday decision making that ultimately determines the nation's course. At first glance, "religious power" seems a self-contradiction at this level as well.

Most studies of community power focus exclusively on the existence, composition, and functioning of political and economic elites. In fact, debate has long revolved around the labels "elitism" and "pluralism" as represented in the works of scholars such as Mills (1956) and Dahl (1961). Once a source of considerable heat, the debate has cooled considerably since Aiken and Mott (1970) noted that it turned more on method than on substance. Political scientists used a decision-making approach that helped lead Dahl (1961) and Polsby (1963) to their pluralist conclusions: in overt decision-making behavior, many individuals participate in different types of decisions. On the other hand, sociologists such as Mills, Hunter (1953), and Domhoff (1978) used more "positional" or "reputational" methods, whose results depicted a social system unified and coherent at the top.

In either case, most community power studies agree on the relatively marginal role of organized religion where power is directly wielded and structured. But these are primarily studies of large cities done mostly by political scientists. There is an equally long tradition of assessing power in smaller communities, and here sociologists predominate. Here also the church seems to play more prominent roles. The Lynds (1929) and Vidich and Bensman (1960) typify this idiom: they portray communities where churches are centers of cultural life, nodes of social networks, and badges of overall community membership and status stratification.

Underwood's (1957) study of Holyoke, Massachusetts, is relevant in this context. He studied the community conflict provoked by the lecture of birth control advocate, Margaret Sanger. But as Underwood documents the ways in which religion is woven into the fabric of everyday social life, it is clear that the Sanger conflict expresses community divisions that are as much economic, ethnic, and social, as religious. This is not to deny the religious component per se; religion is more than a mere symbol. However, rather than an isolated sphere of social life, religion is intertwined with economics and politics.

Although many of these studies are now dated, Caplow, Bahr, and Chadwick (1983) have recently completed a restudy of "Middletown" a half-century following the Lynds. Caplow "discovered" religion alive and well within the community and saw little sign of the secularization that has marked so much of American society and culture. This work has received much criticism for its methodological and theoretical shortcomings. In particular, the authors adopt a restricted definition of secularization and ignore completely religion's relation to community power. However, the study does stand within the community study tradition that places major importance on the cultural role of organized religion. And Roozen, McKinney, and Carroll (1984) have provided an interesting study of religion's public presence in the city of Hartford, Connecticut. The primary focus here is on individual congregations, and while religion is not portrayed as an important locus of city power, it does play a significant role in the city's social and cultural life.

But something is missing in this literature, perhaps fallen between the interests of the political scientists on the one hand, and the sociologists on the other. Political science research on power and decision making have virtually nothing to say about religion's symbolic roles in shaping political debate and a cultural way of life. The community studies tradition within sociology too often neglects the structures of local political power and the involvement, or lack thereof, of organized religions. Both traditions may have their version of the story right, but they have only a partial story. Indeed, we feel this is the case for each perspective we have delineated thus far: secularization and differentiation have indeed diminished American religion's formal and informal political power, but there has also been a resurgence of religious-political issues and interest. Empirical assessments of American politics accurately reflect a disjunction between political structures and political culture. But even these are not unidimensional, either within themselves or in their relationship. Indeed, it is useful to consider their several different dimensions in seeking a broader understanding of the different types of interactions between religion and politics that have been part of the American experience.

Untangling the Web of Religion's Political and Cultural Influence

Few sociological concepts combine such broad applications with such narrow implications as that of "power." Too often we tend to think of it in a specifically political context with reference to governments, laws, and the coercive repertoire of the state. But power occurs in every facet of social life and can be exercised in widely varied ways. While most contemporary treatments tend to concentrate on direct political access to structured relationships, other forms of power involve both the macrolevel of culture including distribution of authority and legitimacy, as well as the microlevel of individual psychology including the manipulation of wants and needs. Even in the political arena, any issue must be shaped and molded before it is acted upon—before, in fact, it even becomes an issue. For any given issue, a political actor can have significant influence by controlling the ways in which basic values and beliefs are mobilized and articulated (see Lukes 1974 for a perceptive critique of the many faces of power). Whether and how an issue is placed on the political agenda is a matter of cultural definition and subject to the power of contending cultural, as well as structural, forces. While cultural forces may have more negative than positive power over short-range policy decisions, this is a critical component of the political process.

Cultural resources are especially important in a political democracy. Here decisions are perennially subject to review, either directly through referenda or indirectly through elections for political representatives. The culturally shaped moods and priorities of the electorate are of enormous consequence to politicians whose careers hang in the balance. In non-democratic societies where power is wielded more autonomously, the culture of the elites is critical. And while the reaction of the masses may be painfully irrelevant in the short term, it too may be significant over the longer run.

At one level, this provides a simple answer to the conflicting images presented previously. As one reconsiders the various interpretations of religion's relationship to power reviewed earlier, religion seems to have retained far more indirect cultural influence than direct political efficacy. Certainly recent religious movements have had greater impact in redefining cultural issues and priorities than in determining actual electoral outcomes or policy decisions. Despite the recent political frenzy of various religious groups, prayer is not legal in the public schools, abortion is still available at the discretion of the woman, and secular humanism has not yet been outlawed. By and large, the United States government has remained remarkably free of the sort of entanglements which would mark a religious establishment or even a religiously responsive system. On the other hand, the free exercise of various religious groups continues to exert cultural claims on the nation's political structures. And, particularly in some geographical regions, religious criteria are so integral to the political culture that some decisions, or candidates, are severely constrained. These cultural themes and political claims ebb and flow, and if religion seems to be experiencing a high-water point today, it is important to note that it has wielded less influence in the past and may have diminished impact in the future.

Note that there is a tension between these two forms of power. The distinction between cultural influence and political efficacy parallels the often noted disjunction between cultural conceptions of what "ought to be" and structural determinations of what "is." It has produced, in American politics, what Huntington (1981) calls the "promise of dishar-mony": an inevitable lack of fit, and a resulting tension, between the nation's ideas (culture) and institutions (political structures). Tiryakian (1982) discusses this conflict in terms of American foreign policy: America's moral self-understanding is rooted in the Puritan calling to bring a "light to all nations"; but this is often dramatically at odds with the realpolitik demands on a world superpower.

But as convenient as it may be to treat religion in terms of cultural influence rather than structural authority, the formulation is simplistic. For one thing, the distinction between culture and structure is too facile. Social structures are not real in the sense that trees and rocks are real; they require cultural resources such as symbols and language to interpret them. Thus political power is as much a cultural product as are moral values of good and right. There is often as much tension among various themes within American culture as there is between culture generally and structure. Further, in any society as complex as the United States, religion's relationship to power varies, depending upon the particular religious group, the particular issue at stake, and the particular cultural and structural context. With more than 200 denominations and a bewildering array of issues and contexts, no simple assertion will suffice. Hence, we want to suggest a typology to facilitate comparisons not only among cases within the United States but also on a more global basis. We have no illusions about the precision of such conceptual devices; typologies can be more a plague than a panacea. Still, we offer the following as a heuristic effort to provoke discussion rather than end it.

Consider figure 22.1. The two basic dimensions which frame the cells are by now familiar: across the top is religion's indirect cultural influence, and down the side is its direct political efficacy. But rather than simply dichotomize each dimension, we have used three categories. First, (Hi +) suggests considerable influence or efficacy that is consistent with (or exhaustive of) secular sources. Second, (Hi −) involves considerable influence but in competition or conflict with secular sources. The third and last category (Lo) represents cases of little appreciable influence in either direction. In effect, then, there are really two variables operating within this figure. In addition to whether religion exerts a political or cultural influence, there is the further question of the direction of that influence relative to prevailing secular tendencies, or the extent to which religion is at odds with its context. Thus by varying the dimensions in these two variables, we can reproduce each of the images of religious-political interaction that we articulated earlier.

Each of the resulting nine cells is labeled primarily with reference to the American religious experience. In fact, America's religious past begins in the upper-left corner (the Covenant Community) and, if the secularization theorists are correct, its future lies in the lower-right cell (the Secular

FIGURE 22.1
Typology of Religious Influence: Cultural Influence

		Hi +	Hi −	Lo
	Hi +	Covenant Community	Coopted Church I	Establishment Elitism
Political Efficacy	Hi −	Prophetic Leadership I	Sacred vs. Secular	Prophetic Leadership II
	Lo	Civil Religion	Coopted Church II	Secular City

Hi + = considerable influence, consistent with (or exhaustive of) secular sources.
Hi − = considerable influence in competition or conflict with secular sources.
Lo   = little appreciable influence.

City). We will describe these types in somewhat greater detail. Meanwhile, they by no means exhaust the range of possibilities. Each of the seven remaining types are also represented on the American scene, both histori- cally and contemporaneously. To ignore them is to overlook important aspects of the relationship between religion and power. Let us consider these types individually, beginning with those along the principle left-right diagonal.

The covenant community In broad theoretical terms, this describes the simple societies of Emile Durkheim's classic *Elementary Forms of the Religious Life* (1965 [1912]). From the perspective of American history, it describes the original communities of colonial New England. In both cases, religion has preeminent cultural and political power. In fact, in neither case is it possible to imagine a nonreligious power base as a viable alternative. To some extent, however, this is an ideal type. In even the most covenanted situations, there is no doubt some underlying tension between sacred and secular. As Bellah (1981) and Reichley (1985) note, church and state were not fused in seventeenth-century New England; a division of institutional labor was maintained, and individuals who held positions of authority in the church were not simultaneously eligible to be officials in the government. Yet ultimately, "Christian" and "citizen" were two ways of saying the same thing. Both appellations were necessary to be a full member of society.

While certain situations in the United States today seem to approximate the covenant model, it remains more a matter of simplistic fantasy than empirical reality. For example, many small communities in the American southeast are dominated by Baptists, both culturally and politically. This may produce an almost monolithic front on behalf of an issue such as the teaching of creationism in the public schools. But as Vidich and Bensman pointed out some years ago (1960), there are few small towns beyond the reach of the nation's mass media as a cultural force. And the outside pressures of state and federal legal restrictions frustrate local legal hegemonies. Even in small northeastern cities, where Catholic domination of political and social processes may provide overwhelming support for public aid to parochial schools, there is a legal limit as to what can be done, at least openly. Hence even a homogeneous religious community is likely to reflect some variation in response to external influences and internal roles. Complete consensus is the stuff of fiction rather than fact. While there are certainly communities which defy decisions of the federal government in order to do things their own way, this is less likely today than in the past, and it tends to involve only those issues that are relatively marginal to the larger political priorities of the nation.

The secular city Of course, this type is in stark contrast to the covenant community. We have borrowed the phrase from theologian Harvey Cox (1965), although he has recently recanted its basic message for the future (1984). We might also have used the title of Richard Neuhaus's recent book *The Naked Public Square* (1984). Here religion has neither indirect cultural influence nor direct political efficacy, although vital religious communities may exist on their own. A number of observers would find this an apt prediction of the future if not an accurate description of the present. Debatable as this may be, it would certainly apply to a number of religious groups as they deal with a number of political issues. Indeed, as once-dominant liberal Protestantism continues to decline, it has moved from the core of a covenant community to the periphery of the secular city.

But perhaps this is too harsh. In most of the towns and cities examined in the community power literature, religion retains a cultural relationship to power even where it lacks direct political access. This is certainly one of the messages of the recent restudy of Middletown religion by Caplow, Bahr, and Chadwick (1983). And because minority religious movements are often most desperate and hence most vociferous, they can sometimes have a cultural impact which goes far beyond that of dominant religious groups in their complacent torpor. Once again then we have an ideal type with only rare approximations to reality.

Earlier we described the shift between America's covenant past and possible secular future. But such a shift may take different routes. Just as no single type captures the society as a whole, nor does any single route between types. Different religious groups have followed different patterns, and some have repeated their tours through the typology as circumstances occasionally reversed themselves. In some cases, the shift follows the main diagonal and involves a major confrontation between sacred and secular forces. In other instances it may move to the right and below as religion loses its cultural influence before its political efficacy. In still other cases the pattern may shift below and to the right as religion's political efficacy shrinks prior to its loss of cultural influence. This last pattern may be more common to the degree that culture is less vulnerable to change and differentiation than political structures. As Huntington (1981) notes, a cultural system is not necessarily coherent by rational standards, hence it can absorb many varied, and occasionally contradictory, elements without producing any noticeable tension or change. This is particularly important in the American case with all its heterogeneity and pluralism. Huntington takes this idea one step further by arguing that there is a particularly "American ideology," based in emotional attachments to certain ideals, and hence noticably impervious to rational contradictions. But let us consider the three quite different intervening types in order; namely, "sacred vs. secular," "established elitism," and "civil religion."

Sacred versus secular   Here religion exerts considerable cultural and political influence but in conflict with contending secular forces. This too is relatively rare. It not only involves religion in strong cultural negation but entails the continuing political efficacy of religion's representatives swimming against the secular tide. Certainly there have been instances in American religious history which fit the type. The potential exists whenever a religious movement is mobilized around a particular issue to produce change, either forward or backward. This would describe some periods of the "great awakenings" in the first halves of the eighteenth and nineteenth centuries, as well as the abolitionism of the 1850s. It might also describe the role of mainline Protestantism in America's brief episode of Prohibition in the 1920s.

Even some aspects of the current surge in political activity on the religious Right qualify, since many of the newly politicized fundamentalists view themselves as occupying final outposts against the secular onslaught. The movement's national political efficacy is overestimated in general, but it has had an undeniable political and cultural presense for some issues in some settings. Its abilities to mobilize extremely committed cadres around a single issue is often impressive. Indeed, much of the movement's momentum is due to the exhilaration of a pitched ideological battle between the "martyrs of light" and the "forces of darkness."

Still, a full split between a society's sacred and secular aspects is almost unimaginable. From Durkheim's perspective, such a split is tantamount to chaotic anomie since society itself must be regarded as sacred if it is to cohere. Many denominations have experienced tension between those who criticize society and those who accommodate to it, but in the long run, the latter are more likely to prevail if the group itself is to endure. The sociological distinction between church and sect revolves around a dynamic in which minority religious sects move from an adversarial to an accepting stance toward their cultural environment, thus joining the ranks of the churches and spawning new sectarian splinter movements of their own (for example, Neibuhr 1929).

Establishment elitism   In some respects this would seem to be the most anomalous type—perhaps the sort of empty cell that is almost inevitable in such typologies. Its combination of low cultural influence and high political efficacy suggests a sociological contradiction in terms. And yet instances do exist. The point is not that there is no religious culture at all here but only that it is not directed overtly towards the exercise of power. Under these terms, religious elites are often given even freer rein in cooperating with and participating in secular political structures, thus enhancing their own status and that of their religious group. Here religious membership confers a kind of broad authority and it is invoked more rhetorically than substantively. The Constitution notwithstanding, this was an important aspect of the Protestant establishment which held sway in this country for almost 150 years until the floodgates of pluralism were truly opened in the 1930s. Protestant leaders from various denominations played highly efficacious roles in determining America's political outcomes. Because they were generally operating under a broad cultural consensus, they rarely acted in the name of a particular religious directive or constituency.

There are also more contemporary instances. Many local communities continue under the spell of religious elites who exert political control on behalf of a religious tradition. Some leaders even rise to national power on this basis, including such pan-Americans as the Reverend Billy Graham, whose political access ultimately came to enhance his religious leadership. Consider too the recent presidential bids of the Reverend Jesse Jackson. Using the mass media to activate and mold his natural constituency, Jackson's participation in a mainstream political process was in some ways the most significant political development of the 1984 campaign. Note, however, that while his religious status is an important source of his legitimacy, little is known or demanded of his specifically religious commitments.

Civil religion   If one had to nominate a single cell in figure 22.1 to describe the current American reality, this might be the obvious candidate. The concept has a double legacy in the works of Rousseau and Durkheim, but it was Robert Bellah's classic article (1967) which gave it the impetus to become a virtual cliché among those presuming to sketch the art of the state in the United States today. Briefly, Bellah argued that American culture has a sacred component that is distinct from any particular religion or faith. This religious sensibility is focused on the nation; national symbols such as the flag, and national events such as presidential inaugurations, are imbued with a sacred quality. Thus, he argued, all Americans can participate in a common religious culture, no matter what their particularistic religious affiliations might be. As one might imagine, the phrase "civil religion" is fraught with connotation. But whatever else is involved, it refers to religion's continued cultural influence over political matters as America's Judeo-Christian heritage imparts a rich sense of the nation as a religious body in its own right. From this perspective, it is not so much that religious leaders have a direct hand in politics, but that political leaders must invoke religion as a set of cultural symbols if they are to have any hopes at all of mobilizing their constituencies and legitimating their authority. Religion's role as a cultural force in shaping the nation's moral sensitivities and political agenda obviates the necessity of violating the Constitution in the pursuit of a structured religious-political establishment.

Like any single concept which attempts to blanket such a sprawling society, this one is inevitably a bit frayed around the edges. For one thing, it is not wholly clear what constitutes the American religious culture or whether America's religious legacy is as homogeneous as Bellah and others suggest. For another, the literatures concerning both the uses of civil religion and the extent of its adherence are somewhat inconclusive. There are times when religious symbols clang and clash cacophonously as political leaders invoke them, at times cynically. The evidence is mixed on whether the American citizenry at large really subscribes to what Herberg (1955) once portrayed as our "religion in general." Many are religiously particularistic; others are more pragmatically instrumental in their religious shopping, and there is a growing and consistently underestimated minority with little religious sensibility at all. American religious and political culture is heterogenous enough to allow both ends of the electoral spectrum—the Reverends Jesse Jackson and Jerry Falwell—to use civil religious imagery in legitimating their own political agendas and portray themselves as heirs to the nation's moral destiny. But to speak of a "civil religion" is to imply the existence of a "civil society." Elsewhere we have examined the prospects of "civil religion in an uncivil society" (Demerath and Williams 1985).

So far we have described the most clearly defined types at the corners and at the center of our nine-cell figure. While it is possible to continue to treat each of the remaining cells separately, this amounts to a bit of specious conceptual precision. They actually divide into two groups of two types each, distinguished more by degree than by kind. Both "prophetic leadership" and the "coopted church" can be described with two-for-one economy.

Prophetic leadership (I and II)   Here religious leadership is highlighted in cutting prophetically against the grain of the dominant secular context. But note that such leaders are often doubly prophetic, for they are also challenging the accommodating position of their own churches, particularly as "churches" are defined in contrast to "sects." This is best represented in type I. But because it is difficult to distinguish between a religious culture that actively supports the secular status quo (Hi +) and one that is supportive by passive default (Lo), the two types can be melded and treated simultaneously.

One sort of instance here involves what Max Weber (1963 [1922]) would have described as the emissary prophet who performs charismatically as a religious virtuoso. Cases here are predictably rare, but by no means nonexistent. Martin Luther King, Jr., is a celebrated American example. There is no doubt of his political efficacy in the primary arenas of government power. What is less appreciated is the extent to which his leadership at least temporarily transformed a black church movement from other-worldly fatalism to this-worldly activism. While no one would suggest that the black churches endorsed the white culture of segregation and racial oppression, they had made deep cultural accommodations. It was a measure of King's prophetic genius that he was capable of effecting a transformation. It is one thing to lead a group that is already marching and quite another to overcome inertia and ideological resistance to help create movement itself.

There are other examples as well. The liberal Protestant Social Gospel Movement of the 1930s and the protest actions of white clergy in the 1960s both qualify. And consider American Catholicism's current positions on several issues. With regard to abortion, surveys of the Catholic laity have demonstrated repeatedly that a solid majority supports freedom of information and freedom of choice. But if the church has been losing the cultural struggle, it has been holding its own in the political wars through the direct pressure of many members of the priesthood and its small but vociferous right-to-life groups. Turning to economic issues and nuclear weapons, once again the Catholic leadership is prophetically at odds with both its laity and the society at large, at least in terms of the American Bishops' recent statements. Here, of course, the leadership has moved more to the political Left than the Right, and it is more difficult to assess its overall political impact.

Clearly not every political force requires a broad cultural mandate, and religious leaders can have influence even if they lack backing from their own religious groups. Elites can be effective when they are at odds with their cultural contexts—at least for a time. Several of the recently celebrated cults fall into this category. For example, Reverend Moon often shared prayer breakfasts with members of Congress, even while his own organization experienced persecution from government bureaucrats and had little or no cultural legitimacy or authority to fall back on. However, this type of contradiction between cultural and political positionings is generally a short-lived and unstable basis for any power relationship, as pointed out by Hadden (1969).

The coopted church (I and II)   Finally, these cells involve religious movements whose cultural position is opposed to prevailing policies but who either participate actively in supportive political arrangements (I) or have a passively compliant political posture (II). Some cynics would leap at the label to describe the dominant pattern in American denominationalism. After all, this is part of the larger church-sect dynamic described earlier, whereby religious groups move from sectarian origins to churchly accommodation and compromise in the interests of institutional stability. Few mainline American churches fully act upon their basic theological and moral doctrines. For many, these doctrines are left partly in the closet as cooperation with prevailing political powers takes precedence. Campbell and Pettigrew (1959) showed that during the southern civil rights struggles, most white churches remained part of the traditional white power structure. Liston Pope (1942) described a similar pattern during the 1930s as southern milltowns faced issues of unionization. Yet it is all too easy to level charges of hypocrisy in such cases. These are adaptations to sociological exigencies which must be understood in sociological terms. Moral judgements about such organizational adaptations are often off the mark, particularly for American religious organizations, whose voluntaristic ethos means that dissatisfied members often vote with their feet.

Conclusion

Each of the above types has some currency in the American religious experience. Surely one could operationalize them more precisely and test them more rigorously in particular situations. But that has not been our objective here. Instead, we have sought to make three basic points. First, the cultural dimension of power is often overlooked as a source of major religious influence in its own right. Second, American religion's relationship to power hangs in the balance between its indirect cultural influence and its direct political efficacy. Third, the typology that results from combining these dimensions—along with positive and negative assessments of the power wielded relative to secular forces—produces a framework for capturing and comparing a wide variety of religious situations. This is so not only within the United States but perhaps in other societies as well. It is tempting to assign whole societies to the different cells in our nine-fold table. But most types are likely to occur within any given society, regardless of its dominant tendencies. Comparative sociology can be a provocative enterprise, but it can also be a procrustean process that distorts under the guise of elucidating.

Certainly it would be a fool's errand to try and find the one and only relationship between religion and power in American society. No single pattern emerges from among the many stereotypes, ideologies, theoretical assessments, and empirical case studies. It is safe to assert that the United States as a whole is no longer a covenant society (if it ever was); indeed, the post–World War II splintering of the white, Protestant social hegemony means that there is little that can currently pass for a dominant culture. In terms of our typology, religion has moved from the upper left towards the lower right. However, religious influence is by no means dismissable as an empty vestige of bygone eras. Religion's power continues to ebb and flow, and it is impossible to locate a single process that has dominated the American historical saga or a single pattern that prevails on the contemporary scene.

In general, mainstream American religion has been more critical to, than critical of, the American political establishment. It helped socialize new immigrants, legitimate foreign policies, pacify working-class alienation, and provide social services a laissez-faire government would not. Recent decades, however, have witnessed changes. Religion has developed increasingly oppositional positions toward the establishment, on both its left and right political flanks. The results have been mixed. America's political scene is so complex that it is rare for any interest group to achieve preeminent power. And yet, recent political debate has often reflected the moral discourse of organized religion, from the left wing's challenge to the Reagan administration's policies on Central America, nuclear weapons, race, and the economy, to the Right's attack on abortion rights and the women's movement. None of these issues can be debated without reference to arguments originating in religious contexts. American religion may not decide the outcome of many national issues, but its cultural influence is a powerful force in shaping issues in the first place and molding their subsequent debate.

The relationship between political power and religion is subject to continual negotiation, and this process itself plays a major role in defining our national history. On balance, we believe that religion exerts less power than most journalists would imply but more power than most social scientists have assumed.

This essay is a revised version of "The Sword and the Spirit: Power and Religion in the U.S.," a paper presented at the XI World Congress of the International Sociological Association, August, 1986; it also appeared in *Society* 26(1) (Jan./Feb. 1989). The authors wish to thank Thomas Robbins and Charles E. Woodhouse for their comments on the earlier draft.

References

Aiken, Michael, and Paul E. Mott, eds., 1970
Bellah, Robert N., 1967, 1981
Campbell, Ernest, and Thomas Pettigrew, 1959
Caplow, Theodore, Howard M. Bahr, and Bruce A. Chadwick, 1983
Cox, Harvey, 1965, 1984
Dahl, Robert A., 1961
Demerath, N. J. III, and Rhys H. Williams, 1985, 1987
Dolbeare, Kenneth M., and Phillip E. Hammond, 1971
Domhoff, G. William, 1978, 1980
Durkheim, Emile, 1965 (orig. 1912)
Flake, Carol, 1982
Hadden, Jeffry K., 1969
Herberg, William, 1955
Hunter, Floyd, 1953
Hunter, James Davison, 1983a
Huntington, Samuel P., 1981
Johnson, Benton, 1985b
Johnson, Stephen D., and Joseph B. Tamney, 1982
Kelley, Dean M., ed., 1982, 1986
Lukes, Steven, 1974
Lynd, Robert S., and Helen Merrell Lynd, 1929
McNamara, Patrick H., 1985
Mills, C. Wright, 1956
Neuhaus, Richard John, 1984
Niebuhr, H. Richard, 1929
Polsby, Nelson W., 1963
Pope, Liston, 1942
Reichley, A. James, 1985
Robbins, Thomas, 1984, 1985b
Roozen, David A., William McKinney, and Jackson W. Carroll, 1984
Shupe, Anson, and William A. Stacey, 1982

Tiryakian, Edward A., 1982
Underwood, Kenneth W., 1957
Vidich, Arthur J., and Joseph Bensman, 1960
Weber, Max, 1963 (orig. 1922)
Wilson, Brian R., 1982
Wuthnow, Robert, 1983

23

Citizens and Believers: Always Strangers?

Harvey Cox

*I promised to write of the rise, progress and
appointed end of the two cities, one of which is
God's, the other this world's, in which, so far as
mankind is concerned, the former is now a
stranger.*

— St. Augustine,
The City of God
bk. 18, chap. 1

Must the citizen of the city of God always be a stranger in the city of man? Is there any legitimate way the believer can be a full and first-class citizen in a kingdom of this passing age? In seeking to address this question in late twentieth-century America, this essay is divided into two parts. The first deals with historical obstacles that have hindered the development of what might be called a "Christian theology of citizenship." The second argues why these obstacles no longer have the weight they once did and thus suggests that it may now be more feasible to forge such a theology.

The topic is the recurrent one of the relation of the secular to the sacred. "Recurrent" because the topic keeps reappearing despite the reigning theory of how the sacred and the secular relate to each other. Every time the discussion seems dead for sure, the rising moon of a new theory of sacred and secular stirs the cadaver to life. The coffin lid creaks open, and the question once thought dead stalks abroad once more.

In the relatively short span of one scholar's career, at least four theories about the relation of the secular to the sacred have come and gone. The first held that secularization was a massive aberration — a falling away from a normative religious or Christian culture. Consequently it interpreted the various expressions of secularization in the light of this larger picture. Next came the theory of secularization as a relentless and unidirectional movement. This linear theory of secularization (Wilson 1985) was related to cognate theories of the stages of economic development and the alleged stages of political maturation. Then came the more sophisticated theory of a dialectical relationship between secularization and revivalism. This theory, ably defended by William Bainbridge at Harvard, amasses considerable data to prove that secularization stimulates a revival of religion, which in turn looses currents of secularization, and so on (Stark and Bainbridge 1985). The movement continues in a challenge-and-response pattern. More recently, even more complex and nuanced theories have emerged. They hold mainly that there can be no global theory of secularization. They contend that patterns of secularization and resacralization have to be studied in very particular and local settings, and that it is misleading to make universal generalizations (Bell 1980; Berger 1982).

Despite all these theories one of the most persistent forms the question takes in the modern world is this: *What is the appropriate role of those persons who are at once both believers and citizens?* It immediately becomes evident that this is a question that has a very different meaning in Japan than in Iran, and that the question has yet another valency when asked within the context of Western Europe and the United States. Nonetheless, the question keeps reappearing. There is a very good reason why it reappears. One may separate church from state by constitutional dictum; one may delineate the religious from the profane in analytical categories; but the dilemma of the "citizen" of a nation state, who is also a religious believer, is not thereby alleviated.

Looking at this from the perspective of Christianity, one is led to observe that ultimately the most enduring tension between the secular and the spiritual runs straight through the soul of the individual, that person who is a citizen of both the kingdom of God and one of the kingdoms of this world. Furthermore, the decisions such citizen-believers must make press in on them every day. They involve not simply an occasional choice of whether or not to pay taxes to Caesar. They include questions of the daily choices churned up by two overlapping realms, both of which make their demands and in both of which one lives out one's existence. Perhaps the most vivid example of such hard choices appears when civil authorities are also Christian believers. Mario Cuomo, the governor of New York, put the matter starkly in the famous speech he gave at Notre Dame University in September, 1983:

> Must politics and religion in America divide our loyalties? Does the separation of church and state imply separation between religion and politics? What is the

relationship of my Catholicism to my politics? Where does one end and one begin? (Cuomo 1984)

In view of this continuing riddle faced by a citizen-believer, one might assume that a general principle would run as follows: the stronger any person's religious commitment, the weaker will be his or her identification with a national state. The evidence, however, does not support this hypothesis. Often quite the opposite occurs. One has only to think, for example, of the intense patriotism exhibited by many American evangelicals and fundamentalists, or of the widely recognized tendency among American ethnic Roman Catholics to underline their loyalty to the American nation. On the other side, one notices the large numbers of upper-middle-class people in the United States and elsewhere whose sense of belonging either to a national state or to a religious community seems increasingly attenuated. Obviously, whatever solutions are chosen to lessen the tension a given person feels when confronted with these two conflicting loyalties, that of identifying more strongly with one while lessening one's sense of belonging in the other, is not one of the most common strategies for solving the riddle. The late Cardinal Spellman of New York was not a man who sensed very much tension between his Roman Catholic faith and his American patriotism, not, that is, until he began to clash with Pope John XXIII and Pope Paul VI about the war in Vietnam. The question remains: how can one be a full, not half-hearted, citizen as well as a full believer?

In a recent paper John Coleman, S.J., has suggested that Christianity has never developed an adequate theology of citizenship. Christian theology has always emphasized, Coleman says, a certain "eschatological reserve." That certainly is an important element, he says, but the question must be asked, what next? What is the *positive* content of being a Christian citizen? (Coleman 1981). Christian theology has never dealt adequately with the relatively modern question of the positive significance of one's participation as a believer in one of the national states. Theologies exist to guide one's behavior in other aspects of the secular: theologies that instruct about being a husband or a wife, about one's professional or vocational work in the world. A vast literature of guidance and admonition has accumulated on the Christian's participation in economic organizations, labor unions, and business life. If Coleman is right that an adequate theology of citizenship in the nation state never appeared, one might well ask why?

This essay argues that the reason why an adequate theological understanding of the appropriate role of the believer in the public sphere has not developed is that the concept "citizen" is itself an ideological construct.

This has created two historical obstacles. However, neither obstacle seems to be as weighty in the present as it once was in the past. This, in turn, may now clear the way for the development of a positive theology of Christian citizenship.

The two historical obstacles are both fused with the concept of citizenship itself. As such, they obscure an important tension between the classical idea of the *civitas* and the more modern bourgeois idea of the *citoyen*. This fusion is due first to the special historical circumstances under which the concept of the national state appeared in the West, a context that generated claims to a higher and prior loyalty. It is also due to the way these same conditions shaped the view of something that came to be called the "public realm" as an area purged of religious references.

The National State

In the eighteenth and nineteenth centuries a tense rivalry developed in the West between church and state, especially in countries within the Catholic realm. The forces representing the state spoke for the interests of a particular and newly emergent class, the bourgeoisie. The increasing tempo of national state development meant that individuals were faced with conflicting claims on their loyalty from the national community on the one side and the religious community on the other.

It is interesting to recall that the victory of this concept of the national state did not occur without considerable opposition and debate. At least three highly significant figures in the international scene opposed the idea vigorously from different perspectives: Lenin, following the teachings of Marx, taught that an international revolution would eventually lead to the withering away of national states; Woodrow Wilson proposed a League of Nations to which various national states would gradually hand over increasing amounts of their sovereignty; and from Pope Leo XIII to Pius XII the papacy taught a vision of a new Christendom in which national states would diminish in importance within the family of the church, a vision that has continued to influence European thinkers.

Post-revolutionary France and late-nineteenth-century Italy are the two prime examples of the bitter clash between church and state in previously Catholic countries. The development in Roman Catholic theology of ultramontanism, culminating in the definition of the infallibility of the pope, represented one response to this rivalry. Historians now largely agree that the infallibility doctrine arose more as the result of an effort to counter the emergence of national state churches than it did for any particular ecclesiological reason within the church.

This conflict between national states and the international community of the Catholic Church continued unabated with various ups and downs until the work of Eugenio Pacelli, first as Vatican Secretary of State and then as Pius XII. He tried to secure treaties with the various national states that recognized the claims of those states but that also sought to ensure the rights of the church. In the 1930s these so-called concordats were worked out even with Fascist Italy and National Socialist Germany. After World War II, it proved difficult but not impossible to negotiate and ratify such arrangements even with states having communist governments. The undergirding theological position in forming the concordats was that Catholics could be both loyal citizens of their various nation states and also loyal Catholics insofar as the rights of the Catholic Church to exercise its pastoral ministry and its authority over such matters as family and religious education were respected by the national state. In return, the church accepted the national state's authority over believers as citizens. But this was a formal arrangement. Its actual content varied from country to country and from time to time. The tensions have never been fully resolved, as can be seen in such figures as Cardinal Sin of Manila, the late Archbishop Romero of El Salvador, and the role of the church in Poland (Holmes 1981; Romero 1985).

In the Protestant realm the effort to define the relationship between the religious community and the national state, and therefore to clarify the predicament of those who were both believers and citizens, largely took the form of various constitutional arrangements to disestablish or "separate" church and state. This separation restricted the power of religious bodies in the public realm and denied them any kind of official status, but it also at least technically delimited the powers of the state and forbade government to intervene in the internal affairs of religious bodies or to impair their right to exercise their religious convictions.

The Public Realm

The second historical development that loaded "citizenship" and made it difficult for the church to develop a Christian theology of citizenship was the understanding of the "public realm" that arose during the appearance of the national states, especially after the French Revolution. As recent commentators such as Karl Adorno and others have pointed out, the idea of such a public realm emerged only with the bourgeois revolutions that created the concept of the national state. It bears definite marks of its historical origin (Mannheim 1951). The triumphant bourgeoisie wanted to make the public sphere free of religion. They claimed that the public realm could be one of "rational" politics and of social emancipation. Therefore, by definition there could be no specifically religious participation in the public sphere. It was to be a realm where only open debate, rational argumentation, and logical persuasion were to be employed in a discussion of public policy issues. It was to be a "value free" realm, based on the economic concept of a free market of ideas, in which authoritarian, superstitious, or religiously legitimated ideas were excluded by their very nature. It is significant that the Declaration of Independence and Adam Smith's *Wealth of Nations* both appeared in the year 1776.

The result of this bourgeois definition of the public sphere was that citizen-believers were forced to develop a kind of "bilinguisticality." In order to speak in the public realms they had to learn the language of that sphere, a tongue that was formed by the anticlerical and nonreligious, sometimes antireligious, philosophies of the bourgeois thinkers who had created it. Any participant in the public realm who could be accused of bringing some kind of religious bias or theologically grounded opinion into that arena risked being excluded or silenced for not following the established rules of the game.

The result of the historic process that created the national state and the public realm was that "citizen" came to mean one who (1) belongs to a national state, and (2) participates in policy debate in a public realm. The trouble was that the two colossal historical formations that underlay the concepts of the national state and the public arena placed those who were both believers and citizens in a doubly difficult situation. Seemingly, they could participate in both the sacred and secular spheres of life but only by donning different hats and operating from different sets of premises. Within the religious community they could assume a set of shared beliefs and symbols nurtured by that community. But in the national community and its public sphere they had to assume a different set of symbols and values. Of course, in some instances, there was a certain overlapping. This area of overlapping came to be known in the United States as the "civil religion." But the problem with the civil religion then as now is that it is neither completely civil nor completely religious. At points it contradicts the symbolic universe of those in religious communities and even risks a form of idolatry. At the same time, it evokes images and values with which most secular participants in the civil community understandably feel uncomfortable.

One result of these developments is that there is no positive Christian doctrine of citizenship. The modern bourgeois concept of citizenship conceals within itself an ideology that is deeply inimical to many Christian and religious values. But all this is now changing. The last decades of the twentieth century have radically altered the global context within which the status of the national state in the public realm exists. Therefore, the problem of the citizen-believer must be worked out in a new setting. This has happened because of the subversion of precisely the two historical formations just described. A new situation has thus been created, one not without its own dangers but also replete with new possibilities for elaborating a theology of Christian citizenship. It will be argued shortly that such a project can best proceed by reclaiming the earlier classical idea of the civitas that was displaced by the more recent notion of the citoyen. But, first, it is necessary to examine why these dislocations in the role of the national state and the nature of the public realm have occurred.

First, the hegemony of the national state as the only accepted way of organizing the international community has suffered severe slippage. The dreams of Wilson and Lenin and the popes have not materialized, but some believe that the national state has reached a certain "crisis of legitimacy." The legitimacy of the national state has been based primarily on two pillars: its capacity to promote the welfare of its citizens and its power to protect them from foreign invasion or attack. But on both these fronts national states now find their legitimacy severely questioned. As for the "general welfare," the internationalization of the market economy has meant that national states are no longer able to guarantee to their citizens the basic necessities of life. Current panicky efforts to curb "free trade" while extolling its merits vividly reveal this inability. At the same time the advent of nuclear weapons and intercontinental delivery systems means that states are not able to offer their citizens even minimal protection from foreign foes. The "Star Wars" fantasy is the last gasp of the dying myth that the national state can protect its citizens from external attack.

The second reason why it is now possible to venture a new and positive theology of Christian citizenship is the massive "return" of religion to the public realm. Commentators on the future of religion not many decades ago frequently conceded that religion might continue to exist for decades or even centuries, but they insisted it would be contained within the private or familial circle. It would have only a lessening impact on public policy formation. This, of course, has not happened. Instead, there has been a massive reappearance of religious personages and institutions in the public political realm in areas as disparate as Japan and Poland, Brazil and Iran, the United States and Israel.

Much of the current discussion about the relationship of religion to the political order in the United States is cast either in terms of the need for more religion and morality in public life or of the danger posed to the commonwealth by fanaticism, bigotry, and divisiveness. But it is possible to examine the issue in a mood that is at once more modest and more positive. Religiously motivated citizens can possibly make a positive contribution to the restoration of the reality of citizenship by reclaiming civitas in a republic where much evidence indicates it is faltering. If religious believers understand and respect the religious pluralism of the United States and the fragile fabric by which persons and groups with different spiritual orientations are bound together in society, then they may be able to bring a gift that will strengthen and deepen citizenship in a democracy rather than diminish it.

At the start one should recall that the word "citizen" or "citoyen" stems from the same root as civility and civilian. It goes back to the notion of the civitas, the classic polity in which each person played a role not as a cleric or as a soldier but as a participant in a publicly defined order.

"Civitas" is also the source of the word "civility." In its original meaning civility meant that form of participation appropriate to this civic community, that is, pertaining to one's citizenship. Only in recent years has the word "civility" taken on the diminished meaning now normally attached to it: that of being deferential or polite, or cultivating the habit of speaking in moderated tones. In its classical sense, however, civility does *not* mean mere propriety. It means that set of skills and commitments appropriate to participation in the civitas.

At the same time that the idea of the public sphere is a recent reductionist redefinition of the much older notion of the civitas, dating only from the bourgeois revolutions of the late eighteenth century, it is also a distortion of civitas because it subtracts something vital and important away from the notion of civitas. It did so originally by trying to make the public sphere a realm free of religious rhetoric, and does so more recently by trying to cleanse it even of values or moral discourse and by declaring it to be an arena governed by a technical expertise that consists of the art of compromise plus an increasing body of administrative science. This is a sharp reversal of what the civitas meant to classical thinkers and to the great political philosophers and theologians of Western history. They also lauded skill and patience in civil debate, but they saw it primarily as a realm of moral discourse.

The proposition that the public realm should be free of value commitment or religious motivation is, in fact, a bourgeois ideology. It was an understandable product of the insistence by the bourgeoisie that their enemies—especially entrenched traditional religion and the customary aristocratic values of their day—should be prevented from dominating the realm of public debate. What has happened, however, is that the ideology of a value free public realm has become a vehicle for the new ruling elites of complex urban industrial societies to secure *their* power. It is an ideology that serves the interests of those elites and subverts justice by often preventing the participation of the less privileged sectors of the society.

The ideological function of the idea of a public sphere becomes particularly clear if one notices where a re-fusing of religious and political values and rhetoric takes place most often, although not always today: it is among oppressed peoples or captive nations or marginated ethnic or racial groups. In Latin America it is the poorest people, organized in base communities, who have created liberation theology, a powerful religious rhetoric, as a way of criticizing the allegedly neutral, technical, secular, and modern ruling elites of their impoverished nations. In the United States the picture is more confused since, despite the legal separation of church and state, the public square has never been naked. Yet, even in the United States the most visible presidential candidate, for more reasons than one, has been Jesse Jackson, who freely combines religious and political language and who represents the social group in the United States that has endured the longest history of oppression and discrimination. If one thinks of captive nations, obviously the country where Catholicism and national liberation are most thoroughly yoked is Poland, which labors under the yoke of an illegitimate and imposed Soviet-sponsored regime.

Because the existing notions of the nation-state and the public realm are now undergoing such severe questioning, the concept of citizenship is in crisis also. This crisis has opened the door to yet another reconsideration of Augustine's old, old question. In the United States itself in recent years a growing chorus of observers has lamented the decline of participation in the American political system. There are various theories of why this decline has set in—a decline suggested, for example, by the relatively small percentage of eligible voters who participate in national elections. Perhaps the increased visibility of religious groups and persons in the American political scene is to be attributed not simply to their growth, which seems statistically insignificant, but as a response to this progressive enfeeblement of the civitas.

Fifteen years ago Wilson Carey McWilliams wrote in his book, *The Idea of Fraternity in America:*

> The great concern of American political philosophy has been the development of "democratic theory." That concern has focused on formal institutions and organizations, even when it rejected "formalism." In so doing, it has neglected the fact that democratic theory must also be a theory about a *demos,* about the character and relation of citizens. (McWilliams 1973)

McWilliams is surely right. The earliest founders of the United States insisted that only with "an informed and active citizenry" would the new republic survive. But, increasingly, recent decades have witnessed a decrease in the level of participation at the polls.

Conservatives trace this decline to the growth of a gigantic national state apparatus that is said to warp and undercut the possibility of genuine citizen participation. This conservative analysis has elements of novelty. Traditionally, conservatives have *opposed* broad participation in the polity. They have feared the excesses of majorities. Therefore, the Moral Majority is something of an anomaly. It is a conservative movement that claims to speak the mind of the "real majority." However, conservatives continue, as they have traditionally, to oppose measures that would genuinely extend the voting rights to other sectors of the society, by simplifying registration or by other means of enlarging voter participation. Advocates of this view would like to diminish the size of the state so that citizen participation presumably can be increased.

A more radical perspective attributes the decline in citizenship to the enormous and growing power of the corporations whose influence on the civitas is to evacuate citizenship and to transform the polis into a market, not a free market except in strictly formal terms, but one in which money talks and wealth controls politics. It is argued from the second perspective that such an evacuation of citizenship removes it from either its classical or its modern definition, and transforms citizens into customers and eventually into consumers.

Whichever of these two diagnoses one accepts as the principal explanation for the decline in participation in the civitas, the result of the decline has been to deepen the chasm between the political world and the world of moral discourse. One institutional expression of this split is the so-called science of public policy formation and the rise of schools to train specialists in public policy. But the idea that public policy formation can be an administrative science from which genuine value conflict has been purged is itself clearly a version of the bourgeois myth of the public sphere.

During the 350th anniversary of Harvard College last fall, faculty members were asked what in their view was the most serious question facing the university in the future. Among those who responded, Professor John Kenneth Galbraith acutely observed that in his mind the university's most dangerous current illusion is that public policy can be a value-free, neutral specialization. He insisted that public policy is always political and that pretending it is not merely obfuscates the actual political powers and motivations that operate within it.

Politics is, of course, always a moral activity. For Aristotle, politics and ethics were two volumes in a single book. The Hebrew prophets directed their polemics against rulers and rich land holders.

When politics is removed from the realm of moral discourse, it becomes a spurious kind of engineering or advanced policy plumbing—or at least that is the image it presents. When ethics and morality are removed from policy formation, they become trivial and marginal. This diminution of the meaning of ethics can be seen if one looks at the pathetic status of the ethics commission in most city and state governments. It monitors elementary honesty on the part of state and city officials, mainly at the level of avoiding obvious conflicts of interest. Ethics commissions never touch the morality of the larger issues these bodies debate. This allows the ideology/myth of a value-free public realm to proceed unchallenged.

Some way must be found to restore the link between morality and politics, and between politics and public policy formation, lest a further enfeeblement and weakening of the American civitas take place. Since for most people in America morality has something to do with religion, this will obviously require a new link between *fides* and civitas. Otherwise large numbers of would-be citizens, who are also believers, will find themselves functionally disenfranchised.

America is religiously pluralistic. Even though the various traditions of Christianity and of Judaism form the majority tradition, any mode of relating religious and moral discourse to public policy formation has to be one that respects the fragile fabric of pluralism that has been created and sustained in this country. Will it be possible to evolve modes of political discourse that draw on *various* religious traditions and bring their insights to bear in the formation of the policies that guide the common life? In recent years various attempts have been made to do this—some more respectful of that pluralism than others. Examining some of these actual attempts may help to clarify the question about citizen-believers.

The Rainbow Coalition and the Jackson candidacy for president represent a remarkable maturation on the part of the black churches in their mode of relating to the American civitas. True to the history of these churches, the Rainbow Coalition focuses on a person, the preacher who "goes downtown to meet the man," and who represents and speaks for that community to the larger society (Baldwin 1965). But there is an irony. The main impact of the Jackson campaign has been to increase the number of registered black voters and also the number of black citizens who hold public office on local, county, and state levels. Consequently, there is now a statistically larger chance that when one finds the "man downtown," he may be black. But the Rainbow Coalition has also gone beyond the personal embodiment stage. The content of its program is a constructive and coherent criticism framed in a religious mode of discourse and directed against the main contours of American domestic and foreign policy over the last decades, and presenting credible alternatives. Jesse Jackson may turn out to be the Norman Thomas of the 1980s and 1990s: never elected to office but watching his ideas and programs taken over by the major parties.

On the so-called religious right, fundamentalists and evangelicals have become increasingly active in electoral politics and in other forms of public policy. Although some would argue that they have not yet learned the necessary art of civility, even to each other, it is interesting to observe that *they are in the process of learning.* They are beginning to notice that in order to accomplish anything in politics one needs to build coalitions and find allies. One cannot insist on a "pure" position unless one is seeking a glorious defeat rather than a partial victory. The Pat Robertson campaign may turn out to be a salutary lesson for his followers in the dynamics of American political life.

Perhaps the most instructive example of a religious community enlivening the public policy realm without imposing a narrow denominational view is represented by the recent pastoral letters issued by the American Roman Catholic bishops on nuclear war and on the economy (Bishops' Letter 1987). The bishops set other religious groups a fine example by circulating drafts of their two letters and encouraging widespread discussion before they were edited into their final forms and published. Also, the perspective the bishops took skillfully combined pluralism and particularity. They insisted that the realm of public policy is not a value-free one of merely technical arrangement. It is one in which moral perspectives (indeed moral perspectives based on underlying theological visions) are relevant and appropriate. They presented their perspective, however, to enrich, deepen, and broaden the discussion rather than to dominate it. The most positive result of their encyclicals was to de-mystify the realm of economic and military policy discussion, thus inviting large numbers of people to engage once more in the activity of being informed citizens.

In each of these three examples, believers are moving beyond either being Augustine's stranger or embracing a bifurcated or schizophrenic bilinguisticality. Both the Roman Catholic bishops and Jesse Jackson and the Rainbow Coalition break taboos of the national state and the public realm. The Catholic bishops do this by reclaiming the biblical ideas of creation, covenant, and world community. Jesse Jackson reaches into the Hebrew prophetic tradition, seeing the United States in relation to Third World peoples and emphasizing God's initial "preferential option for the poor." Both the Rainbow Coalition and the Catholic bishops represent attempts to let a particular tradition speak to a pluralistic community. They go beyond bilinguisticality. The underlying assumption they embody is that the pluralistic community will ultimately profit from a variety of particularities.

All this in turn means that a Christian theology of citizenship must be based on what has traditionally been known as "confession" or "testimony." The Christian can be a full citizen both of his or her national state and of the emerging international community. Indeed, a Christian can help reclaim an older and more wholesome idea of citizenship in the civitas. The believer-citizen may always be a stranger, but in one sense all are always strangers. Still, even strangers can participate, along with others who also testify to the stories of their own particular communities and bring them to the common fund of wisdom. Further, the Christian citizen's particular story has mainly to do with the rights of the oppressed and excluded, the care of the helpless, and a utopian vision that can bring hope even to the darkest hour.

The two major obstacles that have heretofore prevented the development of a credible theology of citizenship have begun to crumble. The once unquestioned legitimacy of the national state as the only sensible way of organizing the international community is waning and is rightly questioned. Other forms of belonging, including communities of faith, are both invaluable in themselves and also vital to the health of national and international communities. Also, the bourgeois notion that the public realm is or should be one free of values or moral argumentation based on religious assumptions is being exposed as one ideology among others.

Is America ready to allow, even welcome, a form of argument about public policy drawn from those moral traditions based on religious worldviews into the public arena? Some fear this entrance would fan bigotry and fanaticism. The evidence of the reception of the Bishops' letters and the Jackson candidacy suggest this need not happen. Indeed, these two events in national life have helped to mitigate the lethal fanaticism of an unchecked nationalism, a heresy that has already exacted a heavy toll in the twentieth century. They have presented a reasonable alternative to the ideology that tries to perpetuate the power of technocratic elites by keeping the public realm pure of religious and moral language and thus depriving citizens whose opinions stem from religiously based moral visions from the opportunity of contributing to the conversation. Must Christians always be strangers in the city of this world? The answer to Augustine's question is yes, at least until the kingdoms of this world become the kingdoms of our Lord and of his Christ. But a stranger can also be a citizen while he or she is passing through. Indeed, perhaps an invaluable citizen. A Christian can serve the state, as Luther and Calvin once so eloquently argued, by preventing it from drifting into idolatry. A point has been reached that makes a new step both necessary and possible. The way is now open for the elaboration of a positive theology of citizenship, one that sees the whole family of God as the highest earthly community, that respects and nourishes religious pluralism, and that makes a contribution to the linking of morality and politics in the activity of public policy debate.

This essay originally appeared in *Transforming Faith: The Sacred and the Secular in Modern History,* edited by Miles Bradbury, Greenwood Press.

References

Baldwin, James, 1965
Bell, Daniel, 1980
Berger, Peter L., 1982
Bishops' Letter, 1987
Coleman, John, 1981
Cuomo, Mario, 1984
Holmes, Derek, 1981
Mannheim, Karl, 1951
McWilliams, W. C., 1973
Romero, Oscar, 1985
Stark, Rodney, and William Bainbridge, 1985
Wilson, Bryan, 1985

24

Conservative Christians, Televangelism, and Politics: Taking Stock a Decade after the Founding of the Moral Majority

Jeffrey K. Hadden

Throughout this century right-wing Christian activism has periodically reappeared. And with each new wave of activism, the press and intellectuals have reacted with expressions of disbelief that religious fanatics could again be entering into the political arena. This tendency to see conservative Christian activism as an aberration in American politics has the quality of cultural schizophrenia. On the one hand there is a cynical snickering at these poor misguided religious extremists. H. L. Mencken and Sinclair Lewis, writing in the third decade of this century, set the tone and style of a genre of lambasting literature that subsequent generations have admired and sought to emulate. But nearly simultaneous to unconcealed mocking are shrill warnings that these fanatical fundamentalist fools pose a grave threat to the health and well-being of the political system. These mixed signals are reminiscent of the old military folk adage: "The situation is desperate, but not serious."

How can we account for the simultaneous presence of these diametrically opposed viewpoints? A good beginning point is the recognition that intellectuals and political pundits largely view religion in the modern world from a perspective that is grounded in secularization theory. While often unarticulated explicitly, this perspective is nevertheless held with considerable confidence. Secularization theory postulates either the eventual erosion of religious sentiment from the modern world or the retreat of religion to the private realm. These unwelcome and unsuited intrusions into the political arena, thus, will eventually pass as aging cohorts of old-time Bible believers die off. In the interim, the periodic reappearance of conservative Christians as a political force amounts to so much noxious noise that disrupts the eighteenth-century accommodation of church and state.

Secularization theory can incorporate the notion that intermittent waves of political activism are to be expected as this archaic belief system moves toward extinction. But this does not explain why the reappearance of Christian political activism produces the hysteria and shrill cries that warn that the fundamentalists are taking over America. Even more ironic is the fact that this reaction tends to come from the same people who steadfastly believe in the inevitability of secularization. Perhaps they experience temporary amnesia. Or perhaps the surges of religious political activism lead to a brief loss of confidence in the inexorableness of the secularization process. The mere contemplation of a dark age in which irrational religious sentiment, rather than reason, guides the ship of state is so horrible that it brings forth a fighting instinct.

However these vacillations are to be explained, America experienced another episode of alarm and amusement during the 1980s. The religious fanatics were called the New Christian Right (NCR), and for most of the decade the undisputed leader was a television preacher named Jerry Falwell who, in 1979, created an organization called the Moral Majority to do battle with the evils of secular humanism.

Seldom in modern history has the emergence of an interest group attracted so much attention. When the 1980 elections were over Ronald Reagan had scored a stunning victory that resulted in the defeat of several ranking liberal Democrats in the House and Senate. Falwell wasted no time in stepping forward to claim responsibility in the name of Moral Majority. Several defeated senators and congressmen agreed with Falwell's assessment, and so did pollster Louis Harris.

Countermovement organizations (for example, Americans for Common Sense and People for the American Way) sprang up all across the nation and joined with traditional liberal organizations (for example, the American Civil Liberties Union and Common Cause) to mobilize resources to do battle with the NCR. After the 1982 congressional elections, the absence of evidence to indicate that the NCR had made further political gains led many to conclude that the movement had been only a brief flash in the pan. Other analysts went even further, contending that the movement never had been anything more than media hype. Downplaying the significance of the NCR took on credibility as both movement and countermovement organizations either closed up shop, or bore evidence of merely being direct-mail organizations.

But Jerry Falwell's ability to gain the attention of the mass media, President Reagan's ongoing courtship of evangelical Christians, and the nagging presence of antiabortion and antipornography protesters made it difficult for the media and scholars to write an obituary and close the books of the NCR.

Then, in early 1986, Jerry Falwell made a surprise announcement that he was abandoning the Moral Majority name in favor of a new organization he would call the Liberty Federation. While he promised that the new organization would tackle a broader range of issues, there was a lot of evidence to indicate that Falwell wanted to move out of the public limelight to concentrate his time and energies on building Liberty University.

Falwell's disestablishment of the Moral Majority corresponded closely with the first national news that fellow Virginia televangelist Pat Robertson was serious about making a bid for the Republican presidential nomination. Robertson, however, had a difficult time persuading the press that his candidacy should be taken seriously. The televangelism scandals that erupted in March of 1987 made his task even more difficult. PTL's Jim Bakker, the focal personality in the sex and financial scandals at Heritage U.S.A., had begun his broadcasting career with Robertson at the Christian Broadcasting Network. Before the PTL scandal began unfolding, the mass media were having a grand time with Oral Roberts' scheme to raise eight million dollars by 1 April 1987 in order to keep God from "calling him home." A few months earlier Roberts had endorsed Robertson's candidacy in a gala occasion in Washington's Constitutional Hall, which was simulcast via satellite in over two hundred auditoriums across the nation.

But as the nation moved closer to the kickoff of the presidential primary sweepstakes, the media became increasingly impressed with Robertson's grass-roots organizational skills. He outorganized Vice President George Bush in Michigan only to lose his grip on the majority of delegates in an unusual and controversial legal maneuver by Bush operatives. Robertson further embarrassed Bush by finishing second in the Iowa caucuses behind Senator Robert Dole. And in Hawaii, where the delegate-selection process was locked-in before the New Hampshire primary, Robertson secured 80 percent of the delegates. For a brief moment, at least, it appeared that Pat Robertson really did have an "invisible army," and that he was staged to make a serious bid for the Republican nomination.

But George Bush's control of the resources of the Republican National Committee led to a swift elimination of all of his rivals. With Bush's nomination early assured, media attention shifted to the Democratic primaries where Jesse Jackson's surprising performance provided good news copy. Little effort was devoted to looking back and assessing the Robertson campaign.

In the brief time span between Robertson's gaining of national visibility and Bush's effective smashing of his opposition on Super Tuesday, several things happened that contributed to undermining Robertson's candidacy. First, candidate Robertson made several gaffs that drew widespread media attention. Then, without warning, another televangelism scandal broke— this one involving Jimmy Swaggert. Robertson, who was already having difficulty shaking the negative image of televangelist, first claimed that the Bush campaign was responsible for the timing of the revelations of Swaggert's involvement with a New Orleans prostitute, and then he traveled to Louisiana to express solidarity with Swaggert. Finally, on the eve of Super Tuesday, Robertson withdrew a libel suit against former Congressman Paul McClosky, who had accused him of using his father's influence to avoid active duty in the Korean War.

These developments led to a hasty conclusion that Pat Robertson had not been a serious candidate. And with his conclusion came yet another swift vacillation in the perceived threat of the NCR. The new conventional wisdom held that the NCR "poli-preachers," as syndicated columnist William Safire (1986) labeled them, never were serious players in the conservative movement of the 1980s. They were merely perceived to be so because of the support the religious broadcasters had received from Ronald Reagan. In the twilight of his administration, and the failed candidacy of Pat Robertson, the NCR seemed destined for oblivion.

This interpretation of the fate of the NCR appeared to have considerable credibility. After eight years of high media visibility, the religious factor seemed to vanish during the general election. If the Robertson and Falwell and Southern Baptist political contingents were working for George Bush, they appeared to be as quiet as church mice. They were neither heard from nor visible in the media. And in the headlines of postelection analyses, there was virtually no mention of the "evangelical vote." At last, it appeared that the skeptics were right.

But once again, the rush to count the NCR down and out was premature. With virtually no fanfare, evangelical Christians played a major role in George Bush's impressive 54 percent to 46 percent victory over Michael Dukakis. While they received virtually no publicity, three major news service exit polls showed that Bush received 80 percent or greater of the evangelical vote (Menendez 1988). The *New York Times/CBS News* exit poll (1988) reported that 81 percent of white fundamentalist or evangelical Christians voted for Bush compared with 78 percent who voted for Reagan in 1984.

Evangelical support for Bush was probably even stronger than indicated by these exit polls. During the 1988 primary and general elections, the Times Mirror Corporation, publishers of the *Los Angeles Times,* using factor analytic techniques, developed a sophisticated method for measuring ten independent sectors of the electorate. The sector they identified as "moralists" is a purer measure of the conservative religious community than the measures "fundamentalists" or "evangelicals" used by most pollsters. In the last Times Mirror poll conducted before the general election, the moralists favored Bush over Dukakis by a margin of 93 percent to 3 percent (Times Mirror 1988). Furthermore, George Gallup, who conducted the polling for Times Mirror, reported that while the moralists constituted 12 percent of the electorate, they were expected to represent 14 percent of all voters (Gallup 1988).

Bush's solid sweep of the South and Southwest, where evangelical Christian concentration is the greatest, was impressive and the margin of victory can substantially be attributed to the evangelical vote. Albert Menendez (1988), an authority on religion and voting who has been reluctant to acknowledge that the NCR has ever had any political clout, concluded that the evangelical vote was also probably the margin of victory for Bush in the tightly contested states of Pennsylvania, Illinois, and Missouri. Menendez reported, for example, that seventeen strongly evangelical counties in Pennsylvania delivered a 134,000 plurality for Bush to offset a Dukakis margin of 34,000 for the rest of the state. And in a sample of campus precincts of ten evangelical colleges, Menendez reported that Bush did almost as well as did Reagan in 1984 (84 percent to 86 percent).

The evangelical vote is not to be equated with the NCR, but neither can we dismiss the role of this political and social movement in the growing alliance between the Republican party and evangelical Christians. In 1980, 63 percent of white evangelicals voted for Reagan, up from 55 percent voting Republican in 1976. Even though critics are right in pointing out that none of the major stated goals of the NCR movement have been achieved—curbing abortion and pornography, reinstating prayer in school, etc.—evangelical Christians seem to be moving toward a consensus that their best chance for achieving these goals is through the Republican party. Their allegiance to the Republican party is now approaching the strength of blacks' allegiance to the Democratic party. This is a remarkable shift of allegiance away from the Democratic party, and it has mostly taken place in a fairly brief time span.

The role of the NCR in this shift of allegiance to the Republican party can't be easily quantified, but the case for the impact of the televangelist-led movement seems more plausible than the argument against this claim. First of all, the moral content of religious broadcasters on television and radio is highly similar; one can virtually say that it is monolithic. Second, very large proportions of evangelicals view some religious broadcasting. Third, the high visibility in the secular media of some politically aroused televangelists has served to heighten evangelical consciousness about politics in general as well as about specific issues.

A serious assessment of the NCR as a social movement, and the role the televangelists have played in forging this movement, must take seriously the presidential candidacy of Pat Robertson. Contrary to the impression created by the media, Robertson achieved some rather remarkable successes in his first bid for political office. Foremost was the fact that he cultivated genuine grass-roots political organization. Until the Robertson candidacy, the NCR had relied primarily on direct-mail and mass media to communicate with adherents and potential adherents. People were enlisted to vote, or occasionally to participate in a demonstration. Aside from contributing to organizations like the Moral Majority or Christian Voice, little was asked of people. There was little development of local organizational chapters. Even piggybacking on existing organizations, primarily churches, was ad hoc.

Robertson effectively utilized churches, but he built organizations independent of local churches. People were enlisted to participate in the political process in a variety of ways at local, congressional district, and state level. To do so, a cadre of local activists had to develop an understanding of both the minutia and complexity of the political process. The degree of success varied, but by the end of the primary season, the Robertson forces were within striking distance of controlling the Republican party in at least ten states. Robertson chose not to flaunt his strength but, rather, to demonstrate that he was a team player.

Robertson is unlikely to win the GOP nomination for the presidency at some future date, but he has established himself as an important player. Furthermore, there are thousands that Robertson drew into active leadership roles who, having learned how the political process works, will remain active in GOP politics.

The alliance between evangelical Christians and the Republican party is an uncomfortable one; one might even say a marriage of convenience. Many traditional Republicans are uncomfortable with the emotionally charged moral agenda of the Christian right. Furthermore, the infusion of newly politicized Christians is viewed as a threat to status-quo party politics at every level. But in spite of the success of the GOP in presidential elections over the past two decades, Republicans remain the minority party. They need the evangelical Christians if they are to build a majority party. The Democratic party, on the other hand, is too staunchly aligned with left-wing special interests to provide an accommodating environment for the Christian right, at least within the foreseeable future. Thus, from a pragmatic perspective, the moralist Christians and the traditional pro-business Republicans are a likely alliance.

The future of the NCR and the Republican party in the immediate future will hinge on whether Republicans seek to accommodate evangelicals mobilized by Robertson or attempt to roust them out of the party. Accommodation will keep NCR movement concerns focused within normal party politics. Hostility toward evangelical Christians could trigger a sustained effort to take over the GOP. But the bitter battles fought by Robertson and Bush forces in states like Michigan and Georgia could leave many alienated from party politics, which could have the effect of renewing more aggressive activity outside of established party politics.

Precisely how the interests of the Christian right will be worked out in the political process during the last decade of the twentieth century is uncertain. What is not in doubt is their presence as a significant interest group. They can no more be ignored than blacks, Catholics, feminists, hispanics, or Jews. While scarcely being recognized as such by the media and the general public, they have already become one of the more politically effective interest groups in American politics.

Unlike previous waves of Christian right-wing politics during this century, the NCR has demonstrated the ability to be politically pragmatic, even in dealing with issues on which they hold absolutist positions. Ronald Reagan is to be credited with having dealt with the NCR in a highly effective manner. From the moment he first addressed the Christian activists during his 1980 presidential campaign, they never doubted his commitment to support their agenda and they, in turn, supported the president's agenda. At the same time, Reagan can probably be credited with having taught them the value of patience and being willing to take what you can get in the political process, recognizing that there will be another day.

Jerry Falwell claims to be the first public figure in America to endorse George Bush's presidential candidacy. This represented both political astuteness and pragmatism. Similarly, once it was evident that the vice president had a lock on the nomination, Pat Robertson moved to heal campaign wounds and to build bridges to Bush and the Republican National Committee.

The most important lesson to be learned about the leadership of the NCR, and what separates it from earlier waves of conservative Christian activists during this century, is the pragmatism that we have seen demonstrated by Falwell, Robertson, and others. They are resolute and determined to be serious players in American politics.

The second most important lesson is to recognize that they have considerable resources to sustain a significant political movement. The single most important resource is the unique access they have to the airwaves (Hadden and Shupe 1988, 291–92). Evangelicals have battled with mainline Protestants for access to the airwaves from the very beginning of radio broadcasting. They developed a clear advantage in 1960 when the Federal Communications Commissions (FCC) ruled that local broadcasters could sell air time and also receive public service "credit." Unlike the mainline churches who have always been dependent upon broadcasters for free air time, Evangelicals have never been hesitant to solicit funds over the air to pay for their broadcast time.

Clearly the televangelism scandals of 1987 and 1988 served to undermine the credibility of all religious broadcasters. Viewing and contributions were down sharply for almost *all* religious broadcasters. Only time will reveal whether the scandals will have a long-term impact on the religious broadcasting industry. But so long as the FCC, the Congress, and the courts do not significantly alter the rules for access to the airwaves, religious broadcasters will communicate both overt and latent political messages. Thus, both directly and indirectly the televangelists will contribute to the mobilization of conservative Christians who are committed to turning back the tide of secular humanism.

This essay began with the assertion that the presence of conservative Christians in the political arena has, for most of this century, been viewed as an aberration. In light of the growing sophistication of conservative Christians during the 1980s, and the large number of U.S. citizens who consider themselves to be fundamentalists or evangelicals, the continued denial of their presence in politics seems itself to be the aberration. But still the idea persists, along with the assumption that conservative Christians constitute a unique threat. How is this to be explained?

It has already been suggested that a subtle commitment to secularization theory has contributed to an assumption that religion can be expected to play a diminishing role in public life. For those who are committed to a liberal social agenda—which includes a fairly large proportion of scholars and political analysts in America—the involvement of liberal Christians in politics should similarly be viewed as an aberration (Williamsburg Charter Foundation 1988). But since they share a common social agenda with liberal Christians, the presence of the latter in politics is not viewed as threatening. Hence, the involvement that is equally anomalous to secularization theory is missed.

Social scientists have frequently addressed the question of how personal values intrude in efforts at objective analysis. Stanley Lieberson, a distinguished scholar of ethnic and race relations, recently explored the issue in his presidential address to the Pacific Sociological Association. Writes Lieberson:

I am convinced that our discipline follows certain implicit rules of thinking that are totally inappropriate, illogical, and ultimately undermine our ability to advance knowledge about society. (1988, 379)

The discipline of sociology, argues Lieberson, carries unspoken social norms regarding what kinds of findings are acceptable and unacceptable with respect to political and social policy issues. When findings are unacceptable, "illogical procedures and inappropriate ways of thinking" are employed to discount or discredit research. Ad hominem arguments and the application of double standards are among several techniques used to discredit "unacceptable" information.

While Lieberson is addressing his sociology colleagues, his argument is equally pungent for the broader community of scholars, intellectuals, and opinion makers in America. Evangelical Christians, and particularly those who would make known their sentiments through the political process, are an anathema to educated secular persons. They are not a phenomenon to be understood, but objects of ridicule and scorn. As long as they are silent and remain on the periphery of society, they can be tolerated. When they threaten to enter the mainstream of political life, they become dangerous. The thought that evangelical Christians might have real political power produces such intense cognitive dissonance (Festinger et al. 1964, 26) that the information suggesting the presence, or even potential for power, is discounted. The bringers of the "bad" news are subjected to ad hominem arguments, double standards are applied to discredit research evidence, etc. "We have a set of illogical but punishing conclusions about those whose results do not meet certain predetermined notions," argues Lieberson (1988, 394).

Evangelical Christians and the political movement they have propagated over the past decade are not well understood because of the immense intellectual barrier to objective analysis. Rather than cool analysis, the introduction of any datum about the Christian right almost automatically produces an ideological response. Some are prone to respond by viewing almost any datum with alarm; others can see the folly in any argument that asserts real or potential political power grounded in evangelical Christian principles. So long as ideology serves as the foundation for understanding the Christian right, our insights will not be very profound and we shall continue to be surprised by their tenacious persistence in the political arena.

References

Festinger, Leon, et al., 1964
Gallup, George Jr., 1988

Hadden, Jeffrey K., and Anson Shupe, 1988
Lieberson, Stanley, 1988
Menendez, Albert J., 1988
New York Times/CBS News Poll, 1988
Safire, William, 1986
Times Mirror, 1988
Williamsburg Charter Foundation, 1988

VII
CONCLUSION

25

Civil Religion and Recent American
Religious Ferment

Dick Anthony and Thomas Robbins

In the 1970s, in the wake of countercultural turbulence of the 1960s, the
United States witnessed the upsurge of new religious movements, cults,
and quasi-religious therapeutic movements (Robbins 1988a, 1988b). In the
1980s spiritual innovation has continued, though there is some ambiguity
as to its prospects: some of the better-known controversial groups, such
as the Unification Church, Hare Krishna, the church of Scientology, the
Children of God, or the Bhagwan Movement, have either experienced
significant declines in membership or are suffering from the impact of
scandals and legal complications such that their future is clouded (Bromley
and Hammond 1987; Robbins 1988a). Authoritarian and totalistic movements may be declining, but there are indications that New Age and occult
beliefs are spreading, and that New Age religiotherapeutic practices are
penetrating conventional business, educational, and even military institutions (Bordewich 1988; Garvey 1985).

At the same time a seemingly opposing trend has been building up for
several decades: the Old Time Religion, in terms of evangelical, fundamentalist, and charismatic-pentecostal spirituality, has been growing steadily
(Kelley 1973; see also several chapters in this volume). This surge has
increasingly manifested an explicit politicization and a strident demand for
the reestablishment, initiation, or augmentation of conservative and pro-
family sociopolitical agendas, including restoration of "prayer in the
schools"; banning of abortion; restigmatization of homosexuality; defeat
of the Equal Rights Amendment and other feminist innovations; resistance
to the spread and stabilization of world communism; mobilization against

New Age and occultist beliefs; promotion of legal restraints on pornography; expulsion of secular humanism from education, media, and other cultural institutions; and enhanced freedom for conservative Christian groups to proselytize, educate children, engage in political activity, raise funds, and control media (Hadden 1987a; Hadden and Shupe 1988; Wuthnow 1988).

The original version of this essay (Anthony and Robbins 1982a) dealt primarily with the spiritual innovation of the 1970s and attempted an analysis in terms of a crisis of American civil religion. Some attention was devoted to the evangelical surge, but it was really a marginal subtopic. In this revised and retitled version we seek to relate the spiritual ferment—innovation and reaction—of the past two decades to vicissitudes of American civil religion and to identify what we and other observers see as a deepening polarization of American religion.

American Civil Religion

Our institutional separation of church and state notwithstanding, religious and political symbols are closely intertwined in American history. Yet our civil religion is more than merely a form of national self-worship. It entails as well "the subordination of the nation to ethical principles that transcend it and in terms of which it should be judged" (Bellah 1970b, 171). Our civil religion thus imparts a religious dimension to the whole fabric of American life, especially the political realm.

An essential element in many conceptions of American civil religion involves a notion of America as a "Redeemer Nation" and Americans as chosen people. Implicit in this notion is the belief in a messianic universal mission, a sort of sacred nationalism that connects manifest destiny with universal ideals. American civil religion interrelates theism, patriotism, competitive individualism, and boundless faith in the potentialities of economic growth and prosperity. In Robert Bellah's view, our civil religion is inherently pluralistic: America's diverse ideological and interest groupings put forward variations of civil religion, or competing "public theologies," that of necessity embody different visions of America's destiny and its relationship to social ideals. Reform movements such as abolitionism, for example, expressed their goals in terms of civil religion and articulated a public theology. There is thus continual conflict and interaction between different public theologies (see Bellah's essay in this volume).

In *The Broken Covenant*, Bellah (1975) talks about a once-dominant communal or covenantal ethos rooted in New England Puritanism and in Old Testament–oriented biblical morality. Early New England political thought was strongly collectivistic, derived partly from classical philosophy and the conception of a *polis,* partly "from the Old Testament notion of the covenant between God and a people held collectively responsible for its actions," and partly "from the New Testament notion of a community based on charity or love and expressed in brotherly affection and fellow membership in one common body." Even the Calvinist emphasis on individual action "only made sense within the collective context. Individual action outside the bounds of religious and moral norms was seen in Augustinian terms as the very archetype of sin" (Bellah 1975, 17–18). Puritanism grounded communal solidarity in moral absolutism.

By mid-nineteenth century, according to Bellah, the biblical covenant ethos began to be seriously threatened by utilitarian individualism, a new ethos that assumed that the pursuit of private materialistic goals by individual citizens would somehow result in a collective public welfare and civic virtue. Utilitarian individualism became the legitimation for burgeoning American capitalism, since it relativized the ends, or goals, of human action and stressed the rationalization of means, or technical reason. This ethos continues its hold over American culture, despite periodic revolts against technical reason such as the counterculture of the 1960s.

Bellah believes that "today the American civil religion is an empty and broken shell," and that the present spiritual ferment is an attempt to bring about a "birth of new American myths" as a response to the decay of civil religion (Bellah 1975, 139–63). The new religions that flourished in the 1970s are survivors of the crisis of meaning that erupted in the 1960s (Bellah 1976). They articulated values of "love" and "raising consciousness," while often evolving composite patterns of symbolic meaning that accommodated countercultural values to resurgent utilitarian individualism (Tipton 1982).

It is arguable that Bellah poses too sharp an antithesis between Puritan biblical absolutism and utilitarian individualism. The legitimation of American capitalism has been tied to a synthesis of both. This synthesis emerged after the Civil War, and was embodied in a culturally dominant ethos, which we have termed "implicit legitimation." The pursuit of selfish goals in the material realm was viewed as conducive to public good so long as egoistic materialism takes place within a framework of moral absolutism in the private expressive realm. Put simply, so long as everyone upholds a limited set of negative moral absolutes—for example, not to murder, steal, fornicate, or drink—each person may pursue selfish materialistic goals and confidently expect that public welfare and civil virtue will arise from such individual egoism. Within an overall framework of moral absolutism, the "invisible hand" will harmonize private egoism in the economic realm. Economic laissez faire is thus a moral as well as an economic imperative. Given moral absolutism and asceticism in private mores, plus economic laissez faire, virtue will become its own reward, and success will come to those who deserve it.

A key feature of the civil religion ethos was the assumption that proscribed acts such as theft were to be strictly and narrowly defined; only then could the prohibition of immoral acts be absolute. Thus theft, narrowly, and negatively defined in relation to property acquisition, meant that other means of acquiring property, technically proper because they were not theft, were implicitly legitimated. Thus, dualistic moral absolutism, which ultimately derives from Puritanism and precapitalist American moral culture, could be used to implicitly legitimate laissez-faire economic entrepreneurial activity free from moral or governmental regulation. "Within this moral system, so long as participants in entrepreneurial capitalism obeyed certain narrowly conceived negative injunctions, they received moral sanction for engaging in economic activities that resulted in social inequality" (Anthony and Robbins 1978a, 81).

The emergent synthesis of covenantal moralism and utilitarian individualism manifested a certain integrity and internal harmony: it was the moral absolutism governing the expressive realm (for example, don't drink, fornicate) and the righteousness of the behavior of proper persons who eschewed certain stigmatized (but narrowly defined) behaviors that sanctified those other problematic behaviors (for example, in the economic realm) that enhanced inequality.[1]

Essential to this synthesis of moral absolutism and utilitarianism was the premise of individual responsibility: individuals were presumed to possess a capacity to choose whether or not to be virtuous, and on that basis were held responsible for their behavior. Virtuous individuals could anticipate success in material endeavors, while those who did not succeed were considered to be morally deficient. This ethos was hostile to collectivist regimentation of the broader economy and society, and because choice and free will were deemed essential to the creation of virtue, regimented virtue could not be true virtue. Competitive individualism was thus given a moral aura.[2]

Finally, the moral dimension of this civil religion ethos entailed a sanctification of American society, its laissez-faire economic processes, its democratic political processes, and its military and international might. The United States was viewed as a country in which equal opportunity— hence free will and the possibility of virtue—were preserved by the nature of our social processes. Moreover, since success was the reward of virtue, American might and power reflected the virtue of American institutions, and ultimately the intervention of Providence. Americans were God's chosen people contending with evil adversaries. In the past, European monarchies whose governments protected hereditary privilege served as contrast symbols vital to American civil religion. More recently, communism has succeeded to this role.

Since the 1930s two factors have operated to undermine or challenge the moral system of implicit legitimation. First, the development of a managed and planned economy and an increasingly bureaucratized society have made the ideas of individualism, free will, and personal autonomy less plausible. Their credibility has been further diminished by a growing acceptance of the notion that any individual's course of action depends to a great extent on his socioeconomic status. Second, the development of a hedonistic, permissive culture has challenged moral absolutism in the private expressive realm. Indeed, in this connection, an inherent partial contradiction involving the combination of privatized moralism and utilitarianism in business and commercialism may have been exposed: a mass consumption capitalist economy inevitably expands into taboo areas and commodifies more and more private behavior, for example, sex. The distinction between business and leisure becomes more problematic.

In the view of some writers (Vidich 1975), a serious legitimation problem has existed for American institutions since the Great Depression. A cultural crisis of legitimation was forestalled by World War II and moral solidarity was created by thematizing the duality of democracy against dictatorship. This solidarity was buttressed in the years after the war by setting "godless communism" over against the idea of God-fearing and individualistic America as the "home of the free and the brave." Arthur Vidich (1975) has commented, "It was only World War Two and the cold war that rescued capitalism from its ideological poverty. The ending of the cold war once again reopens this issue for the capitalist countries and their political systems" (Vidich 1975).

The moral system of implicit legitimation of American capitalism proved to be unstable. As entrepreneurial capitalism was transformed into managerial capitalism, corporate technocracy became increasingly difficult to legitimate in traditional individualist and voluntarist terms. The American economy became increasingly dependent upon a mass-consumption ethic that promised happiness through limitless material acquisition. But this vision contravened Protestant ethic ascetic norms. Finally, the stalemate in Vietnam undercut the faith in American power that had complemented faith in American enterprise.

Responses to the Spectre of Moral Chaos

According to Bellah, the decline of consensual civil religion and the consequent crisis in national identity impinge most heavily on local institutions that are responsible for conveying moral ideologies. The "soft structures" that deal with human motivation—the churches, the schools, the family—have been weakened more than other institutions in recent American upheavals, especially with respect to "their capability to transmit patterns of conscience and ethical values" (Bellah 1981, reprinted as chapter 22 of this volume).

These views are borne out by Wade Clark Roof in a study (1981) that summarizes survey data on religious defection in the early and middle 1970s. According to Roof, the figures for defection from mainline churches are staggering. They suggest that the recent upsurge of unconventional new religions is merely "a small part of a larger climate of unrest taking place in the religious realm," which involves vast numbers of Americans dropping out of conventional churches and synagogues and "breaking with many of their institutional commitments" (Roof 1981).

Roof's findings indicate that defectors from established faiths tend to be young, well educated, and middle class. They are much more likely than nondefectors to be committed to the permissive "new morality" and to have liberal attitudes on issues such as homosexuality and abortion. Roof believes that the large defections from established churches in the 1970s are clearly related to the diffusion of countercultural values. Protestant and Catholic faiths are "internally split over such issues as homosexuality, abortion, and women's ordination." The religious tinge of recent crusades against abortion and homosexuality "reveals the depths of conservative reaction and the close affinity to religious symbols and values."

Extrapolating from Roof's analysis, it can be argued that the Catholic Church and the liberal Protestant denominations are caught between the spread of permissive morality on the one hand and the moralistic evangelical revival on the other. If the churches opt for evangelical absolutism, they may continue to lose members among the well educated and affluent; but if they embrace the new morality, they are, in effect, embracing a modern secular ethos hostile to theism. In the latter case, they are, in a sense, repudiating their own raison d'être. The dilemma may be insoluble, and illustrates the degree to which the churches no longer uphold a moral consensus and embody a national covenant. More recently Elizabeth Hardwick characterizes, "The modesty of the claims of the general Protestant churches, the humbleness of their techniques of propaganda and propagation, the long shadow of relativism lying on the moral ledge, the inscrutable confusion about the Good, with cases to be adjudicated on an infinity of special conditions far more exhausting than Sin or Evil" (Hardwick 1988, 18).

A paradoxical consequence of the present lack of consensual spiritual purpose is a discrediting of the secular ideal of segregating morality from government. The state is asked to adjudicate matters which might otherwise be relegated to the competence of public opinion and social pressure. As Peter Berger notes, in the United States today, "Moral pluralism is becoming increasingly prevalent, and it is much harder to institutionalize than religious pluralism" (Berger 1982, 18). For example:

> The controversy over abortion stems from two sharply differentiated moral positions, one regarding abortion as an act of murder, the other considering it a matter of individual "choice" (a synonym for the denominational term *preference*). . . . Anyone schooled in Durkheimian ideas about the role of moral consensus in the integration of human societies must ask whether American society can survive long with such fundamental moral divisions. In such a society, moral disputes must be referred to the political processes and the courts, self-consciously secular institutions that are ill-equipped to function as sources of a binding common morality. The development of moral pluralism in America, unresolved and probably unresolvable in secular terms, thus contributes to the crisis of secularity (Berger 1982, 18).

Thus, increasing moral pluralism leads to a politicization of morality. The underlying church-supported consensus, which, as Bellah (1981) notes, the Founding Fathers counted on to complement the laissez-faire liberal constitutional state, is no longer present. Moral issues must now be politically adjudicated, a development that is profoundly divisive though it is compatible with the continuous expansion of the apparatus and authority of the state, which now must decide seemingly religious questions such as when life begins and terminates (Robertson and Chirico 1985). In this setting moralists are more or less invited to press their claims in the state and seek to have public authority enforce their moral agendas.

This is then the cultural context in which the political-moral movement of the New Christian Right has gathered steam. Increasing moral pluralism, the commercialization of leisure (including eroticism), and the increasing politicization of morality, are mutually reinforcing developments, which have tended to erode the distinction between private and public normative realms. This erosion was reinforced in the 1970s by the public moral ritual of Watergate and the moralistic candidacy and presidency of an evangelical, Jimmy Carter (who was *not* a right-wing moral zealot but whose Christian public identity and moralistic rhetoric legitimated moralistic religiopolitics). "By the end of the 1970s, what had once been a rather sharp symbolic boundary between private morality and collective life had become so ambiguous that writers and public figures began openly challenging the earlier privatistic notions" (Wuthnow 1988, 201). The Supreme Court's 1973 decision, *Roe v. Wade,* which permitted abortion, was seemingly a defeat for conservative moralism, but it was also a kind of victory. "Many (especially in the evangelical community) recognized it as a statement by the Court that questions of morality could not be divorced from the agencies of government. . . . [M]orality was too important to be decided by individuals alone" (Wuthnow 1988, 200).

The present resurgence of conservative Christian religion and its politicization can thus be seen as a response to the erosion of moral consensus and the disenchantment with secular liberal constitutionalism. Paradoxically, the decline of moral consensus increases the demand for government regulation of morality.

Traditionalist Resurgence

The "Jesus Movement" in the late 1960s and early 1970s reinforced the general rebirth of interest in morally conservative religion. Past decades have witnessed the growth of conservative Protestant denominations, evangelical and Pentecostal movements within liberal denominations, and the Catholic charismatic movement, as well as the surge of neo-Orthodoxy within American Judaism. These developments reflect a widespread repudiation of cultural modernism.

Conservative Christian congregations practice the "cure of souls" within a moral community that shares a transcendent worldview. Yet, despite their rejection of many aspects of secular culture, they basically accept the institutional structure of the everyday world. Traditional religionists, however, may be particularly subject to the alienation that is bred out of relativistic cultural modernism and the impersonal bureaucracies of expanding government and managerial capitalism. Perhaps it is partly for this reason that conservative and Christian evangelical groups increasingly feel a need to alter the political and governmental status quo as a complement to saving individual souls.

Conservative evangelical Protestantism is really tied to a model of society in which the virtuous life is linked to laissez-faire economics and limited government. Indeed, the "sacred cosmos" of biblical Christianity might be viewed as a projection of competitive entrepreneurial capitalism into the realm of ultimacy. Salvation is competitive in the sense that "Many are called, but few are chosen." Spiritual success is possible for a few, but many salvational failures will necessarily be cast into "outer darkness." This quintessentially dualistic conception of salvation approaches a zero-sum game (Anthony and Robbins 1982b; Anthony and Ecker 1987).

Tied to a model of society that bases virtuous life on laissez-faire economics and limited government, conservative evangelical Protestantism has sanctified individualism and rejected collectivism as unholy and inimical to man's obligation to choose righteousness. "The cultural resources available to Americans have emphasized the autonomy of the individual and the individualistic and voluntaristic character of social relations" (Johnson 1981, 57). In the nineteenth century, when the economic life of the nation was carried on primarily through small businesses and farms, such a traditionalist laissez-faire form of civil religion seemed plausible to most people, and social experiences were not too glaringly inconsistent with it. With the growth of both corporations and government in the current era of managerial capitalism, emphasis on personal autonomy and civic virtue as the wellsprings of vocational motivation may actually serve to intensify the frustration of contemporary life. Some radical religious movements attempt to transcend these stresses by developing utopian communal enclaves as models for the coming revolutionary transformation of the larger society.

Civil-Religion Sects—Restored Communities

The new religions that emerged from the counterculture of the late 1960s and 1970s or later can be placed in one of two categories, each of which embodies contrasting strategies for coping with the decline of civil religion. Groups such as the Unification Church of Reverend Sun Myung Moon really promise a revitalized synthesis of political and religious motifs as the basis for crystalizing personal identities. Such "totalistic" groups, which look toward the restoration of a national covenant, might be termed new "civil-religion sects." Jim Jones's ill-fated Peoples Temple approximated this pattern, as did Synanon and, to a lesser degree, some communal or closely knit evangelical groups. The other category of movement involves "privatistic" mystical religions and guru groups (Yogi Bhajan, Meher Baba, Tibetan Buddhism) plus quasi-mystical therapeutic movements such as Scientology, est (now the Forum), Lifespring, and many New Age groups. In part because they often do not manifest overt political or civic emphases, such groups tended to be labeled "narcissistic" by the social critics of the 1970s. These groups are generally noncommunal, but such groups can sometimes form communal enclaves such as the now defunct Rajneesh commune in Oregon (Carter 1987) or the authoritarian "therapy cults" (Reed 1988), which may, however, belong in the category of civil-religion sect.

Civil-religion sects aim ultimately at reconstructing the culture and reordering the polity. This is a difficult, perhaps insuperable task. Because the absolutist ideologies of these movements pose unique problems for the indoctrination of converts, and elicit hostility from outsiders, such movements must often create alternative communities as models of future American society. These morally "pure" and homogeneously integrated minisocieties afford their members escape from daily involvement with a morally chaotic society. But this approach is not without its costs. Part of the exhilaration of membership in a totalistic utopian movement may come from the converts' sense of betting their all on a worthy ideal. Surely it is a high-risk game. A great deal rides on the choice of an organization or leader intended to exemplify civil-religious ideals. As Robert Lifton argues, the embodiment of exalted utopian ideals in a fallible leader creates a contradiction that bedevils authoritarian cults, and results in a "deification of idiosyncracy" that glorifies the leader's eccentricities and suppresses all doubts (Lifton 1979). Thus, one religious fellowship in Illinois was led by an ex-professional football player, a "nutrition fanatic." In emulation of the Leader, "everyone [in the group] had to be physically fit. . . . [P]eople were forced to fast. People were made to stand on scales" (ex-convert quoted by Galloway 1988, A8).

In Peter Berger's (1982) terms, what we have called "civil-religion sects" are sectarian variants of restored communities. Such groups are "movements of both counterpluralism and countersecularity" (1982, 20). The broader New Christian Right might be seen as such a movement, but it represents a nontotalistic version of the quest for a restored community, which hopes to reverse secularism and mitigate pluralism in the broader society rather than enshrine moral and ideological purity in a sectarian communal enclave. The problem of restored communities "is the erection and maintenance of barriers strong enough to keep out the forces that undermine certainty—a difficult feat in the context of modern urban life, mobility, and mass communication" (Berger 1982, 20).

Civil-religion sects or totalistic restored communities such as the Unification Church, the Peoples Temple, or Synanon provisionally heal the split between private feelings and public purpose by influencing their members to withdraw from normal vocational involvements. Members of these movements are encouraged to expend all their energies in developing self-sufficient utopian communities to serve as models for the transformation of America. These movements create moral solidarity only by encouraging a uniformity of opinion and degree of obedience to authority among converts that arguably violate norms of personal autonomy that are integral to a pluralistic and secularized society.

Finally, the civil-religious character of these groups commits them to the attempted total metamorphosis of the nation as a whole. This commitment may encourage confrontations with the larger society. But unfavorable outcomes for these encounters can appear to undermine the plausibility of these groups' missions and render them volatile (see John Hall's paper, chapter 16 in this volume).

A number of well-known authoritarian groups seem to have such features in common. Their differences from each other, however, may be as important as their similarities in predicting a specific movement's course of development and the effects upon members (Richardson 1980). We have studied one such controversial movement (Anthony and Robbins 1978a; Robbins et al. 1978).

Calling America to Unity

The Unification Church of Reverend Sun Myung Moon is nearly unique in the explicit and systematic quality of its extrapolation of public theology. American civil religion has traditionally sanctified the separation of church and state, and legitimated cultural and normative diversity. The erosion of both civil religion and moral consensus in the 1970s set the stage for a sectarian assertion of the authoritarian ideal of the morally purified "virtuous republic." The Unification Church has transformed this ideal into an overtly theocratic vision. The religiopolitical synthesis advocated by the Unification Church entails what Irving Horowitz identifies as "a categorical denial of the Lockean-Jeffersonian principle of the separation of church and state" (Horowitz 1981, 162). The church "searches for the unity rather than the separation of the theological and political. Unification Church members regard their efforts to breach the wall of separation between church and state as not so much an attack on civil liberties as a search for new foundations for the social order" (Horowitz 1981, 163). Attempting to heal the extreme separation of public and private realms and the fragmentation of personal identity in modern society, the Moon movement articulates a provocative authoritarian response to the decline of civil religion. "Reverend Moon's movement can be interpreted as an attempt at a totalitarian response to the cultural fragmentation of mass society" (Robbins et al. 1978, 51).

Although Bellah sees American civil religion at its best functioning to temper chauvinism and to subject American values to moral scrutiny, the Moonist absolutist variant of American civil religion identifies all evil with communist societies and all virtue with the United States. This tendency represents an instance of *exemplary dualism,* which refers to the inclination to perceive contemporary sociopolitical forces and movements as exemplifying absolute moral contrast categories (Anthony and Robbins 1978). Exemplary dualism has frequently characterized Christian millenarian movements—for example, late medieval visions of the papacy as the satanic "whore of Babylon." Exemplary dualism was implicit in the Cold War anticommunism of the 1950s, but it is vividly explicit in the Moon movement, which in the 1970s thought of the United States as a New Rome, providentially ordained to succor and support the chosen land, or

New Israel: anticommunist South Korea (Robbins et al. 1978). The new civil religion of Reverend Moon's Divine Principle is intended to reconstitute the connection between anticommunism and theism, and thus mobilize Americans to accept their country's providential role in sacrificing its wealth and power to combat satanic communism and thereby facilitate the coming of God's kingdom.

But America has allegedly been corrupted by moral relativism, egoism, and permissiveness, and the false hopes of détente. If America does not accept the new civil religion of Divine Principle, Satan and communism will triumph, and the opportunity will be lost to restore harmony between God and man, and to crystalize a universal moral community. A Moonie commented in an interview with one of the authors:

> You know . . . that if America doesn't unite with the Divine Principle, then Divine Principle will find it very hard to spread all over the world and, therefore . . . the world will turn communist, and God will not have a foothold in the world anymore, and the world will go through terrible suffering. (quoted in Anthony and Robbins 1978a, 89)

The Unification movement is seen as the divinely designated absolute contrast category for demonic godless communism. The Moonist system reconstructs the moral absolutism of traditional biblical morality in America, but also redefines it. It stresses "absolute values," but does not equate absolute values with universal moral principles. Instead, moral absolutism is associated with a divinely inspired interpretation of history. Moral categories are viewed as inherent in the historical process, such that the moral choice individuals must make between exemplars of divine and satanic forces in history is absolute.

> It is very unusual to see that you have the truth, because no one has had anything as clear as Divine Principle throughout history, so that if you believe you have something that is universally true, which is universal cosmic truth, then it doesn't make to sense to say, "Well, you know, maybe this is wrong." (quoted, Anthony and Robbins 1978a, 92)

The Manichaean anticommunist ideology of the Moon movement is only slightly more extreme and systematic than the message purveyed by a number of right-wing fundamentalist preachers in contemporary America. What distinguishes Moonism is its capacity to embody its ideology in a communal movement, such that the Moonist synthesis of political and religious values becomes a total identity for the convert, whose commitment is reinforced by the rewards of participation in a "loving" civil-religious community (Parsons 1986). As communism supposedly epitomizes the materialism and corruption that poisons relationships in the contemporary world, Divine Principle is seen as embodying the God-centered values that hold the key to harmony and cooperation in social interaction.

To the potential convert who perceives a lack of harmony and authenticity in interpersonal relationships, the close-knit community and the philosophy of the Unification Church may appear to be a plausible remedy. The ultimate cause of failed relationships is held to be man's fallen nature. The sin of Adam and Eve, conceived by Moon as an unconsecrated sex act, has produced a world peopled by fallen beings, separate from God and incapable of authentic relationships. Through Divine Principle, it is maintained, man's fallen nature can be overcome, and humanity can be reunited into God's harmonious family. The communal solidarity of the movement is defined as a prototype for the loving familial kingdom that is to come. Reverend Moon is "Father," and he and his wife are referred to by devotees as "our True Parents." "The Unification Church constantly emphasizes the breakdown of the American family, corruption and immorality in American life (divorce, pornography, suicide, drugs, and scandal), and, by contrast, the work of the church toward the 'perfect family' in a 'perfect world' " (Doress and Porter 1981, 297).

The Unification Church is a surrogate family but one that is legitimated in terms of universal values. Particularly important here is the theme of sacrifice. A lecturer at a Unification workshop stated, "We in the U.S.A. have relative economic security and welfare, but God may abandon America in a few years unless we reform and create a spiritual revolution. If we can't give up our little things—our privacy, our apartments, cars, record players—all the big things will go" (quoted in Robbins et al. 1978, 65). Young converts see themselves as fighting selflessly for universal ideals of love and harmony and world unity in a world permeated by relativism, cynicism, and selfish egoism.

According to a more recent research report (Parsons 1986) the Unification community has been able to (rather surprisingly) combine a milieu of "expressive personalism" involving interpersonal warmth and evocations of personal authenticity with a strictly authoritarian and hierarchical control system. But the *long-term* effectiveness of the Unification movement as an expressive and therapeutic milieu—and a "restored community"—is open to doubt. Since the early 1980s the American branch of Unificationism has declined in numbers, morale, and internal unity, although its financial and political operations have expanded (Bromley 1985; Mickler 1987; Robbins and Anthony 1984).

Embodied in the totalistic and regimented milieu of the Unification movement may be an insight: in contemporary American society, moral absolutism is viable only if divorced from individualism. The American synthesis of Puritanism and utilitarian individualism may have run its course. It was linked to entrepreneurial capitalism, and has been undercut by the emergence of a bureaucratically regulated society and managed economy, and by the breakdown of moral consensus in a pluralistic culture. Any communally viable reconstitution of moral absolutism must necessarily be authoritarian and collectivist. In this connection, it is significant that Moon objects not to the collectivist character of communism, but to its atheism! Satan is seen as attempting to steer mankind to a premature materialistic socialism. Eventually, however, "there will ultimately have to come a socialistic society centering on God" (Moon 1974, 444).

Dominion versus Tribulation

The political theology of Unificationism is too esoteric and overtly theocratic to elicit much persisting American support. But there are elements of what Berger would call the "Moonist restored community" program that can also be seen in other currents and groups operating under the umbrella of right-wing evangelicism. Christian Reconstructionism (Boston 1988), Theonomy, and the broader movement toward Dominion Theology (Chilton 1985; North 1983) envision Christians employing political activism and education to reconstruct the culture and thus usher in "the Kingdom" and the millennium, which therefore need not await the prior return of Jesus. In contrast, the dominant fundamentalist apocalyptic vision in the twentieth century has been the "premillennial" and "dispensationalist" vision, which foresees Christ returning to bring in the millennium only after Antichrist has ruled the world during the imminent Great Tribulation at the end of which Antichrist will be defeated by heavenly host at the battle of Armageddon. This is the scenario delineated in Hal Lindsey's book, *The Late Great Planet Earth* (1970), which is said to have sold twenty million copies. The premillennial scenario implies that things must get much worse before they can get better (for example, more homosexuality, pornography, communism, etc.) and deliverance will be by an exclusively divine (as opposed to militant Christian) agency, when Jesus comes to overthrow the direct rule of Antichrist, end the suffering of the Tribulation, and set up his kingdom. Apocalyptic premillennial and tribulationist evocations of the imminent "Last Days" and the coming of Antichrist thus tend to be implicitly fatalistic and may provide inadequate reinforcement for Christian political mobilization, since everything will get worse anyway and nothing can stop Antichrist's imminent temporary triumph. Thus, although conservative Christian activists such as Jerry

Falwell are at least nominally premillennial and have not explicitly rejected the apocalyptic tribulationist vision, some observers predict that premillennialism is likely to be quietly shelved by evangelicals becoming more politically activist (Hadden 1987a; Hadden and Shupe 1988).

Today, small but growing evangelical groups, influenced by Calvinism, have explicitly rejected tribulationism and doomsaying apocalypticism and have set forth an alternative vision of Christians building the kingdom themselves.[3] This is also Reverend Moon's vision, although Unificationist doctrine is more complex and esoteric. Dominion theologian Gary North affirms, "We are indeed called to create a politics of transcendence. . . . We are called to execute godly justice as laid down by God" (North 1986, 377). Like premillennialists, or many New Age devotees, North and Christian reconstructionists anticipate imminent cultural disintegration.

> The New Agers, like the Christian reconstructionists, are predicting just such a crumbling. Some of those fundamentalist Christians who hold to a pessimistic eschatology [that is, premillennialists] also think the New Agers will pick up the pieces, at least until Jesus returns physically to establish his kingdom. This prediction is not going to come true. Christians *eventually* are going to pick up the pieces, before Jesus returns physically, just as they picked up the pieces of the Roman Empire, when the "eternal" institution crumbled. (North 1986, 375)

Christian Reconstructionism (Theonomy) and Dominion Theology represent what Berger (1982, 20–21) refers to as the "other, more ambitious form of counterpluralism/countersecularity . . . [which] seeks the restoration of religious and moral community in the society as a whole." This goal may coexist with a communal enclave approach or civil-religion sect reality as in the Unification movement.[4] Catholic Liberation Theology, which could be viewed as a leftist-revolutionary counterpart of right-wing Christian Reconstructionism and Dominion Theology, is seen by some critics as a reactionary medievalist program that seeks "the reconstruction of an all-embracing religious and moral community," what some liberationists have termed "the new Christiandom" (Berger 1982, 21).

The Peoples Temple

The ill-fated Peoples Temple community at Jonestown in Guyana (to which the community had emigrated from California) can also be analyzed as a civil-religion sect or a sectarian version of the restored community enterprise embodying a politicoreligious synthesis entailing the creation of a new covenant (Chidester 1988). According to Hall in chapter 16 of this volume and in his recent monograph (1987), the Temple was poised on the boundary between a totally politicized warring sect, which defines itself as locked in an inescapable struggle with a demonic hostile environment, and an otherworldly millenarian sect. Otherworldly millenarian sects, notes Hall, exist beyond time in the sense that they believe that in a postapocalyptic world they will constitute a saved remnant. They therefore lack the urgency of being personally responsible for bringing about the new dispensation, which will be brought about by a purely spiritual agency. But the increasing fervor of the Marxist and antiracist elements in the movement's ideology weakened the viability of the Peoples Temple as an otherworldly sect. Jones exploited politicized conspiratorial themes to reinforce solidarity within the community. But by emphasizing the persecution of his group by an omnipotent conspiracy, Jones undermined the feeling of autonomy and insulation vital to stabilizing its identity. Yet the movement could not be an authentic warring sect since it saw itself as powerless to prevail over an all-powerful capitalist-racist conspiracy. Mass suicide became a means of realizing a form of immortality; it united the divergent public threads of meaningful existence at Jonestown—those of political revolution and religious salvation.

To restate the analysis in different terms, Jim Jones and his followers were caught between two incompatible tendencies: (1) the desire to provide a communal refuge that would exemplify the new egalitarian and antiracist purity, and (2) the impulse to confront a hostile environment perceived as an implacable and omnipotent conspiracy (Hall 1987; see also Chidester 1988). A confrontation could not be won and a refuge could never be safe (given a posited omnipotent conspiracy), but exemplary suicide could provide an inspirational model through an apocalyptic confrontation. Jones and his close associates were influenced by at least one prior historical incident of collective suicide (Hall 1987), and several scholars have recently made comparisons between the Jonestown holocaust and other historical episodes of collective suicide involving the Russian Old Believers in the late seventeenth century (Chidester 1988; Hall 1987; Robbins 1986a, forthcoming a) and the Circumcellion extremist fringe of the schismatic Donatist "Church of Martyrs" in North Africa in late antiquity (Robbins forthcoming a).

Although seemingly antithetical, Jim Jones's quasi-Marxist ideology and right-wing Unificationism conceal an underlying convergence in terms of exemplary dualism. The capitalist-racist conspiracy fulfilled the same function for Jim Jones as does communism for Sun Myung Moon. Both communism and capitalism-racism embody historically grounded absolute contrast symbols that establish the identity of each civil-religion sect as an exemplary utopia and vanguard of a new and higher civilization. Reverend Moon and his followers tend to interpret opposition to their movement as demonically inspired, in a manner which evokes the "paranoia" of Jim

Jones. Somewhat similar conceptions are held by those fundamentalists and charismatics who see the influence of Satan or the imminent advent of Antichrist underlying the spread of New Age, neopagan, and occult beliefs and practices. Indeed occultism and New Age mysticism may be replacing Godless communism as the central symbolic contrast category which evokes the demonic in the exemplary dualist system of fundamentalist and charismatic Christianity.

The Monistic Alternative

As we have seen, the Moon movement and the Peoples Temple exemplify civil-religion sects that evolve a synthesis of religious and political themes—a revitalized civil religion—as a basis for both total personal identity and close-knit, loving solidarity embodied in authoritarian communal structures. These movements can be contrasted with the many yoga, meditation, and religiotherapy groups. These latter groups are sometimes stigmatized as "narcissistic"—partly because they reject the intermeshing of civic-political and spiritual themes, and relegate utopian visions to the vague anticipation of the New Age that will come after enough individuals have evolved a higher spiritual consciousness. Such movements are usually at least superficially adaptive to conventional social expectations, and their participants only infrequently eschew normal social roles or become encapsulated in communal enclaves.

A key aspect of these groups is their generally monistic meaning systems, which affirm the latent metaphysical unit, or oneness, of all existence and the primacy of consciousness (that is, the illusory quality of phenomenal reality). Monistic ideologies posit a universal self immanent in particular selves, whereby individuals are ultimately harmoniously related to each other and to nature.[5] Such hidden interconnections between people are not dependent upon consciously shared religious or political values; hence, monistic ideologies are usually relatively indifferent to civil religion. Belief in an implicit universal order can provide a value framework that supports conventional participation in a society in which shared values are disintegrating.

For monistic ideologies, progress toward spiritual enlightenment is seen as involving glimpses of the *universal self* behind the apparent chaos of experience. A greater degree of cultural fragmentation makes the relative or arbitrary quality of particular social myths (such as American civil religion) more apparent, and thus provides a basis for individuals to glimpse the unity hidden in life. But the realization of existential unity among persons does not require sociopolitical unity.

Conservative Christians tend to be highly critical of monism and of the

New Age philosophy of which, in their view, monism is a core element. "Monism, the basic premise of the New Age movement, is radically at odds with a Christian view of reality. A Christian world affirms that God's creation is not an undivided unity but rather a created diversity of objects, events and persons" (Groothuis 1986, 19). Monism is also attacked for affirming or implying the divination of man, which "is a denial of the Creator-creation distinction" (North 1986, 335). Finally, monism is criticized from a conservative Christian standpoint for moral relativism and a consequent susceptibility to decadence. "Dostoevski said that anything is permissible if there is no God. Anything is also permissible if everything is God" (Burrows 1987, 93). If all is oneness, the polarities of good/evil and right/wrong must ultimately partake of the quality of illusion (Anthony and Robbins 1982b).

Anthony and Ecker (1987) note that there are levels of monistic sophistication. Unilevel monism assumes that monistic reality can be directly experienced by devotees, who will be able to penetrate illusory world appearances subsequent to undergoing a period of therapy, training, education, ritual purification, or identification with a guru. The best known religiotherapy, oriental, and New Age groups are of this variety, including flamboyant gurus such as Bhagwan Rajneesh, ritualistic groups such as Nicheren Shoshu, some occult-witchcraft groups, and religiotherapy movements such as Scientology, although the monistic premises of some therapeutic movements are implicit rather than overt. But there is also, according to Anthony and Ecker, a multilevel monism which distinguishes between immediate and ultimate levels of reality. Divinization, moral relativity, and immediate experiential oneness pertain only to the ultimate realm and cannot be experienced by devotees who simply learn doctrines and principles or get trained. Multilevel monism does not promise worldly benefits as consequences of involvement and belief. In contrast, unilevel monism is characterized by an epistemological consequentialism whereby enhanced personal efficacy, interpersonal harmony, or success and power are expected to arise from the assimilation of spiritual precepts, and thus become criteria for the validity of the precepts. Such groups appear to justify the views of critics such as North (1986), who sees monistic New Age orientations as exemplifying an irrationalist mystique of occult power, which flourishes in periods of cultural disintegration and decadence.

Anthony and Ecker (1987) argue that these criticisms pertain mainly to unilevel monism, which represents vulgarized monism. As such it is conspicuous for a tendency to be co-opted by popular social motifs such as competitive and utilitarian individualism or permissive-hedonistic orientations. A conspicuous example of this co-optation is "Tantric Freudianism," a composite of vulgarized Freudianism and vulgarized Tantric Buddhism, which has legitimated sexual hedonism in various groups including the Da Freejohn Movement and the Bhagwan movement of Shree Rajneesh (Anthony and Ecker 1987, 67).

The Meher Baba Community

Meher Baba is a movement that we have studied for a number of years (Anthony 1987; Anthony and Robbins 1974, 1982a,b; Robbins and Anthony 1972). Anthony (1987) and America, Ecker, and Wilber (1987) treat the group as coming close to exemplifying multilevel monism.[6]

Avatar Meher Baba is a deceased (d. 1969) Indian spiritual master who claimed to be the most recent manifestation of the Avataric (Hindu messianic) tradition. Baba is said to be the present incarnation of the divine redeemer who was previously incarnated as Zoroaster, Rama, Krishna, Buddha, Christ, and Mohammed. Meher Baba is thus perceived by his followers as a universal savior, the Messiah who incarnates on earth at crucial periods, ''when the earth is sunk in materialism and chaos as it is now,'' and who comes to inspire humanity and lead mankind to a higher level of consciousness. Meher Baba is also universal in a special sense that involves his immanence in all beings. Baba personifies the ultimate realization of the oneness of the universe that all evolving souls will ultimately attain. Salvation as conceived by Meher Baba and his devotees is evolutionary: souls gradually evolve toward God consciousness through numerous earthly reincarnations.

> However, the attainment of this awesome spiritual goal of God-consciousness is so far beyond one's conscious control, and the process so vast and complex over so many lifetimes, that it becomes useless to try and gauge one's own or anyone else's spiritual development univocally or consequentially. For spiritual orientation the aspirant instead must develop his or her own intuitive sense of intrinsic spiritual values, and above all must maximize inner felt contact with Meher Baba as the guiding, indwelling divinity. (Anthony, Ecker, and Wilber 1987, 187)

God realization is thus not seen as something that can be immediately cultivated through mastery of precepts or intensive training. Advanced spiritual masters who have experienced higher levels of cosmic awareness are assumed to be extremely rare and their identities are not assumed to be known to Baba Lovers.[7] The latter cannot therefore presume to act as if they had experientially transcended dualities such as good/evil, male/ female, etc., which the realized soul ultimately transcends. However, such dualities will ultimately be transcended by each evolving soul, as will the ''separative ego'' which defines the (apparent) individuality of each person. Thus, all souls will eventually "succeed" in spiritual terms—no one permanently "fails" or is eternally consigned to Outer Darkness. The stark dualities of saved and damned, serving God or Mammon, etc., are thus obviated by a conception of an inexorable evolutionary spiritual growth. It is such spiritual dualities and their presumed immediacy and urgency that define what Dick Anthony refers to as dualistic religious systems in which there is "a heightened sense of 'contingency,' of individual destinies dividing in two primary directions symbolized by the themes of heaven and hell" (Anthony and Ecker 1987, 38). Such dualism represents a powerful, perhaps dominant, tendency in Jewish, Christian, and Moslem traditions, although within these traditions there have indeed been marginal quasi-monistic currents such as Islamic Sufism, which influenced the thought of Meher Baba.

Unlike the Unification Church or the Peoples Temple, the Baba movement has no clear or unified authority structure. Local Baba groups are more or less autonomous and a bit diffuse. The Baba movement may typify that lack of definite organizational structure and limited capacity for social mobilization that, according to Stark (1987), characterizes many New Age movements and imperils their survival. Baba Lovers often display hostile attitudes toward any kind of formal ritual or procedure, as well as any formal system of authority. Many Baba followers rarely go to meetings, for they view their relationship to Baba as something deeply personal that cannot be collectivized. On the other hand, many Baba followers associate disproportionately (but rarely exclusively) with other Baba Lovers. Baba Lovers in a given area often constitute a definite community and a context for close friendships.

Unlike many monistic or quasi-monistic movements today, the message of Baba is not defined or operationalized in terms of standard spiritual techniques such as a particular mode of meditation (for example, Transcendental Meditation), of chanting (for example, Hare Krishna, Nicheren Shoshu), or of a particular system of training or therapy (for example, Scientology, est). The emphasis on spiritual technology in contemporary mystical programs has led some observers to conclude that mysticism or monism (or unilevel monism) fits with the technical rationality of modern culture and technobureaucratic structures (Anthony and Ecker 1987; Flinn 1983; Wuthnow 1985). The absence of either standardized techniques or a living (that is, fleshly) spiritual identity figure may provide the sociological reason why the Meher Baba movement is not presently as prominent as many other "Eastern" or New Age movements.

Meher Baba's status as the personified embodiment of love is perceived to manifest itself through his relationships with his followers. Movies of Baba shown regularly at meetings depict his loving relationships with people. One shows Baba tenderly washing lepers, whom Baba is said to have called "beautiful birds in ugly cages." Baba is thus perceived as responding to the inner person rather than in terms of one's apparent circumstances or attainments. Although he is the Universal Savior, Baba's followers perceive their relationships with him as one-on-one, and as idiosyncratic in the sense that he deliberately manipulates what happens to them to confront them with important experiences, challenges, or opportunities. Followers sometimes declare that they obtained their jobs or spouses through Baba's intervention. Thus Baba is perceived as intervening in the unique and particular details of each follower's life history, ministering to each person's distinctive spiritual needs, and aiding in the development of his human and spiritual potential.[8]

Meher Baba's universal identity conceptually converts his loving dispositions into universal and archetypal patterns. As such, they are seen to hold the key to overcoming the barriers to spontaneous warmth in relationships. Loving relationships between Baba Lovers are thus seen as emanations of Baba, who is immanent within all the lovers. The harmonizing of interpersonal relationships through Baba's emanations is viewed as a natural process that operates without reference to systematic rules.

The logic of Meher Baba as the "real," universal self of all persons compels a certain tolerance for those who are not followers of Baba or who are very different from Baba Lovers. Baba Lovers do not, therefore, retreat to segregated enclaves, but are active in the world, working side by side with nonbelievers. Relative to civil-religion sects, the Baba movement seems rather more adaptive. On the other hand, the notion that each individual is given those spiritual encounters that his prior evolution has prepared him for militates against urgent proselytization. There is little felt imperative either to convert others or totally transform the world in short order.

The practical ethic of Baba Lovers is one of selfless service through which Baba Lovers try to act lovingly in the world and thus demonstrate the relevance of their meaning system and reinforce their commitment. Meher Baba (1967) advises his followers to act in such a way that their actions are dedicated to the Avatar, and one is inwardly detached from the consequences of one's actions. One must be active in the world but should view one's actions as *Baba's* actions which are consequentially "in the Master's hands." On a mundane level, such inner detachment could make the impersonality of technobureaucratic vocational routines appear less oppressive (Anthony and Robbins 1974). In the late 1960s and early 1970s it was in part through involvement with Meher Baba that many persons emerged from (mainly psychedelic) drug use and marginal hippie lifestyles and became reassimilated to conventional vocational and educational roles (Anthony and Robbins 1974; Robbins and Anthony 1972).

Meher Baba emphasizes the disciple's love for the master as the vital bond of inner contact which promotes spiritual development. "This relational or charismatic path has received little recognition in Western transpersonal studies [for example, 'transpersonal psychology'] and differs significantly from the technique-oriented approaches and apprenticeship types of involvement" (Anthony, Ecker, and Wilber 1987, 189). Yet the example of the Peoples Temple or the quasi-monistic Charles Manson cult suggests that "a spiritual seeker should always remember that charismatic orientations are potentially more dangerous than technical involvements" (Anthony, Ecker, and Wilber 1987, 190). Their very technobureaucratic quality may render the latter less volatile. "One should accept a charismatic master's authority only when wholeheartedly convinced that he or she is completely plausible as a living embodiment of ultimate spiritual truth, love, being and therefore is worthy of unconditional obedience and surrender" (Anthony, Ecker, and Wilber 1987 190).

Monistic Movements and Civil Religion

Although monistic mystiques provide value frameworks that can motivate social participation, such mystiques, almost by definition, implicitly repudiate American civil religion. Traditional American civil religion is dualistic, and exalts the value of our political, economic, and religious institutions vis-à-vis those of other nations. Monism regards all particularistic theologies and ideologies as ultimately arbitrary. This repudiation of America's traditional civil religion may have advantages. Dualistic civil religion defines the nation in terms of the majority's conscious acceptance of a particular rational ideology. It cannot, by definition, be a minority orientation without causing some strain. In a pluralistic society a monistic religion that affirms a hidden social unity beneath the apparent diversity of competing value perspectives has obvious attractions. It might also be argued that the doctrine of karmic determinism (the roots of one's present circumstances are in one's actions in past lives) taught by many such groups is more compatible with participation in impersonal large organizations than is the emphasis on free will associated with traditional civil religion, entrepreneurial capitalism, and dualistic evangelical Christianity.

Religious Ferment, Civil Religion and Cultural Shifts

We have argued that the present climate of moral ambiguity and the consequent polarization of monistic and dualistic worldviews are related to the erosion of a dominant American political-moral ideology or civil religion that we call implicit legitimation. This meaning system combined three key elements into a consistent worldview: (1) stringent moral absolutism reflecting both the Puritan covenantal tradition and subsequent evangelical awakenings, (2) a fervent belief in laissez-faire and competitive individualism in the economic realm, and (3) messianic conceptions of America as an instrument of Divine Providence and an exemplary utopia. This ideology was synthesized from the Puritan tradition and utilitarian individualism. An absolutist and hence narrow conception of theft justified entrepreneurial practices and processes that produced extreme socioeconomic inequality. The dominant civil religion thus combined theistic moral fervor with legitimation of entrepreneurial capitalism; it was America's modernizing ideology.

The moral system of implicit legitimation has been eroding for some time owing to: (1) the negation of laissez faire in an emerging context of state regulation of the economy, (2) a general loss of a sense of personal autonomy in a society dominated by impersonal bureaucratic organizations, (3) the flowering of moral pluralism and hedonism in a mass consumption economy, and (4) recent challenges to American chauvinism growing out of our defeat in Vietnam, Watergate, and United States–Soviet détente as well as more recent anxieties over American economic decline. The results have been political-moral ambiguity and a reactive attempt to reconstruct the traditional civil religion. Innovative and restorative religious movements respond to this growing climate of moral ambiguity and celebrate or repudiate salient elements of the traditional civil religion synthesis.

The politicized evangelical surge and its ally, conservative "Reaganism," can be seen as constituting a drive to reconstruct the system of implicit legitimation and to recreate the synthesis of theistic moral absolutism, economic laissez faire, and messianic interpretation of the meaning and destiny of America. Jerry Falwell and Ronald Reagan share certain basic values that entail a celebration of early entrepreneurial capitalism and its legitimating mix of competitive individualism and evangelical Christianity.

Our analysis, originally developed in the 1982 version of this paper, partly converges with a more recent important formulation by Platt and Williams (1988) in their article, "Religion, Ideology and Electoral Politics." The authors argue that both political conservatives (of the Ronald Reagan–Pat Robertson moralistic stripe) and political left–liberals affirm ideological positions that are "alternately collectivist and individualist" and articulate different combinations of elements of the Puritan covenantal tradition and utilitarian individualism.

America's religious heritage, informed by its Puritan past, links individualism to covenants with God, church and community. The American right has drawn on that heritage advocating a utilitarian individualism regarding economics and politics while simultaneously emphasizing the covenant with God and church concerning moral and cultural issues. Conversely, the political left has drawn upon that same heritage to create an opposing stance—that is, an expressive individualism regarding moral/cultural issues and a vision of a just covenant community in economic and political realms. (Platt and Williams 1988, 44)

In our terms the Reaganite dispensation has entailed an attempt to reconstruct the dualistic ideological system that combines messianic American triumphalism with a moralistic covenant to restrain hedonism and antinomianism in the cultural realm while encouraging utilitarian individualism and laissez faire in the economic sphere. Has this attempt succeeded? Time will tell. But we have suggested above that the essential elements of the traditional synthesis now lack the viability and mutual consistency they once manifested.

From this standpoint it might appear that the re-creation of a national moral community based on a harmonious synthesis of utilitarian individualism and moralistic theism is not a likely possibility. It is for this reason, perhaps, that contemporary American biblical evangelicism appears to waver between an apocalyptic vision in which a hopelessly depraved culture will shortly be destroyed as the world was destroyed "in the days of Noah"—the standard premillennial view—and a contrary triumphalist vision in which evangelicals and their allies will purify the republic through political activism. The latter orientation is presently gaining strength (Boston 1988; North 1986) as the conflict between conservative activism or triumphalism and end-of-the-world doomsaying becomes more apparent (Hadden 1987a); yet a visible failure of the New Christian Right could conceivably reignite a doomsaying tribulationist frenzy!

The ideologies of the less-traditional and more-innovative spiritual movements reflect the diminished viability of the traditional synthesis. Both the Meher Baba movement and the Unification Church provide therapeutic communities for converts in which loving relationships are crystalized and legitimated in terms of universal spiritual mystiques. The warmth and expressivity of childhood familial settings are thereby combined with adult seriousness and idealism. But the values of each movement are sharply divergent. The Meher Baba movement is a monistic system in which ultimate reality is assigned to a realm of consciousness latent within the self. This universal consciousness is personified by a spiritual master, but it cannot be translated into any rigid doctrinal or normative system. Rules and standards may be more or less useful in achieving certain goals, but they are not metaphysical absolutes.[9] Right and wrong are *ultimately* relative. In contrast, Sun Myung Moon pro-pounds a system of stringent moral absolutism and exemplary dualism. As a devotee told one of the authors, "In the Bible, Jesus said, 'I don't come to bring peace on earth, I come to bring a sword.' And what that means is that what he is trying to bring us is a sort of symbolic sword to divide good and evil" (Anthony and Robbins 1978a, 88).

In our view contemporary monistic and dualistic perspectives represent systematized responses to the moral ambiguity that is arising from the decline of traditional civil religion and the moral system of implicit legiti-mation. Moral attitudes seem to be polarizing along a continuum, with systematic monistic relativism at one end and stringent dualistic absolut-ism at the other. The polarity is vividly dramatized by what appears to be an increasing tendency for New Age–occult currents to replace godless communism as the symbolic contrast category that evokes absolute satanic evil for Christian exemplary dualists (North 1986). TV evangelists increas-ingly warn against the New Age threat, which, as one preacher heard by one of the authors proclaimed, really embodies the ancient sin of Adam: the blasphemous presumption that through secret knowledge one can become as God. Another TV evangelist affirms that the conflict between Christianity and New Age religion represents the greatest religious war since the prophet Elijah vindicated Jehovah on the mountain and destroyed the six hundred priests of Baal! Books warning against the spread of New Age philosophy proliferate in Christian bookstores. "New Age ideas have already begun to infiltrate and undermine the Church from within!", announces a bulletin from the Evangelical Book Club. The decisive es-chatological significance of New Age movements is posited by premillen-nial warnings; for example, "Because the New Age is the last age, it will conclude with the emergence of a powerful world teacher, the New Age false 'Messiah,' the famous Antichrist" (Evangelical Book Club Bulletin). An anti-premillennial dominion theologian sees cultural disintegration leading to a final conflict between New Age occultism and a revitalized conservative Christianity (North 1986).

The apocalyptic views of evangelical demonologists receive at least a faint echo from leading social critics, who also perceive a polarizing of the American religions. Could the stark opposites really be mirror opposites? In *Habits of the Heart,* Robert Bellah and his colleagues write:

> Radically individualistic religion, particularly when it takes the form of a belief in cosmic selfhood, may seem to be in a different world from conservative or fundamentalist religion. Yet these are the two poles that organize much of American religious life. To the first, God is simply the self magnified; to the second, God confronts man from the outside the universe. One seeks a self that is finally identical with the world; the other seeks an external God who will

provide order in the world. Both value personal religious experience as the basis of their belief. Shifts from one pole to the other are not as rare as one might think. (Bellah et al. 1985, 234)[10]

This essay represents a substantial revision and extrapolation of an earlier paper, "Spiritual Innovation and the Crisis of American Civil Religion," which appeared in *Daedalus* (vol. 3 (1) 1982) and was reprinted verbatim in Mary Douglas and Steven Tipton, eds., *Religion and America* (Boston: Beacon, 1982).

Notes

1. Our formulation of implicit legitimation does not imply a preexisting well-developed conception of the separation of public-instrumental and private-expressive realms in early- or mid-nineteenth-century America. Implicit legitimation may have facilitated differentiated conceptions of life into moralistic norms for private behavior and utilitarian norms for the business realm.
2. Successive Great Awakenings and continuing revivalism crystalized and consolidated quasi-Arminian conceptions of individual responsibility, free will, and universal grace, which supplanted more deterministic Calvinist notions, and which developed an ideological significance in terms of facilitating internalized social control and labor discipline (Johnson 1978). Conflicting communitarian-democratic and individualistic tendencies in American revivalism tended by the mid-nineteenth century to be resolved in favor of "American society's individualistic bent and middle-class bias" such that "the gap between private interest and communal interest became more severe" (Sweet 1988, 888).
3. These movements and tendencies were the subject of the third installment of a three-part video documentary on *God and Politics* produced and narrated by Bill Moyers and shown on Public Broadcasting Television stations in 1987 and 1988.
4. Interestingly, while Reverend Moon's social philosophy is implicitly collectivist, Christian reconstructionists and dominion theologians such as B. Rushdoony and G. North are fervently laissez faire. Building "the kingdom" will be partly a matter of dismantling government controls over the economy, although God's law will be enforced in the moral realm.
5. On contemporary American monism see Anthony and Ecker (1987) and Anthony and Robbins (1982b). For a Jewish critique of the monist thought of mythologist Joseph Campbell, see Frankiel (1989).
6. Anthony is a devotee and Robbins is sympathetic.
7. In part because the overall movement has such ambiguous organizational parameters and lack of adminstrative structure, particular groups or submovements of Baba Lovers have been able to develop their own characteristics and doctrinal slants, which may diverge from the overall traits adumbrated above. One of the larger subgroups, the reoriented Sufis (Sufism Reoriented), whose group identity existed prior to their reorientation toward Baba as Master, claims that their current leader, or Sufi *Murshid*, is a god conscious master sent to them by Meher Baba. This group and certain smaller groups of Baba Lovers are better organized and more disciplined than the overall movement.
8. There is a superficial similarity here with the "gospel of health and wealth" in

(some) evangelical Christianity. But emphasis here is not on reward for faith but on learning experiences, that is, Baba arranging experiences and encounters that will challenge them spiritually and ultimately enhance growth. Negative experiences may also be viewed in this light. The emphasis is on spiritual learning through encounters and experiences therapeutically controlled by a spiritual master. This is characteristic of American monists, who often view the world as a vast group-encounter session; that is, American culture psychologizes Hindu-Buddhist monism.

9. See the masterly analysis of est by Steven Tipton (1982), who analyzes the way in which "rule egoism" justifies conformity to rules as instrumental in attaining valued psychospiritual states.

10. From the standpoint of Anthony and Ecker (1987) there are salient convergences between unilevel monism and unilevel dualism, for example, a "health and wealth" instrumentalism and a tendency to reinforce utilitarian individualism.

References

Ammerman, Nancy T., 1987
Anthony, Dick, 1987
Anthony, Dick, and Bruce Ecker, 1987
Anthony, Dick, Bruce Ecker, and Ken Wilber, 1987
Anthony, Dick, and Thomas Robbins, 1974, 1978a, 1982a, 1982b
Bellah, Robert N., 1970b, 1975, 1976, 1981
Bellah, Robert, et al., 1985
Berger, Peter L., 1982
Bordewich, Fergus, 1988
Boston, Rob, 1988
Bromley, David, 1985
Bromley, David, and Phillip Hammond, eds., 1987
Bromley, David, and Anson D. Shupe, 1979
Burrows, Robert, 1987
Carter, Lewis, 1987
Chidester, David, 1988
Chilton, James, 1985
Demerath, N. Jay III, and Rhys H. Williams, 1987
Doress, Irving, and Jack Porter, 1981
Frankiel, Tamar, 1989
Flinn, Frank, 1983
Galloway, Paul, 1988
Garvey, Kevin, 1985
Groothuis, Douglas, 1986
Hadden, Jeffrey K., 1987a, 1987b
Hadden, Jeffrey K., and Anson Shupe, 1988
Hall, John R., 1987
Hardwick, Elizabeth, 1988
Horowitz, Irving, 1981
Jacobs, Janet, forthcoming b
Johnson, D. Paul, 1978

Johnson, Benton, 1981
Kelley, Dean M., 1973
Lifton, Robert, 1979
Lindsey, Hal, 1970
Lindsey, Robert, 1986
Martin, David, 1982
Meher Baba, 1967
Mickler, Michael, 1987
Moon, Sun Myung, 1973, 1974
Neitz, Mary Jo, 1987
North, Gary, 1983, 1986
Parsons, Arthur, 1986
Platt, Gerald, and Rhys Williams, 1988
Reed, Susan, 1988
Richardson, James T., 1980
Robbins, Thomas, 1986a, 1988a, 1988b, forthcoming a
Robbins, Thomas, and Dick Anthony, 1972, 1984
Robbins, Thomas, Dick Anthony, Thomas Curtis, and Madeline Doucas, 1978
Robertson, Roland, and Joann Chirico, 1985
Roof, Wade Clark, 1981
Rose, Susan, 1987, 1988
Stark, Rodney, 1987
Sweet, Leonard, 1988
Tipton, Steven M., 1982
Vidich, Arthur J., 1975
Wuthnow, Robert, 1985, 1988

Bibliography

Adler, Margot. 1986. *Drawing down the Moon*. rev. ed. Boston: Beacon.

Adorno, T. W., Else Frenkel-Brunswik, Daniel J. Levinson, and R. Nevitt Sanford. 1950. *The Authoritarian Personality*. New York: Norton.

Ahlstrom, Sydney E. 1972. *A Religious History of the American People*. New Haven: Yale University Press. 2 vols.

Aidala, Angela. 1985. "Social Change, Gender Roles, and New Religious Movements." *Sociological Analysis* 46 (3): 287–314.

Aiken, Michael, and Paul E. Mott, eds. 1970. *The Structure of Community Power*. New York: Random House.

Alexander, Brooks. 1987. "Theology from the Twilight Zone." *Christianity Today* 31 (Sept. 10): 22–26.

Allen, Mike. 1988. "Amway is More Than Business to True Believers Who Came Here." *Richmond Times Dispatch*, 21 Mar.

Allport, Gordon. *The Nature of Prejudice*. Garden City, N.Y.: Doubleday.

Amano, J. Yutaka. 1986. "The Reincarnation of est." *Christianity Today* 21 (16 May).

American Psychiatric Association. 1980. *Diagnostic and Statistical Manual of Mental Disorders*. 3d Ed. Washington, D.C.: APA.

Ammerman, Nancy T. 1987. *Bible Believers: Fundamentalists in the Modern World*. New Brunswick: Rutgers University Press.

Anderson, Robert M. 1979. *Visions of the Disinherited: The Making of American Pentecostalism*. New York: Oxford University Press.

Anderson, Susan. 1985. "Identifying Coercion and Deception in Social Movements." In *Scientific Research of New Religions: Divergent Perspectives*, edited by B. Kilbourne, 12–23. Proceedings of the Annual Meeting of the Pacific Division of the American Association of the Advancement of Science. San Francisco: AAAS.

Anthony, Dick. 1980. "The Fact-Pattern behind the Deprogramming Controversy: An Analysis and an Alternative." New York University Review of Law and Social Change (Spring).

————. 1987. "Meher Baba: An Interview with Dick Anthony." In Anthony, Ecker, Wilber 1987, 153–86.

Anthony, Dick, and Bruce Ecker. 1987. "The Anthony Typology: A Framework for Assessing Spiritual and Consciousness Groups." In Anthony, Ecker, and Wilber 1987, 35–106.

Anthony, Dick, Bruce Ecker, and Ken Wilber. 1987. *Spiritual Choices: The Problem of Recognizing Authentic Paths to Inner Transformation*. New York: Paragon.

Anthony, Dick, and Thomas Robbins. 1974. "The Meher Baba Movement." In *Religious Movements in Contemporary America*, edited by I. Zaretsky and M. Leone, 479–501. New Jersey: Princeton University.

————. 1978a. "The Effect of Détente on the Growth of New Religions: Reverend Moon and the Unification Church." In *Understanding the New Religions*, edited by Jacob Needlemen and George Baker, 80–100. New York: Seabury.

————. 1978b. "New Religions, Families, and 'Brainwashing.'" *Society* 15 (4) (May–June).

————. 1981. "New Religions, Families, and 'Brainwashing.'" In *In Gods We Trust: New Patterns of Religious Pluralism in America*, edited by Robbins and Anthony. New Brunswick, N.J.: Transaction.

————. 1982a. "Spiritual Innovation and the Crisis of American Civil Religion." *Daedalus* 111 (1) (Winter): 215–34. Reprinted in *Religion and America: Spirituality in a Secular Age*, edited by M. Douglas and S. Tipton. Boston: Beacon.

————. 1982b. "Contemporary Religious Ferment and Moral Ambiguity." In *New Religious Movements: A Perspective for Understanding Society*, edited by E. Barka. New York: Edwin Mellon.

Anthony, Dick, Thomas Robbins, and James McCarthy. 1980. "Legitimating Repression." *Society* 17 (3) (Mar.) Reprinted in *The Brainwashing Deprogramming Controversy*, edited by David Bromley and James Richardson. New York: Edwin Mellon. 1983.

Anthony, Dick, Thomas Robbins, and Paul Schwartz. 1983. "Contemporary Religious Movements and the Secularization Premise." In *New Religious Movements*, edited by J. Coleman and G. Baum, 1–7. New York: Seabury.

Anyon, Jean. 1983. "Intersections of Gender and Class: Accommodation and Resistance by Working-Class and Affluent Females to Contradictory Sex-Role Ideologies." In *Gender, Class, and Education*, edited by Stephen Walker and Len Barton. New York: Falmer Press.

Ash, Mary Kay. 1986. *Mary Kay*. New York: Harper & Row.

Aviad, Janet. 1983. *Return to Judaism: Religious Renewal in Israel*. Chicago: University of Chicago Press.

Bainbridge, William Sims, and Daniel H. Jackson. 1981. "The Rise and Decline of Transcendental Meditation." In *The Social Impact of New Religious Movements*, edited by B. Wilson, 135–58. New York: Rose of Sharon Press.

Bainbridge, William Sims, and Rodney Stark. 1982. "Church and Cult in Canada." *Canadian Journal of Sociology* 7 (4): 351–66.

Balch, Robert W. 1980. "Looking behind the Scenes in a Religious Cult." *Sociological Analysis* 41 (2): 137–43.

Baldwin, James. 1985. *Going to Meet the Man*. New York: Dell.

Ballweg, George. 1980. *The Growth and the Number and Population of Christian Schools since 1966*. Ph.D. Dissertation, School of Education, Boston University.

Barker, Eileen V. 1984. *The Making of a Moonie: Choice or Brainwashing?* Oxford: Blackwell.

———. 1986. "Religious Movements: Cult and Anticult Since Jonestown." *Annual Review of Sociology* 12: 329–46.

Barnhart, Joe. 1988. "The Ambivalence of Power among American Evangelicals." Paper presented to the Association for the Sociology of Religion, Chicago.

Barrett, David B. 1982. *World Christian Encyclopedia*. New York: Oxford University Press.

Barton, Bruce. 1925. *The Man Nobody Knows*. Indianapolis: The Bobbs-Merill Co.

Batiuk, Mary Ellen. 1988. "Muslims in Prison." Paper presented to the Society for the Scientific Study of Religion, Chicago.

Basil, Robert, ed. 1988. *Not Necessarily the New Age: Critical Essays*. Buffalo: Prometheus.

Becker, Howard, and Harry Elmer Barnes. 1961. *Social Thought from Lore to Science*. Vol. 2. New York: Dover.

Beckford, James A. 1975. *The Trumpet of Prophecy*. Oxford: Basil Blackwell.

———. 1979. "Politics and the Anticult Movement." *The Annual Review of the Social Sciences of Religion* 3:169–90.

———. 1984. "Holistic Imagery and Ethics in New Religious and Healing Movements." *Social Compass* 31 (2–3): 259–72.

———. 1985a. "The Insulation and Isolation of the Sociology of Religion." *Sociological Analysis* 46 (4): 357–64.

———. 1985b. *Cult Controversies: The Societal Response to New Religious Movements*. London: Tavistock Publications.

Bednarowski, Mary. 1980. "Outside the Mainstream: Women's Religion and Women Religious Leaders in Nineteenth-Century America." *Journal of the American Academy of Religion* 48:207–31.

Bell, Daniel. 1980. "The Return of the Sacred?" In *The Winding Passage: Essays and Sociological Journeys, 1960–1980*, edited by D. Bell, 324–54.

Bellah, Robert N. 1967. "Civil Religion in America." *Daedalus* 96 (1): 1–21.

———. 1970a. "Christianity and Symbolic Realism." *Journal for the Scientific Study of Religion* (Summer): 39–96.

————. 1970b. *Beyond Belief: Essays on Religion in a Post-Traditional World*. New York: Harper and Row.

————. 1970b. "Civil Religion in America." In *Beyond Belief: Essays on Religion in a Post-Traditional World*. New York: Harper and Row.

————. 1975. *The Broken Covenant*. New York: Seabury.

————. 1976. "The New Religious Consciousness and the Crisis of Modernity." In *The New Religious Consciousness,* edited by Charles Glock and Robert Bellah, 335–52. Berkeley, Calif.: University of California.

————. 1981. "Religion and the Legitimation of the American Republic." In *In Gods We Trust,* 1st ed., edited by Thomas Robbins and Dick Anthony, 39–50, and reprinted in the present volume.

Bellah, Robert, Richard Masden, William Sullivan, Ann Swidler, and Steven Tipton. 1985. *Habits of the Heart: Individualism and Commitment in American Life*. Berkeley, Calif.: University of California.

Benedictus, Saint. 1975. (Orig. c. 525?). *The Rule of Saint Benedict*. New York: Doubleday Image.

Berger, Peter L. [1967] 1969. *The Sacred Canopy: Elements of a Sociological Theory of Religion*. Garden City: Anchor Books.

————. 1982. "From the Crisis of Religion to the Crisis of Secularity." In *Religion and America,* edited by M. Douglas and S. Tipton, 14–25.

Bernard, Jessie. 1975. *Women, Wives, Mothers: Values and Options*. New York: Aldine.

Bernstein, Basil. 1976. *Class, Codes and Control: Theoretical Studies towards a Sociology of Language*. New York: Schocken Books.

Berton, Pierre. 1965. *The Comfortable Pew*. New York: Lippincott.

Bibby, Reginald W. 1978. "Why Conservative Churches Really Are Growing: Kelley Revisited." *Journal for the Scientific Study of Religion* 17:129–38.

Bibby, Reginald W., and Merlin Brinkerhoff. 1973. "The Circulation of the Saints: A Study of People Who Join Conservative Churches." *Journal for the Scientific Study of Religion* 12:273–83.

————. 1983. "Circulation of the Saints Revisited: A Longitudinal Look at Conservative Church Growth." *Journal for the Scientific Study of Religion* 22:153–62.

Biderman, Albert. 1962. "The Image of 'Brainwashing.' " *Public Opinion Quarterly* 26:547–63.

Bird, Frederick, and Bill Reimer. 1982. "Participation Rates in New Religious and Para-Religious Movements." *Journal for the Scientific Study of Religion* 21:1–14.

Bird, Frederick, and Frances Westley. 1985. "Constellations and Satellites: Variations in Religious Self-Definition in New Religious Movements." Paper presented at the annual meeting of the Society for the Scientific Study of Religion, Savannah, Ga.

Birmingham, Frederic. 1982. "Rich DeVos: Faith and Family." *The Saturday Evening Post* (July/August): 58–60.

Bishops' Letter. 1987. "Economic Justice for All: Catholic Social Teaching and the U.S. Economy." In *The Catholic Challenge to the American Economy*, edited by T. Gannon. New York.

Bloom, Allan. 1987. *The Closing of the American Mind*. New York: Simon and Schuster.

Bolen, J. S. 1984. *Goddesses in Everywoman*. San Francisco: Harper and Row.

Bordewich, Fergus. 1988. "Colorado's Thriving Cults." *New York Times Magazine* (May 1).

Boston, Rob. 1988. "Thy Kingdom Come: Christian Reconstructionists Want to Take Over America." *Church and State* 41 (8) (Sept): 6–12.

Bouma, Gary. 1979. "The Real Reason One Conservative Church Grew." *Review of Religious Research* 20: 127–37.

Bowart, Walter H. 1978. *Operation Mind Control*. New York: Dell.

Brannigan, Martha. 1989. "Employer's 'New Age' Training Programs Lead to Lawsuits Over Worker's Rights." *Wall Street Journal* (Jan 9).

Brandt, Allen. 1985. *No Magic Bullet*. New York: Oxford.

Braun, Kirk. 1984. *The Unwelcome Society*. Oregon: Scout Creek Press.

Brauns, Timothy. 1988. Review of *Spiritual Choices*. *Cultic Studies Journal* 5 (1): 145–49.

Briffault, Robert. 1931. *The Mothers*. New York: MacMillan.

Bromley, David. 1985. "Financing the Millennium: The Economic Structure of the Unification Movement." *Journal for the Scientific Study of Religion* 24 (3): 253–75.

Bromley, David, and Phillip Hammond, eds. 1987. *The Future of New Religious Movements*. Macon, Ga.: Mercer University.

Bromley, David G., and Anson D. Shupe. 1979. *Moonies in America: Cult, Church, and Crusade*. Beverly Hills, Calif.: Sage Publications.

―――. 1981. *Strange Gods: The Great American Cult Scare*. Boston, Mass.: Beacon Press.

Bromley, David G., Anson D. Shupe, and Donna Oliver. 1982. "Perfect Families: Visions of the Future in a New Religious Movement." In *Cults and the Family*, edited by Florence Kaslow and Marvin B. Sussman. New York: Haworth.

Brown, Peter. 1978. *The Making of Late Antiquity*. Cambridge, Mass.: Harvard University Press.

―――. 1981. *Society and the Holy in Late Antiquity*. Berkeley: University of California Press.

Brumberg, Joan. 1980. *Mission for Life*. New York: The Free Press.

Budapest, Zsuzsanna. 1980. *The Holy Book of Women's Mysteries, Part II*. Los Angeles: Susan B. Anthony Books.

―――. 1986. *The Holy Book of Women's Mysteries*. Vols. 1 and 2, Oakland, Calif.: Susan B. Anthony Coven No. 1.

Burrows, Robert. 1987. "A Christian Critiques the New Age." *Utne Reader* (March/April):86–93. Reprinted from *Christianity Today* (16 May 1986).

Butterfield, Stephen. 1985. *Amway: The Cult of Free Enterprise*. Boston: South End Press.

Campbell, Ernest, and Thomas Pettigrew. 1959. *Christians in Racial Crisis*. Washington, D.C.: Public Affairs Press.

Campbell, Robert J. 1981. *Psychiatric Dictionary*. 5th ed. New York: Oxford University Press.

Caplow, Theodore, Howard M. Bahr, and Bruce A. Chadwick. 1983. *All Faithful People*. Minneapolis: University of Minnesota Press.

Carnegie, Andrew. 1900. *The Gospel of Wealth and Other Timely Essays*. New York: The Century Company.

Carter, Lewis. 1987. "The 'New Renunciates' of the Bhagwan Shree Rajneesh." *Journal for the Scientific Study of Religion* 26 (2): 148–72.

Carter, Paul A. 1968. "The Fundamentalist Defense of the Faith." In *Change and Continuity in Twentieth Century America: The 1920s*, edited by J. Braeman, R. H. Breemer, and D. Brody, 179–214.

Cavanaugh, Michael. 1988. "Puritanism by Way of Mind Cure: Christian Reconstructionism and Religious Differentiation." Paper presented to the Association for the Sociology of Religion, Chicago.

Chaplin, J. 1985. *Dictionary of Psychology*. New York: Dell.

Chalfant, H. Paul, Robert E. Beckley, and C. Eddie Palmer. 1987. *Religion in Contemporary Society*. 2nd ed. Palo Alto, Calif.: Mayfield Publishing Company.

Chidester, David. 1988. *Salvation and Suicide: An Interpretation of the Peoples Temple and Jonestown*. Bloomington: Indiana University.

Chilton, James. 1985. *Paradise Restored: A Biblical Theology of Dominion*. Tyler, Tex.: Reconstruction Press.

Chodroff, Paul. 1966. "Effects of Extreme Coercive and Oppressive Forces: Brainwashing and Concentration Camps." In *The American Handbook of Psychiatry*, chap. 26. New York: Basic Books.

Christ, Carol P. 1987. *The Laughter of Aphrodite*. San Francisco: Harper and Row.

———. 1982. "Why Women Need the Goddess: Phenomenological, Psychological, and Political Reflections." In *The Politics of Women's Spirituality*, edited by C. Spretnak, 71–86. Garden City, New York: Anchor Books.

———. 1985. "Symbols of Goddess and God in Feminist Theology." In *The Book of the Goddess Past and Present*, edited by C. Olsen, 232–51. New York: Crossroad.

Christ, Carol, and Judith Plaskow. 1979. *Womanspirit Rising*. San Francisco: Harper and Row.

Clark, Elizabeth. 1987. "Women and Religion in America." In *Church and State in America: A Bibliographical Guide*, edited by J. Wilson, 373–426. New York: Greenwood.

Clark, Elmer T. 1949. *The Small Sects in America*. 1st rev. ed. New York: Abindon-Cokesbury Press.

Clark, John. 1977. "The Effects of Some Religious Cults on the Health and Welfare of Their Converts." Read into the *Congressional Record* 23(181) Nov. 4: E6894–6895.

Clebsch, William A. 1968. *From Sacred to Profane America: The Role of Religion in American History.* New York: Harper and Row.

Cohen, David. 1979. *J. B. Watson: The Founder of Behaviorism.* London: Routledge and Kegan Paul.

Cohen, Shayle J. D. 1988. "Shifting Boundaries between Jews and Gentiles." American Jewish Committee. No page numbers.

Cohn, Norman. 1961. *The Pursuit of the Millennium.* New York: Harper Torch Books.

———. 1970. Orig. 1957. *Pursuit of the Millennium.* 2d ed. New York: Oxford University Press.

Coleman, John. 1981. "The American Civil Religion Debate: A Source for Theory Construction." *Journal for the Scientific Study of Religion* 20:51–63.

———. 1984. New Religions and the Myth of Mind Control." *American Journal of Orthopsychiatry,* 322, 323.

Collier, Peter, and David Horowitz. 1987. *The Fords: An American Epic.* New York: Summit Books.

Conn, Charles. 1982. *An Uncommon Freedom.* New York: Berkeley Books.

Conrad, Peter. 1986. "The Social Meaning of AIDS." *Social Policy* 17(1): 51–9.

Conway, Flo, and Jim Siegelman. 1978. *Snapping: America's Epidemic of Sudden Personality Change.* Philadelphia: Lippincott.

———. 1982. *Holy Terror: The Fundamentalist War on America's Freedoms in Religion, Politics, and Our Private Lives.* Garden City, N.Y.: Doubleday.

Cox, Harvey. 1965. *The Secular City.* New York: MacMillan.

———. 1984. *Religion in the Secular City.* New York: Simon and Schuster.

Cuddihy, John. 1978. *No Offense: Civil Religion and Protestant Taste.* New York: Seabury.

Cuneo, Michael. 1988. "Revivalist Catholicism in North America." Paper presented to the Association for the Sociology of Religion, Atlanta, Ga.

Cuomo, Mario. 1984. Text of Notre Dame Speech. (Sept. 13).

Currie, Robert, Dan Gilbert, and Lee Horsley. 1977. *Churches and Churchgoers.* Oxford: Clarendon Press.

Dahl, Robert A. 1961. *Who Governs?* New Haven, Conn.: Yale University Press.

Daly, Mary. 1968. *The Church and the Second Sex.* New York: Harper and Row.

———. 1973. *Beyond God the Father.* Boston: Beacon Press.

———. 1978. *Gyn/Ecology.* Boston: Beacon Press.

Daly, Mary, with Jane Caputi. 1987. *Websters' New Intergalactic Wickedary of the English Language.* Boston: Beacon Press.

Davidman, Lynn. 1986. " 'Strength of Tradition in a Chaotic World': Women Turn to Orthodox Judaism." Ph.D. dissertation, Brandeis University. Revised version forthcoming, University of California Press, 1989.

———. 1988. "Gender and Religious Experience." Presented to the Association for the Sociology of Religion, Atlanta, Ga.

———. 1990. "Accommodation and Resistance to Modernity: A Comparison of Two Contemporary Orthodox Jewish Groups." Forthcoming: *Sociological Analysis* 51:1.

Davis, David Brion. 1960. "Some Themes of Counter-Subversion: An Analysis of Anti-Masonic, Anti-Catholic and Anti-Mormon Literature." *The Mississippi Valley Historical Review* 37 (September): 205–24.

Davis, Elizabeth Gould. 1971. *The First Sex*. New York: Putnam.

Dayton, Donald W. 1987. *Theological Roots of Pentecostalism*. Grand Rapids, Mich.: Francis Asbury Press (Division of Zondervan Publishing House).

Delgado, Richard. 1977. "Religious Totalism: Gentle and Ungentle Persuasion under the First Amendment," *Southern California Law Review* 51:1–99.

———. 1979–80. "Religious Totalism as Slavery." *New York University Review of Law and Social Change* 4 (1): 51–68.

———. 1982. "Cults and Conversion: The Case for Informed Consent." *Georgia Law Review* 16 (3): 533–74.

———. 1984. "When Religious Exercise Is Not Free." *Vanderbilt Law Review* 37 (3).

Demerath, N. J. III, and Rhys H. Williams. 1985. "Civil Religion in an Uncivil Society." *The Annals* 480:154–66.

———. 1987. "Church-State Relations: A Mythical Past and Uncertain Future." In Robbins and Robertson 1987, 77–90.

Dessouki, Ali E. Hillel, ed. 1982. *Islamic Resurgence in the Arab World*. New York: Praeger.

Diner, Helen. 1973. *Mothers and Amazons*. Garden City, N.Y.: Anchor Books.

Dolbeare, Kenneth M., and Phillip E. Hammond. 1971. *The School Prayer Decisions: From Court Policy to Local Practice*. Chicago: University of Chicago Press.

Domhoff, G. William. 1978. *Who Really Rules?* Santa Monica, Calif.: Goodyear Publishing Co.

———. ed. 1980. *Power Structure Research*. Beverly Hills, Calif.: Sage.

Doress, Irving, and Jack Porter. 1981. "Kids in Cults." In *In Gods We Trust*, 1st ed., edited by T. Robbins and D. Anthony, 297–302. New Brunswick, N.J.: Transaction.

Douglas, Mary. 1966. *Purity and Danger*. New York: Frederick Praeger.

———. 1970. *Natural Symbols*. Harmondsworth: Penguin Books.

———. 1982. "The Effects of Modernization on Religious Change." In

Religion and America, edited by M. Douglas and S. Tipton, 25–44. Boston: Beacon.

Drucker, Peter. 1986. "The Changed Global Economy." *Foreign Affairs* (Winter).

Dubois, Ann, ed. 1987. *Blindspots and Breakthroughs in Women-In-Ministry Research.* Special issue, *Review of Religious Research,* 28 (4).

Dullea, George. 1986. "New Zeal for Gemstones: Real Search for the Unreal." *New York Times* (10 Dec.).

Durkheim, Emile. 1965. Orig. 1912. *The Elementary Forms of the Religious Life.* New York: Free Press.

———. 1951. *Suicide.* Ontario: Collier-Macmillan Canada.

Edmondson, Brad. 1988. "Bringing in the Sheaves." *American Demographics* (Aug.).

Ehrenreich, Barbara, and Deirdre English. 1973. 2nd ed. *Witches, Midwives, and Nurses: A History of Women Healers.* Westbury, N.Y.: Feminist Press.

———. 1978. *For Her Own Good: 150 Years of the Experts' Advice to Women.* Garden City, N.Y.: Anchor Books.

Ehrenreich, Barbara, Elizabeth Hess, and Gloria Jacobs. 1986. *Re-making Love: The Feminization of Sex.* New York: Doubleday.

Ellenberger, Henre F. 1970. *The Discovery of the Unconscious: The History and Evolution of Dynamic Psychiatry.* New York: Basic Books.

Ellwood, Robert S. 1973. *Religious and Spiritual Groups in Modern America.* Englewood Cliffs, N.J.: Prentice Hall.

Ely, Richart T. 1903. "Economic Aspects of Mormonism." *Harper's Monthly Magazine* (April): 667–78.

Engels, Frederick. 1964a. Orig. 1850. "The Peasant War in Germany." In *Karl Marx and Frederick Engels on Religion,* edited by Reinhold Niebuhr. New York: Shocken.

———. 1964b. Orig. 1850. "The Book of Revelation." In *Karl Marx and Frederick Engels on Religion,* edited by Reinhold Niebuhr. New York: Shocken.

Farber, I. E., H. F. Harlow, and L. J. West. 1957. "Brainwashing, Conditioning, and DDD (Debility, Dependency, and Dread)." *Sociometry* 29:271–85.

Fallding, Harold. 1974. *The Sociology of Religion.* Toronto: McGraw-Hill Ryerson.

Falwell, Jerry. 1980. *Listen, America!* Garden City, N.Y.: Doubleday.

Fenn, Richard K. 1978. *A Theory of Secularization.* Ellington, Conn.: Society for the Scientific Study of Religion.

———. 1981. *Liturgies and Trials.* Oxford: Blackwell.

Festinger, Leon, H. W. Riecken, and S. Schacter. 1964. *When Prophecy Fails.* New York: Harper and Row.

Fiorenza, E. 1979. "Women in the Early Christian Movement." In Christ and Plaskow 1979, 84–92.

Fitzgerald, Frances. 1986. "A Reporter at Large (Rajneeshpuram)." *The New Yorker* (29 September).

Flake, Carol. 1982. *Redemptorama*. New York: Penguin Books.

Flinn, Frank. 1983. "Scientology as Technological Buddhism." In *Alternatives to Mainline Churches,* edited by J. Fichter, 89–112. Barrytown, N.Y.: Unification Seminary.

Foltz, Tanice. 1987. "The Social Construction of Reality in a Para-Religious Healing Group." *Social Compass* 34 (4): 397–413.

Fox, Robin L. 1987. *Pagans and Christians*. New York: Knopf.

Frankiel, Tamara. 1989. "New Age Mythology: A Jewish Response to Joseph Campbell." *Tikkun* 4(3): 23–26, 118–20.

Frankl, Razelle. 1984. *Televangelism: The Marketing of Popular Religion*. Edwardsville, Ill.: Southern Illinois University Press.

Friedan, Betty. 1981. *The Second Stage*. New York: Summit Books.

Friedman, Albert. 1971. "The Usable Myth: The Legends of Modern Mythmakers." In *American Folk Legend: A Symposium,* edited by Wayland Hand, 37–45. Berkeley: University of California Press.

Friedrich, Otto. 1987. "New Age Harmonies." *Time* 130 (7 Dec.): 62–72.

Fuller, Alfred C., and Hartell Spence. 1960. *A Foot in the Door*. New York: McGraw-Hill Book Co.

Fuller Andrew R. 1986. *Americans and the Unconscious*. New York and Oxford: Oxford University.

Furman, D. 1984. *Religion and Social Conflicts in the USA*. English Translation, Moscow: Progress Publishers.

Gabriel, Ralph H. 1949. "The Gospel of Wealth of the Gilded Age." In *Democracy and the Gospel of Wealth,* edited by Gail Kennedy, 55–62. Boston: D.C., Heath.

Galloway, Paul. 1988. "Faith Gone Awry." *Chicago Tribune* (21 June).

Gallup, George Jr. 1977. "U.S. in the Early Stages of a Religious Revival?" *Journal of Current Social Issues* (Spring): 50–55.

———. 1988. "The Impact of Religion in the 1988 National Elections." Address at the annual meetings of the Society for the Scientific Study of Religion, Chicago. (Oct. 29).

Gallup, George and David Poling. 1980. *The Search for America's Faith*. Nashville: Abingdon.

Gans, Herbert, M.D. . "Symbolic Ethnicity: The Future of Ethnic Groups and Cultures in America." *Ethnic and Racial Studies* 2 (Jan.).

Garvey, Kevin. 1985. "Warlocks Among the Warriors: Delta Force and the Myth of Superman." Presented to the conference on "Other Realities, New Religions and Revitalization Movements." Lincoln, Nebr. (April).

Gatewood, Willard B., Jr. ed. 1969. *Controversy in the Twenties: Fundamentalism, Modernism, and Evolution*. Nashville: Vanderbilt University Press.

Gaustad, Edwin Scott. 1962. *Historical Atlas of Religion in America*. New York: Harper and Row.

Geertz, Clifford. 1973. *Interpretations of Culture*. New York: Basic Books.

Gelfand, Howard. 1983. "Fuller Still Keeps a Foot in the Door." *Advertising Age* 23 November, M51–M53.

Gellman, Irving. 1964. *The Sober Alcoholic: An Organizational Analysis of Alcoholics Anonymous*. New Haven, Conn.: College and University Press.

Gerlach, Luther P., and Virginia H. Hine. 1970. *People, Power, and Change: Movement of Social Transformation*. New York: Bobbs Merrill Company.

Gerstner, John H. 1975. "The Theological Boundaries of Evangelical Faith." In Wells and Woodbridge 1975, 21–37.

Glaser, Barney, and Anselm L. Strauss. 1967. *The Discovery of Grounded Theory: Strategies for Qualitative Research*. Chicago: Aldine.

Gleason, Daniel. 1980. "A Study of the Christian School Movement." Unpublished Ph.D. dissertation, University of North Carolina.

Glendinning, C. "The Healing Powers of Women." In Spretnak 1982, 280–93.

Glock, Charles Y. ed. 1973. *Religion in Sociological Perspective*. Belmont, Calif.: Wadsworth Company.

Goffman, Erving. 1961. *Asylums: Essays on the Social Situations of Mental Patients and Other Inmates*. Garden City, N.Y.: Doubleday Anchor.

Goldenber, Naomi. 1979. *The Changing of the Gods: Feminism and the End of Traditional Religions*. Boston: Beacon Press.

Greeley, Andrew, and Michael Hout. 1988. "Musical Chairs: Patterns of Denominational Change." *American Sociological Review* 72 (2): 75–86.

Greenfield, Meg. 1978. "Heart of Darkness." *Newsweek,* 4 December, 132.

Greenleaf, William. n.d. "Preface." In *The Legend of Henry Ford,* Keith Sward. New York: Atheneum.

Greil, Arthur L., and David R. Rudy. 1983. "Conversion to the World View of Alcoholics Anonymous: A Refinement of Conversion Theory." *Qualitative Sociology* 6:5–28.

———. 1984. "Social Cocoons: Encapsulation and Identity Transforming Organizations." *Sociological Inquiry* 54:260–78.

Griffin, Susan. 1978. *Woman and Nature*. New York: Harper and Row.

Groothuis, Douglas. 1986. *Unmasking the New Age*. Downers Grove, Ill.: Inter-varsity Fellowship.

Gross, Rita. ed. 1977. *Beyond Andocentrism: New Essays on Women and Religion*. Decatur, Ga.: Scholars Press.

Gusfield, Joeseph. 1981. "Social Movements and Social Change." In *Research in Social Movements*. Vol. 4, edited by Louis Kreisberger, 299–317. New York: JAI Press.

Hadden, Jeffrey K. 1969. *The Gathering Storm in the Churches*. Garden City, N.Y.: Anchor.

———. 1983. "Televangelism and the Mobilization of a New Christian Right Family Policy." In *Families and Religion: Conflict and Change in Modern Society,* edited by William D'Antonio and Joan Aldous. Beverly Hills: Sage Publishers.

———. 1987a. "Religious Broadcasting and the New Religious Right." *Journal for the Scientific Study of Religion* 26 (1): 1–24.

———. 1987b. "Toward Desacralizing Secularization Theory." *Social Forces* 65 (3): 587–611.

Hadden, Jeffrey K., and Anson Shupe. 1986. "Introduction." In *Prophetic Religions and Politics,* J. Hadden and A. Shupe. New York: Paragon.

———. 1987. "Televangelism in America." *Social Compass* 34 (1): 61–76.

———. 1988. *Televangelism: Power and Politics on God's Frontier.* New York: Henry Holt.

Hadden, Jeffrey K., and Charles Swann. 1981. *Prime Time Preachers: The Rising Power of Televangelism.* Reading, Mass.: Addison-Wesley.

Hadaway, Kirk. 1978. "Denominational Switching and Membership Growth." *Journal for the Scientific Study of Religion* 39:321–37.

Hall, John R. 1978. *The Ways Out: Utopian Communal Groups in an Age of Babylon.* Boston: Routledge and Keegan Paul.

———. *Gone from the Promised Land: Jonestown In American Cultural History.* New Brunswick, N.J.: Transaction Books.

———. 1988a. "The Impact of Apostates on the Trajectories of Religious Movements: The Case of Peoples Temple." In *Falling From the Faith: The Causes, Course, and Consequences of Religious Apostasy,* edited by David G. Bromley. Beverley Hills: Sage.

———. 1988b. "Social Organization and Pathways of Commitment: Ideal types, Rational Choice Theory, and the Kanter Thesis." *American Sociological Review.*

———. Forthcoming. "Bishop Hill and Jonestown: Continuities and Disjunctures in Religious Conflict." In Moore and McGeehee forthcoming.

Hall, N. 1980. *The Moon and the Virgin: Reflections on the Archetypal Feminine.* New York: Harper and Row.

Hammond, Phillip E. 1966. *The Campus Clergyman.* New York, Basic Books.

———. 1983. "Another Great Awakening?" In Liebman and Wuthnow 1983, 207–23.

Hammond, Phillip, and James Davison Hunter. 1984. "On Maintaining Plausibility: The Worldview of Evangelical College Students." *Journal for the Scientific Study of Religion* 23:221–38.

Handy, Robert T. 1971. *A Christian America: Protestant Hopes and Historical Realities.* New York: Oxford University Press.

Hannigan, John. 1988. "Ideological Affinity and Social Movement Networks: The Case of 'New Age' Spirituality." Paper presented to the Association for the Sociology of Religion, Atlanta, Ga.

Hardwick, Elizabeth. 1988. "Church Going." *New York Review of Books*
   xxxv (35) (18 Aug.): 15–17.
Harper, Charles L., and Kevin Leicht. 1984. "Religious Awakenings and
   Status Politics." *Sociological Analysis* 45 (4): 339–53.
Hart, Roderick P. 1977. *The Political Pulpit*. West Lafayette: Purdue
   University Press.
Hatch, Nathan O. 1977. *The Sacred Cause of Liberty*. New Haven: Yale
   University Press.
Haywood, Carol. 1983. "The Authority and Empowerment of Women
   among Spiritualist Groups." *Journal for the Scientific Study of Religion*
   22:157–66.
Heelas, Paul. 1986. "Self, Values, and Corporate Cultures." Paper pre-
   sented to a meeting of the Economic and Social Research Council,
   London.
Heimert, Alan. 1966. *Religion and the American Mind: From the Great
   Awakening to the Revolution*. Cambridge, Mass.: Harvard University
   Press.
Heinerman, John, and Anson Shupe. 1987. *The Mormon Corporate Em-
   pire*. Boston: Beacon.
Heinz, Donald. 1983. "The Struggle to Define America." In Lieberman
   and Wuthnow 1983, 133–48.
Henry, Patrick. 1981. "And I Don't Care What It Is: The Traditional
   History of a Civil Religion." *Journal of the American Academy of
   Religion* 49:35–50.
Herberg, William. 1955. *Protestant, Catholic, and Jew: An Essay in
   American Religious Sociology*. Garden City, N.Y.: Doubleday.
———. 1960. *Protestant, Catholic, Jew*. Garden City, N.Y.: Doubleday.
Heschel, Susannah. ed. 1983. *On Being a Jewish Feminist*. New York:
   Schocken.
Hess, Beth. 1984. "Protecting the American Family: Public Policy, Family
   and the New Right." In *Families and Change: Social Needs and Public
   Policy*, edited by Rosalie Genovese. South Hadley, Mass.: Bergin and
   Garvey.
Hexham, Irving, and Karla Poewe. 1986. *Understanding Cults and New
   Religions*. Grand Rapids: Erdmans.
Hoare, Quintin, and Geoffrey Smith (editors and translators). 1971. *Selec-
   tions from the Prison Notebooks of Antonio Gramsci*. New York:
   International Publishers.
Hoge, Dean R. 1979a. "National Contextual Factors Influencing Church
   Trends." In *Understanding Church Growth and Decline*, edited by
   Dean Hoge and David Roozen, 94–122. New York: The Pilgrim Press.
———. 1979b. "A Test of Denominational Growth and Decline." In
   Understanding Church Growth and Decline, edited by Dean Hoge and
   David Roozen, 179–97. New York: The Pilgrim Press.
Hofstadter, Richard. 1964. *The Paranoid Style in American Politics and
   Other Essays*. Chicago: University of Chicago.

Holmes, Derek. 1981. *The Papacy in the Modern World.* New York: n. p.

Hoover, Stewart. 1988. *Mass Media Religion: The Social Sources of the Electronic Church.* Newbury, Calif.: Sage.

Hopkins, Joseph. 1986. "The Founder of Scientology is Dead at 74." *Christianity Today* 30 (March 7): 52.

Horowitz, Irving. 1981. "The Politics of New Cults." In *In Gods We Trust,* 1st ed., edited by T. Robbins and D. Anthony, 160–71. New Brunswick, N.J.: Transaction.

Huber, Richard. 1971. *The American Idea of Success.* New York: McGraw-Hill Book Co.

Hudson, Winthrop. 1981. *Religion in America.* New York: Charles Scribner's Sons.

Hunter, Edward. 1951. *Brainwashing in Red China.* New York: Vanguard Press.

———. 1960. *Brainwashing: From Pavlov to Powers.*

Hunter, Floyd. 1953. *Community Power Structure.* Chapel Hill: University of North Carolina Press.

Hunter, James Davison. 1983a. *American Evangelicalism: Conservative Religion and the Quandary of Modernity.* New Brunswick, N.J.: Rutgers University Press.

———. 1983b. "The Liberal Reaction." In Liebman and Wuthnow 1983, 150–63.

———. 1987. *Evangelicalism: The Coming Generation.* Chicago: University of Chicago Press.

Huntington, Samuel P. 1981. *American Politics: The Promise of Disharmony.* Cambridge, Mass.: Harvard University Press.

Hurley, Dan. 1988. "Getting Help from Helping." *Psychology Today* 22 (Jan.): 62–67.

Huxley, Aldous. 1958. *Brave New World Revisited.* New York: Harper and Row.

Huxley, Aldous, 1977. *Moksha:* Writings on Psychedelic and the Visionary Experience (1931–1963). Michael Horowitz and Cynthia Palmer, eds., N.Y.: Stonehill.

Inkeles, Alex, and D. H. Smith. 1974. *Becoming Modern.* Cambridge: Harvard University Press.

Jacobs, Janet. 1984. "The Economy of Love in Religious Commitment: The Deconversion of Women From Non-Traditional Movements." *Journal for the Scientific Study of Religion* 23 (2): 155–71.

———. forthcoming a. "The Effects of Ritual Healing on Female Victims of Abuse: A Study of Empowerment and Transformation." (forthcoming *Sociological Analyses*).

———. forthcoming b. "Women-centered Healing Rites." Chapter 20 in this volume.

James, Gene G. 1986. "Brainwashing: The Myth and the Actuality." *Thought* 61: 241–58.

Johnson, Benton. 1963. "On Church and Sect." *American Sociological Review* 28:539–49.

———. 1981. "A Sociological Perspective on New Religions." In *In Gods We Trust*, 1st ed., edited by T. Robbins and D. Anthony, 51–66. New Brunswick, N.J.: Transaction.

———. 1985a. "Liberal Protestantism: End of the Road?" In *The Annals: Religion in America Today*, edited by Wade Clark Roof, 39–52. Beverly Hills: Sage.

———. 1985b. "Religion in American Politics: The Last Twenty Years." In *The Sacred in a Secular Age*, edited by P. Hammond. Berkeley: University of California Press.

Johnson, D. Paul. 1980. "Dilemmas of Charismatic Leadership: The Case of the Peoples Temple." *Sociological Analysis* 40 (4): 315–23.

Johnson, George. 1987. *The Relationship among Organizational Involvement, Commitment, and Success: A Case Study of Amway Corporation*. Unpublished Ph.D. dissertation, Virginia Polytechnic Institute and State University.

Johnson, Stephen D., and Joseph B. Tamney. 1982. "The Christian Right and the 1980 Presidential Election." *Journal for the Scientific Study of Religion* 21:123–31.

Johnson, Stephen D., Joseph B. Tamney, and Ronald Burton. 1988. "Pat Robertson: Who Supports His Candidacy for President." Paper presented at annual meeting of the Association for the Sociology of Religion, Atlanta, Ga.

Jones, Jim. 1978. "Perspectives from Guyana." *Peoples Forum* (January). (Reprinted in Krause, Stern, and Harwood [1978, 205–10]).

Jones, Robert Kenneth. 1970. "Sectarian Characteristics of Alcoholics Anonymous." *Sociology* 4:181–95.

Juth, Carol. 1985. "Structural Factors Creating and Maintaining Illegal and Deviant Behavior in Direct Selling Organizations: A Case Study of Amway Corporation." Paper presented at the annual meeting of the American Sociological Association, Washington, D.C.

Juth-Gavasso, Carol. 1985. *Organizational Deviance in the Direct Selling Industry: A Case Study of the Amway Corporation*. Unpublished Ph.D. dissertation, Western Michigan University.

Kahl, Joseph. 1968. *The Measurement of Modernism: A Study of Values in Brazil and Mexico*. Austin, Tex.: University of Texas Press.

Kanter, Rosabeth Moss. 1972. *Commitment and Community: Communes and Utopias in Sociological Perspective*. Cambridge: Harvard University Press.

Kardec, Allan. 1978. Orig. 1874. *The Book of Mediums*. N.Y.: Samuel Weiser.

Katz v. Superior Court. 1977. 73 Cal. App. 3d 952, 141 Cal. Rptr. 234.

Kaufman, Debra. 1985. "Women Who Return to Orthodox Judaism: A Feminist Analysis." *Journal of Marriage and the Family* (August):543–51.

————. 1987. "Coming Home to Jewish Orthodoxy." *Tikkun* 2 (3): 60–63.
Kautz, William H., and Melanie Branon. 1987. *Channeling: The Intuitive Connection.* San Francisco, Calif.: Harper and Row.
Kelly, Aidan. 1983. *Inventing Witchcraft.* Unpublished manuscript in the collection of the Institute for the Study of American Religion.
Kelly, Aidan. 1987. "An Update on Neopagan Witchcraft in America." Paper presented to the American Academy of Religion, Boston, Mass.
Kelley, Dean M. 1972. *Why the Conservative Churches are Growing.* New York: Harper and Row.
————. 1978. "Comment: Why Conservative Churches Are Still Growing." *Journal for the Scientific Study of Religion* 17:165–72.
————. ed. 1982. *Government Intervention in Religious Affairs.* New York: Pilgrim.
————. ed. 1986. *Government Intervention in Religious Affairs.* Vol. 2. New York: Pilgrim.
Kennedy, Paul. 1987. *The Rise and Fall of the Great Powers.* New York: Random House.
Kern, Louis. 1981. *An Ordered Love.* Chapel Hill: University of North Carolina Press.
Kerns, Phil. 1982. *Fake It til You Make It!: Inside Amway.* Carlton, Oreg.: Victory Press.
Kerr, Peter. 1985. "Singles Seek Social Life at Houses of Worship." *The New York Times* 1 April, 82.
Kiecolt, K. Jill, and Hart M. Nelsen. 1988. "Political Attitudes among Liberal and Conservative Protestants." *Journal for the Scientific Study of Religion* 27(1): 48–59.
Kienel, Paul. 1980. *The Christian School: Why Is It Right for Your Child?* Wheaton, Ill.: Victor Books.
Kilbourne, Brock, and James Richardson. 1986. "Cultphobia." *Thought* 61:258–66.
Kilduff, Marshall, and Ron Javers. 1978. *The Suicide Cult: The Inside Story of the People's Temple Sect and the Massacre in Guyana.* New York: Bantam.
Kingan, Adele. 1982. "Entrepreneur's Corner." *The Executive Female* (Nov./Dec.):12–14.
Klass, Dennis. 1982. "Self-Help Groups for the Bereaved: Theory, Theology, and Practices." *Journal of Religion and Health* 21:307–24.
Klimo, Jon. 1987. *Channeling: Investigations on Receiving Information from Paranormal Sources.* Los Angeles: Jeremy P. Tarcher.
Knox, Ronald. 1950. *Enthusiasm.* London: Collins.
Kramer, Heinrich, and James Sprenger. 1971. Orig. 1484. *The Malleus Maleficarum,* translated by Montague Summers. New York: Dover Publications, Inc.
Krause, Charles, Lawrence M. Stern, and Richard Harwood. 1978. *Guyana Massacre: The Eye Witness Account.* New York: Berkeley Books.

Kropansky in *United States v. Kozminski*. 1987. (6th Cir.) 821 F.2d 1186 cert. granted 108 S.Ct. 225 (No. 86-2000, 1987)

Kuhn, Thomas S. 1970. Orig. 1962. *The Structure of Scientific Revolutions*. Chicago: The University of Chicago Press.

LaHaye, Timothy. 1982. *The Battle for the Family*. Old Tappan, N.J.: Fleming H. Revell.

Lazaris. 1987. *The Sacred Journey: You and Your Higher Self*. Los Angeles: Concept: Synergy.

Larner, Christina. 1984. *Witchcraft and Religion*. Oxford: Blackwell.

Lasch, Christopher. 1977. *Haven in a Heartless World: The Family Besieged*. New York: Basic Books.

———. 1980. (1st ed. 1976). *The Culture of Narcissism*. London: Sphere Books.

Lee, Martin, and Bruce Schlain. 1985. *Acid Dreams: The CIA, LSD and The Sixties Rebellion*. New York: Grove Press.

Lechner, Frank J. 1985. "Fundamentalism and Sociocultural Revitalization in America." *Sociological Analysis* 46 (3): 243–60.

———. 1988. "Fundamentalism and Sociocultural Revitalization: On the Logic of Dedifferentiation." In *Differentiation Theory and Social Change*, edited by Jeffrey Alexander and Paul Colomy. New York: Columbia University Press.

Levitas, Daniel, and Leonared Zeskind. 1987. "The Farm Crisis and the Radical Right." In *Renew the Spirit of My People: A Handbook for Ministry in Times of Rural Crisis*, 23–30. Des Moines: Prairiefire Rural Action, Inc.

Lewis, James. 1986. "Reconstructing the 'Cult' Experience." *Sociological Analysis* 47 (2): 151–59.

Lewy, Gunther. 1974. *Religion and Revolution*. New York: Oxford University Press.

Lehman, Edward C. 1985. *Woman Clergy: Breaking Through the Gender Barriers*. New Brunswick, N.J.: Transaction.

Lidz, Victor M. 1979. "Secularization, Ethical Life, and Religion in Modern Societies." In *Religious Change and Continuity*, edited by Harry M. Johnson, chap. 8, 191–217. San Francisco: Jossey-Bass. (*Sociological Inquiry* 49 [2–3]).

Lieberson, Stanley. 1988. "Asking Too Much, Expecting Too Little." *Sociological Perspectives* 31 (4) (Oct.): 379–97.

Liebman, Robert C., and Robert Wuthnow, eds. 1983. *The New Christian Right: Mobilization and Legitimation*. New York: Aldine.

Lifton, Robert J. 1957. "Methods of Forceful Indoctrination: Psychiatric Aspects of Chinese Communist Thought Reform." In *Symposium 4 (Methods of Forceful Indoctrination: Observations and Interviews)*, 234–49. Group for the Advancement of Psychiatry, New York: G.A.P. Publications Office.

———. 1961. *Thought Reform and the Psychology of Totalism*. New York: Norton and Co.

————. 1968. *Revolutionary Immortality: Mao Tse-Tung and the Chinese Cultural Revolution*. New York: Vintage.

————. 1976. Testimony in the Patty Hearst trial. *The Trial of Patty Hearst*. 314–34. San Francisco: The Great Fidelity Press.

————. 1979. "The Appeal of the Death Trip." *New York Times Magazine* (Jan. 7).

————. 1985. "Cult Processes, Religious Totalism, and Civil Liberties." In *Cults, Culture and the Law*, edited by T. Robbins, W. Shepherd, and J. McBride, 59–70. Chico, Calif.: Scholars Press.

————. 1987. *The Future of Immortality and Other Essays for a Nuclear Age*. New York: Basic Books.

Lightfoot, Sarah Lawrence. 1978. *Worlds Apart: Relationships Between Families and Schools*. New York: Basic Books.

Lindsey, Hal. 1970. *The Late Great Planet Earth*. Grand Rapids: Zondervan.

Lindsey, Karen. 1985. "Spiritual Explorers." *Ms.*, December.

Lindsey, Robert. 1986. "Isolated Strongly Led Sects Growing in U.S." *New York Times* (22 June).

Lindt, Gillian. 1981–82. "Journeys to Jonestown: Accounts and Interpretations of the Rise and Demise of the People's Temple." *Union Theological Seminary Quarterly Review* 37: 159–74.

Lofland, John, and L. N. Skonovd. 1981. "Conversion Motifs." *Journal for the Scientific Study of Religion* 20 (4): 373–85.

Long, Elizabeth. 1985. *The American Dream and the Popular Novel*. Boston: Routledge and Kegan Paul.

Luckmann, Thomas. 1967. *The Invisible Religion: The Problem of Religion in Modern Society*. New York: MacMillan.

Luker, Kristen. 1984. *Abortion and the Politics of Motherhood*. Berkeley: University of California Press.

Lukes, Steven, 1974. *Power: A Radical View*. London, Macmillan.

Lunde and Wilson. 1977. *Brainwashing as a Defense to Criminal Liability: Patty Hearst Revisited. Criminal Law Bulletin* 13.

Lynd, Robert S., and Helen Merrell Lynd. 1929. *Middletown*. New York: Harcourt, Brace and Co.

Lynn, Robert Wood. 1973. "Civil Catechetics in Mid-Victorian America: Some Notes about American Civil Religion, Past and Present." *Religious Education* 68 (1): 5–27.

Lyon, David. 1985. *The Steeple's Shadow: The Myths and Realities of Secularization*. Grand Rapids: Erdmans.

McGraw, Douglas. 1979. "Commitment and Religious Community: A Comparison of a Charismatic and a Mainline Congregation." *Journal for the Scientific Study of Religion* 18: 146–53.

McGuire, Meredith B. 1981. *Religion: The Social Context*. Belmont, Calif.: Wadsworth.

————. 1982. *Pentecostal Catholics, Power, Charisma and Order in a Religious Movement*. Philadelphia: Temple University Press.

———. 1983a. "Words of Power: Personal Empowerment and Healing." *Culture, Medicine, and Psychiatry* 7:140–221.

———. 1983b. "Discovering Religious Power." *Sociological Analysis* 44 (1): 1–10.

———. 1985. "Religion and Healing." In *The Sacred in a Secular Age,* edited by P. Hammon, 268–84. Berkeley, Calif.: University of California.

McGuire, Meredith B., and Debra Kantor. 1988. *Ritual Healing in Suburbia.* New Brunswick, N.J.: Rutgers University Press.

Mackenzie, Brian D. 1977. "Positivism, Realism, and Behaviorist Psychology." In *Behaviorism and the Limits of Scientific Method,* chapter 2. Atlantic Highlands, N.J.: Humanities Press.

MacLaine, Shirley. 1983. *Out on a Limb.* New York: Bantam.

———. 1985. *Dancing in the Light.* New York: Bantam.

———. 1987. *It's All in the Playing.* New York: Bantam.

McLoughlin, William G. 1978. *Revivals, Awakenings, and Reform: An Essay on Religion and Social Change in America 1607–1977.* Chicago: The University of Chicago Press.

McNamara, Patrick H. 1985. "American Catholicism in the Mid-Eighties: Pluralism and Conflict in a Changing Church." *The Annals* 480:63–74.

McWilliams, W. C. 1973. *The Idea of Fraternity in America.* Berkeley, Calif.: University of California.

Mains, Jeremy. 1987. "Trying to Bend Managers' Minds." *Fortune* 116:95–107.

Mannheim, Karl. 1951. *Man and Society in an Age of Reconstruction.* New York: n.p.

Marsden, George M. 1975. "From Fundamentalism to Evangelicalism: A Historical Analysis." In Wells and Woodbridge 1975, 122–42.

———. 1980. *Fundamentalism and American Culture: The Shaping of Twentieth-Century Evangelicalism, 1870–1925.* New York: Oxford University Press.

———. 1982. "Preachers of Paradox: The Religious New Right in Historical Perspective." In *Religion and America,* edited by M. Douglas and S. Tipton, 150–68. Boston, Mass.: Beacon Press.

Martin, David. 1982. "Revived Dogma and New Cult." In *Religion and America,* edited by M. Douglas and S. Tipton, 11–129. Boston: Beacon.

Martin, William. 1981. "God's Angry Man." *Texas Monthly* (Apr.).

———. 1982. "Waiting for the End." *Atlantic Monthly* (April): 31–37.

Marty, Martin E. 1970. *Righteous Empire: The Protestant Experience in America.* New York: The Dial Press.

———. 1975. "Tensions within Contemporary Evangelicalism: A Critical Approach." In Wells and Woodbridge 1975, 170–88.

———. 1976. *A Nation of Behavers.* Chicago: University of Chicago Press.

———. 1979. "Foreword." In *Understanding Church Growth and Decline,* edited by Dean Hoge and David Roozen, 9–15. New York: Pilgrim Press.

————. 1981. "The Revival of Evangelicalism and Southern Religion." In *Varieties of Southern Evangelicalism*, edited by David E. Harrell, Jr., 7–21. Macon: Mercer University Press.

————. 1988. "Front Page Religion." Review of *Spiritual Politics*, Mark Silk (Simon and Schuster), *New York Times Book Review* (3 April): 17.

Marx, Karl, and Friederick Engels. 1959. Orig. 1848. "Manifesto of the Communist Party." In *Marx and Engels: Basic Writings on Politics and Philosophy*, edited by Lewis S. Fewer. Garden City, N.Y.: Doubleday Anchor.

Mauss, Armand L., and Donald W. Petersen. 1974. "Prodigals and Preachers: The 'Jesus Freaks' and the Return to Respectability." *Social Compass* 221 (3).

Mead, Sydney E. 1975. *The Nation with the Soul of a Church*. New York: Harper and Row.

————. 1977. *The Old Religion in the Brave New World: Reflections on the Relations between Christendom and the Republic*. Berkeley: University of California Press.

Meher Baba. 1967. *Discourses*. (3 Vols.) Ahmednegar, India: Adi K. Irani.

Meirs, Michael. forthcoming. *A CIA Experiment in Social Engineering*. Lewiston, N.Y.: Edwin Mellen Press.

Melton, J. Gordon. 1985. "The Revival of Astrology in the United States." In *Religious Movements: Genesis, Exodus, and Numbers*, edited by R. Stark, 279–96. New York: Paragon House.

————. 1987. "How New is New? The Flowering of the 'New' Religious Consciousness Since 1965." In Bromley and Hammond 1987, 46–56.

————. 1988. "A History of the New Age Movement." In Basil 1988, 35–53.

Menendez, Albert J. 1988. "Evangelicals Helped Win It for Bush." *National and International Religion Report* 2(23) (21 Nov.).

Merloo, Joost A. M. 1956. *The Rape of the Mind: The Psychology of Thought Control, Menticide, and Brainwashing*. Cleveland: World Publishing Co.

Mickler, Michael. 1987. "Future Prospects for the Unification Church." In Bromley and Hammond 1987, 175–86.

Miller, Donald E. 1982. "The Future of Liberal Christianity." *The Christian Century* (10 March): 266–70.

Miller, Perry. 1938. "General Introduction—The Puritan Way of Life." In *The Puritans*, edited by Perry Miller and Thomas H. Johnson, 1–63. New York: American Book Company.

————. 1961. "From the Covenant to the Revival." In *The Shaping of American Religion*, edited by James Ward Smith and A. Leland Jamison, 322–68. Princeton, N.J.: Princeton University Press.

————. 1965. *The Life of the Mind in America*. New York: Harcourt, Brace, and World.

Mills, C. Wright. 1956. *The Power Elite*. New York: Oxford University Press.

Moberg, David. 1978. "Prison Camp of the Mind." *In These Times* (13 Dec.): 11–14.

Molko and Leal v. Holy Spirit Association. 1988. 46 California Supreme Court 3d 1092.

Montgomery, Edrene. 1985. "Partners in the Divine Enterprise: Bruce Barton and the Business-Oriented Mythology of the 1920s." Paper presented at the conference: Other Realities: New Religions and Revitalization Movements, University of Nebraska, Lincoln.

Moon, Sun Myung. 1973. *Christianity in Crisis: New Hope.* Holy Spirit for the Unification of World Christianity.

———. 1974. *Divine Principle.* Holy Spirit for the Unification of World Christianity.

Moore, Rebecca. 1985. *A Sympathetic History of Jonestown: The Moore Family Involvement In Peoples Temple.* Lewiston, N.Y.: Edwin Mellon Press.

———. 1986. *The Jonestown Letters: Correspondence of the Moore Family, 1970–1985.* Lewiston, N.Y.: Edwin Mellon Press.

Moore, Rebecca, and Fielding M. McGehee. forthcoming. *New Religious Movements, Mass Suicide and the Peoples Temple: Scholarly Perspectives.* New York: Edwin Mellon.

Moore, R. Laurence. 1985. *Religious Outsiders and the Making of Americans.* New York: Oxford University Press.

Morgan, Robin. 1970. *Sisterhood is Powerful.* New York: Random House.

———. 1977. *Going Too Far.* New York: Random House.

Moyers, Bill. 1987. "On Earth as It Is in Heaven." Transcript. New York: Public Affairs Television, WNET. (Air date, 23 Dec.).

Nash, Dennison. 1968. "A Little Child Shall Lead Them: A Statistical Test of a Hypothesis That Children Were the Source of the American 'Religious Revival.' " *Journal for the Scientific Study of Religion* 7:238–40.

National Youth Survey. 1980. Boulder Research Institute.

Neitz, Mary Jo. 1987. *Charisma and Community: A Study of Religion and Commitment among the Catholic Charismatic Renewal Movement.* New Brunswick, N.J.: Transaction.

———. 1988a. "Sacramental Sex in Modern Witchcraft Groups." Paper presented to the Midwestern Sociological Society, Minneapolis.

———. 1988b. "Women's Mysteries: Menstruation Rituals of Contemporary Witches." Paper presented at the Women and Spirituality Conference, the University of Colorado at Colorado Springs. (10 April).

Nelson, G. K. 1969. *Spiritualism and Society.* New York: Schocken.

Neuhaus, Richard John. 1984. *The Naked Public Square.* Grand Rapids. Mich.: William Erdmann Publishers.

New York Times/CBS News Poll. 1988. "Portrait of the Electorate." *New York Times* (10 Nov.), B6.

Niebuhr, H. Richard. 1929. *The Social Sources of Denominationalism.* New York: Henry Holt Co.

————. 1959. Orig. 1937. *The Kingdom of God in America*. New York: Harper and Row.

Niebuhr, Reinhold. 1940. *Christianity and Power Politics*. New York, Scribners.

Nisbet, Robert. 1980. *History of the Idea of Progress*. New York: Basic Books.

Nock, A. D. 1933. *Conversion*. New York: Oxford University Press.

North, Gary. 1983. *Unconditional Surrender: God's Program for Victory*. Tyler, Tex.: Geneva Divinity School.

————. 1986. *Unholy Spirits: Occultism and New Age Humanum*. Fort Worth, Tex.: Dominion Press.

Novak, Michael. 1974. *Choosing Our King. Powerful Symbols in American Politics*. New York: Macmillan.

Ofshe, Richard. 1980. "The Social Development of the Synanon Cult: The Managerial Strategy of Organizational Transformation." *Sociological Analysis* 41:109–27.

————. 1986. "The Role of Tax Law in the Promotion of Cult Deviance." Paper presented to the American Sociological Association, New York.

Ofshe, Richard, and Margaret Singer. 1986. "Attacks on Peripheral versus Central Elements of Self and the Impact of Thought Reforming Techniques." *The Cultic Studies Journal* 3 (1) (Spring/Summer): 3–24.

Opie, John, Jr. 1965. "The Modernity of Fundamentalism." *The Christian Century* (May) 608–11.

Ortner, Sherry. 1972. "Is Female to Male as Nature is to Culture?" *Feminist Studies* 1 (2): 5–32.

Paddock, Joe, Nancy Paddock, and Carol Bly. 1986. *Soil and Survival: Land Stewardship and the Future of American Agriculture*. San Francisco: Sierra Club Books.

Pagels, Elain. 1979. *The Gnostic Gospels*. New York: Random House.

————. 1988. *Adam, Eve, and the Serpent*. New York: Random House.

Palmer, Susan J. 1986. "Community and Commitment in the Rajneesh Foundation." *Update* (Dec.). Denmark: Aarthus.

————. 1988. "AIDS and the Apocalyptic in Seven Religious Minorities." Paper presented to the Society for the Scientific Study of Religion, Chicago.

Pannikar, K. M. 1965. *Asia and Western Dominance*. London: George Allen & Umwin.

Paris, Ellen. 1985. "Herbalife, Anyone?" *Forbes* (25 Feb.).

Park, Robert. 1930. "Assimilation." In *Encyclopedia of the Social Sciences*. Vol. 2. New York: Macmillan.

Parsons, Arthur. 1986. "Messianic Personalism: A Role Analysis of the Unification Church." *Journal for the Scientific Study of Religion* 25 (2): 141–61.

Parsons, Talcott. 1971. *The System of Modern Societies*. Englewood Cliffs, N.J.: Prentice-Hall.

Perrin, Robin D. 1989. "American Religion in the Post-Aquarian Age: Values and Demographic Factors in Church Growth and Decline." *Journal for the Scientific Study of Religion* (forthcoming).

Peshkin, Alan. 1986. *God's Choice: The Total World of a Fundamentalist Christian School.* Chicago: University of Chicago Press.

Petersen, Donald W., and Armand L. Mauss. 1973. "The Cross and the Commune: A Sociological Interpretation of the 'Jesus Freaks.' " In Glock 1973.

Peven, Dorothy. 1968. "The Use of Religious Revival Techniques to Indoctrinate Personnel: The Home-Party Sales Organization." *The Sociological Quarterly xx:* 97–106.

Platt, Gerald, and Rhys Williams. 1988. "Religion, Ideology, and Electoral Politics." *Society* 25 (5): 38–45.

Pollack, G. H. 1975. "On Mourning, Immortality, and Utopia." *Journal of American Psychoanalytic Association* 23: 334–62.

Poloma, Margaret. 1982. *The Charismatic Movement: Is There a New Pentecost?* Boston, Mass.: Twayne Publishers (G. K. Hall Company).

Polsby, Nelson W. 1963. *Community Power and Political Theory.* New Haven, Conn.: Yale University Press.

Pope, Liston. 1942. *Millhands and Preachers.* New Haven, Conn.: Yale University Press.

Quebedeaux, Richard. 1974. *The Young Evangelicals: Revolution in Orthodoxy.* New York: Harper and Row.

———. 1978. *The Worldly Evangelicals.* New York: Harper and Row.

Radcliffe, Timothy. 1980. "Relativizing the Relativizers: Theologian's Assessment of the Role of Sociological Explanation of Religious Phenomena and Theology Today." In *Sociology and Theology, Alliance or Conflict?,* edited by D. Martin et al., 151–62. Brighton: Harvester Press.

Reed, Susan. 1988. "Two Anxious Fathers Battle a Therapy 'Cult' for Their Kids." *People Magazine* (25 July): 46–48.

Reich, Walter. 1976. "Brainwashing, Psychiatry, and the Law." *Psychiatry* 39 (Nov.).

Reichley, A. James. 1985. *Religion in American Public Life.* Washington, D.C.: The Brookings Institution

Reuther, Rosemary R. 1972. *Liberation Theology.* New York: Paulist Press.

———. 1985. *Women-Church: Theology and Practice.* San Francisco: Harper and Row.

Rich, A. 1976. *Of Woman Born.* New York: W. W. Norton and Company.

Richardson, James T. 1980. "Peoples Temple and Jonestown: A Corrective Comparison and Critique." *Journal for the Scientific Study of Religion* 19 (3): 239–55.

———. 1985a. "Legal and Practical Reasons for Claiming to be a Religion." Paper presented at the annual meeting of the Society for the Scientific Study of Religion, Savannah, Ga.

————. 1985b. "Studies of Conversion: Secularization or Reenchantment." In *The Sacred in a Secular Age,* edited by P. Hammond, 104–21. Berkeley, Calif.: University of California.

————. 1986. "Consumer Protection and Deviant Religions." *Review of Religious Research* 28 (2): 168–79.

Richardson, James T. and Brock Kilbourne. 1983. "Classical and Contemporary Applications of Brainwashing Models: A Comparison and Critique." In *The Brainwashing/Deprogramming Controversy,* edited by Bromley and Richardson. New York: Edwin Mellon.

Richardson, James T., Mary White Stewart, and Robert B. Simmonds. 1979. *Organized Miracles: A Study of a Contemporary Youth, Communal, Fundamentalist Organization.* New Brunswick: Transaction Books.

Richardson, Laurel. 1985. *The New Other Woman: Contemporary Other Women in Affairs with Married Men.* New York: Free Press.

Ridgeway, James. 1986. "The Farm Belt's Far Right." *Sojourners* 15: (9) (Oct.): 22–25.

Robbins, Thomas. 1983. "The Beach Is Washing Away: Controversial Religions and the Sociology of Religion." *Sociological Analysis* 44 (3): 207–14.

————. 1984. "Religious Movements and Boundary Disputes over Church Autonomy." unpublished manuscript.

————. 1985a. "Nuts, Sluts, and Converts: Studying Religious Groups as Social Problems." *Sociological Analysis* 46 (2): 171–78.

————. 1985b. "Government Regulatory Powers over Religious Groups." *Journal for the Scientific Study of Religion* 24 (3): 237–51.

————. 1986a. "Religious Mass Suicide before Jonestown: The Russian Old Believers." *Sociological Analysis* 47: 1–20.

————. 1986b. " 'Uncivil Religions' and Religious Deprogramming." *Thought* 61:277–89.

————. 1988a. "The Transformative Effect of the Study of New Religious Movements on the Sociology of Religion." *Journal for the Scientific Study of Religion* 27 (1): 12–31.

————. 1988b. *Cults, Converts, and Charisma: The Sociology of New Religious Movements.* London: Sage.

————. forthcoming a. "Historical Antecedents of Jonestown." In Moore and McGehee forthcoming.

————. 1989. "Reconsidering Jonestown: A Review Essay." *Religious Studies Review* 15(1): 32–37.

Robbins, Thomas, and Dick Anthony. 1972. "Getting Straight with Meher Baba." *Journal for the Scientific Study of Religion* 11 (2): 122–40.

————. 1979a. "Cults, Brainwashing, and Counter-Subversion." *The Annals of The American Academy of Political and Social Science* 446 (Nov.).

————. 1979b. "Cult Phobia: A Witch Hunt in the Making?" *Inquiry Magazine* (Jan.).

————. 1980a. "Brainwashing and the Persecution of Cults." *Journal of Religion and Health* (Spring).

————. 1980b. "The Medicalization of Deviant Religion: Preliminary Observation and Critique." *Yale Working Paper Series.*

————. 1980c. "The Limits of 'Coercive Persuasion' as an Explanation for Conversion to New Religious Movements." *Journal of Political Psychology* 2 (2).

————. 1980d. " 'Brainwashing' and the Persecution of Cults." *Journal of Religion and Health* 19 (1) (Spring).

————. 1980e. "A Demonology of Cults." *Inquiry Magazine* (1 Sept.): 9–11.

————. 1980f. "Harrasing Cults." *New York Times* Op-Ed Essay (15 Oct.): A15.

————. 1982. "Deprogramming, Brainwashing, and the Medicalization of New Religious Movements." *Social Problems* 29: 283–97.

————. 1984. "The Unification Church." *The Ecumenist* (Sept.–Oct.).

Robbins, Thomas, Dick Anthony, Madeline Doucas, and Thomas Curtis. 1976. "The Last Civil Religion: Reverend Moon and the Unification Church." *Sociological Analysis* 37 (2): 111–25.

Robbins, Thomas, Dick Anthony, Thomas Curtis, and Madeline Doucas. 1978. "The Last Civil Religion: The Unification Church of Reverend Sun Myung Moon." In *Science, Sin and Scholarship,* edited by J. Horowitz, 46–73. Cambridge, Mass.: M.I.T.

Robbins, Thomas, and Roland Robertson, eds. 1987. *Church-State Relations.* New Brunswick: Transaction Books.

Roberts, Keith A. 1984. *Religion in Sociological Perspective.* Homewood, Ill.: Dorsey.

Robertson, Roland. 1970. *The Sociological Interpretation of Religion.* New York: Schocken.

————. 1985a. "Scholarship, Sponsorship, and the 'Moonie' Problem." *Sociological Analysis* 46 (4): 355–60.

————. 1985b. "The Cultural Context of Contemporary Religious Movements." In *Cults, Culture, and the Law,* edited by T. Robbins, W. Shepherd, and J. McBride, 43–58. Chico, Calif.: Scholars Press.

Robertson, Roland, and Joann Chirico. 1985. "Humanity, Globalization, and Worldwide Religious Resurgence: A Theoretical Exploration." *Sociological Analysis* 46 (3): 219–42.

Rochford, E. Burke, Jr. 1985. *Hare Krishna in America.* New Brunswick: Rutgers University Press.

Roman, Sanaya. 1986. *Living with Joy: Keys to Personal Power and Spiritual Transformation.* Tiburon, Calif.: H. J. Kramer.

Roman, Sanaya, and Duane Packer. 1987. *Opening to Channel: How to Connect with Your Guide.* Tiburon, Calif.: H. J. Kramer.

Romero, Oscar. 1985. *Voice of the Voiceless.* New York: Maryknoll.

Roof, Wade Clark. 1981. "Alienation and Apostasy." In *In Gods We*

Trust. 1st ed., edited by T. Robbins and D. Anthony, 87–100. New Brunswick, N.J.: Transaction.

———. 1982. "America's Voluntary Establishment: Mainline Church in Transition." *Daedalus* 111:169–84.

Roof, Wade Clark, and William McKinney. 1985. "Denominational America and the New Religious Pluralism." In *The Annals: Religion in America Today,* edited by Wade Clark Roof, 24–38. Beverly Hills: Sage.

———. 1987. *American Mainline Religion: Its Changing Shape and Future.* New Brunswick, N.J.: Rutgers University Press.

Roozen, David A., William McKinney, and Jackson W. Carroll. 1984. *Varieties of Religious Presence.* New York: Pilgrim Press.

Rose, Susan. 1987. "Woman Warriors: The Negotiation of Gender in a Charismatic Community." *Sociological Analysis* 48 (3): 245–58.

———. 1988. *Keeping Them Out of the Hands of Satan: Evangelical Schooling in America.* New York: Rutledge and Kegan Paul.

Rothenberg, Stuart, and Frank Newport. 1984. *The Evangelical Voter.* Washington: The Institute for Government and Politics of the Free Congress Research and Education Foundation.

Rubin, Lilian. n.d. *Worlds of Pain.* New York: Basic Books.

Rudy, David R., and Arthur L. Creil. forthcoming. "Is Alcoholics Anonymous a Religious Organization?" *Sociological Analysis.*

Ruether, Rosemary Radford. 1975. *New Woman/New Earth: Sexist Ideologies and Human Liberation.* New York: Seabury.

Russell, L. M. 1974. *Human Liberation in a Feminist Perspective.* Philadelphia: Westminster Press.

———. 1976. *The Liberating Word.* Philadelphia: Westminster Press.

Safire, William. 1986. "The Poli-Preachers." *New York Times* (9 June).

Said, Edward W. 1979. *Orientalism.* New York: Random House.

Saliba, Edward. 1985. "Psychiatry and the New Cults: Part I." *Academic Psychology Bulletin* 7 (Spring).

Sandeen, Ernest R. 1970. "Fundamentalism and American History." *The Annals of the American Academy of Political and Social Science* 387 (January): 56–65.

Sargent, William. 1957. *Battle for the Mind: How Evangelists, Psychiatrists, Politicians, and Medicine Men Can Change Your Beliefs and Behavior.* Garden City, N.Y.: Doubleday.

———. 1974. *The Mind Possessed: A Physiology of Possession, Mysticism, and Faith Healing.* Philadelphia: J. B. Lippincott Co.

Scheflin, Alan, and Edward M. Opton. 1978. *The Mind Manipulators.* New York: Paddington Press.

Schein, Edgar H. 1958. "The Chinese Indoctrination Program for Prisoners of War: A Study of Attempted 'Brainwashing.' " In *Readings in Social Psychology,* edited by Maccoby et al. New York: Holt.

———. 1959. "Brainwashing and Totalitarianization in Modern Society." *World Politics* (2): 430–41.

———. 1961. *Coercive Persuasion.* New York: Norton and Co.

———. 1962. "Man against Man's Brainwashing." *Corrective Psychiatry and J. Social Therapy* 8.

Schein, Edgar, W. E. Cooley, and Margaret Singer. 1960. "A Psychological Follow-up of Former Prisoners of War of the Chinese Communists: Part I, Results of Interview Study." Cambridge, Mass.: MIT.

Schiffman, Lawrence H. 1988. "The Limits of Tolerance: Halakha and History." No page numbers.

Schrag, Peter, 1978. *Mind Control.* New York: Dell.

Schussler Fiorenza, Elizabeth. 1983. *In Memory of Her: A Feminist Theological Reconstruction of Christian Origins.* New York: Crossroads Press.

Schwartz, Gary. 1970. *Sect Ideologies and Social Status.* Chicago: University of Chicago Press.

Secretary of Defense. 1955. Advisory Committee on Prisoners of War: Report.

Shapiro, Robert. 1983. "Of Robots, Persons, and the Protection of Religious Beliefs." *Southern California Law Review* 56 (6): 1,277–318.

Shepherd, William C. 1982. "The Prosecutor's Reach: Legal Issues Stemming from the New Religious Movements." *Journal of the American Academy of Religion* 50 (2): 187–214.

Shupe, Anson, and David Bromley. 1980. *The New Vigilantes: Deprogrammers, Anticultists, and the New Religions.* Beverly Hills, Calif.: Sage.

Shupe, Anson, and William A. Stacey. 1983. *Born Again Politics and the Moral Majority.* New York: Edwin Mellon Press.

Sigleman, Lee. 1977. "Multi-Nation Surveys of Religious Beliefs." *Journal for the Scientific Study of Religion* 16:289–94.

Silk, Mark. 1988. *Spiritual Politics: Religion and American Religion since World War II.* New York: Simon and Schuster.

Simpson, John H. 1983. "Moral Issues and Status Politics." In Liebman and Wuthnow 1983, 187–205.

Simpson, John. 1987. "Some Elementary Forms of Authority and Fundamentalist Politics." In *Prophetic Religions and Politics,* edited by J. Hadden and Anson Shupe, 390–409. New York: Paragon.

Singer, Margaret. 1978. "Therapy with Ex-Cult Members." *Journal of the National Association of Private Psychiatric Hospitals* 9 (4): 14–18.

———. 1983. Testimony in *Robin George and Marcia George v. International Society for Krishna Consciousness of California etc. et al.* 27-75-65 Orange County California Superior Court.

———. 1984. Interview in *Spiritual Counterfeits Newsletter* (2) (Mar.–Apr.).

———. 1985a. Deposition testimony, 11–12 Feb., in *Witness Lee et al. v. Neil T. Duddy et al.* Alameda County California Superior Court.

———. 1985b. Testimony in *Julie Christofferson v. Church of Scientology et al.* Multnomah County, Oregon, Circuit Court, Judge Donald Londer.

———. 1986a. Deposition testimony, 23 Jan., in *Larry Wollersheim v. The Church of Scientology of California, a Corporation, et al.* Superior Court of the State of California for the County of Los Angeles.

———. 1986b. Deposition testimony, day 2, 10 Dec., in *Larry Kropinski v. Maharishi Yogi, World Plan Executive Council-United States, Maharishi International University.* Civil Action Nos. 85-2848-85-2854 in the United States District Court for the District of Columbia.

———. 1988a. Deposition testimony in *Pamela Miller v. Lifespring Inc.* Superior Court of the City and County of San Francisco, State of California.

———. 1988b. "List of Cases in Which Dr. Singer Has Testified." Exhibit 10 in *Pamela Miller v. Lifespring Inc.* Superior Court of City and County of San Francisco, State of California.

———. 1988c. "Systems: Similarities and Differences across Several Settings—Families, Couples & Cults." Paper presented at the Annual Convention of the American Psychological Association, October 1, 1988. Summarized in *The Cult Observer: A Review of Press Reports on Cults and Unethical Influence,* September/October 1988, 7 and 9. Also summarized in *The California Psychologist,* newspaper of the California Psychological Association, October 31, 1988, 7 and 10.

Singer, Margaret Thaler, Harold Goldstein, Michael D. Langone, Jesse S. Miller, Maurice K. Temerlin, and Louis J. West. 1987. *Report of the Task Force on Deceptive and Indirect Techniques of Persuasion and Control.* Report to the Board of Social and Ethical Responsibility of the American Psychological Association.

Sklar, Kathryn. 1973. *Catherine Beecher: A Study in American Domesticity.* New York: Norton and Company.

Smith, Elwyn A. 1972. *Religious Liberty in the U.S.: The Development of Church-State Thought Since the Revolutionary Era.* Philadelphia: Fortress Press.

Smith, Jonathan. 1982. *Imagining Religion: From Babylon to Jonestown.* Chicago: University of Chicago Press.

Smith, Rodney. 1984. *Multilevel Marketing: A Lawyer Looks at Amway, Shaklee, and Other Direct Sales Organizations.* Grand Rapids: Baker Book House.

Somit, Albert. 1968. "Brainwashing." *International Encyclopedia of the Social Sciences* 2 (edited by D. L. Sills): 138–42. New York: MacMillan and Free Press.

Sontag, Susan. 1978. *Illness as Metaphor.* Vintage Books.

Spencer, Jim. 1987. "Worshipping the Goddesses." *Chicago Tribune* (25 Oct.).

Spretnak, Charlene, ed. 1982. *The Politics of Women's Spirituality: Essays on the Rise of Spiritual Power within the Feminist Movement.* New York: Doubleday.

Starhawk. 1979. *The Spiral Dance: A Rebirth of the Ancient Religion of the Great Goddess*. San Francisco: Harper and Row.

———. 1982. *Dreaming the Dark: Magic, Sex and Politics*. Boston: Beacon Press.

Stark, Rodney. 1981. "Must All Religions Be Supernatural?" In *The Social Impact of New Religious Movements*, edited by Bryan Wilson. New York: Rose of Sharon Press.

———. 1984. "The Rise of a New World Faith." *Review of Religious Research* 26:18–27.

———. 1985. "Europe's Receptivity to Religious Movements." In *Religious Movements: Genesis, Exodus, and Numbers*, edited by Rodney Stark. New York: Paragon.

———. 1987. "How New Religions Succeed: A Theoretical Model." In Bromley and Hammond 1987, 11–29.

Stark, Rodney, and William Bainbridge. 1979. "Of Churches, Sects and Cults." *Journal for the Scientific Study of Religion* 18:117–33.

Stark, Rodney, and William Bainbridge. 1980. "Secularization, Revival, and Cult Formation." *The Annual Review of the Social Sciences of Religion*, 85–119.

———. 1981. "Secularization and Cult Formation in the Jazz Age." *Journal for the Scientific Study of Religion* 20: 360–373.

———. 1985. *The Future of Religion: Secularization, Revival, and Cult Formation*. Berkeley, Calif.: University of California.

Stark, Rodney, and Charles Glock. 1968. *American Piety: The Nature of Religious Commitment*. Los Angeles: University of California Press.

Stein, D. 1987. *The Women's Spirituality Book*. St. Paul, Minn.: Llewellyn Publications.

Straus, Roger A. 1976. "Changing Oneself: Seekers and the Creative Transformation of Life Experience." In *Doing Social Life*, edited by J. Lofland, 252–72.

———. 1985. "But We *Are* a Religion: 'Religion' and 'Technology' in Scientology's Struggle for Legitimacy." Paper presented at the annual meeting of the Society for the Scientific Study of Religion, Savannah, Ga.

Suro, Roberto. 1989. "Switch by Hispanic Catholics Changes Face of U.S. Religion." *New York Times* (May 14): 1A, 14A.

Swanson, Guy. 1980. "A Basis of Authority and Identity in Post-Industrial Society." In *Identity and Authority*, edited by Robertson and Holzner, 190–217. New York: St. Martin's.

Sweet, Leonard. 1988. "Nineteenth Century Evangelicism." In *Encyclopedia of the American Religious Experience*, vol. 3, 875–900. New York: Scribners.

Tamney, Joseph B., and Stephen D. Johnson. 1987. "Church-State Relations in the Eighties." *Sociological Analysis* 48 (1): 1–16.

Taylor, Rex. 1978. "Marilyn's Friends and Rita's Customers: A Study of Party-Selling as Play and Work." *The Sociological Review* 26: 573–94.

Time. 1982. "Shake-Out in the Skin Game." (11 Oct.) 73.

Times Mirror. 1988. "The Static Dynamic Electorate." *New York Times* (6 Nov.).

Tipton, Steven M. 1982. *Getting Saved from the Sixties: Moral Meaning in Conversion and Cultural Change*. Berkeley, Calif.: University of California.

Tiryakian, Edward A. 1982. "Puritan America in the Modern World: Mission Impossible?" *Sociological Analysis* 43:351–68.

Trebbi, Diana. 1986. *Daughters in the Church Becoming Mothers of the Church: A Study of the Roman Catholic Women's Movement*. Unpublished dissertation thesis, City University of New York Graduate Center.

Trible, P. 1973. "Depatriarchalizing in Biblical Interpretation." *Journal of the American Academy of Religion* 41 (1): 31–33.

Trice, Harrison, Janice Byer. 1984. "Studying Organizational Cultures through Rites and Ceremonials." *Academy of Management Review* 9:653–69.

Trine, Ralph Waldo. 1897. *In Tune with the Infinite*. Indianapolis: Bobbs-Merrill.

Troeltsch, Ernst. 1931. *The Social Teaching of the Christian Churches*. New York: Macmillan.

Tunley, R. 1978. "Mary Kay's Sweet Smell of Success." *Reader's Digest* (Nov.): 17–21.

Turner, Bryan. 1983. *Religion and Social Theory*. London: Heinemann.

Turner, Victor. 1969. *The Ritual Proces*. Ithaca: Cornell University Press.

Tuveson, Ernest Lee. 1968. *Redeemer Nation: The Idea of America's Millennial Role*. Chicago: The University of Chicago Press.

United States v. Kozminski (6th Cir.) 821 F.2d 1186 Cert. granted 108 S.Ct. 225 (No. 86-2000, 1987).

Underwood, Kenneth W. 1957. *Protestant and Catholic*. Boston: Beacon Press.

Vatican. 1977. *Declaration on the Question of the Admission of Women to the Ministerial Priesthood*. Rome: Sacred Congregation for the Doctrine of the Faith. 27 Jan.

Videka-Sherman, Lynn. 1982. "The Effects of Participation in a Self-Help Group for Bereaved Parents." *Prevention in the Human Services* 1:69–77.

Vidich, Arthur J. 1975. "Social Conflict in the Era of Detente." *Social Research* 42 (1): 69–87.

Vidich, Arthur J., and Joseph Bensman. 1960. *Small Town in Mass Society*. Garden City, N.Y.: Doubleday.

Vidich, Arthur J. and Stanford M. Lyman. 1985. *American Sociology: Worldly Rejections of Religion and Their Directions*. New Haven: Yale University Press.

Wagner, Melinda Bollar. 1981. "Spiritual Science: Metaphysics as a Response to 'Rational' Culture." Paper presented at the annual meeting of the Society for the Scientific Study of Religion, Baltimore, Md.

Walker, Barbara. 1987. *The Skeptical Feminist*. San Francisco: Harper and Row.

————. 1983. *Metaphysics in Midwestern America*. Columbus: Ohio State University Press.

Wallace, Anthony F. C. 1966. *Religion: An Anthropological View*. New York: Random House.

Wallis, Roy. 1977. *The Road to Total Freedom*. New York: Columbia University Press.

————. 1979. *Salvation and Protest*. London: Francis Pinter.

————. 1985. "The Dynamics of Change in the Human Potential Movement." In *Religious Movements: Genesis, Exodus, and Numbers*, edited by R. Stark, 129–52. New York: Paragon House.

Wallis, Roy, and Steven Bruce. 1984a. "The Stark-Bainbridge Theory of Religion: A Critical Analysis and Counter Proposals." *Sociological Analysis* 45:11–27.

————. 1984b. "The Stark-Bainbridge Theory of Religion." *Sociological Analysis* 45 (1) 29–40.

————. 1986. *Sociological Theory, Religion, and Collective Action*. Belfast: Queens University.

Watson, John B. 1970. Orig. 1924. *Behaviorism*. New York: W. W. Norton.

Webber, Robert E. 1981. *The Moral Majority: Right or Wrong?* Westchester, Ill.: Cornerstone Books.

Weber, Max. 1963. Orig. 1922. *The Sociology of Religion*. Boston: Beacon Press.

Weber, Max. 1977. Orig. 1922. *Economy and Society,* edited by G. Roth and Claus Wittich. Berkeley and Los Angeles: University of California Press.

Webster, Paula, and Esther Newton. 1975. "Matriarchy: A Vision of Power." In *Toward an Anthropology of Women,* edited by Ryan Reiter. New York: Monthly Review Press.

Webster. 1981. *Third New International Dictionary*.

Weightman, Judith M. 1983. *Making Sense of the Jonestown Suicides: A Sociological History of Peoples Temple*. Lewiston, N.Y.: Edwin Mellon Press.

Weitzman, Lenore. 1985. *The Divorce Revolution*. New York: Free Press.

Wells, David F., and John D. Woodbridge, eds. 1975. *The Evangelicals: What They Believe, Who They Are, Where They Are Changing*. Nashville: Abingdon Press.

Welter, Barbara. 1966. "The Cult of True Womanhood: 1820–1860." *American Quarterly* 18:151–74.

West, Louis J. 1964. "Psychiatry, 'Brainwashing,' and the American Character." *American Journal of Psychiatry* 170 (9).

————. 1976. Testimony in Patty Hearst trial. In *The Trial of Patty Hearst*, 248–89. San Francisco: The Great Fidelity Press.

————. 1982. "Contemporary Cults: Utopian Image and Internal Reality." *The Center Magazine* 13(2):10–13.

West, Louis J., and Margaret Singer. 1980. "Cults, Quacks, and Non-Professional Psychotherapies." In *Comprehensive Textbook of Psychiatry III*, edited by H. I. Kaplan, A. M. Freedman, and B. J. Sadock. Baltimore: Williams and Wilkins.

Westley, Frances. 1983. *The Complex Forms of the Religious Life: A Durkheimian View of New Religious Movements*. Chico, Calif.: The Scholar's Press.

White, T. 1967. *A People for His Name*. New York: Vantage Press.

Whitley, Oliver R. 1977. "Life with Alcoholics Anonymous: The Methodist Class Meeting as a Paradigm." *Journal of Studies on Alcohol* 138:831–48.

Williams, Robin. 1970. *American Society*. New York: Macmillan.

Williamsburg Charter Foundation. 1988. *The Williamsburg Charter Survey on Religion and Public Life*. Washington, D.C.

Wilson, Bryan R. 1966. *Religion in Secular Society*. London: Watts.

————. 1976. *Contemporary Transformations of Religion*. New York: Harper and Row.

————. 1982. *Religion in Sociological Perspective*. New York: Oxford University Press.

————. 1985. "Secularization: The Inherited Model." In *The Sacred and a Secular Age*, edited by P. Hammond, 9–20. Berkeley, Calif.: University of California.

————. 1987. "Factors in the Failure of the New Religious Movements." In Bromley and Hammond 1987, 30–45.

Wilson, John, and Harvey Clow. 1981. "Themes of Power and Control in a Pentecostal Assembly." *Journal for the Scientific Study of Religion* 20 (3): 241–50.

Wollersheim, Larry. 1985. Deposition testimony in *Larry Wollersheim v. The Church of Scientology of California, a Corporation, et al.* Superior Court of the State of California for the County of Los Angeles.

Wrong, Dennis. 1980. *Power, Its Forms, Bases, and Uses*. New York: Harper and Row.

Wuthnow, Robert. 1983. "The Political Rebirth of American Evangelicals." In Liebman and Wuthnow 1983, 167–85.

————. 1985. "The Cultural Context of Contemporary Religious Movements." In *Cults, Culture, and the Law*, edited by T. Robbins, W. Shepherd, and J. McBride, 43–56. Chico, Calif.: Scholars Press.

————. 1988. *The Restructuring of American Religion: Society and Faith since World War II*. Princeton: University of Princeton Press.

Yinger, J. Milton. 1946. *Religion in the Struggle for Power*. Durham, N.C.: Duke University Press.

————. 1970. *The Scientific Study of Religion*. New York: Macmillan.

Zerubavel, Eviatar. 1978. "The Benedictine Ethic and the Spirit of Scheduling." Paper read at the meetings of the International Society for the Comparative Study of Civilizations, Milwaukee, Wisconsin.

Zeskind, Leonard. 1985. *Background Report on Racist and Anti-Semitic Organizational Intervention in the Farm Protest Movement*. Atlanta: Center for Democratic Renewal.

Zuriff, G. E. 1985. *Behaviorism: A Conceptual Reconstruction*. New York: Colombia University Press.

3

Contributors

Dick Anthony is a psychologist who specializes in research on the social and psychological dimensions of involvement in the new religions. While a faculty member of the Department of Psychiatry of the University of North Carolina Medical School, and later at the Graduate Theological Union in Berkeley, he directed a series of funded research projects on this topic. He has reported the results of his research in many articles in professional journals and provides a comprehensive overview in the recent book *Spiritual Choices*.

Earl Babbie earned his B.A. (1960) in Social Relations from Harvard College and his M.A. (1966) and Ph.D. (1969) from the University of California, Berkeley. He is currently Professor and Chair of Sociology at Chapman College. He is the author of numerous textbooks, including *The Practice of Social Research*. Outside of his academic writing, he is the author of a trade book, *You Can Make a Difference,* and he produced an audio cassette album with the same title. He is currently working on a novel, entitled *Doorways to Beyond,* reporting his research on trance channeling.

James A. Beckford is Professor of Sociology at The University of Warwick in England. His publications include *The Trumpet of Prophecy. A Sociological Study of Jehovah's Witnesses* (Oxford: Blackwell, 1975); *Religious Organization* (The Hague: Mouton, 1975); *Cult Controversies* (London: Tavistock, 1985); and *Religion in Advanced Industrial Societies* (London: Unwin Hyman, 1989). He has also edited *New Religious Movements and Rapid Social Change* (London: Sage, 1986) and, with Thomas Luckmann, *The Changing Face of Religion* (London: Sage, 1989). He is currently President of the Association for the Sociology of Religion.

Robert N. Bellah is Elliott Professor of Sociology at the University of California at Berkeley. He was educated at Harvard University, receiving the B.A. in 1950 and the Ph.D. in 1955. His publications include *Tokugawa Religion, Beyond Belief, The Broken Covenant, The New*

Religious Consciousness, and *Varieties of Civil Religion*. In 1985 he published *Habits of the Heart: Individualism and Commitment in American Life* (University of California Press; paperback, Harper and Row), written in collaboration with Richard Madsen, William Sullivan, Ann Swidler, and Steven Tipton. His most recent book is *Uncivil Religion: Interreligious Hostility in America* (Crossroad, 1987), edited with Frederick E. Greenspahn.

David G. Bromley is Professor of Sociology and Senior Project Director at Virginia Commonwealth University in Richmond, Virginia. His recent publications include *Krishna Consciousness in the West*, edited with Larry Shinn (Bucknell University Press, 1988); *Falling from the Faith* (SAGE Publications, 1988); and *The Future of New Religious Movements*, edited with Phillip Hammond (Mercer University Press, 1987).

Harvey Cox was born in Malvern, Pennsylvania, received his B.A. from the University of Pennsylvania, his B.D. from Yale University Divinity School, and his Ph.D. from Harvard University. He presently teaches at Harvard University and Divinity School as the Victor S. Thomas Professor of Divinity at Harvard Divinity School. He is the author of several books, including *The Secular City* (1965), *Religion in the Secular City* (1984), *The Silencing of Leonardo Boff: Liberation Theology and the Future of World Christianity* (Meyer Stone Books, 1988), and *Many Mansions: A Christian's Encounters with Other Faiths* (Beacon Press, 1988).

Lynn Davidman is an Assistant Professor of Sociology and Women's Studies at the University of Pittsburgh. She is the author of the book *Tradition in a Chaotic World: Women Turn to Orthodox Judaism* (forthcoming, University of California Press) and of several articles on women and religion in contemporary America. She has received several fellowships and grants to support her research. Her current work is on gender and religious experience.

N. Jay Demerath III is currently Professor of Sociology at the University of Massachusetts, Amherst, where he and Rhys Williams are currently finishing a book on church-state relations in the American Northeast, and where he is continuing comparative and cross-cultural work on religion and power around the globe. Professor Demerath came to Amherst after two years as Executive Officer of the American Sociological Association and ten years at the University of Wisconsin, Madison. He received his Ph.D. in 1964 from the University of California at Berkeley and his B.A. from Harvard.

Andrew M. Greeley, a distinguished sociologist, journalist, and priest, is Research Associate at the National Opinion Research Center at the University of Chicago, as well as Professor of Sociology at the University of Arizona. His current sociological research focuses on ethnic pluralism, ethnic family structures, and the religious imagination. Fr. Greeley has written scores of books and hundreds of popular and scholarly articles on a variety of issues in sociology, education, and religion.

Arthur L. Greil is Professor of Sociology and Associate Dean of the College of Liberal Arts and Sciences at Alfred University. He received his Ph.D. in 1979 from Rutgers University. He is the author of five scholarly articles on quasi-religious organizations. He has also written about religious conversions and personal change in adulthood. His work has appeared in such journals as *Sociological Analysis, Journal for the Scientific Study of Religion, Religious Research, Qualitative Sociology, Sociological Focus,* and *Sociological Inquiry.*

Jeffrey K. Hadden, who coined the term "televangelism," is Professor of Sociology at the University of Virginia and the author of numerous books, including *Televangelism: Power and Politics on God's Frontier* (1988), *Prime Time Preachers* (1981), and *The Gathering Storm in the Churches* (1969). He is a past president of the Society for the Scientific Study of Religion, the Association for the Sociology of Religion, and the Southern Sociological Society.

John R. Hall is Professor of Sociology at the University of California at Davis, and author of *The Ways Out: Utopian Communal Groups in an Age of Babylon* (Routledge & Kegan Paul, 1978), as well as a series of essays on epistemology, historical sociology, the social interaction perspective, and cultural studies. He has published on religion in *Sociological Analysis* and the *American Sociological Review.*

Barbara Hargrove was Professor of Sociology of Religion at the Iliff School of Theology in Denver. Her many publications include *The Reformation of the Holy, Religion and the Sociology of Knowledge,* and *The Emerging New Class: Implications for Church and Society.* She edited *Sociological Analysis,* served as vice president of the Association for the Sociology of Religion, and was president of the Religious Research Association. The recent death of Barbara Hargrove is deeply regretted by her many friends and colleagues in sociology and religious studies. Her life demonstrated the highest quality of scholarship, intellect, and humane endeavor.

Samuel Heilman is Professor of Sociology on the faculty of Queens College of the City University of New York. Currently, he is Scheinbrun Visiting Professor of Sociology at the Hebrew University of Jerusalem. He is the author of numerous articles and reviews as well as five books: *Synagogue Life, The People of the Book, The Gate behind the Wall, A Walker in Jerusalem,* and, most recently, *Cosmopolitans and Parochials: Modern Orthodox Jews in America* (coauthored with Steven M. Cohen). His book, *The Gate behind the Wall,* was honored with the Present Tense Magazine Literary Award for the best book of 1984 in the "Religious Thought" category. *A Walker in Jerusalem* received the National Jewish Book Award for 1987. Heilman also received a Distinguished Faculty Award from the City University of New York in 1985.

He is listed in *Who's Who in the East* (1978), *Contemporary Authors* (1977), and *Who's Who in World Jewry* (1985). He is a member of the board of the Association for Jewish Studies.

Irving Louis Horowitz is Hannah Arendt Distinguished Professor of Sociology and Political Science at Rutgers University and editor-in-chief of *Transaction Society*. His writings include *Taking Lives: Genocide and State Power*, 3rd ed.; *Beyond Empire and Revolution;* and, most recently, *Persuasions and Prejudices: An Informal Compendium of Modern Social Science*.

Janet L. Jacobs received her Ph.D. in sociology from the University of Colorado where she is now an Assistant Professor in the Women's Studies Program. Her research on gender, religious movements, and spiritual healing has appeared in the *Journal for the Scientific Study of Religion, Sociological Analysis*, and *Signs*. Her forthcoming book, *Divine Disenchantment: The Failure of Charisma in New Religious Movements*, will soon be available from the University of Indiana Press.

Frank J. Lechner is Assistant Professor in the Department of Sociology at Emory University. His research focuses on problems in sociological theory, the sociology of religion, and world system analysis; he has published articles and chapters in all three areas. Publications related to the theme of his contribution to this volume include "Fundamentalism and Sociocultural Revitalization: On the Logic of Dedifferentiation" in *Differentiation Theory and Social Change*, J. Alexander and P. Colomy, eds., Columbia University Press (1989), and "Catholicism and Social Change in the Netherlands" in the *Journal for the Scientific Study of Religion* (1989).

Armand L. Mauss is Professor of Sociology at Washington State University and editor of the *Journal for the Scientific Study of Religion*. His major scholarly interests focus on the rise and evolution of new movements, especially in the religious arena.

Mary Jo Neitz is the author of *Charisma and Community*, a study of charismatic Catholics. This article is part of her current research on Neopagan and feminist witches in contemporary America. She is interested in how religions act as sources for symbolic and material resources in modern society. She teaches sociology and women's studies at the University of Missouri in Columbia.

William McKinney is Director of Educational Programs and Dean, Hartford Seminary. He is co-author of *American Mainline Religion*, Rutgers University Press (1987).

Susan Jean Palmer teaches in the Religion Department of Dawson College in Montreal. She is Canadian because her great-great-grandmothers migrated from Salt Lake City into Alberta to protect their Mormon husbands from antipolygamist persecution. She is involved in early or ethnic music groups and in researching new religions.

Robin D. Perrin recently received his doctorate from Washington State University and is currently Assistant Professor of Sociology at Seattle

Pacific University, Seattle, Washington. He has recently published an article in the *Journal for the Scientific Study of Religion* on value and demographic factors in church growth and decline and is currently serving as assistant editor of the *JSSSR*.

Thomas Robbins received a Ph.D. in sociology from the University of North Carolina and has taught or held research appointments at Yale University, Queens College of the City University of New York, Central Michigan University, the Graduate Theological Union, and the New School for Social Research. He is author of *Cults, Converts and Charisma: The Sociology of New Religious Movements;* and coeditor of *Church-State Relations: Tensions and Transitions,* with Roland Robertson; and the first edition of *In Gods We Trust: New Patterns of Religious Pluralism in America,* with Dick Anthony.

Wade Clark Roof is Professor of Sociology at the University of Massachusetts at Amherst. He is coauthor of *American Mainline Religion: Its Changing Shape and Future* (Rutgers, 1987) and numerous other publications. Currently he is engaged in research on baby boomers and religious change.

Susan D. Rose is Assistant Professor of Sociology at Dickinson College. She has written several articles on evangelicals and the Christian School Movement in the United States and on North American evangelical activity in Guatemala. Her most recent publication is *Keeping Them Out of the Hands of Satan: Evangelical Schooling in America.*

David R. Rudy, Professor and Chair of the Department of Sociology, Social Work, and Corrections at Morehead State University, earned his Ph.D. in sociology at Syracuse University. He is the author of *Becoming Alcoholic: Alcoholics Anonymous and the Reality of Alcoholism* (1986, Southern Illinois University Press). Professor Rudy's prior work has appeared in *Qualitative Sociology, Sociological Inquiry, Sociological Focus, Sociological Analysis,* and the *Journal of Studies on Alcohol.* His current research interests include radical identity transformation, the Adult Children of Alcoholics Movement, and symbol work.

Anson Shupe is Professor and Chair of the Department of Sociology and Anthropology at Indiana University–Purdue University at Fort Wayne. He received his doctorate from Indiana University in 1975 and has taught at Alfred University and the University of Texas at Arlington. His research interests currently include religiopolitical movements, religion and crime, and the meeting of religious faith with medical healing. In addition to voluminous academic publications, he writes for newspapers and magazines such as *The Wall Street Journal, Religious Broadcasting,* and *Geo Magazine.*

Rodney Stark is Professor of Sociology and Comparative Religion at the University of Washington. At present he is completing books on religious competition in the United States (with Roger Finke) and on the rise of Christianity.

Diana Trebbi is a sociologist who undertakes independent research. She has studied the effects of the Times Square adult entertainment industry on an adjacent community, and published her findings in 1980. Since then, she has produced articles for various journals on a variety of topics, and edited *Interfaith Women's News and Network,* a quarterly newsletter for readers interested in advancing women's status in mainstream U.S. religions.

Rhys H. Williams completed his Ph.D. in sociology from the University of Massachusetts, Amherst, in May, 1988 and is currently Adjunct Assistant Professor at that institution. His scholarly interests include American culture, politics, religion, and theory. Along with completing a church-state project with Jay Demerath, he is involved with research projects on organizational change in American seminaries and the role of religion in American political culture, historically as well as contemporarily.

INDEX

543